R. Gupta's®

POPULAR MASTER GUIDE

MANIPUR TET

TEACHER ELIGIBILITY TEST

PAPER-I

Primary Stage (Class I-V)

- Specialised Study & Practice Material Prepared by Experts
- Numerous Solved Multiple Choice Questions (MCQs)
- Solved Question Paper

by

RPH Editorial Board

RAMESH PUBLISHING HOUSE, NEW DELHI

Published by
O.P. Gupta *for* Ramesh Publishing House

Admin. Office
12-H, New Daryaganj Road, Opp. Officers' Mess,
New Delhi-110002 ✆ 23275224, 23245124

E-mail: info@rameshpublishinghouse.com
For Online Shopping: www.rameshpublishinghouse.com

Showroom
• Balaji Market, Nai Sarak, Delhi-110006 ✆ 23282525 📱 9354373464
• 4457, Nai Sarak, Delhi-110006

Book Code: R-1556

ISBN: 978-93-89480-18-4

Price: ₹ 415

Printed by : Repro India Ltd.

CONTENTS

❑❑❑

SCHEME OF PAPER-I EXAM

Primary Stage — Teacher for Classes I to V

PAPER-I will be conducted for candidates who wish to be teachers from Classes I to V.

Subjects	Total Nos. of Questions	Total Nos. of Marks	Duration
Child Development and Pedagogy	30	30	
Language-I (English)	30	30	
Language-II (English-II or Modern Indian Language*)	30	30	2 hours
Mathematics	30	30	
Environmental Studies	30	30	
Total	**150**	**150**	

* Modern Indian Languages recognized by the Board of Secondary Education, Manipur are listed in the Application Form.

Model Paper (Solved)

Manipur TET (Paper-I), Exam 2019

(For Classes I to V)

Child Development and Pedagogy

1. Children have the potential to create knowledge and make meaning. From this perspective the role of a teacher is that of a:
A. Communicator and Lecturer
B. Facilitator
C. Director
D. Negotiator

2. Which one of the following is ***not*** a characteristic of gifted children?
A. High self efficacy
B. Below average mental processes
C. Solving problems insightfully
D. Higher order mental processes

3. According to the pre-conventional level of Kohlberg's theory, to which of the following would an individual turn when making a moral decision?
A. Personal needs and desires
B. Individual values
C. Family expectations
D. Potential punishment involved

4. Regarding learners' individual differences, the teacher should:
A. solve the problems based on deductive method
B. most of the time use algorithms
C. provide facts to students to memorize them
D. provide a variety of learning situations

5. Which one of the following is ***not*** the principle of child development?
A. All areas of development are important
B. All development results from an interaction of maturation and experience
C. All development and learning proceed at an equal rate
D. All development follows a sequence

6. Which one of the following would be the most effective way of conducting assessment?
A. Assessment is an inbuilt process in teaching learning
B. Assessment should be done twice in an academic session – at the beginning and at the end
C. Assessment should be done by an external agency and not by the teacher
D. Assessment should be at the end of the session

7. Which one of the following is related to creativity?
A. Convergent thinking
B. Emotional thinking
C. Egoistic thinking
D. Divergent thinking

8. Which one of the following statements about children would Vygotsky agree with?
A. Children learn when they are offered lucrative rewards
B. Children's thinking can be understood by conducting laboratory experiments on animals
C. Children are born 'evil' and need to be controlled through punishment
D. Children learn through social interaction with peers and adults

9. Children are:
A. adult-like in their thinking and there is a quantitative increase in their thinking as they grow up
B. like empty vessels in which knowledge given by the adults is filled
C. passive beings who can produce exact copies of the information transmitted to them
D. curious beings who use their own logic and abilities to explore the world around them

10. Which of the following statements about children's errors is correct?
A. Children's errors are part of the learning process
B. Children commit errors when the teacher is lenient and does not punish them for mistakes
C. Children's errors are insignificant for the teacher and she should just strike out of the mistakes and not pay any attention to them
D. Children commit errors because they are careless

11. A teacher needs to ensure that all learners in her class feel accepted and valued. To do this, the teacher should:
A. look down upon children from 'disadvantaged' background so that they feel they have to work harder
B. find out students who speak 'good' English and are from 'rich' backgrounds and present them as role models
C. get to know the social and cultural background of her students and encourage diverse opinions in the class
D. make strict rules and punish children who do not follow them

12. Suresh generally likes to study alone in a quiet room whereas Madan likes to study in a group with his friends. This is because of difference in their:
A. Aptitudes B. Learning styles
C. Levels of reflectivity D. Values

13. India has a lot of linguistic diversity. In this context, what is the most appropriate statement about multilingual classrooms at primary level especially class I and II?
A. The schools should admit only those students whose mother tongue is the same as the language of instruction
B. The teacher should respect all languages and encourage children to communicate in all of them
C. The teacher should ignore children who use their mother tongue in the class
D. Students should be penalized for using their mother tongue or local language

14. What is meant by 'nature' in 'nature-nurture' controversy?
A. Biological givens or the hereditary information
B. Temperament of an individual
C. Complex forces of the physical and social world
D. The environment around us

15. Mass Media is becoming a very important agency of socialization. Which one of the following is the most appropriate statement?
A. Socialization is done by the parents and the family only
B. Access to mass media is growing and mass media influences attitudes, values and beliefs
C. Children cannot directly interact with media
D. Media is a very good way to advertise and sell products

16. How children learn? Which one of the following is *not* true with respect to this statement?
A. Children learn when they are cognitively ready
B. Children learn in a number of ways
C. Children learn as they are naturally motivated
D. Children learn in class only

17. Which one of the following strategies should a primary school teacher adopt to motivate her students?
A. Use incentives, rewards and punishment as motivating factors for each activity
B. Help children set goals as per their interests and support them in working towards the same
C. Set standard goals for the entire class and have rigid parameters to assess achievement of those goals
D. Encourage competition for marks amongst individual student

18. Which one of the following is the primary agent of socialization?
A. Computer B. Heredity
C. Political parties D. Family

19. Giving children group work is an effective pedagogic strategy since:
A. it allows some children to dominate the others in small groups
B. children learn from each other and support each other in the learning process
C. children will be able to do their work quickly
D. it helps to reduce the teacher's work

20. A child with normal intelligence shows difficulty in reading and comprehending language. It indicates that the child is showing symptoms of:
A. Dysgraphia B. Dyscalculia
C. Dyspraxia D. Dyslexia

21. The period of infancy is from:
A. birth to 2 years B. birth to 3 years
C. 2 to 3 years D. birth to 1 year

22. According to Piaget, a child between 2 to 7 years is in the .... stage of cognitive development.
A. Formal operational B. Concrete operational
C. Sensorimotor D. Preoperational

23. Development proceeds from .... to ....
A. complex → hard B. specific → general
C. simple → easy D. general → specific

24. When adults adjust to the assistance they provide to facilitate progression of the child from current level of performance to potential level of performance, it is called:
A. Scaffolding B. Participatory learning
C. Collaborative learning D. Proximal development

25. The process of changing the existing schemas to include new information is called:
A. Assimilation B. Accommodation
C. Egocentrism D. Adaptation

26. In middle childhood, speech is more .... rather than ....
A. socialised, egocentric B. animistic, socialised
C. mature, immature D. egocentric, socialised

27. The child centred education involves:
A. children sitting in a corner
B. learning in restricted environment
C. activities that do not include play
D. hands on activities for kids

28. The class teacher observed Raghav in her class playing melodious self-composed music on his keyboard. The class teacher thought that Raghav seemed to be high in .... intelligence.
A. bodily-kinesthetic B. musical
C. linguistic D. spatial

29. When a teacher considers boys as naturally better at mathematics than girls, it shows that the teacher is:
A. gender biased B. moralistic
C. right-minded D. ethical

30. Inclusive education assumes that we should change the .... to fit the ....
A. System / child
B. Environment / family
C. Child / environment
D. Child / system

Language-I : English (Compulsory)

31. Telling interesting stories to young learners is primarily meant for improving their:
A. Writing skills
B. Speaking skills
C. Listening skills
D. Reading skills

32. The best way to sensitize young learners to rhythm and intonation is:
A. by reading out poems in different metres and explaining them
B. by making the learners listen to nursery rhymes and recite them effectively
C. by making the learners copy out simple poems in neat handwriting
D. by explaining the rules of phonetics in simple words

33. An effective language teacher:
A. will make children learn all the answers to the questions given in the textbook
B. will use the textbook as well as other material as resources for teaching
C. will prepare question papers using only the questions given in the textbook
D. will rely entirely on the prescribed textbook

34. The most effective tool to assess values and attitude of learners is:
A. Anecdotal Record
B. Portfolio
C. Unit Test
D. Summative Test

35. A teacher engages her learners in a fun activity before beginning a new lesson. The purpose of this activity is to:
A. discipline the learners before the lesson
B. divert the attention of the learners
C. reduce the workload of the teacher
D. motivate and energise the learners

36. The main purpose of using oral drill is:
A. to assess the comprehension skills of learners
B. to improve pronunciation and accuracy
C. to enhance the speaking skills of learners
D. to improve the retention capacity of learners

37. Continuous and Comprehensive Evaluation should be adopted by all schools because:
A. it is the latest development in the field of education
B. traditional pen-paper tests do not assess and enhance all the attributes and abilities of learners
C. it frees the learners from studies and hard work
D. it affords teachers opportunities to test learners frequently

38. Knowledge of more than one language:
A. becomes a burden to the teacher in the language classroom
B. confuses the learners while learning a new language
C. is very helpful in teaching and learning a new language
D. causes interference in learning a new language

39. Seating arrangement should be flexible so that:
A. many group, pair and whole-class activities can be conducted easily
B. children do not form permanent friendship groups
C. the teacher ensures equality prevails in her classroom
D. children have the freedom to move their seats wherever they want

40. Curriculum is an educational programme which does *not* state:
A. the number of lessons to be taught in a term
B. the means of evaluating whether the educational objectives have been achieved or not
C. the content (material etc.), teaching strategies and learning experiences which will be necessary to achieve this purpose
D. the educational purpose of a programme

41. Which of the following is an important stage in the writing process?
A. Editing B. Memorisation
C. Calligraphy D. Comprehension

42. A 'sight word' is a vocabulary item:
A. that needs proper visual understanding of the context
B. that is to be learned by heart
C. that helps in judging the effectiveness of the author's style
D. that the reader recognizes and finds meaningful on sight without a complicated analysis

43. Scanning means darting over much of a text to search for:
A. the opinion of the author
B. difficult words
C. a specific item or piece of information that we wish to discover
D. the central idea

44. We use real objects to teach young learners new words because:
A. it helps in teaching the correct spelling of words
B. we can teach vocabulary only through objects
C. young learners are not capable of abstract thinking
D. it helps learners associate words with objects they see in real life

45. A good introduction to a text should be:
A. telling the students anything that they can find out for themselves by reading the text
B. a detailed explanation of the meaning of the text
C. blocking the student's active involvement by means of questioning
D. short and to the point

Directions (Q. No. 46 to 51) : *Read the poem given below and answer the questions that follow by selecting the* **most** *appropriate option.*

Night

The sun descending in the west,
The evening star does shine;
The birds are silent in their nest,
And I must seek for mine.
The moon, like a flower,
In heaven's high bower,
With silent delight
Sits and smiles on the night.
Farewell, green fields and happy groves,
Where flocks have took delight.
Where lambs have nibbled, silent moves
The feet of angels bright;
Unseen they pour blessing,
And joy without ceasing,
On each bud and blossom,
And each sleeping bosom.
They look in every thoughtless nest,
Where birds are covered warm;
They visit caves of every beast,
To keep them all from harm.
If they see any weeping
That should have been sleeping,
They pour sleep on their head,
And sit down by their bed.

46. The evening star rises when:
A. the sun descends in the west
B. the birds leave their nests
C. it is midnight
D. it is dawn

47. Here, 'bower' represents:
A. a flower vase
B. a potted plant
C. a framework that supports climbing plants
D. a bouquet of flowers

48. The poet compares moon to:
A. an angel
B. a flower
C. a bird in the nest
D. an evening star

49. The angels come down on earth to:
A. take blessing and joy
B. spread moonlight
C. give blessing and joy
D. make people dance and have fun

50. Birds' nest is described as 'thoughtless' because:
A. the occupants are asleep without any care
B. the angels are blessing the birds to be happy
C. the birds are covered in the warmth of their nest
D. it is made without any thought

51. The figure of speech used in the line 'In heaven's high bower' is:
A. Simile B. Metaphor
C. Personification D. Alliteration

Directions (Q. No. 52 to 60) : *Read the passage given below and answer the questions that follow by selecting the* **most** *appropriate option.*

Our body is a wondrous mechanism and when subjected to unusual stress over a period of time, it adapts itself to deal more effectively with that stress. Therefore, when you exert you muscles against resistance, they are forced to adapt and deal with this extraordinary workload. This is the principle of weight training. Strands of muscle fibres become thicker and stronger in response to the demands placed on them.

One of the great merits of weight training is the strength of your heart. During weight training, your heart is forced to beat faster and stronger in order to pump sufficient blood to the muscles being worked. In time, your heart, like your body, will adapt to this extra-work had by becoming stronger and more efficient. Since your body needs a given amount of blood to perform its daily tasks, your heart will now need fewer beats to pump the same quantity of blood. Sounds good? There's more. Your entire circulatory system is given a thorough workout every time you exercise, which increases its overall efficiency. Even the neural paths from your brain's command centres to each individual muscle become more effective, enabling easier recruitment of muscle fibres for carrying out physical tasks. In essence, your body becomes a well-oiled and finely-tuned piece of machinery, whirring along without any breakdown. In today's stress-filled world, you need all the help you can get.

52. The principle of weight training is:
A. training muscles to exert more pressure
B. disposing extra workload
C. thickening of body through extra consumption
D. helping the body adapt to increased stress

53. Weight training makes the muscles:
A. resist workload
B. thicker and stronger
C. become stranded
D. become intense

54. During weight training, the heart pumps:
A. more blood
B. required blood
C. an extraordinary amount of blood
D. less blood

55. A stronger and more efficient heart:
A. needs fewer beats to pump the same amount of blood
B. can rest longer, reducing its workload
C. is assisted by muscles of the body
D. beats faster and more often to pump blood

56. When neural paths become more effective:
A. the brain opens new pathways for communication
B. the brain employs various muscles easily for physical tasks
C. the muscles function effectively and independently
D. the brain functions at extraordinary speed

57. What does the term 'well-oiled' in the passage denote?
A. Serviced B. Massaged
C. Greased D. Healthy

58. Which one of the following is the most appropriate title for the passage?
A. Stress-busting
B. The Mechanics of Weight Training
C. How to retain your health?
D. Health is Wealth

59. What does the above passage suggest?
A. Physical exercise is necessary occasionally
B. We should ignore physical exercise
C. We should subject our body to as much exercise as it can withstand
D. We should carry out physical exercise as a routine

60. The word 'wondrous' (first line) is:
A. a noun B. an adverb
C. an adjective D. a verb

Language-II : English

Directions (Q. Nos. 61 to 69): *Read the passage given below and answer the questions that follow by selecting the **most appropriate** options:*

One Sunday morning, I was travelling on a subway in Mumbai. People were sitting quietly–some reading news-papers, some lost in thought. It was a calm, peaceful scene.

Then suddenly, a man and his children entered the subway car. The children were so loud and rambunctious that instantly the whole climate changed.

The man sat next to me and closed his eyes, apparently oblivious to the situation. The children were yelling back and forth, throwing things, even grabbing people's papers. It was very disturbing. And yet, the man sitting next to me did nothing.

It was difficult not to feel irritated. I could not believe that he could be so insensitive as to let his children run wild and do nothing about it. It was easy to see that everyone else on the subway felt irritated, too. So finally, I turned to him and said, "Sir, your children are really disturbing a lot of people. I wonder if you couldn't control them a little more?"

The man lifted his gaze as if to come to a consciousness of the situation for the first time and said softly, "Oh, you're right. I guess I should do something about it. We just came from the hospital where their mother died an hour ago. I don't know what to think and I guess they don't know how to handle it either".

Can you imagine what I felt at that moment. My paradigm shifted. Suddenly I saw things differently, and because I saw things differently, I thought, felt and behaved differently. My irritation vanished; my heart was filled with the man's pain. Feelings of sympathy and compassion flowed freely. "Your wife just died? Oh, I am sorry! Can you tell me about it? What can I do to help?" Everything changed in an instant.

61. The primary purpose of the author is to:
A. narrate an amusing incident
B. show how indulgent parents spoil their children
C. show a radical shift in attitude
D. highlight the problems of subway travellers

62. The word 'oblivious' (Para 3) means:
A. unaware B. neglectful
C. inconsiderate D. insensitive

63. The word which is opposite in meaning to 'compassion' (para 6) is:
A. coarseness B. dislike
C. wildness D. cruelty

64. 'I *felt* differently.'
Tense of the above sentence has been correctly changed into present continuous in:
A. I am feeling differently
B. I had been feeling differently
C. I was feeling differently
D. I have been feeling differently

65. 'My irritation vanished.'
The sentence given above has been correctly changed into interrogative form in:
A. Couldn't my irritation vanish?
B. Hadn't my irritation vanished?
C. Didn't my irritation vanish?
D. Did my irritation vanish?

66. The children's behaviour on the subway was:
A. irritating B. disgusting
C. shocking D. amusing

67. How did the man (children's father) react to the unruly behaviour of his children?
A. He rebuked them
B. He tried to control them
C. He did nothing
D. He enjoyed their antics

68. It can be inferred from the man's behaviour that he was:
A. an indulgent parent B. mentally distrubed
C. unsocial D. insensitive

69. When the writer learnt the truth:
A. his heart was filled with the man's suffering
B. he was angry with himself for being judgemental
C. he decided to help the man out
D. he felt apologetic

Directions (Q. Nos. 70 to 75): *Read the passage given below and answer the questions that follow by selecting the most appropriate options:*

Your attitudes are the perspectives from which you view life. Some people seem to have a good attitude towards most things. Some people seem to have a bad attitude towards everything. But when you look closer, you will find that most of us have a combination of attitudes, some good, some not so good.

Whatever attitude we have towards anything will affect how we feel about it, which in turn determines whether or not we will do well. So our right attitudes play a very important part in helping us become successful.

In fact, as we can see, a good attitude is essential for achievement of any kind ! We so often hear of someone who is said to have a "bad attitude". The term is often applied to young people, especially to teenagers who frequently get into trouble, but we often hear it about adults, too. The implication is always that the individual in question is not going to make it if he doesn't change his attitude.

I would agree, without a good attitude it is not possible to see the opportunities ahead and set one's sights to reach them. But even more important is the fact that in order to possess the kind of feelings which work for us, we've got to have the right attitude to start with.

But where do we get our attitudes from? Are we born with them or do they just appear out of nowhere? Our attitudes are no accident. They don't just happen. Our attitudes are created and influenced entirely by our beliefs.

70. Which one of the following statements is correct?
A. Our attitudes are influenced by our parents only
B. Our attitudes are created and controlled by our beliefs
C. Our attitudes are the results of our personal experience
D. We are born with our attitudes

71. The word 'determine' most nearly means:
A. influence B. overcome
C. engage D. govern

72. Which part of speech is the **bold** word in the sentence given below?
'Some people seem to have a good attitude **towards** most things.'
A. Preposition B. Adjective
C. Conjunction D. Adverb

73. A/An .... attitude is absolutely necessary for attainment of any kind.
A. cheerful B. optimistic
C. good D. virtuous

74. The term "bad attitude" is used for young people because they:
A. behave irresponsibly
B. often get into difficulty
C. are unpredictable
D. defy all kinds of authority

75. Right attitudes are absolutely essential to:
A. win the goodwill of our peers and superiors
B. have harmonious relations with others
C. promote our mental well-being
D. succeed in life

76. Which of the following is the highest level of cognitive ability?
A. Knowing B. Understanding
C. Evaluating D. Analysing

77. Why is story telling most important in an English language class at primary level?
A. It is useful for developing integrated language skills
B. It develops moral values among the students
C. It improves students' vocabulary
D. It creates fun in the class

78. A good teacher is one who:
A. gives them ample opportunities to learn
B. gives them useful information
C. explains concepts and principles
D. gives printed notes to students

79. Which of the following helps in learning the second language without using the printed text?
A. Situational approach
B. Natural approach
C. Language immersion
D. Grammar-translation method

80. A person, who is a fluent speaker, is likely to possess:
A. Logico-mathematical ability
B. Bodily-kinesthetic ability
C. Musical ability
D. Verbal-linguistic ability

81. Which approach emphasizes interaction as the means and the goal of learning a language?
A. Communicative B. Oral-aural
C. Immersion D. Silent way

82. Maximum participation of students during teaching in a language class-room is possible through:
A. Lecture method
B. Translation method
C. Inductive method
D. Discussion and demonstration methods

83. Dyslexia is an intellectual disability that negatively affects the understanding abilities in terms of:
A. Oral language
B. Sign language
C. Dialect
D. Reading

84. The Linguist, Noam Chomsky maintains that every child has an innate Language Acquisition Device (LAD) that he/she uses for:
A. Phonemes B. Universal Grammar
C. Complex words D. Semantics

85. The structural approach advocates:
A. resorting to fluency
B. selection and gradation of material
C. assessing learners' performance
D. using mother tongue

86. According to socio-cultural theory of Vygotsky:
A. Self-directed speech is the lowest stage of the scaffolding
B. Children can think in abstract terms if abstract material is provided at a lower age
C. Children think in different domain and do not take a complete perspective
D. Culture helps in language development

87. What is the main purpose of poetry recitation in a language classroom?
A. To appreciate and enjoy the poem
B. To give their opinions about the poem
C. To become aware of the poet and her works
D. To know the historical background of the poem

88. Who strongly maintains that language is learnt by imitation of stimuli and reinforcement of correct responses?
A. Albert Bandura B. Kurt Lewin
C. Tolman D. B.F. Skinner

89. Under which activity do recognising sounds and deducing meanings from them come?
A. Speaking B. Listening
C. Reading D. Writing

90. During the process of language learning, students lack confidence in their pronunciation. How can one overcome this?
A. Providing scope for special activities with the help of language experts for removing speaking defects
B. Correcting mistakes immediately
C. Reading aloud in the classroom
D. Organizing play like tasks in which children can talk to one another

Mathematics

91. The Perimeter of a square is 20 cm. A rectangle has the same width as the square. The length of the rectangle is double its width. The area, in square cm, of the rectangle is:
A. 30 B. 50
C. 100 D. 25

92. The internal length, breadth and height of a rectangular box A are 20 cm, 18 cm and 5 cm respectively and that of box B are 18 cm, 12 cm and 5 cm respectively. The volume of box A is how many times that of box B?
A. 4 B. 5
C. 6 D. 3

93. Which of the following is ***not*** correct?
A. Area of a square of side 10 cm = Area of a rectangle of length 10 cm and breadth 0.1 m
B. 1 metre 5 centimetre ≠ 1.5 metre
C. 0.40 is same as 0.4
D. Rupee $\frac{3}{4}$ = Rupee 0.75

94. One orange costs five and half rupees and one kg apple costs ₹ 80. Then the total cost of one and half dozen of oranges and one and three-fourth kg of apples is:
A. ₹ 219 B. ₹ 229
C. ₹ 239 D. ₹ 209

95. NCF, 2005 states that Mathematics teaching should be ambitious, coherent and important. Here, 'ambitious' refers to achievement of:
A. narrow goals of Mathematics
B. linking of Mathematics with other subjects
C. application of Mathematics
D. higher goals of Mathematics

96. In Class II, concept of even number and odd number was introduced by activity of pairing the given number with concrete objects. Then teacher asked the students to check
(*i*) whether the total number of crayons in their colour boxes is even in number or odd in number
(*ii*) whether the number of pages in their Maths notebook is odd or even.
This task of finding even or odd number of crayons/pages is:
A. assessment for learning
B. assessment as learning
C. assessment at the end of learning
D. assessment of learning

97. After explaining the operation of subtraction in Class II, teacher drew the following diagram on the board and asked the students to fill in the circles:

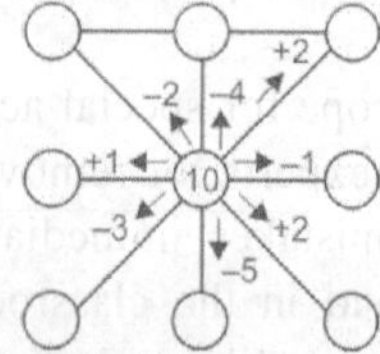

The purpose of the exercise is:
A. strengthening skill of addition and subtraction
B. summative assessment
C. arranging fun activity for the students
D. mathematization of mind

98. How many rectangles are there in the following figure?

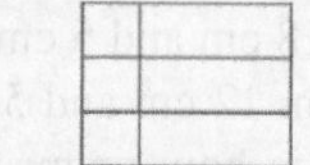

The above question is testing
A. knowledge of learner
B. understanding of learner
C. creativity of learner
D. memory of learner

99. Which of the following activities is meant to enhance problem-solving abilities of students of Class III?
A. A crossword puzzle containing clues for all key terms learnt like even number, odd number, composite number, prime number, etc.
B. A group project : How the students of primary wing shall be distributed equally in four houses (house system of school) so that every house has talented students from sports, arts, cultural and academic activities?
C. Conduct an interclass quiz in the class on 'numbers and operations'
D. A worksheet containing problems on four basic operations like—Find 25 × 34, 451 ÷ 11, etc.

100. The recommended key concept in the unit of 'multiplication' in Class III is:
A. multiplication of 2-digit number with 2-digit number
B. properties of multiplication–order property and group property
C. word problem based on multiplication
D. multiplication of 3-digit numbers by 10

101. From the unit of 'fraction', teacher asked the students to list any five fractions.
This question refers to:
A. higher level of thinking
B. analytical thinking
C. spatial thinking
D. lower level of thinking

102. In an exercise, the question was—Measure the lengths of the line segments P •———• Q and R •———• S.
The child answered—
length of AB = 5 cm, length of AB = 3 cm
This refers to:
A. conceptual error
B. procedural error
C. error due to habit of naming line segment as AB
D. reading error

103. A teacher distributed newspaper in Class V and asked the students to read the cricket scores of Indian team in latest match. Then she asked them to draw bar graph of the scores. The teacher is trying to:
A. help the students to make connections between mathematical concepts and real life
B. teach them through project approach
C. make the class joyful and communicating
D. enhance reasoning power of the students

104. The following word problem was given to a child of Class IV:
Mumbai has 336 bus stops. Delhi has 127 more bus stops than Mumbai. How many bus stops are there in all, in Delhi?

The child's response to the above problem is recorded as:

336 Mumbai
336 127 Delhi

Total bus stops in Delhi are 336 + 127 = 463.

The teacher shall report about his performance as:

A. the child can find the answer correctly but his expression is poor
B. the child is good at visualizing and analyzing, and his problem-solving ability is appreciable
C. the child has not adopted the right procedure. He needs to practice more
D. the child is not able to write all steps required properly

105. A student was asked to read the following numbers : 306, 408, 4008, 4010

He read as follows:

Thirty six, forty eight, four hundred eight, forty ten

The reason for error in reading is that:

A. the student does not like Maths class and finds the class boring
B. the student has understood the concept of place value but does not know how to use it
C. the student is not fit for study of Maths
D. the student is not able to understand the concept of place value and feels comfortable using two-digit numbers only

106. The parameter(s) of assessment for 'time' for Class IV shall be:

A. reading time on analogous clock only
B. reading time on digital and analogous clock, concept of half past, quarter past, quarter to, a.m., p.m., relation between minutes and seconds
C. reading time on digital clock, concept of a.m. and p.m. only
D. reading time on digital clock only

107. 'Tall shape of Mathematics' mentioned in NCF, 2005 refers to:

A. solving challenging problems
B. creating Maths game
C. providing hands-on experience
D. building of one concept on other

108. Consider the following:

5 + 3 = ?

The open-ended question corresponding to the above close-ended question is:

A. Find the sum of 5 and 3.
B. What shall be added to 5 to get 8?
C. Give any two numbers whose sum is 8.
D. What is the sum of 5 and 3?

109. Farhan went to school library and found that 100 books kept in story section are spoiled. 20 books are missing. 219 are kept in shelf and 132 were issued to students. How many story- books were there in the library?

Teacher can teach the following value through this question:

A. Helping others
B. Sharing books with others
C. Taking good care of books
D. Sense of cooperation

110. The product of the place values of 5 and 6 in 70560 is:

A. 300 B. 3000
C. 30000 D. 30

111. When 3010301 is divided by 43, the quotient is:

A. 70707 B. 70007
C. 7077 D. 7007

112. What should be subtracted from the product 3001 × 101 to get 300311?

A. 2790 B. 2090
C. 2970 D. 270

113. (Smallest common multiple of 36 and 60) + (Biggest common factor of 18 and 45) is equal to:

A. 20 B. 30
C. 40 D. 10

114. (10 tens + 11 hundreds + 12 ones) equals:

A. 1213 B. 111012
C. 101112 D. 1212

115. The number of factors of 42 is:

A. 7 B. 8
C. 9 D. 6

116. When 3488 is divided by 12 and 2478 is divided by 11, the difference between the remainders in both cases is:

A. 5 B. 6
C. 7 D. 3

117. A train leaves station P at 8:18 a.m. and reaches station Q at 10:28 p.m. on the same day. The time taken by the train to reach Q is:

A. 14 hours 10 minutes B. 14 hours 46 minutes
C. 18 hours 46 minutes D. 13 hours 10 minutes

118. 14 L 280 mL of orange juice and 18 L 830 mL of carrot juice were mixed together. This mixture was filled in 15 bottles each containing 1.5 L. How much mixture was left?

A. 11 L 105 mL B. 9 L 610 mL
C. 11 L 605 mL D. 10 L 610 mL

119. One-fourth of a pizza was eaten by Renu. The rest was equally distributed among 12 children. What part of the pizza did each of these children get?

A. $\frac{1}{16}$ B. $\frac{1}{32}$
C. $\frac{3}{16}$ D. $\frac{1}{8}$

120. The number of seconds in 6 hours equals the number of minutes in:

A. 4 days B. 10 days
C. 15 days D. 2 days

Environmental Studies

121. These are the chemical substances which reduce body temperature during high fever:
A. Laxatives
B. Antacids
C. Tranquillizer
D. Antipyretics

122. Which of the following is not a fossil fuel?
A. Crude oil B. Wood
C. Hydrogen D. Coal

123. The milk, which is packed in pre-sterilized brick-style cartons and can be stored without refrigeration for about six months is:
A. Pasteurized
B. Skimmed
C. Condensed
D. Ultrapasteurized

124. Milky Way is:
A. An elliptical galaxy
B. An irregular galaxy
C. A spherical galaxy
D. A spiral galaxy

125. Which of the following is used as biofertilizer?
A. Ammonia B. Urea
C. Azospirillum D. Bagasse

126. The Mukurthi National Park is located in ....
A. Kerala B. Karnataka
C. Tamil Nadu D. Odisha

127. Which of the following highways did not pass through Manipur?
A. NH-39 B. NH-53
C. NH-150 D. NH-35

128. Which one of the following is not a tributary of Barak river?
A. Jatinga B. Chiri
C. Madhura D. Teesta

129. Which one of the following districts covers largest geographical area?
A. Sanapati
B. Tamenglong
C. Ukhrul
D. Chandel

130. Acid rain contains:
A. Sulphuric acid and Nitric acid
B. Carbon dioxide and Carbon monoxide
C. Methane and Sulphuric acid
D. Nitric acid and Hydrochloric acid

131. Manipuri language was inserted in the 8th Schedule of the Constitution of India by:
A. The Constitution (90th Amendment) Act
B. The Constitution (71st Amendment) Act
C. The Constitution (72nd Amendment) Act
D. None of the above

132. Special provisions with respect to State to Manipur are provided in Indian Constitution under _______ .
A. Article 371-A
B. Article 370-B
C. Article 371-C
D. Article 372-D

133. What is the correct sequence of the States in terms of the length of the International Border with Myanmar in descending order?
A. Arunachal Pradesh, Mizoram, Manipur, Nagaland
B. Nagaland, Manipur, Mizoram, Arunachal Pradesh
C. Mizoram, Nagaland, Arunachal Pradesh, Manipur
D. Manipur, Mizoram, Nagaland, Arunachal Pradesh

134. Who among the following persons from Manipur has been selected for the prestigious Sangeet Natak Akademi Award 2015?
A. Gangmei Aluna Kabuini and W. Lokendrajit Singh
B. Ningombam Ibobi Singh and L. Ibohalmacha Singh
C. Amusana Devi and M.K. Saroja
D. Ibopishak Sharma and H. Ngangbi Devi

135. Manipuri folk dance 'Thabal Chongba' is associated with which festival?
A. Lai Haraoba
B. Yaoshang
C. Rath Yatra
D. Heikru

136. In rural areas, cow dung is used to coat the floor and walls of huts to:
A. keep the insects away
B. make them smooth and clean
C. make them rough to increase friction
D. give a natural colour to the floor

137. A farmer wanted to separate the grains from the chaff. This can be achieved by the process called:
A. Handpicking
B. Threshing
C. Winnowing
D. Harvesting

138. Which one of the following is ***not*** an objective of including riddles and puzzles in the EVS textbook?
A. To develop curiosity and ability to think creatively
B. To develop critical thinking ability in students

C. To develop reasoning ability in students
D. To confuse the mind of the students and let them enjoy the confusion

139. Giving importance to individual experiences of children in an EVS class will benefit the teacher:
A. to save her energy as children enjoy talking
B. to know the unique experiences of children
C. to help and improve the language and communication skills of the children
D. to connect the subject to the learners' experiential world and promote reflection and learning

140. To make children aware of different kinds of fuel, a teacher can:
A. discuss with children about possible kinds of fuel that can be used for cooking, along with a short film
B. show pictures of fuels on a chart
C. ask children to list different fuels
D. show some samples of fuels in the class

141. The skills required to read a map include:
A. ability to understand relative position of places, distances and directions
B. excellent drawing and painting skills
C. ability to use calculations and sketch positions on a globe
D. excellent communication skills to draw out the expressive ability

142. It has been observed that the process of digestion is faster inside the stomach than outside because:
A. the food is churned in the stomach thereby increasing the surface area for quicker enzyme action
B. the digestive juices inside the stomach are acidic, while outside they are alkaline
C. the amount of digestive juices produced in the stomach in the presence of food is much more
D. the digestive juices when kept outside the stomach become inactive

143. The idea of showing a sample of a railway ticket in the EVS textbook is to:
A. give them an opportunity to interact with real information and develop the skill of observation
B. give the students an idea of the rail fare
C. provide them the knowledge of various abbreviations used in the ticket
D. enhance the skills of students to arrive at conclusions

144. Which of the following statements is ***not*** an objective of teaching EVS at the primary level?
A. To internalise the values of concern for life and environment
B. Arouse curiosity about the natural and social environment
C. Engage in exploratory and hands-on activities that lead to the development
D. To load learners with terms and definitions for assessment

145. An egret bird is often seen on a buffalo's back. This is because the egret:
A. feeds on insects present in the grass
B. loves to sing while sitting on the buffalo's back
C. rests after flying for a while
D. feeds on parasites on the buffalo's back

146. Which of the following represents one of the objectives of teaching EVS at Primary School?
A. To connect the experiences of the learners in school with the outside world
B. To make learners aware of technical terms and definitions
C. To assess technical terms related to EVS
D. To inform the learners about the books they should read to expand their knowledge

147. The difference between boiling and evaporation is that:
A. changing of boiling liquid into vapour can be seen but evaporation cannot be seen
B. boiling causes a change of state of water while evaporation does not
C. evaporation can take place at any temperature while boiling cannot
D. boiling causes reduction in volume of liquid while evaporation does not

148. A man blood group 'O' marries a woman with blood group 'A'. The chance of their first child having blood group 'O' is:
A. 75% B. 50%
C. 100% D. 25%

149. A Shooting Star is a:
A. star which moves with a constant speed
B. shining object which moves with a constant speed in the atmosphere
C. star with a tail at the end
D. meteoroid which catches fire as it enters the Earth's atmosphere

150. At the primary stage, assessments should consist of:
A. home assignments and class assignments every week to rate young learners under the categories of pass or fail
B. continuous and unstructured teacher observations to be shared with learners and parents
C. formal tests and games done every week and recorded in the Report Card
D. half-yearly and annual examinations at the end of the year

Answers

1	2	3	4	5	6	7	8	9	10
B	B	D	D	C	A	D	D	D	A
11	**12**	**13**	**14**	**15**	**16**	**17**	**18**	**19**	**20**
C	B	B	A	B	D	B	D	B	D
21	**22**	**23**	**24**	**25**	**26**	**27**	**28**	**29**	**30**
A	D	D	A	B	A	D	B	A	A
31	**32**	**33**	**34**	**35**	**36**	**37**	**38**	**39**	**40**
C	B	B	B	D	B	B	C	A	A
41	**42**	**43**	**44**	**45**	**46**	**47**	**48**	**49**	**50**
D	D	C	D	D	A	A	B	C	A
51	**52**	**53**	**54**	**55**	**56**	**57**	**58**	**59**	**60**
B	A	B	B	A	B	B	B	D	C
61	**62**	**63**	**64**	**65**	**66**	**67**	**68**	**69**	**70**
C	A	D	A	C	A	C	B	A	B
71	**72**	**73**	**74**	**75**	**76**	**77**	**78**	**79**	**80**
D	A	C	B	D	C	A	A	B	D
81	**82**	**83**	**84**	**85**	**86**	**87**	**88**	**89**	**90**
A	D	D	B	B	D	A	D	B	C
91	**92**	**93**	**94**	**95**	**96**	**97**	**98**	**99**	**100**
B	B	B	C	D	A	A	B	B	B
101	**102**	**103**	**104**	**105**	**106**	**107**	**108**	**109**	**110**
D	C	A	B	D	B	D	C	C	C
111	**112**	**113**	**114**	**115**	**116**	**117**	**118**	**119**	**120**
B	A	A	D	B	A	A	D	A	C
121	**122**	**123**	**124**	**125**	**126**	**127**	**128**	**129**	**130**
D	C	D	D	C	C	D	D	C	A
131	**132**	**133**	**134**	**135**	**136**	**137**	**138**	**139**	**140**
B	C	A	A	B	A	C	D	D	A
141	**142**	**143**	**144**	**145**	**146**	**147**	**148**	**149**	**150**
A	A	A	D	D	A	C	B	D	B

Explanatory Answers

1. Though a traditional pedagogical teaching approach gives emphasis on the teacher's role as the holder of the wisdom, the teacher as facilitator, puts the onus on the students to become involved in their own learning, which is by virtue of their potential to create knowledge and make meaning by their own efforts and application of I.Q. The facilitator's is supposed to introduce subjects of discussion, encourage sharing of perspectives, and integrate students' share experiences. A good facilitator stimulates his/her students' thinking, encourage exploration, make associations and be a connector.

2. A gifted child is identified by his/her educational performance in school as to how talented or laudable he/she is in his/her studies. As far as the characteristics of gifted children are concerned, below average mental processes cannot be a characteristic of such children because it pertains to their mental ability to perceive the things taught to them or what appears to them. Mental process or mental functions are terms often used interchangeably for all the things that children can do with their minds. Of course, the event of perceiving something is different from the entire process, or capacity of perception, i.e., one's ability to perceive things.

4. Students come to learning situations with already formulated knowledge, ideas and understandings they have. Such previous knowledge works as the raw materials for the new knowledge they create. However,

if they are provided with the situations that prompt them to learn, it helps them a lot in solving the problems put before them. For example, a teacher presents a class problem to measure the length of the "Mayflower". Rather than starting the problem by introducing the ruler, the teacher allows students to reflect and to construct their own methods of measurement. It is a sort of providing a learning situation to students. Thus, the teacher should provide a variety of learning situations.

5. It will be incorrect to say that all development and learning in a child proceed at an equal rate; rather development proceeds at varying rates from child to child as well as unevenly within different areas of each child's functioning. Each child is a unique person with an individual pattern and timing of growth, as well as individual personality, temperament, learning style, and experiential and family backgrounds. They have their own individual strengths, needs, and interests; for some children, special learning and developmental needs or abilities are identified.

6. Assessment is essential to allow the students to get the educational support they need to succeed, to see the effectiveness of different educational methods, and to ensure that education budgets are being spent effectively. Inevitably, assessment also risks marking teachers, learners and institutions as successes or failures. In today's world, we have very good multimedia (Computer based) resources which have inbuilt assessment tasks in the concept presentation and teachers should try to use these resources.

7. Divergent thinking is a thought process or method used to generate creative ideas by exploring many possible solutions. It is often used in conjunction with its cognitive opposite, convergent thinking, which follows a particular set of logical steps to arrive at one solution, which in some cases is a 'correct' solution. By contrast, divergent thinking typically occurs in a spontaneous, free-flowing, 'non-linear' manner, such that many ideas are generated in an emergent cognitive fashion.

8. According to Lev Vygotsky (1962), a Russian teacher and psychologist, man learns through his interactions and communications with others. He examined how people's social environments influence the learning process. He suggested that learning takes place through the interactions students have with their peers, teachers, elders and other experts. Consequently, teachers can create a learning environment that maximizes the learner's ability to interact with each other through discussion, collaboration, and feedback.

9. Children are curious beings who use their own logic and abilities to explore the world around them, as they use their sense, their minds and their bodies to find out about and make sense of what they feel and experience in the world around them. They demonstrate their ability to reason, negotiate and think logically. They make decisions and take increasing responsibility for their own learning.

10. Errors made by children are a part of the learning process, as errors are the basis of application and they allow for experimentation. If children are afraid of making errors or mistakes, then they will also be afraid of trying anything new, of being creative, of thinking in a different way to know and explore something. By committing mistakes, they come to know as to where they need to avoid what and where they need to adopt what, as that would enable them to succeed in their efforts to reach the desired goal.

12. Learning styles are just a subset of a much wider range of individual differences affecting the process of language learning. Age, aptitude, motivation, general intelligence, sensory preferences and sociocultural conditions are all examples of other important factors influencing the way learners react to classroom instruction.

Individual-vs group-oriented: The former learners are likely to be independent also in terms of self-esteem and personal identity; they tend to work on the basis of intrinsic motivation, and may like to establish their own working plan; on the other hand, group-oriented people may be more dependent on a group or an external authority to define their personal identity and social role; they tend to be motivated by extrinsic motivations; they may benefit by being provided with a clearly described working plan.

14. In describing age old nature-nurture controversy, by nature, we mean inborn biological givens—the hereditary information we receive from our parents at the moment of conception. By nurture, we mean the complex forces of the physical and social world that influence our biological makeup and psychological experiences before and after birth.

15. Since the advent of television, mass media have become prominent socialization agents. The use of more personalized forms of media, such as text messaging and participation in social networking sites, has expanded exponentially in recent years. Media are rich sources of information about government, politics, and current affairs. Media also establish linkages between leaders, institutions, and citizens. In contrast to typing and mailing a letter, it is easier than ever for people to contact leaders directly using e-mail and Facebook.

17. A primary school teacher should adopt a Instructional Behaviours That Motivate Students by helping them to set achievable goals for themselves. Failure to atain unrealistic goals can disappoint and frustrate students. Encourage students to focus on their continued improvement, not just on their grade on any one test or assignment. Help students evaluate their progress by encouraging them to critique their own work, analyze their strengths, and work on their weaknesses. For example, consider asking students to submit self-evaluation forms with one or two assignments.

18. Socialization is the process by which human infants begin to acquire the skills necessary to perform as a functioning member of their society, and is the most influential learning process one can experience. The family is the primary agency of socialisation. It is here that the child develops an initial sense of self and habit-training—eating, sleeping etc. To a very large extent, the indoctrination of the child, whether in primitive or modem complex society, occurs within the circle of the primary family group. The child's first human relationships are with the immediate members of his family—mother or nurse, siblings, father and other close relatives.

20. Dyslexia, also known as reading disorder, is characterized by trouble with reading despite normal intelligence. Different people are affected to varying degrees. Problems may include difficulties in spelling words, reading quickly, writing words, "sounding out" words in the head, pronouncing words when reading aloud and understanding what one reads.

21. The period from birth to two years of age is a critical time for an infant's health, growth and development. New parents and parents-to-be will find information here to help their children with the best possible start in life.

23. Growth and development is one of the important subject of psychology. Development implies changes in shape, form or structure resulting in improved working. It implies qualitative changes.

Development proceeds from general to specific responses: It moves from a generalized to localized behaviour. The newborn infant moves its whole body at one time instead of moving only one part of it. It makes random kicking with its legs before it can coordinate the leg muscles well enough to crawl or to walk.

25. Accommodation: A part of adaptation involves changing or altering our existing schemas in light of new information, a process known as accommodation. Accommodation involves altering existing schemas, or ideas, as a result of new information or new experiences.

91. Perimeter of square = 20 cm

$\therefore$ Side of square $= \frac{20}{4} = 5\text{cm}$

Breadth of rectangle = 5 cm

Length of rectangle = 5 × 2

= 10 cm

Area of rectangle $= l \times b$

= 10 × 5

= 50 cm^2.

92. Volume of box A = 20 × 18 × 15 cm^3

= 5400 cm^3

Volume of box B = 18 × 12 × 5 cm^3

= 1080 cm^3

Clearly, 1080 × 5 = 5400

$\therefore$ Volume of box A is 5 times the volume of box B.

93. A. Area of square = 10 × 10

= 100 cm^2

Area of rectangle $= 10 \times \frac{1}{10} \times 100 = 100\text{cm}^2$

B. 1 m 5 cm = 105 cm

1.5 m = 150 cm

C. $0.40 = \frac{40}{100} = \frac{4}{10}$

$0.4 = \frac{4}{10}$

D. $₹\frac{3}{4} = \frac{300}{4}$paise

= 75 paise

$₹ 0.75 = \frac{75}{100} \times 100 = 75$ paise

Clearly, 1 m 5 cm ≠ 1.5 m.

94. Cost of 1 orange $= ₹ 5\frac{1}{2}$

$= ₹\frac{11}{2}$

$\therefore$ Cost of 18 oranges $= ₹\frac{11}{2} \times 18$

= ₹ 99

Again cost of 1 kg of apple = ₹ 80

Cost of $\frac{7}{4}$ kg of apples $= ₹ 80 \times \frac{7}{4}$

= ₹ 140

Total cost = 140 + 99

= 239.

110. Given number = 70560

The place value of 5 = 500

The place value of 6 = 60

The product of 500 × 60 = 30,000.

111. 43) 3010301 (70007

```
301
 301
 301
  ×
```

∴ Quotient = 70007.

112. The product of 3001 × 101 = 303101

```
 303101
-300311
   2790
```

∴ Required number = 2790

113. LCM of 36 and 60 = 180

HCF of 18 and 45 = 9

According to the question

$$\frac{180}{9} = 20.$$

114. 10 tens + 11 hundreds + 12 ones

= 10 × 10 + 11 × 100 + 12 × 1

= 100 + 1100 + 12 = 1212.

115. 1 × 42 = 2 × 3 × 7

2 × 21

3 × 14

6 × 7

∴ factors of 42 are 1, 2, 3, 6, 7, 14, 21 & 42

Hence, number of factors of 42 is 8.

116. 12) 3488 (290

```
 24
 108
 108
   8
```

11) 2478 (225

```
 22
 27
 22
  58
  55
   3
```

Difference between the remainders in both cases = (8 – 3) = 5.

117. 8 : 18 a.m. P ———— Q 10 : 28 p.m.

Time taken by the train to reach Q

= 12 hrs + 2 hrs 10 minutes

= 14 hrs 10 minutes.

118.

14 L	280 mL
18 L	830 mL
33 L	110 mL

$$15 \times \frac{3}{2} L = \frac{45}{2} L$$

$$= 22.5 \text{ L}$$

33 L + 110 mL – 22.5 L = 10.5 L + 110 mL

∴ Mixture left = 10 L 610 mL

119. $\text{Rest} = 1 - \frac{1}{4}$

$$= \frac{3}{4}$$

$$\frac{3}{4} \div \frac{12}{1} = \frac{3}{4} \times \frac{1}{12}$$

$$= \frac{1}{16}$$

∴ Required part $= \frac{1}{16}$.

120. The number of seconds in 6 hrs

= 6 × 60 × 60

= 21600

$$\text{Required days} = \frac{21600}{60 \times 24}$$

= 15 days.

130. Acid rain is a result of air pollution. When any type of fuel is burnt, lots of different chemicals are produced. The smoke that comes from a fire or the fumes that come out of a car exhaust don't just contain the sooty grey particles that you can see - they also contains lots of invisible gases that can be even more harmful to our environment.

Power stations, factories and cars all burn fuels and therefore they all produce polluting gases. Some of these gases (especially nitrogen oxides and sulphur dioxide) react with the tiny droplets of water in clouds to form sulphuric and nitric acids. The rain from these clouds then falls as very weak acid - which is why it is known as "acid rain".

131. The **Seventy-first Amendment** of the Constitution of India, officially known as **The Constitution (Seventy-first Amendment) Act, 1992**, amended the Eighth

Schedule to the Constitution so as to include Konkani, Manipuri and Nepali languages, thereby raising the total number of languages listed in the schedule to eighteen. The Eighth Schedule lists languages that the Government of India has the responsibility to develop.

132. 371-C: Special provision with respect to the State of Manipur

1. Notwithstanding anything in this Constitution, the President may, by order made with respect to the State of Manipur, provide for the constitution and functions of a committee of the Legislative Assembly of the State consisting of members of that Assembly elected from the Hill Areas of that State, for the modifications to be made in the rules of business of the Government and in the rules of procedure of the Legislative Assembly of the State and for any special responsibility of the Governor in order to secure the proper functioning of such committee.
2. The Governor shall annually, or whenever so required by the President, make a report to the President regarding the administration of the Hill Areas in the State of Manipur and the executive power of the Union shall extend to the giving of directions to the State as to the administration of the said areas.

137. Winnowing is the process of separating lighter components of a mixture from the heavier ones by using wind or moving air is known as winnowing.

142. Stomach churns the food to mix digestive juices. The food in the stomach is churned into semi solid. The churned semi-solid food is called chime. Gastric juice is secreted from the wall of stomach and mixed with food. Gastric juice contains some enzymes and hydrochloric acid. The enzymes present in the gastric juices break down protein from food. The hydrochloric acid kills the harmful bacteria present if any in the food and helps the gastric enzymes to work.

147.

S.No.	Boiling	Evaporation
1.	It occurs at specific temperature.	It occurs at all temperatures.
2.	It requires heat energy to be supplied by external sources.	In general liquid absorbs heat energy from its surroundings.
3.	It takes place throughout the liquid.	It is a surface phenomenon and occurs only at the surface of the liquid.
4.	It is not accompanied by cooling. Temperature of liquid has increased.	In this process the region surrounding the evaporating liquid gets cooler.
5.	It is rapid and noisy process.	It is slow and quiet process.
6.	Temperature of the liquid remains constant at the boiling point.	Usually the temperature of liquid drops.

149. Meteoroid: A small chunk of rock, no larger than a few feet in diameter, that is travelling through space and enters the Earth's atmosphere; commonly known as a shooting star.

Previous Paper (Solved)

Manipur TET (Paper-I), Exam 2012

(For Classes I to V)

Child Development and Pedagogy

Directions: *Answer the following questions by selecting the most appropriate option.*

1. Development implies
A. Improvement in physical
B. Improvement in emotional
C. Improvement in social
D. All of these

2. According to Ryburn's divisions, stages of later childhood is?
A. 0–3 yrs B. 3–6 yrs
C. 6–8 yrs D. 8–12 yrs

3. The number of chromosomes in human cells are
A. 23 pairs B. 24 pairs
C. 46 pairs D. 48 pairs

4. Environment, training and education affects intelligence.
A. True B. False
C. True to an extent D. Not valid

5. Intelligence does not differ due to sex differences.
A. True B. False
C. True to an extent D. Not valid

6. Gifted or Genius I.Q. is
A. 140 and above B. 120 to 140
C. 110 to 120 D. 90 to 110

7. A good teacher should not be
A. sincere B. impartial
C. dominating D. competent

8. How many stages of moral development are associated with Koblberg?
A. 7 stages B. 4 stages
C. 2 stages D. 6 stages

9. Whose name is associated with the ideas of general intelligence ("g" factor)?
A. Charles Spearman B. Robert Sternbery
C. Howard Gardner D. E.L. Thorndrike

10. "Interest may refer to the motivating force that impels us to attend to a person, a thing, or an activity" was said by
A. Freemen B. Craw and Crow
C. Sorenson D. Froebel

11. The reliability of a good evaluation process is one
A. which actually tests what is set out of test
B. which produces the same result under differences but comparable conditions
C. which is realistic, practical and efficient
D. which provides feedback to the students

12. Army Beta Test is used for
A. Group test B. Individual test
C. Personality test D. Performance test

13. The Standford-Binet Intelligence scale is arranged by
A. Age levels B. Types of items
C. Both A and B D. None of these

14. Which of the following is use as an audio visual aid in the classroom?
A. Tape recorder B. T.V.
C. Radio D. Chalkboard

15. Intelligence means ________ capacity.
A. innate B. memory
C. skill D. acquired

16. The main aim of inclusive education is
A. to conduct the test
B. to prepare the result
C. to know the diversity of class
D. to organise materials to be targeted

17. A creative child has
A. a good academic record
B. a large vocabulary
C. fluency of expression
D. I.Q. above normal

18. Dyslexia is a
A. reading disorder
B. behaviour disorder
C. mathematical disorder
D. mental disorder

19. Script of blind is
A. Greek B. Arabic
C. Braille D. Italy

20. If the students do not understand what is taught in the class, the teacher should
A. proceed to the next lesson
B. check the previous knowledge

C. teach the lesson again giving more example
D. ask question relating to the lesson

21. Learning by observing is learning by
A. watching B. thinking
C. imitation D. doing

22. What is the best techniques of teaching at primary level?
A. Self-learning
B. Game technique
C. Practical technique
D. Traditional blackboard and chalk techniques

23. Motivation is release of ________ by proceeding towards a goal.
A. tension B. power
C. pride D. knowledge

24. The mental elements that make up our problem-solving experience includes
A. perception B. images
C. symbol D. All of these

25. Memory involves the mental functions of
A. learning B. retaining
C. remembering D. All of these

26. Attention is determined largely by
A. the external objects B. their situations
C. their conditions D. All of these

27. Factors on which interest depends are
A. individual affairs
B. typical individual interest
C. certain individual psycho-physical condition
D. All of these

28. Artificial and extrinsic motivation are
A. drives
B. learning activity
C. knowledge of progress
D. praise and blame

29. Who said, "Personality is the sum total of innate and acquired dispositions"?
A. Boring B. Cattell
C. Valentine D. Munn

30. Which behaviour could not be predicted by measures of a personality traits?
A. Actual behaviour
B. Individual behaviour
C. Good behaviour
D. Abnormal behavour

Language-I : English-I

Directions: *Read the following passages and answer the questions that follow:*

PASSAGE-1

All over the countryside, wherever one goes, indication of techniques are visible to the seeing eye. By technique is meant an exercise of skill acquired by practice and directed to a well-foreseen end. It is the name for the action of any of the powers after they have been so improved by training as to perform that action with certainty and success.

31. 'Skill' in the passage means
A. the ability to do things by hand
B. the ability to master technique
C. the ability acquired by experience to make success sure
D. the ability to practise

32. 'Technique' in the passage means the use of skill
A. for handling tools and machinery
B. for a definite purpose
C. for improving the countryside
D. for observation and analysis

33. The word which has the same meaning as 'aim' in the passage is
A. exercise B. practice
C. success D. end

PASSAGE-2

It is this neighbourly feeling that binds society together. In very olden times, however, people did not think like this. They were then savages, little better than beasts and fought with one another. But gradually men became civilized. They saw that if they behaved in this way, society would be destroyed. So they made certain rules to guide them.

34. People in the olden times saw that society would be destroyed
A. if they fought one another
B. if they let neighbourly feeling bind society
C. if they became civilized
D. if they made rules to guide them

35. Early men made rules to guide them because
A. they were savages
B. they became civilized
C. they were little better than beasts
D. they wanted to continue fighting in a civilized way

36. The word from the passage that have the opposite meaning of 'Vague' is
A. feeling B. better
C. certain D. conduct

Directions: *Choose the correct answers:*

37. When a noun or pronoun is used as the subject of a verb, it is in the

A. nominative case B. dative case
C. instrumental case D. ablative case

38. Verbs which require objects are called
A. finite verbs B. non-finite verbs
C. intransitive verbs D. transitive verbs

39. How many genders are there in English?
A. 5 B. 4
C. 3 D. 2

40. Inanimate objects or abstract qualities which denote strength, courage, might and greatness are said to be of ________.
A. masculine gender
B. feminine gender
C. both masculine and feminine gender
D. no gender

Directions: *Choose the correct modal verbs to fill in the blanks in each of the given sentences:*

41. ______ danger come, we shall remain united.
A. Will B. Would
C. Should D. May

42. He asked me whether the news ______ be true.
A. should B. could
C. would D. may

43. It is quiet late, I ______ go home now.
A. must B. would
C. could D. need

Directions: *Choose the correct conjunctions to fill in the blanks in each of the following sentences:*

44. He has not written any letter ______ he went to Mumbai.
A. so B. therefore
C. since D. while

45. Work hard ______ you will fail.
A. or B. but
C. and D. though

Directions: *In each of the following questions there are four sentences. Only one of them has correct punctuation marks. Choose it in each sentence:*

46. A. He said, "has Mary come?"
B. He said, "Has Mary come?"
C. He said has Mary come?
D. He said, "Has Mary come"?

47. A. I passed my M.A. in Manipur University.
B. I passed my M.A. at Manipur University.
C. I passed my M.A. from Manipur University.
D. I passed my M.A. with Manipur University.

Directions: *In each of the following questions there are four sentences. Only one of them is correct. Choose the correct sentence in each of them:*

48. A. The subject has been treated in a masterly way.
B. The subject has been treated masterly.
C. The subject has been treated masteringly.
D. The subject has been treated in a mastering way.

49. A. This pen is more preferable than that pen.
B. This pen is more preferable to that pen.
C. This pen is preferable than that pen.
D. This pen is preferable to that pen.

Directions: *Choose the correct sounds produced by the following animals:*

50. Jackals
A. bray B. howl
C. growl D. squeal

51. Sheep
A. bleat B. trumpet
C. low D. grunt

Directions: *Choose the young ones of the following:*

52. Elephant
A. kid B. calf
C. cub D. fawn

53. Eagle
A. eaglet B. eagling
C. leveret D. baby eagle

Directions: *Choose the one word substitute for the following:*

54. That cannot be corrected
A. incorrectable B. illegible
C. incorrigible D. incredible

55. Easily breakable
A. flexible B. brittle
C. fragile D. delicate

Directions: *Choose the correct answers:*

56. Which of the following is the last step in programmes for effective teaching?
A. Follow up B. Assignment
C. Appraisal D. Farewell function

57. How many phases are involved in the teaching of English?
A. Two B. Three
C. Four D. Five

58. Which of the following is accepted in all parts of the world as the standard form of English?
A. British Received Pronounciation
B. American English
C. Australian English
D. Indian English

59. Which of the following grammar is taught incidentally?
A. Prescriptive Grammar B. Theoretical Grammar
C. Functional Grammar D. Traditional Grammar

60. Which of the following types of grammar lay more emphasis on rules?
A. Transformational-Generative
B. Scholarly
C. Prescriptive
D. Descriptive

Mathematics

Directions: *Answer the following questions by selecting the most appropriate option.*

61. The difference between the place-value and face-value of the digit 7 in the number 22750 is
A. 6993 B. 693
C. 63 D. 0

62. The sum of the greatest and smallest 5-digit numbers formed by the digits 1, 0, 9, 6, 7 (without repeating the digits) is
A. 108289 B. 97610
C. 98289 D. 107610

63. The digital root of any 5-digit number cannot be
A. 1 B. 4
C. 12 D. 7

64. The smallest 5-digit number that has 9 and 11 as factors is
A. 10701 B. 10098
C. 10890 D. 10089

65. The number of prime numbers lying between 62 and 100 is
A. 5 B. 6
C. 7 D. 8

66. By selling a watch for ₹ 1125 a dealer loses ₹ 50. Had he sold it for ₹ 1200, he would have
A. a loss of ₹ 25
B. a profit of ₹ 25
C. a profit of ₹ 50
D. neither loss nor profit

67. A girl has a 14 m 35 cm long ribbon. From it she cuts 12 pieces each of length 1 m 5 cm. The length of the remaining portion is
A. 1 m 75 cm B. 2 m 25 cm
C. 1 m 25 cm D. 2 m 65 cm

68. The product of two numbers is 23985 and three times one of them is 615. The other number is
A. 39 B. 117
C. 156 D. 127

69. A sum of money is divided among three persons A, B and C. If A and B together get ₹ 180, B and C together get ₹ 169 and C and A together get ₹ 191, then the sum of money is
A. ₹ 540 B. ₹ 500
C. ₹ 270 D. ₹ 250

70. The sum of two numbers is five times their difference. If the smaller number is 234, then the greater number is
A. 468 B. 368
C. 432 D. 351

71. The greatest number which when diminished by 5 will divide each of the number 50, 74 and 122 leaving the same remainder 2 in each case, is
A. 19 B. 24
C. 28 D. 29

72. The cost of 12 copies of a book is ₹ 1140. The cost of 17 copies is
A. ₹ 1615 B. ₹ 1620
C. ₹ 1632 D. ₹ 1637

73. The average weight of eight students in a school is 56 kg. Three of the students weight 52 kg, 57 kg and 69 kg. The average weight of the other five is
A. 57 kg B. 56 kg
C. 55 kg D. 54 kg

74. $2\frac{1}{4} \div 1\frac{1}{2}$ of $\frac{3}{7} - 1\frac{1}{2} =$
A. 0 B. 2
C. $\frac{3}{4}$ D. $-\frac{1}{2}$

75. A girl after giving away $\frac{1}{3}$ of her pocket money to one of her friends and $\frac{2}{3}$ of the remainder to another friend has ₹ 50 left with her. The total amount of her pocket money is
A. ₹ 135
B. ₹ 216
C. ₹ 225
D. ₹ 243

76. The difference between 5.16 and $4\frac{1}{4}$ is
A. 0.90 B. 0.91
C. 1.09 D. 1.01

77. The population of a village is 8400. If the population increases by 5% every year, then after two years the population of the village will be
A. 9240 B. 9265
C. 9261 D. 9288

78. To cover a distance of 400 m, a boy has to run 5 times around a square park. The area of the square park is
A. 400 m^2 B. 441 m^2
C. 576 m^2 D. 625 m^2

79. The measure of an angle when 2 times its supplement exceeds 4 times its complement by 70°, is
A. 45° B. 40°
C. 35° D. 30°

80. Observe the succession of numbers
2, 5, 10, 17, ...
The next two numbers will be
A. 26, 37 B. 25, 37
C. 25, 36 D. 26, 36

81. When asked to measure the distance between your school and its gate by pace, two students A and B gave different answers of 35 paces and 31 paces respectively. It can be concluded that
A. B misses 4 counts
B. A counts twice in each of 4 of his paces
C. A's pace is longer than that of B
D. A's pace is shorter than that of B

82. In the following addition sum, the letters stand for distinct digits:

	A	D	A
+	E	B	C
C	A	C	B

If A stands for 7, then D, E stand respectively for
A. 9, 3 B. 3, 9
C. 8, 4 D. 4, 8

83. How many lines of symmetry are there for a circle?
A. 1 B. 2
C. 3 D. Infinite

84. To round a given number to the nearest 100 means
A. to find the greatest multiple of 100 which is less than or equal to the number
B. to find the smallest multiple of 100 which is greater than or equal to the number
C. to find the multiple of 100 which is nearest to the number, if the number is not midway between two consecutive multiples of 100 and to find the larger of the two consecutive multiples of 100 if the number is midway between them
D. to replace each of the digits in ones place and tens place by zero

85. How old is a child whose mental age is 9 and I.Q. is 75?
A. 12 years B. 10 years
C. 9 years D. 8 years

86. The body temperature of a patient suffering from viral fever is found to be 39°C. This temperature is higher than the body temperature 98.6°F of a normal person by
A. 3.5°F B. 3.6°F
C. 2.5°F D. 2.6°F

87. Two angles of a triangle are complementary and their difference is 16°. The smallest angle of the triangle is
A. 32° B. 35°
C. 36° D. 37°

88. 45% of 55 exceeds 32% of 75 by
A. $\frac{1}{4}$ B. $\frac{1}{2}$
C. $\frac{3}{4}$ D. $\frac{3}{5}$

89. When asked to give an example of a pair of perpendicular lines a student's response was 'opposite edges of a table'. It implies that the student:
A. misunderstands parallelism as perpendicularity
B. has no concept of line
C. is misinformed
D. does not read well

90. Study the pattern:

$$1 + 2 + 3 + ... + 10 = 55$$
$$11 + 12 + 13 + ... + 20 = 155$$
$$21 + 22 + 23 + ... + 30 = 255$$

If you continue the pattern, the right hand side of the 10th equation will be
A. 955 B. 1055
C. 1155 D. 1255

Environmental Studies

Directions: *Answer the following questions by selecting the most appropriate option.*

91. Which of the following internal organs of our body helps in the digestion of fats?
A. Large intestine B. Small intestine
C. Stomach D. Liver

92. Which one of the following is a true statement?
A. Food should be eaten hurriedly
B. Vegetables should first be cut and then washed
C. We should eat all types of food items
D. All vegetables should be eaten raw

93. When a disaster happens, the first responders are
A. The State Government
B. The Non-Government Organisation
C. The Disaster Response Force
D. The local people

94. Which is the nearest star to the earth?
A. Pole Star B. Great Bear
C. Sun D. Proxima Centauri

95. The blood is circulated to different parts of the body by the
A. kidney B. heart
C. lungs D. cerebrum

96. For better results, dry-cleaning method should be used in cleaning
A. woollen clothes B. nylon clothes
C. cotton clothes D. acrylic clothes

97. Which one of the following is not considered as a sense?
A. Sense of hearing B. Sense of thinking
C. Sense of smell D. Sense of taste

98. One of the serious diseases caused by the polluted air is
A. Asthma B. Dysentry
C. Cholera D. Jaundice

99. Industries take major share in causing
A. land pollution B. water pollution
C. air pollution D. noise pollution

100. The condition of temperature, rainfall and wind of a place at a particular time is known as
A. climate B. precipitation
C. condensation D. weather

101. Which of the following is **not** a characteristic of natural resource?
A. All the gifts of nature are natural resources
B. Man gets valuable resources from nature
C. Our natural resources are limited
D. Availability of resources differs from country to country

102. What benefit will Manipur get best if the railway line from Jiribam is further extended up to Imphal?
A. Bulk movement of goods and passengers
B. Inclusion in the railway map of India
C. Improvement in State economy
D. Easy contact with other States

103. In order to help us grow and repair our body we should take food containing
A. Vitamins B. Proteins
C. Minerals D. Carbohydrates

104. We should eat plenty of vegetables, fresh fruits and sprouted grains because they are rich
A. energy giving foods
B. body-building foods
C. bone strengthening foods
D. disease protective foods

105. Which one of the following may be taken as a socio-natural disaster?
A. Earthquake
B. Flood
C. Environmental pollution
D. Road accident

106. Which of the following internal organs helps in keeping our body properly moist?
A. Kidneys B. Arteries
C. Veins D. Intestine

107. Some children suffer from a disease called Night Blindness. This is caused due to lack of
A. vitamin-A B. vitamin-B
C. vitamin-C D. iodine

108. To locate any place on the earth we should find out
A. its longitude and latitude
B. the major city lying near it
C. its relevant State and Country
D. its distance from the equator

109. In order to read maps easily, one must be fully acquainted with
A. the conventional symbols
B. the scale of the map
C. its latitudinal extent
D. its relief features

110. How was the Imphal Valley formed?
A. Uplift of the ocean floor
B. Wearing down of highland area
C. Sedimentation of an ancient lake
D. Draining out of stagnant water

111. To which State does the Indira Gandhi Canal provide water?
A. Tamil Nadu B. Punjab
C. Kerala D. Rajasthan

112. The northern part of the western coastal plain of India is known as the
A. Northern Circars B. Konkan Coast
C. Coromandel Coast D. Malabar Coast

113. Which one of the following valleys lies close to Mt. Iso, the highest peak in Manipur?
A. Khoupum valley B. Barak valley
C. Imphal valley D. Dzuko valley

114. Choose the odd one out of the following pair
A. National Bird – Peacock
B. National Flower – Lotus
C. National Animal – Lion
D. National Anthem – Jana Gana Mana

115. An area protected generally for conservation of rare species of wildlife is termed as
A. Zoological Garden B. National Park
C. Biosphere Reserve D. Wildlife Sanctuary

116. In the Anglo-Manipur War of 1891, Manipur fell into the hands of the British troops and the British occupied Kangla on–
A. 22nd March B. 24th March
C. 27th April D. 13th August

117. Which one of the following activities happened on the life of Hijam Irabot is **not** related to the second Nupi Lal of Manipur?
A. 3 years imprisonment at Imphal Jail
B. Influence of Marxist ideology at Sylhet Jail
C. Foundation of the Manipur Praja Sammelini
D. Creation of the Nikhil Manipuri Mahasabha

118. Haipou Jadonang was sentenced to death by the British authorities for–
A. the revolt against the British
B. the unification of Zemeis, Liangmeis and Rongmeis
C. becoming a follower of Mahatma Gandhi
D. Standing against the propagation of Christianity

119. In the course of freedom movement in India, the formation of the Provisional Government of Free India was proclaimed by
A. Mahatma Gandhi
B. Jawaharlal Nehru
C. Shaheed Bhagat Singh
D. Subhas Chandra Bose

120. Name the person who received all the three prestigious National and International Awards, namely, Padmasri, Bharat Ratna and Nobel Prize.
A. Satyajit Roy
B. Hargobind Khurana
C. Mother Teresa
D. Rabindranath Tagore

Language-II : English-II

Directions: *Read the following passages and answer the questions that follow:*

PASSAGE-1

Pasteur made a very useful experiment to show the difference between pure and impure air. He filled some glasses with broth. He exposed some of them to the stuffy air in the room and sealed them again. He exposed some to fresh air of the field and sealed them up. Finally he opened some on the top of a mountain and sealed them up too. What was the result? The broth in the glasses opened in the stuffy room had decayed, the broth opened in the field had not decayed very much and the broth opened on the mountain was free from germs.

121. Pasteur made the experiment to show
A. he was a great scientist
B. broth can be opened anywhere
C. the difference between pure and impure air
D. how to seal glasses with broth

122. The experiment shows that
A. there is no difference between stuffy air and fresh air
B. air on the mountain is pure
C. we should go to mountains to take food
D. we should build our houses on mountains to get pure air

123. The broth in the glasses opened in the stuffy room had decayed because
A. the glasses were dirty
B. the broth was mixed with germs as part of the experiment
C. the air in the stuffy room was impure
D. Both A and B

124. Find the word from the passage that has the same meaning as "outcome".
A. Useful B. Stuffy
C. Free D. Result

PASSAGE-2

India is wedded to democracy. She is the largest democracy in the world. There is the 'rule of the people'. But unfortunately, the elected leaders soon lose their contacts with the people. They also do not care to keep contact with their party under whose banner they won the electoral battle. They give up their party at the slightest hint of a possible gain. Defection was not in vogue up to Shastri's time. However, there were hundreds of defections during Indira Gandhi's glorious decade in the states as well as at the centre. Defection knew no bounds during the Janata rule.

125. India is the largest democracy in the world because
A. she has the second largest population in the world
B. there is the 'rule of the people'
C. elected rulers lose contact with the people
D. defection is in vogue

126. The unfortunate thing of Indian democracy is that
A. she is wedded to democracy
B. the rulers are elected by the people
C. the elected leaders soon lose their contacts with the people
D. defection was not in vogue up to Shastri's time

127. Elected rulers in India defect because
A. they are selfish
B. democracy is not possible without political defections
C. India is the largest democracy in the world
D. the people who elect them tell them to do so

128. Find the word from the passage that has the opposite meaning of "infamous".
A. Wedded B. Glorious
C. Banner D. Possible

Directions: *Choose the correct determiners:*

129. I have got ________ milk.
A. any B. some
C. few D. more

130. How ________ cows do you have?
A. much B. few
C. many D. any

131. She has ________ confidence in herself.
A. many B. few
C. little D. any

Directions: *Choose the correct prepositions:*

132. I cannot approve ________ such a heinous act.
A. with B. by
C. for D. of

133. She is brooding ________ her past life.
A. at B. over
C. about D. of

134. Lai Haraoba is indigenous _______ Manipur.
A. in B. to
C. from D. of

Directions: *Choose the correct meaning of the phrases:*

135. Dead beat
A. Beaten to death
B. A person who never pays his debts
C. A person who beats people to death
D. to be very tired

136. An open book
A. A book which is kept open
B. Someone or something which is easy to understand
C. A book which everybody can read freely
D. None of these

137. Swan song
A. A beautiful song
B. Song sung by a swan
C. Final appearance
D. A song sung to trap swans

Directions: *Choose the correctly spelt words:*

138. A. Abbreviation
B. Abriviation
C. Abbriviation
D. Abreviation

139. A. Appendisitis
B. Apendicitis
C. Apendisitis
D. Appendicitis

140. A. Diferrentiate
B. Differrentiate
C. Diferentiate
D. Differentiate

Directions: *Choose the correct answers to replace the bold words and improve the sentences:*

141. Seeing a little boy crying I asked him **that why was he crying**.
A. why he was crying
B. that he crying why
C. that was why he was crying
D. why was he crying

142. Please do not object **to me watching** while you work.
A. against me watching
B. against me to watch
C. to my watching
D. at my watching

143. The only furniture in the room was a **wooden and broken chair**.
A. broken wooden
B. wooden, broken
C. broken, wooden
D. broken and wooden

Directions: *In the following questions, a sentence has been broken into five parts and jumbled up. Choose the correct order of parts to make meaningful sentences:*

144. a. lies
b. is too limited
c. to say
d. scientific understanding
e. where the truth
A. a b d e c B. a b c d e
C. d b c e a D. b a e c d

145. a. to send b. not needed
c. to me d. these books
e. it is
A. b a c e d B. c b e a d
C. e b a d c D. e b a c d

146. a. cannot be b. endured
c. what d. must be
e. cured
A. a b c d e B. c a e d b
C. c d e a b D. c a e b d

Directions: *Choose the correct answers which can substitute the following words/phrases:*

147. A person who says one thing and does another.
A. Liar B. Cheater
C. Vagabond D. Hypocrite

148. A woman who has never married.
A. Widow B. Spinster
C. Maid D. Dame

149. A place where coins are made.
A. Coinery B. Mint
C. Bank D. Coinage

150. A bag for carrying school books.
A. Suitcase B. Carry-bag
C. Satchel D. Hand-bag

Answers

1	**2**	**3**	**4**	**5**	**6**	**7**	**8**	**9**	**10**
D	D	C	A	C	A	B	D	A	B
11	**12**	**13**	**14**	**15**	**16**	**17**	**18**	**19**	**20**
B	A	A	B	A	C	D	A	C	C
21	**22**	**23**	**24**	**25**	**26**	**27**	**28**	**29**	**30**
A	B	A	D	D	D	D	D	C	A
31	**32**	**33**	**34**	**35**	**36**	**37**	**38**	**39**	**40**
C	B	D	A	B	C	A	D	B	A
41	**42**	**43**	**44**	**45**	**46**	**47**	**48**	**49**	**50**
C	B	A	C	A	B	C	B	D	B
51	**52**	**53**	**54**	**55**	**56**	**57**	**58**	**59**	**60**
A	B	A	C	C	B	B	A	C	C
61	**62**	**63**	**64**	**65**	**66**	**67**	**68**	**69**	**70**
B	A	D	B	C	B	A	B	C	D
71	**72**	**73**	**74**	**75**	**76**	**77**	**78**	**79**	**80**
B	A	D	B	C	B	C	A	C	A
81	**82**	**83**	**84**	**85**	**86**	**87**	**88**	**89**	**90**
D	B	D	C	A	B	D	C	B	A
91	**92**	**93**	**94**	**95**	**96**	**97**	**98**	**99**	**100**
D	C	D	C	B	A	B	A	B	D
101	**102**	**103**	**104**	**105**	**106**	**107**	**108**	**109**	**110**
B	D	B	D	B	B	A	A	A	C
111	**112**	**113**	**114**	**115**	**116**	**117**	**118**	**119**	**120**
D	B	D	C	D	C	D	A		C
121	**122**	**123**	**124**	**125**	**126**	**127**	**128**	**129**	**130**
C	B	C	D	A	C	A	B	B	C
131	**132**	**133**	**134**	**135**	**136**	**137**	**138**	**139**	**140**
C	D	B	B	D	D	C	A	D	D
141	**142**	**143**	**144**	**145**	**146**	**147**	**148**	**149**	**150**
A	C	C	C	C	B	D	B	B	C

Explanatory Answers

61. Given number = 22750
Place value of 7 = 700
Face value of 7 = 7
Difference = 700 − 7 = 693.

62. Given number = 1, 0, 9, 6, 7
Greatest number = 97610
Smallest number = 10679
Sum = 97610 + 10679 = 108289
∴ Sum of greatest and smallest 5-digit numbers = 108289.

64. 10098 is the factor of both 9 and 11
10890 is the factor of both 9 and 11
But smallest number is 10098.

65. Prime numbers lying between 62 and 100 are 67, 71, 73, 79, 83, 89, 97
there are 7 prime numbers lying between 62 and 100.

66. SP = ₹ 1125, Loss = ₹ 50
CP = Loss + SP = 50 + 1125 = ₹ 1175
Now, SP = ₹ 1200, CP = ₹ 1175
Profit = SP − CP = 1200 − 1175 = ₹ 25.

67. Total length = 14.35 m
Length of 12 pieces = 12 × 1.05 m = 12.60 m
Length of remaining = 14.35 − 12.60 = 1.75 m = 1 m 75 cm.

68. Let numbers are x and y

$$xy = 23985$$

According to the question,

$$3x = 615 \Rightarrow x = \frac{615}{3} = 205$$

$$y = \frac{23985}{205} = 117$$

Hence, other number = 117.

69. $A + B = 180$ ...(*i*)

$B + C = 169$ ...(*ii*)

$C + A = 191$ ...(*iii*)

Adding (*i*), (*ii*) and (*iii*)

$2(A + B + C) = 540$

$A + B + C = \frac{540}{2} = 270$

Hence, sum of money = ₹ 270.

70. Let greater number = x, and

Smaller number = y

$x + y = 5(x - y)$

$\Rightarrow x + 234 = 5x - 5 \times 234$

$\Rightarrow x + 234 = 5x - 1170 \Rightarrow 4x = 1404$

$\Rightarrow x = \frac{1404}{4} = 351$

Hence, greater number = 351.

71. $50 - 2 = 48$, $74 - 2 = 72$, $122 - 2 = 120$

HCF of 48, 72 and 120 = 24

Required no. = 24.

72. Cost of 12 copies of a book = ₹ 1140

Cost of 17 copies of a book = ₹$\frac{1140}{12} \times 17$

= ₹ 95 × 17 = ₹ 1615.

73. Total weight of 8 students = 56 × 8 = 448 kg

Weight of 3 students = 52 + 57 + 69 = 178 kg

Weight of 5 students = 448 − 178 = 270 kg

Average weight of 5 students = $\frac{270}{5}$ = 54 kg.

74. $2\frac{1}{4} \div 1\frac{1}{2}$ of $\frac{3}{7} - 1\frac{1}{2} = \frac{9}{4} \div \frac{3}{2} \times \frac{3}{7} - \frac{3}{2}$

$= \frac{9}{4} \div \frac{9}{14} - \frac{3}{2} = \frac{9}{4} \times \frac{14}{9} - \frac{3}{2} = \frac{7}{2} - \frac{3}{2} = \frac{4}{2} = 2$

75. Let total amount of pocket money = ₹ x

According to the question,

$\frac{x}{3} + \frac{2x}{3} \times \frac{2}{3} + 50 = x$

$\Rightarrow \frac{3x + 4x + 450}{9} = x \quad \Rightarrow 9x - 7x = 450$

$\Rightarrow 2x = 450 \Rightarrow x = 225$

∴ Total amount of her pocket money = ₹ 225.

76. $5.16 - 4\frac{1}{4} = 5.16 - 4.25 = 0.91$.

77. Population after 1 year $= \frac{5}{100} \times 8400 + 8400$

$= 420 + 8400 = 8820$

Population after 2 years $= 8820 + \frac{5}{100} \times 8820$

$= 8820 + 441 = 9261$

Hence, after 2 years the population of the village will be 9261.

78. Perimeter of square $= \frac{400}{5} = 80$ m

Side of square $= \frac{80}{4} = 20$ m

Area of square $= (20)^2 = 400$ m^2.

79. Measure of an angle = $x°$

its supplement angle = $(180 - x)°$

its complement angle = $(90 - x)°$

According to the question,

$2(180 - x) = 4(90 - x) + 70$

$\Rightarrow 360 - 2x = 360 - 4x + 70$

$\Rightarrow 2x = 70 \Rightarrow x = \frac{70°}{2} = 35°$.

80.

2,	5,	10,	17,	26,	37
↓	↓	↓	↓	↓	↓
1^2+1	2^2+1	3^2+1	4^2+1	5^2+1	6^2+1

The next two numbers will be 26, 37.

82. Put A = 7, B = 8, D = 3, E = 9, C = 1

```
  A D A        7 3 7
+ E B C      + 9 8 1
-------      -------
C A C B      1 7 1 8
             C A C B
```

Hence, D, E stand respectively for 3, 9.

85. Actual age $= \frac{\text{Mental age}}{\text{I.Q.}} \times 100 = \frac{9}{75} \times 100$

= 12 years.

86. We have, $\frac{C}{5} = \frac{F-32}{9}$

$\Rightarrow \frac{39}{5} = \frac{F-32}{9} \Rightarrow 5F - 160 = 351$

$\Rightarrow 5F = 351 + 160 = 511$

$\Rightarrow F = \frac{511}{5} = 102.2°F$

Difference = 102.2°F – 98.6°F = 3.6°F.

87. Let smallest angle = $x°$

According to the question,

$x + x + 16 = 90$

$\Rightarrow 2x = 90 - 16 = 74 \Rightarrow x = 37°$

$\therefore$ Smallest angle of the triangle = 37°.

88. 45% of 55 = 32% of 75 + x

$\Rightarrow \frac{45}{100} \times 55 = \frac{32}{100} \times 75 + x$

$\Rightarrow \frac{99}{4} = \frac{96}{4} + x$

$\Rightarrow x = \frac{99}{4} - \frac{96}{4} = \frac{3}{4}$

90. 1 + 2 + 3 + ... + 10 = 55

11 + 12 + 13 + ... + 20 = 155

21 + 22 + 23 + ... + 30 = 255

....

....

91 + 92 + 93 + ... + 100 = 955.

Child Development & Pedagogy

CHILD DEVELOPMENT (PRIMARY SCHOOL CHILD)

CONCEPT OF DEVELOPMENT AND ITS RELATIONSHIP WITH LEARNING

The discipline of Child Development is concerned with the changes in the behaviour of children over time and explains why and how they occur. It aims to describe and explain development in the areas of physical, social, emotional, language and cognitive functioning.

Development and Growth

The term 'development' is used for changes in a person's physical and behavioural traits that emerge in orderly ways and last for a reasonable period of time. The three main characteristics of these changes are progressive, orderly and long lasting. Development refers to both quantitative as well as qualitative changes. It includes changes not only in structure but also in function.

'Growth' refers to physical increase in the size of the body. Increase in weight, height and internal organs is growth. Growth refers to a quantitative change, that is, a change that can be measured.

Growth is only one aspect of the larger process of development. Development continues even when physical changes are not visible. Physical growth slows down considerably after adolescence but development does not.

Stages of Development

The human life span has been divided into the stages of infancy, childhood, adolescence and adulthood.

The period from birth to two years of age is referred to as the period of infancy. In this period the child is totally dependent on the caregiver for the fulfilment of his needs. After birth, this is the period of most rapid growth and development. The child's skills and abilities increase. By the end of infancy he is able to walk, run, communicate his needs verbally, feed himself, identify family members, recognise himself and venture confidently in familiar surroundings.

The period of childhood is from two to twelve years of age. Development at this stage is not as rapid as during infancy. During this period the child refines the skills he has acquired during infancy and learns new skill as well. During childhood he also learns the ways of behaviour that are considered appropriate by the society. The child meets many people outside the family and forms attachments with more people. As the child grows and his thinking capacities mature, he realises that he can do many things. This gives him a feeling of confidence. During this period he becomes more independent though adult guidance is constantly needed. The period of childhood is divided into two stages : the period of early childhood (2–6 years) and middle childhood (6–12 years). The period of early childhood is also referred to as the preschool age because at this age the child is learning skills that will help him to do tasks associated with schooling. The preschooler has mastered the words to ask questions about things and people. He learns about numbers, colours, shapes and the reasons for everyday events. All these concepts develop from actually seeing things and doing various activities. The child in the age group 6–12 years has matured a great deal and is expected to behave more responsibly than the preschooler.

The next stage is referred to as the period of adolescence (12–18 years). The beginning of this period is marked by puberty. Puberty refers to the stage around 11–14 years of the age, when there is a spurt in physical growth. This results in a rapid increase in height and weight and the emergence of secondary sexual characteristics. These rapid physical changes lead to a need for emotional readjustment.

At this age the peer group becomes very important and the adolescent follows the rules and the codes of her group. Feelings of loyalty and pride for the group are very strong. At times the values of the peer group may become more important than those of the family. During adolescence thinking develops further and becomes more complex. The individual can understand and deal with varied situations. He can think of abstract problems and work out their solutions. All this helps him to prepare for the roles and responsibilities, which he will be expected to carry out as an adult.

After the age of 18 years the person is referred to as an adult. Physical changes are completed in this stage and person becomes mature.

Areas of Development

The various developments that take place during the life span of an individual can be classified thus: physical and motor development, social development, emotional development, cognitive and language development.

Physical development refers to the physical changes in the size, structure and proportion of the parts of the body that take place from the moment of conception.

Motor development means the development of control over body movements. This results in increasing coordination between various parts of the body. As a result of physical and motor development the child acquires many abilities. These developments will bring about the change from an infant who at the time of birth is capable of only lying on his back to one who learns to roll over, hold his head, sit, walk, run and climb stairs. The improving coordination between the eye and the hand movements will help him to eat food without smearing it on his face. Gradually he will learn to clothe himself, draw, skip, paint, ride a bicycle and type. As he grows he will refine the skills already acquired as well as develop new ones.

Language development refers to those changes that make it possible for an infant, who in the early months uses crying for communication, to learn words and then sentences to converse fluently. How the child learns to speak grammatically correct sentences is amazing! At first the child indicates his need for water through crying. Then he learns to say ''water''. A little later he says, ''Mummy water'' and finally he speaks a complete sentence, ''Mummy, I want to drink water''. He will be about three years by this time.

Cognitive development concerns the emergence of thinking capabilities in the individual. We can see how the child's thinking develops and changes from one age to the next. The infant is not born with the reasoning and thinking, abilities of adults. In fact, the infant acts as if an object that is removed from his sight has ceased to exist. Gradually he learns that objects and people are permanent and they exist even if he cannot see them. Around five years of age he can understand concepts such as heavy and light, fast and slow, colours and sizes which he did not comprehend earlier. Exploration of the surroundings and the questions regarding the 'why' and 'how' of things result in an increasing store of information. His thought develops but he is still unable to see a situation from another person's point of view. For example, he is unable to understand why another child cannot climb the tree when he can do so. He thinks that everybody else should be able to do what he can and feel the way he does. He believes that all things have life and feelings like him including the sun, stone, pencil and table. A ten year old has learnt to reason and analyze but this ability is limited to real life concrete situations. He cannot usually think in abstract terms or predict future event. The capacity for abstruct thinking develops fully during the period of adolescence. He can now handle complex situations. Thus at each stage of a person's life, the ability to think is qualitatively different and more developed compared to the earlier stage.

Cognitive development is the process of mental development from infancy to adulthood. Cognition refers to the process of 'coming to know', which is accomplished through the gathering and processing of information. It includes perceiving, learning, remembering, problem solving, and thinking about the world. Intelligence is a term difficult to define. Nevertheless, according to a well known definition, it refers to the individual's ability to ''act purposefully, think rationally and deal effectively with the environment''.

Social development refers to the development of those abilities that enable the individual to behave in accordance with the expectations of the society. It is concerned with the child's relationships with people and his ways of interaction with them. The infant instinctively reaches out to the person who approaches him with love and affection. Gradually he learns to recognize his mother and other caregivers and forms attachment to them.

Emotional development refers to the emergence of emotions like anger, joy, delight, happiness, fear, anxiety and sorrow and the socially acceptable ways of expressing them. As the child grows up and becomes aware of acceptable ways of behaviour, a variety of emotions also emerge. As an infant he expresses only discomfort and delight. As he grows older, expressions of joy, happiness, fear, anger and disappointment appear. He learns to express these emotions in a healthy manner. For example, initially the child hits out when angry. Gradually he learns to control this and expresses anger in other ways.

Theories of Child Development and Learning

Maturationist Theory

The maturationist theory was advanced by the work of Arnold Gessell. Maturationists believe that development is a biological process that occurs automatically in predictable, sequential stages over time. This perspective leads many educators and families to assume that young children will acquire knowledge naturally and automatically as they grow physically and become older, provided that they are healthy.

School readiness, according to maturationists, is a state at which all healthy young children arrive when they can perform tasks such as reciting the alphabet and counting; these tasks are required for learning more complex tasks such as reading and arithmetic. Because development and school readiness occur naturally and automatically, maturationists believe the best practices are for parents to teach young children to recite the alphabet and count while being patient and waiting for children to become ready for kindergarten. If a child is developmentally unready for school, maturationists might suggest referrals to transitional kindergartens, retention, or holding children out of school for an additional year. These practices are sometimes used by schools, educators, and parents when a young child developmentally lags behind his or her peers. The young child's underperformance is interpreted as the child needing more time to acquire the knowledge and skills needed to perform at the level of his or her peers.

Environmentalist Theory

Theorists such as John Watson, B.F. Skinner, and Albert Bandura contributed greatly to the environmentalist perspective of development. Environmentalists believe the child's environment shapes learning and behaviour in fact, human behaviour, development, and learning are thought of as reactions to the environment. This perspective leads many families, schools, and educators to assume that young children develop and acquire new knowledge by reacting to their surroundings.

Kindergarten readiness, according to the environmentalists, is the age or stage when young children can respond appropriately to the environment of the school and the classroom (*e.g.*, rules and regulations, curriculum activities, positive behaviour in group settings, and directions and instructions from teachers and other adults in the school). The ability to respond appropriately to this environment is necessary for young children to participate in teacher-initiated learning activities. Success is dependent on the child following instructions from the teacher or the adult in the classroom. Many environmentalist-influenced educators and parents believe that young children learn best by rote activities, such as reciting the alphabet over and over, copying letters, and tracing numbers. This viewpoint is evident in kindergarten classrooms where young children are expected to sit at desks arranged in rows and listen attentively to their teachers. At home, parents may provide their young children with workbooks containing such activities as colouring or tracing letters and numbers—activities that require little interaction between parent and child. When young children are unable to respond appropriately to the classroom and school environment, they often are labelled as having some form of learning disabilities and are tracked in classrooms with curriculum designed to control their behaviours and responses.

Constructivist Theory

The constructivist perspective of readiness and development was advanced by theorists such as Jean Piaget, Maria Montessori, and Lev Vygotsky. Although their work varies greatly, each articulates a similar context of learning and development. They are consistent in their belief that learning and development occur when young children interact with the environment and people around them. Constructivists view young children as active participants in the learning process. In addition, constructivists believe young children initiate most of the activities required for learning and development. Because active interaction with the environment and people are necessary for learning and development, constructivists believe that children are ready for school when they can initiate many of the interactions they have with the environment and people around them.

Constructivist-influenced schools and educators pay a lot of attention to the physical environment and the curriculum of the early childhood classroom. Kindergarten classrooms often are divided into different **learning centers** and are equipped with developmentally appropriate materials for young children to play with and manipulate. Teachers and adults have direct conversations with children, children move actively from one center to another, and daily activities are made meaningful through the incorporation of children's experiences into the curriculum. At home, parents engage their young children in reading and storytelling activities and encourage children's participation in daily household activities in a way that introduces such concepts as counting and language use. In addition, parents may provide young children with picture books containing very large print, and toys that stimulate interaction (such as building blocks and large puzzles). When a young child encounters difficulties in the learning process, the constructivist approach is neither to lable the child nor to retain him or her; instead, constructivists give the child some individualized attention and customize the classroom curriculum to help the child address his or her difficulties.

Today, most researchers have come to understand child development and the learning process as articulated by the constructivists. However, this view has not been widely translated into practice. Many kindergarten teachers and parents still believe that young children are not ready for school unless they can recite the alphabet, count, and have the ability to follow instructions from adults.

PRINCIPLES AND THEORIES OF CHILD DEVELOPMENT

Studying and understanding child growth and development are important parts of teaching young children. No two children are alike. Children differ in physical, cognitive, social and emotional growth patterns. Even identical twins, who have the same genetic makeup, are not exactly alike. They may differ in the way they respond to play, affection, objects and people in their environment.

Knowledge of the areas of child development is basic to guiding young children. Linked to this is the understanding of healthy brain development. These stimuli begin at birth. Therefore, it is vital for children to have loving caregivers. Young children need dependable, trusting relationships. They thrive in environments that are predictable and nurturing. Understanding theories about how people develop helps form your knowledge base in caring for young children.

Child Development

Development refers to change or growth that occurs in children. It starts with infancy and continues to adulthood. By studying child development, you will form a profile of what children can do at various ages.

Different names are used to describe young children at different ages. From birth through the first year, children are called **infants. Toddlers** are children from age one up to the third birthday (Because of an awkward style of walking, the name toddler describes this age group). The term **preschooler** is often used to describe children ages three to six years of age.

Areas of Development

The study of child development is often divided into three main areas. These include physical, cognitive and social-emotional development. Dividing development into these areas makes it easier to study.

Physical development refers to physical body changes. It occurs in a relatively stable, predictable sequence. It is orderly, not random. Changes in size and weight are also part of physical development.

Physical skills, such as crawling, walking and writing, are the result of physical development. These skills fall into two main categories:

1. **Grossmotor development :** It involves improvement of skills using the large muscles in the legs and arms. Such activities as running, skipping and bike riding fall into this category.
2. **Fine-motor development :** It involves the small muscles of the hands and fingers. Grasping, holding, cutting and drawing are some activities that require fine-motor development.

Environmental factors also affect what children can do physically. These factors include proper nutrition and appropriate toys and activities.

Cognitive development, sometimes called **intellectual development,** refers to processes people use to gain knowledge. Language, thought, reasoning and imagination are all included. Identifying colours and knowing the difference between one and many are examples of cognitive tasks.

Language and thought are a result of cognitive development. These two skills are closely related. Both are needed for planning, remembering and problem solving. As children mature and gain experience with their world, these skills develop.

The third area of development is called social-emotional development. These two areas are grouped together because they are so interrelated. Learning to relate to others is social development. Emotional development, on the other hand, involves feelings and expression of feelings. Trust, fear, confidence, pride, friendship and humor are all part of social-emotional development. Other emotional traits include timidity, interest and pleasure.

Learning to express emotions in appropriate ways begins early. Caregivers promote this learning when they positively model these skills. A person's self-concept and self-esteem are also part of this area. As children have success with all skills confidence flourishes. This leads to a healthy self-concept and sense of worth.

The physical, cognitive and social-emotional areas of development are linked to one another. Development in one area can strongly influence another area. For instance, writing words requires fine-motor skills. It also requires cognitive development. Language, a part of cognitive development, is needed to communicate with others. It is also necessary for growing socially and emotionally.

Principles of Development

Although each child is unique, the basic patterns or principles of growth and development are universal, predictable and orderly. Through careful observation and interaction with children, researchers and those who work with children understand the characteristics of the principles that follow:

1. Development tends to proceed from the head downward. This is called the **cephalocaudal principle.** According to this principle, the child first gains control of the head, then the arms, then the legs. Infants gain control of head and face movements within the first two months after birth. In the next few months, they are able to lift themselves up using their arms. By 6 to 12 months of age, infant start to gain leg control and may be able to crawl, stand or walk.
2. Development also proceeds from the center of the body outward according to the **proximodistal principle**. Accordingly, the spinal cord develops before other parts of the body. The child's arms develop before the hands and the hands and feet develop before the fingers and toes. Fingers and toes are the last to develop.
3. Development also depends on maturation. **Maturation** refers to the sequence of biological changes in children. These orderly changes give children new abilities. Much of the maturation depends on changes in the brain and the nervous system. These changes assist children to improve their thinking abilities and motor skills. A rich learning environment helps children develop to their potential.

Children must mature to a certain point before they can gain some skills. For instance, the brain of a four-month-old has not matured enough to allow the child to use words. A four-month-old will babble and coo. However, by two years of age, with the help of others, the child will be able to say and understand many words. This is an example of how cognitive development occurs from simple tasks to more complex tasks. Likewise, physical skills develop from general to specific movements. For example, think about the way an infant waves its arms and legs. In a young infant, these movements are random. In several months, the infant will likely be able to grab a block with his or her whole hand. In a little more time, the same infant will grasp a block with the thumb and fore finger.

INFLUENCE OF HEREDITY AND ENVIRONMENT

Heredity and environment greatly influence the growth, development and behaviour of a child. Each child inherits certain capacities for growth. The way in which these capacities develop is influenced by the opportunities afforded by the environment, for example, the height to which the individual is capable of growing is determined by heredity. The environment cannot change the limits imposed by heredity. Whereas a poor environment *i.e.*, lack of exposure will slow down a child who is genetically clever, a rich environment which provides and exposes a child to a lot of educational facilities will not change a child who is genetically born not clever to become clever. A good environment will enable the individual to reach these limits. The environment influences the speed with which the child develops. The environment shapes the individual's development in the sense that it promotes the growth of certain capacities and neglects the growth of others. For instance, if the child experiences more emphasis on academic and no attachment to physical education, the child's capacity to develop certain skills will be neglected.

Effects of Heredity and Environment on Development of Personality

Before discussing the contribution of hereditary factors let us see what is meant by heredity when we talk of heredity we usually have biological heredity in mind. The term 'heredity' may also be used in another sense, for example, if a child is brought up in a particular social environment say of a tribe, the value of that tribe and the norms of that tribe are inculcated in him through other members of that social group and we call it **social heredity.** In the same way, a student in a classroom situation brings with him a specific cultural heredity also. Here our discussion will be focused on the influence of only biological heredity on individual differences. Each individual has a specific set of potentials which are developed through the environment. These potentialities and characteristics possessed by the individual are the result of his biological heredity. The influence of heredity is so strong that twins brought up in drastically different environment show very much similarity in terms of their mental abilities and other traits. This shows that even drastically different environments are not capable of overcoming hereditary influences.

Hereditary, or the genetic transmission of characteristics from parents to offspring, determine personality to a certain extent. Hereditary characteristics manifest at birth such as hair and eye colour, skin colour and body type. Hereditary also includes aptitude or the capacity to learn a skill or inclination for a particular body of knowledge. It establishes the limits of one's personality traits that can be developed. This aptitude creates the desire for a person to learn something. For instance, the son of a sports hero like a boxer superstar is expected to inherit the genes of his father. His capacity for growth in the boxing arena is immense because he is born with the ability.

Behavioural geneticists, Dr. David Reiss and colleagues from George Washington University, conducted a thorough and long-term study on the effects of genetics to a person's personality. The result of their study revealed that 'it seems that genetic influences are largely responsible for how 'adjusted' kids are : how well they do in school, how they get along with their peers, whether they engage in dangerous or delinquent behaviour'.

Effect of Environment on Personality Development

Apart from heredity, environment also effects the child development. The concept of environment needs little clarification when we say the environment of the child is not good, sometimes we mean that he is living in a locality which does not have desirable people or we mean that he is living in the rural area where he does not have access to many things which an urban environment may provide. As has rightly been said, the psychological environment consists of the sum total of the stimulation the individual receives from conception till death. This is an active concept of environment *i.e.*, the physical presence of objects does not in itself constitute environment unless the objects serve as stimuli for the individual.

The role of the prenatal environment on the development of the child is well known and has been demonstrated through various experiments. The diet a mother takes at the time of pregnancy, her mental status, glandular secretions and even the thinking process influence the development of the child. Environmentalists firmly believe that, under favourable circumstances, every individual is almost infinitely improvable.

Newman, Freeman and Holzinger conducted thorough research on nineteen pairs of identical twins reared in different environments. Initially they found that the pairs reared apart show mere differences in I.Q. But Woodworth (1941) in his analysis of the results pointed out a factor called error of measurement that is always involved in intelligence testing. When this factor was taken into account and results interpreted, Woodworth concluded that environmental differences do operate to produce I.Q. differences in persons with exactly the same hereditary potentialities. But the magnitude of these differences is not as large as those found among children whose heredity is not alike.

Environment and its Interaction with Hereditary Factors

Nature refers to what a child has inherited genetically, from the parents (*e.g.* eye colour, appearance, etc). The influence of environment on the development of the child (*e.g.* liking for a type of music) is referred to as nurture. The earlier view of child development focused either entirely on nature or nurture. Many favoured heredity, and believed that we are born with certain talents and personalities. These determine who we are and what we become.

In the other view, the focus was on the role of environment. We learn to do things for which we get rewards (or praises) and do not do things for which we are punished (including disapproval from elders). Both views contained some truth but neither is complete. To understand the development of a person, we have to study the complex interaction between nature and nurture (or heredity and environment).

Let us consider an example. A child is born with a talent for music. In the child's family, this talent for music is expressed by the child at an early age, through his activities of singing and listening to music. The parents notice the child's interest in music and expose the child to more music and give him a toy musical instrument (*e.g.* ek tara or flute). The child's interest in music grows further and his talent develops and this make the parents offer even more musical experiences (*e.g.* playing music on stage, attending music concerts etc.). This has a further positive effect on the child's talent and his desire to play music.

It is thus clear that both the child's inherited talent and environment shaped his/her development. The child had the talent for music, but this led to a change in the environment by making her parents provide more musical experiences at home. Now these experiences in the environment further developed the child's talent and motivation and made the parents introduce more musical experiences to the child. The process goes on and on like this in a form of transaction. This approach to understanding development is called a transactional model (TA).

The TA model is able to explain why brothers and sisters, though physically in the same environment, always grow up in 'different' ways. This simply means that the environment of family life is always changing in the process of adjusting to the personalities of its members. A first born child grows up with very different experiences than a middle born or youngest child. A child who displays temper tantrums (getting angry easily, without sufficient cause) has a very different experience with her parents as compared to her easy going brother.

Let us take another example to make the point more clear. Suppose you as a parent (if not today, then in the future) are facing difficulty with your argumentative 12-year-old. The TA model reminds you that you must first think about the factor which has brought your child to this point. Is it a personality trait that is troubling you? Is she stubborn (does not listen to others) all the time and is thus part of her nature? Does she resist any change in her usual routine? Does she lack the ability to talk to you about what's troubling her, and could that be upsetting her? The child represents one part of the puzzle or problem which has to be solved.

The next questions you have to ask are : What is my role in all this? Am I somehow rewarding the very behaviours? Am I trying to stop by paying too much attention to them? Am I having too much expectation from a 12-year old? Am I reminded of my younger sister with whom I had faced a similar problem, and could be causing irritation in me now? The environment which includes you forms the other-part of the picture.

Finally, you need to put the two together to obtain a full picture of what is going on and how to bring about a positive change. In which way my behaviour is affecting my child? And most importantly, what do I need to change to break this pattern of behaviour (argumentation in the child) located in its transactions with nurture? How can I better understand the forces behind my child's behaviour so as to improve my response to it?

This may sound very theoretical to some of you but it's exactly the questions which many parents are always asking themselves, even if they are not aware of it. By understanding the TA-model you will be in a better position to understand the interaction between nature and nurture which is responsible for your child's behaviour and development. This will help you in deciding which role you can play for effective development and improve the child's behaviour.

In summary according to the transactional model of development, the child changes the environment which in turn changes the child. The child's development is like a complex dance in which nature and nurture both lead, and are led.

SOCIALISATION PROCESS

As a child grows up, there is a deliberate and conscious effort made through active training to make the child learn the values and expectations of the society he or she lives in. The child has to learn to adjust and accommodate her behaviour according to the rules for appropriate behaviour in the society. Parents, teachers, elders as well as the peers (same age group children) all influence and control the behaviour of a child.

According to the Indian view, a child comes to this world with certain behavioural tendencies which carry over from previous birth. The role of the family is to bring up the child in such a way that her positive capacities are developed fully and negative tendencies are controlled. Apart from the family, there are also other influences on the child from the outside environment. The important agents of socialisation include media, day-care centers, peer group, school and religion.

Parents have the most direct effect on the socialisation of the child. They are role models for children. Their responses to child behaviour, giving approval or disapproval etc. mould the personality of child and plays a very important role in acquiring rules. In addition, parents arrange the environment of a children in different ways. They take the child outside in specific settings like museum, church, temple, mosque, hill station, sea beach. The grand parents and aunts and uncles of the child also contribute in the socialisation process. Children learn manners and skills by observing parents. During the life span of a person, at different ages, specific rituals are performed. These rituals represent the changes in the child from one stage to another. They contribute in forming the identity of the child.

The influence of the **peer group** of the child, particularly during middle childhood is very important. In the interactions with the children of the same age group, a child learns the importance of team work, sharing and trust. One of the significant effects of this is that the child learns to adjust and accommodate to the view point of the others.

The school which the child attends is another very important socializing agent. The child learns different types of social, intellectual and physical skills in school. The school provides the child with a miniature society where he or she has to learnt the right values and rules and follow them. Values such as honesty, democracy and fairness etc. are learnt in the school setting.

Now-a-days, children search and know the world through TV, magazines, books, comics, radio and films. This media influences the socialisation of the child in significant ways. A positive influence can be learning the importance of family values by watching good and informative programmes. Watching aggressive programmes and programmes based on violence can influence the child negatively.

In the present way of life, when both parents are doing jobs, very young children have to be left at day-care centers. These centers, therefore, play an important role in the socialisation of the child because the child will learn many things about appropriate behaviour in the society. For children from poor background the Aganwadis under the programme of Integrated Child Developments (ICDs) help children to learn about appropriate social behaviour and the importance of community life.

Theories of Development

Psychologists continue to study human development. They are learning more about what people are like and how they develop. Over the past century, many psychologists have provided theories that are considered practical guides. A theory is a principle or idea that is proposed, researched and generally accepted as an explanation. Developmental theories provide insights into how children grow and learn. Theories are helpful for understanding and guiding developmental processes.

Theories can be useful decision-making tools. Since a variety of theories exists, teachers need to understand these different approaches for working with children. Theories will help you understand strategies for promoting children's development. Four major theories about how children learn are important. These include theories of mid-twentieth century psychologists Erik Erikson, Jean Piaget and Lev Vygotsky. The final theorist, Howard Gardner, is a twenty first century developmental psychologist. These theories are based on observation and experiences with children.

Erikson's Psychosocial Theory

Erik Erikson proposed a theory of psychosocial development. He believed development occurs throughout the life span. His theory provided new insights into the formation of a healthy personality. It emphasizes the social and emotional aspects of growth. Children's personalities develop in response to their social environment. The same is true of their skills for social interaction.

Erikson's theory includes eight stages. At each stage, a social conflict or crisis occurs. These are not generally tragic situations; however, they require solutions that are satisfying both personally and socially. Erikson believed that each stage must be resolved before children can ascend to the next stage.

Maturity and social forces help in the resolution of the crisis or conflict. Therefore, teachers and parents play a powerful role in recognizing each stage. By providing social opportunity and support, teachers and parents can help children overcome each crisis. Following table contains the first four stages of Erikson's theory. These stages occur during the early childhood years. The paragraphs that follow give a brief overview of these early stages.

Erikson's Stages of Development During Early Childhood

Stage	Approximate Age	Psychosocial Crisis
I	Birth–18 months	Trust versus mistrust
II	18 months–3 years	Autonomy versus shame and doubt
III	3–5 years	Initiative versus guilt
IV	6–12 years	Industry versus inferiority

Note : *The first four stages of Erikson's theory concern children from birth to twelve years.*

Stage 1 : Trust Versus Mistrust

During the first eighteen months of life, children learn to trust or mistrust their environment. To develop trust, they need to have warm, consistent, predictable, and attentive care. They need caregivers who will accurately read and respond to their signals. When infants are distressed, they need to be comforted. They also need loving physical contact, nourishment, cleanliness, and warmth. Then they will develop a sense of confidence and trust that the world is safe and dependable. Mistrust will occur if an infant experiences an unpredictable world and is handled harshly.

Stage 2 : Autonomy Versus Shame and Doubt

This second stage occurs between eighteen months and three years of age. During this stage, toddlers use their new motor and mental skills. They want to be independent and do things for themselves. They are in the process of discovering their own bodies and practicing their developing locomotor (physical movement) and language skills.

The objective of this stage is to gain self-control without a loss of self-esteem. Fostering independence in children is important. At this age, toddlers start to become self-sufficient. They need to learn to choose and decide for themselves. To do this, toddlers need a loving, supportive environment. Positive opportunities for self-feeding, toileting, dressing and exploration will result in *autonomy,* or independence. On the other hand, overprotection or lack of adequate activities results in self-doubt, poor achievement, and shame.

Stage 3 : Initiative Versus Guilt

Between three and five years of age, the third stage occurs. According to Erikson, it emerges as a result of the many skills children have developed. Now children have the capacity and are ready to learn constructive ways of dealing with people and things. They are learning how to take initiative without being hurtful to others. They are also busy discovering how the world works. Children begin to realize that what they do can have an effect on the world, too. Challenged by the environment, children are constantly attempting and mastering new tasks. Aided by strong initiative, they are able to move ahead energetically and quickly forget failures. This gives them a sense of accomplishment.

Children at this stage need to develop a sense of purpose. This happens when adults direct children's urges toward acceptable social practices. If children are discouraged by criticism, feelings of incompetence are likely to emerge. This can also occur if parents demand too much control.

Stage 4 : Industry Versus Inferiority

The major crisis of this stage occurs between six and twelve years of age. At this time, children enjoy planning and carrying out projects. This helps them learn society's rules and expectations. During this stage, children gain approval by developing intellectual skills such as reading, writing, and math.

The way family, neighbours, teachers, and friends respond to children affects their future development. Realistic goals and expectations enrich children's sense of self. Children can become frustrated by criticism or discouragement, or if parents demand too much control. Feelings of incompetence and insecurity will emerge.

PIAGET'S COGNITIVE DEVELOPMENT THEORY

Jean Piaget's thinking has challenged teachers to focus on the *ways* children come to know as opposed to *what* they know. His theory of cognitive development focuses on predictable cognitive (thinking) stages. Piaget believed that thinking was different during each stage of development. His theory explained mental operations. This includes how children perceive, think, understand and learn about their world.

Piaget believed that children naturally attempt to understand what they do not know. Knowledge is gathered gradually during active involvement in real-life experience. By physically handling objects, young children discover that relationships exist between them. Terms Piaget used to describe these processes were *schemata, adaptation, assimilation* and *accommodation.* These processes occur during each stage of development.

Schemata are mental representations or concepts. As children receive new information, they are constantly creating, modifying, organizing and reorganizing schemata.

Adaptation is a term Piaget used for children mentally organizing what they preceive in their environment. When new information or experiences occur, children must adapt to include this information in their thinking. If this new information does not fit with what children already know, a state of imbalance occurs. To return to balance, adaptation occurs through either assimilation or accommodation.

Assimilation is the process of taking in new information and adding it to what the child already knows.

Accommodation is adjusting what is already known to fit the new information. This process is how people organize their thoughts and develop intellectual structures.

Piaget's stages of cognitive development are the same for all children. Most children proceed through the stages in order. Each stage builds on a previous stage. However, the age at which a child progresses through these stages is variable due to differences in maturation.

Although Piaget did not apply his theory directly to education, he did strongly influence children's early education. Many teaching strategies have evolved from his work. Caregivers and teachers now know that learning is an active process. Providing children with stimulating, hands-on activities helps them build knowledge. Piaget's theory includes four stages: sensorimotor, preoperational concrete, and formal operations. The first three stages occur during early childhood and the early school-age years. The following paragraphs describe these stages.

Piaget's Stages of Development

The **sensorimotor stage** takes place between birth and two years of age. Infants use all their senses to explore and learn. In this way, sensory experiences and motor development promote cognitive development. Babies' physical actions, such as sucking, grasping and hitting, help them learn about their surroundings. Movements are random at first. Gradually they become intentional as behaviours are repeated. Children begin to learn that objects still exist even when they are out of sight. This is known as *object permanence.* Through exploration and exposure to new experiences, new concepts are learned.

The **preoperational stage** takes place between ages two and seven. Children during this stage are very *egocentric*. This means that they assume others see the world the same way they do. Children do not yet have the ability to see others' points of view. During this time, representation skills are learned. These skills include language, symbolic play, and drawing. Children learn to use symbols and internal images, but their thinking is illogical. It is very different from that of adults. Children begin to understand that changing the physical appearance of something does not change the amount of it. They are able to recognize the difference between size and volume. For example, a ball of clay can be stretched into a long rope. Even if the physical appearance changes, the amount of the object does not change. This skill is called *conservation.* At this stage, children can also classify groups of objects and put objects in a series in order.

During the ages of seven to eleven years, **concrete operations** begin. Children develop the capacity to think systematically, but only when they can refer to actual objects and use hands-on activities. Then they begin to internalize some tasks. This means they no longer need to depend on what is seen. They become capable of reversing operations. For example, they understand that 3 + 1 is the same as 1 + 3. When real situations are presented, they are beginning to understand others' points of view.

The fourth stage, *formal operations,* takes place from eleven years of age to adulthood (the age range you are in right now). According to Piaget, young people develop the capacity to think in purely abstract ways. They no longer need concrete examples. Problem solving and reasoning are key skills developed during this stage.

VYGOTSKY'S SOCIOCULTURAL THEORY

Both Jean Piaget and Lev Vygotsky believed that children build knowledge through experiences. Piaget believed this happened through exploration with hands-on activities. Vygotsky, on the other hand, believed that children learn through social and cultural experiences. Interactions with peers and adults help children in this process. While interacting with others, children learn the customs, values, beliefs, and language of their culture. For this reason, families and teachers should provide plently of social interaction for young children.

Vygotsky believed language is an important tool for thought and plays a key role in cognitive development. He introduced the term ***private speech***, or self-talk. This refers to when children ''think out loud''. After learning language, children engage in this self-talk to help guide their activity and develop their thinking. Generally, self-talk continues until children reach school age.

One of Vygotsky's most important contributions was the *zone of* ***proximal development*** (ZPD). This concept presents learning as a scale. One end of the scale or ''zone'' includes the tasks that are within the child's current development level. The other end of the scale includes tasks too difficult for children to accomplish, even with help. In the middle are the tasks children cannot accomplish alone. These are achieved with help from another knowledgeable peer or adult. The term used for this assistance is ***scaffolding***. Just as a painter needs a structure on which to stand and point a building, scaffolding provides the structure for learning to occur. For example, a teacher could scaffold a child's learning while constructing a puzzle. The teacher might demonstrate how a piece fits or provide clues regarding colour, shape or size. The ''zone'' is constantly changing. In contrast to Piaget, Vygotsky believed that learning was not limited by stage or maturation. Children move forward in their cognitive development with the right social interaction and guided learning.

KOHLBERG'S THEORY OF DEVELOPMENT

According to him moral development of the child proceeds in sequential but distinctive stages. These stages are given below:

(a) **Stage-I :** In the early years of a child's life (from zero-four years) the physical consequences of an action determines its goodness or badness. If fire burns the child, he does not touch it. The child is ego-centric and standards of morality are external here.

(b) **Stage-II :** The child gives importance to his own point of view, (his self) and is able to take account of other's roles insofar as he can use them in his own way. This is a period of make belief. Right action is what which satisfies the needs of the child. The role of others is also important in the sense that a child does only what can bring approval of others. Thus, only that behaviour is moral which can satisfy not only self needs of the child but it must please others also.

(c) **Stage-III :** At this stage the child adopts the view pints of others on the basis of their consequences. He does not question the views of others. The child considers only that thing as right which are considered as right by others. Thus, the child is totally conformist to the standard of the society.

(d) **Stage-IV:** At this stage, the child is able to make any moral decision on his own without caring for the thinking of others. Though he considers laws and regulations set by the society as the essence of morality, yet he develops his own principles of morality on various occasions. Thus, he is a non-conformist to the norms of the society to a great extent.

(e) **Stage-V :** Standards and norms are more internalized here. The adolescents examine various view points prepared by different societies and recognize them. They think that the laws prepared by their own society are correct. Other societies may have good moral principles that must be adopted after careful appraisal.

(f) **Stage-VI :** This is the last stage of moral development according to Kohlberg. Here the universality of the view points of the individual is seen. He formulates his own universal moral principles which he thinks that all societies should adhere to it. True understanding of right and wrong is developed at this stage.

Gardner's Multiple Intelligences Theory

Howard Gardner has helped teachers rethink how they work with young children. Traditional intelligence tests mainly focus on language and math/logic skills. In contrast, Gardner's theory of **multiple intelligences** emphasizes that there are different kinds of intelligences used by the human brain. Gardner believes intelligence is the result of complex interactions between children's heredity and experiences. This theory focuses on how cultures shape human potential.

Gardner claims that children learn and express themselves in many different ways. In the process, they are using several types of intelligence. Each intelligence functions separately, but all are closely linked. According to Gardner, a potential intelligence will not develop unless it is nurtured. Learning can best be achieved by using a child's strongest intelligence. Gardner claims, however, that all children need opportunities to develop all areas of intelligence.

The multiple intelligence theory allows teachers to see the positive attributes of all children. Teachers also view Gardner's theory as a meaningful guide for making curriculum decisions. It gives them a chance to assess children's learning strengths. From this data, teachers can plan a wide variety of learning experiences. Following chart lists Gardner's eight intelligences. The paragraphs that follow explain these intelligences in detail.

(i) Bodily-Kinesthetic Intelligence

Bodily-kinesthetic intelligence involves the ability to control body movements. This includes using parts of the body to solve problems, handle objects, and express emotions. People with this type of intelligence typically enjoy sports, dance or creative drama. They are able to express themselves with their entire bodies. Children will benefit from creative-movement experiences and role-playing.

Children with this type of intelligence process knowledge through sensation. They enjoy touch and creating with their hands. Therefore, daily opportunities should be provided for hands-on activities. Clay, sand, dough, feely boxes and other sensory activities help them develop fine-motor skills. Movement is also needed for gross-motor skills and coordination. It is important for caregivers and teachers to provide activities involving physical challenges. These may include playing kickball, jumping rope, and moving to music.

(ii) Musical-Rhythmic Intelligence

Musical-rhythmic intelligence involve the ability to recognize musical patterns. It also includes the ability to produce and appreciate music. Since music evokes emotion, this is one of the earliest intelligences to emerge. Composers and musicians are examples of people with this type of intelligence.

Children with this type of intelligence love listening to music. They are drawn to the art of sound and appreciate all forms of musical expression. They have a well-developed auditory sense and can discriminate tone, pitch and rhythmic patterns. As a result, they often cannot get songs out of their minds. You will hear them repeatedly singing or humming. This helps them understand concepts and remember information.

Activities to support musical intelligence can be included throughout the day. Offer opportunities for sound exploration through listening and singing. Use songs for directions and moving children from one activity to another. Play background music during self-selected play. Include songs during large and small group activities. Record the children creating their own music while singing or chanting. Explore rhythm by moving to recorded music. Use different instruments and instruments from other cultures to add variety.

(iii) Logical-Mathematical Intelligence

Logical-mathematical intelligence is more than just the ability to use math. It is the ability to use logic and reason to solve problems. Math experts have this form of intelligence. Scientists and composers may also have it. This intelligence involves the ability to explore categories, patterns and other relationships. It includes applying the principle of cause and effect. It also involves the skill to make predictions about patterns.

Children with this type of intelligence take pleasure in finding patterns and relationships. They enjoy discovering similarities and differences. Manipulatives for matching, measuring, and counting should be provided. Blocks can encourage the children's problem-solving and reasoning skills. Storybooks that show a sequence of events hold appeal for this type of intelligence. Water and sand activities with different-size containers help teach the concept of volume.

(iv) Verbal-Linguistic Intelligence

Verbal-linguistic intelligence involves the ability to use language for expression. People with this type of intelligence have well-developed language skills. They demonstrate sensitivity to the meaning, sound and rhythm of words. Lawyers, poets, public speakers and language translators have this type of intelligence.

Young children with this intelligence learn best by talking, listening, reading and writing. These children quickly learn the words to new stories, songs and finger plays. They enjoy talking to other people and are able to speak in an interesting and engaging manner. They are also able to learn a second language with ease.

This intelligence can be nurtured by environments rich with language opportunities. Children learn language in setting where it is used. Teachers need to follow the children's interests. They can then use these interests to engage children in meaningful conversations. Children's storybooks, songs, poetry, chants, and rhymes can serve as means for learning new vocabulary words. Listening to and telling stories can also promote language development.

(v) Interpersonal Intelligence

People with *interpersonal intelligence* display excellent communication and social skills. These people have a gift for understanding the feelings, behaviours, moods and motives of others. They make friends easily. They use language to develop trust and bonds with others. They are also skilled in supporting others and empathizing with them. These skills are important for teachers, politicians, salespeople and people working in the service industry.

These skills are nurtured in young children when caring behaviours are modeled for them. Teachers should keep this in mind. They can share experiences and provide the children with chances for verbal interaction. Books focusing on emotions can be acted out.

(vi) Intrapersonal Intelligence

Intrapersonal intelligence is the ability to understand the inner self. This is also known as *self-awareness.* It involves knowing your skills, limits, and feelings. It includes understanding your desires and motives. The ability to organize groups of people is part of this strength. Communicating needs clearly is another aspect. Psychologists, social workers, religious leaders, and counsellors are examples of people with this type of intelligence.

How can you foster this type of intelligence? In the classroom, share emotions that all children experience. These include joy, sadness, regret and disappointment. Classroom examples should be shared as well as storybooks that contain emotional concepts.

(vii) Visual-Spatial Intelligence

Visual-spatial intelligence allows people to use their vision to develop mental images. People who have this type of intelligence show a preference for pictures and images. Photographers and artists are some examples. Architects, engineers, and surgeons also need this ability. They use it to see the relationship of objects in space.

Teachers can foster this intelligence by providing children with unstructured materials. Building blocks and puzzles strengthen this type of intelligence, 4-18. Make and use visual aids wherever possible. For example, classroom schedules, recipes, and stories can all be displayed on charts. Shelving units can be labelled with pictures cut from equipment catalogs.

(viii) Naturalistic Intelligence

Naturalistic intelligence is developed from the need to survive. This is the ability to classify objects in nature such as animals and plants. It depends on a type of pattern recognition. This strength also includes the ability to distinguish among types and brands of objects. Sailors, gardeners, chefs, and farmers are people who have this intelligence.

To build on this intelligence, provide cooking activities and nature walks. These help develop use of the senses to gather information. Planting and growing a garden helps the children observe cycles. Rocks, seashells, flowers, leaves, seeds, and coins can also be collected. In the classroom, they can be sorted and classified. Post picture collections and share books about natural events.

CONCEPTS OF CHILD-CENTERED AND PROGRESSIVE EDUCATION

Child-Centered Education

Child-centered education is the idea that the needs and desires of the child should take precedence in structuring the learning day. The whole idea is that learning should be fun and engaging for the child, and is most likely to be that way if the child is incharge of the learning experience, rather than the adult parent or teacher.

Child-centered education is most characterised by learning 'centers' in a classroom that promote hands-on, active participation by the child. There may be magnifying glasses and bug slides in the science center, books and puppets that could be used to re-tell the stories in the language arts center, and wood blocks and shapes in the math center. The children are free to manipulate the objects in these centers. It is the process, the activity, the experience, that is valuable, not the facts, ideas, concepts or skills.

It is a relatively new approach to education. For centuries past, adults defined what education should be and children were the ones who did the adjusting. Education was considered work, not play.

Then came the softening influences of child psychologist Jean-Jacques Rousseau, as well as Dr. Marria Montessori, John Dewey, Jean Piaget and Lev Vygotsky, who all contended that a child's self-esteem and self-concept should be built up in order to create a better learner. Soon, the colleges of education were promoting child-centered education instead of instructionally centered education.

Role of Learner in Child-Centered Education

Learners are active as opposed to passive recipients of knowledge. Learners may assume a decision-making role in the classroom. Learners often decide what is to be learned, through which activities and at what pace. Learners can also produce materials and provide activities for the classroom.

Role of Teacher in Child-Centered Education

To put this approach into practice, teachers need to help students set achievable goals; they encourage students to assess themselves and their peers; help them to work co-operatively in groups and ensure that they know how to make use of all the available resources for learning.

Progressive Education

During most of the twentieth century, the term 'progressive education' has been used to describe ideas and practices that aim to make schools more effective agencies of a democratic society. Although there are numerous differences of style and emphasis among progressive educators, they share the conviction that democracy means active participation by all citizens in social, political and economic decisions that will affect their lives. The education of engaged citizens, according to this perspective, involves two essential elements: (1) respect for diversity, meaning that each individual should be recognised for his or her own abilities, interests, ideas, needs, and cultural identity, and (2) the development of critical, socially engaged intelligence, which enables individuals to understand and participate effectively in the affairs of their community in a collaborative effort to achieve a common good. These elements of progressive education have been termed 'child-centered' and 'social reconstruction' approaches, and while in extreme forms they have sometimes been separated, in the thought of John Dewey and other major theorists they are seen as being necessarily related to each other.

The term 'progressive' arose from a period (roughly 1890–1920) during which many Americans took a more careful look at the political and social effects of vast concentrations of corporate power and private wealth. Dewey, in particular, saw that with the decline of local community life and small scale enterprise, young people were losing valuable opportunities to learn the arts of democratic participation, and he concluded that education would need to make up for this loss. In his Laboratory School at the University of Chicago, where he worked between 1896 and 1904, Dewey tested ideas he shared with leading school reformers such as Francis W. Parker and Ella Flagg Young. Between 1899 and 1916 he circulated his ideas in works such as The School and Society, The Child and the Curriculum, Schools of Tomorrow, and Democracy and Education, and through numerous lectures and articles. During these years other experimental schools were established around the country, and in 1919 the Progressive Education Association was founded, aiming at "reforming the entire school system of America".

Therefore, progressive education is a reaction against the traditional style of teaching which teaches facts largely at the expense of understanding what is being taught. According to **John French,** "The progressive school teaches the child to think for himself instead of passively accepting stereotyped ideas. It keeps always in mind that each child is different from every other, and that what makes an educated person useful in his particular walk of life, what makes him interesting, what makes him an individual, is not his resemblance to other people, but his differences".

Philosophies and Practices of Progressive Education

1. Curriculum is strongly influenced by what the children are interested in, and is child-centered rather than adult driven.
2. Learning is 'hands-on', experiential and the emphasis is on process rather than product children are 'learning to learn'.
3. Children learn through integrated, theme-based units or inquiry projects and the 'theme' often emerges from the children.
4. Assessment is authentic and holistic. Children are well known by their teachers and peers.

There are no tests or letter grades. Instead, narrative reports are written about children that cover all aspects of their development: social, emotional, personal, physical and intellectual level.

5. Classes are usually of mixed ages and no ability grouping is used. Children are able to work at their own pace and cross-age friendships are encouraged.
6. Progressive education practices a developmental approach which holds that each child is a unique being unfolding and developing at their own pace according to a specific pattern. At each stage of development there are things that can be learned and things that should not be learned. Respecting a child's development is central to progressive education.

Types of Progressive Education

1. **Humanistic :** The humanistic form of progressive education focuses on the humanities, arts and social sciences. Its emphasis is on the individual child and not the curriculum. This type of progressivism aims to build a well-rounded individual with highly developed critical thinking and reasoning skills. The children learn think for themselves instead of accepting everything teachers tell them. Social development and interaction among the students are seen as valuable learning techniques.
2. **Constructivism :** Constructivism is a type of child-centered progressivism. It focuses on the child's creativity and learning abilities. Teachers should build the curriculum around the requirements and interests of the child. It maintains that education should consider children's developmental stages. Swiss psychologist **Jean Piaget** influenced the theories of constructivist education. Experiential learning, or learning by doing, allows students to construct their own knowledge.
3. **Montessori :** Italian doctor Marria Montessori started the Montessori progressive educational system. She developed her teaching theories by clinical observation and analysis of how children learn. Her method of education focused on how children naturally learn, all by themselves, without the help of adults. Maria Montessori concluded that children teach themselves, and it's the job of teachers to facilitate this process, not dominate it. Montessori teachers provide a sensory-rich environment and hands-on activities.

CRITICAL PERSPECTIVE OF THE CONSTRUCT OF INTELLIGENCE

Introduction

The most important variable that affects schooling or performance on a job is intelligence. Psychologists have interpreted the term intelligence in different ways and there is no consensus among them on the term even so far. In psychology this term is treated as a construct whose structure is different in different individuals.

The vagueness of the term arises due to the fact that intelligence is not a concrete material. It is rather abstraction from the behaviour of the individual which is indirectly inferred and elaborated as an adjective.

The dictionary meaning of term "intelligence" is the capacity to acquire and apply knowledge. **Boring** defines intelligence as intelligence is what an intelligence test measures.

Definitions of Intelligence

Several psychologists have classified and defined intelligence in several ways. Some of them are given below:

1. Vernon's Classification of Intelligence

(a) *Biological Approach:* Man is an organism among millions living on earth. Environment works as a foe for him. Intelligence is the capacity to adapt to the environment or new situations of life at every moment.

This definition of intelligence can be criticized on the ground that there have been many intelligent and renowned persons who were ill adapted to their social and physical environment. Besides, if we want to study individual differences in a society, this definition serves no practical purpose.

(b) *Psychological Approach* : According to psychologists intelligence is the relative effects of heredity and environment both. An English psychologist, **C. Burt** defined intelligence as the innate general cognitive ability.

In support of psychological definitions of intelligence **Hebb** and **R.B. Catell** distinguished two kinds of intelligence. The first is intelligence "A" which is Fluid intelligence and which is related to genetic potentialities or innate qualities of the individual's nervous system. Second is intelligence "B" which is crystalised "intelligence" and which is related to experiences, learning and environmental factors. These two types of intelligence in normal circumstances so much overlap on each other that they are practically indistinguishable.

(c) *Operational Approach :* These definitions help us to understand the concept of intelligence in clear and definite terms. In this approach scientific terms are first of all defined operationally and then observations are conducted with reference to these terms. For example, in order to determine a child's IQ, we first administer a test of a specific kind. Then we observe his performance on the test and finally draw certain conclusions in the context of the pre-determined objectives.

2. Freeman's Classification

(a) *Ability of adjustment :* An individual is intelligent to the extent to which he is able to adjust to new situations and problems of life. The more a person is intelligent, the more he is able to adapt to his environment in antagonistic conditions. The person who is low in intelligence has less capacity to adjust to the new situations of life.

(b) *Ability of learning :* Learning ability is also an index of intelligence. The more a person is intelligent, the more he will be able to learn new things.

(c) *Ability to carry on abstract thinking :* This category of definitions of intelligence is related to the effective use of concepts and symbols in dealing with situations and solving the problems through the use of verbal and numerical symbols. According to **Terman**, an individual is intelligent to the extent he is able to carry on abstract thinking.

3. E.L. Thorndike's Classification

(a) *Concrete intelligence :* The intellectual ability in relation to concrete materials is called concrete intelligence. It is the ability of a person to comprehend the actual situations and react to them adequately. This kind of intelligence is measured by using performance tests or picture tests in which the subject manipulates the concrete materials.

(b) *Abstract intelligence :* It is the ability to respond to words, letters, numbers or symbols. This type of intelligence is required in all academic activities in schools or outside the schools. The highest level of abstract intelligence is manifested in the thoughts of philosophers or in the inventions of scientists and mathematicians.

(c) *Social intelligence :* It is the ability of an individual to react to social situations of life. It is the ability to understand others and to react to them in such a manner that they may not feel unjust attitude regarding them.

4. Intelligence as a Global Capacity

A comprehensive definitions of intelligence : **Stoddard** (1943) and **Wechsler** (1944) have defined intelligence in the following words :

"Intelligence is the aggregate or the global capacity of the individual to act purposefully, to think rationally and to deal with the environment effectively".

Stoddard further elaborated that intelligence is the capacity of a person to undertake such activities which are: (*i*) difficult (*ii*) complex (*iii*) abstract (*iv*) economical (*v*) goal directed (*vi*) valuable from social view points (*vii*) original. These activities demand concentration of energy and a resistance to emotional forces.

Characteristics of Intelligence

From the above definitions of intelligence, we can draw the following characteristics of intelligence:

(*i*) Intelligence is the composite of several intellectual skills, such as thinking, doing, reasoning, dealing, learning etc.

(*ii*) Intelligence is displayed by the behaviour of the individual as a whole and intelligent behaviour is always goal directed.

(*iii*) Intelligence is the ability to adjust to abnormal and challenging situations of life.

(*iv*) Intelligence is not related to ordinary tasks of life. It is always related to extra ordinary manipulation.

(*v*) Wechsler has included the concepts of drive and incentive which are implied in his statement. "To act purposefully" and "to deal effectively". But many psychologists are of the view that drive and incentive are non-intellectual traits of personality and if they are included in a test of mental ability, more confusions will be created thereof.

(*vi*) There are seven fundamental elements of intelligence according to **Stoddard.** Intelligent person can undertake difficult and abstract tasks with ease. He can manipulate and deal the abstract ideas and concepts efficiently. Similarly, economy refers to the rate at which a mental task is done or a problem is solved. If "A" solves a problem sooner than 'B' then 'A' will be considered more intelligent than 'B'. The term social value indicates whether a mental task performed by a person is in accordance with the socially desirable and acceptable norms or not. The last term original refers to a person's, ability to discover something new and different, *i.e.*, this term is directly related to creative potential of a person. Discovery of some new facts and principles and inventions of new concrete materials by the scientists are few examples of originality.

Stoddard's definition of intelligence has been criticized on two grounds :

(a) It includes social values in intelligence, *i.e.*, intelligent task must be socially desirable. Psychologists criticize this point by saying that social value is a subjective phenomenon, *i.e.*, what is desirable for me, may not be necessarily desirable for others. So, there is no scope of subjectivity in an objective intelligence test.

(b) He has included two conditions of intelligent behaviour in his definition. First is concentration of energy and second is resistance to emotional forces. Psychologists say that these elements are non-intellectual traits and hence they should not be included in mental abilities at any cost.

Theories of Intelligence

1. Faculty theory of intelligence:

This is the oldest theory of intelligence given during the period of pre-experimental psychology. According to this theory mind is made up of different faculties like reasoning, logic, memory, imagination and discrimination. These faculties are independent of each other and can be developed by rigorous mental exercises of the difficult subject-matter.

This theory does not take the hereditary factors of intelligence into account and thus this theory was discarded by the later psychologists who believed that we can never improve the intellectual capacity of a person if he is mentally slow by birth.

2. Unifactor theory:

According to Alfred Binet (1916) intelligence is a general intellectual ability which is made up of several discrete abilities. These abilities include

(i) to reason well with abstract material

(ii) to comprehend well

(iii) to have a clear direction of thoughts

(iv) to relate thinking with the attainment of a desirable end and

(v) to be self-critical.

All these abilities combined together is called general mental ability. Thus, intelligence is a single but complex mental process which can be measured by different kinds of materials designed for the purpose.

3. Two factors theory:

This theory was developed by an English psychologist, **Charles Spearman** in 1904. According to him, intellectual abilities consist of two factors, general ability known as 'G' factors and specific abilities known as 'S' factors.

Characteristics of G factors

(i) It is universal inborn ability.

(ii) It is general mental energy.

(iii) It is constant, *i.e.*, it remains the same in all the individuals and does not change with time.

(iv) The amount of G differs from person to person depending on his genes.

(v) It is used in every life activity.

(vi) Greater the amount of G in an individual, larger is the chance of his success in life.

Characteristics of 'S' factors

(i) It is learnt and hence acquired in the environment.

(ii) It varies from activity to activity in the same individual.

(iii) The amount of S also differs from person to person due to his accessibility to learning situations.

(iv) 'S' factors are related to the specific activity. A low correlation between two or more functions or activities indicates the presence of 'S' factor involved in the activity. A person can be expert only in one or few activities because of the specific factors involved in the activity.

According to Spearman, out of these two factors 'G' factor is more important and thus it is an important measure of intelligence. So, any intelligence test should measure only 'G' factor because it provides most important basis of predicting a person's behaviour in different situations. Raven's Progressive Matrices and Catell's Culture Fair Test both measure 'G' factor.

Spearman has explained his theory with the help of a tetrad equation which is given below :

$$rap \times rbq - raq \times rbp = 0$$

Here,

a = opposites
b = discrimination
p = completion
q = cancellation

Thus, rap means correlation between opposites and completions, rbq means correlation between cancellation and discrimination, raq means correlation between opposite and cancellation and rbp means correlation between discrimination and completion. This theory can also be explained with the help of a diagram given below :

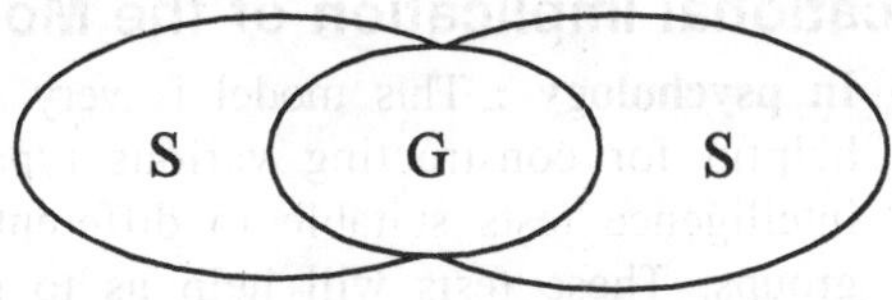

4. Multi-factors theory :

This theory was developed by an American psychologist, **E.L. Thorndike.** He opposed the theory of general intelligence by saying that there are specific stimuli and specific mental responses. Intelligence is nothing more than a potential specific connections between these stimuli and responses. Differences of intelligence among people are due to the different number of such connections in the neurological system. This theory is also called **atomistic theory** of intelligence. There are **four attributes of intelligence** according to him:

(a) *Level :* It refers to the difficulty of a task that can be removed by using intelligence. If different tasks are arranged in increasing difficulty order, then the height that a person can attain determines his level of intelligence. It is a kind of power test.

(b) *Range :* It refers to the number of tasks of the same difficulty value that a person can do in a certain period of time. Theoretically, an individual possessing a certain level of intelligence should be able to solve the whole range of tasks at a given level. It is a kind of speed test.

Range and level can not be completely isolated from each other. We can not measure range without altitude (level) and vice versa.

(c) *Area :* It refers to the total numbers of situations at each level to which the individual is able to respond. Area is the summation of all ranges at each level of intelligence. Area = Level × Range.

(d) *Speed :* It refers to the rapidity with which an individual can respond to a test items. Speed and level are positively correlated. It is different from range in the sense that no specific time is given here to complete a task.

Every intelligence test should consist of these four attributes.

5. Group factor structure of intelligence (PMA Test) :

This theory was developed by **L.L. Thurstone.** According to him, intelligence is not an expression of general factor but a combination of group of traits. They are intermediate factors, *i.e.*, they are not so universal as 'G' factor and they are not so specific as 'S' factor. This primary group of factors give the common mental abilities, a functional cohesiveness and then constitute a group. Another group of common mental abilities is said to have another primary factor and so on. In this way, there are a number of groups of mental abilities each of which has its own primary factors. On the basis of factor analysis of these groups, Thurstone identified the following seven group factors which are termed as primary mental abilities (PMA).

1. Number factor (N) : It is the ability to do numerical calculations rapidly and accurately.
2. Verbal factor (V) : They are related to the operations involving verbal comprehension.
3. Space factor (S) : It is related to the tasks in which subject manipulates an object imaginary in space.
4. Word fluency factor (W) : It is involved to the situation when the subject is asked to think of isolated words at a fast rate.
5. Reasoning factors (R) : It is used in those tasks that require the subject to discover a rule or principles involved in series or groups of letters.
6. Rote memory (M) : It is the ability to memorize a fact quickly.
7. Perceptual speed (P) : It is the ability to note perceptual (visual) details rapidly.

   The point to be noted here is that these seven abilities are significantly correlated with each other.

6. Structure of intelligence (SI) model :

This model was given by **J.P. Guilford** in 1966 in the University of California on the basis of factor analysis of many tests. According to him human mind is composed of at least three dimensions—operations, contents and products, and each dimension of intellect is sufficiently distinct which can be detected by factor analysis. These three dimensions of mind are given below:

(A) **Operations :** Operations can be divided into five major groups of intellectual abilities.

- **Cognition :** It includes discovery, recognition of informations and new understanding of the facts.
- **Memory :** It is the ability to recognize or recall previously learnt material.
- **Divergent thinking :** This operation is closely associated with creative potential.

It refers to the ability to search out and think in a novel out of track way.

- **Convergent thinking :** It refers to the generation of information from given information and drawing conclusion from the given facts.
- **Evaluation :** It is the ability to make judgement on the basis of merits and demerits of a phenomenon. Here, value judgement on knowledge and thoughts is placed after critically examining them.

(B) **Contents :** Five kinds of contents are involved here. Operations are performed on these contents.

- **Figural content :** It is the concrete material perceived through the senses. Visual materials have three properties, size, form and colour.
- **Auditory content :** It includes nature and characteristics of sound perceived.
- **Symbolic content :** It includes letters, digits and other conventional signs usually organised in general pattern.
- **Semantic content :** It refers to those verbal meanings, ideas and concepts for which no examples are necessary.
- **Behavioural content :** It includes knowledge regarding other persons.

(C) **Products :** When five operations are applied to five types of contents, six kinds of products are made.

- **Units :** It refers to the production of a single word, definition or isolated bits of informations.
- **Classes :** It refers to the production of a concept.
- **Relations :** It refers to the production of any form of relationship, such as, analogy, opposite or similar ones.
- **System :** It refers to the production of internally consistent set of classification of various forms.
- **Transformation :** It refers to the production of changes in meaning, organisation or some other arrangement.
- **Implication :** It refers to the production of such information which is beyond the data given.

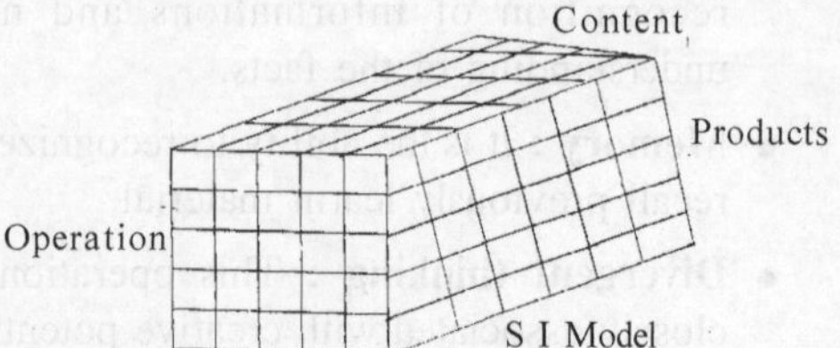

S I Model

On the basis of the model given above it can be stated that there are 5 × 5 × 6 = 150 factors involved in intelligent acts.

Educational Implication of the Model

(a) **In psychology :** This model is very much helpful for constructing various types of intelligence tests suitable to different age groups. These tests will help us to study individual differences in the society. This model is taxonomic in nature and has discovered many abilities which were not known before. If test maker has included items representing contents and operations, he can see whether products are same or different. Conversely, if products are shown by the subject through the test, the test maker can find out the content and operation and match them with the items given in the test.

(b) **In vocational testing :** This model shows that there are 150 intellectual abilities. This model predicts five kinds of mental abilities classified as content. This means that different kinds of test items are needed in vocational testing. Six types of products are also tested on the basis of items representing the products. For example, if a person is able to deal with items of figural contents, he can deal with machines, operators, engineers etc. and any or all of the six types of products can be made by him, such as, he can define a machine or any operator. He can give clear concept about how a machine is operated and so on.

(c) **In the field of education :** Conventionally, learner was considered to be a kind of stimulus response device. Once the stimulus is given to him, he will respond but the new conception of the learner in the light of SI model is that of electronic computer which not only stores information but uses that information to generate new information either by divergent or convergent thinking.

Thus, this model gives the idea that learning is not merely the association of informations but it is the discovery of information as well. Model suggests that in order to understand human learning and higher mental processes of thinking, some drastic modifications are to be made in our theory of curriculum construction and pedagogy of instruction. Similarly, education is no longer considered to be the training of mind. Now, main emphasis on education is given to the learning of specific skills and modification of behaviour and all these materials are not taught merely for the purpose of training the mind of humans.

7. Two Level Process Theory of Intelligence :

This theory was developed by **Jensen** in 1968. According to him intelligence is a combination of two levels of processes. One is associative intelligence and the other is abstract intelligence. Associative intelligence includes those kinds of tests that depend upon memory and simple verbal association. Abstract intelligence includes those factors as concept learning, thinking, problem solving skills, multiple discrimination, principle learning etc.

8. Burt and Vernon's hierarchy theory :

Burt (1940) separated four factors of intelligence by using statistical techniques :

- General factors (common to all traits)
- Group factors (common to some of the traits)
- Specific factors (limited to few traits)
- Error factors (limited to a particular trait when it is measured)

When human mind is put at the top, there will be 5 level hierarchical model of intelligence where general factors will come next to intelligence and error factors will come in the last.

Vernon, on the other hand, suggested that intelligence tests measure an overall factor G as well as two other mental abilities. First are related to verbal, numerical and educational. Second are related to practical, mechanical, spatial and physical. These two major factors can be divided into minor group factors. These minor factors can further be divided into various specific factors and so on.

MEASUREMENT OF INTELLIGENCE

Historical development of mental testing can be divided into three periods for the purpose of convenience.

(A) Pre-Binet Period :

In the 19th century, there was a good deal of interest in the field of psychophysics in which attempts were made to develop general rule of sensory judgement. The functioning of sensory reactions of the typical individuals is actually studied in psycho-physics. Method of limits procedure was used here to measure the extent to which people were able to differentiate between stimuli. But the limitation of these experiments was that accurate generalization of the result was not possible.

Francis Galton was the first psychologist who took interest in studying whether individual characteristics are acquired or inherited. For this purpose, he studied the lives of prominent English men and in his book "Hereditary Genius" he demonstrated that personal characteristics, (mental and physical) of men are inherited. He developed a series of tests to measure these characteristics. It was the starting point of mental measurement.

The first laboratory of experimental psychology was established by **Wundt** in 1879 in Leiping. He employed two methods to test vision, hearing, reaction time and psychosomatic problems—*(i)* psycho-physical method *(ii)* Introspection method. He also developed mental tests which could measure the keenness of vision and hearing, muscular strength, reaction time and other sensory motor functions of body.

Many of **Galton's** ideas were brought to USA by an American psychologist **J.M. Catell.** Like **Galton** he also believed that intellectual functions can best be measured by the reaction time and sensory discrimination tests.

In the last quarter of the 19th century, many psychological laboratories came into existence and studies of individual differences in mental abilities started.

The word "**Mental Test**" was first used by Catell in 1890 but his tests were actually tests of sensory discrimination, speed of motor responses and the like.

Thus, upto this period mental ability was identified as sensory acuity of an individual. The correlation between mental abilities and academic achievements was not known at the time.

Drawbacks of this period:

- Psychologists were unable to identify and define the nature of intelligence. Keenness of sensory motor reactions were related to intelligence.
- They were unable to measure the complex functions of the body.
- Intelligence tests developed during this period were measuring other than intelligence.

(B) Binet Period :

An important incident led the people to think about mental measurement during this period. In the beginning of the 20th century in France, a large number of students failed in the examination. For this teachers and students blamed each other. Seeing this, superintendent of public instruction appointed a committee to device some techniques to screen out slow learners in the schools. Binet and Simon were among members of the committee. They developed a variety of paper pencil tests in their psychological laboratory established in 1889, to administer them on children of different ages. Through these tests Binet tried to measure more complex mental functions such as power of judgement and reasoning, memory, arithmetic ability, etc.

An important contribution of Binet and Simon is that they categorised their tests in terms of age levels by administering their test items to children of different ages. In this way, an age scale of intelligence was also developed. For example, if an item was correctly answered by majority of seven years old children but only few six years old children could respond it correctly, then this item was reserved for seven years old children. In this way, Binet and Simon developed separate tests for different ages.

Similarly, if an item suited to eight years old child was correctly answered by a child of 6 years and if the same trend was shown by the six years old child in most of the cases of a test, then the mental age of the child was considered to be eight years not six years, though his chronological age is six years only. Thus, the concept of mental age was also introduced by Binet and Simon for the first time in the history of mental testing and with the help of this concept we could assess the intellectual ability of a person. Some of the tests developed during this period are given below:

Binet-Simon Scale

The first scale of Binet-Simon was published in 1905. This scale consisted of 30 items arranged in increasing order of difficulty. This scale was a crude measure of intelligence of school going children.

In order to remove some of its defects they revised their scale in 1908. It was the first age based scale and it created a lot of interest among the psychologists across the world. The items in the tests were grouped according to the appropriate age levels from 3 to 13 years.

Some items for three years age

- Point to your nose, eyes and mouth.
- Repeat two digits 3, 5.
- Repeat sentences of six syllables.
- Enumerate objects in a picture.
- Give family names.

Some items of eight years age

- Read a passage and remember two lines.
- Add up the value of five coins.
- Name four colours.
- Count reverse from 20 to zero.
- Give differences between two objects.

1908 revision of Binet-Simon Scale was adopted by many psychologists of America, Switzerland and Germany and many suggestions were given by them for the improvement of the scale. Binet-Simon accepted their suggestions and revised their scale again in 1911.

Some sample items of 1911 scale are given below:

(A) Age = 8 years

- Gives difference between two objects.
- Counts reverse from 20 to zero.
- Points out omissions from unfinished pictures.
- Tells the dates correctly.
- Repeats the digits.

(B) Age = 10 years

- Arranges five blocks in order of increasing weights.
- Reproduces two geometric designs by using memory.
- Criticizes absurd statements.
- Comprehends and answers difficult questions.
- Uses three given words in two sentences.

Main Features of Binet-Simon Scale

(i) They are really scales, *i.e.*, items of the tests are arranged in the increasing difficulty order. Easiest items are put in the beginning and the most difficult item is put in the last. Thus, these scales measure the level or aptitude of an examinee and not their speed.

(ii) These tests measure the general abilities of intelligence instead of specific abilities.

(iii) They can also measure the mental growth of the subject because they are arranged according to different ages from 3 to 14 years.

(iv) They are administered on subjects individually.

(v) Their system of scoring is tied to age norms. A child's performance on the scale will be compared to that of children of his own age.

L.M. Terman's revision of Binet–Simon Scale: L.M. Terman of **Stanford** University revised this scale in 1916 to adapt to American situations. He introduced one new concept which was intelligence Quotient (IQ) in his revision. His scale consisted of 90 items ranging from 3 to 14 years of age. Some items of this scale are given below:

Age = 7 years

- Knows number of fingers on both hands.
- Describes pictures.
- Repeats five digits.
- Gives differences between paired objects.
- Ties a bowknot.

1937 Revision of Binet-Simon Scale : Terman along with his associate Merill revised 1916 scale again in 1937. This revision had two equivalent forms L and M. The number of items in the test was raised to 129 in each L M. forms. A new change was also introduced in the test which was the calculation of chronological age. Upto 13 years CA was taken to be as original but after 13 years CA was computed in the following manner.

At 14 years = 13 yrs+2/3 of 14th year = 13 2/3 years.

At 15 years = 13+2/3 of 2 years = 14 1/3 years.

At 16 years = 13+2/3 of 3 years = 15 years.

Besides, 16 years was taken to be the last age for calculation of IQ. After that, CA was taken to be constant.

LM form revision of 1960 : Binet-Simon scale was last revised in 1960 in which items of both L and M forms were included in the scale. This revision has a range of 2 years of mental age scores to 22 years and 11 months of mental age score. This form of the test measures abilities from 7 categories namely, language, memory, reasoning, social intelligence, conceptual phenomenon, numerical, reasoning and visual motor. Test items are in the form of words, objects and pictures and the responses given by the examinees are in the form of drawing, calculating, writing and speaking. Administration of the test requires one full hour. In this revision intelligence is expressed in terms of standard scores of the deviation IQ.

Wechsler Scale : This scale may be considered an improvement over Binet-Simon scale as it can measure the intelligence of adults very effectively. David Wechsler developed this scale in 1939. This scale was developed in two equivalent forms, each form consisted of ten subtests of which five tests were verbal and five were non-verbal or performance type. This scale was revised in 1955 and was renamed as Wechsler Adult Intelligence Scale (WAIS). It comprised of 11 sub tests of which six were verbal and five were non-verbal. This scale is used on persons above 16 years of age upto 64 and administration time of the scale is one hour. The detail of these 11 subtests are given below:

(a) Verbal subtests :

1. *Information* : 29 questions are given here to test the recall of knowledge concerning wide varieties of information.
2. *Comprehension* : 14 questions are given here to test understanding of knowledge concerning a particular subject or event.
3. *Arithmetic* : 14 questions are given here to test numerical ability. These questions are solved orally without using paper and pencil at all.
4. *Similarity* : 13 questions are given here to measure abstract verbal reasoning. Examinees are required here to compare two objects and find out the relationship between them.
5. *Digit span* : Memory for digits are measured here. In the first half, the examinee is asked to repeat in the same order, three to nine digits presented in the forward directions and in the second half, the digits are repeated in a backward direction.
6. *Vocabulary* : 40 words of increasing difficulty value are presented before the examinees here and they are asked to tell the meaning of these words.

(b) Non-verbal or performance subtests:

1. *Digit symbol* : Nine digits each with different digit symbols are given to the examinees here and they are asked to give the right code for each digits or symbols.
2. *Picture completion* : This subtest measures the ability of the examinees to analyse the parts from the whole. Examinees are given 21 cards containing incomplete pictures and they are asked to fill the missing part of each picture.
3. *Block design* : Its purpose is to measure the ability to analyse the complex whole. There are only 7 designs in these blocks which have red, white and red-white sides. Examinees are asked to produce a given design with the help of these blocks.
4. *Picture arrangement* : Its purpose is to measure the ability to identify the whole from the parts. Here six set of pictures are given to the examinees and they are asked to arrange them in an order which tells a meaningful story.
5. *Object assembly* : Its purpose is to measure the ability to synthesise the whole with the help of parts. Here examinees are given some puzzle pictures each representing some parts of the human body and they are asked to assemble them in the form of a complete man.

Speed and accuracy factors are also scored in Arithmetic, digit symbol, block design, picture arrangement and object assembly. Raw scores of each subject are converted into normalized standard scores with a mean of 10 and SD of 3. This makes the scores of each sub tests comparable. Separate IQ for verbal and non-verbal subtest forms is calculated by adding up the respective subtests of the two forms and if we add up scores on all the 11 subtests, we obtain total scale score. These standard scores are expressed in the form of deviation IQ with a mean of 100 and SD of 15.

Wechsler developed another scale known as Wechsler intelligence Scale for Children in 1949 to test the intelligence of children from 5 to 15 years of age. It also takes one hour to administer, though there are 12 subtests in this scale. Maze test is the only test which is extra in WISC. Maze subtest has eight mazes to be traced by the examinee with a pencil. These mazes are given in increasing order of difficulty.

The scoring system of both the tests WAIS and WISC are the same. Here also the total scores are converted into deviation IQ with a mean of 100 and SD of 15.

Advantages of Wechsler Scales

(i) Though Binet's scale and Wechsler's scale both are individual scales, yet the later can be administered on small groups of children and adults.

(ii) Wechsler's scale is easier to administer than Binet's Scale and its scoring is also less complex than the former.

(iii) Wechsler has prepared separate scales for children and adults Binet's scale does not possess this advantage.

Other differences of Wechsler Scales and Stanford Binet Scale

(i) In Wechsler scale, items are not grouped in terms of mental age as is the case of Stanford-Binet scale. Points are given here for all correct responses. Thus, WAIS or WISC is a point scale.

(ii) In Stanford-Binet scale items are interpreted in terms of different age levels of the examinees but in WAIS or WISC similar types of items are grouped together to form subtests.

(iii) WAIS has separate age norms for adults but in SB Scale all the individuals above 18 are treated in a similar manner as far as computation of IQ is concerned. Thus, people of all age levels are treated as 18 years of age after 18.

(iv) In SB tests items are varied, unrelated and upgraded but in WAIS and WISC tests, items are graded according to various range of ages.

(v) SB scale is internally standardized and rigid but WAIS is externally standardized and flexible.

(vi) SB scale refers to qualitative evaluation while WAIS refers to quantitative evaluation.

(vii) Slight chance of statistical treatment is possible in SB scale but WAIS is fully subject to all statistical analysis.

(c) Post Binet period :

This period is particularly known for testing intelligence in groups and thus group test of intelligence became popular during this periods.

A group test is one that can be given to a number of subjects at a time by a single examiner. This type of test came into being during first World War for the purpose of classifying soldiers for various jobs in accordance with their mental abilities. Army Alpha and Army Beta, two tests were developed during this period. Army Alpha is a verbal group test of intelligence meant for literate people. Army beta is a non-verbal group test of intelligence meant for illiterate persons.

We will discuss here some more group test of intelligence :

1. **Catell's Culture Fair Test :** This test was developed by RB Catell and was published by IPAT (Institute for Personality and Ability Testing) in 1961. The test has three scales and can be administered on children and adults both.

   Scale I meant for 4-8 years

   Scale II meant for 8-15 years

   Scale III meant for 15 years and above

   This test measures the general intelligence factor and takes 30-60 minutes to administer. The test has been prepared in such a manner that previously learnt skill or knowledge does not help the examinee to score more on this test. That is why, it is said to be independent of school achievement, social advantages and environmental influences.

2. **Large Thorndike's Intelligence Test :** This test is meant for primary and secondary school children graded into five different levels. The purpose of the test is to measure verbal comprehension, numerical skill and reasoning abilities. Test has verbal as well as non-verbal items. Only non-verbals items are, however, included at the lower levels. The administration of the test takes 30 minutes in all.

3. **Raven Progressive Matrices Test :** This test was developed in England. It consists of geometric figures and designs. The subjects find out the relationship between figures and select appropriate parts for completion of each pattern of relations.

Classification of Intelligence Test

(A) Classification from the point of view of administration

1. **Individual intelligence test :** An individual intelligence test is one which is administered to only one person at a time. Binet-Simon is an example.

2. **Group intelligence test :** A group intelligence test is one which can be administered to more than one persons at a time. Army Alpha and Army Beta are two examples of such tests.

Some general characteristics of group intelligence tests are as follows :

(i) They have been developed on the assumption that intelligence is a general capacity and can be measured by sampling a variety of mental activities.

(ii) In group tests the similar types of items are pooled together in different subtests.

(iii) Every group test is standardized for a special range of ages or school grades.

(iv) Construction of individual test is also very difficult and costly as compared to group tests. Their scoring and standardization is also time consuming process.

(v) It is very difficult to establish rapport between the examiner and the examinees and hence examinees can not be motivated properly in group tests of intelligence. These two limitations are not seen in individual tests.

(vi) Group tests are superior to individual tests in the sense that norms established here are more dependable than that of individual tests. It is because these norms are calculated on the basis of a very large sample.

(vii) Individual test provides qualitative performance of the individual while group tests are mostly point scale and express the performance in quantities.

(B) Classification from the point of view of nature of items of the test

1. **Verbal test :** Verbal test of intelligence is one in which instructions and items are produced before the examinees through the written language. So, examinees must be literate to take these tests. Mohsin's General intelligence Test, Joshi's General Mental Ability test and Jalota's Group General Mental Ability Test are some examples of verbal tests of intelligence of Indian origin.

2. **Non-verbal test :** A non-verbal test is one which requires the use of language only to impart instructions. The examinees are asked to manipulate the test materials in their own way. Since language is not needed to respond to items here, it can be administered to illiterate persons as well. They are also culturally free and hence they can be applied to any situation representing any culture. Test items are usually of figured relation type. Army Beta is a good example of non-language test.

3. **Performance test :** A performance test is one in which a subject has to perform some thing or to manipulate some concrete materials without much use of the language ability. Non-verbal and performance tests are useful for the following groups of people:

   (a) *Deaf and Dumb :* Those children who cannot hear or speak can be tested with the help of performance test.

   (b) *Illiterates :* Verbal test of intelligence is useless for those who cannot read or write. Performance test is useful for them.

   (c) *Shy children :* Many withdrawn children are hesitant to express before others. Performance and non-verbal test of intelligence will suit them very much.

   (d) *Educationally deficient children :* Verbal test of intelligence generally measure learning along with intelligence. If children are educationally poor, they will perform poorly on intelligence test too and thus they will be wrongly declared as children of below average intelligence. Such a problem can be overcome by using performance test or non-verbal intelligence test.

   (e) *Useful for children of other culture :* A particular culture dominates in every verbal intelligence test and thus the test can not be adopted by other cultures. Due to free from culture, performance test is suitable for these foreign students.

Some performance tests of intelligence are given below :

(a) **Pintner Paterson Scale :** This is the first systematic performance test. This scale was standardized in 1917. It consists of 15 subtests.

(b) **Goodenough Drawing Test :** This scale was developed by Florence Goodenough in 1926. Here child is asked to draw the picture of a man as best as possible without any time limit. This is especially useful for those children who are suspected to be mentally retarted.

Weaknesses of performance test :

- Here the subject can score high due to practice effect and chance success is more frequent than verbal tests. Because of this reason, reliability coefficient is very low.
- They fail to distinguish between gifted and average children due to limited scope of these tests.
- These scales fail to test fine mental abilities such as, ability to make abstraction or concept formation or evaluation abilities of mind.

Interpretation of Intelligence Test Scores : Intelligence test scores can be interpreted in the following three ways:

1. **Mental age :** This concept was first introduced by **Afred Binet** of France in 1908. It refers to a score that is determined by comparing a child's score with the scores obtained by younger or older children in the norming group. Here a child's score is compared with the average score of his own age. For example, if a 9-year-old child scores 60 on an

intelligence test and suppose mental age norms for that scale are as follows:

Mental age of 8 years = 60

Mental age of 9 years = 70

Mental age of 10 years = 80

Then, in that case, mental age of the child will be considered as 8 years instead of 9 though his chronological age is 9 years.

Similarly, if another child of 8 years obtains a score of 80, then his mental age will be 10 years, though his chronological age is 8 years only.

Thus, we can say that the mean performance of each age level becomes the mental age for that age level.

2. **Intelligent Quotient (IQ) :** IQ is also based on the concept of mental age. It is the ratio of mental age to the chronological age multiplied by 100.

$$IQ = \frac{MA}{CA} \times 100.$$

Suppose, the mental age of a 10-year-old child is 12 years on the basis of his scores on an intelligence test, his IQ will be

$$\frac{12}{10} \times 100 = 120.$$

Similarly, if mental age of a person is nine years two months and his age is 12 years 6 months, then his IQ will be

$$\frac{110}{150} \times 100 = 73.3.$$

General classification of persons in terms of IQ

IQ	Classification
140 and above	Genius
130-140	Very superior
120-130	Superior
110-120	Bright
90-110	Average
80-90	Dull
70-80	Borderline
Below 70	Mentally retarded.

Shortcomings of IQ: Some of the main short comings of IQ are as follows:

(i) It is a well-known fact that after 18 years, the mental age of a person tends to stabilize. Thus, if IQ is calculated after this age, the result will be misleading, *i.e.*, a person will be less intelligent if he grows in age.

(ii) Variability of IQ scores from one test to another is not the same. As a result IQ scores for different tests would not be directly comparable.

(iii) It has also been found that variability in IQ scores for the different age levels on the same test is not the same. In that case IQ scores would be a misleading index because it would indicate that a person's IQ may increase or decrease as he grows in age. An example will illustrate this point.

Age	IQ	SD
9 years old child	120	12
7 years old child	120	9

Here IQ of 120 of both the children is not the same due to difference in SD.

3. **Deviation IQ :** Now-a-days IQ ratio is converted into a normalized standard score with a fixed mean of 100 and SD of 15. This is known as DIQ. This fixed mean and SD remain constant through all the age levels. It means that if a child's score is 1 SD above the mean his DIQ will be 100 + 15 = 115. Similarly, if his score is 1 SD below the mean his DIQ will be 100 – 15 = 85 and so on. Thus, with the help of these **DIQ** scores inter age comparison is also possible.

Uses of Intelligence Test

Intelligence tests can be applied in the following situations.

1. **Measurement of general learning abilities:** Intelligence and achievement in schools are highly correlated. If a person is high on an intelligence test, he is expected to score high on school achievements also. Conversely if a person scores high on an intelligence test and still his school achievement is very poor, we can find out other reasons for his educational backwardness.
2. **Assessment of individual differences and categorization :** With the help of intelligence tests we can categories a particular class into several convenient groups and plan our instructional strategies accordingly. Thus, intelligence testing is very useful for educational guidance.
3. **Exact definition of mental retardation is possible :** It is said that those who are below 70 in IQ are retarded but to what extent they are mentally retarded can further be studied with the help of higher screening. We may define the three groups of mentally retarted in the following ways.

Category	IQ level
Morons	45-69
Imbeciles	25-45
Idiots	Below 25

4. **Identification of gifted children :** Gifted children are the treasure of the society. They must be identified in the earlier stages of their lives so that they can be fully guided and helped for their better advancement which is directly related to the advancement of the society as well. Intelligence testing will help the concerned organisations to chalk out plans in the desired manner.

5. **Vocational guidance :** Some children are very forward in verbal abilities and some are superior in non-verbal abilities. This identification is possible only with the help of intelligence tests. Since academic subjects need verbal intelligence and technical subjects need non-verbal or performing abilities, hence children may be guided accordingly.

6. **Screening :** In today's age of competition and rush, screening has become a necessity. Every school has limited seats of admission and it has to select only those students who can raise the academic level of the school high and get name for it. Same is the case with appointments in jobs. For all these purposes, intelligence testing is a must.

7. **Study of mental growth :** Mental abilities develop in a sequential order onward. We can use intelligence tests for studying the trends of mental development of individuals. Intelligence tests have made it clear that mental development of children is a steady consistent process from year-to-year till the age of 25. Intelligence tests show that mind does not develop rapidly in the period of adolescence like the physical and emotional development, but in childhood, it develops rapidly.

Limitations of Intelligence Tests

1. Generally intelligence test shows what a person can do at a certain point of time. These abilities are tested on the basis of certain items included in the test. In order to make the results dependable, a proper size of the sample must be selected for standardization of the test.

2. Some people may be fatigued earlier than others when take a test. This extent of fatigue may reduce their scores and hence intelligence testing will not be accurate. So scores should be taken with caution.

3. No intelligence test is fully free from cultural influences. So, home or school background may affect the intelligence test scores of subjects.

4. Administration of the test also affects the scores of subjects. If proper rapport is there between the examiner and the examinee. IQ scores may be high. On the other hand, if children are frightened with the testing situation as is case of slow learners they will perform poorly on the test.

5. Taking intelligence scores in absolute form is misleading. Intelligence tests do not reveal all the mental abilities in most of the cases. So, intelligence test must be supplemented with clinical setting and case history method to collect detailed information about a subject as is done in clinics by physician who does not entirely believe in physical investigations. He rather takes the help of clinical diagnosis before giving remedial treatment to the patients.

THOUGHT AND LANGUAGE

In this section we examines the relationship between language and thought: that language determines thought, that thought determines language, and that thought and language have different origins. Let us examine these three viewpoints in some detail.

Language as Determinant of Thought

In Hindi and other Indian languages we use a number of different words for various kinship relationships. We have different terms for mother's brother, father's elder brother, father's younger brother, mother's sister's husband, father's sister's husband and so on. An English person uses just one word *uncle* to describe all these kinship relationships. In the English language there are dozens of words for colours whereas some tribal languages have only two to four colour terms. Do such differences matter for how we think? Does an Indian child find it easier to think about and differentiate between various kinship relationships compared to her English-speaking counterpart? Does our thinking process depend on how we describe it in our language?

Benjamin Lee Whorf was of the view that language determines the contents of thought. This view is known as **linguistic relativity hypothesis**. In its strong version, this hypothesis holds what and how individuals can possibly think is determined by the language and linguistic categories they use **(linguistic determinism).** Experimental evidence, however, maintains that it is possible to have the same level or quality of thoughts in all languages depending upon the availability of linguistic categories and structures. Some thoughts may be easier in one language compared to another.

Thought as Determinant of Language

The noted Swiss psychologist, Jean Piaget believed that thought not only determines language, but also precedes it. Piaget argued that children form an internal representation of the world through thinking. For example, when children see something and later copy it (a process called imitation), thinking does take place, which does not involve language. A child's observation of other's behaviour and imitation of the same behaviour, no doubt involves thinking but not language. Language is just one of the vehicles of thinking. As actions become internalised, language may affect children's range of symbolic thinking but is not necessary for the origins of thought. Piaget believed that though language can be taught to children, understanding of the words require knowledge of the underlying concepts (*i.e.* thinking). Thus, thought is basic, and necessary if language is to be understood.

Different Origins of Language and Thought

The Russian psychologist, Lev Vyogotsky, argued that thoughts and language develop in a child separately until about two years of age, when they merge. Before two years thought is preverbal and is experienced more in action (Piaget's sensory motor stage). The child's utterances are more automotic reflexes—crying when uncomfortable—than thought-based. Around two years of age, the child expresses thought verbally and her/his speech reflects rationality. Now children are able to manipulate thoughts using soundless speech. He believed that during this period the development of language and thinking become interdependent; the development of conceptual thinking depends upon the quality of inner speech and vice versa. Thought is used without language when the vehicle of thinking is non-verbal such as visual or movement-related. Language is used without thought when expressing feelings or exchanging pleasantries, for example "Good morning! How are you?" "Very well, I am fine". When the two functions overlap, they can be used together to produce verbal thought and rational speech.

Development of Language

Language is a complex system and unique to human beings. Psychologists have tried to teach sign language, use of symbols to chimpanzees, dolphins, parrots, etc. But it is observed that, human language is more complex, creative, and spontaneous than the system of communication other animals can learn. There is also a great deal of **regularity** with which children all over the world seem to be learning the language or languages to which they are exposed. When we compare individual children, we find that they differ a great deal in the rate of their language development as well as in how they go about it. But when we take a general view of children's acquisition of language all over the world we find some *predictable pattern* in which children proceed from almost no use of language to the point of becoming competent language users. Language develops through some of the stages discussed below.

Newborn babies and young infants make a variety of sounds, which gradually get modified to resemble words. The first sound produced by babies is crying. Initial crying is undifferentiated and similar across various situations. Gradually, the pattern of crying varies in its pitch and intensity to signify different states such as hunger, pain, and sleepiness, etc. These differentiated crying sounds gradually become more meaningful *cooing sounds* (like 'aaa', 'uuu', etc). usually to express happiness.

At around six months of age children enter the *babbling* stage. Babbling involves prolonged repetition of a variety of consonants and vowel sounds (for example, da—, aa—, ba—). By about nine months of age these sounds get elaborated to strings of some sound combinations, such as 'dadadadadada' into repetitive patterns called *echolalia.* While the early babblings are random or accidental in nature, the later babblings seem to be imitative of adult voices. Children show some understanding of a few words by the time they are six months old. Around the first birthday (the exact age varies from child-to-child) most children enter the *one-word-stage.* Their first word usually contains one syllable—*ma or da*, for instance. Gradually they move to one or more words which are combined to form whole sentences or phrases. So they are called *holophrases.* When they are 18 to 20 months of age, children enter a *two-word stage* and begin to use two words together. The two-word stage exemplifies *telegraphic speech.* Like telegrams (got admission, send money) it contains mostly nouns and verbs. Close to their third birthday, *i.e.* beyond two-and-a-half years, children's language development gets focused on rules of the language they hear.

How is language acquired? You must be wondering: "How do we learn to speak?" As with many other topics in psychology, the questions of whether a behaviour develops as a result of inherited characteristics (nature) or from the effects of learning (nurture) has been raised with regard to language. Most psychologists accept that both nature and nurture are important in language acquisition.

Behaviourist B.F. Skinner believed we learn language the same way as animals learn to pick keys or press bars. Language development, for the behaviourists follow the learning principles, such as association (the sight of bottle with the word 'bottle'), imitation (adults use of word ''bottle''), and reinforcement (smiles and hugs when the child says something right). There is also evidence that children produce sounds that are appropriate to a language of the parent or care-giver and are reinforced for having done so. The principle of shaping leads to successive approximation of the desired responses so that the child eventually speaks as well as the adult. Regional differences in pronunciation and phrasing illustrate how different patterns are reinforced in different areas.

Linguist Noam Chomsky put forth the innate proposition of development of language. For him the *rate at which children acquire words and grammar* without being taught can not be explained only by learning principles. Children also *create all sorts of sentences* they have never heard and, therefore, could not be imitating. Children throughout the world seem to have a *critical period*—a period when learning must occur if it is to occur successfully—for learning language. Children across the world also go through the same stages of language development. Chomsky believes language development is just like physical maturation given adequate care, it ''just happens to the child''. Children are born with ''universal grammar''. They readily learn the grammar of whatever language they hear.

Skinner's emphasis on learning explains why infants acquire the language they hear and how they add new words to their vocabularies. Chomsky's emphasis on our built-in readiness to learn grammar helps explain why children acquire language so readily without direct teaching.

GENDER AS A SOCIAL CONSTRUCT; GENDER ROLES, GENDER-BIAS AND EDUCATIONAL PRACTICE

Gender refers to the social distinctions between boys and girls and men and women that are socially constructed rather than biologically determined. These distinctions are reflected in the roles that boys and girls play in society and the status that they occupy within it. Gender roles tend to be dynamic. They vary from one culture and time period to another and are characterized by unequal power relationships.

Ending gender bias and discrimination is crucial to the empowerment of women and girls and to the achievement of gender equality in education. Applying a gender perspective helps to make differences in power relations visible. It also helps us to see more clearly the needs and rights of girls and boys in particular geographical, cultural and economic contexts.

The ultimate goal is to eliminate gender biases and discriminatory practices and policies, both overt and covert. This is at the heart of gender analysis. Gender analysis should therefore be a prerequisite for identifying and understanding problems as they relate to education, and especially to the continued exclusion of girls from quality schooling. Gender analysis guides the process of finding viable and sustainable solutions to the problems of access, quality and learning achievement.

Gender analysis of what learners bring to education (including early childhood socialization, feeding and health access, cultural heritage and language), the content of education, teaching and learning processes, learning environments and learning outcomes help to highlight bad (and good) educational practices and policies. This analysis, in turn, should form the basis for educational interventions that are sensitive to both gender and human rights.

Gender Bias in Teaching

A common response from teachers when asked about gender inequity in classrooms is that they treat all their students the same. There are two problems with this statement. First, students are diverse and have different learning issues, thus treating all students in the same way means that some students will have a better learning experience than their peers. Second, teachers may be ignoring their unconscious gender biases towards their students, their schools and themselves. If ignored, these gender biases, which may have developed from cultural norms, may lead to bias in the classroom.

Gender bias occurs when people make assumptions regarding behaviours, abilities or preferences of others based upon their gender. Because there are strong gender role stereotypes for masculinity and femininity, students who do not match them can encounter problems with teachers and with their peers. For example, the expectation is that boys naturally exhibit boisterous, unruly behaviour, are academically able, rational, and socially uncommunicative, whereas girls are quiet, polite, and studious. Girls are also expected to possess better social skills than boys and to excel at reading and the language arts. So girls who present discipline problems for teachers, or quiet, studious boys, may encounter a lack of understanding from peers and teachers. Within the classroom, these biases unfold in students' practices and teachers' acceptance of certain behaviours from one student or another based upon the students' gender. Also, bias due to a person's gender is not mutually exclusive of other social categories such as race, ethnicity, class, religion, and language. For example, some teachers may perceive African American or other Black girls as loud and uncontrollable because the girls do not exhibit the feminine behaviours associated with White women, such as quiet, self-effacing and malleable.

Gender bias can occur within subject areas and school activities. For example, in subjects such as mathematics and the sciences, there are different participation patterns for girls and boys. Gender bias promulgates a myth that boys are naturally better at mathematics and science than girls. The implications are that if girls succeed in these subjects it is due to their hard work, not their intelligence, whereas boys' success is credited to their natural talent. There are some signs that gender bias in schools may be decreasing in some areas. The percentage of girls participating in science has increased and achieved parity with boys in biology, chemistry and algebra. However, subjects that are prerequisites for college majors such as engineering or physics remain dominated by men. Only 25% of high school students enrolled in physics are female. Moreover, there has been little increase in the percentage of women in engineering programs.

Males are also more likely than females to be in remedial programs and students' race also impacts these patterns. For example, African American males are more likely than White or female peers to enroll in remedial reading and mathematics courses. And non-White students have a higher representation in vocational and noncollege preparatory courses than their White peers. Teachers are critical components in challenging gender bias in schooling, but they also can be major contributors to it as well, through their pedagogical practices, curriculum choices, and assessment strategies.

Gender Bias in Teachers

Teachers' unconscious gender biases can produce stereo-typic expectations for students' success and participation in the classroom. Teachers view male students' domination of the classroom and their time as typical masculine behaviour. However, these biases have consequences for the students and the classroom climate. More than two decades ago, researchers identified and named groups of students who dominated the teacher's time and the classroom resources as ''target students'' (Tobin & Gallagher, 1987). Target students were typically white and male. They answered most of the teacher's questions and also asked most of the questions. This behaviour pattern was particularly insidious in mathematics and science classrooms because teachers did not expect girls to have competent knowledge in these subject areas. Classroom observations documented that target students typically called out answers to the teacher's questions, thus denying other students the opportunity to engage in dialogue with the teacher or get to grips with the subject matter. Furthermore, because boys are perceived as having natural talent in science, teachers asked boys harder and more complicated questions than girls. If girls attempted to answer more difficult questions than boys and faltered, teachers often repeated the question and asked that another student, typically a boy, provide the answer. However, if a boy failed to answer correctly, teachers reframed the question or broke it into a series of simpler questions that could help the student find the answer. Teachers' unconscious stereotyped gender bias that boys are smarter than girls, especially in mathematics and the sciences, meant they were willing to work with boys to reach the answer because they perceived boys were capable of achieving that goal but girls were not. Conversely, teachers of subjects perceived as feminine will spend more time engaged with girls.

Teachers' gendered perceptions of students' ability is also reflected in the type of praise and expectations they have of their students. Teachers often give girls less meaningful and less critical praise than boys. Boys' work is described as unique or brilliant, while girls' work is often undervalued, critically ignored and praised for its appearance. This aspect of teachers' behaviour is particularly detrimental to girls because it means they do not receive feedback on their work that could help them develop deeper understandings of concepts (Liu, 2006).

Teachers also use target students to maintain the tempo and pace of classroom instruction. For example, in a lecture or whole class discussion when a teacher is posing questions to the class, he or she may encourage target students to call out answers in order to keep the lesson moving, rather than wait for the other students to process the question and provide an answer. This short ''wait time'' may be detrimental to learning. More than three decades ago, researchers found that if teachers waited three to five seconds before accepting a student's answer, more students became engaged in the classroom and also improved their understanding of the content. Moreover, the longer wait time meant that teachers began to ask more cognitively challenging questions. However, the existence of target students in classes who often call out answers without direction from teachers meant that fewer students, especially girls, engaged in the lessons. In the absence of proactive teacher intervention, these patterns in which males dominate classroom interactions also occur in mixed-gender, small groups.

Target students dominate classroom interactions and exchanges at all education levels. In the early

2000s, researchers identified these same patterns of engagement in a professional development program for science teachers. When alerted to the invasive behaviours of the male teachers in the cohort, faculty began using overt breaching strategies to stop the target students calling out answers, dominating the human and materials resources of the classroom, and showing disrespect to their peers (Martin Milne & Scantlebury, 2006).

Teachers' gender bias towards students can also extend to their response to students who challenge their authority. Such risk-taking behaviour in boys is expected and at times praised, but assertiveness in girls is viewed negatively and labelled unfeminine. Similarly, boys who do not exhibit stereotypic masculine behaviours may be ridiculed (Renold, 2006).

Teachers use gender expectations as a means of maintaining classroom control. For example, teachers will seat undisciplined boys next to girls as a classroom management strategy. Further, teachers use the gendered expectation that girls' nurturing characteristics will lead them to place others' needs before their own. In other words, teachers often ask girls to assume mothering roles towards students who have fallen behind with learning because of inattentiveness, absenteeism through truancy, or in-school disciplinary procedures, and often those students are male.

Effects of Gender Bias

Gender bias can impact students' attitudes towards learning and their engagement with the subject. If affected by gender bias, girls will tend to believe that any success they have is due to hard work rather than any innate talent or intelligence. Boys may be encouraged to believe that success in science and mathematics should come easily to them because of their gender. Some males report dropping out of college science and mathematics programs because they no longer perceive these subjects as easy. Overall, teachers have lower expectations for girls' academic success compared to boys, and their attitudes are shown through the type and quality of the student-teacher interaction. The type and quality of critique teachers give their students can also have an impact. Teachers' comments on girls' work focuses on its appearance but with boys' work teachers focus on the content. Girls often do not receive substantive comments or criticism from teachers from which they could improve their ability to learn. During the many hours spent in classrooms, girls receive less time and attention from teachers than their male peers. Teachers usually ask girls easier questions than they ask boys. Typically, girls receive fewer opportunities to engage in classroom discourse, use equipment and assert their knowledge in classrooms.

Reducing Gender Bias

Gender bias in education is a series of microinequities whose impact is cumulative and often ignored. Girls are rewarded and praised for compliant behaviour. Teachers do not challenge girls with questions and rarely offer criticisms of their works. Teachers can reduce and challenge gender bias through an examination of their pedagogical practices and by posing simple questions about their practices. For example, which students do they frequently interact with? Are target students evident in their classroom? If so, how does the teacher deal with those students? What questioning techniques does the teacher use to engage students? Does the teacher ask complicated questions to girls as well as boys? Does the teacher use a variety of pedagogical and assessment practices? Which students are engaged with the curriculum?

Another way of reducing gender bias would be for teachers to videotape their classes and review their interactions with the students. Or they could invite a colleague to watch their teaching and record which students are being asked questions and what type of questions. However, teachers must also prepare for the consequences of changing their practices. Girls are conditioned to receiving less of the teacher's attention, and they do not usually cause discipline problems if they are not receiving their fair share, but boys can react negatively to losing the teacher's attention, causing disruption to lessons and becoming discipline problems. Moreover, research has also shown that boys avoid written work and often have poor communication skills when asked to work in singlesex groups.

However, the gains in reducing gender bias in education may disappear with the requirements of high-stakes testing required by No Child Left Behind (NCLB). NCLB requires that states report academic achievement data in most social categories, except gender (Kahle, 2004). This may result in less attention being placed on gender bias and less data that might reveal it. Continued monitoring of gender bias is necessary to minimize its impact on students' opportunities for learning and achievement.

INDIVIDUAL DIFFERENCES AMONG LEARNERS

It is not unusual to find a wide range of differences among students in a class or a group. These differences are invariably identified in terms of student's characteristics such as physical (appearance, height, size, sex, colour, etc.), demographic (age, caste, socio-economic status, etc.) and cognitive behaviour (thinking, remembering, problem solving, creating idea, etc.). The differences that exist among students due to physical, demographic, affective behaviour and cognitive behaviour characteristics are referred to as individual differences.

Differences due to physical and demographic characteristics are conspicuous and easy to identify. However, the differences that exist in the way they solve problem in Mathematics or in their ability to interpret and explain ideas are not easily visible but are identified through their performance. Let us examine, for instance, the answers given by Bitto and Neha, two students of the same class to the following proverb.

Interpret the saying, ''Pen is mighter than the sword''.

Bitto's Interpretation

It means that writing had always been able to influence mankind more than any amount of sheer physical strength; writing undoubtedly makes a more lasting impact in the minds of the people than any form of physical demonstration. In the case of the latter the impact might be forceful though less lasting. Great thinkers, writers and philosophers have from time immemovial been able to hold sway over the minds of the people by means of their profound knowledge through their writings. For example, Socrates won the wrath of a powerful state, because of his great ability to hold spellbound the young through his discourses. Similarly, the writing of Voltaire and Rousseau inspired the French to rise up in revolt.

Neha's Interpretation

It is a common proverb which simply means that through writing it is possible to win more victories than by using physical force and weapons. When any good book is read it is possible to retain in our memory the message it contains. On the other hand, success achieved through physical might is not for mankind.

The above illustration reflects the differences between Bitto and Neha in their interpretation of the proverb. While Bitto delves deep in her interpretation, Neha states only the meaning.

According to Skinner, individual differences in learner behaviours are the result of the organism's genetic endowment and reinforcement. Thus, Skinner believed that defective genetic endowment and/or defective reinforcement contingencies in an individual's experience result in a failure to acquire a variety of learned behaviours.

The process of an individual's mental activities such as remembering, analysing, interpreting, reasoning, problem solving and thinking are cognitive domain behaviours and are essential for learning and achievement. How we think, what and how we remember, how we solve problem and how we create ideas are cognitive domain behaviours and individuals differ by these behaviours. Such differences are often identified by psychologists in terms of intelligence, aptitude, creating and academic achievement.

Individual differences are crucial for teachers who are responsible for guiding all forms of learning. In fact, many educators would suggest that the primary role of teachers is to provide education to meet the individual differences and to develop student cognitive process.

Do Individuals Differ in Intelligence?

Well, they do differ. But how? Differences are due to the differences in the level of general intellectual ability and the underlying cognitive process among individuals.

How do we identify differences in intelligence?

Using suitable intelligence tests we can measure and identify the difference. An intelligence test may contain sub-tests (sub-sections) and each sub-test represents a different set of ability. The scores obtained in all sub-tests are added up to obtain a single score to represent the general ability of the student. Thus, the single score obtained for each individual in a test is expressed in terms of **intelligence quotient** (IQ). IQ is a measure of intelligence and is defined as the ratio of mental age (average age of children who give correct responses/ answers in an intelligence test) to the chronological age (actual age) multiplied by 100 (to avoid fraction). Thus mental age is:

$$IQ = \frac{\text{Mental age}}{\text{Chronological age}} \times 100$$

IQ scores help us estimate individual differences by categorising individuals on the basis of their IQs. These differences have important consequences for learning and performance. Let us examine the different categories of students based on their intelligence level.

Gifted : Those students who possess IQs of 130 or above are called gifted students. They are superior in intelligence and have high ability to reason. As compared to other children, they can perform academic activities grasping concepts, memorising, perceiving, seeing relationships, generalising, dealing with abstract ideas, critical thinking and solving problems more effectively and quickly. They have a broad attention span that permits concentration and the ability for a high level of academic performance. They take initiative in intellectual work and follow complex directions. Such individuals are small in number as compared to normal or average children. Normal groups have those children whose IQs range from 90 to 110 and they are able to profit from regular school programmes with varying degrees of effort.

Disabled : There are children with **disability** due to low level to intellectual functioning or specific learning deficits. Children with low level or below-average intellectual functioning are called mentally retarded. The children with inadequate level of intelligence are impaired in their ability to learn and to adapt to the demands of society. Mentally retarded children are of different categories. They can be:

- **Border line** (IQ ranges 90-70) and **educable mentally retarded** (IQ ranges 70-50) children can perform academic activities but are slow in their learning. Special instructional strategies can help them to profit from learning activities. They can take care of themselves and live independently as adults.
- **Trainable mentally retarded** (IQ ranges 50-35) are capable of learning only certain rudimentary literacy materials and simple occupational skills. They possess some ability to take care of their personal needs and can be trained in daily living skills. Such children require special classes or schools to study in.
- **Severely retarded** (IQ below 35) have quite limited adaptive behaviour and are never found in school. They are dependent on their families for their personal needs.

Children with specific learning defects are called learning disabled group. They are normal to above-average on intelligence but have difficulties in one or more psychological processes involved in understanding or in using language or numbers (written or spoken). The difficulties manifest in their ability to listen, think, speak, read, write, spell or do mathematical calculations. These difficulties are identified as **aphasia** (difficulty in grasping spoken language), **dylesia** (difficulty in reading), **hyperlexia** (little or no comprehension), **dyscalculia** (difficulty in doing arithmetic) and **dysgraphia** (difficulty in writing). Some are hyperactive in the sense that they are excessively active inattentive and behave impulsively. They follow instructions poorly and do not often complete the assigned tasks.

Instructional Strategies for Handling Individual Differences

- Organise instruction for the development of cognitive process.
- Use existing cognitive level as base.
- Strengthen memory.
- Formulate level specific instructional strategy.
- Use individual meeting.
- Provide instructions to overcome learning disability.

Do Individuals Differ in Aptitude?

Yes, they do differ. An individual may have a mechanical aptitude, another may have an aptitude for mathematics or yet another may have an aptitude for language, music or athletics. Such differences are due to the differences in the combination of abilities related to the cognitive processes, and the sensory and psychomotor components. For instance, when we talk of mechanical aptitude, we may deal with ability for spatial relations, ability to acquire information on mechanical matters and ability to comprehend mechanical relations, besides sensory and psychomotor abilities. Similarly, when we discuss aptitude in music, we may identify ability for musical memory, pitch discrimination, loudness discrimination, time discrimination and judgement of rhythm. Likewise, abilities required for science or mathematics are different and each requires a separate set of abilities.

The differences in aptitude can be identified using aptitude tests. Aptitude tests for areas such as mechanical skills, mathematics, science, language, music and graphic art can be used to identify the aptitude of students in each area of performance. You might have heard of the use of aptitude tests in medicine, engineering, business management, law or teacher training for selection of students for studies in the respective fields. The aptitude test, in fact, provides a measure of the candidates promise or teachability in a field of study, say, medicine. In other words, the test would tell whether the candidate possesses the required aptitude or readiness to profit from studies in the concerned field of study.

Instructional Strategy for Handling Individual Differences

The suggested approach for handling individual differences is **adaptive instructional system**. In this approach at least two alternative instructional treatments are needed to ensure academic success. Which is the most appropriate instructional treatment for the student depends upon his or her existing level of aptitude (learning readiness). Students with high aptitude may choose unstructured instructional strategy. With minimum guidance from teacher, they may be encouraged to learn through the discovery oriented approach. You may use the inductive process but instructional treatment is essentially learner-centered.

In contrast, highly structured instructional treatment for low aptitude learners is designed in small units through sequential steps and feedback. Frequent summary and review with simplified illustration, analogy and precise explanation of concepts and principles to be learned will facilitate progressive learning. Periodic achievement and aptitude assessments and comparison of these scores with the aptitude scores obtained at the start of instruction would tell the degree to which each learner in the specific treatment group has achieved.

However, for those who are unable to profit from either of the alternative treatments presented above, **compensatory aptitude training** is suggested. This consists of directed reading skill, study habits, self-learning skills, note taking and related activities. The main aim of compensatory aptitude training is to develop readiness for entry into structured treatment. Periodic monitoring should be formulated to identify the students who reach the required level for entry into alternative treatment.

Do Learners Differ in their Academic Achievements?

They do differ, but how? We have seen that those who possess appropriate pre-requisite knowledge learn more effectively than those who lack such knowledge. Differences in pre-requisite knowledge possessed by students create differences in the attainment of knowledge. Further, knowledge is attained progressively. Progressive differences in knowledge attainment leads to cumulative differences in knowledge attainment and this form of differences is often called **Mathew Effect.** It means that academically rich get richer and those who are poor continue to be poor. Thus, differences in pre-requisites and cumulative knowledge lead to differences in the knowledge possessed by the students likewise, they also differ in their capabilities to manipulate the knowledge in a given situation and the differences are identified in terms of the abilities to apply, analyse, synthesise and evaluate knowledge. In fact, ability is an essential condition for learning and the abilities related to intelligence, aptitude and creativity are important for academic achievement. We have seen the instructional strategies for meeting the differences in intelligence, aptitude and creativity through classroom situations. It means that differences in intelligence, aptitude and creativity do create differences in academic achievement.

The differences in academic achievement can be identified using an achievement test in the concerned subject. However, if the achievement test contains only knowledge level items (questions), it tells only knowledge level differences. On the other hand, if it contains items (questions) on knowledge and capabilities—comprehension, application, analysis, synthesis and evaluation—the various levels of differences can be identified. Besides, the total marks, each level-wise total is needed to identify the strengths and weaknesses of every student as well as the differences among students. As a teacher, if you know the strengths and weaknesses of your students in a subject, you may be able to adopt appropriate instructional strategies to suit their strenghts and weaknesses in that subject.

Apart from these achievement differences are quite often identified in terms of categories of achievers by classifying students as high, average and low achievers. Though there is no strict cut-off points, these categories can be created using marks. High achievers are those who possess higher level of knowledge and capabilities (say, with marks 66% and above) than the rest and those who possess average level of knowledge and capabilities (say, with marks 36% to 65%) are called average achievers. On the other extreme, you may find learners with low level knowledge and capabilities (with 35% and below marks). They are called low achievers. If you are interested in identifying the high, average and low achievers in a subject, say Science or language, the categories are created using the marks obtained in the concerned subject. However, categories can also be created based on the overall achievement in a class.

As a teacher, you may be curious to know the strategies for meeting the achievement differences in your classroom or the challenges posed by the strengths and weaknesses of the students in teaching-learning situations. Let us discuss important instructional strategies.

What are Instructional Strategies?

Let us discuss the major strategies to cope up with the differences in academic achievement.

- Provide appropriate pre-requisites to organise and learn new information.
- Use visual aids.
- Use analogy, example and illustration.
- Ensure learner's active involvement in learning.
- Periodic assessment.

EVALUATION AND ASSESSMENT

Evaluation

Evaluation, particularly educational evaluation is a series of activities designed to measure the effectiveness of the teaching-learning systems as a whole. According to Mary Thorpe (1980), "Evaluation is the collection, analysis and interpretation of information about any aspect of a programme of education." Teaching-learning process is a continuous activity. It needs to be evaluated from beginning to end. Evaluation during the learning process (continuous assessment), often termed as ''formative evaluation'', is important for learners and teachers alike.

The bases of evaluation are learning objectives, performance standards and achievement tests on the one hand, and learners' and experts' opinions on the other. Evaluation helps to build an educational programme, assess its achievement and improve upon its effectiveness. It also provides valuable feedback on the design, development and implementation of the programme. It is, of course, an important component of the teaching-learning process. It helps in making the value judgement, determining educational status, or measuring achievement of learners.

The scope of evaluation in schools extents to almost all the areas of learner's personality development. It includes both scholastic and non-scholastic areas. It reveals the strengths and weaknesses of the learners, so that the learners have better opportunity to understand and improve themselves.

Evaluation is helpful to teachers also. It provides feedback to them to reshape their teaching strategies according to the needs of the learners. Evaluation in education in general and in distance education in particular becomes imperative to know as to what extent the goals of education have been achieved.

Thus, evaluation is not merely assigning grades to learners. It is a continuous process of acquiring and processing information in order to improve one's learning and to assess decisions made in designing an instructional system. If we analyse the above statement we easily notice that it has three important implications for the entire teaching-learning system. They are as follows:

1. Evaluation is a continuous process and not a one time performance measurement, effected at the end of a course/programme. It starts at the stage of curriculum development and continues until the instruction ends.
2. Evaluation process is goal-directed. It is aimed at finding ways and means to improve learning and thereby to achieve learning objectives more effectively and more efficiently.
3. Evaluation requires the use of accurate and appropriate measuring instructions to collect information for taking decisions about the quality and operation of education.

It is clear that in designing an effective learning system, one of the earliest steps we need to take is to prepare a comprehensive evaluation plan, which should be developed soon after the learning objectives have been formulated. This practice will help us to:

- determine whether the objectives are attainable or need revisions before we start designing the instructional system;
- collect data/information in a form that suits our purposes adequately and at a time when it is available, otherwise the opportunity to collect specific information may be lost; and
- have sufficient time to test the effectiveness of a design.

Continuous and Comprehensive Evaluation (CCE)

Continuous and Comprehensive Evaluation (CCE) refers to a system of school based evaluation of a student that covers all aspects of a student development. It is a developmental process of student which emphasizes on two fold objectives. These objectives are continuity in evaluation and assessment of broad based learning and behaviourial outcomes on the other.

The term **'continuous'** is meant to emphasise that evaluation of identified aspects of students **'growth and development'** is a continuous process rather than an event, built into the total teaching-learning process and spread over the entire span of academic session. It means regularity of assessment, frequency of unit testing, diagnosis of learning gaps, use of corrective measures, retesting and feedback of evidence to teachers and students for their self evaluation.

The second term **'comprehensive'** means that the scheme attempts to cover both the scholastic and the co-scholastic aspects of the students' growth and development. Since abilities, attitudes and aptitudes can manifest themselves in forms other than the written word, the term refers to application of variety of tools and techniques (both testing and non-testing) and aims at assessing a learner's development in areas of learning, like:

- Knowledge
- Understanding
- Applying
- Analyzing
- Evaluating
- Creating

Objectives of CCE

- To help develop cognitive, psychomotor and affective skills.
- To lay emphasis on thought process and de-emphasise memorization.
- To make evaluation an integral part of teaching-learning process.
- To use evaluation for improvement of students achievement and teaching-learning strategies

on the basis of regular diagnosis followed by remedial instructions.

- To use evaluation as a quality control device to maintain desired standard of performance.
- To determine social utility, desirability or effectiveness of a programme and take appropriate decisions about the learner, the process of learning and the learning environment.
- To make the process of teaching and learning a learner-centered activity.

Features of CCE

- The **'continuous'** aspect of CCE takes care of **'continual'** and **'periodicity'** aspect of evaluation.
- Continual means assessment of students in the beginning of instructions (placement evaluation) and assessment during the instructional process (**formative evaluation**) done informally using multiple techniques of evaluation.
- Periodicity means assessment of performance done frequently at the end of unit/term (**summative evaluation**).
- The **'comprehensive'** component of CCE takes care of assessment of all round development of the child's personality. It includes assessment in **Scholastic as well as Co-Scholastic** aspects of the pupil's growth.
- Scholastic aspects include curricular areas or subject specific areas, whereas Co-Scholastic aspects include Life Skills, Co-Curricular Activities, Attitudes and Values.
- Assessment in Scholastic areas is done informally and formally using multiple techniques of evaluation continually and periodically. The diagnostic evaluation takes place at the end of unit/term test. The causes of poor performance in some units are diagnosed using diagnostic tests. These are followed with appropriate interventions followed by retesting.
- Assessment in Co-Scholastic areas is done using multiple techniques on the basis of identified criteria, while assessment in Life Skills is done on the basis of Indicators of Assessment and Checklists.

Functions of CCE

- It helps the teacher to organize effective teaching strategies.
- Continuous evaluation helps in regular assessment to the extent and degree of Learner's progress (ability and achievement with reference to specific Scholastic and Co-Scholastic areas).
- Continuous evaluation serves to diagnose weaknesses and permits the teacher to ascertain an individual learner's strengths and weaknesses and her needs. It provides immediate feedback to the teacher, who can then decide whether a particular unit or concept needs a discussion again in the whole class or whether a few individuals are in need of remedial instruction.
- By continuous evaluation, children can know their strengths and weaknesses. It provides the child a realistic self assessment of how he/she studies. It can motivate children to develop good study habits, to correct errors, and to direct their activities towards the achievement of desired goals. It helps a learner to determine the areas of instruction in where more emphasis is required.
- Continuous and comprehensive evaluation identifies areas of aptitude and interest. It helps in identifying changes in attitudes and value systems.
- It helps in making decisions for the future, regarding choice of subjects, courses and careers.
- It provides information/reports on the progress of students in Scholastic and Co-Scholastic areas and thus helps in predicting the future success of the learner.

Continuous evaluation helps in bringing awareness of the achievement to the child, teachers and parents from time-to-time. They can look into the probable cause of the fall in performance if any, and may take remedial measures of instruction in which more emphasis is required. Many times, because of some personal reasons, family problems or adjustment problems, the children start neglecting their studies, resulting in sudden drop in their performance. If the teacher, child and parents do not notice the sudden drop in the performance of the child in academics, it could result in a permanent deficiency in the childs' learning.

The major emphasis of CCE is on the continuous growth of students ensuring their intellectual, emotional, physical, cultural and social development and therefore, it will not be merely limited to assessment of learner's scholastic attainments. CCE uses assessment as a means of motivating learners to provide feedback and follow up work to improve upon the learning in the classroom and to present a comprehensive picture of a learner's profile. It is this that has led to the emergence of the concept of **School Based Continuous and Comprehensive Evaluation.**

Scholastic and Co-Scholastic Assessment

In order to have Continuous and Comprehensive Evaluation, both Scholastic and Co-Scholastic aspects need to be given due recognition. Such a holistic assessment requires maintaining an ongoing and comprehensive profile for each learner that is honest, encouraging and discreet. While teachers frequently reflect, plan and implement remedial strategies, the child's ability to retain and articulate what has been learned over a period of time also requires periodic assessment. These assessments can take many forms but all of them should be as comprehensive and discreet as possible. **Weekly, fortnightly**, or **quarterly** reviews (depending on the learning area), that do not openly compare one learner with another are generally recommended. The objective is to promote and enhance not just learning and retention among children, but their soft skills as well.

Scholastic Assessment

The objectives of the Scholastic domain are:-

- Desirable behaviour related to the learner's knowledge, understanding, application, evaluation, analysis and the ability to apply it in an unfamiliar situation.
- To improve the teaching learning process.
- Assessment should be both **Formative** and **Summative**.

Summative and Formative Assessment

Assessment is often divided into formative and summative categories for the purpose of considering different objectives for assessment practices.

Summative Assessment

Summative assessment is intended to measure learning outcomes and report those outcomes to students, parents and administrators. In an educational setting, it generally occurs at the conclusion of a class, course, semester or academic year. In the context of a course summative assessments are typically used to assign students a course grade. It is also referred to in a learning context as **"assessment of learning". Performance-based assessment** is similar to summative assessment, as it focuses on achievement. A well-defined task is identified and students are asked to create, produce, or do something, often in settings that involve real-world application of knowledge and skills. Proficiency is demonstrated by providing an extended response. Performance formats are further differentiated into products and performances. The performance may result in a product, such as a painting, portfolio, paper, or exhibition, or it may consist of a performance, such as a speech, athletic skill, musical recital, or reading.

Definitions of Summative Assessment

- "Good summative assessments—tests and other graded evaluations—must be demonstrably reliable, valid, and free of bias" (Angelo and Cross, 1993).
- '...assessment (that) has increasingly been used to sum up learning' (Black and William, 1999).
- '...looks at past achievements ... adds procedures or tests to existing work ... involves only marking and feedback grades to student ... is separated from teaching ... is carried out at intervals when achievement has to be summarized and reported.' (Harlen, 1998).

Features of Summative Assessment

- Assessment of learning.
- Generally taken by students at the end of a unit or semester to demonstrate the **"sum"** of what they have or have not learned.
- Summative assessment methods are the most traditional way of evaluating student work.

Formative Assessment

Formative assessment is generally carried out throughout a course or project. In an educational setting, formative assessment is used by teachers to consider approaches to teaching and next steps for individual learners and the class, and would not necessarily be used for grading purposes. Formative assessment, also referred to as **"educative assessment"** or **"assessment for learning",** is used to aid learning. Assessment for learning is defined as "all those activities undertaken by teachers and/or students, which provide information to be used as feedback to modify the teaching and learning activities in which they are engaged" (Black and William 2004).

Definitions of Formative Assessment

- '... often means no more than that the assessment is carried out frequently and is planned at the same time as teaching'. (Black and William, 1999)
- '... provides feedback which leads to students recognizing the (learning) gap and closing it ... it is forward looking ...' (Harlen, 1998).
- '... includes both feedback and self-monitoring'. (Sadler, 1989)
- '... is used essentially to get a feedback into the teaching and learning process.' (Tunstall and Gipps, 1996)

Features of Formative Assessment

- Is diagnostic and remedial.
- Makes provision for effective feedback.

- Provides a platform for the active involvement of students in their own learning.
- Enables teachers to adjust teaching to take account of the results of assessment.
- Recognizes the profound influence assessment has on the motivation and self-esteem of students, both of which are crucial influences on learning.
- Recognizes the need for students to be able to assess themselves and understand how to improve.
- Builds on students' prior knowledge and experience in designing what is taught.
- Incorporates varied learning styles to decide how and what to teach.
- Encourages students to understand the criteria that will be used to judge their work.
- Offers an opportunity to students to improve their work after they get the feedback.
- Helps student to support their peer group and vice-versa.

A common form of formative assessment is **"diagnostic assessment"**. Diagnostic assessment measures a student's current knowledge and skills for the purpose of identifying a suitable program of learning. **"Self-assessment"** is a form of diagnostic assessment which involves students assessing themselves. **"Forward-looking assessment"** asks those being assessed to consider themselves in hypothetical future situations.

Co-Scholastic Assessment

The desirable behaviour related to learner's life skills, attitudes, interests, values, co-curricular activities and physical health are described as skills to be acquired in co-scholastic domain.

The process of assessing the students' progress in achieving objectives related to scholastic and co-scholastic domain is called comprehensive evaluation. It has been observed that usually under the scholastic domain such as knowledge and understanding of the facts, concepts, principles etc. of a subject are assessed. The Co-Scholastic elements are either altogether excluded from the evaluation process or they are not given adequate attention. For making the evaluation comprehensive, both Scholastic and Co-Scholastic aspects should be given importance. Simple and manageable means of assessment of Co-Scholastic aspects of growth must be included in the comprehensive evaluation scheme.

Comprehensive evaluation would necessitate the use of a variety of tools and techniques. This will be so because both different and specific areas of learner's growth can be evaluated through certain special techniques.

School Based CCE

School based Evaluation is held at school level unlike external examination conducted by the Boards of School Education. This is done by the teachers according to the schedule developed by the school and guidelines given by the Board. Though this evaluation has been done at school level all along, certain shortcomings have crept into this system. These shortcomings can be attributed to various factors. The basic factor is the misconception of teachers regarding the place of evaluation and its importance in the educational process. The other factor has been the imitation of the practice of external examination which is generally held at the end of the session.

In the School Based System of evaluation, the focus on the purpose of assessment has changed. Now, it includes readiness testing, screening of development, evaluation of performance in cognitive, affective and psychomotor domains more frequently, systematically and effectively.

In other words, School Based Evaluation is child-centred, school-centred and multidimensional evaluation. Hence, in its true spirit, it triggers an all round development of the learner. It encourages all kinds of learning in life both inside the school as well as outside it. It is child-centered as it attempts to consider the learner as a unique entity for its individual pattern of development. It builds on individual child's abilities, progress and development in achieving already set goals and objectives of education as an individual and not just his/her position in relation to other learners.

Further, this evaluation helps a learner to use his/her potential in a better manner and also provides insight to the teachers to discover the methods which may be helpful to the individual learner in resolving his/her problems and difficulties.

Besides being ***child-centred,*** this evaluation is ***school-centred*** as well. It means that no outside agency interferes in this evaluation process. It is entirely school based and done by the teacher. The teacher is trusted and given full responsibility of evaluating students with the brief that the teacher knows best about his/her students.

School Based Evaluation is ***multidimensional***. Its multidimensional nature is reflected in recognizing and taking care of learners' social, emotional, physical, intellectual and other areas of development which are interrelated and cannot be considered in isolation. It also calls for the use of multiple techniques and tools of evaluation.

Aim of School Based CCE

- Elimination of chance element and subjectivity (as far as possible), de-emphasis on memorization, encouraging comprehensive evaluation incorporating both Scholastic and Co-Scholastic aspects of learners development.
- Continuous evaluation spread over the total span of the instructional time as an integral built-in aspect of the total teaching-learning process.
- Functional and meaningful declaration of results for effective use by teachers, students, parents and the society.
- Wider uses of test results for purposes not merely of the assessment of levels of pupils' achievements and proficiencies, but mainly for their improvement, thorough diagnosis and remedial/enrichment programmes.
- Improvement in the mechanics of conducting examinations for realizing a number of other allied purposes.
- Introduction of concomitant changes in instructional materials and methodology.
- Introduction of the semester system.
- The use of grades in place of marks in determining and declaring the level of pupil performance and proficiency.

Its Characteristics

School Based Evaluation has the following characteristics:

- Is broader, more comprehensive and continuous than traditional system.
- Aims primarily to help learners for systematic learning and development.
- Takes care of the needs of the learner as responsible citizens of the future.
- Is more transparent, futuristic and provides more scope for association among learners, teachers and parents.

School based evaluation provides opportunities to teachers to **know the following about their learners:**

- What they learn?
- How they learn?
- What type of difficulties/limitations they face in working in tandem?
- What do the children think?
- What do the children feel?
- What are their interests and dispositions?

The focus has shifted to developing a deep learning environment. There is a paradigm shift in the pedagogy and competencies from 'controlling' to 'enriching' to 'empowering' schools.

Traditional Schooling	**Enriching Schooling**	**Empowering Schooling**
• Teacher centred	• Student centred	• Experience centred
• Subjects and classes-teacher directed	• Self directed	• Virtual authenticity
• Sorting and ranking individuals	• Continuous assessment	• Multi literacies
Competency:	**Competency:**	**Competency:**
• Memory	• Critical thinking	• Risk taking
• Competitive	• Collaborative	• Ethical
	• Creative	• Interactive

Implementing School Based Assessment would mean:

- Elimination of chance element and subjectivity (as far as possible), de-emphasis of memorization, encouraging Comprehensive evaluation incorporating both scholastic and co-scholastic aspects of learners development.
- Continuous evaluation spread over the total span of the instructional time as an integral built-in aspect of the total teaching-learning process.
- Functional and meaningful declaration of results for effective use by teachers, students, parents and the society.
- Wider uses of test results for purposes not merely of the assessment of levels of pupils' achievements and proficiencies, but mainly for its improvement, through diagnosis and remedial/enrichment programmes.
- Improvements in the mechanics of conducting examinations for realizing a number of other allied purposes.
- Introduction of concomitant changes in instructional materials and methodology.

- Introduction of the semester system from the secondary stage onwards.
- The use of grades in place of marks in determining and declaring the level of pupil performance and proficiency.

The above goals are relevant for both external examination and evaluation in schools.

Shortcoming of Traditional External Examination

- It is a one shot examination at the end of a year at the terminal stage of schooling.
- It mainly evaluates only the scholastic aspects of learning of the students.
- It does not evaluate all the abilities of the children. On the basis of marks obtained in written examination the students are declared pass or fail and further classified into predetermined divisions.
- Pass and fail system causes frustration and is inhumane because the failed candidates come to feel that they are good for nothing.
- Co-scholastic areas are almost totally ignored and have no place in the currently prevalent scheme of education and evaluation.
- The practice of testing of untaught content also reflects poor learning achievement.
- Only limited techniques of evaluation without potential for judging a student are being used.
- The aim of evaluation is to improve learner's quality which is not served by external examination.
- The current practice of awarding marks suffers from many discrepancies due to variety of errors.
- The varied ranges of obtained scores of students in different subjects create the problem in declaring reliable results.
- Analysis and interpretation of test results is not done in a scientific way.

School Based Continuous and Comprehensive Evaluation System should be Established to:

- reduce stress on children.
- make evaluation comprehensive and regular.
- provide space for the teacher for creative teaching.
- provide a tool of diagnosis and remediation.
- produce learners with greater skills.

Four Assessment Paradigms

Assessment *of* Learning

The 'assessment **of** learning' is defined as a process whereby someone attempts to describe and quantify the knowledge, attitudes or skills possessed by another. Teacher direction is paramount and the student has little involvement in the design or implementation of the assessment process in these circumstances.

- Teacher designs learning
- Teacher collects evidence
- Teacher judges what has been learnt (and what has not been learnt)

Assessment *for* Learning

The 'assessment **for** learning' involves increased level of student autonomy, but not without teacher guidance and collaboration. The assessment **for** learning is sometimes seen as being akin to 'formative assessment'. There is more emphasis towards giving useful advice to the student and less emphasis on the giving of marks and the grading function.

- Teacher designs learning
- Teacher designs assessment with feedback to student
- Teacher judges what has been learnt (student develops insight into what has not)

Assessment *as* Learning

The 'assessment **as** learning' is perhaps more connected with diagnostic assessment and can be constructed with more of an emphasis on peer learning. Assessment **as** learning generates opportunities for self assessment and peer assessment. Students take on increased responsibility to generate quality information about their learning and that of others.

- Teacher and student co-construct learning
- Teacher and student co-construct assessment
- Teacher and student co-construct learning progress map

Assessment **for** learning and assessment **as** learning activities should be deeply embedded in teaching and learning and be the source of interactive feedback, allowing students to adjust, re-think and re-learn.

Assessment *in* Learning

The 'assessment **in** learning' places the question at the centre of teaching and learning. It deflects the teaching from its focus on a 'correct answer' to a focus on 'a fertile question'. Through enquiry students engage in processes that generates feedback about their learning, which come from multiple sources and activities. It contributes to the construction of other learning activities, line of enquiry and the generation of other questions.

- Student as the centre of learning

- Student monitors, assesses and reflects on learning
- Student initiates demonstration of learning (to self and others)
- Teacher as coach and mentor.

Teachers and students need to understand the purpose of each assessment strategy. The overall assessment 'package' being used by learners and teachers should accurately capture, generate and use meaningful learning information to generate deep learning and understanding.

ASSESSING LEARNERS

Any meaningful report on the quality and extent of a child's learning needs to be comprehensive. We need a curriculum whose creativity, innovativeness, and development of the whole being, the hallmark of a good education makes uniform tests that assess memorised facts and textbook-based learning obsolete. We need to redefine and seek new parameters for and ways of evaluation and feedback. In addition to the learner's achievements in specific subject areas that lend themselves to testing easily, assessment would need to encompass attitudes to learning, interest, and the ability to learn independently.

ASSESSMENT IN THE COURSE OF TEACHING

Preparing report cards is a way for the teacher to think about each individual child and review what she/he has learnt during the term, and what she/he needs to work on and improve. To be able to write such report cards, teachers would need to think about each individual child, and hence pay attention to them during their everyday teaching and interaction. One does not need special tests for this; learning activities themselves provide the basis for such ongoing observational and qualitative assessments of children. Maintaining a daily diary based on observation helps in continuous and comprehensive evaluation. An extract from the diary of a teacher for a week notes the following: ''Kiran enjoyed his work. He took an instant liking to the books that were informative and brief. He says that he likes simple and clear language. In noting down facts, he goes for short answers. He says that it helps him understand things easily. He favours a practical approach.'' Similarly, keeping samples and notes of the child's work at different stages provides both the teacher and the learner herself or himself with a systematic record of his/her learning progress.

The belief that assessment must lead to finding learning difficulties to then be remediated is often very impractical and not founded on a sound understanding of pedagogic practice. Problems regarding conceptual development cannot and do not wait for formal tests in order to be detected. A teacher can, in the course of teaching itself, come to know of such problems by asking questions that make children think or by giving them small assignments. She can then attend to them in the process of teaching—by ensuring that her planning is flexible and responsive to the learners and their learning.

CURRICULAR AREAS THAT CANNOT BE 'TESTED FOR MARKS'

Each area of the curriculum may not lend itself to being 'tested'; it may even be antithetical to the nature of learning in the curricular area. This includes areas such as work, health, yoga, physical education, music and art. While the skill-based component of physical education and yoga could be tested, the health aspect needs continuous and qualitative assessments. Currently, this has the effect of making these subjects and activities 'less important' in the curriculum; these areas are inadequately provided for in terms of material resources and curricular planning, and marked by a lack of seriousness. Further, the time allocated for them is also frequently sacrificed to accommodate special classes. This is a serious compromise with parts of the curriculum that have deep educational significance and potential.

Even if 'marks' cannot be given, children can be assessed for their development in these areas. Participation, interest, and level of involvement, and the extent to which abilities and skills have been honed, are some markers that can help teachers to gauge the benefits of what children learn and gain through such activities. Asking children to self-report on their learning can also provide teachers with insight into children's educational progress and give them feedback on improving curriculum or pedagogy.

DESIGN AND CONDUCT OF ASSESSMENT

Assessments and examinations must be credible, and based on valid ways of gauging learning.

As long as examinations and tests assess children's ability to remember and recall textbook knowledge, all attempts to redirect the curriculum towards learning will be thwarted. First, tests in knowledge-based subject areas must be able to gauge what children have learnt, and their ability to use this knowledge for problem solving and application in the real world. In addition, they must also be able to test the processes of thinking to gauge if the learner has also learnt where to find information, how to use new information, and to analyse and evaluate the same.

The types of questions that are set for assessment need to go beyond what is given in the book. Often children's learning is restricted as teachers do not accept their answers if they are different from what is presented in the guidebooks.

Questions that are open-ended and challenging could also be used. Designing good test items and questions is an art, and teachers should spend time thinking about and devising such questions. The interest and ability of teachers to design good questions can be promoted through district—or state-level competitions. All question papers must be designed graded for difficulty in order to permit all children to experience a level of success, and to gain confidence in their ability to answer and solve problems.

Trying to devise a good and effective open-book examination can be a challenge that we must try to take up in our curricular efforts at all levels of school. This would require teachers and examination setters to emphasise the interpretation and application of learning over the arguments and facts that can be located in the book. There have been successful demonstrations that such examinations can be carried out on a large scale, and that teachers can themselves be trusted with moderating the results of such examinations. In this way, the assessment of projects and lab work can also be made credible and sound.

It is important that after receiving their corrected papers, children rewrite the answers and that these are again reviewed by teachers to ensure that children have learnt and gained something out of the ordeal.

Competition is motivating, but it is an extrinsic rather than intrinsic form of motivation. It is, of course, much easier to establish and to manipulate, and therefore frequently resorted to by teachers and school systems as a way creating and nurturing the drive for excellence. Schools begin 'ranking' children as early as their pre-primary years as a way of inculcating in them a competitive spirit. Such a competitive drive has several negative side effects on learning, often superficial learning is sufficient to create and maintain impressions, and over time students lose their ability to take initiative or do things for the fulfilment of one's own interest; hence, areas that cannot be 'marked' are neglected. This has unhealthy consequences for classroom culture, making children individualistic and unsuited to team work. There is an absurd and unnecessary importance given to term examinations, often accompanied by extreme arrangements of invigilation and secrecy. While the physical and psychological effects of this may not be readily visible until middle school, they frequently lead to high levels of stress in children, and cause early burnout. Schools and teachers need to ask themselves whether there is really much to be gained out of such practices and to what extent learning requires such systems of marking and ranking.

SELF-ASSESSMENT AND FEEDBACK

The role of assessment is to gauge the progress that both learner and teacher have made towards achieving the aims that have been set and appraising how this could be done better. Opportunity for feedback, leading to revision and improvement of performance, should constantly be available, without exams and evaluations being used as a threat to study.

Grading and correction carried out in the presence of students and providing feedback on the answers they get right and wrong, and why. Asking children about why they answered what they did assists teachers in going beyond the written answer to engage with children's thinking. Such processes also take away the frightening judgemental quality of marks obtained in a test, and enable children to understand and focus on their mistakes and learn through these mistakes. Sometimes head teachers object, claiming that correction in the presence of the child reduces 'objectivity'. This is a misplaced concern for 'objectivity', stemming from a competitive system that believes in judging children. Such a concern for 'objectivity' is misplaced in evaluation, which is consistent with educational goals.

Not only learning outcomes but also learning experiences themselves must be evaluated. Learners happily comment on the totality of their experience. Exercises, both individual and collective, can be designed to enable them to reflect on and assess their learning experiences. Such experiences also provide them with self-regulatory capabilities essential for 'learning to learn'. Such information is also valuable feedback to the teacher, and can be used to modify the learning system as a whole.

Every classroom interaction with children requires their evaluation of their own work, and a discussion with them about what should be tested and the ways of finding out whether the competencies are being developed or not. Even very young children are able to give correct assessments of what they can or cannot do well. The role of teaching is to provide an opportunity to each child to learn to the best of his or her ability and provide learning experiences that develop cognitive qualities, physical well-being and athletic qualities, as also affective and aesthetic qualities.

Report cards need to present to children and parents a comprehensive and holistic view of the child's development in many fields. Teachers must be able to say things about each child/student, that conveys to them a sense of individualised attention, reaffirms a positive self-image, and communicates personal goals for them to work towards. Whether it is marks or grades that are reported, a qualitative statement by the teacher is necessary to support the assessment. Only through such a relationship with each child can any teacher succeed in influencing him/her, and contributing to his/her learning. Along with the teacher assessing each child, each student could also assess himself or herself and include this self-assessment in the report card.

Currently, many report cards carry information on subject areas and have nothing to say about other aspects of the child's development, including health, physical fitness and abilities in games, social skills, and abilities in art and craft. Qualitative statements about these aspects of children's education and development would provide a more holistic assessment of educational concerns.

AREAS THAT REQUIRE FRESH THINKING

There are many areas of the curriculum that can be assessed but for which we still do not have reliable and efficient instruments. This includes assessing learning that is carried out in groups, and learning in areas such as theatre, work and craft where skills and competencies develop over longer time scales and require careful observation.

Continuous and comprehensive evaluation has frequently been cited as the only meaningful kind of evaluation. This also requires much more careful thinking through about when it is to be employed in a system effectively. Such evaluation places a lot of demand on teachers' time and ability to maintain meticulous records if it is to be meaningfully executed and if it is to have any reliability as an assessment. If this simply increases stress on children by reducing all their activities into items for assessment, or making them experience the teacher's 'power', then it defeats the purpose of education. Unless a system is adequately geared for such assessment, it is better for teachers to engage in more limited forms of evaluation, but incorporating into them more features that will make the assessment a meaningful record of learning.

Finally, there is a need to evolve and maintain credibility in assessment so that they perform their function of providing feedback in a meaningful way.

ASSESSMENT AT DIFFERENT STAGES

ECCE and Classes I and II of the Elementary Stage: At this stage, assessment must be purely qualitative judgements of children's activities in various domains and an assessment of the status of their health and physical development, based on observations through everyday interactions. On no account should they be made to take any form of test, oral or written.

Class III to Class VIII of the Elementary Stage: A variety of methods may be used, including oral and written tests and observations. Children should be aware that they are being assessed, but this must be seen by them as a part of the teaching process and not as a fearful constant threat. Grades or marks along with qualitative judgements of achievement and areas requiring attention are essential at this stage. Children's own self-evaluation can also be a part of the report card from Class V onwards. Rather than examinations, there could be short tests from time-to-time, which are criterion based. Term-wise examinations could be commenced from Class VII onwards when children are more psychologically ready to study large chunks of material and, to spend a few hours in an examination room, working at answering questions. Again, the progress card must indicate general observations on health and nutrition, specific observations on the overall progress of the learner, and information and advice for the parents.

Class IX to Class XII of the Secondary and Higher Secondary Stages: Assessment may be based more on tests, examinations and project reports for the knowledge-based areas of the curriculum, along with self-assessment. Other areas would be assessed through observation and also through self-evaluation.

Reports could include much more analysis about the students, various skill/knowledge areas and percentiles, etc. This would assist them by pointing out the areas of study that they need to focus on, and also help them by providing a basis for further choices that they make regarding what to study thereafter.

CONCEPT OF INCLUSIVE EDUCATION & UNDERSTANDING CHILDREN WITH SPECIAL NEEDS

INCLUSIVE EDUCATION: DEFINITION AND CONCEPT

Inclusive Education denotes that all children irrespective of their strengths and weaknesses will be part of the mainstream education. Thus, inclusive education means, "the act of ensuring that all children despite their differences, receive the opportunity of being part of the same classroom as other children of their age, and in the process get the opportunity to being exposed to the curriculum to their optimal potential."

Every child is special for his/her parent and, every child has a special need for love, acceptance and a feeling of belongingness. Here, we call **children with special needs** to those who are "different" from their cohorts. They are born equal with some limitations and with the help of inclusion be able to actively participate as equal citizens in all aspects of society and community life. Thus, children with special needs refer to "all those children who require adaptations to the normal process of education due to problems of vision, hearing, movement, learning and intellect." In other words, these children have some kind of **disability**.

Disability: Definitions

Disability refers to any limitations experienced by the disabled in comparisons to able persons of similar age, sex and culture. The UN Declaration on the Rights of Disabled Persons has defined disabled person as "any person unable to ensure by himself or herself, wholly or partly, the necessities of a normal individual and/or social life, as a result of a deficiency, either congenital or not, in his or her physical or mental capabilities".

DISTINCTIONS AMONG IMPAIRMENT, DISABILITY AND HANDICAP

The World Health Organisation (WHO) has made distinctions between the definitions of impairment, disability and handicap as follows:

- Impairment is any loss or abnormality of psychological, physiological or anatomical structure or function generally taken to be at organ level. Impairment is a damage to tissue due to disease or trauma.
- A disability is any restriction or lack of ability (resulting from an impairment) to perform an activity in the manner or within the range considered normal for a human being.
- A handicap is a disadvantage for an individual, resulting from impairment or disability that limits or prevents fulfilment of a role that is normal (depending on age, sex and social cultural factors) for that individual. Handicap is a condition or burden, which is imposed on the person confronted with the disability.

Types of Disability According to PWD Act, 1995

The PWD Act, 1995 has given the following seven types of disability as:

1. Blindness
2. Low Vision
3. Leprosy-cured
4. Hearing impairment
5. Locomotor disabilities
6. Mental retardation
7. Mental illness

EDUCATIONAL PROVISIONS FOR CHILDREN WITH SPECIAL NEEDS

The last two decades of the 19th century has witnessed the knowledge and processes of educating the disabled children through Christian Missionaries. The first school for the deaf was established in Mumbai in 1883 and the first school for the blind in Amritsar in 1887. At that time, it was believed that children with disabilities could not be educated alongwith normal children. Therefore, education to disabled children was offered through special school. This trend continued early sixties of the last century with the help of some international agencies who developed programme of integrated education. Here, children disabilities were placed in regular school so that they could study alongwith their non-disabled 'peers". The integrated education adopts various models for service deliver. Presently the emphasis is on the need to provide education for all in appropriate environment with inclusive philosophy through inclusive education.

Integrated Education for the Disabled Children (IEDC)

With the development of science and technology and improvement in Medical Services and Aggressive neo-natal intervention has ensured that a large number of babies who would earlier have not survived but often with different abilities. The number of differently abled children is on the increasing trend but it is not possible to create the required number of special schools throughout the country to meet this challenge due to the high cost and also due to the fact that the population is so scattered. The best alternative under these situations is to make use of the infrastructural facilities already present in terms of regular schools and integrate children into the mainstream of education.

Consequent on the success of international institutions in introducing differently abled children in regular schools, the planning commission, Govt. of India, in 1971 includes in its plan a programme for integrated education. In 1974, the Union Government introduced a scheme called "Integrated Schools" to do just this. This scheme was later revised and a plan of action formulated. The important aims of IEDC includes:

- Provide educational opportunity to differently abled children in regular schools.
- Facilitate retention of differently abled in the school system.
- Integrate children from special school to common schools.

The scope of the scheme of IEDC includes pre-school training, counselling for the parents, and special training in skills for all kinds of differently abled children. It provides facilities in the form of books, stationary, uniforms and allowances for transport, reader and escort etc.

Project Integrated Education for the Disabled (PIED)

This scheme was launched by MHRD Govt. of India in collaboration with UNICEF in 1987 to strengthen the integration of differently abled into regular schools. Under this scheme, a cluster instead of individual school is given importance. This scheme is an improvement over the special schools in one or many ways and provides a way towards universalisation of elementary education and Education for All including for differently abled children.

ASSUMPTION ABOUT INTEGRATED EDUCATION

Integrated education assumes a process of bringing disabled children into mainstream schools, where the system remains the same. As per the system, the child is the problem. So, it is essential to change the child where the resources are focused on the individual child. The failure is due to the child's problem; he is not able, not ready, not good enough to cope up with the system.

In integrated education; it is the children with disabilities who are seen as the problem, who must be "fixed", "changed" & "adapted" to suit the existing regular, mainstream school. It is the disabled child who is seen as a square peg in a round table. The system remains the same. The onus for successful integration therefore, is on the disabled child.

ASSUMPTION ABOUT INCLUSIVE EDUCATION

Assumptions of inclusive education is opposite to integrated education. Inclusive education assumes that changes the system to fit the child. It is essential to addresses all types of individual needs, not just disability. Teachers and schools are held responsible for children's learning. It focuses on flexibility of curriculum, teacher training and change in environmental. Failure is the problem with the system not with the child. It is quite essential to assumes that all children can learn and that all children need their learning to be supported in diverse ways.

In this model of inclusive education, it is not the child, but the education system, which is seen as a problem. Therefore, it is the system (with all its components) with should be changed, modified & made flexible enough to accommodate the diverse needs of all learners, including children with disabilities. The onus for success is therefore on the flexibility of the system. It focuses on the environment, as the "disabling" cause because it fails to provide appropriate access to equal opportunities for all persons to participate fully in social life.

Though integrated education of differently abled children has gained momentum all over the country since 1974, there are some other possibilities too for these children to get education. For example, the NIOS (National Institute of Open Schooling) offers education which have the advantage of being specially adopted to the needs of every child as well as aimed at giving the child every opportunity to progress at his/her pace. Another example is alternative schooling and community-based rehabilitation programmes.

EDUCATION FOR A COHESIVE SOCIETY

Despite more than half a century of independence, India is struggling for freedom from various kinds of biases and imbalances such as rural/urban, rich/poor, and differences on the basis of caste, religion, ideology, gender etc. Education can play a very significant role in minimising and finally eliminating these differences by providing equality of access to quality education and opportunity.

Equality of opportunity means ensuring that every individual receives suitable education at a pace and through methods suited to his/her being. Children of the disadvantaged, and socially discriminated groups and also those suffering from specific challenges must be paid special attention.

Provision for equal opportunity to all not only in access, but also in the conditions for success is a precondition for the promotion of equality. The curriculum must create an awareness of the inherent equality of all with a view to removing prejudices and complexes transmitted through the social environment and the factor of birth.

EDUCATION OF GIRLS

Equality among sexes is a fundamental right under the constitution of India. The state, however, also has the right to exercise positive protective discrimination in favour of the disadvantaged population groups including women. Emphasis in education has moved from 'Equality of Educational Opportunity' (NPE, 1968) to 'Education for Women's Equality and Empowerment' (1986). As a result, the curricular and training strategies for the education of girls now demand more attention. Besides, making education accessible to more and more girls, especially rural girls, removing all gender discrimination and gender bias in school curriculum, textbooks and the process of transaction is absolutely necessary. There is a need to develop and implement gender inclusive and gender sensitive curricular strategies to nurture a generation of girls and boys who are equally competent and are sensitive to one another, and grow up in a caring and sharing mode as equals, and not as adversaries.

EDUCATION OF LEARNERS FROM DISADVANTAGED GROUPS

For achieving a cohesive society it would be essential to respond to specific educational needs of learners from different sections of the society with special emphasis on the Scheduled Castes, the Scheduled Tribes and the other socially and economically disadvantaged groups. In order to do so, there is a need for integrating the socio-cultural perspectives partly by showing concern for their linguistic specificities and pedagogic requirements. Implications of the multilingual and multicultural environment shall have to be taken care of through specifically devised methodology. Contextualisation of curriculum shall have to be effected through curricular materials. The fundamental rights of the disadvantaged groups have to be consciously incorporated in the curriculum. Even the problem of educating the migrating population shall have to be handled through specific condensed educational programmes based on the main ingredients of the national curriculum.

EDUCATION OF THE GIFTED AND TALENTED

An educational system has the dual role of promoting equality as well as excellence. Education is increasingly called upon to liberate all the creative potentialities of human consciousness. Man essentially fulfils himself in and through creation. It is in the context of this, that education of gifted and talented children assumes great importance. A curricular programme while on the one hand should identify such children, on the other it should also nurture their diverse creative abilities by paying them special attention. It is also important that the identification and nurturance begins right from the earliest stage of education. Moreover, the task of identifying the gifted and talented must be accomplished on the basis of a broad conceptualisation of the process from multiple perspectives rather than as a search for a unitary human attribute. Not only their IQ (Intelligence Quotient) but also their EQ (Emotional Quotient) and SQ (Spiritual Quotient) ought to be assessed.

NATIONAL LEVEL POLICY AND LEGISLATION

Kothari Commission (1964-66)

The Kothari Commission first suggested that the education of handicapped children has to be organised not merely on humanitarian grounds, but also an aspects of utility. The commission emphasised that the education of children with disability should be "an inseparable part of the general education system. The commission also specifically emphasised that the education of children with disability should be "an inseparable part of the general education system. The commission also specifically emphasised. the importance of integrated education in meeting this target as it is cost effective and useful in developing mutual understanding between children with and without disabilities.

National Policy on Education (1986)

The National Policy on Education was adopted by Indian Parliament in 1986. The policy emphasized the removal of disparities, and ensuring equalisation of educational opportunity under its para education of the disabled.

National Policies for Persons with Disabilities (2006)

This recognises that persons with disabilities are valuable human resources for the country and seek to create an environment that provides them equal opportunities, protection of their rights and full participation in society.

Persons with Disabilities (Equal Opportunities, Protection of Rights & Full Participation) Act, 1995

Landmark legislation in the history of special education in India is the persons with Disabilities Act, 1995. This comprehensive Act covers seven disabilities, namely blindness, low vision, hearing impaired, loco-motor impaired, mental retardation, leprosy cured and mental illness.

The Rehabilitation Council of India (RCI) Act, 1992

This Act was passed in 1992 for the purpose of constituting the Rehabilitation Professionals and for maintenance of a Central Rehabilitation Register. It was amended by Rehabilitation Council of India (Amendment) Act, 2000 to provide for monitoring the training of rehabilitation professionals and personal, promoting research in rehabilitation and special education as additional objectives of the council.

LEARNING AND PEDAGOGY

HOW CHILDREN THINK AND LEARN

Children learn from anything and everything they see and act upon. They have learnt a lot before they join school, and they continue to learn outside the school hours. If we believe that children learn only in school, it is because of what we wrongly regard as learning. When a child spends hours on trying to solve a Jigsaw puzzle (say), he/she is often reprimanded by adults for wasting study time. Little do the grown-ups realise that it is through such interesting games that this child may be increasing his/her understanding of shapes and size. And, this learning is taking place outside the school hours, without formal instruction. A curriculum built upon assumptions about children's learning, that ignore this aspect, is also responsible for children losing interest in mathematics or in any formal learning.

From the time a child is born, his/her interaction with the world around his/her starts. He/she perceives things around his/her, and gradually makes sense of them. He/she slowly begins to recognise people and objects, relate more and more to the environment, and observe things through the senses of touch, sight, taste, smell and sound. There are **four different stages** of learning or development that each child goes through.

Sensorimotor

This is from the ages of birth to about two years old. During this time the child's primary mode of learning occurs through the five senses. He/she learns to experience environment. The child touches things, holds, looks, listens, tastes, feels, bangs, and shakes everything in sight. When the child adds motor skills such as creeping, crawling and walking, his/her environment expands by leaps and bounds. The child is now exploring their environment with both senses and the ability to get around.

Preoperational

This is the stages between ages two and seven. During this stage the child is busy gathering information or learning, and then trying to figure out ways that they can used what they have learned to begin solving problems.

During this stage of his/her life child will be thinking in specifics and will find it very difficult to get generalise anything. This is the time when a child learns by asking questions. The child generally will not want a real answer to his question at this point. When he asks why do we have grass .... He simply wants to know that it is for him to play in. No technical answers for know. The child in this age group judges everything on the 'me' basis—How does it affect me? Do I like it?

Concrete Operations Period

This is the period of time when child is between the ages of seven to ten. This is a wonderful age as this is when children begin to manipulate data mentally. They take the information at hand and begin to define, compare and contrast it. They, however, still think concretely.

The concrete operational child is capable of logical thought. This child still learns through their senses, but no longer relies on only them to teach him. He now thinks as well. A good teacher for this age group would start each lesson at a concrete level and then more toward a generalised level. The child, during this period, is very literal in their thinking.

Formal Operations Period

The period begins at about age eleven. At this time the child will break through the barrier of literalism and more on to thinking in more abstract terms. He no longer restricts thinking to time and space. This child now starts to reflect, hypothesize and theorize.

In the formal operation period, children need to develop cognitive abilities. The following is a list of six simple categories of cognitive abilities. The following is a list of six simple categories of cognitive abilities:

1. **Knowledge of facts and principals:** This is the direct recall of facts and principals. **Examples:** memorisation of dates, name, definition, vocabulary words.
2. **Comprehension:** Understanding of facts and ideas.
3. **Application:** Needs to know, rules, principles, and procedures and how to use them.
4. **Analysis:** Breaking down concepts into parts.
5. **Synthesis:** Putting together information or ideas.
6. **Evaluation:** Judging the value of information.

BASIC PROCESSES OF TEACHING AND LEARNING

Teaching-learning process is the heart of education. On it depends the fulfilment of the aims & objectives of education. It is the most powerful instrument of education to bring about desired changes in the students. Teaching learning are related terms. In teaching-learning process, the teacher, the learner, the curriculum & other variables are organised in a systematic way to attain some pre-determined goal.

Essential Aspects of the Teaching-learning Process

According to Diana Laurillard, there are four aspects of the teaching-learning process:

1. **Discussion**—between the teacher and learner.
2. **Interaction**—between the learner and some aspect of the world defined by the teacher.
3. **Adaptation**—of the world by the teacher and action by the learner.
4. **Reflection**—on the learner's performance by both teacher and learner.

According to **Burton** in the figure above

1. Teaching can become effective only by relating it to process of learning.
2. Teaching objective cannot be realised without being related to learning situation.
3. We may create and use teaching aids to create some appropriate learning situation.
4. The strategies and devices of teaching may be selected in such a manner that the optimal objectives of learning area achieved.
5. To understand principles, goals, objectives of education in right perspective.
6. Appropriate learning situation condition may be created for congenial and effective teaching.

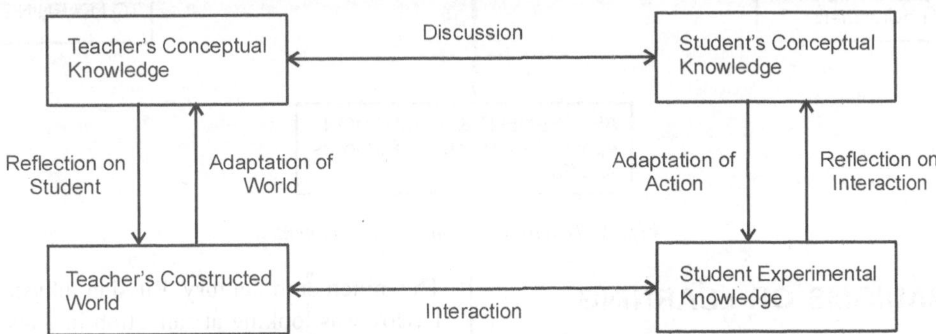

Fig. 1: *Essential aspects of the ideal teaching-learning process*

Approaches to Learning Theories

Aspect	Behaviourist	Cognitivist	Humanist
Learning theorists	Thorndike, Pavlov, Watson, Guthrie, Hull, Tolman, Skinner	Koffka, Kohler, Lewin, Piaget, Ausubel, Bruner, Gagne	Maslow, Rogers
View of the learning process	Change in behaviour	Internal mental process (including insight, information processing, memory, perception)	A personal act to fulfil potential
Locus of learning	Stimuli in external environment	Internal cognitive structuring	Affective and cognitive needs

Aspect	Behaviourist	Cognitivist	Humanist
Purpose in education	Produce behavioural change in desired direction	Develop capacity and skills to learn better	Become self-actualized autonomous
Educator's role	Arranges environment to elicit desired response	Structures content of learning activity	Facilitates development of the whole person
Manifestations in adult learning	Behavioural objectives	Cognitive development	Andragogy
	Competency-based education	Intelligence, learning and memory as function of age	Self-directed learning
	Skill development and training	Learning how to learn	

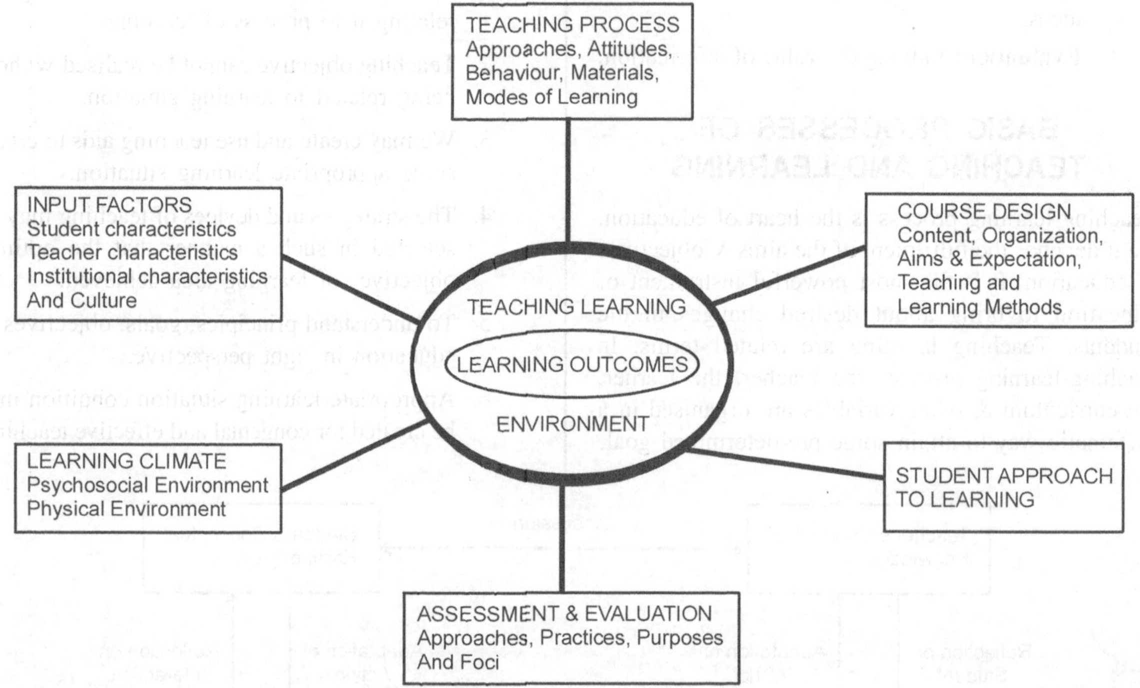

Fig. 2: *Teaching-Learning Environment*

PARADIGMS OF LEARNING

Learning takes place in many ways. There are some methods that are used in acquisition of simple responses while other methods are used in the acquisition of complex responses. The simplest kind of learning is called conditioning. Two types of conditioning have been identified. The first one is called classical conditioning and the second instrumental/operant conditioning. In addition, we have observational learning, cognitive learning, verbal learning, concept learning and skill learning.

Classical Conditioning

This type of learning was first investigated by Ivan P. Pavlov. Like many great scientific advances, classical conditioning was discovered accidentally. The nineteenth-century Russian physiologist Ivan Pavlov was looking at salivation in dogs in response to being fed, when he noticed that his dogs would begin to salivate whenever he entered the room, even when he was not bringing them food. However, when Pavlov discovered that any object or event which the dogs learnt to associate with food (such as the food bowl) would trigger the same response, he realised that he had made an important scientific discovery, and he devoted the rest of his career to studying this type of learning.

Classical conditioning is 'classical' in that it is the first systematic study of basic laws of learning. Classical conditioning involves learning to associate an unconditioned stimulus that already brings about a particular response (*i.e.* a reflex) with a new (conditioned) stimulus, so that the new stimulus brings about the same response. The unconditioned stimulus (or UCS) is the object or event that originally produces the reflexive/natural response.

Once the neutral stimulus has become associated with the unconditioned stimulus, it becomes a conditioned stimulus (CS). The conditioned response (CR) is the response to the conditioned stimulus. Thus, learning situation in classical conditioning is one of S-S learning in which one stimulus becomes a signal of another stimulus.

Determinants of Classical Conditioning

How quickly and strongly acquisition of a response occurs in classical conditioning depends on several factors. Some of the major factors influencing learning a CR are described below:

1. Time Relations between Stimuli: The classical conditioning procedures, discussed below, are basically of four types based on the time relations between the onset of conditioned stimulus (CS) and unconditioned stimulus (US). The first three are called forward conditioning procedures, and the fourth one is called backward conditioning procedure. The basic experimental arrangements of these procedures are as follows:

(*a*) When the CS and US are presented together, it is called simultaneous conditioning.

(*b*) In delayed conditioning, the onset of CS precedes the onset of US. The CS ends before the end of the US.

(*c*) In trace conditioning, the onset and end of the CS precedes the onset of US with some time gap between the two.

(*d*) In backward conditioning, the US precedes the onset of CS.

It is now well established that delayed conditioning procedure is the most effective way of acquiring a CR. Simultaneous and trace conditioning procedures do lead to acquisition of a CR, but they require greater number of acquisition trials in comparison to the delayed conditioning procedure. It may be noted that the acquisition of response under backward conditioning procedure is very rare.

2. Type of Unconditioned Stimuli: The unconditioned stimuli used in studies of classical conditioning are basically of two types, *i.e.* appetitive and aversive. Appetitive unconditioned stimuli automatically elicits approach responses, such as eating, drinking, caressing, etc. These responses give satisfaction and pleasure. On the other hand, aversive US, such as noise, bitter taste, electric shock, painful injections, etc. are painful, harmful, and elicit avoidance and escape responses. It has been found that appetitive classical conditioning is slower and requires greater number of acquisition trials, but aversive classical conditioning is established in one, two or three trials depending on the intensity of the aversive US.

3. Intensity of Conditioned Stimuli: This influences the course of both appetitive and aversive classical conditioning. More intense conditioned stimuli are more effective in accelerating the acquisition of conditioned responses. It means that the more intense the conditioned stimulus, the fewer are the number of acquisition trials needed for conditioning.

Operant/Instrumental Conditioning

B.F. Skinner is regarded as the father of operant conditioning, but his work was based on **Thorndike's law of effect.** In the late nineteenth century, psychologist Edward Thorndike proposed the law of effect. The law of effect states that any behaviour that has good consequences will tend to be repeated, and any behaviour that has bad consequences will tend to be avoided. In the 1930s, B.F. Skinner, extended this idea and began to study operant conditioning. Operant conditioning is a type of learning in which responses come to be controlled by their consequences.

Operants are those behaviours or responses, which are emitted by animals and human beings voluntarily and are under their control. The term operant is used because the organism operates on the environment. Conditioning of operant behaviour is called operant conditioning. Skinner conducted his studies on rats and pigeons in specially made boxes, called the Skinner Box.

Determinants of Operant Conditioning

The operant or instrumental conditioning is a form of learning in which behaviour is learned, maintained or changed through its consequences. Such consequences are called **reinforcers**. A reinforcer is defined as any stimulus or event, which increases the probability of the occurrence of a (desired) response. A reinforcer has numerous features, which affect the course and strength of a response. They include its type—positive or negative, number or frequency, quality—superior or inferior, and schedule—continuous or intermittent (partial).

Reinforcement may be positive or negative. Positive reinforcement involves stimuli that have pleasant consequences. They strengthen and maintain the responses that have caused them to occur. Positive reinforcers satisfy needs, which include food, water, medals, praise, money, status, information, etc. Negative reinforcers involve unpleasant and painful stimuli. Responses that lead organisms to get rid of painful stimuli or avoid and escape from them provide negative reinforcement. Thus, negative reinforcement leads to learning of avoidance and escape responses. For instance, one learns to put on woollen clothes, burn firewood or use electric heaters to avoid the unpleasant cold weather. One learns to move away from dangerous stimuli because they provide negative reinforcement. It may be noted that negative reinforcement is not punishment. Use of punishment reduces or suppresses the response while a negative reinforcer increases the probability of avoidance or escape response. For instance, drivers and co-drivers wear their seat belts to avoid getting injured in case of an accident or to avoid being fined by the traffic police.

Classical and Operant Conditioning : Differences

1. In classical conditioning, the responses are under the control of some stimulus because they are reflexes, automatically elicited by the appropriate stimuli. Such stimuli are selected as US and responses elicited by them as UR. Thus Pavlovian conditioning, in which US elicits responses, is often called respondent conditioning.

   In instrumental conditioning, responses are under the control of the organism and are voluntary responses or 'operants'. Thus, in the two forms of conditioning different types of responses are conditioned.
2. In classical conditioning, the CS and US are well-defined, but in operant conditioning CS is not defined. It can be inferred but is not directly known.
3. In classical conditioning, the experimenter controls the occurrence of US, while in operant conditioning the occurrence of the reinforcer is under the control of the organism that is learning. Thus, for US in classical conditioning the organism remains passive, while in operant conditioning the subject has to be active in order to be reinforced.
4. In the two forms of conditioning, the technical terms used to characterise the experimental proceedings are different. Moreover what is called reinforcer in operant conditioning is called US in classical conditioning. An US has two functions. In the beginning, it elicits the response and also reinforces the response to be associated and elicited later on by the CS.

OBSERVATIONAL LEARNING

The other form of learning takes place by observing others. Earlier this form of learning was called **imitation**. Bandura and his colleagues in a series of experimental studies investigated observational learning in detail. In this kind of learning, human beings learn social behaviours, therefore, it is sometimes called **social learning**. In many situations individuals do not know how to behave. They observe others and emulate their behaviour. This form of learning is called **modelling**.

Examples of observational learning abound in our social life. Fashion designers employ tall, pretty, and gracious young girls and tall, smart, and well-built young boys for popularising clothes of different designs and fabrics. People observe them on televised fashion shows and advertisements in magazines and newspapers. They imitate these models. Observing superiors and likeable persons and then emulating their behaviour in a novel social situation is a common experience.

The children observe adults' behaviours, at home and during social ceremonies and functions. They enact adults in their plays and games. For instance, young children play games of marriage ceremonies, birthday parties, thief and policeman, house keeping, etc. Actually they enact in their games what they observe in society, on television, and read in books.

Children learn most of the social behaviours by observing and emulating adults. The way to put on clothes, dress one's hair, and conduct oneself in society are learned through observing others. It has also been shown that children learn and develop various personality characteristics through observational learning. Aggressiveness, prosocial behaviour, courtesy, politeness, diligence, and indolence are acquired by this method of learning.

COGNITIVE LEARNING

Some psychologists view learning in terms of cognitive processes that underlie it. They have developed approaches that focus on such processes that occur during learning rather than concentrating solely on S-R and S-S connections. Thus, in cognitive learning, there is a change in what the learner knows rather than what he/she does. This form of learning shows up in insight learning and latent learning.

Insight Learning

Kohler demonstrated a model of learning which could not be readily explained by conditioning. He performed a series of experiments with chimpanzees that involved solving complex problems. Kohler placed chimpanzees in an enclosed play area where food was kept out of their reach. Tools such as poles and boxes were placed in the enclosure. The chimpanzees rapidly learned how to use a box to stand on or a pole to move the food in their direction. In this experiment, learning did not occur as a result of trial and error and reinforcement, but came about in sudden flashes of insight. The chimpanzees would roam about the enclosure for some time and then suddenly would stand on a box, grab a pole and strike a banana, which was out of normal reach above the enclosure. The chimpanzee exhibited what Kohler called insight learning—the process by which the solution to a problem suddenly becomes clear.

In a normal experiment on insight learning, a problem is presented, followed by a period of time when no apparent progress is made and finally a solution suddenly emerges. In insight learning, sudden solution is the rule. Once the solution has appeared, it can be repeated immediately the next time the problem is confronted. Thus, it is clear that what is learned is not a specific set of conditioned associations between stimuli and responses but a cognitive relationship between a means and an end. As a result, insight learning can be generalised to other similar problem situations.

Latent Learning

Another type of cognitive learning is known as latent learning. In latent learning, a new behaviour is learned but not demonstrated until reinforcement is provided for displaying it. Tolman made an early contribution to the concept of latent learning. To have an idea of latent learning, we may briefly understand his experiment. Tolman put two groups of rats in a maze and gave them an opportunity to explore. In one group, rats found food at the end of the maze and soon learned to make their way rapidly through the maze. On the other hand, rats in the second group were not rewarded and showed no apparent signs of learning. But later, when these rats were reinforced, they ran through the maze as efficiently as the rewarded group.

Tolman contended that the unrewarded rats had learned the layout of the maze early in their explorations. They just never displayed their latent learning until the reinforcement was provided. Instead, the rats developed a cognitive map of the maze, *i.e.* a mental representation of the spatial locations and directions, which they needed to reach their goal.

LEARNING AS A SOCIAL ACTIVITY

Learning is a social activity. Our learning is intimately associated with our connection with other human beings, our teachers, our peers, our family as well as casual acquaintances, including the people before us or next to us. We are more likely to be successful in our efforts to educate, if we recognise this principle rather than try to avoid it. Much of traditional education, as Dewey pointed out, is directed towards isolating the learner from all social interaction, and towards seeing education as a one-on-one relationship between the learner and the objective material to be learned. In contrast, progressive education (to continue to use Dewey's formulation) recognizes the social aspect of learning and uses conversations interaction with others, and the application of knowledge as an integral aspect of learning.

SOCIAL CONTEXT OF LEARNING

Social Learning theory

Social learning theory focuses on the learning that occurs within a social context. It considers that people learn from one another, including such concepts as observational learning, imitation, and modelling. Among others **Albert Bandura** is considered the leading proponent of this theory.

General Principles of Social Learning Theory Follows:

1. People can learn by observing the behaviour is of others and the outcomes of those behaviours.
2. Learning can occur without a change in behaviour. Behaviourists say that learning has to be represented by a permanent change in behaviour, in contrast social learning theorists say that because people can learn through observation alone, their learning may not necessarily be shown in their performance. Learning may or may not result in a behaviour change.
3. Cognition plays a role in learning. Over the last 40 years social learning theory has become increasingly cognitive in its interpretation of human learning. Awareness and expectations of future reinforcements or punishments can have a major effect on the behaviours that people exhibit.
4. Social learning theory can be considered a bridge or a transition between behaviourist learning theories and cognitive learning theories.

How the Environment Reinforces and Punishes Modelling:

People are often reinforced for modelling the behaviour of others. Bandura suggested that the environment also reinforces modelling. This is in several possible ways:

1. The observer is reinforced by the model. For example, a student who changes dress to fit in with a certain group of students has a strong likelihood of being accepted and thus reinforced by that group.
2. The observer is reinforced by a third person. The observer might be modelling the actions of someone else, for example, an outstanding class leader or student. The teacher notices this and compliments and praises the observer for modelling such behaviour thus reinforcing that behaviour.
3. The imitated behaviour itself leads to reinforcing consequences. Many behaviours that we learn from others produce satisfying or reinforcing results. For example, a student in my multimedia class could observe how the extra work a classmate does is fun. This student in turn would do the same extra work and also receive enjoyment.
4. Consequences of the model's behaviour affect the observers behaviour vicariously. This is known as vicarious reinforcement. This is where in the model is reinforced for a response and then the observer shows an increase in that same response. Bandura illustrated this by having students watch a film of a model hitting a inflated clown doll. One group of children saw the model being praised for such action. Without being reinforced, the group of children began to also hit the doll.

Contemporary Social Learning Perspective of Reinforcement and Punishment

1. Contemporary theory proposes that both reinforcement and punishment have indirect effects on learning. They are not the sole or main cause.
2. Reinforcement and punishment influence the extent to which an individual exhibits a behaviour that has been learned.
3. The expectation of reinforcement influences cognitive processes that promote learning. Therefore, attention pays a critical role in learning. And attention is influenced by the expectation of reinforcement. An example would be, where the teacher tells a group of students that what they will study next is not on the test. Students will not pay attention, because they do not expect to know the information for a test.

Cognitive Factors in Social Learning

Social learning theory has cognitive factors as well as behaviourist factors (actually operant factors).

1. **Learning without performance:** Bandura makes a distinction between learning through observation and the actual imitation of what has been learned.
2. **Cognitive processing during learning:** Social learning theorists contend that attention is a critical factor in learning.
3. **Expectations:** As a result of being reinforced, people form expectations about the consequences that future behaviours are likely to bring. They expect certain behaviours to bring reinforcements and others to bring punishment. The learner needs to be aware however, of the response reinforcements and response punishment. Reinforcement increases a response only when the learner is aware of that connection.
4. **Reciprocal causation:** Bandura proposed that behaviour can influence both the environment and the person. In fact each of these three variables, the person, the behaviour, and the environment can have an influence on each other.
5. **Modelling:** There are different types of models. There is the live model, and actual person demonstrating the behaviour. There can also be a symbolic model, which can be a person or action portrayed in some other medium, such as television, videotape, computer programs.

Behaviours that can be learned through modelling:

Many behaviours can be learned, at least partly, through modelling. Examples that can be cited are, students can watch parents read, students can watch the demonstrations of mathematics problems, or seen someone acting bravely and a fearful situation. Aggression can be learned through models. Much research indicate that children become more aggressive when they observed aggressive or violent models. Moral thinking and moral behaviour are influenced by observation and modelling. This includes moral judgments regarding right and wrong which can in part, develop through modelling.

Conditions Necessary for Effective Modelling to Occur:

Bandura mentions four conditions that are necessary before an individual can successfully model the behaviour of someone else:

1. **Attention:** the person must first pay attention to the model.
2. **Retention:** the observer must be able to remember the behaviour that has been

observed. One way of increasing this is using the technique of rehearsal.

3. **Motor reproduction:** the third condition is the ability to replicate the behaviour that the model has just demonstrated. This means that the observer has to be able to replicate the action, which could be a problem with a learner who is not ready developmentally to replicate the action. For example, little children have difficulty doing complex physical motion.
4. **Motivation:** the final necessary ingredient for modelling to occur is motivation, learners must want to demonstrate what they have learned. Remember that since these four conditions vary among individuals, different people will reproduce the same behaviour differently.

Effects of Modelling on Behaviour:

Modelling teaches new behaviours.

Modelling influences the frequency of previously learned behaviours.

Modelling may encourage previously forbidden behaviours.

Modelling increases the frequency of similar behaviours. For example, a student might see a friend excel in basketball and he tries to excel in football because he is not tall enough for basketball.

Educational implications of social learning theory:

Social learning theory has numerous implications for classroom use.

1. Students often learn a great deal simply by observing other people.
2. Describing the consequences of behaviour is can effectively increase the appropriate behaviours and decrease inappropriate ones. This can involve discussing with learners about the rewards and consequences of various behaviours.
3. Modelling provides an alternative to shaping for teaching new behaviours. Instead of using shaping, which is operant conditioning, modelling can provide a faster, more efficient means for teaching new behaviour. To promote effective modelling a teacher must make sure that the four essential conditions exist; attention, retention, motor reproduction, and motivation.
4. Teachers and parents must model appropriate behaviours and take care that they do not model inappropriate behaviours.
5. Teachers should expose students to a variety of other models. This technique is especially important to break down traditional stereotypes.
6. Students must believe that they are capable of accomplishing school tasks. Thus, it is very important to develop a sense of self-efficacy for students. Teachers can promote such self-efficacy by having students receive confidence-building messages, watch others be successful, and experience success on their own.
7. Teachers should help students set realistic expectations for their academic accomplishments. In general in my class that means making sure that expectations are not set too low. I want to realistically challenge my students. However, sometimes the task is beyond a student's ability, example would be the cancer group.
8. Self-regulation techniques provide an effective method for improving student behaviour.

CHILD AS A PROBLEM SOLVER AND A SCIENTIFIC INVESTIGATOR

Problem solving is the foundation of a young child's learning. It must be valued, promoted, provided for and sustained in the early childhood classroom. Opportunities for problem solving occur in the everyday context of a child's life. By observing the child closely, teachers can use the child's social, cognitive, movement and emotional experiences to facilitate problem solving and promote strategies useful in the lifelong process of learning.

Problem solving is thinking that is goal-directed. Almost all our day-to-day activities are directed towards a goal. Here, it is important to know that problems are not always in the form of obstacles or hurdles that one faces. It could be any simple activity that you perform to reach a defined goal, for example, preparing a quick snack for your friend who has just arrived at your place. In problem solving there is an initial state (*i.e.* the problem) and there is an end state (the goal). These two anchors are connected by means of several steps or mental operations. Following table would clarify our understanding of various steps through which one solves a problem.

Table: Mental Operations Involved in Solving a Problem

Let us look at the problem of organising a play in school on the occasion of Teachers' Day. Problem solving would involve the following sequence.

Mental operation	Nature of problem
1. Identify the problem	A week is left for teachers' day and you are given the task of organising a play.
2. Represent the problem	Organising a play would involve identification of an appropriate theme, screening of actors, actresses, arranging money, etc.
3. Plan the solution: Set sub-goals	Search and survey various available themes for a play, and consult teachers and friends who have the expertise. The play to be decided, based on such considerations as cost, duration, suitability for the occasion, etc.
4. Evaluate all solutions (plays)	Collect all the information/stage rehearsal.
5. Select one solution and execute it	Compare and verify the various options to get the best solution (the play).
6. Evaluate the outcome	If the play (solution) is appreciated, think about the steps you have followed for future reference for yourself as well as for your friends.
7. Rethink and redefine problems and solutions	After this special occasion you can still think about ways to plan a better play in future.

Learning Through Problem Solving

By exploring social relationships, manipulating objects, and interacting with people, children are able to formulate ideas, try these ideas out, and accept or reject what they learn. Constructing knowledge by making mistakes is part of the natural process of problem solving. Through exploring, then experimenting, trying out a hypothesis, and finally, solving problems, children make learning personal and meaningful. Piaget states that children understand only what they discover or invent themselves. It is this discovery within the problem solving process that is the vehicle for children's learning. Children are encouraged to construct their own knowledge when the teacher plans for problem solving; bases the framework for learning in problem solving; and provides time, space, and materials.

Teacher's Role

Changing through problem solving is modelled by adults and facilitated by the teacher in the classroom environment. When teachers articulate the problems they face and discuss solutions with children, children become more aware of the significance of the problem-solving process. Being a problem solver is modelled by the teacher and emulated by the children. The teacher's role is two-fold: first, to value the process and be willing to trust the learner, and second, to establish and maintain a classroom environment that encourages problem solving. It is the attitude of the teacher that must change first in the problem-solving classroom. Values and goals must be clearly defined to include a child-centered curriculum, the development of communication skills, promotion of cooperative learning, and inclusion of diverse ideas.

The teacher must be willing to become a learner, too. By being curious, observing, listening, and questioning, the teacher shares and models the qualities that are valued and promoted by the problem-solving process.

Planning for Problem Solving

A curriculum that accommodates a variety of developmental levels as well as individual differences in young children sets the stage for problem solving. Choices, decision-making, and a curriculum framework that integrates learning, such as Katz and Chard's project method, are especially appropriate for young learners. The project approach facilitates cooperative learning and promotes diverse ideas. Donna Ogle's K-W-L (what you KNOW, what you WANT to know, and what you have LEARNED) is another method of organizing work that promotes problem solving. Themes, units, webbing, and the KWL method are all ways of organizing curriculum that can support problem solving. Beginning with the needs and interests of the children, problem solving develops from meaningful experiences important to the children. The teacher-designed curriculum provides the classroom basis for these experiences.

For example, a second grade investigation of waste materials from a classroom led one group of young children to explore the topic in an integrated way. Reading, writing, counting, measuring, interviews of community people, and science experiments were planned, initiated and reported. Solutions to many problems posed during the investigation were tried out and some were found to be successful. Through group work, individuals were able to participate and communicate as cognitive and social needs were met. Each child, at individual levels and in individual ways, was successful within the group experience. Problem solving empowers children.

Providing for Problem Solving

Problem solving is a skill that can be learned and must be practiced. It is facilitated by a classroom schedule that provides for integrated learning in large blocks of time, space for ongoing group projects, and many open-ended materials. The teacher provides the time, space, and materials necessary for in-depth learning.

1. Time: Teachers can provide for problem solving by enlarging blocks of learning time during the school day. Because making choices, discussing decisions, and evaluating mistakes takes time, large time blocks best suit the problem-solving process. It is important that children know they have time to identify and solve problems.

2. Space: Projects and group meetings may require an assessment of classroom space. Moving desks and tables together facilitates communication and cooperation in the classroom. Once the teacher has observed the patterns of traffic in the classroom, equipment can be moved or eliminated to promote problem solving.

3. Materials: The open-ended materials that are needed for the construction and concrete solving of problems should be safe, durable, and varied. Well-marked storage units should be easily accessible to children, and materials should be available for ongoing exploration and manipulation. Access to a variety of materials encourages children to use materials in new and diverse ways. This freedom promotes problem solving.

The Problem-Solving Model

Individuals or groups can solve problems. Group problem solving is important to young children because many diverse ideas are generated. Both individual and group processes should be included in the early childhood classroom. Becoming skillful at problem solving is based on the understanding and use of sequenced steps. These steps are:

1. Identifying the problem,
2. Brainstorming a variety of solutions,
3. Choosing one solution and trying it out, and
4. Evaluating what has happened.

Choosing Good Problems

Goffin provides teachers with guiding questions that will help them identify appropriate problems for young children. Some of these are:

1. Is the problem meaningful and interesting?
2. Can the problem be solved at a variety of levels?
3. Must a new decision be made?
4. Can the actions be evaluated?

Problem solving is a way to make sense of the environment and, in fact, control it. The process allows children in an increasingly diverse world to be active participants and to implement changes. By including problem solving in the early childhood classroom, we equip children with a life-long skill that is useful in all areas of learning.

Obstacles to Solving Problems

Two major obstacles to solving a problem are mental set and lack of motivation.

Mental Set

Mental set is a tendency of a person to solve problems by following already tried mental operations or steps. Prior success with a particular strategy would sometimes help in solving a new problem. However, this tendency also creates a mental rigidity that obstructs the problem solver to think of any new rules or strategies. Thus, while in some situations mental set can enhance the quality and speed of problem solving, in other situations it hinders problem solving. You might have experienced this while solving mathematical problems. After completing a couple of questions, you form an idea of the steps that are required to solve these questions and subsequently you go on following the same steps, until a point where you fail. At this point you may experience difficulty in avoiding the already used steps. Those steps would interfere in your thought for new strategies. However, in day-to-day activities we often rely on past experiences with similar or related problems.

Like mental set, **functional fixedness** in problem solving occurs when people fail to solve a problem because they are fixed on a thing's usual function. If you have ever used a hardbound book to hammer a nail, then you have overcome functional fixedness.

Lack of Motivation

People might be great at solving problems, but all their skills and talents are of no use if they are not motivated. Sometimes people give up easily when they encounter a problem or failure in implementing the first step. Therefore, there is a need to persist in their effort to find a solution.

ALTERNATIVE CONCEPTIONS OF LEARNING

When teachers provide instruction on concepts in various subjects, they are teaching students who already have some pre-instructional knowledge about the topic. Student knowledge, however, can be erroneous, illogical or misinformed. These erroneous understandings are termed alternative conceptions or misconceptions (or intuitive theories). Alternative conceptions (misconceptions) are not unusual. In fact, they are a normal part of the learning process. We quite naturally form ideas from our everyday experience, but obviously not all the ideas we develop are correct with respect to the most current evidence and scholarship in a given discipline. Moreover, some concepts in different content areas are simply very difficult to grasp. They may be very abstract, counterintuitive or quite complex. Hence, our understanding of them is flawed. In addition, things we have already learned are sometimes unhelpful in learning new concepts/theories. This occurs when the new concept or theory is inconsistent with previously learned material. Accordingly, as noted, it is very typical for students (and adults) to have misconceptions in different domains (content knowledge areas). Indeed, researchers have found that there is a common set of alternative conceptions (misconceptions) that most students typically exhibit. There is one class of alternative theories (or misconceptions) that is very deeply entrenched. These are "ontological misconceptions," which relate to ontological beliefs (*i.e.*, beliefs about the fundamental categories and properties of the world).

Alternative conceptions (misconceptions) can impede learning for several reasons. First, students generally are unaware that the knowledge they have is wrong. Moreover, misconceptions can be very entrenched in student thinking. In addition, new experiences are interpreted through these erroneous understandings, thereby interfering with being able to correctly grasp new information. Also, alternative conceptions (misconceptions) tend to be very resistant to instruction because learning entails replacing or radically reorganizing student knowledge. Hence, conceptual change has to occur for learning to happen. This puts teachers in the very challenging position of needing to bring about significant conceptual change in student knowledge. Generally, ordinary forms of instruction, such as lectures, labs, discovery learning, or simply reading texts, are not very successful at overcoming student misconceptions. For all these reasons, misconceptions can be hard nuts for teachers to crack. However, several instructional strategies have been found to be effective in achieving conceptual change and helping students leave their alternative conceptions behind and learn correct concepts or theories.

Instructional strategies that can lead to change in students' alternative conceptions (misconceptions) and to learning of new concepts and theories

1. Present new concepts or theories that you are teaching in such a way that students see as plausible, high-quality, intelligible and generative.
2. Use students' correct conceptions and build on those by creating a bridge of examples to the new concept or theory that students are having trouble learning due to misconceptions they hold.
3. Use model-ased reasoning, which helps students construct new representations that vary from their intuitive theories.
4. Use diverse instruction, wherein you present a few examples that challenge multiple assumptions, rather than a larger number of examples that challenge just one assumption.
5. Help students become aware of (raise student metacognition about) their own alternative conceptions (misconceptions).
6. Present students with experiences that cause cognitive conflict in students' minds. Experiences (as in strategy 3 above) that can cause cognitive conflict are ones that get students to consider their erroneous (misconception) knowledge side-by-side with, or at the same time as, the correct concept or theory.
7. Engage in Interactive Conceptual Instruction (ICI).
8. Develop students' epistemological thinking, which incorporates beliefs and theories about the nature of knowledge and the nature of learning, in ways that will facilitate conceptual change. The more naive students' beliefs are about knowledge and learning, the less likely they are to revise their misconceptions.
9. Help students "self-repair" their misconceptions.
10. Once students have overcome their alternative conceptions (misconceptions).

Presenting new concepts or theories

In presenting new concepts or theories, teachers should be sure to show these theories or concepts as:

1. Plausible: The new information should be shown to be consistent with other knowledge and able to explain the available data. Learners must see how the new conception (theory) is consistent with other knowledge and a good explanation of the data.

2. High quality: Of course, the theory/concept to be taught is of high quality from a scientific point of view, since it is a correct theory. However, the presented theory should take a better account of the data than what students currently have available to them. For example, the instructor should deal with the problem from the perspective of the students (*e.g.*, students for whom a "flat earth" theory provides a better account of the data available than does a "spherical earth" theory). Hence, the quality of the new theory must be considered along with the kind of data that students know about.

3. Intelligible: Teachers should do what they can to increase the intelligibility of the new theory. Learners must be able to grasp how the new conception works. To increase intelligibility, teachers can use methods such as use of:

(*a*) analogies,

(*b*) models, and

(*c*) direct exposition.

4. Generative/fruitful: Teachers should show that the new concept/theory can be extended to open up new areas of inquiry. Learners must be able to extend the new conception to new areas of inquiry. Teachers might accomplish this by illustrating the application of the new concept/theory to a range of problems. These problems can include familiar ones and new ones.

UNDERSTANDING CHILDREN'S 'ERRORS' AS SIGNIFICANT STEPS IN THE LEARNING PROCESS

The legacy of Jean Piaget to the world of early childhood education is that he fundamentally altered the view of how a child learns. And a teacher, he believed, was more than a transmitter of knowledge she was also an essential observer and guide to helping children build their own knowledge.

As a university graduate, Swiss-born Piaget got a routine job in Paris standardizing Binet-Simon IQ tests, where the emphasis was on children getting the right answers. Piaget observed that many children of the same ages gave the same kinds of incorrect answers. What could be learned from this?

Piaget interviewed many hundreds of children and concluded that children who are allowed to make mistakes often go on to discover their errors and correct them, or find new solutions. In this process, children build their own way of learning. From children's errors, teachers can obtain insights into the child's view of the world and can tell where guidance is needed. They can provide appropriate materials, ask encouraging questions, and allow the child to construct his own knowledge.

Piaget's continued interactions with young children became part of his life-long research. After reading about a child who thought that the sun and moon followed him wherever he went, Piaget wanted to find out if all young children had a similar belief. He found that many did indeed believe this. Piaget went on to explore children's countless "why" questions, such as, "Why is the sun round?" or "Why is grass green?" He concluded that children do not think like adults. Their thought processes have their own distinct order and special logic. Children are not "empty vessels to be filled with knowledge" (as traditional pedagogical theory had it). They are "active builders of knowledge-little scientists who construct their own theories of the world."

COGNITION & EMOTIONS

What is Cognition?

Cognition is the ability to preceive, memorise, reason and understand. These abilities change with age. As the child grows, her thinking becomes more mature and efficient. Therefore, cognition can simply be defined as the process of acquiring, processing, organising and using knowledge. The development of cognition means development of all these abilities. A child's thinking changes as result of both age (maturation) and increased experiences.

Major Cognitive Characteristics of Children

Infancy

It is interesting to see the number of changes that take place in the first two years. Children at this stage are very active learners. Even when it seems the child is only lying and looking at nothing (e.g. 2 month old) she is actually looking at and trying to understand the things around her.

The first two years children begin by exploring their own bodies and move to the outside objects. Children at 2/3 months discover their thumb or hand or occasionally their own foot. These fascinate them they try to play with them. For a two month old a toy is not as satisfying as her/his own thumb in her/his mouth. Gradually, by about six months, children begin to play with objects outside the body. This could be the toy, the sheet, the bottle, etc. Later, by two years they can even indulge in pretend play [example doctor-doctor, house-house, etc.].

What children also achieve by two years is the understanding of object permanance. **Object**

permanance is the understanding that things exist even if you can not see them. Let us take an example. If you show a five month old a toy she gets excited. If you hide the toy the child soon forgets that any toy even existed. This is because she thinks out of sight is out of mind. Do the same thing with a 1½ year old and you will find the child is either looking for it or asks you to find it. This is because she knows the toy exists even if she can not see it. This understanding, that things exist even if you can not see them, is called object permanance.

The other major development that happens by two years is that children begin to learn the symbols. What are symbols? A two year old can convey her thoughts and desires through language. All these are essential processes of cognition.

Early Childhood

This is a period when the childs mastery in use of symbols increases. We can observe this in the everyday behaviour and activities of the child, *i.e.* in what she plays, her language etc. Gradually her representations of objects become more flexible and less self centred. A one year old while playing does not need a toy phone to pretend speaking on the phone. She can use any object. This is indicative of flexibility in thinking. Gradually, children also start directing play between dolls, *e.g.,* one doll is the mother and the other doll the child. This is indicative of the child moving away from self to becoming less self centred.

Children at this stage also believe that all objects have feelings like human beings. That is why you will often see the child feeding her teddy bear.

Children at this stage can also focus on only one aspect of a situation and can not go back. Let us now take an example. You offer cola to a 4 yr old in a tall glass. You then change your mind and pour the coke from the tall glass to a short glass and give it to the child. You will find the child will say I want the big glass. This is because she can only focus on one aspect (height) at a time. Also, she is not able to go back mentally and realise that in the process of pouring from big to small glass, no cola was taken away.

Similarly, take two plates and put in one 6 pieces of chocolate spreadout and in the other make a tower of 6 pieces of chocolate. You will find the child thinking the spread out chocolate is more. This is because the child can only focus on one aspect at a time. This limitation seriously restricts the problem solving and logical thinking abilities of the child.

It also indicates the child's inability to understand that another point of view different from her own can exist, *e.g.,* you often find children responding to your question by nodding their heads, even if they are not in the same room as you. This is because they do not see another's point of view.

Middle Childhood

During this period, children begin to understand that another view point can exist. They are also able to focus on more than one aspect of a situation and go back and forth on their thinking. This makes their thinking more logical and efficient. However, children are only comfortable with concrete ideas/objects. It means, something that is real for them, *i.e.,* either something they have seen, *e.g.,* a house or something is in front of them, a plant or something linked to what they know, *e.g.,* blue like the sky. They are not able to think about abstract ideas, *e.g.,* what would happen if everyone could fly?

Emotion

Emotions, put simply, are feelings. In infants we can see these very clearly in the form of joy, anger and fear. These are similar to the emotions that adults have.

1. **The variety of emotions increases with age:** The basic emotions of joy, fear, anger are visible in infants. Gradually, as a sense of self develops; children begin to relate with people around them and value their opinions. Then we can see the emotion like pride, shame, sympathy, guilt also developing in them.
2. **The expression of emotion also changes with age:** Emotions are both innate and learnt. The instinctive response to a stimulus is innate but how to express that feeling is learnt, *e.g.* taking away of a toy makes the child angry (innate) but instead crying she is encouraged to ask for it back (learnt). Frustration tolerance increases with age. As children grow older, their responses change in both as well as instinctive method of expression, *e.g.,* when 2 year old falls downs she cries loudly and later forgets quickly. A 6 year old on the other hand, may not cry but forgets far less easily.
3. **The triggers or cause of emotions change with age:** The stimuli that elicit emotion also change with age, *e.g.,* an infant may cry on hearing the loud explosion of a cracker but a middle childhood child may laugh. Sucking a thumb may give great joy to an infant but provides no pleasure to a child is middle childhood.
4. **The coping techniques change with age:** Methods of coping with frustration and stress change with age. While a younger child may cry, or cling to the adult, an older child is likely to suppress the emotion.

Factors Affecting Emotional Development

If we look round in our environment, we will find that people differ in the emotions they experience and express. Some are happy, some are angry, some moody, some helpful. What then affects our emotional development?

1. **Parenting style:** Democratic parenting where induction is used as a method of disciplining allows for more mature emotional development and also for development of personal behaviour.
2. **Role model:** There are two factors which influence what a child ultimately learns:
   (i) How adults and others in the child's environment handle their emotions.
   (ii) How successful is the emotional expression in achieving their needs.
3. **Violence in the child's environment:** The kind of behaviour the child see in the community (*e.g.* during riots) or on TV will affect her expressions of emotions.
4. **Cultural norms:** Emotional expressions are learnt from the environment. It is the environment that tells us how to react in a situation (*e.g.* some people feel the emotion of fear when a black cat crosses their path). It is also the environment that tells us the acceptable way of expressing ones emotions (*e.g.* in many families it is unacceptable for boys to express their distress by crying). Therefore, our cultural beliefs and values also influence our emotional development.

MOTIVATION AND LEARNING

Motivation

Motivation is the heart of the learning process. It generates the will in an individual to do something. Adequate motivation not only engages the student in an activity which results in learning, but also sustains and directs learning. Two types of motivation are commonly recognised. These are: intrinsic and extrinsic motivation.

Intrinsic motivation arises when the resolution of tension is to be found in mastering the learning task itself; the material learned provides its own reward. For example, the student who studies the construction of model aeroplanes diligently so that he can make a model, is experiencing a kind of intrinsic motivation.

Extrinsic motivation occurs when a student pursues a learning task, but for reasons which are external. If a student engages in construction of model aeroplanes because he thinks it will please his father, who is an ex-pilot, rather than because of intrinsic motivation. We should remember that in most learning situations motivation can not be dichotomised so neatly. It is the function of the total learning situation and hinges on some blend of personal concern for the work itself and the concern for some extrinsic factors as well. As a working principle, motivation is probably a function of an interactive situation where reward to a particular action acts as an incentive. Some of the common forms of extrinsic motivation are:

- **Purposive striving, goals and ideals:** The goal and purposes of learning clearly perceived by the individual, provide strong motivation for better action and learning.
- **Knowledge of results:** Knowledge of results in terms of success and failure provides incentive for greater efforts on the part of the student. If a student practices a task without knowing the accuracy or inaccuracy of his performance, he may practise wrong task. In such a case, all learning will be futile. Therefore, if results of performance are known to the student, he learns better as compared to when he does not know about the results. Mere repetition of a task without knowledge of its results fails to bring about learning. Knowledge of results serves two purposes: (i) it enables the subject to evaluate his efficiency and to change his responses in the direction of greater accuracy, and (ii) it adds to the satisfaction in reaching a goal, one tends of repeat rewarded responses.
- **Punishment and rewards:** Punishment can be understood as an act of inflicting pain deliberately with the purpose of affecting the future conduct of an individual being punished. Punishment is based on fear of physical pain, embarrassment and loss of status. Thus, punishment of fear of being punished is one of the common and obvious methods of keeping under control and guiding the students. Punishment or fear is a very strong stimuli, a negative incentive to learning especially when errors occur. Thorndike showed that generally punishment speeds up learning and reduces the number of errors as it produces emotional excitement which tends to fix at punished response. But it does not mean that punishment under all the circumstances and with all the students is equally effective. For example, it may prove disastrous and destructive when task is very difficult.

  Contrary to punishment, rewards are certainly better and positive incentives to learning. They are responsible for initiative, energy, competition, self-expression and creative ability. According to law of effect, reward is satisfying and pleasant, thus reward strengthens learning. Rewards may in the form of gifts, prizes, money, badges, cups, certificates of merit, or other objects of some value. Motivation through such objects feeds the natural drive in all the human beings. But, when these rewards are too much strived for, they degenerate the whole learning.

- **Praise and blame:** These are also strong incentives for effective learning. Praise stimulates average and inferior children, but has less effect on those of superior intelligence. Reproof is felt most by superior children, but girls seem more susceptible to praise than do boys. Regardless of age sex, or initial ability, praise is the most effective of the incentives. Reproof seems to be less effective for all students. Chase (1932) reported praise to be less effective than blame with young children, but Hurlock (1920) generalised, still accepted by contemporary investigators, that praise is more effective stimulus in motivating both immediate and long-continued tasks.
- **Rivalry:** The rivalry between students which leads to resentment, jealousy, etc., or rivalry between groups of students which creates hatred, is the least desirable type of incentive to be encouraged in the schools. Self-rivalry or rivalry in the form of healthy competition is the most valuable type. This tendency should be developed in the student. Though experimental researchers have shown rivalry to be a powerful motivation influence, the emotional and social consequences of rivalry must be considered by the teacher.

Functions of Motivation

The major functions of motivation in learning are as follows:

- To energies the students in learning
- To direct behaviour
- To select behaviour
- To help capture the attention
- To help in acquiring knowledge
- To help in character formation
- To develop social qualities

Attention in Relation to Motivation

Attention is the basic pre-requisite of all learning in the classroom. Learning is possible only if students concentrate their attention on the object or stimuli to be learnt. Attention increases the amount and rate of learning, and also the efficiency of work.

Attention is closely related to motivation. Attention is motivated behaviour, in which the student makes a variety of efforts for achieving the goal. Thus motivation helps in capturing attention. You can help your students by motivating them to concentrate their attention on the tasks to be learnt by them.

Between the two types of motivation, intrinsic motivation should be preferred to extrinsic motivation. It produces better learning because it is related to interest. The learner pursues the activity in which he has interest without waiting for any external pressure. When the learner does not show any intrinsic motivation or interest in learning we have to resort to extrinsic motivation by the use of 'incentives'—whether financial or non-financial (monetary or non-monetary)—such as rewards, awards, prizes, competitions, praise, etc.

In-built Motivation

Another type of motivation is called in-built motivation. Whatever may be the type of motivation, it should be an in-built component of the whole programme of education/training. Right type of trainers, attractive and need-based reading materials, supportive training methodologies, constant awareness of the new dimensions of the programme will facilitate motivation in an in-built manner.

Theories of Motivation

The main theories of motivation are: (a) Psycho-analytic Theory, (b) Maslow's Theory of Self-actualisation, (c) Physiological Theory and (d) Achievement-Motivation Theory.

Psycho-Analytic Theory

According to this theory, motivation gives the vital life forces which are the prime mover of life and its activities. 'It is will power that motivates a person', *i.e.*, 'no will power—no activity'. All these versions agree on one point *i.e.*, 'building ego of man'.

Maslow's Theory of Self-Actualisation

This theory is based on human needs and their satisfaction. Maslow (1998) has arranged man's basic needs in a hierarchy, *i.e.*, some needs are strong or more important than others. According to him the five basic needs, progressing from physiological needs through safety needs, love, esteem needs and the need for self-actualisation. These basic needs are described here under:

- **Physiological needs:** Maslow states that physiological needs are undoubtedly the most powerful of all needs. Examples are the needs for food, sleep or rest. Until the biological needs are met, an individual may lack awareness of other needs. When a person is gratified he/she is released and higher needs can emerge. Some potential adult learners from low-economic background actually have unmet physiological needs, such as hunger, which prevent them from learning. An old person may not be able to see or hear well and he might not be open to satisfying other needs.

- **Safety Needs:** When physiological needs are satisfied, safety needs emerge, such as need for security, for physical safety, for stability in one's life. Safety needs are seen when a person prefers the familiar over the unfamiliar. An adult would rather go to a meeting in a building with which he is familiar than in a building new to him.
- **Love or Belongingness:** If both the physiological and safety needs are gratified, the needs for love, affection and belongingness emerge. Love needs involve both giving and receiving love. They involve the feeling of being wanted. The person who does not feel he belongs, no matter what the reason, probably will not continue with the group and discontinue his participation in adult education programme. The teacher should be affectionate towards adult learners and develop a group spirit among learners.
- **Esteem:** All people in our society have a need, a desire, for self-respect or self-esteem and for the esteem of others. There are two types: The desire for achievement and the desire for prestige or recognition from others. Satisfaction of the need for self-esteem leads to feelings of self-confidence and of being useful to the society. Thwarting of these needs produce feelings of inferiority or weakness. Fear or failure or lack of self-esteem might prevent an adult from participating in educational activities.
- **Self-Actualisation:** Even after the earlier needs are satisfied a person might still feel restless unless he becomes everything he is capable of becoming. This is called self-fulfilment or self-actualisation. The specific form of this needs varies from person-to-person. One person might desire to be an ideal mother or an ideal leader.
- **Implications for Adult Learning:** Before starting the adult education class, the basic needs of the learners should be studied. It may be possible that due to poverty and less per capita income, the basic biological needs of the learners may not be fulfilled. Then the main aim of adult education should be to provide regular income to the learners. This can be done by starting various income generating projects. The educators should also help by marketing of such products produced by the learners. The officials connected with adult education should take steps to start such programmes. This will make the classes more interesting to the learners. The teacher needs to strengthen the group spirit among learners and should identify himself/herself with the group. The learning experiences in the centres should promote the talents, attitudes capacities and potentialities of adults.

Physiological Theory of Motivation

This theory has been developed by Clifford Morgan and William James. According to this theory of the body determines attitudes and interests and explains activities and behaviour of people.

Implications for Adult Education: Participa-tion in physical activities decrease with age so also interests change as a person becomes older. Many physical limitations affect the amount of time an adult has for educational activities. After working all day at a job, some adults are too tired to participate in educational activity, such people can be motivated giving them work which gives them relaxation. Hearing and vision also decrease with age. The ages of the group members will determine the size of letters that a teacher writes on a black board, the colour of the chalk used, the size of the articles he holds for the adults to see, and how loudly and distinctly he speaks. The size, type and quality of handout material are also important.

Achievement-Motivation Theory

This theory has been developed by McClelland (1985). According to this theory all human behaviour is intended to reduce tension and reach a state of physiological and psychological equilibrium. It is a desire to do better, to achieve unique accomplishment, to compete with a standard of excellence and to involve oneself with long term achievement goals. It can be identified on the basic of individual expectation of success. It applies only when the individual knows that his/her performance will be evaluated by himself or by others in terms of excellence, and that the consequences of his action will either succeed or fail.

FACTORS CONTRIBUTING TO LEARNING

Introduction

Learning, can be considered as the process by which skills, attitudes, knowledge and concepts are acquired, understood, applied and extended. All human beings, whether grown ups or children engage in the process of learning, either consciously, sub-consciously or subliminally. It is through learning that their competence and ability to function in their environment get enhanced. It is important to understand that while we learn some ideas and concepts through instruction or teaching, we also learn through our feelings and experiences. Feelings and experiences are a tangible part of our lives and these greatly influence what we learn, how we learn and why we learn.

Learning has been considered partly a cognitive process and partly a social and affective one. It qualifies as a cognitive process because it involves the functions of attention, perception, reasoning, analysis, drawing of conclusions, making interpretations and giving meaning to the observed phenomena. All of these are mental processes which relate to the intellectual functions of the individual. Learning is a social and affective process, as the societal and cultural context in which we function and the feelings and experiences which we have, greatly influence our ideas, concepts, images and understanding of the world. These constitute inner subjective interpretations and represent our own unique, personalized constructions of the specific universe of functioning. Our knowledge, ideas, concepts, attitudes, beliefs and the skills which we acquire are a consequence of these combined processes.

CLASSIFICATION OF FACTORS: PERSONAL & ENVIRONMENT

To understand how we categorise the factors affecting learning, let us begin by considering the following examples:

- Ravi is sixteen year old and wants to please his mother by getting good results in his board examinations. He is so eager to please her, that he spends long hours of concentrated time and energy on his studies. He consciously tries to control other sources of distraction in his life and reduces the time spent on watching television, playing games and chatting with his friends.
- Rita Williams wants to be a famous tennis player. To achieve her goal, she practices tennis whenever she can, even though she gets no encouragement from her family. She makes it a point to watch tennis matches and maintain a good rapport with her sports teacher.
- Yuvraj is a good student, but lately he has been scoring very low marks at school. He is not able to concentrate or pay attention and his class work and home assignments reflect a very poor quality. Sources revealed that his parents fight a lot with each other and are about to get divorced.
- Arti and Kavita are two sisters. Arti is very good at art and craft and can sketch just about anything she sees. Kavita has a ear for music. She knows most songs and can sing them even if she has heard them only once. Both of them spend hours together pursuing their respective interest areas.
- Sayeeda is tall, attractive and has a very good figure. She wants to be a model or an air-hostess and nurtures this secretly as her dream. She is too scared to share her wishes with her family, since she belongs to an orthodox family, where girls at best can pursue teaching as a career. When she tries telling her mother what she wants, she is firmly told that she can only do her B.Ed and can go to the coaching classes for these.

The above cited examples illustrate that learning is a universal phenomenon mediated by a number of factors, both personal and environmental in nature. The dictum "everybody learns" is as true as its corollary, *i.e.*, everybody learns in accordance with his/her unique, individualized blend of personal and environmental factors. For example, in case of Ravi, the desire to please his mother, striving to do well in his board exams and managing his life situations appropriately constitute the key factors which influence him. For Rita Williams, it is her intrinsic desire to be a good tennis player which is paramount. She is not deterred by the lack of family support and continues to make efforts to promote her love for tennis on her own and fulfil her desire to be successful.

In case of Yuvraj, in spite of his innate capacity to study and perform well, his lack of achievement can be attributed to the emotional insecurity stemming from his parents' divorce. As far as Arti and Kavita are concerned, their special interests and talent in art and music respectively, seem to guide their activities.

For Sayeeda, the home environment and family culture and values determine her professional choice. Her own inner interests, desires and wishes are not to be taken into cognizance.

In all the examples cited, we can find evidence of both personal and environmental factors influencing the process of learning. Learning can thus be defined as a function of the interaction of personal and environmental factors.

$$L = f\,(EF \times PF)$$

L = learning; f = function; EF = environmental factors; PF = personal factors.

Personal factors are the intra individual factors like motivation, interests, abilities etc which predispose an individual towards learning as in the case of Rita Williams, Arti and Kavita. Environmental factors on the other hand, are those contextual factors which highlight the role of the environment in learning, such as the socio-emotional, societal and cultural factors as seen in the case of Yuvraj and Sayeeda. Although the two factors represent different categories, they operate in a common system. The environmental factors provide the context within which the personal factors, operate. The learner and the learning process can only be completely understood with reference to the interaction of both environmental and personal factors. This may be diagrammatically represented as follows:

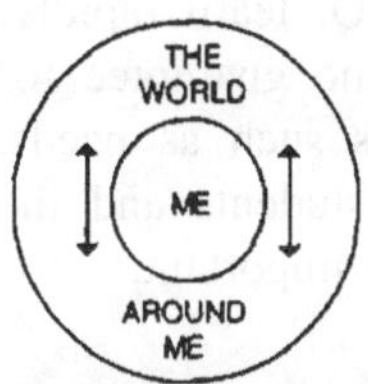

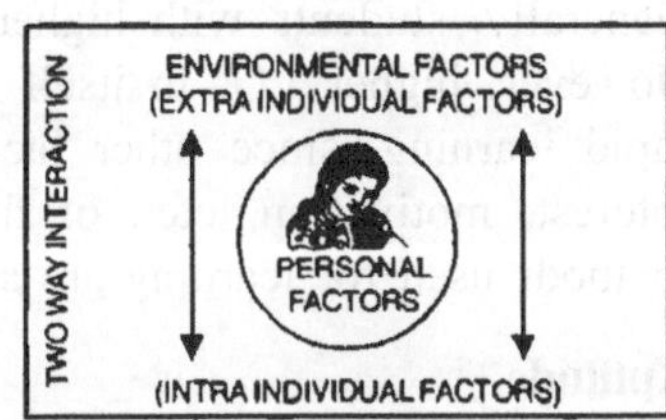

Fig: *Factors affecting learning*

Personal Factors Influencing Learning

The process of learning is influenced by a variety of personal factors. A thorough knowledge of these factors will prove very helpful for teachers and parents in understanding and guiding their children's learning. Some of the personal factors that influence the learning process may be classified as under : sensation and perception, fatigue and boredom, maturation, emotional condition, needs, interests, motivation, attention, intelligence, aptitude, attitude, etc. Let us discuss the important personal factors in the following sub-sections.

Sensation and Perception

Apart from the general health of the students, sensation and perception are the psychological factors which help in learning. Sensation is at the core of perception. There are five sense organs *i.e.*, skin, ears, tongue, eyes and nose. These sense organs are the gateways of knowledge and help in perception of various stimuli in the environment. Any defect in any of the sense organs will affect learning and hence acquisition of knowledge. For example, defects of vision such as myopia, hypermetropia, astigmatism, etc., cause headaches, nausia and general disinclination to study. A blind person depends upon the sense of touch or skin for learning and thus acquires knowledge and skills, as he can not visualise the objects. The stimuli are preceived and assimilated, and hence learnt through various sense organs. In this way we can say that sensation and perception is the bases of knowledge and learning.

Fatigue and Boredom

It is virtually boredom or lassitude rather than fatigue which bothers the students. The difference between the two is that fatigue is mental or physical tiredness which decreases in efficiency and competency to work. Boredom, on the other hand, is a lack of desire on an aversion to work. Such an aversion makes one feel fatigued without being actually fatigued. Studying seldom causes fatigue. It is mainly boredom which, besides causing the impression of fatigue, decreases student efficiency in learning.

Age and Maturation

Learning is directly dependent upon age and maturation. No learning can take place unless individual is matured enough to learn. Some children can learn better at earlier age while others take more time to learn the same content.

Mental age increases with the chronological age and ceases at about the age of sixteen years. Increase in age means intellectual maturation which helps in solving difficult problems. The principle of maturation warns us against enforcing learning on a child when he is not mature enough to learn the specific skills. Teachers should explain this principle to parents who are over ambitious or over enthusiastic in sending their children to school at the very early age.

Emotional Conditions

Desirable emotional conditions enhance the quality and speed of learning. Happiness, joy and satisfaction are always favourable for any type of learning. Adverse emotional conditons, on the other hand, hinder learning. Many studies have established the fact that emotional strain, stress, tensions, disturbances, etc., are extremely inimical to scholastic pursuits.

Needs

A need is the lack of something which, if provided, would facilitate child's usual behaviour. The lack of something is experienced by the child. The child then tries to perform that activity which culminates in the satisfaction of the need. Thus, the needs are associated with goals. Among human beings, the needs are realtively permanent tendencies which seek satisfaction in achieving certain specific goals. When these goals are achieved, the particular need is satisfied or met for the time being, but it recurs sooner or later and energises further activity. The needs in human beings can be physiological such as need for oxygen, food, water, etc. They may be social such as the need for affection, recognition, self-regard, etc. Social needs are however, quite different from physiological needs. Social needs might originate after physiological needs are satisfied. These needs have a complex structure and dominate the individual's behaviour.

There is not equal urgency in the satisfaction of all needs. Some have to be satisfied before others can manifest themselves.

In schools, children are not expected to do any intellectual thinking unless their physiological needs are satisfied. Poor, starved children may concentrate less on attainment of knowledge than on food. Similarly, very cold or hot classrooms or over-crowded seats will not be conducive to good learning. Likewise the need for safety, love and esteem, all act as powerful motives in the learning situations. If the child is afraid of the teacher or feels unsafe while in the school on account of too much beating or some other form of punishment, no learning can take place. Similarly, his needs for warmth and affection are very stimulating and hence results in effective learning.

Interests

Various types of interests of the students can be exploited to facilitate their learning. The interests during early infancy are mostly limited and short lived. As the child grows older his interests diversify and stabilize. You, a school teacher, should have thorough knowledge of children's interests. You can eliminate much drudgery, monotony and boredom from the school work if you make your instruction lively and stimulating and arouse student interest in it.

Once the students' interest is aroused in an activity you should expend more effort on it. No learning can be achieved without proper expenditure of effort on it. Students can even overcome distraction, fatigue and boredom if they feel interested in your instruction and class activities. It has often been found that, in most cases, fatigue in reality is loss of interest in the learning activity. Interest, should be exploited to yield results of greater quantity and quality learning in school.

Life is so exciting that many interesting things and activities often clamor to attract our attention. Children frequently face the dilemma of mutually conflicting interests. Immediate interests often seem to be clashing with the remoter ones. A student might be in a quandary at least for the time being when his interest in sports impels him towards the play-field and his interest in studies force him to concentrate on books.

In such cases of conflicting interests a lot of hesitancy, wastage, frustration and unhappiness is bound to follow. What is needed is education at home and school which helps/trains children to achieve a healthy balance in their interests. They should be trained to budget their time in such a manner as to pay a reasonable attention to various interests, scholastic, athletic, social etc., within the time at their disposal.

Motivation

Motivation is the heart of the learning process. It generates the will in an individual to do something. Adequate motivation not only engages the student in an activity which results in learning, but also sustains and directs learning. Two types of motivation are commonly recognised. These are: intrinsic and extrinsic motivation.

Intelligence

Intelligence as expressed by an I.Q. score on an intelligence test is positively related to learning. Generally, students with higher I.Q. learn rapidly. However, higher I.Q. in itself is no guarantee for rapid learning, since other factors such as needs, interest, motivation, etc., of the students and the methods used for learning are also important.

Aptitude

A student who possesses appropriate aptitude for a particular subject of study or skill, will learn better and retain it for a longer time. On the other hand, he will require relatively longer time to study a subject for which he lacks natural aptitude. He is liable to forget it soon besides feeling bored and unhappy all the time while learning it. Hence, it is extremely desirable to analyse the aptitude of students before prescribing courses of study for them.

Attitude

The learning process is also influenced considerably by the attitude of the student. If he is alert, attentive and interested in the material to be learnt, he is bound to have a favourable attitude towards it. Such an attitude will enable him to tackle the learning situation economically, pleasantly and effectively. Conversely, if he is inattentive and is uninterested in the material his attitude is bound to be unfavourable. This will hinder the smooth learning of the material in hand besides involving undue strain and tension in the learner.

Environmental Factors

Environmental influences begin since the time of the conception of the child in the womb of the mother. Mother's mental, physical and emotional conditions influence the development of foetus in the womb. The external environment starts from the time of birth of the child. It (external environment) refers to the surroundings which prevail in home, school and locality. At these places, the child interacts with members of the family, teachers, classmates or peers and neighbours and establishes relationship with them. The relationship with the members of the society, and the surroundings may affect the development of the child and also the way he learns. Some of the environmental factors are discussed as follows:

Surrounding : Natural, Social and Cultural

As the title of the sub-section indicates, we shall discuss here natural, social and cultural environment the child interacts with and get influenced.

Natural surrounding covers the climatic and atmospheric condition. These conditions affect learning directly. It has been found that high temperature and humidity reduces mental efficiency. For a limited time, humidity and high temperature can be tolerated but prolonged humidity and high temperature become unbearable and decrease mental efficiency. The intellectual productivity and creativeness of people living in hot regions are much low. Likewise, the morning time is always better for mastering difficult tasks. Mental efficiency decreases due to increased humidity and temperature. Studies on the academic progress of evening school students shows losses of efficiency varying from one to six per cent.

Social surrounding includes especially the environment of home, school and locality. Physical conditions at home such as large family, small family, (specific place of the study), insufficient ventilation, improper lighting, uncomfortable temperature, noisy home environment due to use of radio, TV, etc., noisy neighbourhood, constant visits by friends or relatives, etc., influence the intellectual learning of the student. The socio-emotional factors such as child rearing practices, reward and punishment, scope for freedom and independence in activities and decision making, play and study facilities, ambitions and aspirations of the parents, disorganisation and discord among birth positions such as eldest, youngest or single child have their definite influence on learning. For example, a student who comes from a very poor family and never had any intellectual stimulation at home remains dull and unresponsive in the class. In some societies there is a strong sex bias. Girls are directly or indirectly told that education is not meant for them. In the middle class families, on the other hand, parents are rather over-ambitious. They wish their children to make quick academic progress, grow-up and find a respectable vocation preferably a white collar job. Such children, therefore get sufficient incentive from their families. This, of course, is most favourable to scholastic learning, although an overdose of family emphasis on acquiring academic excellence might affect the child's mental and physical health adversely. Similarly, school activities, study facilities and teaching methods and behaviour of teachers, principals and non-teaching staff have an impact upon learning. If the school atmosphere is unconducive, it adversely affects the learning process. Locality also has an influence on a child. If the locality is bad, the learning will be ineffective to some extent.

Cultural demands and social expectations also influence learning. The spirit of culture is reflected in its social and educational institutions. Children's learning, therefore, is greatly determined by the demands and expectations of their culture. Thus, for instance, in an industrialized culture the emphasis mostly centres mechanical sciences and preparing children for highly mechanised vocations. In an agriculture based community, on the other hand, the educational process focusses on preparing its members for those skills which are suited to the needs of an agrarian community.

The philosophical elements of culture also influence the spirit of children's learning. Children in a democratic culture tend to acquire democrative and values and attitudes. A feudal, aristocratic or dictatorial culture, on the other hand, promotes autocratic modes of thought and behaviour.

Relationship with Teacher, Parents and Peers

The teacher is an important constituent in the instructional process. She/he plays an important role in shaping the behaviour of students. The way he teaches and manages the students has an affect on their learning. An authoritarian teacher will create an aggression and hostility among students while a democratic teacher will create a participatory climate for learning. The democratic environment leads students to constructive, thoughtful and cooperative behaviour. Generally, students learn better in a democratic set up because they like democratic procedures. The teacher is no more an instructor or the director of learning in a democratic set up. She/he helps his/her students in their learning. The teachers no more dominate the scene, they can get better results by decentralizing authority, increasing independence of students. They can attend to the comments and questions of the students. They can encourage students to participate in learning activities in and outside the class. There should be more emphasis on activity-centred classroom where student's active participation in the teaching-learning process is encouraged and the teacher acts as a guide to promote learning.

Relationship with parents plays a vital role in the learning process of the student. If the child-parents relationship is based on mutual respect and faith, it can provide the child a congenial atmosphere which in turn can facilitate his/her learning. A distorted and unhealthy environment, on the other hand, adversely affects the learning of the student. The upward mobility brings resistance on the part of the student to learn. Students in such families find themselves unable to cope up. A subtle but powerful influence on the growing child arises from his/her position among the children in the family. The parents of the first born expect the child to act like miniature adults and hence the first-born are found to encounter a variety of expectations and stresses. Whereas parents tend to be more relaxed in their do's and dont's with the last-born. Factors like traumatic events at home, separation or death can also precipitate learning problems in the normal child.

A healthy peer group relationship also plays an important role in learning. Student-student relationship in the classroom, school, society, etc., create a particular type of emotional climate. The climate solely depends upon their relationships. A sound relationships provides a tension free environment to the student to learn more and to compete in the class. If the relationship among peers is not good, it adversely affects their learning. Therefore, to improve the classroom learning climate, free discussion should be there. You should help your students understand each other in formal or informal meetings. They should be encouraged to meet each other and their teachers freely. If any misunderstanding is created or developed, it should be immediately clarified so as to maintain the healthy climate and cordial relationship among peers.

Media Influence on Learning

Media has been considered an important component of transmitting information. Media can be divided into two broad categories—print and non-print media. Print media refers to texts or printed materials. It is economical and has traditionally been used for pedagogical purposes.

But, it may not be the only or the perfect medium to impart education. Non-print media, also known as modern electronic media, have certain unique qualities which, in certain cases, facilitate learning much more faster than the print medium. These helps meet diverse learning objectives more efficiently than the printed matter.

Certain non-print media formats and delivery systems contribute well to student's learning actitivies, For example, audio tapes or computers can be used effectively to drill and practice in language and learning arithmatic. Electronic media can help promote the discovery approach to learning. For example, a film can be exploited for discovery teaching in the physical sciences. Students keep watching the various sections of the film until they perceive the relationships between the visuals. Then they are curious to find out the principles that explain those relationships. Likewise, in the social sciences various media can be used to present students with visual and auditory experiences that provide related inquiry. Films and stimulation are often used to present real-life or laboratory learning situations to students.

The role of the electronic media has proved effective for teaching students. These excite the student psychologically and prepare/motivate them to participate in teaching-learning activites. Non-print media perform following fuctions:

- direct attention,
- arouse motivation,
- increase student's concentration, and
- help them actively involve in the learning process.

PRACTICE PAPER

1. Mass media, cinema and library are passive agencies of education because
   (*a*) learner can not react to the feedback system of these agencies directly
   (*b*) they provide informal education
   (*c*) they can not come closer to the educant
   (*d*) all of these
2. Education of a child really begins
   (*a*) Once he takes birth
   (*b*) Once he attains the age of three
   (*c*) Once he is admitted to post nursery schools
   (*d*) Once he learns to speak
3. Family is the original social institution from which all other institutions emerged, who said this
   (*a*) Brown (*b*) Ballard
   (*c*) Machiver (*d*) None of them
4. Which of the following is not the primary function of schools
   (*a*) reorganization and reconstruction of Human experiences
   (*b*) all-round development of the child
   (*c*) to make the children self reliant
   (*d*) advancement of culture
5. In a democratic country, school should reflect
   (*a*) National aspirations
   (*b*) Community related local aspirations
   (*c*) Both of these
   (*d*) None of these
6. The best teacher in a village school is he who
   (*a*) carries community experiences to the class room
   (*b*) prepares instructional programmes in the interest of the community
   (*c*) carries classroom experiences to the community
   (*d*) all of these
7. Universalisation of education is the concept adopted by
   (*a*) modern state (*b*) democratic state
   (*c*) totalitarian state (*d*) religious state
8. Secular education in India means
   (*a*) an education opposed to religion
   (*b*) an education indifferent to religion
   (*c*) an education emphasizing equality of religions
   (*d*) none of these
9. School works as a social sub system for
   (*a*) transmission of culture
   (*b*) preservation of culture
   (*c*) advancement of culture
   (*d*) all of these
10. "Society is nothing but a process of interaction among people." Who said this?
    (*a*) Lapier (*b*) Cuber
    (*c*) Reuter (*d*) Payne
11. The best model of schooling is
    (*a*) Close interaction between education of society
    (*b*) Self reliant society by education
    (*c*) Reflection of openness by schools
    (*d*) All of these
12. Special provisions have been made for socially and educationally backward classes of the nation under article
    (*a*) 29 (*b*) 31
    (*c*) 15 (*d*) 19
13. Religious education is prohibited in government schools and colleges under Article
    (*a*) 29 (*b*) 28 (1)
    (*c*) 39 (2) (*d*) 15 (a)
14. Religious and linguistic minorities shall have the right to establish and administer their own educational institutions under Article
    (*a*) 30(1) (*b*) 31(2)
    (*c*) 40 (*d*) 41
15. Article 351 is about
    (*a*) education of tribals
    (*b*) promotion of Hindi
    (*c*) promotion of secularism
    (*d*) English as official language
16. Status of central university is given to any educational institution under union list of
    (*a*) Entry 65 (*b*) Entry 63
    (*c*) Entry 66 (*d*) None of these
17. Entry 25 of concurrent list states about
    (*a*) vocational and technical training of labour
    (*b*) the education of working class
    (*c*) the education of disabled
    (*d*) none of the above

18. Education in the mother tongue at primary stage to children belonging to linguistic minorities has been mentioned in Article
(*a*) 250 (*b*) 350
(*c*) 349 (*d*) 351

19. Educational and economic interests of SCs and STs have been safeguarded under Article
(*a*) 46 (*b*) 45(a)
(*c*) 351 (*d*) 52

20. Education of union territories is administered by the central government under Article
(*a*) 350 (*b*) 229
(*c*) 239 (*d*) 50

21. Education was transferred from state list of subjects to concurrent list in
(*a*) 1976 (*b*) 1972
(*c*) 1980 (*d*) 1950

22. Which of the following statements about growth and development is not correct?
(*a*) Growth generally refers to quantitative changes while development refers to qualitative changes
(*b*) Growth is a function of the environment
(*c*) Growth is not possible without development and vice versa
(*d*) Growth is determined by intrinsic and genetic factors of the organism

23. The limit of growth is fixed by
(*a*) internal factors of the organism
(*b*) nutrition and exercise
(*c*) both of these
(*d*) none of these

24. Development is
(*a*) Maturation
(*b*) Learning
(*c*) Synthesis of abilities
(*d*) All of these

25. Development takes place when
(*a*) environmental forces work on the organism
(*b*) environmental forces interact with the hereditary forces in an organism
(*c*) both of these
(*d*) none of these

26. Which of the following statements about development is correct?
(*a*) Process of development can be improved by exercise and nutrition
(*b*) Development may be positive and negative both
(*c*) Development proceeds from general to specific
(*d*) All of these

27. The son of a goldsmith becomes an expert goldsmith. It is an example of a
(*a*) biological heredity
(*b*) social heredity
(*c*) transfer of instinct
(*d*) none of these

28. All humans contain .... chromosomes.
(*a*) 26 (*b*) 36
(*c*) 46 (*d*) 42

29. DNA test helps us to know
(*a*) the genetic traits of a person
(*b*) nature of personality and its composition
(*c*) both of these
(*d*) none of these

30. The law of inheritance was discovered by Gregor Mendel in
(*a*) 1866 (*b*) 1911
(*c*) 1888 (*d*) 1920

31. Which of the following statements regarding personality traits is correct?
(*a*) Traits of personality can not be developed in isolation without taking the help of environment
(*b*) Subjective traits of the individual are determined by genetic factors
(*c*) Bad environment can surpass good inheritance but good environment is not a substitute for poor heredity
(*d*) All of these

32. Which of the following characteristics denote infancy period?
(*a*) Physical growth is curvilinear
(*b*) Physical growth is rapid
(*c*) Head grows at relatively slower rate as compared to other parts of the body
(*d*) All of these

33. Which of the following is not the characteristic of infancy period?
(*a*) From bilateral to unilateral trend in motor organs
(*b*) From general to specific trend in motor organs
(*c*) Emotional/social development is not associated with motor development
(*d*) Steady mental development

34. Which of the following illustrates conceptual development?
(*a*) Perception is the beginning of concept formation
(*b*) Concept changes with changes in experiences
(*c*) Concept changes with age
(*d*) All of these

35. There is one thing common in language and physical development what is that?
(*a*) Spurts of development at different ages
(*b*) Dependence on experience
(*c*) Dependence on training
(*d*) None of these

36. Which of the following characteristics is not associated with emotional development?
(*a*) Emotion is accompanied by physiological changes
(*b*) Emotions start immediately after birth
(*c*) Intense form of emotions are seen during early childhood period
(*d*) Emotions are unrelated to physical development

37. The child acquires about three fourth of the brain weight by the age of
(*a*) 2½ years (*b*) 2 years
(*c*) 6 years (*d*) 8 years

38. Social development of an infant depends on
(*a*) his chance of interaction with others
(*b*) love and affection shown to the child
(*c*) the extent to which he is able to attract the attention of others
(*d*) all of the above

39. In which of the following stages the child looks self centred?
(*a*) Infancy (*b*) Early childhood
(*c*) Adolescence (*d*) Adulthood

40. In the period of infancy, emotions are
(*a*) intense, frequent and unstable
(*b*) like an open book(overt)
(*c*) need based
(*d*) all of these

41. Which of the following organs of the body shows rapid growth in infancy?
(*a*) growth of hands (*b*) growth of head
(*c*) growth of legs (*d*) growth of fingers

42. In normal learning environment, forgetting is caused
(*a*) due to back of practice for a long time
(*b*) due to the interference of other learnt material
(*c*) due to lack of consolidation of memory traces
(*d*) all of these

43. Clear conception of size, weight, colour, time etc., is seen at the age of
(*a*) six (*b*) four
(*c*) four and half (*d*) five

44. Which of the following is not the characteristics of intellectual development of early childhood?
(*a*) increased span of attention
(*b*) exploration of the environment
(*c*) ability to verbalize all known concepts
(*d*) ability to distinguish past, present and future

45. Social development by the end of early childhood is marked by
(*a*) the feeling of autonomy
(*b*) the end of solitary plays
(*c*) the temperament of co-operation and friendliness
(*d*) all of these

46. Fictional world of the child starts at the age of
(*a*) 5-6 (*b*) 6-8
(*c*) 3-4 (*d*) 4-5

47. Girls are more dominating than boys in social situations in which of the following periods?
(*a*) pre-adolescent period
(*b*) early childhood period
(*c*) both of these
(*d*) none of these

48. In the period of early childhood, child is
(*a*) helpless to hide his emotions
(*b*) seen shifting his emotions very rapidly and frequently
(*c*) guided by his innate tendencies and instincts
(*d*) all of these

49. A nursery teacher should organize
(*a*) group games in the school
(*b*) those games which involve motor organs of the body
(*c*) those games which help the child to manipulate the environment
(*d*) all of these

50. Later childhood is called latency period because
(*a*) creative potentials are dormant
(*b*) sex remains dormant
(*c*) it is a period of inactivity
(*d*) all of these

51. Physical development of later childhood is marked by
(*a*) Auscification of bones
(*b*) Permanent teeth
(*c*) Excessive motor activity
(*d*) All of these

52. Girls surpass boys physically in
(*a*) infancy
(*b*) later childhood
(*c*) early childhood
(*d*) adolescence

53. The period of later childhood is marked by
(*a*) intellectual maturity
(*b*) high muscular energy
(*c*) hero worship
(*d*) all of these

54. Which of the following is not the characteristics of intellectual development of later childhood?
(*a*) High interest in science fiction
(*b*) Increased logical power
(*c*) Careful for future
(*d*) End of imaginary fears

55. Children are very much hateful or indifferent to opposite sex at the age of
(*a*) 11-12 (*b*) 13-14
(*c*) 10-11 (*d*) 15-16

56. Period of later childhood is marked by
(*a*) slow and steady physical growth
(*b*) stability in emotions
(*c*) anger against injustice
(*d*) all of these

57. At the end of later childhood period, the child
(*a*) feels himself superior to girls
(b) becomes independent of his family
(c) wants to become hero
(d) all of these

58. The best place of social development for a 12 years old child is
(*a*) neighbourhood
(*b*) family
(*c*) playground
(*d*) school

59. Group activities and group loyalties are at its peak at the age of
(*a*) 10-12 (*b*) 13-15
(*c*) 8-10 (*d*) 18-20

60. A teacher should not let a 12 years old child any time free because
(*a*) child is always interested to get involve in physical or mental activities
(*b*) spurts of creativity are seen at this age
(*c*) child is frustrated
(*d*) all of these

61. Elektra complex refers to
(*a*) daughter comes closer to the father
(*b*) son comes closer to the mother
(*c*) inferiority complex in the presence of girls
(*d*) none of these

62. According to Freud, super ego is properly developed during
(*a*) latency period (*b*) anal period
(*c*) phallic period (*d*) none of these

63. Development is a process of observable social interaction. This is the opinion of
(*a*) Erikson (*b*) Skinner
(*c*) Robert Sears (*d*) None of these

64. The secondary behaviour of the child according to Robert Sears starts with
(*a*) reinforcement (*b*) imitation
(*c*) modelling (*d*) none of these

65. The period of sensory motor adoptation of Piaget is
(*a*) 0-2 years (*b*) 1-3 years
(*c*) 3-5 years (*d*) 4-6 years

66. The child adopts the view points of others on the basis of consequences of these views in the
(*a*) third stage of Kohlberg's theory
(*b*) second stage of Kohlberg's theory
(*c*) fourth stage of Kohlberg's theory
(*d*) fifth stage of Kohlberg's theory

67. Which of the following is not the view point of cognitive theories of development?
(*a*) moral principles are acquired automatically with age
(*b*) super ego is formed during the period of adolescence
(*c*) Moral values are determined by culture
(*d*) Mural principles are universal

68. Organization of sensory experiences about a particular object is called
(*a*) percepts (*b*) reasoning
(*c*) concept (*d*) none of these

69. The concept building in a person depends on
(*a*) the age and maturity of the person
(*b*) past experiences of the learner
(*c*) intelligence of the learner
(*d*) all of these

70. Agreement on a concept is possible because
(*a*) concepts are subjective
(*b*) concepts are objective
(*c*) concepts are hierarchical
(*d*) b and c both

71. Which of the following statements about concepts is correct?
(*a*) Some concepts are more powerful than others
(*b*) All concepts are universal
(*c*) Concepts are differentiated on the basis of their attributes
(*d*) None of these

72. Which is the highest level of concept formation?
(*a*) formal level (*b*) sensory level
(*c*) concrete level (*d*) none of these

73. How many steps of problem solving has been given by Gates?
(*a*) Six (*b*) Seven
(*c*) Five (*d*) Ten

74. Freeman considers intelligence as an ability
(*a*) to adjust in an adverse situation
(*b*) to learn better and faster
(*c*) to manipulate abstract materials
(*d*) all of these

75. Single factor theory of intelligence was given by
(*a*) Alfred Binet (*b*) Thorndike
(*c*) Freeman (*d*) None of them

76. Which of the following is not the characteristics of 'S' factor according to Spearman ?
(*a*) It is the acquired capacity of the individual
(*b*) Specialization in only one trade is possible
(*c*) It varies from activity to activity in the same individual
(*d*) Individuals differ only in 'S' factor of intelligence

77. In multifactor theory, range is related to
(*a*) Number of tasks that a person can do in a limited period of time

(*b*) Difficulty level of items
(*c*) General intelligence of learners
(*d*) None of these

78. SI model of intelligence was given by I P Guilford in
(*a*) 1911 (*b*) 1904
(*c*) 1966 (*d*) 1975

79. Hierarchy theory of intelligence was given by
(*a*) Jenson
(*b*) Thorndike
(*c*) Burt and Vernon
(*d*) None of them

80. In the pre-Binet period, intelligence was considered as
(*a*) Sensory acuity of the individual
(*b*) Verbal ability of the individual
(*c*) Associative ability of the individual
(*d*) All of these

81. An age scale of intelligence was first developed by
(*a*) Spearman (*b*) Terman
(*c*) Binet-Simon (*d*) None of them

82. Binet-Simon scale of intelligence measures
(*a*) General mental abilities not specific ones.
(*b*) Mental growth of the individual over a period of time
(*c*) The aptitude or level of an examinee not their speed
(*d*) All of these

83. WAIS came into being in
(*a*) 1939 (*b*) 1955
(*c*) 1960 (*d*) 1964

84. Wechsler developed an intelligence test for children in
(*a*) 1939 (*b*) 1949
(*c*) 1955 (*d*) 1956

85. Catell's culture fair test of intelligence was developed in
(*a*) 1960 (*b*) 1961
(*c*) 1965 (*d*) 1955

86. Non-verbal test of intelligence is suitable for
(*a*) deaf and dumb
(*b*) illiterates
(*c*) backward children
(*d*) all of these

87. Intelligence testing is useful for knowing
(*a*) individual difference
(*b*) mental retardation
(*c*) educational backwardness
(*d*) all of these

88. Scores on intelligence tests can not be fully relied on because
(*a*) fatigue level can influence the performance
(*b*) cultural factors can influence the score
(*c*) they generally do not reveal all the mental abilities of a person
(*d*) all of these

89. Who among the following psychologists is of the view that a learner can be motivated by satisfying his needs?
(*a*) Henry Murray (*b*) Abraham Maslow
(*c*) Both of these (*d*) None of these

90. Permanent change in behaviour brought about by experience or training is called.
(*a*) Learning (*b*) Motivation
(*c*) Assimilation (*d*) None of these

91. The book **"Theory of Motivation"** has been written by
(*a*) K B Madson (*b*) Maslow
(*c*) Murray (*d*) None of them

92. Motivated behaviour of a person is
(*a*) Well directed and well guided towards the goal
(*b*) Agitated until the goal is achieved
(*c*) Both of these
(*d*) None of these

93. Factors affecting motivations are
(*a*) Physiological factors only
(*b*) Psychological factors only
(*c*) Psycho-social factors
(*d*) All of these

94. Process of motivation is affected by all except
(*a*) Habits
(*b*) Mental sets and values
(*c*) Physical factors
(*d*) None of these

95. Which of the following does not come under the category of social motives?
(*a*) Prestige and Status
(*b*) Social approval
(*c*) Personal goal
(*d*) Money hoarding

96. Our action and behaviour is motivated by the desire for getting pleasure and avoiding pain. This is the opinion of
(*a*) Thomas Hobbes (*b*) Descartes
(*c*) Kant (*d*) John Locke

97. Fundamental instincts of humans are inherited rather than acquired. These instincts are the spring of human behaviour. The above opinion was held by
(*a*) Charles Darwin (*b*) Mc Dougall
(*c*) Both of these (*d*) None of these

98. Instinct theory of behaviour was rejected by psychologists on which of the following grounds?
(*a*) Adult behaviour is guided by experience and learning also. It is not always guided by instinct
(*b*) Human behaviour is affected by the cultural factors also

(*c*) Human being is a rational animal. He is not supposed to be directed by instincts only
(*d*) All of these

99. Central motive state was explained by
(*a*) Morgan
(*b*) Mc Dougall
(*c*) Murray
(*d*) None of them

100. Abraham Maslow was basically a
(*a*) Pragmatist (*b*) Humanist
(*c*) Realist (*d*) All of them

101. A self actualized person is one who
(*a*) Does not accept restrictions imposed by the society
(*b*) Always seeks perfection
(*c*) Is very good in inter personal relationship with others
(*d*) All of these

102. The theory of achievement motivation was developed by Mc Clelland of Harward University in
(*a*) 1949 (*b*) 1951
(*c*) 1965 (*d*) 1944

103. Achievement motive in a child can be developed by
(*a*) Proper guidance and high expectation from the child
(*b*) Telling the stories of great men to the child
(*c*) Setting a realistic goal for the child
(*d*) All of these

104. Which of the following is not a characteristic of learning?
(*a*) Learning is a relatively permanent change in behaviour
(*b*) Learning is a growth of the organism
(*c*) Learning is directly observed
(*d*) Learning is a goal directed process

105. In the beginning of life, the baby is guided by
(*a*) maturation
(*b*) instincts
(*c*) learning
(*d*) none of these

106. Accumulation of knowledge or facts becomes learning when
(*a*) It is applied in real life situation
(*b*) It is done by the learner himself
(*c*) It is provided by the teacher
(*d*) None of these

107. Dancing, driving, writing etc are the examples of
(*a*) Mechanical learning
(*b*) Perceptual motor learning
(*c*) Psychomotor learning
(*d*) both (*b*) and (*c*)

108. In Gagne's hierarchy, learning has been divided into
(*a*) eight parts (*b*) nine parts
(*c*) seven parts (*d*) none of the above

109. Match the following:

(A)	(B)
(*i*) Classical conditioning	1. Kohler
(*ii*) Drive reduction	2. Hull
(*iii*) Sign gestalt	3. Pavlov
(*iv*) Learning by insight	4. Tolman

	(*i*)	(*ii*)	(*iii*)	(*iv*)
(*a*)	1	2	3	4
(*b*)	3	2	4	1
(*c*)	2	1	3	4
(*d*)	4	3	2	1

110. Reflexes are of two types according to Pavlov. They are physiological and
(*a*) Psychic (*b*) Neural
(*c*) Mental (*d*) None of these

111. In classical conditioning, extinction will take place when
(*a*) Organism is poor in generalization
(*b*) CS is given without UCS for a long time
(*c*) CS > UCS
(*d*) None of these

112. Backward conditioning will take place when
(*a*) UCS is presented prior to CS
(*b*) CS is presented prior to UCS
(*c*) Reward is not given to the organism
(*d*) None of these

113. When connection is not established between a CS and CR, due to any factor, that is called
(*a*) Spontaneous recovery
(*b*) Extinction
(*c*) Inhibition
(*d*) None of these

114. When a child responds to all women who wear black suit because of the black suit of her mother, it is the example of
(*a*) internal inhibition
(*b*) generalization
(*c*) assimilation
(*d*) all of these

115. Which of the following is not a behaviourist?
(*a*) Watson
(*b*) Skinner
(*c*) Pavlov
(*d*) Lewin

116. Learning according to Watson is
(*a*) the shifting of old responses to the new stimuli
(*b*) the result of connection between S-R formed in the brain
(*c*) both of these
(*d*) none of these

117. Which of the following points differentiates the theories of Watson and Guthrie?
(*a*) law of contiguity
(*b*) law of recency
(*c*) generalization
(*d*) law of frequency

118. In operant conditioning reward works as motives but in Guthrie's theory motives are
(*a*) Stimuli given to the learner
(*b*) Actions done by the learner
(*c*) Both of these
(*d*) None of these

119. We forget something not by disuse but by other learning. This is the theory of
(*a*) contiguity
(*b*) trial and error
(*c*) learning by insight
(*d*) perception

120. Which of the following is not an essential requirement for trial and error learning?
(*a*) Drive
(*b*) Barrier
(*c*) Chance success
(*d*) Selective movement of the organism

121. According to the law of trial and error, learning occurs when
(*a*) it is satisfying for the learner
(*b*) bond between S-R is strengthened by the repeated use
(*c*) drive is there in the learner to act
(*d*) all of these

122. Which of the following facilitates learning according to Thorndike?
(*a*) Transfer of training
(*b*) Mental set of the learner
(*c*) Law of contiguity
(*d*) All of these

123. In Hull's theory, for learning to occur, the S-R connection must be associated with the
(*a*) cognitive field of the learner
(*b*) diminution of the need
(*c*) both of these
(*d*) none of these

124. Reinforcement in Skinner's theory is similar to drive reduction in which theory
(*a*) Hull's theory
(*b*) Guthrie's theory
(*c*) Lewin's theory
(*d*) None of these

125. Which of the following theories is most quantitatively measurable?
(*a*) Pavlov's
(*b*) Skinner's
(*c*) Hull's
(*d*) None of these

126. In drive reduction theory, the effective stimulus in learning is the trace. It is formed
(*a*) in the brain
(*b*) by the bond of S-R
(*c*) in the nervous system
(*d*) none of these

127. In drive reduction theory, habit formation is a function of
(*a*) stimulus potential
(*b*) stimulus generalization
(*c*) reaction potential
(*d*) all of these

128. Hull may be considered superior to other S-R Theorists in the sense that he was able to measure
(*a*) latency of response
(*b*) reinforcement potential
(*c*) both of these
(*d*) none of these

129. Which of the following points differentiates Skinner from other S-R theorists?
(*a*) His operant conditioning (type R learning)
(*b*) His schedule of reinforcement
(*c*) His way of shaping behaviour
(*d*) All of these

130. Skinner's theory is more objective in nature than the others because
(*a*) operant behaviour is external
(*b*) reflexes never have zero strength
(*c*) reinforcement is followed by responses
(*d*) all of these

131. Aversive stimuli in operant conditioning means
(*a*) individual will not do a particular act because of fear of such stimuli
(*b*) individual will not do a particular act because of the disapproval from others
(*c*) both of these
(*d*) none of these

132. In Skinner's theory, reinforcement is given to the learner when
(*a*) his response is 100% correct
(*b*) his response is closer to the correct behaviour
(*c*) both of these
(*d*) none of these

133. Which of the following statements regarding S-R theories is not correct?
(*a*) Man behaves like a machine
(*b*) Behaviour is overt and can be objectively measured
(*c*) Learning proceeds from simple to complex
(*d*) Things are perceived in the context of figure ground *i.e.*, in relation to other things

134. Which of the following statements regarding field theories are correct?
(*a*) Learning is not additive

(b) Molar approach of behaviour is followed here
(c) Interaction between organism and the environment is essential for learning
(d) All of these

135. Operant conditioning is different from respondent conditioning in which of the following points
(a) In OC reinforcement is given after the response is made
(b) In operant conditioning, behaviour is controlled by central nervous system
(c) A chain of responses is needed for shaping the behaviour (learning)
(d) All of these

136. Thorndike and Skinner do not differ at all in
(a) the law of effect
(b) law of readiness
(c) law of contiguity
(d) all of these

137. According to gestalt psychologists, behaviour can not be quantified because
(a) it is always changeable
(b) it is governed by the configuration produced in the mind
(c) it is rarely overt
(d) all of these

138. Law of pragnanz is the other name of the law of
(a) continuity
(b) closure
(c) contiguity
(d) none of these

139. How does the law of similarity work according to field theorists?
(a) Similar ideas and experiences get associated to form a whole
(b) Similar objects or experiences are easily learnt
(c) Both of these
(d) None of these

140. Learning by insight looks similar to some extent to which of the following theories?
(a) Need reduction theory
(b) R type of learning
(c) Trial and error theory
(d) None of the above

141. The other name of conditioned reflexes is
(a) psychic reflexes
(b) motor reflexes
(c) physiological reflexes
(d) none of the above

142. According to Renzuli, a gifted child is one
(a) Who possesses above average ability in almost every field
(b) Who is committed to task and highly motivated
(c) Who is definitely creative
(d) All of these

143. Gifted and talented children must be identified as early as possible because
(a) If their potentials are not developed by proper guidance of the teacher, it is a loss of the society
(b) They are likely to create problems for others, if they are not given work according to their ability
(c) Ordinary level of curriculum will not suit to these children
(d) All of these

144. Achievement test can be a good indicator of intellectual power if
(a) It is conducted immediately after the teaching is over
(b) A student shows good performance consistently on different achievement test
(c) Both of these
(d) None of these

145. Which of the following skills does not require high intellectual ability?
(a) Technical skills
(b) Mechanical skills
(c) Teaching skills
(d) Management skills

146. Cognitive abilities related to giftedness are all except
(a) High comprehensive and analytical abilities
(b) High level of verbal intelligence
(c) High retention power
(d) None of these

147. A superior child is advanced to a normal child by at least
(a) 2½ years
(b) Four years
(c) 1 years
(d) 1½ years

148. A gifted child is
(a) realistic in his approach
(b) highly interested in solving social problems
(c) more frequently chosen by his age mates and peers
(d) all of these

149. Which of the following enrichment programmes is suitable for gifted children in the school?
(a) Mathematics or Science Olympiad
(b) Challenging home assignments
(c) Map work during studies
(d) All of these

150. Which of the following does not come under the category of acceleration for gifted children?
(a) Skipping of classes

(*b*) Early admission
(*c*) Extra laboratory work
(*d*) Organizing summer camps

151. Under achievers are those who
(*a*) Score low on intelligence tests
(*b*) Achieve low in the class consistently despite their superior intelligence
(*c*) Are unable to correspond their achievement to the level of their innate abilities
(*d*) Both (*b*) and (*c*)

152. Which of the following conditions must be satisfied in order to designate a person mentally retarded?
(*a*) Sub-normal intellectual functioning
(*b*) Very poor adaptive ability
(*c*) Dependability on others
(*d*) All of these

153. The best measure of identifying mildly mentally retarded is
(*a*) Administration of standardized intelligence test
(*b*) Administration of behaviour test
(*c*) Administration of adjustment test
(*d*) A combination of all

154. Physical trauma during pregnancy may cause
(*a*) Mental retardation
(*b*) Blindness
(*c*) Deafness
(*d*) All of these

155. All of the following may cause mental retardation except
(*a*) Blood incompatibility
(*b*) Action of toxic agent
(*c*) Radio-activity
(*d*) None of these

156. Which of the following is an important postnatal cause of mental retardation?
(*a*) Brain injury
(*b*) Infection
(*c*) Severe malnutrition
(*d*) All of these

157. Dullers do not differ from normal children in
(*a*) Physical characteristics
(*b*) Level of social expectancy
(*c*) Both of these
(*d*) None of these

158. Which of the following things is not required for educating mildly mentally retarded children?
(*a*) Regular counseling
(*b*) Remedial teaching
(*c*) Modification in the curriculum
(*d*) Regular evaluation

159. Teaching of which of the following skills is not suitable to borderline cases?
(*a*) Electric fitting
(*b*) Repairing of electric or electronic equipments
(*c*) Oratory skills
(*d*) Activity based skills

160. IQ range of morons are in the range of
(*a*) 60-90 (*b*) 50-75
(*c*) 60-80 (*d*) 30-50

161. Morons are slow in
(*a*) Physical growth
(*b*) Thinking and planning
(*c*) Taking initiative
(*d*) All of these

162. Unsatisfactory relation of a mentally retarded child with the environment is technically called
(*a*) Autism
(*b*) Maladjustment
(*c*) Pseudo-dullness
(*d*) None of these

163. All of the following are characteristics of morons except
(*a*) They are restricted to unskilled or semi skilled occupations
(*b*) They are likely to be delinquent more easily
(*c*) They have stronger sex drives than the normals
(*d*) They are educable upto normal level but at a slower rate

164. Which of the following modifications in the curriculum is needed for morons?
(*a*) Activity based curriculum
(*b*) Skill dominated curriculum
(*c*) Emphasis on social training
(*d*) All of these

165. Which of the following things can not be taught to Imbeciles?
(*a*) Self help skills
(*b*) Unskilled job to be performed under supervision
(*c*) Writing skills
(*d*) Social skills

166. In which of the following cases divergent thinking is required?
(*a*) Attempting a multiple choice items
(*b*) Writing an essay
(*c*) Doing a research activity
(*d*) Both (*a*) and (*c*)

167. Which of the following tests is similar to Guilford's test of cognitive abilities?
(*a*) Word association test
(*b*) Things test
(*c*) Hidden shapes test
(*d*) None of these

168. In Hidden shapes test of creativity, which of the following things is used?
(*a*) Pictures

(*b*) Words
(*c*) Things
(*d*) None of them

169. A creative child in the class can not be satisfied unless
(*a*) He is given freedom to manipulate ideas or things
(*b*) He is allowed to ask questions in his own way
(*c*) Both of these
(*d*) None of these

170. A creative child is one who
(*a*) Is ideationally productive and unconventional
(*b*) Does not stick to social and religious norms in a hard manner
(*c*) Is all the time restless to do something uncommon and unique
(*d*) All of these

171. For the development of creative potential of a child, the teacher should
(*a*) Allow him to be critical to ideas and people
(*b*) Give them chance of problem solving
(*c*) Both of these
(*d*) None of these

172. New ideas (Eureka) suddenly comes in the minds of the creative children in the stage of
(*a*) Preparation
(*b*) Illumination
(*c*) Revision
(*d*) Incubation

173. The technique to foster creativity in children is
(*a*) Brain storming
(*b*) Problem solving
(*c*) Both of these
(*d*) None of these

174. A teacher can foster creativity in children by
(*a*) Developing confidence in them
(*b*) Giving them opportunity to express
(*c*) Both of these
(*d*) None of these

175. Learning disabled children are
(*a*) Deficient in using potentials
(*b*) Low in intelligence
(*c*) Slow in activity
(*d*) None of these

176. Learning disabled children perform very poorly in
(*a*) academic areas
(*b*) technical areas
(*c*) both of these
(*d*) none of these

177. Problem of learning disability is more complex than that of other disabilities because
(*a*) Its causes can not be easily ascertained by applying usual tests
(*b*) It is associated to behaviour problems
(*c*) Both of these
(*d*) None of these

178. Educationally, learning disabled look similar to
(*a*) dullers
(*b*) backward children
(*c*) both of these
(*d*) none of these

179. In which of the following physical characteristics learning disabled children differ from the normal ones?
(*a*) They are all the time clumsy and awkward
(*b*) Poor coordination of motor abilities
(*c*) Height, weight and health
(*d*) All of these

180. Which of the following methods is most suitable for learning disabled children?
(*a*) Behaviour guidance method
(*b*) Remedial teaching
(*c*) Brain storming
(*d*) None of them

181. In order to improve work habits of learning disabled what should be done?
(*a*) Unattending behaviour should be penalized
(*b*) Close monitoring of the behaviour is needed
(*c*) Cues and prompt should be given
(*d*) All of these

182. Those who are normal in intelligence but slow in academic achievement due to psycho-social reasons are called
(*a*) Backward children
(*b*) Gifted under achievers
(*c*) Both of these
(*d*) None of these

183. Consistent low achievement leads to low intelligence because
(*a*) 50% intellectual ability is expressed in verbal form
(*b*) Learning develops thinking and reasoning power
(*c*) Both of these
(*d*) None of these

184. Which of the following situations may lead to educational backwardness?
(*a*) Sensory impairment
(*b*) Motor disability
(*c*) Long diseases and health problems.
(*d*) All of these

185. Emotional disturbances may lead to educational backwardness because
(*a*) Proper emotional development is necessary for social interactions
(*b*) Emotions will develop intellectual power, *i.e.*, emotional intelligence

(c) Both of these
(d) None of these

186. Which of the following factors will not lead to educational backwardness?
(a) Poor socio economic status of the family
(b) Poor educational environment of the school
(c) Occupation of the family
(d) Poor emotional climate of the family

187. Which of the following is an important cause of educational backwardness at primary level of education in India?
(a) Poor school organisation
(b) Lack of accountability
(c) Attitude of the masses towards education
(d) All of these

188. Which of the following measures should be adopted by the teacher to check educational backwardness?
(a) Continuous evaluation and regular feedback
(b) Remedial teaching
(c) Adjustment and behaviour training
(d) All of these

189. Teaching by small steps and frequent short assignment techniques are useful for
(a) Slow learners
(b) Learning disabled
(c) Educationally backward children
(d) Children of all types of disabilities

190. Special schools are required for backward children when
(a) Backwardness is due to any serious physical handicap
(b) The size of population of backward children in the society is very large as is the case of Gujarat where the achievement of students in mathematics is always seen very low
(c) Both of these
(d) None of these

191. Which of the following should be considered the most important quality of a teacher at primary level?
(a) Patience and perseverance
(b) Competence in methods of teaching and knowledge of subjects
(c) Competence to teach in highly standardised language
(d) Eagerness to teach

192. A teacher, because of his/her democratic nature, allows students to sit all over the class. Some sit together and discuss or do group reading. Some sit quietly and read themselves. A parent does not like it. Which of the following may be the best way to handle the situation?
(a) Parents should request the principal to change the section of their ward
(b) Parents should show trust in the teacher and discuss the problem with the teacher
(c) Parents should take away the child from that school
(d) Parents should complain against the teacher to the principal

193. The stage in which a child begins to think logically about objects and events is known as
(a) Formal operational stage
(b) Pre-operational stage
(c) Concrete operational stage
(d) Sensori-motor stage

194. 'Mind mapping' refers to
(a) a plan of action for an adventure
(b) drawing the picture of a mind
(c) researching the functioning of the mind
(d) a technique to enhance comprehension

195. The best way, specially at primary level, to address the learning difficulties of students is to use
(a) expensive and glossy support material
(b) easy and interesting textbooks
(c) story-telling method
(d) a variety of teaching methods suited to the disability

196. Which of the following will foster creativity among learners?
(a) Providing opportunities to question and to nurture the innate talents of every learner
(b) Emphasizing achievement goals from the beginning of school life
(c) Coaching students for good marks in examination
(d) Teaching the students the practical value of good education

197. According to Piaget, at which of the following stages does a child begin to think logically about abstract propositions?
(a) Formal operational stage (11 years and up)
(b) Sensori-motor stage (Birth–02 years)
(c) Pre-operational stage (02–07 years)
(d) Concrete operational stage (07–11 years)

198. Learning can be enriched if
(a) more and more teaching aids are used in the class
(b) teachers use different types of lectures and explanation
(c) due attention is paid to periodic tests in the class
(d) situations from the real world are brought into the class in which students interact with each other and the teahcer facilitates

199. Which of the following statements ***cannot*** be considered as a feature of the process of learning?
(a) Learning is a comprehensive process
(b) Learning is goal-oriented
(c) Unlearning is also a learning process
(d) Educational institutions are the only place where learning takes place

CHILD DEVELOPMENT & PEDAGOGY

200. A student of V-grade with 'visual deficiency' should be
(*a*) helped with his/her routine-work by parents and friends
(*b*) treated normally in the classroom and provided support through Audio CDs
(*c*) given special treatment in the classroom
(*d*) excused to do a lower level of work

201. Which of the following is ***not*** related to the socio-psychological needs of the child?
(*a*) Need for emotional security
(*b*) Regular elimination of waste products from the body
(*c*) Need for company
(*d*) Need for appreciation or social approval

202. Which is the place where the child's 'cognitive' development is defined in the best way?
(*a*) School and classroom environment
(*b*) Auditorium
(*c*) Home
(*d*) Playground

203. .... is considered a sign of motivated teaching.
(*a*) Remedial work given by the teacher
(*b*) Questioning by students
(*c*) Pin drop silence in the class
(*d*) Maximum attendance in the class

204. Which of the following is ***not*** a sign of an intelligent young child?
(*a*) One who has the ability to communicate fluently and appropriately
(*b*) One who carries on thinking in an abstract manner
(*c*) One who can adjust oneself in a new environment
(*d*) One who has the ability to cram long essays very quickly

205. "Children actively construct their understanding of the world" is a statement attributed to
(*a*) Pavlov (*b*) Kohlberg
(*c*) Skinner (*d*) Piaget

206. Kritika who does ***not*** talk much at home, talks a lot at school. It shows that
(*a*) teachers demand that children should talk a lot at school
(*b*) she does not like her home at all
(*c*) her thoughts get acknowledged at school
(*d*) the school provides opportunities to children to talk a lot

207. A teacher should make an attempt to understand the potentialities of her/his students. Which of the following fields is related to this objective?
(*a*) Social Philosophy
(*b*) Media – Psychology
(*c*) Educational Psychology
(*d*) Educational Sociology

208. Motivation, in the process of learning,
(*a*) differentiates new learning from old learning
(*b*) makes learners think unidirectionally
(*c*) creates interest for learning among young learners
(*d*) sharpens the memory of learners

209. The term 'curriculum' in the field of education refers to
(*a*) overall programme of the school which students experience on a day-to-day basis
(*b*) evaluation process
(*c*) text-material to be used in the class
(*d*) methods of teaching and the content to be taught

210. At lower classes, play-way method of teaching is based on
(*a*) principles of methods of teaching
(*b*) psychological principles of development and growth
(*c*) sociological principles of teaching
(*d*) theory of physical education programmes

211. "A young child responds to a new situation on the basis of the response made by him/her in a similar situation as in the past." This is related to
(*a*) 'Law of Effect' of learning
(*b*) 'Law of Attitude' of learning process
(*c*) 'Law of Readiness' of learning
(*d*) 'Law of Analogy' of learning

212. .... is ***not*** considered a sign of 'being gifted'.
(*a*) Fighting with others
(*b*) Novelty in expression
(*c*) Curiosity
(*d*) Creative ideas

213. Education of children with special needs should be provided
(*a*) by methods developed for special children in special schools
(*b*) in special schools
(*c*) by special teachers in special schools
(*d*) along with other normal children

214. To make assessment a 'useful and interesting' process, one should be careful about
(*a*) labelling students as intelligent or average learners
(*b*) using a variety of ways to collect information about the student's learning across the scholastic and co-scholastic boundaries
(*c*) using technical language to give feedback
(*d*) making comparisons between different students

215. 'Dyslexia' is associated with
(*a*) Mathematical disorder

(b) Reading disorder
(c) Behavioural disorder
(d) Mental disorder

216. Parents should play a .... role in the learning process of young children.
(a) proactive
(b) sympathetic
(c) neutral
(d) negative

217. "Development is a never ending process." This idea is associated with
(a) Principle of continuity
(b) Principle of integration
(c) Principle of interaction
(d) Principle of interrelation

218. The 'insight theory of learning' is promoted by
(a) Pavlov
(b) Jean Piaget
(c) Vygotsky
(d) 'Gestalt' theorists

219. In which of the following stages do children become active members of their peer group?
(a) Adulthood
(b) Early childhood
(c) Childhood
(d) Adolescence

220. Four distinct stages of children's intellectual development are identified by
(a) Erikson (b) Skinner
(c) Piaget (d) Kohlberg

ANSWERS

1	2	3	4	5	6	7	8	9	10
(a)	(a)	(b)	(d)	(c)	(d)	(a)	(c)	(d)	(c)
11	12	13	14	15	16	17	18	19	20
(a)	(c)	(b)	(a)	(b)	(b)	(a)	(b)	(a)	(c)
21	22	23	24	25	26	27	28	29	30
(a)	(b)	(a)	(d)	(c)	(d)	(b)	(c)	(c)	(a)
31	32	33	34	35	36	37	38	39	40
(d)	(d)	(c)	(d)	(a)	(d)	(b)	(d)	(a)	(d)
41	42	43	44	45	46	47	48	49	50
(c)	(d)	(a)	(c)	(d)	(a)	(c)	(d)	(d)	(b)
51	52	53	54	55	56	57	58	59	60
(d)	(b)	(d)	(c)	(a)	(d)	(d)	(c)	(a)	(a)
61	62	63	64	65	66	67	68	69	70
(a)	(a)	(c)	(b)	(a)	(a)	(c)	(a)	(d)	(d)
71	72	73	74	75	76	77	78	79	80
(b)	(a)	(c)	(d)	(a)	(d)	(a)	(c)	(c)	(a)
81	82	83	84	85	86	87	88	89	90
(c)	(d)	(b)	(b)	(b)	(d)	(d)	(d)	(c)	(a)
91	92	93	94	95	96	97	98	99	100
(a)	(c)	(d)	(d)	(c)	(a)	(c)	(d)	(a)	(b)
101	102	103	104	105	106	107	108	109	110
(d)	(b)	(d)	(c)	(b)	(a)	(d)	(a)	(b)	(a)
111	112	113	114	115	116	117	118	119	120
(b)	(a)	(c)	(b)	(d)	(c)	(d)	(a)	(a)	(d)
121	122	123	124	125	126	127	128	129	130
(d)	(d)	(b)	(a)	(c)	(c)	(a)	(a)	(d)	(a)
131	132	133	134	135	136	137	138	139	140
(a)	(c)	(d)	(d)	(d)	(a)	(b)	(b)	(a)	(c)
141	142	143	144	145	146	147	148	149	150
(a)	(d)	(d)	(c)	(a)	(d)	(a)	(d)	(d)	(c)
151	152	153	154	155	156	157	158	159	160
(d)	(d)	(d)	(d)	(d)	(d)	(c)	(c)	(c)	(b)

161	162	163	164	165	166	167	168	169	170
(d)	(a)	(d)	(d)	(d)	(d)	(b)	(a)	(c)	(a)
171	172	173	174	175	176	177	178	179	180
(c)	(b)	(c)	(c)	(d)	(a)	(a)	(b)	(b)	(a)
181	182	183	184	185	186	187	188	189	190
(d)	(a)	(c)	(d)	(c)	(c)	(d)	(d)	(d)	(c)
191	192	193	194	195	196	197	198	199	200
(a)	(b)	(c)	(c)	(d)	(a)	(d)	(d)	(d)	(b)
201	202	203	204	205	206	207	208	209	210
(b)	(a)	(b)	(d)	(d)	(c)	(c)	(c)	(a)	(b)
211	212	213	214	215	216	217	218	219	220
(a)	(a)	(d)	(b)	(b)	(a)	(a)	(d)	(d)	(c)

GLOSSARY

Accommodation : Piaget used this term for modification or reorganisation of existing cognitive structure (schemata) to deal with environmental demands. Accommodation is the adjustment the individual makes when incorporating external reality. Piaget uses this concept in conjunction with assimilation, which is the individual's response to the immediate and compelling environmental demands that have been and are being assimilated.

Advance organisers : Introductory information intended to facilitate a student's learning by providing a framework and organisation for the material to be learned.

Affective domain : One of the categories of educational objectives for students attitudes, values and emotional growth. The affective domain includes five basic categories: receiving, responding, valuing, organisation and characterisation by a value.

Assimilation : Assimilation is the process of taking within or internalising, one's environmental experience. The term is used by Piaget for the process of making sense of experiences and perceptions by fitting them into previously established cognitive structure (schemata). Assimilation is used by Piaget in conjunction with the concept of accommodation. Piaget believes that assimilation is a spontaneous process on the part of the child.

Attitudes : A learned predisposition to respond either positively or negatively to persons, situations, or things. Attitudes carry a strong emotional component and therefore can never be neutral.

Attribution theory : The term attribution refers to the explanation a person gives for his or her own or another person's actions or beliefs. An attribution based on internal factors is called a dispositional attribution, and one based on external factors is called a situational attribution.

Behaviourism : A school of thought in Psychology usually considered to have originated in the work and writings of John B. Watson in 1913. Watson argued against the use of introspection in gathering psychological data. He considered observable behaviour the only valid data in Psychology. According to Watson, any concepts, like mind or consciousness, that have mentalistic overtones must be purged from the field of psychology. The most famous current representative of this tradition is Harvard University's B.F. Skinner.

Classical conditioning : A procedure in which the conditioned stimulus after being paired with the unconditioned stimulus often enough, can then be substituted for it. It is often called "stimulus substitution."

Cognition : The process of faculties by which knowledge is acquired and manipulated (*e.g.*, thinking or remembering).

Cognitive domain : A part of Bloom's Taxonomy of educational objectives. Bloom divided the objectives in the cognitive domain into six categories: knowledge, comprehension, application, analysis, synthesis and evaluation.

Cognitive style : The consistent way in which an individual responds to a wide range of perceptual tasks.

Computer-assisted instruction (CAI) : The use of a computer as tutor to present information, give students opportunities to practice what they learn, evaluate student achievement, and provide additional instruction.

Concept learning : The acquisition of pattern-recognition knowledge involving the learning of a rule or rules for classifying a number of objects into mutually exclusive categories based on one or more salient characteristics of the objects.

Conditioned response : A response elicited by a conditioned stimulus. The response is similar but not identical to its associated unconditioned response.

Cognitive learning : The view that learning is based on a restructuring of perceptions and thoughts occurring within the organism is called cognitive learning. This restructuring allows the learner to perceive new relationships, solve new problems and gain understanding of a subject area. Cognitive learning theorists stress the reorganisation of one's perceptions in order to achieve understanding, as opposed to the behaviourist theorists, who stress the importance of associations formed between stimuli and responses.

Conditioned response : The term is used both in classical conditioning, and in operant conditioning. In classical conditioning, the conditioned response is the response being elicited by the conditioned stimulus. The stronger the conditioning, the greater the magnitude of the conditioned response and the shorter its latency. In Pavlov's experiment the conditioned response was the dog's salivation to the tone.

In operant conditioning, since the response must precede the reinforcer, the conditioned response is defined not in terms of magnitude or latency, but in terms of either the rate of response or its resistance to extinction. For example, a strongly conditioned operant will occur for more rapidly than one that has been only weakly conditioned. Also, a strongly conditioned operant will be far more difficult to extinguish.

Conditioned stimulus : In classical conditioning, the previously neutral stimulus takes on the power to elicit the response through association with an unconditioned stimulus. For this to occur, the conditioned stimulus must precede the unconditioned stimulus on enough occasions to cause the conditioned stimulus to serve as a signal that the unconditioned stimulus will follow. In Pavlov's experiment on conditioning the dog, the tone was used as the conditioned stimulus. The tone was consistently followed by the meat powder, until the dog began salivating to the tone alone.

Conditioning : Process of learning whereby stimuli and responses become associated through training. There are two general types of conditioning, classical and operant. In classical conditioning a conditioned stimulus is presented, followed by an unconditioned stimulus. Conditioning is exhibited when the organism learns to respond to the conditioned stimulus alone. In operant conditioning the operant is allowed to occur and then is followed by a reinforcing stimulus. Operant conditioning is exhibited when the rate of responding increases over the original, preconditioned rate.

Convergent thinking : A term used by Guilford to describe the type of thinking in which an individual produces a single response to a specific question or problem.

Creativity : The capacity of individuals to produce novel or original answers or products.

Culture : The ways in which a group of people think, feel, and react in order to solve problems of living in their environment.

Cumulative records : A file on a student that includes such information as family data, health, academic grades, standardized test scores, attendance and teacher comments.

Discovery learning : Term is used to describe a form of learning that results not from rote memorisation or conditioning but from the active exploration of alternatives on the part of the learner. This learning is largely a result of learner's own efforts. Learning attained through discovery is more meaningful and long-lasting than that from memorisation.

Divergent thinking : A term used by Guilford to describe the type of thinking wherein an individual produces multiple responses or solutions (often non-traditional) to a single question or problem. Divergent thinking is associated with creativity.

Egocentrism : Piaget's term for describing children in the preperational stage, who have difficulty in assuming the point of view of others.

Enactive : Bruner's first stage of cognitive development, in which children understand the environment through physical action on that environment.

Encoding : The short-term memory process of transforming incoming information into episodic or semantic form and associating it with old knowledge for storage in long-term memory.

Entry behaviour : The knowledge, skills, or attitudes that a learner brings into a new learning situation.

Formal-operations stage : This is a stage of cognitive development according to Jean Piaget, occurring during early adolescence. The period of formal operations (eleven to sixteen years) is the last of Piaget's stages and is characterised by the youth's ability to develop full, formal patterns of thinking based on abstract symbolism. The youth is able to reason things out logically at the abstract level, develop symbolic meanings, and generalize to other situations. This is the highest level of thinking and according to Piaget, must await the maturation of certain structures in the brain for its full development.

Equilibration : A motivation principle in Piaget's theory that identifies human beings as active and exploratory in attempting to impose order and meaningfulness on experiences. This order or balance occurs through the processes of assimilation and accommodation.

Evaluation : This is a process of obtaining information to form judgments so that educational decisions can be made.

External locus of control : A feeling that one has little control over one's and the failure to perceive a cause-and-effect relationship between actions and consequences.

Extrinsic motivation : Motivation influenced by external events such as grades, marks or money.

Gestalt psychology : A school of thought maintaining that the organised whole, configuration, or totality of psychological experience should be the proper object of study. Founded in Germany by Max Wertheimer in the early 1900s, gestalt psychology's first interest was in the field of perception. Later, under Wolfgang Kohler's direction, studies were done in the area of learning, and under Kurt Lewin's direction, in the area of motivation. Gestalt psychologists tend to emphasize cognitive processes in the study of learning. They stress that true understanding occurs only through the reorganisation of ideas and perceptions, not through memorisation or conditioning.

Information processing : Theory of learning and remembering that is based on the computer as a model. Information is seen as following into and within the organism. The sense organs respond to incoming information, and it is passed along and encoded in the memory and nervous system. The encoded information may then be stored and processed and finally retrieved and acted on. As with the computer, there is information input, storage and/or processing, and output.

Insight : A suddenly realised solution to a problem, sometimes called the ''a-ha! phenomenon''. Introduced by Wolfgang Kohler, the concept of insight is used to explain the apparently spontaneous appearance of a solution to a problem. Insight results from the reorganisation of ideas and perceptions rather than from simple trial-and-error behaviour. The concept of insight is used typically by gestalt psychologists.

Inquiry learning : A process that is similar to discovery learning. Students learn strategies to manipulate and process information, test hypothesis and apply their conclusions to new content or situations.

Intelligence : The capacity, or a set of capacities that allows an individual to learn, solve problems, and/or interact successfully with his or her environment. As hypothetical construct, intelligence has come to mean higher-level thought processes, or intellectual abilities. Statistical studies of intelligence utilise the concept of measured intelligence, which is the score received on a standardised intelligence test.

Intelligence Quotient (IQ) : Originally, a measure of intelligence calculated by dividing a student's mental age (MA) by the chronological age (CA) and multiplying by 100, that is, IQ = MA/CA × 100. This is called the ratio method of obtaining an IQ.

More recently, IQ has been computed by the deviation method. One's deviation IQ is defined by one's relative standing among peers. The deviation IQ is computed on the basis of how far one's score deviates from the mean score obtained for the entire group of individuals of the same chronological age. This technique is based on the standard, or z-score concept and assumes a normal distribution for each age group.

Law of effect : This is one of E.L. Thorndike's main laws of learning. It states that when an association between a stimulus and response is followed by a satisfying state of affairs, the association (or connection) is strengthened. When the association is followed by an annoying state of affairs, it is weakened. In brief, reward strengthens and punishment weakens any connection between stimuli and responses. In a later version of the law, Thorndike soft-pedaled the importance of punishment of a weakening agent. Thorndike's law of effect is considered by many psychologists to be the cornerstone on which B.F. Skinner built his system of operant conditioning.

Law of exercise : One of E.L. Thorndike's three main laws of learning. It states that the more frequently a stimulus response connection occurs, the stronger the resulting association and hence, the stronger the learning. The repetition of a learned response strengthens the bond between stimulus situation and the response. The law was later amended to incorporate the importance of the consequences of the action; thus, practice without knowledge of results is not nearly as effective as when the consequences become known to the learner.

Law of readiness : One of E.L. Thorndike's three main laws of learning. It states that learning occurs when the student is mentally ready to learn. The reference here is to momentary readiness rather than maturational readiness.

Learning : Learning is a very general term refering to a process that leads to a relatively permanent change in behaviour resulting from experience. Thus, such activities as acquiring physical skills, memorizing poems, acquiring attitudes, etc., are all examples of learning. Learning may be conscious or unconscious, adaptive or maladaptive, overt or covert. Although the learning process is typically measured on the basis of a change in performance, most psychologists agree that an accompanying change occurs within the nervous system. Though there are a great many theories and explanations concerning learning, there is general agreement regarding its definition.

Locus of control : The concept identifies the type of personal control used by an individual. When the locus of control is internal, individual views himself as personally in charge of his own destinies. When the locus of control is external, the person feels he is at the mercy of external circumstances.

Long-term memory (LTM) : In the information-processing system, LTM is the second of the two main storage systems. Information that is in short-term memory may, under certain conditions, be passed along for processing and consolidation into a more permanent storage site, long-term memory. Long-term memory has the potential for holding encoded information for long periods.

Mental age : Term first used by Alfred Binet as the unit for measuring intelligence. Binet defined mental age in terms of the age at which a given number of test items are passed by an average child. If, for example, the average six-year-old could correctly answer a certain number of items, then any other child correctly answering the same number of items would be assigned at least a mental age of six.

Motivation : A general psychological term used to explain behaviour initiated by needs and directed towards a goal. Motives may be biogenic (that is stemming from tissue needs within the organism) or acquired (that is, learned through interaction with the environment, especially the social environment).

Among learning theorists, Jerome Bruner makes much of the principle of motivation, assuming that almost all children have a built-in "will to learn".

Nature-nurture controversy : Debate over which component, nature (heredity) or nurture (environment), is more influential in determining behaviour. In Psychology the behaviourists consistently argued on behalf of nurture, and the intelligence testers favoured nature. Educational Psychology has long been the battleground on which this issue has been fought, since the psychologists primarily concerned with this issue were the learning theorists (largely behaviourists).

Need hierarchy : Theory proposed by Abraham Maslow that suggests that human beings place their needs on the following universal, order-of-importance scale: (*i*) physiological needs, (*ii*) safety needs, (*iii*) love needs, (*iv*) esteem needs, and (*v*) self-actualising needs.

Needs : The part of the motivational cycle seen as deficits that lie within the individual. These may be physiological (*e.g.*, the needs for food) or psychological (*e.g.*, the need for approval).

Non-verbal behaviour : Body language. Based largely on the theroy of Charles Galloway and some research by Robert Rosenthal, the teacher's non-verbal behaviour represents an important avenue for the transmission of teacher expectations. Galloway has shown how non-verbal behaviour can promote or reduce student learning. Rosenthal has shown how his test (Profile of Non-verbal Sensitivity) can identify the channels for communicating how teachers really feel about their students.

Operants : Responses, according to B.F. Skinner, for which the original stimuli are either unidentified or non-existent are called operants. The consequences of operant behaviour can be observed even though the stimulus is not known. For example, if a rat presses the lever in a Skinner box and this results in reinforcement, an increase in operant rate will be observed despite the fact that no stimulus could be identified as initiating the original stimulus could be identified as initiating the original lever pressing. In operant conditioning, reinforcement is contingent on the operant's first being emitted. The organism must in some way "operate" on the environment in order that the reinforcement will follow. Operant responding at one time was called instrumental responding by some psychologists.

Operant conditioning : A type of learning that involves an increase in the probability that a response will occur as a function of reinforcement. This is a forn of conditioning, described by B.F. Skinner, in which the free operant is allowed to occur and is followed by a reinforcing stimulus that is, in turn, followed by an increased likelihood of the operant's occurring again. For optimum conditioning the reinforcing stimulus should follow the operant immediately. The rate of responding for a conditioned operant may jump dramatically over the preconditioned rate (operant level).

Operant level : The original, or preconditioned, rate of operant responding before any reinforcing stimuli have been introduced. If a rat happens to press the lever in a Skinner box four times an hour (without being reinforced), the operant level for that response is established at four per hour. Thus, the operant level is the rate at which the free operant is typically emitted prior to conditioning.

Positive reinforcement : A procedure that maintains or increases the rate of a response by presenting a stimulus (a positive reinforcer) following the response.

Preoperational stage : The second stage in Piaget's theory of cognitive development, in which the lack of logical operations forces children to make decisions bases on their perceptions.

Primary reinforcement : The process of using a stimulus that is reinforcing in the absence of any learning. Such stimuli as food and water are primary reinforcers.

Programmed instruction (PI) : PI is an arrangement of instructional material in a step-by-step sequence designed to lead the student to a specified goal. The material being presented is broken down into small steps called frames. There are two general approaches to programming: (*i*) linear programmes, in which all students go through the entire programme and the frames gradually increase in difficulty, and (*ii*) branched programmes, in which the student skips forward or backward in the programme (the order of the frame presentation varies) as a result of the success or failure experienced in responding.

PI can be in book form, or it can be presented through the use of a teaching machine and/or computer. The concept of programmed instruction is credited to B.F. Skinner.

Psychoanalytic theory : This reveals the theory/method of studying and treating mental illness presented by Sigmund Freud. The theory attempts to give a rational explanation for irrational thoughts and responses. Psychoanalytic theory states (*i*) that all behaviour is determined by specific motives; (*ii*) that most human motives lie at the unconscious level, and therefore people are unaware of the reasons for most of their own behaviour; (*iii*) that neurotic symptoms result from an individual's inner conflicts; and (*iv*) that inner conflicts are a product of childhood trauma and anxiety. The technique is based on the therapist's revealing to the patient the source of his or her anxiety and helping the patient achieve insight and emotional release.

Puberty : The biological changes that lead to reproductive maturity. Its onset is identified by such factors as the growth of body hair, voice changes in males, and menstruation and breast development in females.

Punishment : A method for controlling behaviour through the use of aversive stimulation. In other words, punishment is a procedure in which an aversive stimulus is presented immediately following a response, resulting in a reduction in the rate of response. Punishment, though not itself causing the extinction of a conditioned response, does severely reduce the rate of responding while the punishment is in force. Punishment should not be confused with negative reinforcement.

Reinforcement : Any stimulus that increases the likelihood of a response's recurring. Reinforcement, as a Skinnerian concept, should not be confused with reward, feelings of pleasure, or any other concept with subjective of mentalistic overtones. Reinforcement may be used in either classical (respondent) or operant conditioning. In respondent condition the unconditioned stimulus serves as the reinforcement. In operant conditioning the presentation of any stimulus following the emitted response can be considered a reinforcement if it results in a higher response rate.

Schemata : Cognitive structures created through the abstraction of previous experience. Schemata function in the comprehension and recall of data and can aid learning or be responsible for many types distortion in recall.

Secondary reinforcement : A process that uses a stimulus that is not originally reinforcing but that acquires reinforcing properties when paired with a primary reinforcer. Money is a secondary reinforcer.

Self-actualization : Maslow's term for the psychological need to develop one's capabilities and potential in order to enhance personal growth. It refer to a person's constant striving to realise the potential within and to develop inherent talents and capabilities.

Self-concept : The total organisation of the perceptions individuals have of themselves.

Self-esteem : The value, or judgement, individuals place on their behaviour. Self-esteem and self-concept are often used interchangeably in educational literature.

Self-reinforcement : A procedure in which individuals reinforce their own behaviour.

Sensitive period : This is a time period when an organism is susceptible to a change in behaviour due to certain kinds of environmental stimulation. The sensitive periods typically occur early in the organism's life and tend to produce behaviour changes that are relatively long-lasting. The process of mother-infant bounding is said to occur only during the baby's first three days of life.

Short-term memory (STM) : In the information processing system, STM is the first of two main storage systems. Sometimes it is called working or active memory. Estimates of how long information may be retained in short-term memory vary from about twenty seconds to over a minute.

Social facilitation : The concept from the field of social psychology is used to explain the fact that in some circumstances individuals perform more quickly when in a group situation than when alone. Social facilitation is most pronounced in the case of fairly simple mechanical tasks. The more difficult and the more intellectual the task, the less the effect of social facilitation.

Social learning theory : Theory, proposed by Albert Bandura, suggests that a large part of what a person learns occurs through imitation or modelling. Bandura's major concern is with learning that takes place in the context of a social situation in which individuals come to modify behaviour as a result of how others in the group respond. Social learning does not require primary reinforcement.

Stimulus-response : A theory that stresses the importance of the build up of stimulus response associations in defining learning. Most behaviourists adhere to stimulus response learning theories, the major exception being E.C. Tolman. The leading stimulus response theorists are E.L. Thorndike, Ivan Pavlov, J.B. Watson, Edwin Guthrie, C.L. Hull, and B.F. Skinner. Stimulus response theorists stress the importance of nurture in the nature-nurture debate. Most theories of learning during the first half of the twentieth century were stimulus response theories. The cognitive-gestalt position, however, was not based on a stimulus-response theory.

Stimulus variety : Variation, at all sensroy modes, of stimulus inputs. Stimulus variety was seen by many early-experience theorists as the crucial ingredient in intellectual development. The more the child hears, sees, and touches, the more he or she will want to hear, see, and touch and the more intellectual growth will occur.

Teaching machine : A device used to present an instructional programme one step (or frame) at a time. The student either writes in answers or presses a button corresponding to the correct alternative. The advantages of the teaching machine are that (*i*) the student can proceed at his or her own pace; (*ii*) the student receives immediate feedback; (*iii*) for many students the machines are intrinsically motivating.

Unconditioned response : An unconditioned response is any response that can be elicited automatically by the presentation of a certain stimulus, without any training or learning. The term is used in classical conditioning and in Ivan Pavlov's original experiment the unconditioned response was salivation to the stimulus of meat powder being placed in the dog's mouth.

Unconditioned stimulus : Any stimulus that will elicit a given response automatically, without any training or learning. The term is used in classical conditioning and in the case of Ivan Pavlov's own experiment, the unconditioned stimulus was meat powder placed in the dog's mouth.

Mathematics

MATHEMATICS

NUMBERS

INTRODUCTION

In our System of numeration, numbers are written by using the symbols 0, 1, 2, 3, 4, 5, 6, 7, 8 and 9 with each symbol getting a value depending on the place it occupies. These symbols are called digits. A number related to the objects in a collection gives an idea of how many objects are there in the collection.

The number 789345126 can be represented as:

Ten crores	Crores	Ten Lacs (Millions)	Lacs	Ten Thousands	Thousands	Hundreds	Tens	Units
10^8	10^7	10^6	10^5	10^4	10^3	10^2	10^1	10^0
7	8	9	3	4	5	1	2	6

This number can be read and written in words as : "Seventy-eight crores, ninety-three lacs, forty-five thousands, one hundred twenty six". The above pattern is known as Indian/Hindu Arabic System.

There is an another pattern of number system. It is called International System. It is most commonly used system in the world. In this system the number is written as 562 785 326. The number can be represented as:

Hundred Millions	Ten Millions	Millions	Hundred Thousands	Ten Thousands	Thousands	Hundreds	Tens	Units
10^8	10^7	10^6	10^5	10^4	10^3	10^2	10^1	10^0
5	6	2	7	8	5	3	2	6

TYPES OF NUMBER

1. **Natural Numbers or Positive Integers (N = 1, 2, 3, 4, 5 .....):** These are also called counting numbers. When two natural numbers are added or multiplied together, the result is always a natural number. Therefore, all positive integers, used for counting objects, are always **natural numbers** whereas zero together with negative integers and fractional numbers are not natural numbers.
2. **Whole Numbers: (W = 0, 1, 2, 3, 4, 5, ...):** The number '0' together with the natural numbers gives us the numbers which are called **whole numbers,** *e.g.,* 0, 1, 2, 3, 4 ..... etc. whereas –10, –15, –12 ..... or $\frac{1}{5}, \frac{2}{9}, \frac{4}{5}$..... etc. are not whole numbers.
7. **Even Numbers:** All those numbers which are exactly divisible by 2, are called 'even numbers', *e.g.,* 2, 8, 14, 28, 52 etc. are even numbers.
8. **Odd Numbers:** All those numbers which are not exactly divisible by 2, are called 'odd numbers', *e.g.,* 1, 3, 5, 7, 9, 19 etc. are odd numbers.
9. **Composite Numbers:** The numbers which are divisible not only by 1 or themselves, but by some other numbers also, are called the 'composite numbers'. In other words, the numbers which have more than two factors are called 'composite numbers.', *e.g.,* 4, 9, 15, 18, 27, ... etc. are composite numbers.

10. **Prime Numbers:** The numbers which have only two factors, 1 and the number itself are called 'prime numbers', *e.g.,* 2, 5, 11, 19, 23, 31, ... etc. are prime numbers.
11. **Co-primes:** Two numbers which have only 1 as the common factor are called 'co-primes'. 5 and 7 are co-primes. So are 15 and 16.
12. **Twin Primes:** Two prime numbers which differ by 2, are called 'twin primes', *e.g.,* 3, 5; 5, 7; 11, 13; 71, 73 are some pairs of twin primes.
13. **Consecutive Numbers:** The numbers which are following or coming after other numbers in regular order, are called consecutive numbers. 4, 6, 8, 10 are consecutive even numbers and 9, 11, 13, 15 are consecutive odd numbers. 3, 4, 5, 6, 7 ..... etc. are consecutive numbers in the natural order of the number series.

PROPERTIES OF NUMBERS

(a) The product of two consecutive numbers is exactly divisible by 2.
e.g., $3 \times 4 = 12$ which is exactly divisible by 2.

(b) The product of three consecutive numbers is exactly divisible by 6.
e.g., $2 \times 3 \times 4 = 24$, which is exactly divisible by 6.

(c) The product of four consecutive numbers is exactly divisible by 24.
e.g., $2 \times 3 \times 4 \times 5 = 120$, which is exactly divisible by 24.

(d) The product of five consecutive numbers is exactly divisible by 120.
e.g., $2 \times 3 \times 4 \times 5 \times 6 = 720$, which is exactly divisible by 120.

(e) The difference between the squares of two consecutive odd numbers is always exactly divisible by 8.
e.g., $5^2 - 3^2 = 25 - 9 = 16$, which is exactly divisible by 8.

(f) If 1 is added to the product of either two odd consecutive numbers or two even consecutive numbers, the result obtained will be a perfect square number,
e.g., $5 \times 7 + 1 = 35 + 1 = 36 = 6^2$, which is a perfect square number.

(g) The sum of two consecutive numbers is equal to the difference between their squares.
e.g., $4 + 5 = 9 = 5^2 - 4^2 = 9$

(h) The sum of the cubes of three consecutive numbers is exactly divisible by their own sum.
e.g., $4^3 + 5^3 + 6^3 = 64 + 125 + 216 = 405 = (4 + 5 + 6) \times 27$

Ascending Order: If in a given number series, numbers are written in increasing order, then the number series is said to be written in ascending order. *e.g.,* 25, 30, 41, 50 or –10, –8, –6, –2 etc. are series in ascending order.

Descending Order: If in a given number series, numbers are written in decreasing order, then the number series is said to be written in descending order. *e.g.,* 50, 41, 30, 25, or –2, –6, –8, –10 etc. are series in descending order.

Place Value: Numbers are written by using the symbols 0, 1, 2, 3, 4, 5, 6, 7, 8 and 9 called digits, with each digit getting a value depending on the place it occupies. This value assigned to the digit due to its placement, is called place value. For example, in the number 56, digit 6 is placed in unit's place and 5 in ten's place. Therefore, place value of 6 in 56 is $6 \times 1 = 6$ and that of 5 is $5 \times 10 = 50$.

Face Value: In a number, face value of a digit is the digit itself. For example, in 42, the face value of digit 2 is 2 and that of digit 4 is 4.

Larger and Smaller Numbers: We can determined larger and smaller number by comparing one number to another number.

e.g., In a numbers 4074, 765 and the larger number is 4074.

Change the Value of Number by Interchanging the Digits: To change the digits of any number, the value of that number is changed.

e.g., Let number be 712.

If we interchanged the unit and hundred place digits, the new numbers will be 217.

Expression Form of Numbers: Any number can be expressed as a place value form.

e.g., 7562 = 7000 + 500 + 60 + 2

Formation of a Number by Given Digits: If some digits are given, then a different number can be made with the given digits.

Example–From digits 375, the number 375, 357, 573, 537, 753 and 735 can be made.

TESTS FOR DIVISIBILITY OF NUMBERS

1. **Divisibility by 2:** A number is divisible by 2, if its units digit is 0, 2, 4, 6 or 8. For example, each of the numbers 130, 244, 566, 278, ... etc. is divisible by 2.
2. **Divisibility by 3:** A number is divisible by 3, if the sum of its digits is a multiple of 3. For example, each of the numbers 312, 213, 456 is divisible by 3 since sum of digits in each of these numbers is (3 + 1 + 2 = 6), (2 + 1 + 3 = 6)

and (4 + 5 + 6 = 15) respectively, each of which is a multiple of 3.

3. **Divisibility by 4:** A number is divisible by 4, if the number formed by its digits in ten's and unit's places is divisible by 4. For example, numbers formed by ten's and unit's digits of 1132, 1312, 1400 and 1348 are 32, 12, 00 and 48 respectively which are divisible by 4. Hence, these numbers also are divisible by 4.
4. **Divisibility by 5:** A number is divisible by 5, if its unit's digit is either 0 or 5. For example, each of the numbers 100, 205, 315, 435 is divisible by 5 since unit's digit in each of these numbers is either 0 or 5.
5. **Divisibility by 6:** A number is divisible by 6, if it is divisible by both 2 and 3.
6. **Divisiblity by 8:** A number is divisible by 8, if the number formed by its digits in hundred's, ten's and unit's places is divisible by 8. For example, numbers formed by hundred's, ten's and unit's digits of 1864, 1024, 2008 and 5000 are 864, 024, 008 and 000 respectively which are divisible by 8. Hence, these numbers also are divisible by 8.
7. **Divisibility by 9:** A number is divisible by 9, if the sum of its digits is a multiple of 9. For example, each of the numbers 23409, 454554, 66636 is divisible by 9 since sum of digits in each of these numbers is (2 + 3 + 4 + 0 + 9 = 18), (4 + 5 + 4 + 5 + 5 + 4 = 27) and (6 + 6 + 6 + 3 + 6 = 27) respectively, each of which is a multiple of 9.
8. **Divisibility by 10:** A number is divisible by 10, if its unit's digit is zero. For example, each of the numbers 50, 80, 1310, 1400 is divisible by 10 since unit's digit in each of these numbers is 0.
9. **Divisibility by 11:** A number is divisible by 11, if the difference of the sum of its digits in even places and the sum of its digits in odd places (starting from unit's place) is either 0 or a multiple of 11. For example, each of the numbers 909183, 540045 and 184712 is divisible by 11 since in each of the numbers difference of the sum of digits in even places and sum of the digits in odd places is [(9 + 9 + 8) – (0 + 1 + 3) = 22], [(5 + 0 + 4) – (4 + 0 + 5) = 0] and [(8 + 7 + 2) – (1 + 4 + 1) = 11] respectively, each of which is either '0' or a multiple of '11'.

FACTS AND FORMULAE

(i) The smallest natural number or positive integer is (+1).

(ii) The greatest negative integer is –1.

(iii) The number '0' is neither positive nor negative integer.

(iv) 1 is only such number which is neither a prime number nor a composite number.

(v) 2 is only such number which is an even number as well as a prime number.

(vi) 2 is the smallest prime number.

(vii) The number of prime numbers between 1 to 100 is 25.

(viii) A square number may have 0, 1, 4, 5, 6 or 9 in its unit's place.

(ix) A cubic number may have any digit from 0 to 9 in its unit's place.

Things to remember while solving problems on whole numbers

(a) Sum of numbers from 1 to $n = \frac{n(n+1)}{2}$ (where n is the number of terms)

(b) Number of odd numbers from 1 to n $= \left(\frac{\text{Last odd number} + 1}{2}\right)$

(c) Sum of odd numbers from 1 to n = (Number of odd numbers)^2

(d) Number of even numbers from 1 to n $= \left(\frac{\text{Last even number}}{2}\right)$

(e) Sum of even numbers from 1 to n = Number of even numbers × (Number of even numbers + 1)

EXAMPLES

Example 1 : Is 979 a prime number?

Solution: The approximate square root of 979 is 32.

Prime numbers less than 32 are 2, 3, 5, 7, 11, 13, 17, 19, 23, 29, 31. We observe that 979 is divisible by 11, so it is not a prime number.

Example 2 : What is the difference in face value and local value (Place value) of 5 in 7501?

Solution: The local value of 5 in 7501 = 500 and intrinsic value of 5 in 7501 = 5.

∴ Required difference = 500 – 5 = 495.

Example 3 : Which digits cannot be on the place of unit digit when any number is squared?

Solution: If a number is squared, it will end with one of these numbers *i.e.*, 0, 1, 4, 5, 6 or 9.

Hence it will never end with 2, 3, 7 or 8.

Example 4 : What will be the sum of odd numbers between 110 to 320?

Solution: Sum of odd numbers between 1 to 320 $= (160)^2 = 25600$.

No of odd numbers between 1 to 110 $= \frac{110}{2} = 55$

$\therefore$ Sum of odd numbers between 1 to 110 $= (55)^2 = 3025$

$\therefore$ Sum of odd numbers between 110 to 320 $= 25600 - 3025 = 22575$

Example 5 : What will be the sum of even numbers between 1 to 40?

Solution: Number of even numbers between 1 to 40 $= \frac{40}{2} = 20$

$\therefore$ Sum of even numbers between 1 to 40 $= 20(20 + 1) = 20 \times 21 = 420$.

MULTIPLE CHOICE QUESTIONS

1. If 30*x* 0103 is divisible by 11 then what is the value of *x*?

A. 4 B. 6
C. 7 D. 5

2. What least value must be given to * so that the number 91876*2 is divisible by 8?

A. 1 B. 2
C. 3 D. 0

3. If the number 135*7 is completely divisible by 9, then which number should replace the asterisk (*)?

A. 0 B. 1
C. 2 D. 3

4. The value of 387 million in Indian place value system is:

A. Three crores eighty seven lakhs
B. Thirty eight crores seventy lakhs
C. Thirty eight crores seven lakhs
D. None of these

5. The value of six arabs ninety two crores fifty four lakhs in International place value system is:

A. six billions ninety two millions and fifty four thousands
B. sixty nine billions twenty five millions and four hundred thousands
C. six billions nine hundred twenty five millions and four hundred thousands
D. None of these

6. Which one of the following is co-primes?

A. 9, 18 B. 10, 12
C. 27, 28 D. None of these

7. Which one of the following is twin primes?

A. 22, 24 B. 2, 5
C. 17, 19 D. None of these

8. Which of the following are true statements?

(*i*) Greatest negative number can not be determined.
(*ii*) 2 is a prime number
(*iii*) 1 is a prime number
(*iv*) Smallest positive number is (+1)

A. (*ii*) and (*iii*) B. (*ii*) and (*iv*)
C. (*i*), (*ii*) and (*iv*) D. (*ii*), (*iii*) and (*iv*)

9. If the difference of the sum of the digits in even places and the sum of the digits in odd places of a number is zero. Then the number is divisible by:

A. 2 B. 9
C. 13 D. 11

10. Which of the following are true?

(*i*) The number of prime numbers between 1 to 50 is 15.
(*ii*) A cubic number may have any digits from 0 to 9.
(*iii*) Sum of number from 1 to $n = \frac{(n \times n)+1}{2}$
(*iv*) A square number may have 0, 1, 4, 5, 6, or 9 in its units place.

A. (*ii*), (*iii*) and (*iv*) B. (*iii*) and (*iv*)
C. (*ii*) and (*iv*) D. All the above

11. What is the difference in face value and place value of 5 in 7501?

A. 459 B. 594
C. 495 D. 496

12. The least prime number of 3 digits is:

A. 100 B. 101
C. 103 D. 999

13. The sum of even numbers between 1 to 40 is:

A. 401 B. 410
C. 402 D. 420

14. The digits in units place in the product of 36* × 39 × 967 × 951 is 1. Which numbers should replace asterisk * ?

A. 3 B. 9
C. 5 D. 7

15. Correct formula for sum of even number where number of even numbers is '*n*' is:

A. $n \times (n + 1)$ B. $n \times \frac{(n+1)}{2}$
C. $(n \times n) + 1$ D. None of these

ANSWERS

1	2	3	4	5	6	7	8	9	10
A	C	C	B	C	C	C	B	D	C
11	12	13	14	15					
C	B	D	D	A					

SOME SELECTED EXPLANATORY ANSWERS

1. If a number is divisible by 11, the difference between the sum of the digits at the even places and sum of digits at odd places should be zero or a multiple of 11.

$\because$ The sum of the digits in the even places = 0 and the sum of the digits in the odd places

$$= 3 + x + 1 + 3 = 7 + x$$

$$\therefore \quad (7 + x) - 0 = 11$$

$$x = 11 - 7 = 4.$$

2. By hit and trial method, we find that 632 is divisible by 8. Hence * must be replaced by 3.

3. We know that a number is divisible by 9 only if the sum of its digits is a multiple of 9.

In the given number 135 * 7, sum of all other digits except the digit in place of (*) is (1 + 3 + 5 + 7 = 16). Hence, digit 2 should replace the asterisk to form the sum of the digits of the number a multiple of 9.

4. 387 million = 387000000 units
= 38 crores 70 lakhs.

5. Six arabs ninety two crores fifty four lakhs
= 6,92,54,00,000 units
= 6 billions 925 millions and 400 thousands.

11. Place value of 5 in 7501 = 500
Face value of 5 in 7501 = 5
Hence, difference = 495.

12. Least number of 3 digits = 100
But it is not a prime number. Hence, the least three digits number which is prime is 101.

13. Number of even numbers between 1 to 40

$$= \frac{40}{2} = 20$$

$\therefore$ Sum of even numbers between 1 to 40

$$= 20(20 + 1)$$
$$= 20 \times 21 = 420.$$

14. Unit's digits in numbers 39, 967 and 951 are 9, 7 and 1 respectively.

$\therefore$ Product of 9, 7 and 1 = $9 \times 7 \times 1 = 63$ in which unit digit is 3.

but by the question 36* $\times$ 39 $\times$ 967 $\times$ 951, unit digit is 1

$\therefore$ 7 should be replaced the asterisk because $7 \times 3 = 21$ in which digit in unit's place is 1.

MATHEMATICS

ADDITION

Addition is the concept of putting two or more groups together to get the total number. Here attention is focused on the number of objects in the collection.

To develop the concept of addition, there are three stages—

1. Objects of each collection are counted, the collections are combined and the objects of the resulting collection are counted.

2. Objects of the first collection are counted. Objects of the second collection are counted beyond the number of objects of the first collection and so on.

3. Objects of collections are not used. Instead, the numbers of objects of the collections are used.

METHODS OF ADDITION

Column-wise Addition:

6 5 7 4 9
\+ 7 2 3 8
Total = 7 2 9 8 7

Row-wise Addition:

7 5 6 9 3 + 1 3 4 8 + 2 7 3

= 77314.

Addition of Fractional Numbers

Two or more fractional numbers are added with the following process.

(*i*) If the denominators (Lower part of the fraction) are same then add the numerators (upper part of the fraction) and put the denominator below it.

Example: $\frac{7}{10}+\frac{3}{10}+\frac{1}{10}=\frac{11}{10}$

(*ii*) If the denominators are different then find the LCM of the denominators. Divide the LCM with the different denominators, multiply the quotients with correspondings numerators, add these calculation and put the LCM as the denominator of the fraction.

Example: $\frac{4}{5}+\frac{3}{10}+\frac{5}{6}=\frac{24+9+25}{30}=\frac{58}{30}$

EXAMPLES

Example 1 : Add the following—

(*a*) 763827, 62783 and 27253

(*b*) 700759 and 275832

Solution:

(*a*)
$$\begin{array}{r} 763827 \\ +62783 \\ +27253 \\ \hline 853863 \end{array}$$

(*b*)
$$\begin{array}{r} 700759 \\ +275832 \\ \hline 976591 \end{array}$$

Example 2 : Add the following—

(*a*) 5.382 and 63.27

(*b*) 972.386, 52.0624 and 0.38

Solution:

(*a*)
$$\begin{array}{r} 5\cdot382 \\ 63\cdot27 \\ \hline 68\cdot652 \end{array}$$

(*b*)
$$\begin{array}{r} 972\cdot386 \\ 52\cdot0624 \\ 0\cdot38 \\ \hline 1024\cdot8284 \end{array}$$

Example 3 : $3\frac{3}{5}+2\frac{7}{10}+4\frac{5}{6}$

Solution: $(3+2+4)+\frac{3}{5}+\frac{7}{10}+\frac{5}{6}$

$$= 9+\left(\frac{18+21+25}{30}\right)=9+\frac{64}{30}$$

$$= 9+2\frac{4}{30}=11\frac{4}{30}$$

Second Method

$$\frac{18}{5}+\frac{27}{10}+\frac{29}{6}=\frac{108+81+145}{30}$$

$$= \frac{334}{30}=11\frac{4}{30}$$

MULTIPLE CHOICE QUESTIONS

1. Sum of 3827, 7938 and 5738 is:
A. 17504 B. 17403
C. 17305 D. 17503

2. Sum of 5.807, 0.39 and 5.4 is:
A. 10.850 B. 11.507
C. 11.597 D. None of these

3. $3\frac{5}{12}+7\frac{3}{4}+\frac{2}{9}$ is equal to:
A. $\frac{74}{25}$ B. $11\frac{7}{18}$
C. $\frac{401}{36}$ D. None of these

4. Addition is the concept
A. of putting two or more groups together side by side.
B. of putting two or more groups together to get the total number of digits.
C. of putting two or more groups together to get the total number.
D. None of these.

5. 5 + 19 + 509 + 4075 + 87003 equals to:
A. 9611 B. 91611
C. 61911 D. 247653

6. $\frac{7}{12}+\frac{3}{8}+\frac{5}{9}+\frac{6}{10}+\frac{1}{4}+\frac{2}{3}+\frac{4}{5}$ equals to:
A. $\frac{1397}{360}$ B. $\frac{3299}{360}$
C. $3\frac{299}{360}$ D. None of these

7. 5 + 12 + 7 + 25 + 39 + 8 + 37 + 92 + 16 + 20 equals to:
A. 216 B. 612
C. 261 D. 126

8. Sum of two odd numbers is always:
A. a prime number B. an odd number
C. an even number D. either odd or even

9. Sum of two odd prime numbers is always:
A. a prime number
B. an odd number
C. a composite number
D. None of these

10. 0.72 + 3.0 + 0.1 + 9.738 + 6.003 equals to:
A. 19.561 B. 91.561
C. 0.165 D. 19.615

ANSWERS

1	2	3	4	5	6	7	8	9	10
D	C	B	C	B	C	C	C	C	A

SOME SELECTED EXPLANATORY ANSWERS

2.
```
 5.807
 0.39
 5.4
------
11.597
```

3. $3\frac{5}{12}+7\frac{3}{4}+\frac{2}{9} = \frac{41}{12}+\frac{31}{4}+\frac{2}{9}$

$= \frac{123+279+8}{36} = \frac{410}{36} = 11\frac{7}{18}$

5.
```
      5
    + 19
   + 509
  + 4075
 + 87003
 -------
  91611
```

6. $\frac{7}{12}+\frac{3}{8}+\frac{5}{9}+\frac{6}{10}+\frac{1}{4}+\frac{2}{3}+\frac{4}{5}$

$= \frac{210+135+200+216+90+240+288}{360}$

$= \frac{1379}{360} = 3\frac{299}{360}.$

10.
```
  0.720
+ 3.000
+ 0.100
+ 9.738
+ 6.003
-------
 19.561
```

MATHEMATICS

SUBTRACTION

Subtraction is the concept of removing or taking away some from bigger to make it smaller. It is just inverse of addition.

To develop the concept of subtraction there are four aspects—

***(i)* Taking away :** A man has 7 shirts. He gives 3 shirts to a poorman. How many shirts are left with him? Here is an action of removing some objects and finding out how many are left.

***(ii)* Comparision :** Madhu has 5 skirts and her friend has 3 skirts. How many more skirts does Madhu have than her friend? It clears that how much one is greater than the other.

***(iii)* Complementary addition :** Saurabh has 9 toys. Bhanu has 5 toys. How many more must Bhanu take to have the same number of toys as Saurabh? It tells that how many objects should be added to one number to get the other.

***(iv)* Reduction:** Lalit had 16 pencils yesterday but today he has 6 pencils only. How many pencils has he lost? It tells that when the original amount and the left amount is given, how can be found the amount that is to be subtracted.

Subtraction of Simple Numbers and Decimals

(*a*) 3827 – 1926 (*b*) 17.283 – 11.257

$$\begin{array}{r} 3827 \\ -1926 \\ \hline 1901 \end{array} \qquad \begin{array}{r} 17.283 \\ -11.257 \\ \hline 6.026 \end{array}$$

(*c*) 3.4 – 0.976

$$\begin{array}{r} 3.400 \\ -0.976 \\ \hline 2.424 \end{array}$$

Subtraction of Fractional Numbers

A fractional number is subtracted from the other with following process—

Find the LCM of the denominators. Divide the LCM with the denominators, multiply the quotients with corresponding numerators, write the difference of two calculations and put the LCM as the denominators of the fraction.

Example: $\frac{17}{20} - \frac{7}{12} = \frac{51-35}{60} = \frac{16}{60}$

EXAMPLES

Example 1 : Find the difference—

(*a*) 13.87 and 16.07

(*b*) 0.007 and 6.4

Solution: (*a*) $\begin{array}{r} 16.07 \\ -13.87 \\ \hline 2.20 \end{array}$ (*b*) $\begin{array}{r} 6.400 \\ -0.007 \\ \hline 6.393 \end{array}$

Example 2 : Simplify—

(*a*) 4638 + 3875 – 3869 – 2714

(*b*) 8527 – 3824 – 1234

Solution: (*a*) 4638 + 3875 – (3869 + 2714)

= 8513 – 6583 = 1930

(*b*) 8527 – (3824 + 1234)

= 8527 – 5058 = 3469.

Example 3 : Subtract—

(*a*) $\frac{17}{24} - \frac{7}{18}$ (*b*) $\frac{12}{20} - \frac{3}{8}$

Solution: (*a*) $\frac{17}{24} - \frac{7}{18} = \frac{51-28}{72} = \frac{23}{72}$

(*b*) $\frac{12}{20} - \frac{3}{8} = \frac{24-15}{40} = \frac{9}{40}$

MULTIPLE CHOICE QUESTIONS

1. 873827 – 3824 – 75280 equals to :

A. 945283 B. 802371

C. 794723 D. None of these

2. Difference of 87.13 and 70.007 is:

A. 7.123 B. 17.123

C. 71.123 D. None of these

3. 4627 – 5380 + 7518 + 2007 equals to :
A. 87172 B. 8772
C. 8227 D. None of these

4. Difference of $\frac{22}{40}$ and $\frac{18}{30}$ is:
A. $\frac{6}{20}$ B. $\frac{11}{20}$
C. $\frac{1}{20}$ D. None of these

5. $3\frac{4}{5}+7\frac{3}{8}-2\frac{1}{4}-7\frac{1}{2}+3\frac{2}{3}$ equals to:
A. $\frac{-494}{120}$ B. $\frac{494}{120}$
C. Either A or B D. None of these

6. Difference between sum of 0.007 and 5.07 and difference of 13.607 and 8.156 is:
A. 10.528 B. 0.374
C. 3.086 D. None of these

7. Difference of two consecutive number
A. can not be determined
B. is always 1
C. equals to the first number
D. None of these

8. Difference of two odd number
A. is always on odd number
B. is always a prime number
C. is always an even number
D. can not be determined

9. Subtraction is a concept of
A. adding some to make it bigger
B. taking away some from bigger to make it smaller
C. Both the above
D. None of these

10. Abhinav has ₹ 1665, he lost ₹ 550 but his father gave him ₹ 1256 and he bought a book for ₹ 2000. Now Abhinav has the remaining money:
A. ₹ 2921 B. ₹ 2550
C. ₹ 371 D. ₹ 731

11. Reeta refilled 65 litre petrol in her car and consumed 43.6 litre. Again she refilled 16.9 litre and went 60 km. How much petrol is left in her car now?
A. 38.3 litres B. 36.3 litres
C. None of these D. Can not be found

12. Adams bought 3827 kg of sugar. He kept 426 kg for use and sold 2856 kg of sugar. How much sugar is left now?
A. 340 of kg B. 545 kg
C. 971 kg D. None of these

13. Difference of two even number is always :
A. an odd number B. a prime number
C. an even number D. None of these

14. Difference of twin primes is always:
A. 2 B. odd number
C. prime number D. None of these

15. Substraction is:
A. inverse of itself
B. inverse of addition
C. inverse of division
D. inverse of multiplication

ANSWERS

1	2	3	4	5	6	7	8	9	10
C	B	B	C	D	B	B	C	B	C
11	**12**	**13**	**14**	**15**					
D	B	C	A	B					

SOME SELECTED EXPLANATORY ANSWERS

4. Since $\frac{18}{30} > \frac{22}{40}$

Hence,

$$\text{difference} = \frac{18}{30} - \frac{22}{40} = \frac{72-66}{120} = \frac{6}{120} = \frac{1}{20}.$$

5. $$\frac{19}{5}+\frac{59}{8}-\frac{9}{4}-\frac{15}{2}+\frac{11}{3}$$
$$= \frac{456+885-270-900+440}{120} = \frac{611}{120}.$$

6. Sum of 0.007 and 5.07 = 5.077
Difference of 13.607 and 8.156 = 5.451
Hence, required difference = 5.451 – 5.077
= 0.374.

10. Abhinav has the money = ₹ 1665
His father gave = ₹ 1256
Total money he has = ₹ 2921
He lost the money = ₹ 550
He bought the book for = ₹ 2000
Total = ₹ 2550
Hence, remaining money = ₹ 2921 – ₹ 2550
= ₹ 371.

11. It is not clear that how much petrol had consumed to cover 60 km distance.
Hence, left quantity of petrol can not be found.

MULTIPLICATION

Multiplication is a repeated addition. It tells that how many times a number is added to itself. Also, if a number is added repeatedly then what is the result of the repeated addition.

Multiplication of Simple Numbers and Decimals

(*a*) 382 × 76 =

$$\begin{array}{r} 382 \\ \times 76 \\ \hline 2292 \\ 2674 \\ \hline 29032 \end{array}$$

(*b*) 3.827 × 15.24 =

$$\begin{array}{r} 3.827 \\ \times 15.24 \\ \hline 15308 \\ 7654 \\ 19135 \\ 3827 \\ \hline 58{\cdot}32348 \end{array}$$

Multiplication of Fractional Numbers

(*a*) $\frac{7}{8}\times\frac{16}{21}=\frac{2}{3}$

(*b*) $4\frac{2}{3}\times4\frac{1}{8}=\frac{14}{3}\times\frac{33}{8}=\frac{7}{4}\times11=\frac{77}{4}$

EXAMPLES

1. Multiply : (*a*) 4382 × 536
(*b*) 7.382 × .34

Solution: (*a*)

$$\begin{array}{r} 4382 \\ \times 536 \\ \hline 26292 \\ 13146 \\ 21910 \\ \hline 2348752 \end{array}$$

(*b*)

$$\begin{array}{r} 7.382 \\ \times .34 \\ \hline 29528 \\ 22146 \\ \hline 2.50988 \end{array}$$

2. Multiply : (*a*) $\frac{6}{10}$ and $\frac{22}{24}$ (*b*) $\frac{11}{15}$ and $\frac{7}{8}$

Solution: (*a*) $\frac{6}{10}\times\frac{22}{24}=\frac{11}{20}$

(*b*) $\frac{11}{15}\times\frac{7}{8}=\frac{77}{120}$

3. Alok hired a taxi, the fare of the taxi is ₹ 8 for first three km. ₹ 6 for next four km. and ₹ 1.50 per km for the next journey. If he travelled 15 km. and gave ₹ 40 then find the amount of tips given by Alok to the taxidriver

Solution: Total fare = 8 + 6 + (8 × 1.5) = ₹ 26.

Alok gave Rs. 40 and tips is included in that amount

∴ Amount for tips = 40 – 26 = ₹ 14

MULTIPLE CHOICE QUESTIONS

1. Product of 382 and 784 is:
A. 294988 B. 299488
C. 299848 D. None of these

2. 7.872 × 5.07 equals to:
A. 29.91104 B. 39.91104
C. 39.19104 D. None of these

3. Product of 0.002 and 0.07 is:
A. 0.14 B. 0.00140
C. 0.00014 D. 0.14000

4. $3\frac{3}{4}\times5\frac{3}{5}\times\frac{1}{12}\times\frac{4}{7}$ equals to:
A. 0 B. 1
C. 12 D. $\frac{1}{12}$

5. Product of 3.1 × 0.001 and 5.38 – 5.34 is
A. 0.00142
B. 0.00124
C. 0.000124
D. None of these

6. $\frac{9}{4}\times\frac{15}{6}\times\frac{3}{4}\times\frac{12}{5}\times\frac{8}{9}\times\frac{3}{8}\times\frac{4}{5}$ equals to:

A. $2\frac{7}{10}$ B. $7\frac{2}{10}$

C. $\frac{10}{27}$ D. None of these

7. 38.27 × 9200 equals to:

A. 352048 B. 350284

C. 352084 D. None of these

8. 5.92 × 0.507 × 0.01 equals to:

A. 0.030144 B. 0.0300144

C. 30144 D. None of these

9. Product of 17.382 and 58 is:

A. 1080.156 B. 108.126

C. 1008.156 D. None of these

10. Product of 0.724 + 2.4 and 6.369 – 6.269 is :

A. 3124 B. 3.1240

C. 30.124 D. 0.3124

11. The digits in units place in the product of 588, 357, 39 and 24 is:

A. 4 B. 6

C. 2 D. 3

12. Product of two even numbers is always:

A. an even number

B. an odd number

C. can not be determined

D. None of these

13. Product of two prime numbers is always :

A. a prime number

B. an even number

C. a composite number

D. None of these

14. Product of two odd numbers is always :

A. an odd number B. an even number

C. a prime number D. None of these

15. If the number of negative integers is odd then their product will be:

A. always negative

B. always positive

C. sometimes negative and sometimes positive

D. None of these

16. If the number of negative integers is even then their product will be:

A. always positive

B. always negative

C. sometimes negative and sometimes positive

D. None of these

ANSWERS

1	2	3	4	5	6	7	8	9	10
B	B	C	B	C	A	C	B	C	D
11	12	13	14	15	16				
B	A	C	A	A	A				

SOME SELECTED EXPLANATORY ANSWERS

1.
```
   382
 × 748
  1528
 3056
2674
299488
```

2.
```
   7.872
  × 7.06
   55104
   0000
 39360
39.91104
```

4. $\frac{15}{4}\times\frac{28}{5}\times\frac{1}{12}\times\frac{4}{7}=1.$

5. 3.1 × 0.001 = 0.0031, 5.38 – 5.34 = 0.04

Hence, required product = 0.0031 × 0.04

= 0.000124.

6. $\frac{9}{4}\times\frac{15}{6}\times\frac{3}{4}\times\frac{12}{5}\times\frac{8}{9}\times\frac{3}{8}\times\frac{4}{5} = \frac{27}{10}=2\frac{7}{10}.$

8.
```
   5.92          3.00144
 × 0.507          × 0.01
   4144        0.0300144 .
  000
2960
3.00144
```

9.
```
  17.382
  × 58
 139056
 86910
1008.156
```

10.
```
  0.724       6.369
+ 2.400     – 6.269
  3.124       0.100
```

Hence, 3.124 × 0.1

= 0.3124

Units digits in numbers 588, 357, 39 and 24 are 8, 7, 3 and 4 respectively.

∴ product of 8, 7, 9 and 4 = 2016

Hence, 6 will be the in the unit place in the product of given numbers.

DIVISION

Division is the inverse of multiplication. If any two of product / (Dividend), Multiplicant / (Divisor) and Multiple (Quotient) are given then third can be found.

Division Based Formulae

Dividend = Divisor × Quotient + Remainder

$$\text{Quotient} = \frac{\text{Dividend} - \text{Remainder}}{\text{Divisor}}$$

$$\text{Divisor} = \frac{\text{Dividend} - \text{Remainder}}{\text{Quotient}}$$

Remainder = Dividend − Divisor × Quotient

Division of Simple Numbers and Decimals

(*a*) 5829 ÷ 24 = 24) 5829 (242

```
48
---
102
 96
---
  69
  48
---
  21
```

Here Dividend = 5829, Divisor = 24, Quotient = 242, Remainder = 21

(*b*) 75.28 ÷ 12 = 12) 75.28 (6.27

```
72
--
 32
 24
---
  88
  84
---
   4
```

Here, Dividend = 75.28, Divisor = 12, Quotient = 6.27, Remainder = 4.

Division of Fractional Numbers

(*a*) $\frac{15}{16} \div \frac{5}{4} = \frac{15}{16} \times \frac{4}{5} = \frac{3}{4}$

(*b*) $\frac{3}{4} \div \frac{9}{10} \div \frac{3}{20} = \frac{3}{4} \times \frac{10}{9} \times \frac{20}{3} = \frac{50}{9}$

EXAMPLES

1. Divide : (*a*) 3867 ÷ 32
(*b*) 7634 ÷ 52

Solution: (*a*) 32) 3867 (120

```
32
--
 66
 64
---
 27
```

Here, Dividend = 3867, Divisor = 32, Quotient = 120, Remainder = 27

(*b*) 52) 7634 (146

```
52
---
243
208
---
 354
 312
----
  42
```

Here, Dividend = 7634, Divisor = 52 Quotient = 146, Remainder = 42

2. (*a*) If divisor is 14, remainder is 9 and quotient is 11, then find the dividend.

(*b*) Find the remainder if quotient is 12, divisor is 25 and dividend is 311.

Solution: (*a*) Dividend = Divisor × Quotient + Remainder = 14 × 11 + 9 = 154 + 9 = 163

(*b*) Remainder = Dividend − Divisor × Quotient = 311 − 25 × 12 = 311 − 300 = 11.

3. Divide : (*a*) $\frac{24}{35} \div \frac{27}{28}$ (*b*) $\frac{26}{40} \div \frac{24}{65} \div \frac{13}{15}$

Solution: (*a*) $\frac{24}{35} \times \frac{28}{27} = \frac{32}{45}$

(*b*) $\frac{26}{40} \times \frac{65}{24} \times \frac{15}{13} = \frac{195}{96} = \frac{65}{32}$

MULTIPLE CHOICE QUESTIONS

1. If 4879 is divided by 27 the remainder is:
A. 39 B. 29
C. 19 D. 91

2. If 8497 is divided by 72 the quotient is:
A. 78 B. 181
C. 186 D. None of these

3. If quotient is 53, divisor is 28 and remainder is 16 the dividend is:
A. 1484 B. 5100
C. 1500 D. None of these

4. If quotient is 248, dividend is 5604 and remainder is 148 then divisor is:
A. 42 B. 22
C. 32 D. None of these

5. If a number is divided by 899 gives a remainder of 63. If the same number is divided by 29 then what will be remainder?
A. 5 B. 15
C. 51 D. None of these

6. What least number must be subtracted from 1294, so that the remainder when divided by 9,11,13, will leave in each case the same remainder 6?
A. 0 B. 1
C. 2 D. 3

7. If in a question of division divisor is 9, quotient 114 and remainder is 5 then what will be the dividend?
A. 1301 B. 1103
C. 1310 D. 1031

8. In a division sum, the divisor is ten times the quotient and five times the remainder. If the remainder is 46 then the dividend is:
A. 3556 B. 6335
C. 5336 D. None of these

9. Sarita got 384 chocolates on her birthday and distributed these in her 38 class-mates equally. How many chocolates she have how?
A. 14 B. 4
C. 24 D. None of these

10. 36.333 ÷ 2.6 equals to (approx):
A. 31.974 B. 13.794
C. 13.974 D. None of these

11. $\frac{1}{8} \div \frac{2}{7} \div \frac{5}{6} \div \frac{3}{8} \div \frac{7}{5}$ equals to:
A. 0 B. 2
C. 3 D. 1

12. $\frac{27}{35} \div \frac{45}{49} \div \frac{25}{36}$ equals to:
A. $\frac{12}{7}$ B. 1
C. $\frac{7}{12}$ D. None of these

13. (360 ÷ 45) ÷ (144 ÷ 16) equals to:
A. 8 B. 16
C. 0 D. 1

14. 288 ÷ (144 ÷ 16) equals to:
A. $\frac{1}{8}$ B. 8
C. 23 D. 32

15. Sushma gives gifts to her 28 colleague. She has ₹ 10000. How much maximum money does she spend on her colleagues and how much money remains to her?
A. ₹ 350, ₹ 300 B. ₹ 200, ₹ 350
C. ₹ 530, ₹ 200 D. None of these

ANSWERS

1	2	3	4	5	6	7	8	9	10
C	D	C	B	A	B	D	C	B	C
11	**12**	**13**	**14**	**15**					
D	C	D	D	D					

SOME SELECTED EXPLANATORY ANSWERS

1. $27\overline{)4879}$ quotient 180; 4879 − 27 = 217; 217 − 216 = 19

Hence, quotient = 180, and remainder = 19

2. $72\overline{)8497}$ quotient 118; 84 − 72 = 129; 129 − 72 = 577; 577 − 576 = 1

Hence, quotient = 118.

3. Dividend = divisor × quotient + remainder
= 28 × 53 + 16
= 1500

4. Divisor = $\frac{\text{Dividend} - \text{Remainder}}{\text{Quotient}} = \frac{5604 - 148}{248}$
$= \frac{5456}{248} = 22$

5. Number = D × Q + R
= 899 × K + 63
= 31 × 29 × K + 29 × 2 + 5
= 29 (31K + 2) + 5

∴ The remainder when the number is divided by 29 is 5.

6. The number when divided by 9, 11, 13 leaving remainder 6
= (L.C.M. of 9, 11, 13) + 6 = 1287 + 6 = 1293
∴ Required number = 1294 – 1293 = 1.

7. Dividend = Divisor × Quotient + Remainder
= 9 × 114 + 5
= 1026 + 5 = 1031

8. Let the quotient be Q and the remainder be R. According to the question,
Divisor = 5 × 46 = 230

$$\text{Quotient} = \frac{230}{10} = 23$$

∴ Dividend = Divisor × Quotient + Remainder
= 230 × 23 + 46 = 5290 + 46
= 5336

9. If 384 is divided by 38 then remainder is 4. Hence, she has remaining 4 chocolates.

10. $$\frac{36333}{1000} \div \frac{26}{10} = \frac{36333}{1000} \times \frac{10}{26}$$

$$= \frac{36333}{26} \times \frac{1}{100} = 1397.423 \times \frac{1}{100}$$

= 13.97423.

11. $$\frac{1}{8} \times \frac{7}{2} \times \frac{6}{5} \times \frac{8}{3} \times \frac{5}{7} = 1.$$

12. $$\frac{27}{35} \times \frac{44}{45} \times \frac{36}{25} = \frac{7}{12}.$$

13. (360 ÷ 45) ÷ (224 ÷ 28) = 8 ÷ 8 = 1

14. 288 ÷ (144 ÷ 16) = 288 ÷ 9 = 32.

15. If 10000 is divided by 28 the quotient is 350. Hence, Shushma spends ₹ 350 on her each colleagues and remainder is 200, hence ₹ 200 remains to her. Therefore answer should be ₹ 350, ₹ 200.

SIMPLIFICATION

When simplification of fractions involving addition, subtraction, multiplication and division (all in one question together) is done, the VBODMAS rule is followed,

The seven of VBODMAS indicate as under:

V = Vinculum (Bar);

B = Bracket;

O = Of;

D = Division;

M = Multiplication;

A = Addition;

S = Subtraction.

Remember the following points:

(i) **If the given expression contains brackets, simplify terms within the *brackets* first. Brackets are of three kinds:**
(a) ( ) *(b)* { } *(c)* [ ]
They may be used together in the following manner:
[{( )}].
First simplify ( ), then { } and finally [ ].

(ii) **After the brackets, simplify 'Of', 'Of' is multiplication.**

(iii) **After brackets and of, simplify division.**

(iv) **Next, simplify multiplication.**

(v) **And thereafter do addition and subtraction.**

If these points (stages of operations in indicated order) are not followed in actual application, the answer is bound to be wrong.

We shall have some examples to show how non-application of these points, may give wrong answers.

Example. 1. 6 + 5 × 3 = ?

Sol.: The sum has plus sign (+) and multiplication sign (×).

As per rule, first simplify the multiplication and then add.

5 × 3 = 15

6 + 15 = 21 (correct answer)

In case the rule is not followed and first addition is done and then multiplication is done the result will be wrong.

6 + 5 = 11

11 × 3 = 33 (incorrect answer)

Therefore, the rule must be followed in proper order.

Example 2. $\frac{3}{4} \div \frac{1}{2} + \frac{1}{4} - \frac{1}{8} = ?$

Sol. As per rule, first divide, then add and then subtract.

$$\frac{3}{4} \div \frac{1}{2} + \frac{1}{4} - \frac{1}{8} = \frac{3}{4} \times \frac{2}{1} + \frac{1}{4} - \frac{1}{8} = \frac{3}{2} + \frac{1}{4} - \frac{1}{8}$$

(here '+' and '–' can be simplified together)

$$= \frac{3}{2} + \frac{1}{4} - \frac{1}{8} = \frac{12+2-1}{8} = \frac{13}{8} = 1\frac{5}{8}$$

Example 3. $\frac{1}{2}$ of $\frac{4}{3} \times 3\frac{1}{2} + \frac{7}{4} - \frac{1}{2} = ?$

Sol.: As per rule, first 'of', then ×, then +, and at the end –.

$$\frac{1}{2} \text{ of } \frac{4}{3} \times \frac{7}{2} + \frac{7}{4} - \frac{1}{2} = \frac{2}{3} \times \frac{7}{2} + \frac{7}{4} - \frac{1}{2}$$

$$= \frac{7}{3} + \frac{7}{4} - \frac{1}{2} = \frac{28+21-6}{12}$$

$$= \frac{49-6}{12} = \frac{43}{12}$$

Example 4. $3 - \left[1 + \left\{1 - \left(\frac{2}{5} + \frac{1}{5}\right)\right\}\right]$.

Sol.: As per rule, first ( ), then { } and at the end [ ].

$$3 - \left[1 + \left\{1 - \left(\frac{2}{5} + \frac{1}{5}\right)\right\}\right]$$

$$= 3 - \left[1 + \left\{1 - \left(\frac{2+1}{5}\right)\right\}\right] = 3 - \left[1 + \left\{1 - \left(\frac{3}{5}\right)\right\}\right]$$

$$= 3 - \left[1 + \left\{\frac{5-3}{5}\right\}\right] = 3 - \left[1 + \frac{2}{5}\right]$$

$$= 3 - \left[\frac{5+2}{5}\right] = 3 - \frac{7}{5} = \frac{15-7}{5} = \frac{8}{5} = 1\frac{3}{5}$$

MULTIPLE CHOICE QUESTIONS

1. If 45 – [28 – {37 – (15 – ?) }] = 58, then which of the following should replace the sign of interrogation (?)?

   A. 18 B. 17
   C. 13 D. 19

2. The value of $8\frac{1}{3}+5\frac{1}{4}\times13\frac{1}{5}\div6\frac{3}{5}$ is:

   A. $19\frac{1}{3}$ B. $18\frac{5}{6}$
   C. $21\frac{1}{3}$ D. $22\frac{1}{2}$

3. The value of $\frac{14}{3}$ of $\frac{5}{8}$ of 72 is:

   A. 209 B. 217
   C. 210 D. 199

4. 1150 ÷ 50 ÷ 23 + 15 = ?

   A. 16 B. 20
   C. 22 D. 18

5. What is the value of $1+\cfrac{1}{1+\cfrac{1}{1+\cfrac{9}{16}}}$?

   A. $\frac{44}{31}$ B. $\frac{55}{41}$
   C. $\frac{66}{41}$ D. $\frac{77}{51}$

6. What is the value of

   $22\div\left[(28-13)\div\{(32-8)\div\left(5+\frac{1}{3}\right)\}\right]$?

   A. 7.9 B. 6.8
   C. 6.6 D. 5.7

7. What is the value of

   $11^2 - 6^2 \div 6 \times \frac{5}{2} + 2$ of 10?

   A. 126 B. 108
   C. 110 D. 125

8. What is the value of $\frac{25}{3}-\frac{4}{7}$ of $\frac{7}{5}+\frac{11}{3}\div\frac{2}{3}-4$?

   A. $8\frac{1}{15}$ B. $9\frac{1}{30}$
   C. $7\frac{1}{30}$ D. $9\frac{1}{5}$

9. What is the value of 35 × .07 – 21 × .03?

   A. 2.75 B. 1.72
   C. 1.82 D. 2.13

10. What is the value of

    $60 \times [35 - \{25 - (18 - \overline{9-3}) \div 11\}]$?

    A. $566\frac{5}{7}$ B. $665\frac{5}{11}$
    C. $665\frac{8}{11}$ D. $765\frac{5}{11}$

11. What is the value of $\frac{19}{17}$ of $\frac{28}{5}$ of $\left(\frac{17}{3}\div\frac{5}{3}\text{of }6\frac{1}{3}\right)$?

    A. $4\frac{9}{25}$ B. $3\frac{8}{23}$
    C. $3\frac{9}{24}$ D. $3\frac{9}{25}$

12. What is the value of $1+\cfrac{1}{1+\cfrac{1}{1+\cfrac{1}{3}}}$?

    A. $1\frac{4}{7}$ B. $2\frac{4}{7}$
    C. $3\frac{4}{7}$ D. $4\frac{4}{7}$

13. A man has some hens and cows. If the number of heads be 48 and the number of feet equals 140. Then find the number of hens.

    A. 26 B. 24
    C. 23 D. 22

14. A man has Rs. 480 in the denominations of one-rupee notes, five-rupee notes and ten-rupee notes. The number of notes of each denomination is equal. Find the total number of notes he has:

    A. 90 B. 75
    C. 60 D. 45

15. N number of persons decided to raise Rs. 3 lakhs by equal contributions from each. Had they contributed Rs. 50 each extra, the contribution would have been Rs. 3.25 lakhs. Find the value of N.

    A. 600 B. 550
    C. 400 D. 500

ANSWERS

1	2	3	4	5	6	7	8	9	10
D	B	C	A	C	C	A	B	C	B
11	**12**	**13**	**14**	**15**					
D	A	A	A	D					

SOME SELECTED EXPLANATORY ANSWERS

1. $\because \quad 45 - [28 - \{37 - (15 - ?)\}] = 58$

$\Rightarrow \quad 45 - [28 - \{37 - 15 + ?\}] = 58$

$\Rightarrow \quad 45 - [28 - \{22 + ?\}] = 58$

$\Rightarrow \quad 45 - [28 - 22 - ?] = 58$

$\Rightarrow \quad 45 - 28 + 22 + ? = 58$

$\Rightarrow \quad 39 + ? = 58$

$\Rightarrow \quad ? = 58 - 39$

$= 19$

Therefore, the interrogation sign should be replaced by 19.

2. $\because 8\frac{1}{3} + 5\frac{1}{4} \times 13\frac{1}{5} \div 6\frac{3}{5}$

$= \frac{25}{3} + \frac{21}{4} \times \frac{66}{5} \div \frac{33}{5} = \frac{25}{3} + \frac{21}{4} \times \frac{66}{5} \times \frac{5}{33}$

$= \frac{25}{3} + \frac{21}{2} = \frac{50+63}{6} = \frac{113}{6} = 18\frac{5}{6}.$

3. $\because \frac{14}{3}$ of $\frac{5}{8}$ of $72 = \frac{14 \times 5 \times 72}{3 \times 8} = 210.$

4. $1150 \div 50 \div 23 + 15 = \frac{1150}{50} \div 23 + 15 = 23 \div 23 + 15$

$= \frac{23}{23} + 15 = 1 + 15 = 16.$

5. This type of question is solved starting from the bottom.

$\therefore \; 1 + \cfrac{1}{1 + \cfrac{1}{1 + \cfrac{9}{16}}} = 1 + \cfrac{1}{1 + \cfrac{1}{\frac{25}{16}}}$

$= 1 + \cfrac{1}{1 + \frac{16}{25}} = 1 + \cfrac{1}{\frac{41}{25}} = 1 + \frac{25}{41} = \frac{66}{41}.$

6. $22 \div \left[(28-13) \div \left\{(32-8) \div \left(5 + \frac{1}{3}\right)\right\}\right]$

$= 22 \div \left[15 \div \left\{24 \div \frac{16}{3}\right\}\right]$

$= 22 \div \left[15 \div \cfrac{24}{\frac{16}{3}}\right] = 22 \div \left[15 \div \frac{9}{2}\right] = 22 \div \cfrac{15}{\frac{9}{2}}$

$= 22 \div \frac{10}{3} = \frac{22 \times 3}{10} = 6.6$

7. $11^2 - 6^2 \div 6 \times \frac{5}{2} + 2$ of 10

$= 11^2 - 6^2 \div 6 \times \frac{5}{2} + 20$

$= 11^2 - 6 \times \frac{5}{2} + 20 = 11^2 - 15 + 20$

$= 121 + 5 = 126$

8. $\frac{25}{3} - \frac{4}{7}$ of $\frac{7}{5} + \frac{11}{3} \div \frac{2}{3} - 4$

$= \frac{25}{3} - \frac{4}{5} + \frac{11}{3} \div \frac{2}{3} - 4 = \frac{25}{3} - \frac{4}{5} + \frac{11}{2} - 4$

$= \frac{83}{6} - \frac{24}{5} = \frac{415-144}{30} = \frac{271}{30} = 9\frac{1}{30}.$

9. $35 \times .07 - 21 \times .03 = 2.45 - .63 = 1.82.$

10. $60 \times [35 - \{25 - (18 - \overline{9-3}) \div 11\}]$

$= 60 \times [35 - \{25 - (18 - 6) \div 11\}]$

$= 60 \times [35 - \{25 - 12 \div 11\}]$

$= 60 \times \left[35 - \left\{25 - \frac{12}{11}\right\}\right] = 60 \times \left[35 - \frac{263}{11}\right]$

$= 60 \times \frac{122}{11} = 665\frac{5}{11}$

11. $\frac{19}{17}$ of $\frac{28}{5}$ of $\left(\frac{17}{3} \div \frac{5}{3} \text{ of } 6\frac{1}{3}\right)$

$= \frac{19}{17}$ of $\frac{28}{5}$ of $\left(\frac{17}{3} \div \frac{5}{3} \text{ of } \frac{19}{3}\right)$

$= \frac{19}{17}$ of $\frac{28}{5}$ of $\left(\frac{17}{3} \div \frac{95}{9}\right)$

$= \frac{19}{17}$ of $\frac{28}{5}$ of $\frac{153}{285}$

$= \frac{19}{17} \times \frac{28}{5} \times \frac{153}{285} = \frac{84}{25} = 3\frac{9}{25}$

12. This type of questions is solved starting from the bottom.

$1 + \cfrac{1}{1 + \cfrac{1}{1 + \frac{1}{3}}} = 1 + \cfrac{1}{1 + \cfrac{1}{\frac{4}{3}}}$

$= 1 + \cfrac{1}{1 + \frac{3}{4}} = 1 + \cfrac{1}{\frac{7}{4}} = 1 + \frac{4}{7} = \frac{11}{7} = 1\frac{4}{7}$

13. Let the number of hens and cows be x and y respectively.

Then, $\quad x + y = 48$

$\therefore \quad y = (48 - x) \quad$ ...(i)

Again, $2x + 4(48 - x) = 140$

$\Rightarrow \quad 2x - 4x = 140 - 192$

$\Rightarrow \quad 2x = 52 \quad \therefore \quad x = 26$

14. $x \times 1 + x \times 5 + x \times 10 = 480$

$\Rightarrow \quad 16x = 480 \quad \therefore \quad x = 30$

Hence, total number of notes $= 3x = 3 \times 30 = 90$

MEASUREMENT

Mathematics is the calculation of units. Maximum calculations in mathematics require unit. These units represent length, time, weight, area, volume etc. Measurement is calculation of units.

MEASUREMENT OF LENGTH

Through this process we can compare two or more objects in the relation of big-small, far-near, above-below etc.

We can make an idea to see the objects (rods, logs, bricks etc) that which is bigger or smaller which is farther or nearer. It may be different in the views of different persons. But Mathematics requires the exact length. So to get the exact length we use some measure divices like metre rod, inch tape, scale etc.

MEASURES OF LENGTH

10 Millimetres	=	1 Centimetre
10 Centimetres	=	1 Decimetre
10 Decimetres	=	1 Metre
10 Metres	=	1 Decametre
10 Decametres	=	1 Hectometre
10 Hectometres	=	1 Kilometre

MEASUREMENT OF WEIGHT

Through this process we can compare two or more objects in relation to heavier or lighter.

If we lift two objects then we get an idea about these that which one of the two is heavier or lighter. But it is not enough in Mathematics. Because idea may be different. Therefore we get exact weight through the different type of balances.

MEASURES OF WEIGHTS

10 Milligrams	=	1 Centigram
10 Centigrams	=	1 Decigram
10 Decigrams	=	1 Gram
10 Grams	=	1 Decagram
10 Decagram	=	1 Hectogram
10 Hectogram	=	1 Kilogram
100 Kilograms	=	1 Quintal
10 Quintals	=	1 Metric ton
1000 Kilograms	=	1 Metric ton

MEASUREMENT OF VOLUME

Through the measurement of volume we can know about the space occupied by the object. We also compare the two or more object in relation to the space occupied by it. To measure the capacity of three dimensional objects we use the different type of measuring utensils.

MEASURES OF VOLUME (CAPACITY)

10 Millilitres	=	1 Centilitre
10 Centilitres	=	1 Decilitre
10 Decilitres	=	1 Litre
10 Litres	=	1 Decalitre
10 Decalitres	=	1 Hectolitre
10 Hectolitres	=	1 Kilolitre

ARTICLES

12 Articles	=	1 Dozen
12 Dozen	=	1 Gross
144 Articles	=	1 Gross
24 Sheets	=	1 Quire
480 Sheets	=	1 Ream
20 Quires	=	1 Ream
500 Sheets	=	1 Ream (Commercial)

e.g., 500 Sheets are counted in a ream instead of 480 Sheets.

MEASUREMENT OF TIME

Punctuality is an essential factor of our life. We have to finish our work within the time. We measure the period in hours, minutes and seconds and use the clock to measure the time.

TIME

60 Seconds	= 1 Minute
60 Minutes	= 1 Hour
24 Hours	= 1 Day
7 Days	= 1 Week
4 Weeks or 30 days	= 1 Month

12 Months	= 1 Year
365 Days	= 1 Year
366 Days	= 1 Leap year

TRANSFORMATION OF DIFFERENT UNITS

1 Mile	= 1.61 Kilometres
1 Kilometre	= 0.6214 Mile (approx.)
1 Metre	= 3.2802 Feet
1 Foot	= 0.3048 Metre
1 Metre	= 39.37 Inches
1 Inch	= 2.54 Centimetres
1 Centimetre	= 0.3937 Inch
1 Decimetre	= 4 Inches (approx.)
8 Kilometres	= 5 Miles (approx.)
1 Yard	= 0.9137 Metre
1 Metre	= 1.0936 Yards
1 Pound	= 0.4536 Kilogram
1 Kilogram	= 2.2046 Pounds
1 Carat	= 0.2 Gram
1 Gram	= 5 Carats
1 Tone	= 2240 Pounds
1 Ounce	= 28.35 Grams
1 Gram	= 0.0353 Ounce
1 Gallon	= 3.7854 Litres
1 Litre	= 0.2641 Gallon
1 Cubic Foot	= 6.23 Gallons
1 Cubic Inch	= 16.4 Cubic Centimetres
1 Cubic Centimeter	= 0.061 Cubic Inch
1 Cubic Metre	= 35.3146 Cubic feet
1 Cubic Foot	= 0.28 Cubic Metre
	= 28.317 Letres

IMPORTANT FORMULAE OF MEASUREMENT

Area of Rectangle = $l \times$ b square unit

Area of Square = $(\text{side})^2$ square unit

Area of Circle = πr^2 square unit

Area of Semicircle = $\frac{\pi r^2}{2}$ square unit

Area of Triangle = $\frac{1}{2} \times$ base $\times$ height square unit

Area of Sphere = $4 \pi r^2$ square unit

Area of Cilinder = $2 \pi r (r + h)$ square unit

Area of Cube = $6 \times (\text{side})^2$ square unit

Area of Cuboid = $2 (l \times b + b \times h + l \times h)$ square unit

Area of Cone = $\pi r (l + r)$ square unit

Volume of Rectangular Room = $l \times b \times h$ cubic unit

Volume of Cubical Object = $(\text{side})^3$ cubic unit

Volume of Spherical Object = $\frac{4}{3} \pi (r)^3$ cubic unit

Volume of Cylindrical Object= $\pi r^2 h$ cubic unit

Volume of Conical Object = $\frac{1}{3} \pi r^2 h$ cubic unit.

EXAMPLES

Example 1 : How many articles are there in 20 gross, 5 dozens and 10 units?

Solution:

20 gross	= 20 × 144	=	2880
5 dozens	= 5 × 12	=	60
10 unit	= 10 × 1	=	10
Total			**2950**

Example 2 : Convert 7508 grams into kilograms and grams.

Solution: 1000 grams = 1 kg

$$7508 \text{ grams} = \frac{1}{1000} \times 7508$$

= 7 kg 508 grams.

Example 3 : Convert 15 litres 775 millilitres into millilitres.

Solution: 1 litre = 1000 ml

15 litre = 15000 ml

Now, 15000 ml + 775 ml = 15775 ml

MULTIPLE CHOICE QUESTIONS

1. Convert 5.5 quintals into kilograms.

A. 55 kg B. 5500 kg
C. 550 kg D. 65 kg

2. How many days are there in 5 months, 6 weeks and 15 days?

A. 217 B. 227
C. 207 D. 213

3. Convert 5 metres 1503 centimetres into centimetres.

A. 2030 cm

B. 1508 cm

C. 2003 cm

D. 1553 cm

MATHEMATICS

4. Add 15 kilograms 400 grams and 16 kilograms 80 grams.
A. 31.408 kg B. 31.480 kg
C. 31.840 kg D. 30.408 kg

5. Convert 15 kilograms 8 Hectograms and 80 grams into grams.
A. 18508 gms B. 15808 gms
C. 15088 gms D. 15880 gms

6. One litre is equivalent of:
A. 100 ml B. 10 desilitres
C. 110 centimetres D. 1 kilolitre

7. 1000 cm is equivalent of:
A. 1 metre B. 100 metres
C. 110 metres D. 10 metres

8. Convert 10 inch into centimetre.
A. 2.54 cm B. 25.4 cm
C. 254 cm D. None of these

9. Convert 72 km/h into m/s.
A. 20 m/s B. 27 m/s
C. 30 m/s D. 18 km/s

10. What is the weight of 1 cu cm of a iron in gram, if weight of 1 cu m of the same iron is 4060 kg?
A. 406 g B. 40.6 g
C. 4.06 g D. 0.406 g

11. What is the weight of 3.5 kL milk in kilogram, if weight of 1 cu cm milk is 1 g?
A. 35 kg B. 350 g
C. 3500 g D. 3500 kg

12. Covert 10 ream papers into quire.
A. 20 B. 100
C. 200 D. 1000

13. Convert 1 s into hour.
A. 0.00028 h B. 0.00032 h
C. 0.0028 h D. 0.0032 h

14. In a container, 3.52 kL of water can be filled. Find the capacity of container in millilitre.
A. 3.52×10^4 mL B. 3.52×10^5 mL
C. 3.52×10^6 mL D. None of these

15. If 1 m = 39.37 inch, then conversion of 1 sq cm in square inch is
A. 0.155 sq inch B. 0.165 sq inch
C. 0.175 sq inch D. 0.185 inch

ANSWERS

1	2	3	4	5	6	7	8	9	10
C	C	C	B	D	B	D	B	A	C
11	12	13	14	15					
D	C	A	C	A					

SOME SELECTED EXPLANATORY ANSWERS

1. 1 quintal = 100 kg
5.5 quintal = 5.5 × 100 = 550 kg.

2. 5 months = 5 × 30 = 150 days
5 weeks = 6 × 7 = 42 days
15 days = 15 × 1 = 15 days
207 days.

3. 1 metre = 100 cm
5 metre = 5 × 100 = 500 cm
∴ 500 cm + 1503 cm = 2003 cm.

4. 15 kg 400 gm
16 kg 080 gm
31 kg 480 gm.

5. 1 kg = 1000 gm
15 kg = 15 × 1000 gm
1 Hg = 100 gm
8 Hg = 8 × 100 gm
Total = 15000 + 800 + 80
= 15880 gm.

6. One litre is equivalent of 10 decilitre

7. 100 cm = 1 metre
$$1000 \text{ cm} = \frac{1000}{100} = 10 \text{ metres.}$$

8. ∵ 1 inch = 2.54 cm
∴ 10 inch = 10 × 1.54 cm
= 25.4 cm

9. 72 km = 72 × 1000 m = 72000 m
and 1 h = 60 min = 60 × 60 s
= 3600 s
$$\therefore \; 72 \text{ km/h} = \frac{72000}{3600}$$
= 20 m/s.

10. We know that,
1 cu m = 1000000 cu cm
∴ Weight of 1 cu m = Weight of 1000000 cu cm
Again, 4060 kg = 4060 × 1000 g

$\therefore$ Weight of 1 cu cm= $\frac{4060 \times 1000}{1000000}$ g

= 4.06 g

11. 3.5 kL = 3.5 × 1000 L = 3500 L

$\because$ 1L = 1000 cu cm

$\therefore$ 3500 L = 1000 × 3500 cu cm

$\because$ 1 cu cm = 1 g

$\therefore$ 1000 × 3500 cu cm = 1000 × 3500 g

$= \frac{1000 \times 3500}{1000}$

= 3500 kg.

12. $\because$ 1 ream = 20 quire

$\therefore$ 10 ream = 200 quire.

13. 1s = $\frac{1}{60}$min

$= \frac{1}{60 \times 60}$h

$= \frac{1}{3600}$h

= 0.00028 h.

14. $\because$ 1 kL = 10^6 mL

$\therefore$ 3.52 kL = $10^6 \times 3.52$ mL.

15. $\because$ 1 m = 39.37 inch

$\therefore$ 1 sq m = $(39.37)^2$ sq inch

= 1549.9969 sq inch

$\Rightarrow$ 10000 sq cm = 1549.9969 sq inch

$\Rightarrow$ 1 sq cm = $\frac{1549.9969}{1000}$ sq inches

= 0.155 sq inch.

MONEY

This units is meant to provide people experience in dealing with collection of coins and notes.

Indian currency is known as rupee. It is sub-divided into 100 paise. The Indian currency is available in normal value of ₹ 1, 2, 5, 10, 20, 50, 100, 500 and 1000. The coins of ₹ 10, 5, 2, 1 and 50 paise is also in vogue today.

Indian currency is counted in hundreds, thousands, lakhs and crores.

EXAMPLES

Example 1 : Convert (*a*) ₹ 38 into paise.
(*b*) 6000 paise into rupees.

Solution: (*a*) ₹ 38 = 38 × 100 = 3800 paise.

(*b*) 6000 paise = $\frac{6000}{100}$ = ₹ 60.

Example 2 : Find the value in paise of the following.

(*a*) ₹ 27.75 (*b*) ₹ 53.50
(*c*) ₹ 90.60

Solution: (*a*) ₹ 27.75 = 27 × 100 + 75
= 2775 paise

(*b*) ₹ 53.50 = 53 × 100 + 50
= 5350 paise

(*c*) ₹ 90.60 = 90 × 100 + 60
= 9060 paise

Example 3 : Suneeta has 3 thousand-rupee note, 7 five-hundred-rupee note, 4 hundred rupee note and 6 twenty-rupee note. Her mother gave her 3 hundred-rupee note, 7 fifty-rupee note 3 ten-rupee note, 6 five-rupee note, 3 coins of 2 rupee, 5 coins of one rupee and 18 coins of fifty paise. How much money does she have?

Solution: Total money = 3 × ₹ 1000 + 7 × ₹ 500 + 4 × ₹ 100 + 6 × ₹ 20 + 3 × ₹ 100 + 7 × ₹ 50 + 3 × ₹ 10 + 6 × ₹ 5 + 3 × ₹ 2 + 5 × ₹ 1 + 18 × 50 paise.
= ₹ 3000 + ₹ 3500 + ₹ 400 + ₹ 120 + ₹ 300 + ₹ 350 + ₹ 30 + ₹ 30 + ₹ 6 + ₹ 5 + ₹ 9 = ₹ 7750.

Example 4 : Seema had Rs. 58.50. Roma had Rs. 45.50 and Veena had Rs. 38.00. Then how much money did they have in all?

Solution: Seema had Rs. 58.50
Roma had Rs. 45.50
Veena had Rs. 38.00
Total Rs. 142.00

Example 5 : Sonam bought a cinema ticket for Rs. 162.50. She gave a 500 rupee note. How much money will she get back with the ticket?

Solution:
Rs. 500.00
– Rs. 162.50
Rs. 337.50

Hence, she will get Rs. 337.50 rupees back with the ticket.

Example 6 : Shabnam and her friends went to shopping. She bought things for Rs. 158, Rs. 137 and Rs. 22. Shabnam had four 50 rupee note. How much money should she borrow from her friends to pay the bill?

Solution:

	four 50-rupee note = Rs. 200
Rs. 158	Rs. 317
+ Rs. 137	– Rs. 200
+ Rs. 22	
Rs. 317	Rs. 117

Hence, she should borrow Rs. 117 from her friends to pay the bill.

MULTIPLE CHOICE QUESTIONS

1. Shankar has 320 rupees. He bought a bat for 170 rupees, a ball for 105 rupees. Now how much money is left with him?
A. 54 rupees B. 145 rupees
C. 45 rupees D. None of these

2. Sonalika bought biscuits for 157 rupees and a packet of chips for 126 rupees. How much money will she pay to shopkeeper?
A. 283 rupees B. 238 rupees
C. 183 rupees D. 328 rupees

3. Fateh Singh had 640 rupees. He spent 380 rupees at the fair, and 130 rupees at bus-fare. How much money is left with him?
A. 310 rupees B. 103 rupees
C. 130 rupees D. None of these

4. Three friends wanted to buy a cricket bat and a ball. Bhola gave ₹ 48.50, Ramu gave ₹ 55.50 and Hari gave ₹ 38.00. How much money did they gave in all?
A. ₹ 124 B. ₹ 142
C. ₹ 412 D. None of these

5. Shyam booked railway ticket for ₹ 262.50. He gave a 500 rupee note. How much money will he get back with the ticket?
A. ₹ 235.70 B. ₹ 237.70
C. ₹ 235.50 D. ₹ 237.50

6. Namrata and her friends went to shopping. She bought T-shirt, school bag and a pair of shoes for ₹ 580, ₹ 370 and ₹ 420 respectively. She had two five hundred rupee note. How much money should she borrow from her friends to pay the bill?
A. ₹ 307 B. ₹ 370
C. ₹ 730 D. None of these

7. ₹ 368 is equal to:
A. 3680 paise B. 36800 paise
C. 38600 paise D. None of these

8. 4873 paise is equal to:
A. 487 rupees and 39 paise
B. 48 rupees and 37 paise
C. 48 rupees and 73 paise
D. None of these

9. Sum of ₹ 82.34 and 57.28 is:
A. ₹ 193.62 B. ₹ 139.26
C. ₹ 130.62 D. None of these

10. Difference of ₹ 384.39 and ₹ 254.57 is:
A. ₹ 129.82 B. ₹ 129.28
C. ₹ 182.29 D. None of these

11. Sharmajee distributed his cash property to his three children. Gaurav got two fifth of the property. Saurabh got $\frac{5}{8}$ of the rest and Sudha got ₹ 1,80,000 then Gaurav got:
A. ₹ 3200000 B. ₹ 2300000
C. ₹ 32000 D. ₹ 320000

12. If ₹ 6548 is distributed equally in 5 person then each will get:
A. ₹ 1306.90 B. ₹ 1903.60
C. ₹ 1309.60 D. None of these

13. Vinod has 368 rupees and his elder brother gave him 467 rupees. He went to shopping and bought a shirt and two paints. But he found that he has lost 660 rupees of them. How much money is needed to pay the bill?
A. 835 rupees
B. 1495 rupees
C. Can not be determined
D. None of these

14. What is the value of ₹ 71.87 in paise?
A. 1787 paise B. 7178 paise
C. 1778 paise D. None of these

ANSWERS

1	2	3	4	5	6	7	8	9	10
C	A	C	B	D	B	B	C	D	A
11	12	13	14						
D	C	C	D						

SOME SELECTED EXPLANATORY ANSWERS

1. Price of bat = 170 rupees
Price of ball = 105 rupees
Total = 275 rupees
Hence, left money = 320 – 275 = 45 rupees.

6. Total expenditure = ₹ 580 + ₹ 370 + ₹ 420
= ₹ 1370
She had the amount = 2 × 500 = ₹ 1000
Hence, required money to pay the bill
= 1370 – 1000 = ₹ 370
Hence, She should borrow ₹ 370 to pay the bill.

11. Gaurav got $\frac{2}{5}$ part of property

∴ rest part $= 1-\frac{2}{5}=\frac{3}{5}$

Saurabh got $\frac{5}{8}$ of the rest part $=\frac{3}{5}\times\frac{5}{8}=\frac{3}{8}$

Hence, Sudha got $1-\left(\frac{2}{5}+\frac{3}{8}\right)=\frac{9}{40}$

From question, $\frac{9}{40}$ = ₹ 180000.

∴ Whole property $= 180000\times\frac{40}{9}$ = ₹ 800000

Hence, Gaurav got $= 800000\times\frac{2}{5}$ = ₹ 320000.

PATTERNS

A similar image turns of figure of series is known as pattern. The study of patterns helps the students in learning to observe relationships to find connections and to make predictions, generalisations and deductions. Understanding of patterns nourish the kinds of mathematical thinking that helps students in problem solving. One who understands the patterns well; he may become a good thinker. Understanding of patterns is used as a problem solving tool.

EXAMPLES

Example 1 : Which of the following will be the next term of the given pattern?

(*a*) 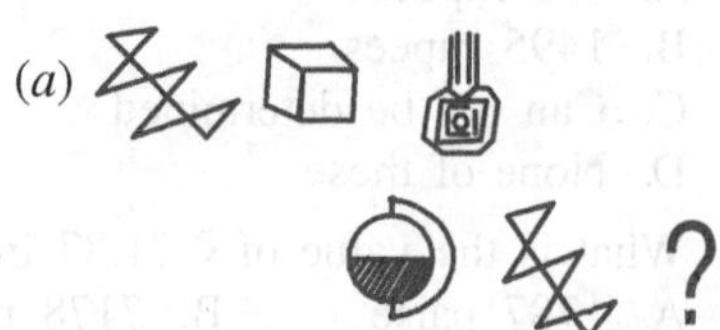

(*b*) 

Solution: (*a*) It is clear from the given pattern that the next term will be [cube].

(*b*) Obviously, the next turn will be [umbrella].

Example 2 : Study the patterns and fill in the missing numbers.

(*a*) 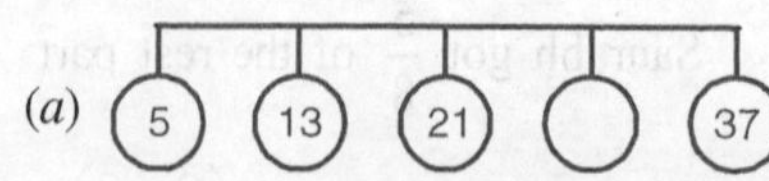

(*b*) 

(*c*) 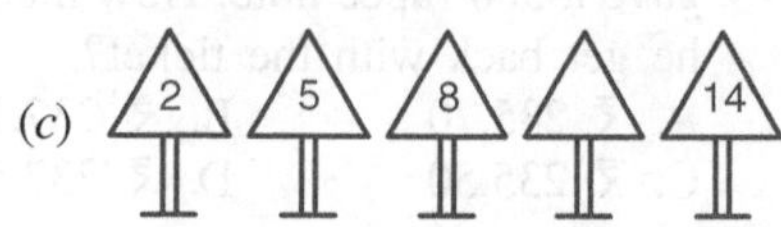

(*d*) 

(*e*) 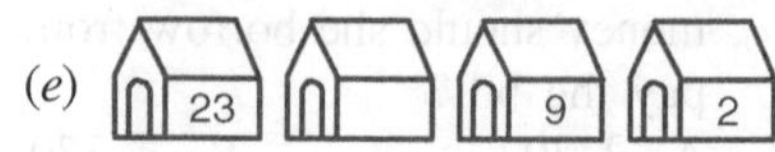

(*f*) 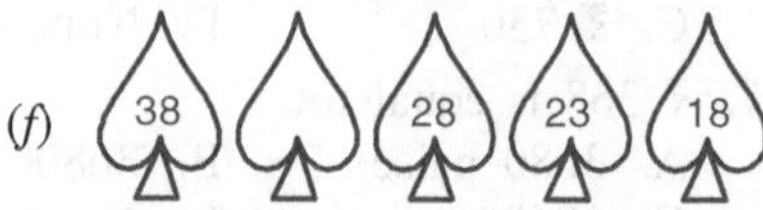

Solution : (*a*) 5 + 8 = 13, 13 + 8 = 21

21 + 8 = 29, 29 + 8 = 37

(*b*) 5 + 5 = 10, 10 + 5 = 15

15 + 5 = 20

(*c*) 2 + 3 = 5, 5 + 3 = 8

8 + 3 = 11, 11 + 3 = 14

(*d*) 7 + 5 = 12, 12 + 5 = 17

17 + 5 = 22, 22 + 5 = 27

(*e*) 23 – 7 = 16, 16 – 7 = 9

9 – 7 = 2

(*f*) 38 – 5 = 33, 33 – 5 = 28

28 – 5 = 23, 23 – 5 = 18

MULTIPLE CHOICE QUESTIONS

1. Problem Figures

Answer Figures

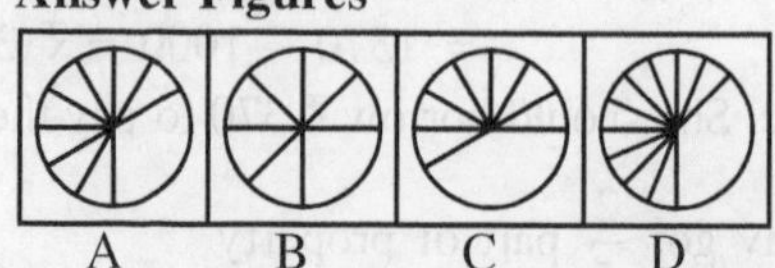

2. Problem Figures

Answer Figures

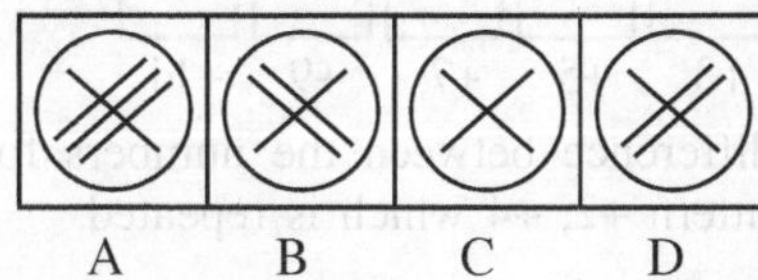

A B C D

3. Problem Figures

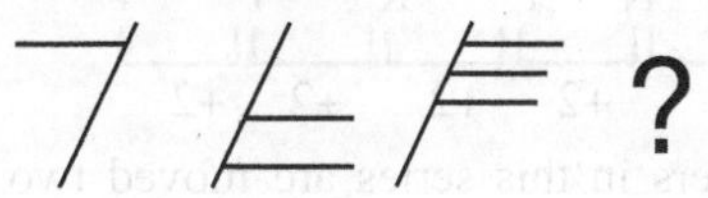

Answer Figures

A B C D

4. Problem Figures

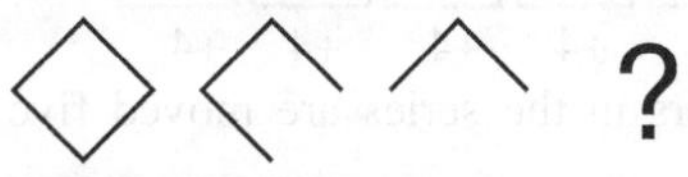

Answer Figures

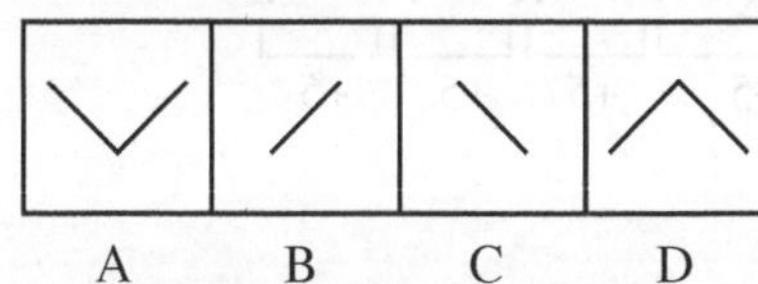

A B C D

5. Problem Figures

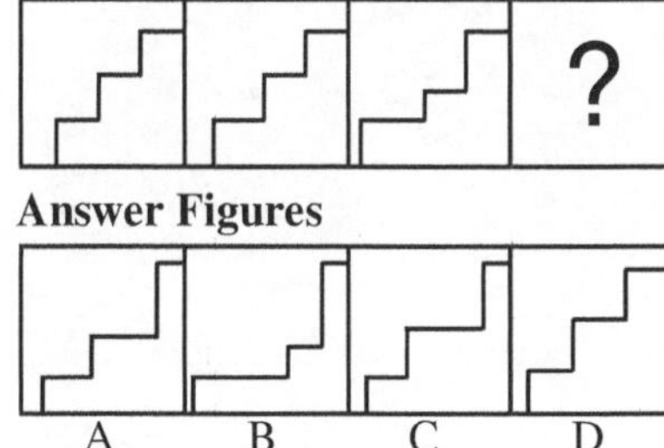

Answer Figures

A B C D

6. Problem Figures

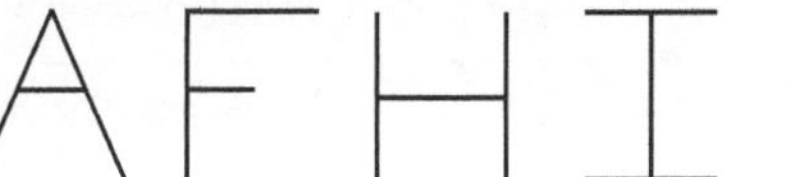

Answer Figures

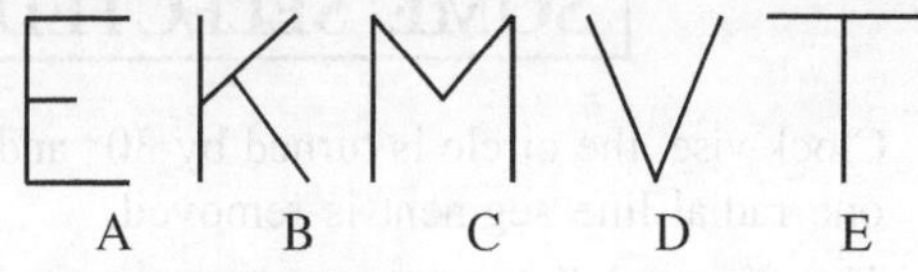

A B C D E

7. Problem Figures

Answer Figures

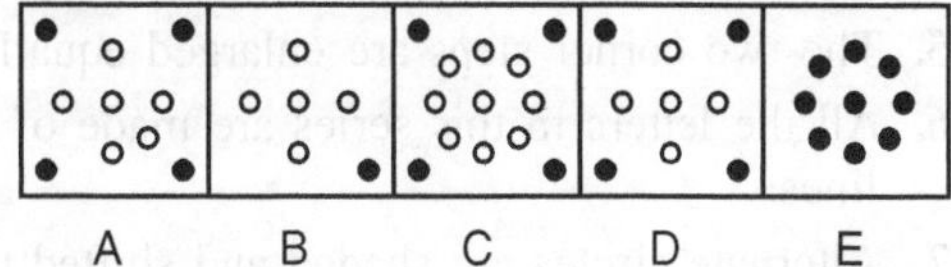

A B C D E

8. 1, 6, 12, 19, 27, ?

A. 38 B. 35
C. 36 D. 54

9. 2, 6, 14, 30, 62, ?

A. 126 B. 128
C. 120 D. 130

10. 4, 7, 12, 19, 28, ?

A. 35 B. 37
C. 39 D. 41

11. 11, 13, 17, 19, 23, ?

A. 37 B. 31
C. 25 D. 41

12. L N P R T ?

A. U B. V
C. W D. Y

13. Z X V T ?

A. Q B. S
C. R D. P

14. A E I M Q ?

A. T B. U
C. V D. W

15. A F K P ?

A. T B. U
C. W D. X

ANSWERS

1	2	3	4	5	6	7	8	9	10
C	D	A	C	B	B	D	C	A	C
11	**12**	**13**	**14**	**15**					
C	B	C	B	B					

MATHEMATICS

SOME SELECTED EXPLANATORY ANSWERS

1. Clockwise, the circle is turned by 30° and also one radial line segment is removed.
2. The diagonal line segments are removed one by one in a set order.
3. In alternate figures, the horizontal line is moved to the other side of the slanting line and two more horizontal lines are then added.
4. Anticlockwise, one side of the' rhombus is removed at each step.
5. The two corner steps are enlarged equally.
6. All the letters in this series are made of three lines.
7. Alternate circles are shaded and shifted to the corners anticlockwise.
8. The difference between the numbers in the series increases by 1, after beginning from 5, *i.e.,*

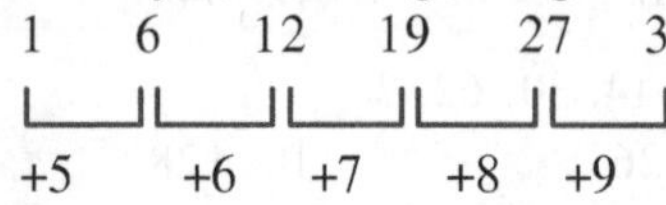

9. The difference between the numbers in the series doubles each time, after beginning from 4, *i.e.,*

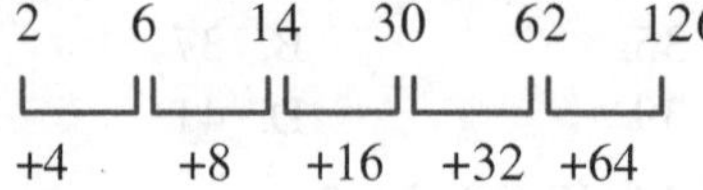

10. The difference between the consecutive numbers in the series increases by 2 at each step.

    4 7 12 19 28 39

    +3 +5 +7 +9 +11

11. The difference between the numbers follows the pattern +2, +4 which is repeated.
12. The series follows the +2 pattern. *i.e.*

    L N P R T V

    +2 +2 +2 +2 +2

13. The letters in this series are moved two steps backward.

    Z X V T R

    −2 −2 −2 −2

14. The letters in the series are moved four steps forward.

    A E I M Q U

    +4 +4 +4 +4 +4

15. The letters in the series are moved five steps forward.

    A F K P U

    +5 +5 +5 +5

DATA HANDLING

Data handling is a tool to express or depict the given information using various types of symbols. In our day to day life we come across several kinds of information such as—

(*i*) Distance covered by a car in 10 hours.

(*ii*) Books sold by a shopkeeper in the last week.

(*iii*) Runs scored by Sachin in World Cup. etc.

The information collected in all such cases is called 'data'. In other words, "Data is a collection of numbers gathered to give some information." It is usually gathered in the context of a situation that we want to study. To give a clear idea of what it represents the data is represented in graphic form.

Organising Data

Generally data is given in unorganised or raw form. We organise it systematically to draw meaningful conclusions. *e.g.,* the temperature of 30 days of a city was given as : 30º, 25º, 29º, 28º, 25º, 30º, 30º, 26º, 29º, 28º, 30º, 30º, 28º, 26º, 30º, 28º, 22º, 29º, 28º, 30º, 26º, 28º, 30º, 27º, 30º, 25º, 28º, 29º, 30º and 29º then how many days the city faced the highest temperature?

It's not easy to answer the question looking at the given temperatures which are written haphazardly. So we arrange the data using tally marks. Thus we easily give the answer.

Temperatures	Tally makrs	No. of Days
25º	|||	3
26º	|||	3
27º	|	1
28º	~~||||~~ |||	8
29º	~~||||~~	5
30º	~~||||~~ ~~||||~~	10
		N = 30

Thus, we can easily determine that the city faced the highest temperature 30º till 10 days.

Grouping Data

In the above example we have seen that same degree of temperatures occurs frequently *e.g.,* 30º occurs 10 days, 28º occurs 8 days, 29º occurs 5 days and so on. This information can depicted graphically.

In our daily life we often deal with different type of data. Some of them are small but some of them are large data. For example, following is the daily attendence of employees of an office in April. 14, 16, 46, 24, 22, 43, 25, 24, 32, 43, 14, 30, 27, 31, 32, 28, 18, 19, 30, 27, 16, 25, 11, 12, 31, 30, 17, 48, 19, 23.

The frequency distribution table of the above observations would be so long. So, it is convenient to prepare groups of observations *e.g.,* 0-10, 10-20, 20-30 and so on. Then we obtain a frequency distribution of the groups of observations using tally marks.

Groups	Tally Marks	Frequency
10-20	~~||||~~ ~~||||~~	10
20-30	~~||||~~ ||||	9
30-40	~~||||~~ ||	7
40-50	||||	4
		N = 30

Data arranged in this manner is known as the grouped and the distribution is called a grouped frequency distribution. Now we can derive many meaningful inferences like—

(*i*) Most of the days the attendences were poor.

(*ii*) Only four days the attendence were maximum and so on.

Variate: The quantity that we measure from observation to observation is called a variate.

Class Interval: Every data is generally divided into small group using some interval is said to be in class-interval, *e.g.,* 0-5, 5-10, 10-15, etc.

Class-size: The difference between the true upper limit and true lower limit of a class gives the size of the class-interval, *e.g.,* class-size of the class interval 0-5 is 5.

Mid-value: The variable value which is midway between the lower and upper limit of a class is called its mid-value, *e.g.,* mid-value of class interval 0-5 is

$$\frac{0+5}{2} = 2.5$$

Frequency: The number of observations corresponding to particular class is said to be the frequency of that class, *e.g.,* frequency of the interval

5-10 is 6. It means 6 persons have got 5 or more articles but less than 10.

Cumulative Frequency: The sum of the preceding frequencies is called cumulative frequency. Last frequency of cumulative frequency column is equal to the sum of the frequencies.

Class Limits: Every interval has two limits. Lower number of the interval is called lower limit while upper number of the interval is called upper limit, *e.g.,* in interval 0-5, 0 is the lower limit while upper number of the interval 5 is called upper limit.

Diagrammatic representation of data

(a) One-dimensional diagrams are (i) Bar diagram, (ii) Sub-divided bar diagram, (iii) Multiple bar diagram.
(b) Two-dimensional diagrams are (i) Squares, (ii) Circles, (iii) Pie-diagrams.
(c) Three-dimensional diagrams are (i) Cubes, (ii) Cylinders, (iii) Spheres.
(d) Pictograms.
(e) Cartograms.

Graphical representation of data

(a) Histogram
(b) Frequency polygon
(c) Frequency curve
(d) Cumulative frequency curve or ogive.

Histogram: A statistical graph that represents by the height of a rectangular column the number of times that each class of result occurs in a sample or experiment, *e.g.,* the following table presents the number of matured persons in the age group (15-50) in a city.

Age Group	No. of Persons	Age Group	No. of Persons
15-20	200	35-40	750
20-25	350	40-45	900
25-30	475	45-50	100
30-35	600		

Then the histogram of the data is given below:

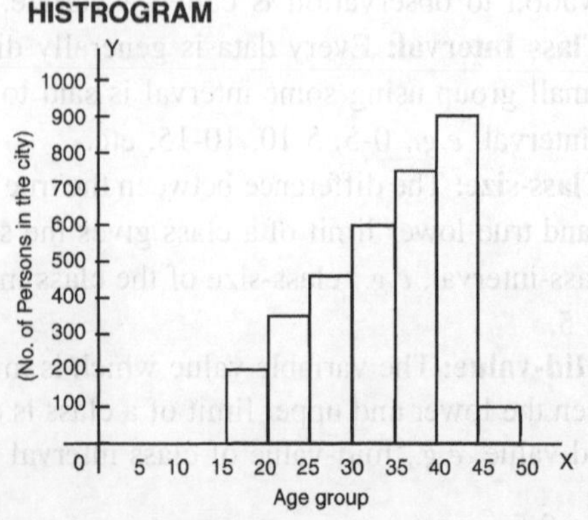

Frequency Polygon: The graph obtained when the mid-point of the tops of the rectangle in a histogram with equal class interval are joined by line segment. The area under the polygon is equal to the total area of the rectangle, *e.g.,* the frequency polygon of above given data is shown in figure.

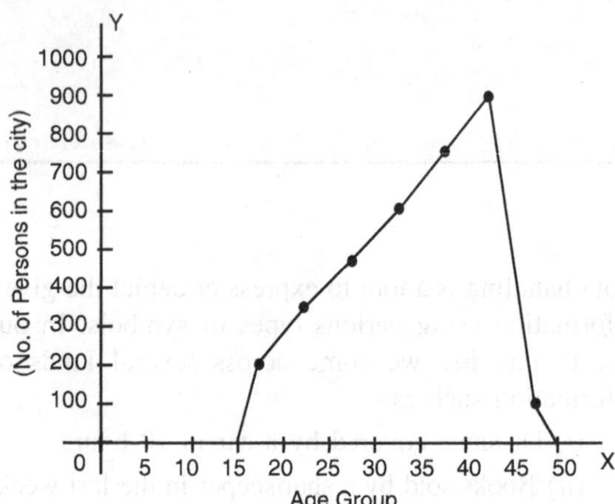

Bar Graph: A graph consisting of bars whose lengths are proportional to quantities in a set of data. It can be used when one axis cannot have a numerical scale, *e.g.,* to show how many different columns of flowers grow from a packet of mixed seeds given in figure.

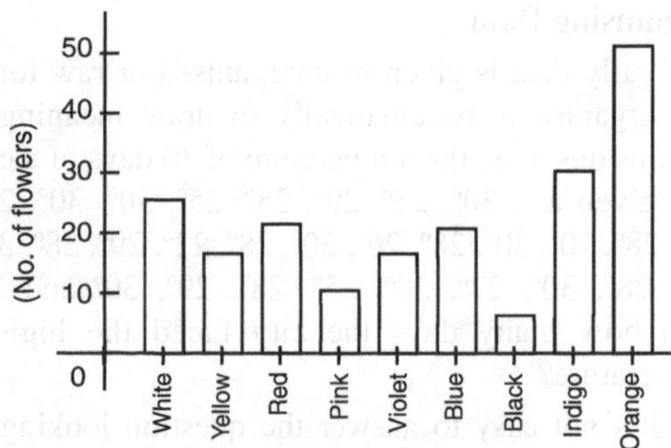

Pie-chart: A diagram in which proportions are illustrated as sectors of a circle. The relative area of the sectors representing the different proportions, *e.g.,* if out of 100 military personnels 25 personnels use tank, 30 personnels use warship, 40 personnels use aircraft and rest of them use rifles. Then pie-chart of the above data is

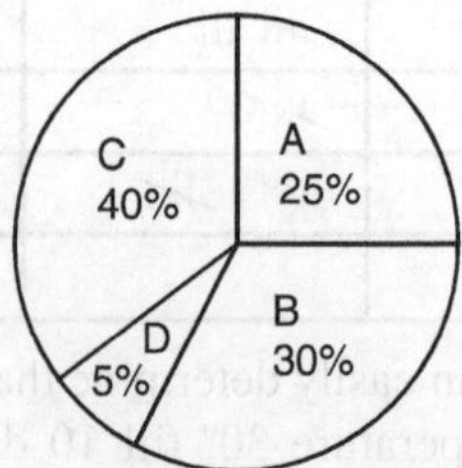

$$\text{A use tank} = \frac{25 \times 360}{100} = 90°$$

$$\text{B use warship} = \frac{30 \times 360}{100} = 108°$$

$$\text{C use aircraft} = \frac{40 \times 360}{100} = 144°$$

$$\text{D use rifles} = \frac{5 \times 360}{100} = 18°$$

THE MEAN

Arithmetic Mean (Raw Data)

The arthmetic mean is commonly used as average. All of us are familiar with the "average of the data". The arithmetic mean is obtained by adding the values of the items and dividing by the number of items.

For example : The marks obtained by 10 students are 22, 35, 37, 38, 29, 27, 34, 36, 28, 34. The mean of marks is:

Solution: No. of students = 10

$$\text{Mean } (\bar{x}) = \frac{22+35+37+38+29+27+34+36+28+34}{10}$$

$$= \frac{320}{10} = 32 \text{ marks.}$$

Arithmetic Mean (Grouped Data)

If the data is grouped with no class interval. If x_i (i = 1, 2, 3 .... n) are n observations to which weights attached are f_i (i = 1, 2, 3 .... n), then weighted mean is:

$$\bar{x} = \frac{\sum_{i=1}^{n} f_i x_i}{\sum_{i=1}^{n} f_i}$$

Again, if the data is grouped with class interval and frequencies are gien with these then,

$$\text{mean } \bar{x} = \frac{\Sigma fx}{\Sigma f} \qquad \text{where, } f = \text{frequency}$$

$$x = \text{mid-value}$$

For example: Calculate the mean for the following distribution:

Marks	Frequency
10-20	6
20-30	8
30-40	15
40-50	7
50-60	3
60-70	0
70-80	1

Solution:

Marks	Mid-value (x)	Frequency (f)	$f \times x$
10-20	15	6	15 × 6 = 90
20-30	25	8	25 × 8 = 200
30-40	35	15	35 × 15= 525
40-50	45	7	45 × 7 = 315
50-60	55	3	55 × 3 = 165
60-70	65	0	65 × 0 = 0
70-80	75	1	75 × 1 = 75
		$\sum f = 40$	$\sum fx = 1370$

$$\text{Mean } \bar{x} = \frac{\sum fx}{\sum f} = \frac{1370}{40} = 34.25$$

THE MEDIAN

It is defined as the value of that item of the arrayed series which divides the whole series into two equal parts. The middle item of the array is called the median. For example, in the 3, 5, 9, 13, 15, 21, 22, 25, 29, the median is 15. When the data is ungrouped and the number of items is odd, the median is $\left(\frac{n+1}{2}\right)$ th value. If n is even, there will be two central items, *i.e.,* $\left(\frac{n}{2}\right)$ th item and $\left(\frac{n}{2}+1\right)$ th item. The average value of these two items will be median in such case.

When the data is grouped,

$$\text{Median} = l + \frac{\frac{N}{2} - C}{f} \times i$$

Where l is the lower limit of the class in which median lies. N is the sum of frequencies, i is the magnitude of class interval, f is the frequency of the median class and C is the cumulative frequency of the class preceding the median class.

Example: 1. The median of the scores 25, 28, 20, 8, 10, 15, is:

Solution: Ascending order:
8, 10, 15, 20, 25, 28

$$\text{Median} = \frac{15+20}{2} = \frac{35}{2} = 17.5$$

Example: 2. Calculate the median of the following:

Income in Rs :	20	21	22	23	24
No. of persons :	2	4	4	3	6

Solution:

Income (x)	Frequency (f)	C. frequency (c)
20	2	2
21	4	6
22	4	10
23	3	13
24	6	19

Here N = 19, which is odd.

$\therefore$ Median = Income of $\left(\frac{n+1}{2}\right)$th term

= Income of $\left(\frac{19+1}{2}\right)$th term

= Income of 10th term

= Rs 22.

THE MODE

Mode is defined as that item of the series which occurs most frequently. In a frequency distribution, mode is that variable which has the maximum frequency. When we say that average age of Indians is 60 years, it means that model age of the people in India is 60 years *i.e.* most of the people in India die after 60 years.

For example: Find the mode of given set of numbers: 2, 2, 3, 5, 4, 3, 2, 3, 3, 3, 5

Solution: Arranging the number with same value together, we get, 2, 2, 2, 3, 3, 3, 3, 4, 5, 5 mode of this data is 3 because it occurs more frequently then other observations.

In case of grouped data the formula to be used is

$$l+\frac{f-f_1}{2f-(f_1+f_2)}\times i$$

Where l = lower limit of the model class
f = frequency of the model class
f_1 = frequency of the class preceding the model class
f_2 = frequency of the class succeeding of the model class
i = class interval

For example: Find the mode of the following frequency distribution.

Class interval	Frequency
24.5-29.5	1
29.5-34.5	1
34.5-39.5	3
39.5-44.5	4
44.5-49.5	7
49.5-54.5	9
54.5-59.5	3
59.5-64.5	8
64.5-69.5	4

Solution: Mode = $l+\frac{f-f_1}{2f-(f_1+f_2)}\times i$

$= 49.5+\frac{9-7}{2\times 9-7-3}\times 5$

= 49.5 + 1.2 = 50.7.

MULTIPLE CHOICE QUESTIONS

1. Rain fall (in mm) of 25 days of a city is given below:
38, 27, 36, 40, 20, 24, 36, 28, 22, 25, 36, 40, 27, 38, 26, 30, 28,, 32, 37, 38, 39, 27, 25, 28, 30. The average daily rainfall is:
A. 30.08 mm B. 32.08 mm
C. 31.80 mm D. 31.08 mm

2. The temperature (in degree) of 30 days is given below:
38, 36, 26, 42, 38, 27, 40, 30, 36, 35, 28, 25, 42, 40, 28, 38, 41, 28, 25, 32, 38, 36, 26, 30, 38, 30, 36, 40, 32.
The mean of the temperature (in degree) is:
A. 33.366 B. 33.663
C. 33.633 D. None of these

3. The number of observation corresponding to particular class is called:
A. Class-Interval B. Class-Limit
C. Class-Size D. Frequency

4. The median of 7, 11, 23, 36, 42, 50, 61, 73, 110 and 120 is:
A. 54.5 B. 5.55
C. 55.5 D. None of these

5. The mode of the date 14, 11, 16, 22, 14, 23, 17, 14, 26, 28, 11, 14, 26 is:
A. 0.14 B. 1.4
C. 14.0 D. 140

6. In a frequency distribution, the variable which has the maximum frequency is called:
A. Mean B. Histogram
C. Mid value D. Mode

Directions (Q.No. 7-9): *The pie chart, drawn here, shows the spending of a country on various sports during a particular year. Study the pie-chart carefully and answer the questions that follow:*

Per cent of Money Spent on Various Sports for One Year

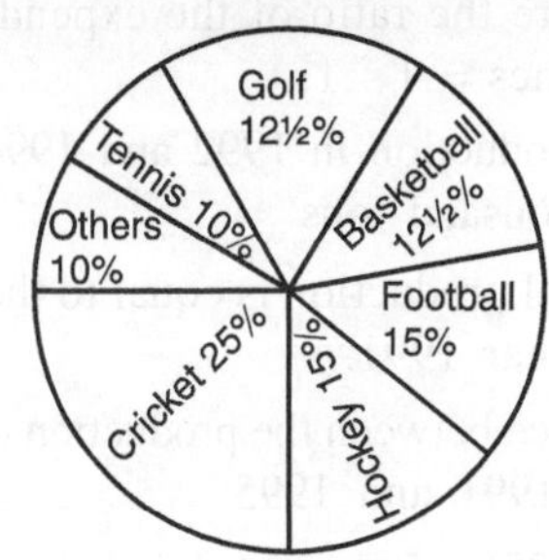

7. Graph shows that the most popular game of the country is:
   A. Football
   B. Hockey
   C. Cricket
   D. Tennis

8. Out of the following the country spent the same amount on:
   A. Hockey and Cricket
   B. Hockey and Football
   C. Hockey and Golf
   D. Tennis and Golf

9. The ratio of the total amount spent on football to that spent on hockey is:
   A. 2 : 1 B. 1 : 1
   C. 1 : 2 D. 3 : 2

Directions (Q.No. 10-12): *The following bar graph shows the production of food grains in India during certain year. Study the graph carefully and answer the questions given below:*

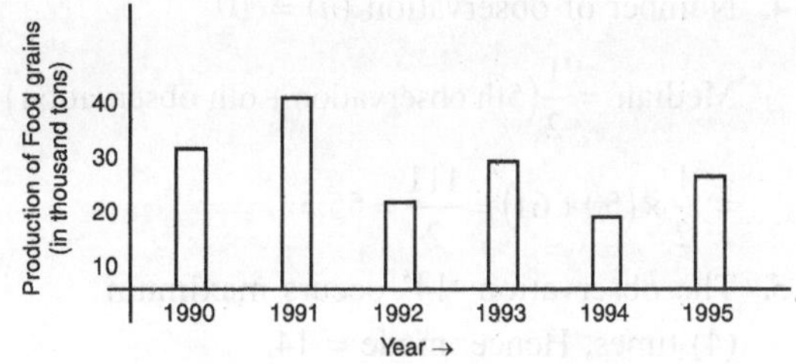

10. Total food grain production in 1992 and 1994 is equal to the production during which of the following years?
    A. 1990 B. 1991
    C. 1993 D. 1995

11. The difference between the foodgrain productions of 1991 and 1995 is:
    A. 500 tons B. 1000 tons
    C. 5000 tons D. 10000 tons

12. Percentage increase in the production of foodgrains in the year 1995 over the year 1994 is:
    A. 15% B. 30%
    C. 50% D. 100%

13. We organise the data:
    A. to fulfil our hobbey
    B. because it is said to do
    C. to get a meaningful conclusion
    D. None of these

14. To arrange the data we use:
    A. tally mark B. mean
    C. median D. None of these

15. Difference between upper limit and lower limit is called:
    A. Class interval B. Class-size
    C. Mid-value D. Class-limit

ANSWERS

1	2	3	4	5	6	7	8	9	10
D	C	D	C	C	D	C	B	B	B
11	**12**	**13**	**14**	**15**					
C	D	C	A	B					

SOME SELECTED EXPLANATORY ANSWERS

1. Average daily rainfall

$$= \frac{\begin{array}{c}20\times1+22\times1+24\times1+25\times2+26\times1\\+27\times3+28\times3+30\times2+32\times1+36\times3\\+37\times1+38\times3+39\times1+40\times2\end{array}}{1+1+1+2+1+3+3+2+1+3+1+3+1+2}$$

$$= \frac{777}{25} = 31.08 \text{ mm.}$$

2. Mean of the temperature

$$= \frac{\begin{array}{c}25\times2+26\times2+27\times1+28\times4\\+30\times3+32\times2+35\times1+36\times4\\+38\times5+40\times3+41\times1+42\times2\end{array}}{2+2+1+4+3+2+1+4+5+3+1+2}$$

$$= \frac{1009}{30} = 33.633 \text{ degree.}$$

MATHEMATICS

4. Number of observation (n) = 10

Median = $\frac{1}{2}$(5th observation + 6th observation)

$= \frac{1}{2} \times (50 + 61) = \frac{111}{2} = 55.5$

5. The observation '14' occurs maximum (4) times, Hence, mode = 14.

7. According to the graph, expenditure on cricket is the maximum. Therefore cricket is the most popular game.

8. According to the graph, equal amount has been spent on Hockey and Football.

9. Expenditure on the game of Football = 15% of total amount spent

   Expenditure on the game of Hockey = 15% of total amount spent

   Therefore the ratio of the expenditure on the two games = 1 : 1.

10. Total production in 1992 and 1994 = 20 + 15 = 35 thousand tons

    This total production is equal to the production in the year 1991.

11. Difference between the production of foodgrains during 1991 and 1995

    = 35 – 30 = 5 thousand tons.

12. Percentage increase in foodgrain production = $\frac{30-15}{15} \times 100 = 100\%$.

GEOMETRY

(*i*) **Point:** A minute geometrical figure that only determines a location is known as point. Point is a tiny dot which has no lenght or breadth.

Example: Tip of a compass, the pointed end of a needle etc.

(*ii*) **Line Segment:** A geometrical figure which has length but no breadth. It has two end points. Line segment is a part of line. It is the shortest route between two points. If a line segment has two end points X and Y then it is denoted as $\overline{XY}$ or $\overline{YX}$.

Example: An edge of box, An edge of book, pencil etc.

(*iii*) **Line:** If a line segment is extended endlessly in both directions is known as line. We can not draw a complete line and also can not determine its length because it has no end point in the both directions. So we put arrow marks to indicate its endlessness.

e.g., A B

We put minimum two points to determine the line and indicate the line as $\overleftrightarrow{AB}$ or $\overleftrightarrow{BA}$.

(*iv*) **Ray:** A ray is a portion of a line. It has only one end point. It start from a point and goes endlessly to the another direction. Length of ray is also can not be determined. Ray is drawn as A B and indicated as $\overrightarrow{AB}$.

Examples: Sun rays, Ray of light from a torch etc.

(*v*) **Intersecting line:** If two lines have a common point they are called intersecting lines.

Examples: X (the letter of english alphabet; the sign of mathematical operation.)

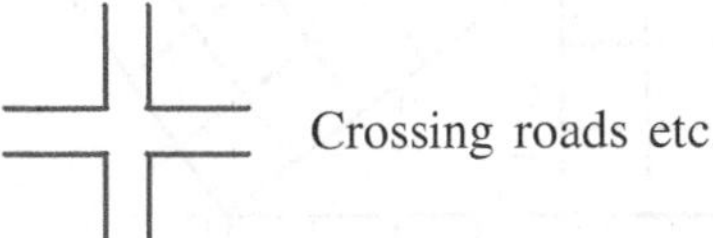

Crossing roads etc.

(*vi*) **Parallel lines:** If two lines do not intersect up to thier endless points is called parallel lines. In other words, lines like these which do not meet to each-other are said to be parallel; these lines are called parallel lines.

Examples: Railway tracks, opposite edges of scale, opposite edges of table etc.

(*vii*) **Curves:** The doodling line is called curve. If we draw some drawing without lifting the pencil from the paper and without using a rular, all are curves.

(*a*) **Simple curve:** If a curve does not cross itself. It is also known as open curve.

(*b*) **Closed curve:** If a curve crosses to each other and surround some space is called closed curve.

(*viii*) **Concurrent Lines:** The point where three or more lines intersect.

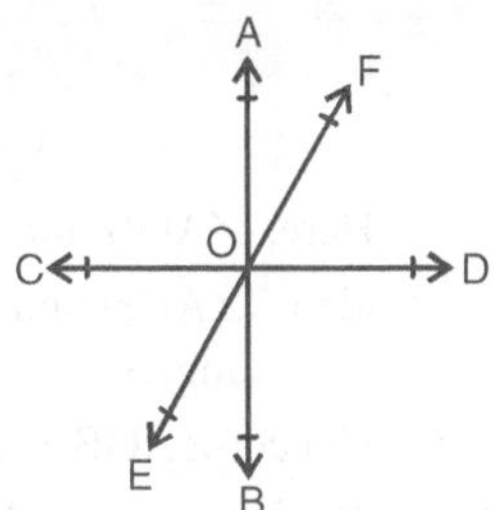

(*ix*) **Angle:** A geometrical figure which have two rays with single end point is called angle.

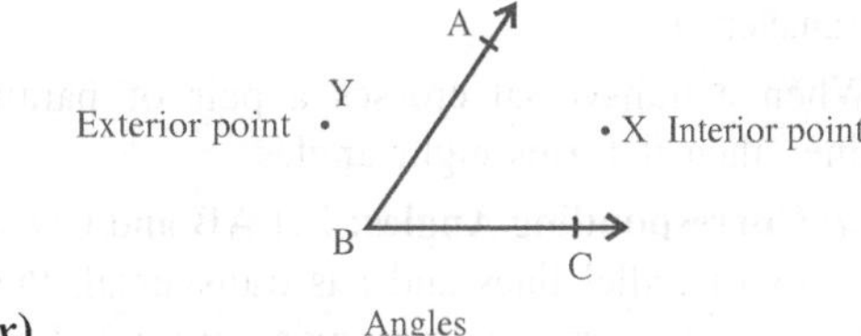

(*x*) Angles

- Acute angle (Between 0° and 90°)
- Right angle (Equal to 90°)
- Reflex angle (Between 180° and 360°)
- Obtuse angle (Between 90° and 180°)
- Straight angle (Equal to 180°)
- Complete angle (Equal to 360°)

(*xi*) **Complementary Angles:** Two angles whose sum is 90º is said to be complementary to each other *i.e.*, complement of $\theta = (90^\circ - \theta^\circ)$.

(*xii*) **Supplementary Angles:** Two angles whose sum is 180º is said to be supplementary to each other. *i.e.*, supplementary of $\theta = (180^\circ - \theta^\circ)$.

(*xiii*) **Adjecent Angles:** If two angles have a common vertex then they are said to be adjecent.
Here, ∠BAC and ∠CAD are adjacent angles.

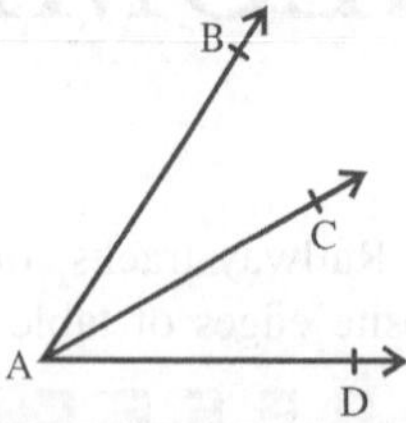

(*xiv*) **Linear pair:** If the pair of adjacent angles are also the supplementary to each-other then it is said to be a linear pair.
Here, ∠ABC and ∠CBD are adjacent and ∠ABC + ∠CBD = 180º

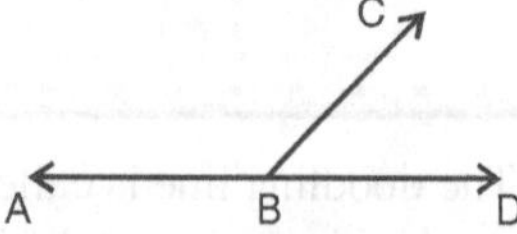

Hence, both the angles are linear pair.

(*xv*) **Vertically opposite Angles:** If two lines intersect at a point, the pair of alternative angles is called vertically opposite angles.
Vertically opposite angles are always equal.

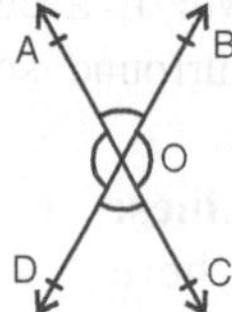

Here, ∠AOB and ∠DOC
also ∠AOD and ∠BOC are vertically opposite angles.

Hence, ∠AOB = ∠DOC and ∠AOD = ∠BOC

(*xvi*) **Angles on parallel lines:**
Transversal: If a straight line crosses two or more than two parallel lines then it is called transversal.
When a transversal crosses a pair of parallel lines then it forms eight angles.

(*a*) **Corresponding Angles:** Let AB and CD are two parallel lines and *l* is transversal, then, pair of corresponding angles are equal *i.e.*,

∠1 = ∠6 ∠3 = ∠8
∠2 = ∠5 ∠4 = ∠7

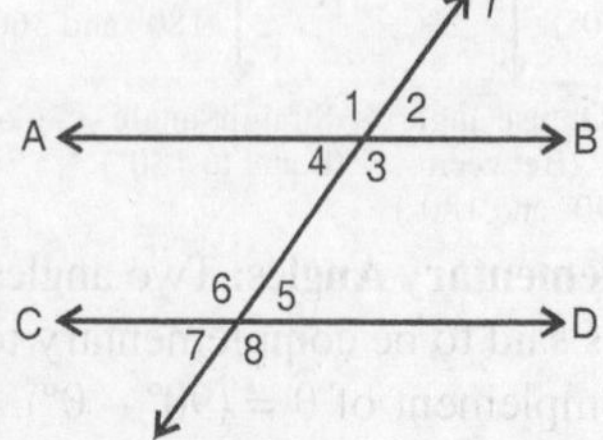

(*b*) **Alternate Interior Angles:** In the above figure ∠4 and ∠5 also ∠3 and ∠6 are the pairs of alternate interior angles. The pair of alternate interior angles are equal.

Hence, ∠4 = ∠5 and ∠3 = ∠6

* **The sum of interior angles on the same side of transversal is 180°.**

i.e., ∠3 + ∠5 = 180° also ∠4 + ∠6 = 180°.

TRIANGLE

A closed figure with three sides which has three angles and three vertices is called triangle.

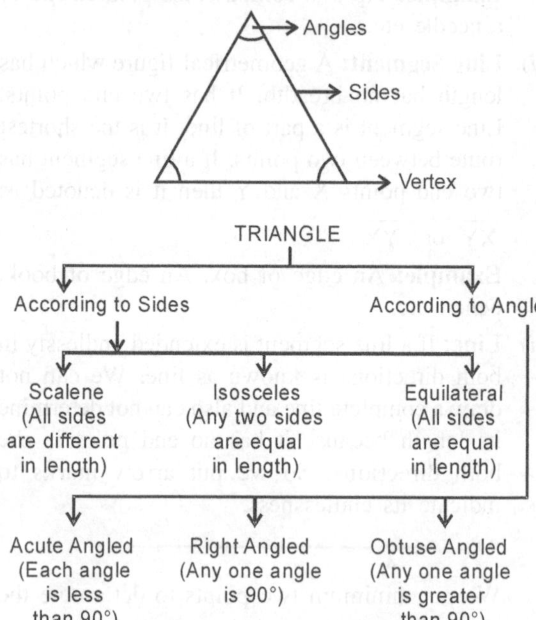

Pythagoras Theorem: In a right angled triangle the square of the hypotenuse equals the sum of the square of its sides.

i.e., $AC^2 = AB^2 + BC^2$

$\Rightarrow \quad b^2 = c^2 + a^2$

$= a^2 + c^2$

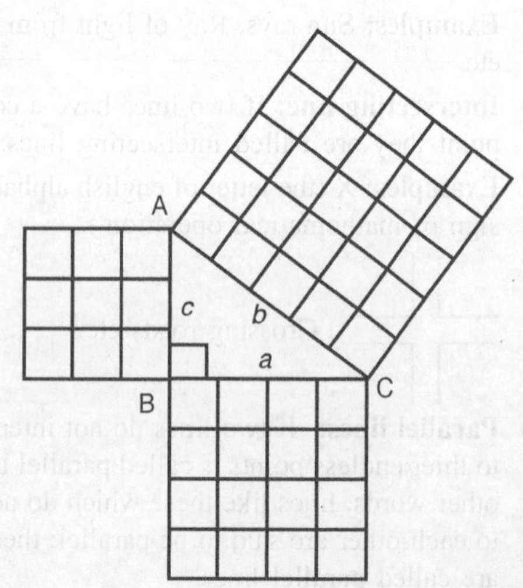

Axiom & Theorems on lines and angles

Axioms:

1. If a ray stands on a line, then the sum of two adjacent angles so formed is 180º.
2. If the sum of two adjacent angles is 180º, then the non-common arms of the angles form a line.
3. If a transversal intersects two parallel lines, then each pair of corresponding angles is equal.
4. If a transversal intersects two lines such that a pair of corresponding angles is equal, then the two lines are parallel to each other.

Theorems

1. If two lines intersect each other, then the vertically opposite angles are equal.
2. If a transversal intersects two parallel lines, then each pair of alternate interior angles is equal.
3. If a transversal intersects two lines such that a pair of alternate interior angles is equal, then the two lines are parallel.
4. If a transversal intersects two lines, then each pair of interior angles on the same side of the transversal is supplementary.
5. If a transversal intersects two lines such that a pair of interior angles on the same side of the transversal is supplementary, then the two lines are parallel.
6. Lines which are parallel to the same line are parallel to each other.
7. The sum of the angles of a triangle is 180º.
8. If a side of a triangle is produced, then the exterior angle so formed is equal to the sum of the two interior opposite angles.

Axiom and Theorems on Triangles

Axiom 1. (SAS congruence rule) : Two triangles are congruent if two sides and the included angle of one triangle are equal to the corresponding two sides and the included angle of the other triangle.

Theorems

1. **(ASA congruence rule):** Two triangles are congruent if two angles and the included side of one triangle are equal to two angles and the included side of other triangle.
2. Angle opposite to equal sides of an isosceles triangle are equal.
3. The sides opposite to equal angles of a triangle are equal.
4. **(SSS congruence rule):** If three sides of one triangle are equal to the three sides of another triangle, then the two triangles are congruent.
5. **(RHS congruence rule):** If in two right triangles the hypotenuse and one side of one triangle are equal to the hypotenuse and one side of the other triangle, then the two triangles are congruent.
6. If two sides of a triangle are unequal, the angle opposite to the longer side is larger (or greater).
7. In any triangle, the side opposite to the larger (greater) angle is longer.
8. The sum of any two side of a triangle is greater than the third side.

QUADRILATERAL

A figure which is made up of joining four non-collinear points called quadrilateral. Or, A figure which is made up of four sides, angles and four vertices is called quadrilateral. The sum of all angles of a quadrilateral is 360°.

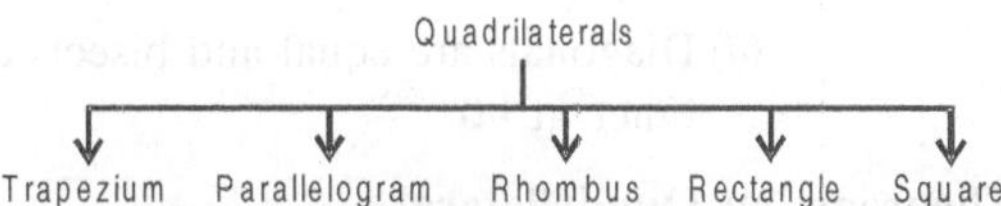

(*i*) **Parallelogram:** If both pairs of opposite angles of a quadrilateral are equal and both pair of opposite sides are equal and parallel is called parallelogram.

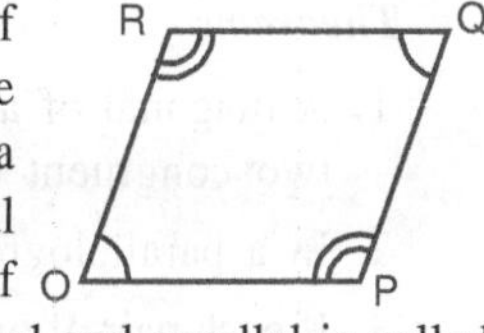

Here, (*a*) QR || OP and OR || PQ

(*b*) ∠ORQ = ∠QPS and ∠ROP = ∠PQR

(*c*) RQ = OP and OR = PQ

(*d*) diagonals bisect each other.

(*ii*) **Trapezium:** If one pair of opposite sides are parallel of a quadrilateral, then it is called a trapezium.

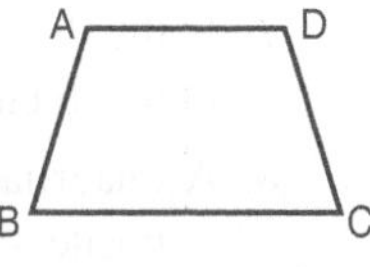

Here, AD || BC

(*iii*) **Rhombus:** A parallelogram in which all the sides are equal is called a rhombus.

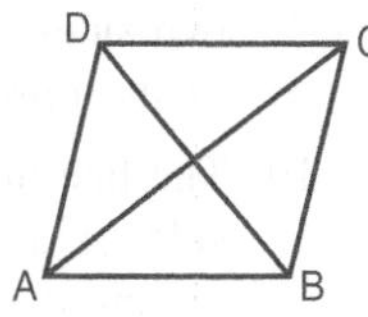

Here, (*a*) □ ABCD is a parallelogram

(*b*) AB = BC = CD = AD

(*c*) Diagonals bisect each-other at 90°.

(*iv*) **Rectangle:** A parallelogram in which each angles is right angle and pair of opposite sides are equal is called rectangle.

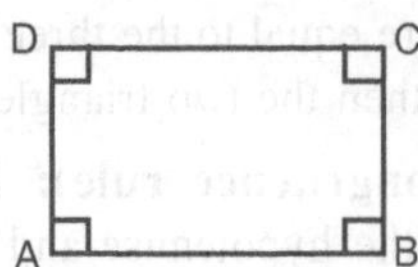

Here, (*a*) ABCD is a parallelogram.

(*b*) AB = CD and AD = BC

(*c*) Angles are right angle

(*d*) Diagonals are equal and bisects each-other.

(*v*) **Square:** A parallelogram which have all sides equal and each angle is right angle is called a square.

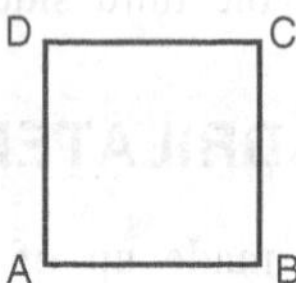

Here, (*a*) AB = BC = CD = AD

(*b*) AB || CD and AD || BC

(*c*) Angles are right angle

(*d*) Diagonals are equal and bisects each-other at 90°.

Theorems on Quadrilateral

Theorems

1. A diagonal of a parallelogram divides it into two congruent triangles.
2. In a parallelogram, opposite sides are equal.
3. If each pair of opposite sides of a quadrilateral is equal, then it is a parallelogram.
4. In a parallelogram, opposite angles are equal.
5. If in a quadrilateral, each pair of opposite angles is equal, then it is a parallelogram.
6. The diagonals of a parallelogram bisect each other.
7. If the diagonals of a quadrilateral bisect each other, then it is a parallelogram.
8. A quadrilateral is a parallelogram if a pair of opposite sides is equal and parallel.
9. The line segment joining the mid-points of two sides of a triangle is parallel to and half of the third side.
10. The line drawn through the mid-point of one side of a triangle, parallel to another side bisects the third side.

Theorems on Areas of Parallelograms and Triangles

Theorems

1. Parallelograms on the same base and between the same parallels are equal in area.
2. Two triangles on the same base (or equal bases) and between the same parallels are equal in area.
3. Two triangles having the same base (or equal bases) and equal areas lie between the same parallels.

CIRCLE

A circle is a set of points in a plane which are at a constant distance from a given fixed point.

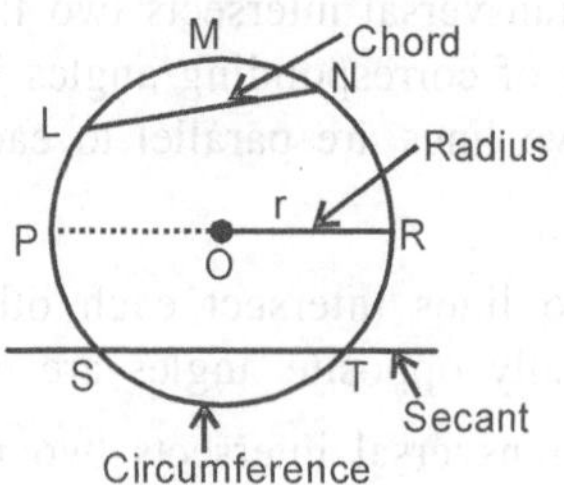

Here, The Fixed point O is called the centre. The constant distance is called radius. PR is the diameter of the circle.

Diameter is twice of radius.

Arch: A continuous part of a circle.

Secant: A line which intersect a circle in two distinct points.

Chord: A line segment joining any two points on the circle.

Segment: A chord divides the circle into two parts and each parts is called segment.

Semicircle: A diameter divides the circle into two equal parts and each part is called semicircle.

Central Angle: An angle whose vertex is centre of a circle is called central angle.

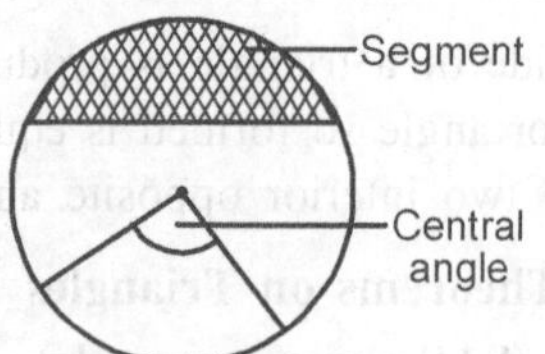

Cyclic Quadrilateral: If all four vertices of a quadrilateral lie on the circumference of a circle, then such a quadrilateral is called a cyclic quadrilateral.

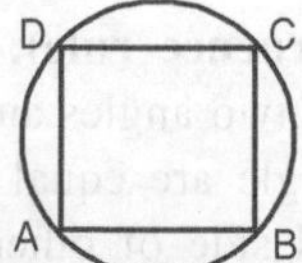

SOME IMPORTANT RESULTS

- The perpendicular from the centre to any chord bisects the chord.

- The line joining the centre of the mid point to any chord of a circle is perpendicular to the chord.
- Equal chords of congruent circles are equidistant from the corresponding centres.
- Chords of congruent circles which are equidistant from the corresponding centres, are equal.
- Equal chords of a circle are equidistant from the centre.
- Equal chords of a circle subtend equal angle at the centre.
- The angle subtended by an arc at the centre of a circle is double the angle subtended by it at any point on the remaining part of the circle.
- Angles in the same segment of a circle are equal.
- If the sum of any pair of opposite angles of a quadrilateral is 180°, then the quadrilateral is cyclic.
- The angle made in a semicircle is always a right angle.
- The arc of a circle subtending a right angle at any point of the circle in its alternate segment is a semicircle.

Theorems on Circles

1. Equal chords of a circle subtend equal angles at the centre.
2. If the angles subtended by the chords of a circle at the centre are equal, then the chords are equal.
3. The perpendicular from the centre of a circle to a chord bisects the chord.
4. The line drawn through the centre of a circle to bisect a chord is perpendicular to the chord.
5. There is one and only one circle passing through three given non-collinear points.
6. Equal chords of a circle (or of congruent circle) are equidistant from the centre (or centres).
7. Chords equidistant from the centre of a circle are equal in length.
8. The angle subtended by an arc at the centre is double the angle subtended by it at any point on the remaining part of the circle.
9. Angles in the same segment of a circle are equal.
10. If a line segment joining two points subtends equal angles at two other points lying on the same side of the line containing the line segment, the four points lie on a circle (*i.e.* they are concyclic).
11. The sum of either pair of opposite angles of a cyclic quadrilateral is 180º.
12. If the sum of a pair of opposite angles of a quadrilateral is 180º, the quadrilateral is cyclic.

EXAMPLES

Example 1. If AB || CD and CD || EF. Also EA ⊥ AB. If ∠ BEF = 55º, find the values of x, y and z.

Solution : $y + 55° = 180°$

(Interior angles on the same side of the transversal ED)

Hence, $y = 180° - 55° = 125°$

Again $x = y$

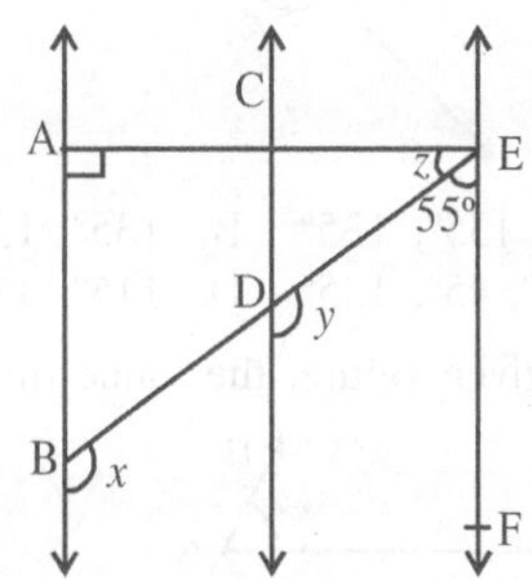

(AB || CD, Corresponding angles axiom)

Hence $x = 125°$

Now, since AB || CD and CD || EF, so, AB || EF,

So, $\angle EAB + \angle FEA = 180°$

Hence, $90° + z + 55° = 180°$

Which gives $z = 35°$

Example 2. If ABCD is a cyclic quadrilateral and ∠ DBC = 55º and ∠ BAC = 45º, find ∠ BCD.

Solution : $\angle CAD = \angle DBC = 55°$

(Angles in the same segment)

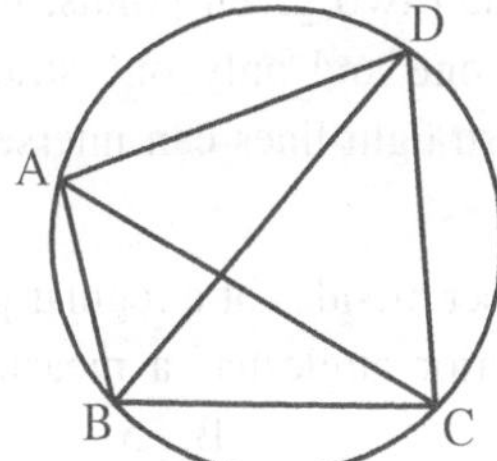

Hence, $\angle DAB = \angle CAD + \angle BAC$

$= 55° + 45° = 100°$

But $\angle DAB + \angle BCD = 180°$

(Opposite angles of a cyclic quadrilateral)

So, $\angle BCD = 180° - 100° = 80°$

Example 3. Measure x in given figure.

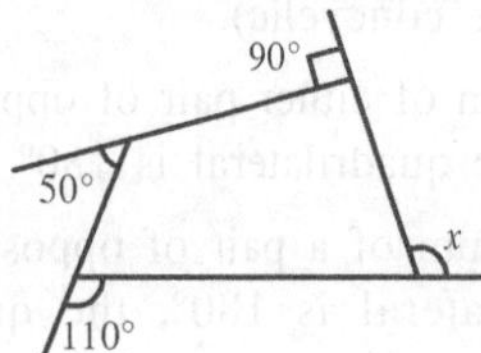

Solution :

$$x + 90° + 50° + 110° = 360°$$
$$x + 250° = 360°$$
$$x = 110°$$

MULTIPLE CHOICE QUESTIONS

1. Lines l and m intersect at O, forming angles as shown in figure. If $x = 45°$, then values of y, z and u are

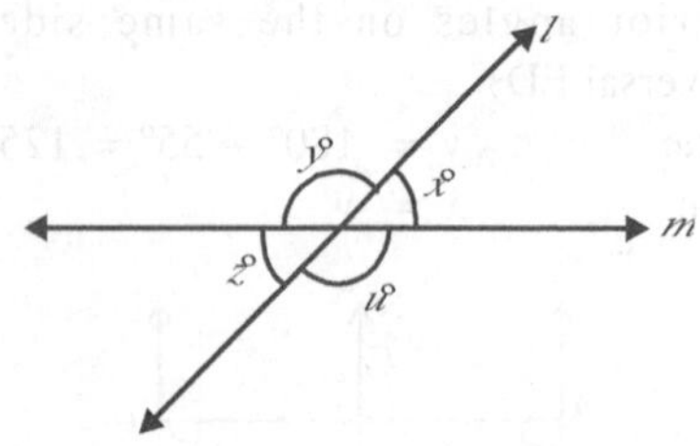

A. 45º, 135º, 135º B. 135º, 135º, 45º
C. 135º, 45º, 135º D. 115º, 45º, 115º

2. In the given figure, the value of x and y are

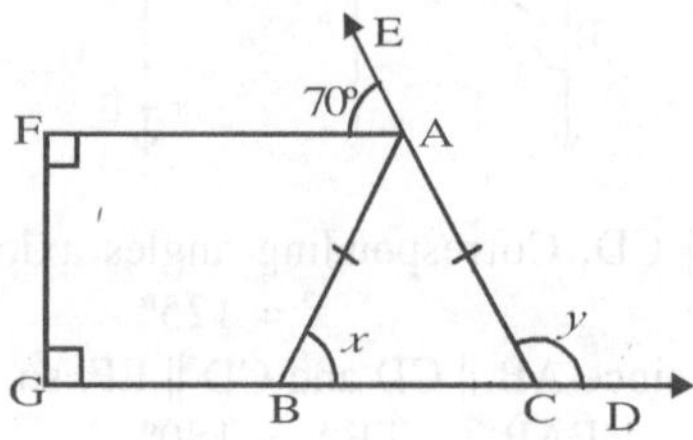

A. 70º, 110º B. 110º, 70º
C. 120º, 60º D. 70º, 90º

3. Which of the following statements is false?

A. A line segment can be produced to any desired length

B. Through a given point, only one straight line can be drawn

C. Through two given points, it is possible to draw one and only one straight line

D. Two straight lines can intersect in only one point

4. The number of sides of a regular polygon whose each exterior angle has a measure of 45° is:

A. 7 B. 5
C. 10 D. 8

5. ABCD is a parallelogram. The values of x, y and z are:

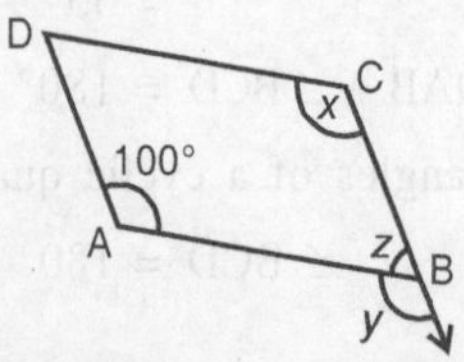

A. 80º, 100º, 100º B. 80º, 80º, 100º
C. 80º, 100º, 180º D. 100º, 100º, 80º

6. In a parallelogram RSTU if $m\ \angle R = 70°$, then all the other angles x, y, z are:

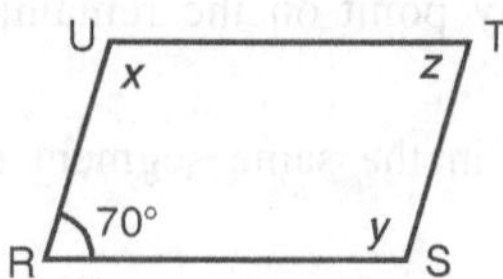

A. 101º, 101º, 70º B. 110º, 70º, 110º
C. 110º, 110º, 70º D. None of these

7. If ABCD is a parallelogram, OB = 4 and AC is 5 more than BD. Then OA equal to:

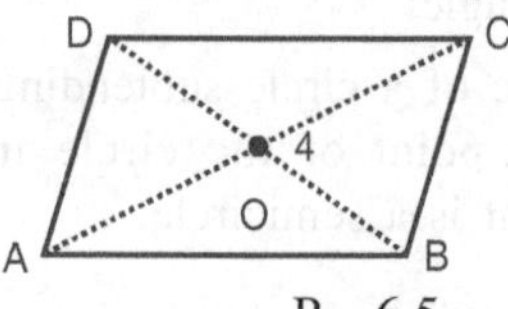

A. 6.6 B. 6.5
C. 5.5 D. 5.6

8. ABCD is a rectangle. Its diagonals meet at O. Find x, if OA = $2x + 4$ and OD = $3x + 1$.

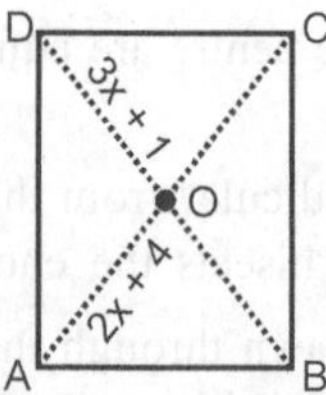

A. 3
B. 4
C. 5
D. None of these

9. If an angle equals to two-third of its complementary then the measurement of the angle is:

A. 45º B. 63º
C. 90º D. 36º

10. According to the given figure the value of x is:

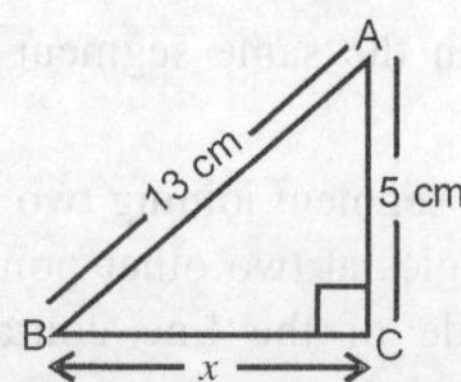

A. 13 cm B. 5 cm

C. 12 cm D. None of these

11. The length of the chord which is at a distance of 6 cm from the centre of the circle and the radius of the circle is 10 cm is:

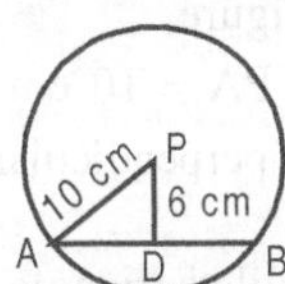

A. 8 cm B. 16 cm

C. 6 cm D. None of these

12. If, ∠PQR and ∠RQS form a linear pair then the value of x is:

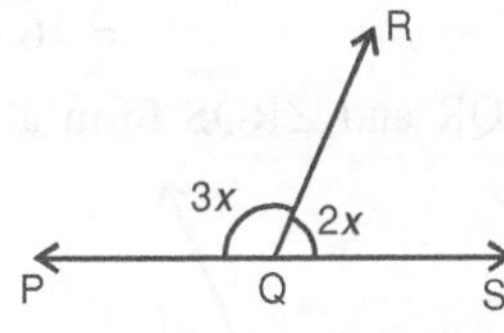

A. 45° B. 54°

C. 63° D. 36°

13. Lines l and n intersect at the point O. The value of x, y and z if a = 72° is:

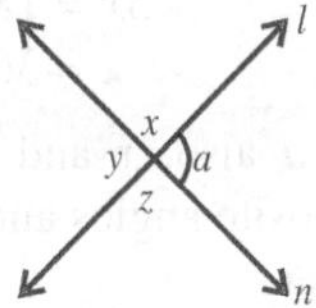

A. 72°, 72°, 108°

B. 108°, 108°, 72°

C. 72°, 108°, 72

D. 108°, 72°, 108°

14. In the given figure, ΔXYZ is an isosceles triangle with XY = XZ and ∠XYZ = 60°. Then ∠YPZ equal to:

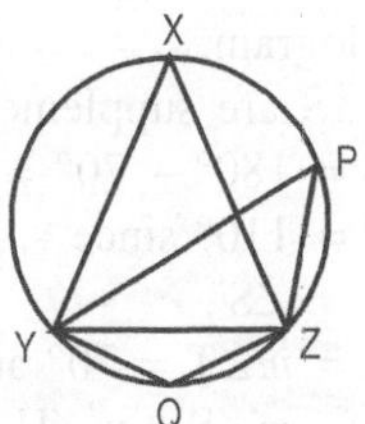

A. 120°

B. 60°

C. can not be determined

D. None of these

15. According of the given figure then the value of x if $\overline{AB} \| \overline{CD}$ is:

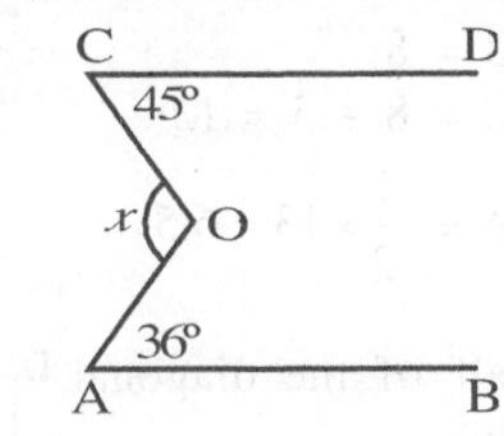

A. 9° B. 90°

C. 80° D. 81°

ANSWERS

1	2	3	4	5	6	7	8	9	10
C	A	B	D	D	C	B	A	D	C
11	**12**	**13**	**14**	**15**					
B	D	D	B	D					

SOME SELECTED EXPLANATORY ANSWERS

1. $x = z$ [∵ vertically opposite angles]

⇒ $x = 45°$ ⇒ $z = 45°$

$y + x = 180°$ [∵ linear pair]

⇒ $y = 180° - 45°$

∴ $y = 135°$

Also, $y = u$ [∵ vertically opposite angles]

⇒ $u = 135°$.

2. In Δ ABC,

∠ ABC = ∠ ACB = x

and $x + y = 180°$

Now, ∠ EAF = ∠ ACB = 70° [corresponding angles]

∴ $x = 70°$

⇒ $y = 180° - 70°$

∴ $y = 110°$.

3. Since, an infinite number of straight lines can be drawn through a given point.

Hence, (b) is false statement.

4. Total measure of all exterior angles = 360°

Measure of each exterior angles = 45°

Therefore, the number of exterior angles

$$= \frac{360}{45} = 8$$

Hence, The polygon has 8 sides.

5. C is opposite to A.

Hence, $x = 100°$ (opposite angles property)

$y = 100°$ (measure of angle corresponding to ∠x)

$z = 80°$ (since ∠y, ∠z is a linear pair).

6. Given $m\angle R = 70°$

Then $m\angle T = 70°$

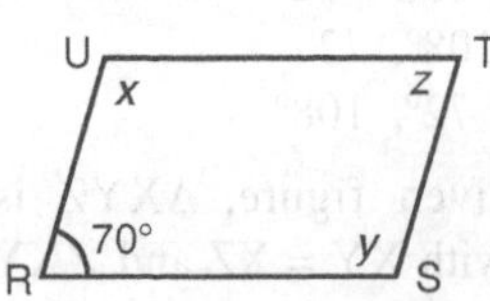

Since, $\angle R$ and T are opposite angles of a parallelogram.

and $\angle R$ and $\angle S$ are supplementary,

$m\angle S = 180° - 70° = 110°$

Also, $m\angle U = 110°$ since – $\angle U$ is opposite to $\angle S$

Thus, $m\angle R = m\angle T = 70°$ and

$m\angle S = m\angle U = 110°$.

7. OB = 4 then OD also is 4

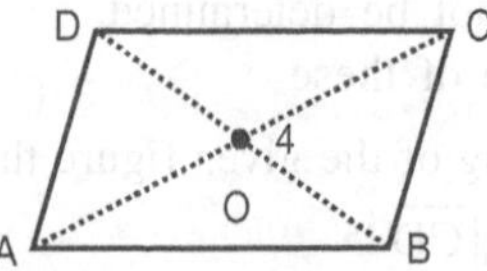

So, PB = 8,

Hence, AC = 8 + 5 = 13

Hence, $OA = \frac{1}{2} \times 13 = 6.5$

8. $\overline{OD}$ is half of the diagonal $\overline{DB}$, $\overline{OA}$ is half of the diagonal $\overline{AC}$. Diagonals are equal.

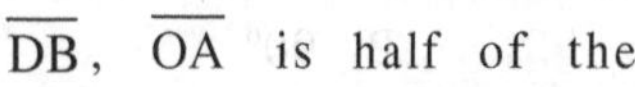

Hence, their halves are also equal.

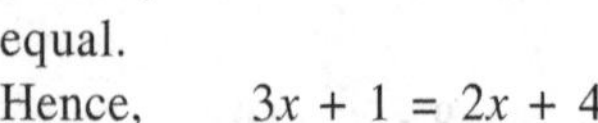

Hence, $3x + 1 = 2x + 4$

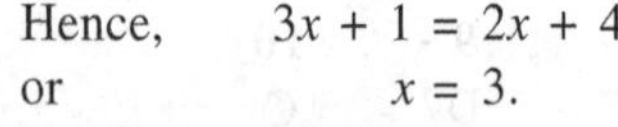

or $x = 3$.

9. Let the angle be $x°$

According to question, $x° = \frac{2}{3}(90° - x)$

$\Rightarrow \quad x = \frac{180° - 2x°}{3}$

$\Rightarrow \quad 3x° = 180° - x°$

$\Rightarrow \quad 5x° = 180°$

$\therefore \quad x° = \frac{180°}{5} = 36°$.

10. From Pythagoras theorem,

$AC^2 + BC^2 = AB^2$

$\Rightarrow \quad 5^2 + x^2 = 13^2$

$\Rightarrow \quad x^2 = 169 - 25$

$\therefore \quad x = \sqrt{144} = 12$ cm.

11. Let AB is the chord of the circle with centre P and radius 10 cm.

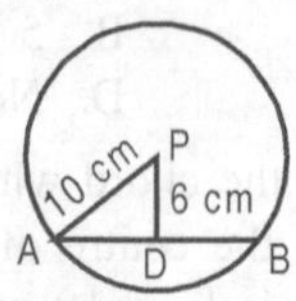

According to figure,

PD = 6 cm and PA = 10 cm.

As we know that perpendicular from centre bisect the chord.

Now in right angled triangle ADP,

$AD = \sqrt{AP^2 - PD^2} = \sqrt{10^2 - 6^2} = \sqrt{100 - 36}$

$= \sqrt{64} = 8$ cm

Hence, Length of chord AB = 2AD = 2 × 8 = 16 cm.

12. Since $\angle PQR$ and $\angle RQS$ form a linear pair

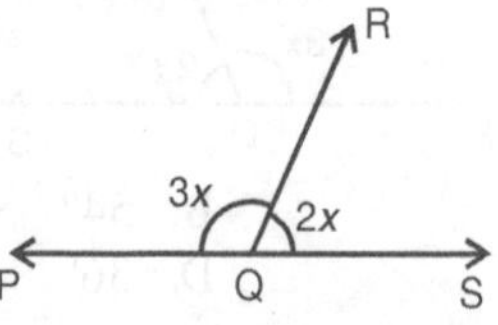

Hence, $\angle PQR + \angle RQS = 180°$

$\Rightarrow \quad 3x + 2x = 180°$

$\Rightarrow \quad 5x = 180°$

$\therefore \quad x = 36°$.

13. Since, y and a also, x and z are the pairs of vertically opposite angles and it is always equal to each - other

Hence, $\angle y = 72°$

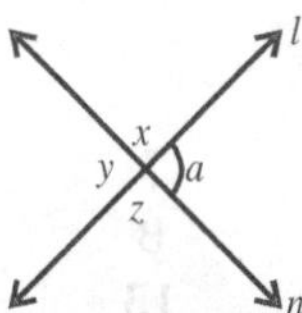

Again since, $\angle x$ and $\angle y$ are linear pair

Hence, $\angle x + \angle y = 180°$

$\therefore \quad x = 180° - 72° = 108°$

And $\angle z = 108°$ (Vertically opposite angle).

14. Since XY = XZ

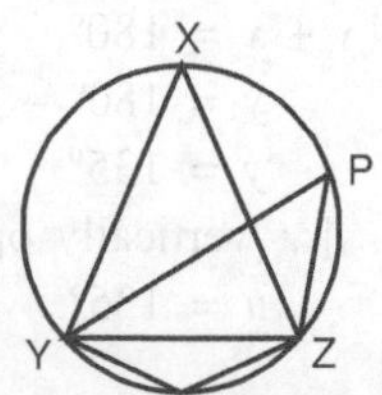

$\Rightarrow \quad \angle XYZ = \angle XZY = 60°$

In ΔXYZ,

$\angle YXZ = 180° - (60° + 60°) = 60°$

$\therefore \quad \angle YPZ = \angle YXZ = 60°$

(angle in the same segment).

SOLID AROUND US

We are familiar with the solid things in our day-by-day life. We use these things in playing, eating, drinking and in many other works *e.g.*, Book, cups, bricks, dices, glasses etc. We can differenciate these things in different kinds.

Name of shape	*Examples*
Sphere	Ball, Marble
Cylinder	Water bottle, Glass
Cube	Dice
Cuboid	Bricks, Box
Cone	Cone of ice-cream Conical cap

Cuboid : A cuboid has six faces, each one a rectangle. It has 12 edges. For example, a rectangular brick.

Let Length = l, Breadth = b and Height = h, then,

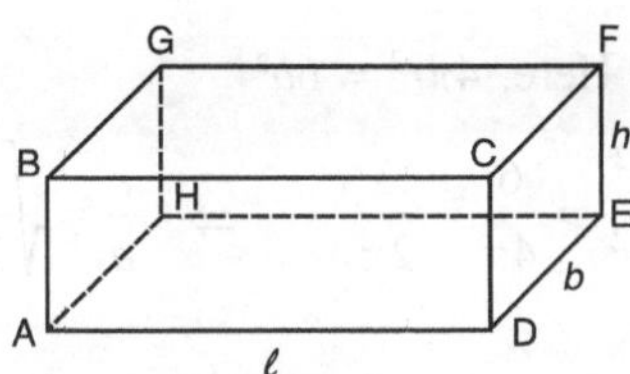

1. Volume = (Length × Breadth × Height) = lbh
2. Whole Surface Area = $2(lb + bh + lh)$
3. Diagonal = $\sqrt{l^2 + b^2 + h^2}$
4. Area of 4 walls of a room = $2 \times h\ (l + b)$

Cube : In a cube, Length = Breadth = Height

1. Volume = $(l)^3$
2. Length = $\sqrt[3]{\text{Volume}}$
3. Whole Surface Area = $6\ l^2$

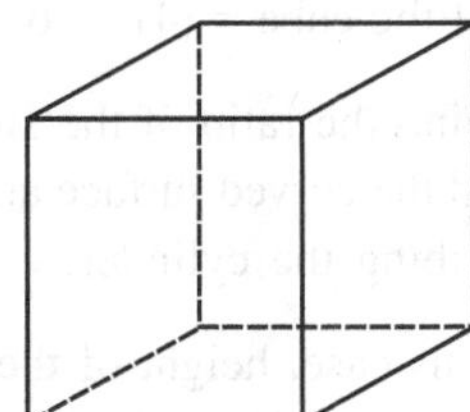

4. Diagonal = $l \times \sqrt{3}$
5. Lateral Surface Area = $4\ l^2$

Cylinder

1. Volume = $\pi r^2 h$
2. Curved Surface Area = $2\pi rh$
3. Total Surface Area = $2\pi r(r + h)$

where r = radius,
h = height

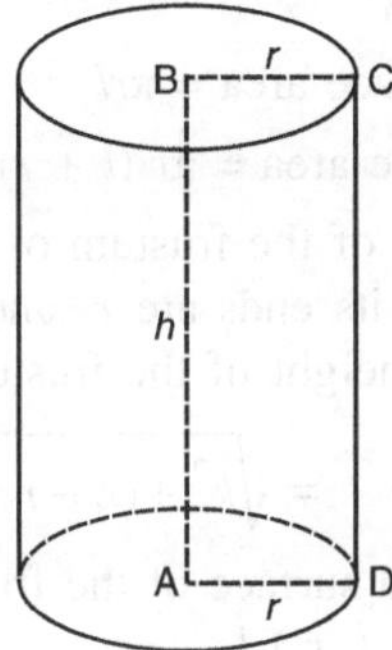

Spherical shell

1. Volume = $\frac{4}{3}\pi\left(R^3 - r^3\right)$
2. Total Surface Area = $4\pi(R^2 - r^2)$

where R = Outer radius
r = Inner radius

Sphere

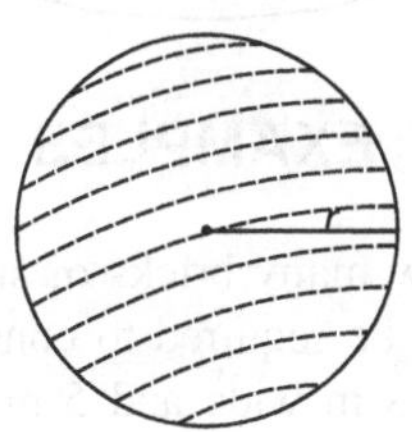

1. Volume = $\frac{4}{3}\pi r^3$
2. Surface Area = $4\pi r^2$

Semi-sphere

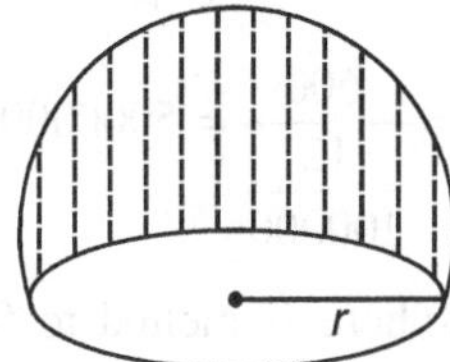

1. Volume = $\frac{2}{3}\pi r^3$
2. Curved surface area = $2\pi r^2$
3. Total surface area = $3\pi r^2$

Cone

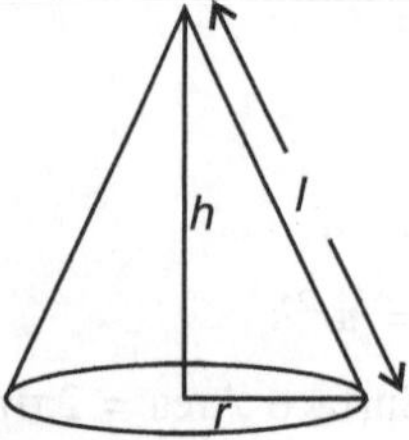

1. Slant height (l) = $\sqrt{r^2 + h^2}$
2. Volume = $\frac{1}{3}\pi r^2 h$
3. Curved surface area = πrl
4. Total surface area = $\pi r\,(l + r)$
5. If the depth of the frustum of a cone be k and the radii of its ends are r_1 and r_2, then
   (i) Slant height of the frustum of a cone
   $$= \sqrt{k^2 + (r_1 - r_2)^2}$$
   (ii) Curved surface of the frustum
   $= \pi(r_1 + r_2)\, l.$
   (iii) Volume = $\frac{\pi k}{3}\left(r_1^2 + r_1 r_2 + r_2^2\right)$

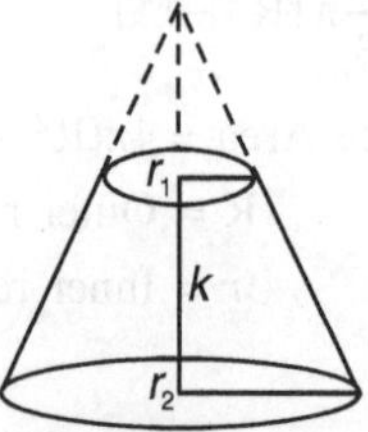

EXAMPLES

Example 1. How many bricks of size 6 cm × 5 cm × 4 cm will be required to construct a platform 15 m long, 8 m wide and 5 m high.

Solution: Volume of the platform = 15 × 8 × 5
= 600 cu m

Volume of one brick

$$= \frac{6}{100} \times \frac{5}{100} \times \frac{4}{100} = \frac{12}{100000} \text{ cu m}$$

∴ Number of bricks required to construct the

$$\text{platform} = \frac{600}{\frac{12}{100000}} = 5000000 = 5 \times 10^6.$$

Example 2. A sphere is melted to form a cylinder whose height is $4\frac{1}{2}$ times its radius. What is the ratio of radii of sphere to the cylinder?

Solution: Here, $\frac{4}{3}\pi r_1^3 = \pi r_2^2 \times \frac{9}{2} r_2$

$$\Rightarrow \frac{r_1^3}{r_2^3} = \frac{9}{2} \times \frac{3}{4} \quad \therefore \frac{r_1}{r_2} = \frac{3}{2}$$

Hence, required ratio = 3 : 2.

Example 3. Find the length of canvas 1.1 m wide required to build a conical tent of height 14m and the floor area of 346.5 m².

Solution: Here, $\pi r^2 = 346.5$

$$\Rightarrow r^2 = \frac{346.5 \times 7}{22} = 110.25 \quad \therefore r = 10.5 \text{ m}$$

Now, slant height,

$$l = \sqrt{(14)^2 + (10.5)^2} = \sqrt{306.25} = 17.5 \text{ m}$$

Curved surface area of conical tent

$$= \frac{22}{7} \times 10.5 \times 17.5 = 577.5 \text{ m}^2.$$

Hence, length of canvas required

$$= \frac{577.5}{1.1} = 525 \text{ m}$$

Example 4. A sphere and a cube have equal surface area. Find the ratio of their volumes?

Solution: Here, $4\pi r^2 = 6a^2$

$$\Rightarrow \frac{r^2}{a^2} = \frac{6}{4\pi} = \frac{3}{2\pi} \qquad \Rightarrow \frac{r}{a} = \sqrt{\frac{3}{2\pi}}$$

$$\text{Now, } \frac{\frac{4}{3}\pi r^3}{a^3} = \frac{4\pi}{3} \times \left(\sqrt{\frac{3}{2\pi}}\right)^3 = \frac{4\pi}{3} \cdot \frac{3\sqrt{3}}{2\pi\sqrt{2\pi}} = \frac{\sqrt{6}}{\sqrt{\pi}}$$

Hence, required ratio = $\sqrt{6} : \sqrt{\pi}$

Example 5. Find the volume of a cube whose diagonal measures $4\sqrt{3}$ cm.

Solution: Side of the cube = $\frac{4\sqrt{3}}{\sqrt{3}} = 4$ cm

Volume of the cube = $(4)^3 = 64$ cm³

Example 6. Find the ratio of the surface area of the sphere and the curved surface area of the cylinder circumscribing the cylinder.

Solution: In this case, height of the cylinder, $h = 2r$ (diameter of the sphere)

Hence, required ratio = $\frac{4\pi r^2}{2\pi r . 2r} = \frac{1}{1} = 1 : 1.$

MULTIPLE CHOICE QUESTIONS

1. A reservoir is 3 m long, 2 m wide and 1 m deep. Its capacity in litres is

A. 8000 litres B. 10000 litres
C. 6500 litres D. 6000 litres

2. Surface area of a cube is 1014 sq. cm. Its volume will be

A. 2197 cu cm B. 2297 cu cm
C. 2179 cu cm D. 2117 cu cm

3. If the volumes of two cubical blocks are in the ratio of 8 : 1, what will be the ratio of their edges?

A. 1 : 2 B. 2 : 1
C. 4 : 1 D. 2 : 3

4. Two spheres have their surface areas in the ratio 9 : 16. Their volumes are in the ratio of

A. 64 : 27 B. 27 : 64
C. 16 : 27 D. 11 : 27

5. The length of the longest rod that can be placed in a room 12 m long, 9 m broad and 8 m high is

A. 17 m B. 18 m
C. 25 m D. 16 m

6. If two cubes each of 10 cm side are kept close to each other, then the cuboid so formed will have surface area equal to

A. 1200 sq. cm B. 5000 sq. cm
C. 1000 sq. cm D. 1250 sq. cm

7. Diameter of a roller is 2.4 m and it is 1.68 m long. If it takes 1000 complete revolutions once over to level a field, the area of the field is

A. 12672 sq. m B. 12671 sq. m
C. 12762 sq. m D. 11768 sq. m

8. If each edge of a cube is increased by 10%, then by how much per cent will the surface area of this cube be increased?

A. 21% B. 18%
C. 15% D. 20%

9. A room is in the form of a cube of side 10 m. How many bales of cotton can be kept in it if each bale covers 5 cu m space?

A. 100 B. 175
C. 200 D. 225

10. The surface area of a cube is 600 sq. m. Its diagonal is

A. $10\sqrt{3}$ cm B. $5\sqrt{3}$ cm
C. $4\sqrt{2}$ cm D. $10\sqrt{2}$ cm

11. If the whole mass of a sphere can be tightly placed in a cube, then the volume of the cube and the volume of the sphere are in the ratio

A. 7 : 12 B. 22 : 21
C. 21 : 11 D. 20 : 7

12. A cone and a sphere have the same radius and the same volume. The ratio of the diameter of the sphere to the height of the cone is

A. 1 : 3 B. 3 : 2
C. 1 : 2 D. 2 : 3

13. The ratio of radii of two cylinders is 2 : 3 and the ratio of their heights is 5 : 3. Find the ratio of their volumes.

A. 4 : 9 B. 9 : 4
C. 20 : 27 D. 27 : 20

14. A tank is of the shape of a cuboid whose length is 7.2 m and breadth is 2.5m. Water flows into it through a pipe whose cross-section is 5 cm × 3 cm at the rate of 10 m/s. Find the height to which water level will rise in the tank in 40 minutes.

A. 1m B. 2m
C. 3m D. 4m

15. A well with 7m inside diameter is dug 22.5 m deep. Earth taken out of it is spread all around to a width of 10.5 m to form an embankment. Find the height of the embankment. $\left(\text{Use } \pi = \frac{22}{7}\right)$

A. 1m B. 1.5m
C. 2m D. 2.5m

ANSWERS

1	2	3	4	5	6	7	8	9	10
D	A	B	B	A	C	A	A	C	A
11	**12**	**13**	**14**	**15**					
C	C	C	B	B					

SOME SELECTED EXPLANATORY ANSWERS

1. Volume of the reservoir = $l \times b \times h$

$= 3 \times 2 \times 1 = 6$ cu. m

($\because$ 1 cu m = 1000 litre)

$\therefore$ Capacity of the reservoir = 6 × 1000 = 6000 litre.

MATHEMATICS

2. Here, $6 \times (\text{side})^2 = 1014$

$\Rightarrow \quad (\text{side})^2 = \frac{1014}{6} = 169$

$\therefore \quad \text{side} = \sqrt{169} = 13$ cm

Hence, Volume of the cube = $(\text{side})^3 = (13)^3$
$= 2197$ cu cm.

3. Here, $a_1^3 : a_2^3 = 8 : 1$

$\therefore \quad \left(\frac{a_1}{a_2}\right)^3 = \left(\frac{2}{1}\right)^3 \Rightarrow a_1 : a_2 = 2 : 1$

Therefore, ratio of their edges = 2 : 1.

4. Here, $4\pi r_1^2 : 4\pi r_2^2 = 9 : 16 \Rightarrow r_1^2 : r_2^2 = 9 : 16$

$\Rightarrow \left(\frac{r_1}{r_2}\right)^2 = \left(\frac{3}{4}\right)^2 \Rightarrow r_1 : r_2 = 3 : 4$

$\Rightarrow \frac{r_1^3}{r_2^3} = \frac{27}{64} \Rightarrow r_1^3 : r_2^3 = 27 : 64.$

Therefore, ratio of their volumes

$= \frac{4}{3}\pi r_1^3 : \frac{4}{3}\pi r_2^3 = r_1^3 : r_2^3 = 27 : 64$

5. The longest rod that can be placed in the cuboidal room = Length of the diagonal

$= \sqrt{l^2 + b^2 + h^2} = \sqrt{(12)^2 + (9)^2 + (8)^2}$

$= \sqrt{144 + 81 + 64} = \sqrt{289} = 17$ m

6. Here, length of the cuboid = Edge of the first cube + Edge of the second cube
$= 10 + 10 = 20$ cm

$\therefore$ Surface area of the cuboid
$= 2(20 \times 10 + 10 \times 10 + 10 \times 20)$
$= 2(200 + 100 + 200)$
$= 2 \times 500 = 1000$ sq. cm.

7. Surface area of the roller = $2\pi rh$

$= 2 \times \frac{22}{7} \times 1.2 \times 1.68 = 12.672$ sq. m

In one complete revolution, the roller covers 12.672 sq. m.

$\therefore$ It will cover in 1000 revolutions
$= 12.672 \times 1000 = 12672$ sq. m
Hence, area of the field = 12672 sq. m.

8. Percentage increase in the surface area of the cube = $\left(x + y + \frac{xy}{100}\right)\%$

$= \left(10 + 10 + \frac{10 \times 10}{100}\right)\% = 21\%.$

9. Volume of the cubical room = $(10)^3$
$= 1000$ cu m

Number of cotton bales which can be placed in the room

$= \frac{\text{Volume of the room}}{\text{Volume of each cotton bale}} = \frac{1000}{5} = 200.$

10. Here, $6 \times (\text{side})^2 = 600$

$\Rightarrow \quad \text{side}^2 = 100$

$\Rightarrow \quad \text{side} = \sqrt{100} = 10$ cm

$\therefore$ Diagonal of the cube

$= \sqrt{3} \times \text{side} = \sqrt{3} \times 10 = 10\sqrt{3}$ cm.

11. The sphere can be completely fitted in the cube. It means side of the cube is equal to the diameter of the sphere.

Volume of the sphere= $\frac{4}{3}\pi (r)^3$

And volume of the cube = $(\text{side})^3$

$\therefore$ Ratio of the volumes of the cube and the sphere = $(\text{side})^3 : \frac{4}{3}\pi r^3$

$\Rightarrow (2r)^3 : \frac{4}{3}\pi r^3 = 6 : \frac{22}{7} = 21 : 11$

12. Here, $4/3\pi r^3 = \frac{1}{3}\pi r^2 h \Rightarrow 4r = h$

$\Rightarrow \quad 2d = h \quad \therefore \frac{d}{h} = \frac{1}{2}$

Hence, required ratio = 1 : 2

13. Here, $\frac{V_1}{V_2} = \frac{\pi \times 2^2 \times 5}{\pi \times 3^2 \times 3} = \frac{20}{27}$

Hence, required ratio = 20 : 27.

14. Here, length of water column in 40 min
$= 10 \times 40 \times 60$ m

Since, $7.2 \times 2.5 \times h = \frac{5}{100} \times \frac{3}{100} \times 10 \times 40 \times 60$

$\Rightarrow \quad h = \frac{36 \times 100}{72 \times 25} = 2\text{m}$

15. Here, $\pi\left[(10.5 + 3.5)^2 - (3.5)^2\right]h = \pi(3.5)^2 \times 22.5$

$\Rightarrow (196 - 12.25)h = 12.25 \times 22.5$

$\therefore h = \frac{12.25 \times 22.5}{183.75} = 1.5$ m.

SHAPES AND SPATIAL UNDERSTANDING

We have learnt about plane shapes and solid shapes. Plane shapes are also called two dimensional shapes which have two measurements *i.e.*, length and breadth. Whereas solid shapes has three dimensions and it has three measures *i.e.*, lengths, breadth and height or depth. So the solid shapes are called three dimensional shapes. Two dimensional shapes are indicated as 2D, similarly three dimensional shapes are indicated as 3D. Following is the details of two dimensional and three dimensional shapes and its examples in our daily life.

Types of shape	Name of shape	Examples
Two Dimen-sional	Square	Surface of carom board
	Rectangle	Surface of book or copy
	Triangle	Surface of signpost
	Polygon	A paper cutting for decoration
	Circle	Surface of compact disk (CD)
Three Dimen-sional	Cube	Dice
	Cuboid	Bricks, Box.
	Cylinder	Water bottle, Glass.
	Cone	Cone of ice-cream, Conical cap
	Sphere	Ball, Marble

Concepts of spatial understanding

(*i*) small - big

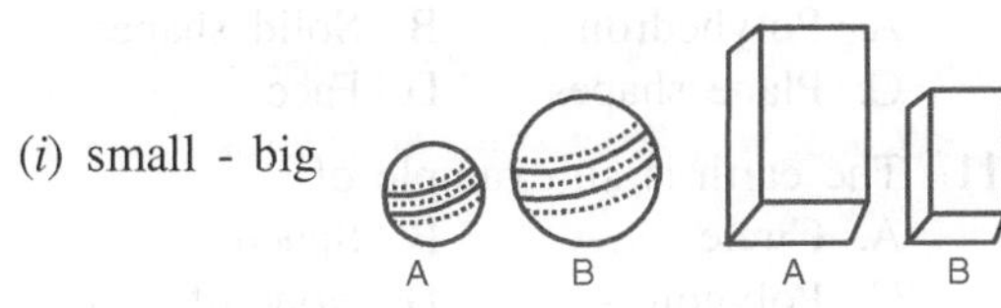

(*ii*) smallest - biggest

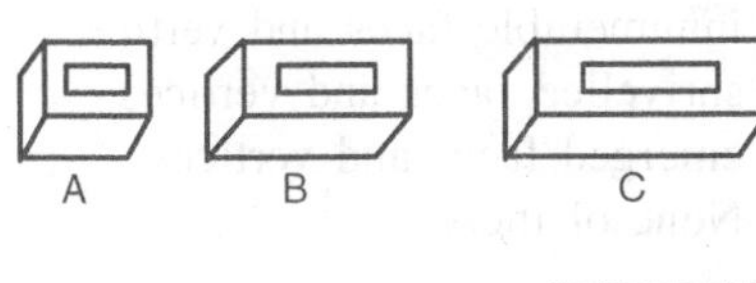

(*iii*) in - out

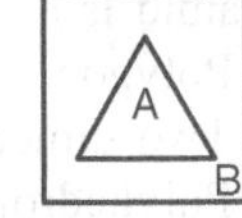

(*iv*) near - far

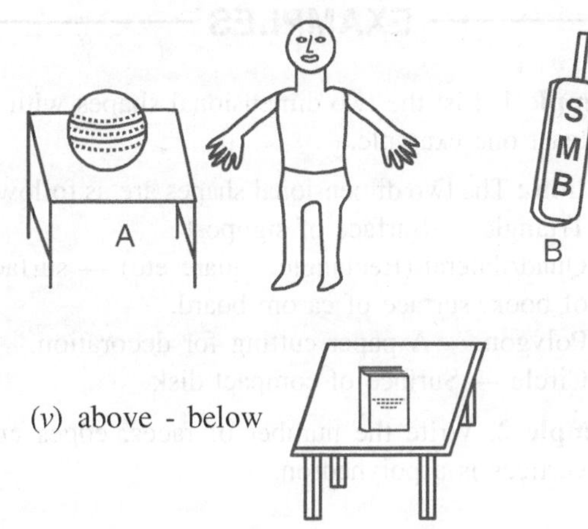

(*v*) above - below

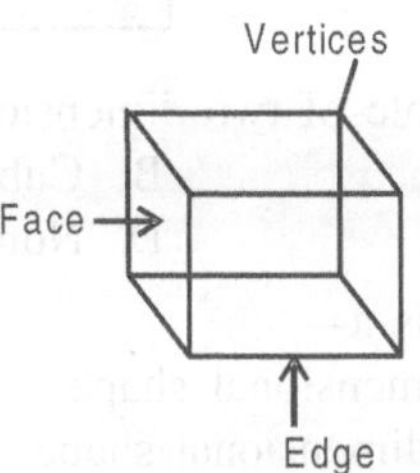

Faces, Edges and Vertices

Faces: The polygonal regions of a solid surface called faces.

Edges: Where two faces meet that is called edge.

Vertices: Where two or more edges meet that point is called vertex.

Polyhedron: The solid which have faces, edges and vertices is called polyhedron.

Polyhedrons: Cube, cuboid, prism, pyramid.

Non-polyhedron: Sphere, cone, cylinder.

Convex-Polyhedron: This type of polyhedrons have emerged faces and vertices *e.g.*,

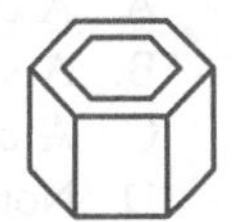

Non convex-polyhedron: This type of polyhedrons have shrivelled faces and vertices *e.g.*,

Regular polyhedron: If polyhedron is made up of regular polygons and same number of faces meet at each vertex. Then it is called regular polyheron.

e.g.,

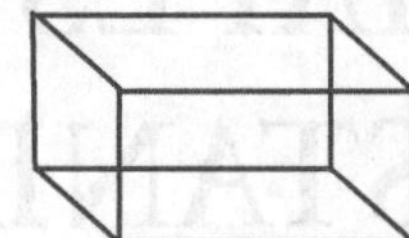

This is regular polyhedron. Its faces are congruent, regular polygon. Vertices are formed by the same number of faces.

EXAMPLES

Example 1. List the two dimensional shapes with at least one example.

Solution : The two dimensional shapes are as follows.

Triangle — Surface of signpost

Quadrilateral (Rectangle, square etc) — surface of book, surface of carom board.

Polygon — A paper cutting for decoration.

Circle — Surface of compact disk.

Example 2. Write the number of faces, edges and vertices is a polyhedron.

Solution : A polyhedron has six faces, twelve edges and eight vertices.

Example 3. Match with List I to List II.

List-I	List-II
(*i*) cube	(*a*) foot ball
(*ii*) sphere	(*b*) bricks
(*iii*) cylinder	(*c*) dice of ludo
(*iv*) cone	(*d*) tube light
(*v*) cuboid	(*e*) cap of magician

Solution : (*i*) — (*c*), (*ii*) — (*a*), (*iii*) — (*d*), (*iv*) — (*e*), (*v*) — (*b*)

Example 4. A convex polyhedron has—

(*a*) emerged faces (*b*) shrivelled faces
(*c*) flat faces (*d*) narrow faces

Solution : A convex polyhedron has emerged faces.

Example 5. In regular polyhedron the vertices are formed by—

(*a*) odd number of faces
(*b*) even number of faces
(*c*) indifinite number of faces
(*d*) same number of faces

Solution : In regular polyhedron vertices are formed by same number of faces.

MULTIPLE CHOICE QUESTIONS

1. An example of two dimensional shape is—
A. Cone B. Cube
C. Circle D. None of these

2. Triangle is a—
A. Unidimensional shape
B. Two dimensional shape
C. Three dimensional shape
D. None of these

3. Two dimensional shapes do not have—
A. Existance B. Length
C. Depth D. Breadth

4. Brick is an example of—
A. Rectangle B. Cube
C. Cuboid D. Square

5. Which of the following statement is true?
A. A cube has eight faces
B. A sphere has no vertices
C. A cuboid has six edges
D. None of these

6. Which of the following is false
A. Two dimensional shapes have maximum four vertices
B. Dice is an example of cube
C. A polyhedron has faces, edges and vertices
D. None of these

7. An example of circle is—
A. Ice cream cone
B. Ball
C. Surface of black-board
D. Surface of Compact Disk (CD)

8. 3D term is used for—
A. 3 Diameters B. 3 Data
C. 3 days D. 3 Dimensional

9. Where two faces of a solid shape meet is called
A. Shape B. Edge
C. Vertex D. Polyhedron

10. Two dimensional shapes are called .... also
A. Polyhedron B. Solid shapes
C. Plane shapes D. Face

11. The earth is an example of
A. Circle B. Sphere
C. Polygon D. None of these

12. A convex-polyhedron has—
A. innumerable faces and vertices
B. shrivelled faces and vertices
C. emerged faces and vertices
D. None of these

13. Pyramid is a
A. Polygon
B. Two dimensional shape
C. Polyhedron
D. Four dimensional shape

14. A box has

A. four faces, twelve edges and eight vertices

B. Six faces, eight edges and twelve vertices

C. Six faces, twelve edges and eight vertices

D. None of these

ANSWERS

1	2	3	4	5	6	7	8	9	10
C	B	C	C	B	D	D	D	B	C
11	**12**	**13**	**14**						
B	C	C	C						

SECTION 6 PEDAGOGICAL ISSUES

NATURE OF MATHEMATICS

WHAT IS MATHEMATICS?

Mathematics is the science of measurement and calculations. It is the science of logical reasoning. It is a systesmatically organised and exact branch of science.

A universal definition of mathematics can not be given due to its immensity (wide extent). Many mathematicians have defined the mathematics as a subject. But they could not even touched the every factors of mathematics.

e.g., ''Mathematics is the science of measurement, quantity and magnitude''

—Oxford dictionary

''Mathematics may be defined as the subject in which we never know what we are talking about nor wheather what we are saying true.''

—Bertrand Russel

''Mathematics is the language in which God has written the universe.''

—Galeleo

''Mathematics is the study of abstract system built of abstract elements. These elements are not described in concrete fashion.''

—Marshal H. Stone

''Mathematics is a way to settle in mind of children a habit of reasoning.''

—Locke

''Mathematics is the science that draws necessary conclusions.''

—Benjamin Peirce

''As far as the laws of mathematics refer to reality they are not certain; and as far as they are certain, they do not refer to reality.''

—Albert Einstien

According to above definitions we can conclude that

(*i*) Mathematics is the science that draws necessary conclusions.

(*ii*) It is a systematic, organised and exact branch of science.

(*iii*) It settles in the mind a habit of reasoning.

(*iv*) It is a science of logical reasoning.

(*v*) It is a science of number and calculation also.

(*vi*) Mathematics is the science of space, measurement, magnitude and quantity.

(*vii*) It deals with relationships and quantitative facts.

(*viii*) Mathematics is an abstract experimental and inductive science.

IMPORTANCE OF MATHEMATICS

Mathematical thinking is a very significant factor in a modern society as a habit of mind for its usage at the workplace, business and finance; and for personal decision-making. Mathematics is essential for the prosperity of a nation in providing devices for comprehending science, engineering, technology and other related subjects. It is a very important tool in public decision-making and for involvement in the knowledge economy. Mathematics provides students with great and powerful ways to describe, analyse and transform the world. It has the power to create moments of pleasure and wonder for all students when they solve a problem for the very first time, discover a better solution, or observe hidden links. Pupils who are very good at mathematics and capable of intelligent thinking are able to think independently in applied and abstract ways, and can reason, solve problems and calculate risk. In fact education should always begin with mathematics because it creates well designed brains that are capable of reasoning right. It is even proved that those who have learned math from their childhood should be trusted, for they have procured solid foundation for arguing which becomes to them a kind of second nature.

Mathematics is not a mere subject that prepares students for higher academic attainment or job qualification in the future. It is not all about practicing calculations in algebra, statistics and algorithms that, after all, computers are capable of doing. It is more about how it compels the human brain to formulate problems, theories and methods of solutions. It prepares children to face a variety of simple to multifaceted challenges every human being encounters on a daily basis. Irrespective of your status in life and however basic your skills are, you apply mathematics. Daily activities including the mundane things you do memorizing phone numbers, buying groceries, cooking food, balancing a budget, paying bills, estimating gasoline consumption, measuring distance and managing your time. In the fields of business and economy, including the diverse industries existing around you, basic to complex math applications are crucial.

Anywhere in the world, mathematics is employed as a key instrument in a diversity of fields such as medicine, engineering, natural science, social science, physical science, tech science, business and commerce, etc. Application of mathematical knowledge in every field of study and industry produces new discoveries and advancement of new disciplines. All innovations introduced worldwide, every product of technology that man gets pleasure from is a byproduct of Science and Math. The ease and convenience people enjoy today from the discoveries of computers, automobiles, aircraft, household and personal gadgets would never have happened if it were not for this essential tool used in technology.

Every branch of Mathematics has distinct applications in different types of careers. The skills enhanced from practicing math such as analyzing patterns, logical thinking, problem solving and the ability to see relationships can help you prepare for your chosen career and enable you to compete for interesting and high-paying jobs against people around the globe. Even if you do not take up math-intensive courses, you have the edge to compete against other job applicants if you have a strong mathematical background, as industries are constantly evolving together with fast-paced technology.

Since mathematics encompasses all aspects of human life, it is unquestionably important in education to help students and all people from all walks of life perform daily tasks efficiently and become productive, well-informed, functional, independent individuals and members of a society where Math is a fundamental component.

NATURE OF MATHEMATICS

Students must understand aims and objectives of the subjects which are included in the curriculum. Because it decides the nature of the subject. Mathematics has an unbreakable and strong position as compared to other subjects. It is more stable and important also than the other subjects which is taught in school curriculum. These are the factors which decide the structure, truthfulness, prediction and reliability of the subject. The nature of mathematics is also determined on the basis of these factors like the other subjects.

Mathematics relies on both logic and creativity, and it is pursued both for a variety of practical purposes and for its intrinsic interest. For some people, and not only professional mathematicians, the essence of mathematics lies in its beauty and its intellectual challenge. For others, including many scientists and engineers, the chief value of mathematics is how it applies to their own work. Because mathematics plays such a central role in modern culture, some basic understanding of the nature of mathematics is requisite for scientific literacy. To achieve this, students need to perceive mathematics as part of the scientific endeavor, comprehend the nature of mathematical thinking, and become familiar with key mathematical ideas and skills.

Mathematics is the science of patterns and relationships. As a theoretical discipline, mathematics explores the possible relationships among abstractions without concern for whether those abstractions have counterparts in the real world. The abstractions can be anything from strings of numbers to geometric figures to sets of equations. In addressing, say, "Does the interval between prime numbers form a pattern?" as a theoretical questions, mathematicians are interested only in finding a pattern or providing that there is none, but not in what use such knowledge might have. In deriving, for instance, an expression for the change in the surface area of any regular solid as its volume approaches zero, mathematicians have no interest in any correspondence between geometric solids and physical objects in the real world.

A central line of investigation in theoretical mathematics is identifying in each field of study a small set of basic ideas and rules from which all other interesting ideas and rules in that field can be logically deduced. Mathematicians, like other scientists, are particularly pleased when previously unrelated parts of mathematics are found to be derivable from one another, or from some more general theory. Part of the sense of beauty that many people have perceived in mathematics lies not in finding the greatest elaborateness or complexity but on the contrary, in finding the greatest economy and simplicity of representation and proof. As mathematics has progressed, more and more relationships have been found between parts of it that have been developed separately — for example, between the symbolic representations of algebra and the spatial representations of geometry. These cross-connections enable insights to be developed into the various parts; together, they strengthen belief in the correctness and underlying unity of the whole structure.

Mathematics is also an applied science. Many mathematicians focus their attention on solving problems that originate in the world of experience. They too search for patterns and relationships, and in the process they use techniques that are similar to those used in doing purely theoretical mathematics. The difference is largely one of intent. In contrast to theoretical mathematicians, applied mathematicians, in the examples numerical information, rather than as an abstract problem. Or they might tackle the area/volume problem as a step in producing a model for the crystal behavior.

The results of theoretical and applied mathematics often influence each other. The discoveries of theoretical mathematicians frequently turn out—sometimes decades later—to have unanticipated practical value. Studies on the mathematical properties of random events, for example, led to knowledge that later made it possible to improve the design of experiments in the social and natural sciences. Conversely, in trying to solve the problem of billing long-distance telephone users fairly, mathematicians made fundamental discoveries about the mathematics of complex networks. Theoretical mathematics, unlike the other sciences, is not constrained by the real world, but in the long run it contributes to a better understanding of that world.

Because of its abstractness, mathematics is universal in a sense that other fields of human thought are not. It finds useful applications in business, industry, music historical scholarship, politics, sports, medicine, agriculture, engineering, and the social and natural sciences. The relationship between mathematics and the other fields of basic and applied science is especially strong. This is so for several reasons, including the following:

- The alliance between science and mathematics has a long history, dating back many centuries. Science provides mathematics with interesting problems to investigate, and mathematics, provides science with powerful tools to use in analyzing data. Often, abstract patterns that have been studied for their own sake by mathematicians have turned out much later to be very useful in science. Science and mathematics are both trying to discover general patterns and relationships, and in this sense they are part of the same endeavor.
- Mathematics is the chief language of science. The symbolic language of mathematics has turned out to be extremely valuable for expressing scientific ideas unambiguously. The statement that $a = F/m$ is not simply a shorthand way of saying that the acceleration of an object depends on the force applied to it and its mass; rather, it is a precise statement of the quantitative relationship among those variables. More important, mathematics provides the grammar of science—the rules for analyzing scientific ideas and data rigorously.
- Mathematics and science have many features in common. These include a belief in understandable order; and interplay of imagination and rigorous logic; ideas of honesty and openness; the critical importance of peer criticism; the value placed on being the first to make a key discovery; being international in scope; and even, with the development of powerful electronic computers, being able to use technology to open up new fields of investigation.
- Mathematics and technology have also developed a fruitful relationship with each other. The mathematics of connections and logical chains, for example, has contributed greatly to the design of computer hardware and programming techniques. Mathematics also contributes more generally to engineering, as in describing complex systems whose behaviour can then be simulated by computer. In those simulations, design features and operating conditions can be varied as a means of finding optimum designs. For its part, computer technology has opened up whole new areas in mathematics, even in the very nature of proof, and it also continues to help solve previously daunting problems.

It is not necessary that all subjects should be same nature. Comparatively mathematics has unique nature thus on the basis of which we generally compare it with other subjects. Of course, the basis of comparision of two or more subjects is their nature. Understanding the nature of mathematics may be easy on the basis of following features—

(*i*) Mathematics relies on logic and creativity.

(*ii*) It is pursued for a variety of practical purposes and for its intrinsic interest.

(*iii*) Mathematics plays a central role in modern culture.

(*iv*) It is the science of patterns and relationships.

(*v*) Mathematics explores the possible relationships among abstractions as a theoretical discipline.

(*vi*) It is an applied science.

(*vii*) The result of theoretical and applied mathematics influence each - other.

(*viii*) Mathematics is universal in a sense that other fields of human thought are not.

(*ix*) It finds useful applications in business, music industry, politics, sports, medicines, agriculture, engineering, historical scholarship, social and natural science and many other region of human life.

(*x*) The relationship between mathematics and the other fields of basic and applied science is especially strong.

(*xi*) Mathematics is the chief language of science.

(*xii*) Mathematics and science have many common features.

(*xiii*) It involves conversion of abstract concepts into concrete form.

(*xiv*) It draws numerical inferences on the basis of given information and data.

(*xv*) Mathematical rules, law and formulae are universal.

(*xvi*) It has its own language and the language is well defined useful and clear. The language consists mathematical terms, concepts, formulae, theories, principles and signs etc.

(*xvii*) It helps to develop the habit of self confidence and self reliance.

(*xviii*) It provides doubtless and errorless theories, principles, concepts etc.

(*xix*) It helps in the development of sense of appreciation and scientific attitude.

(*xx*) It provides the training of scietific method.

(*xxi*) It provides accurate and reliable knowledge based on sense-organs.

Now, we can understand the nature of mathematics and conclude that really the structure of mathematics is the basis of its nature. It is stronger than the other subjects. Roger Becon has also said that Mathematics is the gateway and key of all sciences.

LOGICAL THINKING

Logical thinking is the process in which one uses reasoning consistently to come to a conclusion. Problems or situations that involve logical thinking call for structure, for relationships between facts, and for chains of reasoning that make sense.

According to Dr. Karl Albrecht sequential thought is the basis of all logical thinking. The process involves taking the important ideas, facts, and conclusions involved in a problem and arranging them in a chain-like progresssion that takes on a meaning in and of itself. To think logically is to think in steps.

It has been proven that specific training in logical thinking processes can make people smarter. Logical thinking allows a child to reject quick answers, such as "I don't know," or "this is too difficult," by empowering them to delve deeper into their thinking processes and understand better the methods used to arrive at a solution and even the solution itself.

Logical thinking is also an important foundational skill of math. Learning mathematics is a highly sequential process. If you don't grasp a certain concept, fact, or procedure, you can never hope to grasp others that come later, which depend upon it. For example, to understand fractions you must first understand division. To understand simple equations in algebra requires that you understand fractions. Solving 'world problems' depends on knowing how to set up and manipulate equations, and so on.

Logical thinking is not a magical process or a matter of genetic endowment, but a learned mental process.

One of the aims of the mathematics is to teach a child to think logically. Logical thinking exercises are carefully graded. For example, in the first example of *Logical Thinking exercise* a child would be asked to arrange a sequence of coloured blocks in front of them, from left to right.

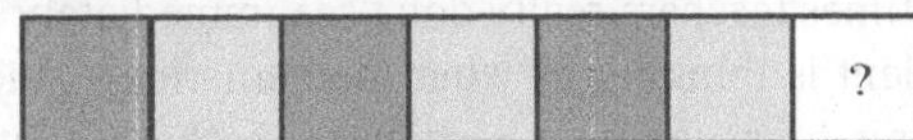

One would then ask the child : "If you had to add one more colour to the above sequence, which colour would you choose?" The answer, of course, is dark.

UNDERSTANDING CHILDREN'S THINKING

One of the fundamental characteristics of "mathematics reform pedagogy is that teachers are encouraged to understand the mathematics thinking of each of their students and then use that knowledge in instructional planning. As compared to typical pedagogy of 25 years ago, explanation/demonstration by the teacher is relatively less important and using questions to probe students' thinking is relatively more important. One implication of this shift is that teachers have the burden of making sense of what students say in their explanations of their thinking. Making sense requires understanding not only the relevant mathematics that might underlie an explanation but also the trajectory of development of students' (*i.e.*, novices') mathematical understanding. Understanding each student's mathematical development becomes a critical focus of a teacher's attention.

Questioning

Teachers can get information about students' thinking in a variety of ways, for example, questioning, observation, analysis of students' writing, tests, and project work. Probably the most important of these is questioning, since that is the most interactive of these techniques. Through a series of questions, a teacher can accomplish one or more of several different goals. First, carefully sequenced questions can lead students to a correct answer. Indeed, many teachers are very good at getting students to say almost anything desired, by "leading the student down the garden path." The down side of this, though, is that it may not be clear to the student why those questions were asked or what the final, correct answer means.

Second, questions can help a student process, or even self-correct, an answer. Teachers regularly recognize when a mistake has been made in computing or processing or choice of operation, etc. Asking a question about the student's work may have the effect of "slowing the student down" in order to re-analyze that work. That rethinking may be sufficient reflection for the student to see the error and correct it.

Third, questions can help expose a student's thinking so that the teacher can understand it. Sometimes teachers really don't see immediately how a student is thinking or what mathematics a student is using to generate a response. In that situation, questions can help reveal a student's thinking so that the teacher can determine whether the thought process is acceptable. It is this kind of questioning that is probably most useful for teachers to use as they learn to understand students' thinking, but this is also the kind of questioning that is least familiar to teachers. It is this kind of questioning that teachers need the most help at learning how to do.

Questioning has to occur in real time during face-to-face interactions; teachers have to create questions immediately and with very little reflection time. Teachers, obviously, have more time outside of class than they do in class, so an alternate, though perhaps not as effective, technique for understanding students' thinking is analysis of students' writing. Students might record solutions to problems in a journal, respond to specific prompts posed by the teacher, create reports of projects, or maintain portfolios of their work over time. In many ways, the easiest way for teachers to get students to respond to prompts, particularly in middle and high school classes, is to include those prompts on a test. Probably the most frequently used of these prompts is "show your work." The difficulty with this prompt is that teachers and students often do not share a common perspective on what constitutes work. It is important that as part of instruction, teachers and students reach an agreement on what should be written down so as to allow the teacher to understand the thinking that lies behind the solution to a particular problem.

The usefulness of writing as a window into thinking is influenced by the language and writing ability of the students. It is less useful in primary grades than in high school, and it is less useful when students are expected to write in their second language. We must consider, however, that mathematical symbolism is itself a second language for most students. Effort must be put forth, both by teachers in teaching and by students in learning, to master this form of written communication.

Professional Development Focused on Understanding Students' Thinking

There are several professional development projects that have helped teachers gain the skill and knowledge of processes for understanding students' thinking. The one we are most familiar with is Cognitively Guided Instruction (CGI). CGI is an approach to teaching mathematics in which knowledge of children's thinking is central to instructional decision making. Teachers use research-based knowledge about children's mathematical thinking to help them learn specifics about individual students and then to adjust instruction to match students' performance. Teachers learn to assess students' thinking and then use that knowledge to plan instruction.

Learning as development seems critical if teachers are going to help students increase the level of sophistication of their thinking. Teachers need to have both a vision of what level of sophistication they want students to attain and a sense of where each student is along the path toward that vision. In addition, teachers need to be thinking about how to organize instruction so that students move in the direction of the desired goals.

Reflective abstraction is important as a mechanism by which teachers can improve their instruction. It is also important for children, in the sense that the children must reflect on their own mathematical development. Thus, teachers have to reflect on their own work and to help students reflect on their thinking. In grades K-3, there would seem to be a special obligation to help students develop the skills necessary for reflection; for example, through listening to their peers explain solutions, learning to ask questions to clarify those presentations of solutions, and keeping written records of their solutions that can form data for reflection.

Dialogue is especially important in CGI classrooms, but for dialogue (as opposed to multiple monologues) to occur, all parties involved must listen to each other. Within the implementation of CGI, teachers have special responsibilities for listening. During early implementation of CGI, teachers tend to listen to children's explanations with the expectation that they (the teachers) are supposed to understand children's thinking simply on the basis of what the children say; this type of listening can be called "passive listening." In contrast, teachers who are especially effective at implementing CGI seem to understand that making sense of children's thinking is a joint responsibility; both the teacher and the children must contribute to generating shared knowledge about that thinking. These teachers often engage children in conversation about solution strategies so that both the teacher and the children come to understand how what is being said reflects real thinking. This type of listening can be called "active listening." A teacher's development of either passive or active listening skills is consistent with allowing students to develop personal meaning.

One other advantage of listening is that it provides time, both for the students and the teacher. When a teacher chooses to listen, all of the children in the class have time to think and to develop meaning. When listening is combined with questioning, the time required increases further, since students need time to respond to those questions. The teacher has the opportunity to use the questions to focus students' attention on particular aspects of a solution, so that their reflection on those aspects of thinking is more intense. Having patience to allow students to internalize deep understanding of mathematics concepts is an essential characteristic of effective teachers.

Recent curriculum projects have also attempted to help teachers understand students' thinking; these materials can be an effective vehicle for professional development. For example, in Investigations materials there are dialogue boxes, which illustrate how children might respond to particular questions, lists of questions that teachers can use to probe students' thinking, and suggestions for what to look for during observations. In Connected Mathematics Project materials a launch/explore/summarize strategy is suggested for the activities, and within the notes for each of these there are numerous suggestions for ways to assess what students know and can do. These aids for teachers are designed to help teachers use classroom interactions to deepen their understanding of children's thinking, with the hope that teachers will then use this information to make better instructional decisions. This process is what has been called classroom assessment. The pay-off for helping teachers become better at classroom assessment is better instructional planning, which in turn should lead to greater student learning.

Much research has tried to help understand the trajectory of students' thinking. The research underlying CGI, for example, indicates a consistent pattern of development of students' thinking as revealed in their solution strategies. When teachers understand this path of development, they can interpret where a child's thinking is and can project ways of helping that child move to a more sophisticated level of thinking. Making instructional decisions based on a clear understanding of children's thinking seems to have significant pay-off for improved learning of mathematics. Unfortunately, not much seems to be known about how to recreate these effects across all levels of mathematics instruction.

Professional development materials and programs should help teachers understand more about students' thinking. In addition to the obvious pay-off for student learning, teachers themselves also seem to be renewed and become more excited about being successful teachers. Such renewal is certainly a worthy goal in itself, but the more important outcome is better student learning that follows from teachers' renewed excitement about teaching.

PLACE OF MATHEMATICS IN CURRICULUM

CURRICULUM EXPECTATIONS

The expectations identified for each course describe the knowledge and skills that students are expected to acquire, demonstrate, and apply in their class work, on tests, and in various other activities on which their achievement is assessed and evaluated. Two sets of expectations are listed for each strand, or broad curriculum area, of each course.

- The overall expectations describe in general terms the knowledge and skills that students are expected to demonstrate by the end of each course.
- The specific expectations describe the expected knowledge and skills in greater detail. The specific expectations are arranged under subheadings that reflect particular aspects of the required knowledge and skills and that may serve as a guide for teachers as they plan learning activities for their students. The organization of expectations in subgroupings is not meant to imply that the expectations in any subgroup are achieved independently of the expectations in the other subgroups. The subheadings are used merely to help teachers focus on particular aspects of knowledge and skills as they develop and present various lessons and learning activities for their students.

Importance of Mathematics in Curriculum

''Science and Mathematics should be taught on a compulsory basis to all pupils as a part of general education during first ten years of schooling.

—Kothari Commission (1964-66)

''The progress of Mathematics is linked to the prosperity of the state.''

—Nepolean

''Mathematics is a queen of all sciences without any king.''

—Unknown

Mathematics is most important subject in curriculum. Actually except our mother tongue there is no other subject which is such closely related to our daily life but mathematics. Now-a-days it has been given an important position in curriculum. Because it not only has the utility in daily life but also the social and cultural importance. It is helpful in the development of mental descipline. Mathematics has own desciplinary value and it does not need any special evaluation or testing to get a place in curriculum. When one sends his or her child to school he or she generally expects that the child will be able to cash the knowledge, skills, attitude and ideas. Parents expects that the child will earn intellectual habits and different powers *i.e.* discipline, value, morality etc. Of course matematics helps the child to achieve the aforesaid qualities. Moreover there are many advantage of giving due importance to mathematics and making it compulsory subject.

PLACE OF MATHEMATICS IN CURRICULUM

Everybody stands in need of some knowledge of mathematics. But in the case of an ordinary citizen, it is felt that the knowledge acquired during the primary and middle stage will suffice. Consequently there is some controversy over the place of mathematics in the school curriculum.

Some people are also of the view that mathematics is an exceptionally difficult subject, *i.e.*, its study demands special ability and intelligence. It is felt that everybody is not able enough to learn it successfully. Therefore, everybody should not be burdened with the study of this tough subject. References are also made to low pass percentage and heavy failures in this subjects in examinations. These poor results also support the view that mathematics should be made an optional subject.

There appears some justification for the view that mathematics should be made an optional subject at the high school stage. Since mathematics is primarily taught for its disciplinary value and mental discipline being a myth, no mathematics need be taught beyond the middle school stage.

It is also true that mathematics is indispensable in various sciences and professions. But everybody is not going to become an engineer or a statistician. Only those who have to go to such vocations may continue to study it. There is no need of burdening an average student with the study of this subjects, especially when an average citizen can lead to a successful life with the help of an elementary knowledge of mathematics and without any specialised or advanced knowledge in it.

If we take a broader view of the situation, we can infer that the belief of the critics is erroneous.

So far as the need of special ability in the learning of mathematics is concerned, it has been established with the help of experiments that in mathematics more of general intelligence (G) than specific ability (S) is needed.

Mathematics is a useful subject for most of the vocations and specialised courses. Although everybody studying in the school is not going to become an engineer or a scientist, but at a very early stage, it may not be possible to determine finally as to who is not going to join a profession like that. Therefore, the duty of the school is to give to the high school student a broad view of what he is capable of achieving in future. He should get a broader view of what he is capable of achieving in future. To deprive the student of the knowledge of this subject at the high school stage means narrowing the choice of semi-vocational courses, preparatory courses, vocational courses and vocations for him. Ignorance of mathematics will be a great handicap in the way of his future studies and occupations.

Educationists have begun to feel that education upto middle standard is not sufficient for the citizen of today. The period of compulsory education needs to be extended from the middle to the high school standard. After this extension of the period of compulsory education from eight to ten or eleven years, mathematics will have to be retained as a compulsory subject for as many number of years.

When foreigners talk of making this subject optional, they do so on a different fotting. Their pupils are two years older at the high school stage. In India, the pupils at high school stage are too young and immature to choose subjects and vocations for themselves. The parents being mostly illiterate are also not in a position to make any final choice at this stage regarding the future education and occupation.

While keeping it compulsory the interests of both types of students will have to be safeguarded. So the syllabus shall contain such subject matter as it useful for those who are going to discontinue their education after the high school stage and are entering into life. It shall also contain such knowledge as elucidates mathematical principles and processes so that the students who will later join a university course, shall not feel handicapped because of sudden rise in standard.

However, there cannot be any two opinions about the necessity of diversification and specialization in the final year of the higher secondary school stage. Here mathematics has to be treated as an optional or specialized subject like other subject of study.

The unprecedented changes that are taking place in today's world will profoundly affect the future of today's students. To meet the demands of the world in which they will live, students will need to adapt to changing conditions and to learn independently. They will require the ability to use technology effectively and the skills for processing large amounts of quantitative information. Today's mathematics curriculum must prepare students for their future roles in society. It must equip them with essential mathematical knowledge and skills; with skills of reasoning, problem solving, and communication; and, most importantly, with the ability and the incentive to continue learning on their own. This curriculum provides a framework for accomplishing these goals.

The choice of specific concepts and skills to be taught must take into consideration new applications and new ways of doing mathematics. The development of sophisticated yet easy-to-use calculators and computers is changing the role of procedure and technique in mathematics. Operations that were an essential part of a procedures-focused curriculum for decades can now be accomplished quickly and effectively using technology, so that students can now solve problems that were previously too time-consuming to attempt, and can focus on underlying concepts. "In an effective mathematics program, students learn in the presence of technology. Technology should influence the mathematics content taught and how it is taught. Powerful assistive and enabling computer and handheld technologies should be used seamlessly in teaching, learning, and assessment." This curriculum integrates appropriate technologies into the learning and doing of mathematics, while recognizing the continuing importance of students' mastering essential numeric and algebraic skills...

The development of mathematical knowledge is a gradual process. A coherent and continuous program is necessary to help students see the "big pictures", or underlying principles, of mathematics... These courses reflect the belief that students learn mathematics effectively when they are initially given opportunities to investigate ideas and concepts and are then guided carefully into an understanding of the abstract mathematics involved...

A balanced mathematics program at the secondary level includes the development of algebraic skills. This curriculum has been designed to equip students with the algebraic skills they need to understand other aspects of mathematics that they are learning, to solve meaningful problems, and to continue to meet with success as they study mathematics in the future. The algebraic skills required in each course have been carefully chosen to support the other topics included in the course. Calculators and other appropriate technology will be used when the primary purpose of a given activity is the development of concepts or the solving of problems, or when situations arise in which computation or symbolic manipulation is of secondary importance.

WHY MATHEMATICS IS KEPT IN CURRICULUM?

Before starting to teach a particular subject it is essential to know why we are goint to teach the subject. Aimlessness makes a work uninteresting and it is wastage of time, energy and other resourses. Hence we first determine aims and objectives of a work. Thus, teaching mathematics also has some aims and objectives. Because aimless teaching of mathematics may be uninteresting and it will be wastage of time, energy and other resourses for both the pupil and the teacher. Some aims of teaching mathematics are as follows—

(*i*) To develop their intellectual powers and disciplines.

(*ii*) To enable to make use of the learning in mathematics in their daily life.

(*iii*) To help the student in recieving social and moral virtues.

(*iv*) To help in the study of other subjects and future learning in mathematics.

(*v*) To give the insight to recognise relationships between different branches and topics of mathematics.

(*vi*) To meet this different interests, to develop their aesthetic abilities and to help them in their power of utilisation of their leisure time.

(*vii*) To help them in becoming self-dependent for mastering new topics and problems of mathematics.

(*viii*) To make them understand the contribution of mathematics in the development of culture and civilizaiton.

(*ix*) To prepare for the future vocation or occupation.

LANGUAGE OF MATHEMATICS

WHAT IS A LANGUAGE?

Here are some definitions of language:

1. A set (finite or infinite) of sentences, each finite in length and constructed out of a finite set of element —Noam Chomsky
2. The code we all use to express ourselves and communicate to others—Speech & Language Therapy Glossary of Terms
3. A systematic means of communicating by the use of sounds or conventional symbols —Word Net
4. A system of words used in a particular discipline —Word Net

These definitions describe language in terms of the following components:

- A vocabulary of symbols or words
- a grammar consisting or rules or how these symbols may be used
- A community of people who use and understand these symbols
- A range of meanings that can be communicated with these symbols

Each of these components also found in the language of mathematics.

The language of mathematics is the system used by mathematicians to communicate mathematical ideas among themselves. This language consists of a substrate of some natural language (for example English) using technical terms and grammatical conventions that are peculiar to mathematical discourse, supplemented by a highly specialized symbolic notation for mathematical formulas.

Like natural languages in general, discourse using the language of mathematics can employ a scala of registers. Research article in academic journals use a more formal tone than oral exchanges over a scribbled-upon napkin in the university cafeteria.

THE VOCABULARY OF MATHEMATICS

Mathematical notation has assimilated symbols from many different alphabets and typefaces. It also includes symbols that are specific to mathematics, such as $\forall \exists \nabla \wedge \infty$

Mathematical notation is central to the power of modern mathematics. Though the algebra of Al-Khwarizmi did not use such symbols, it solved equations using many more rules than are used today with symbolic notation, and had great difficulty working with multiple variables (which using symbolic notation can simply be called *x, y, z*, etc.). Sometimes formulas cannot be understood without a written or spoken explanation, but often they are sufficient by themselves, and sometimes they are difficult to read aloud or information is lost in the translation to words, as when several parenthetical factors are involved or when a complex structure like a matrix is manipulated.

Like any other profession, mathematics also has its own brand of technical terminology. In some cases, a word in general usage has a different and specific meaning within mathematics—example are group, ring, field, category, term, and factor etc.

In other cases, specialist terms have been created which do not exist outside of mathematics—examples are tensor, fractal, functor. Mathematical statements have their own moderately complex taxonomy, being divided into axioms, conjectures, theorems, lemmas and corollaries. And there are stock phrases in mathematics, used with specific meanings, such as *"if and only if"*, *"necessary and sufficient"* and *"without loss of generality"*. Such phrases are known as mathematical jargon.

When mathematicians communicate with each other informally, they use phrases that help to convey ideas. Examples of some of the more idiomatic phrases are "kill this term", "vanish this interval" and "grow this variable".

The vocabulary of mathematics also has visual elements. Diagrams are used informally on blackboards, as well as more formally in published work. When used appropriately, diagrams display schematic information more easily. Diagrams also help visually and aid intuitive calculations. Sometimes, as in a visual proof, a diagram even serves as complete justification for a proposition. A system of diagram conventions may evolve into a mathematical notation.

THE GRAMMAR OF MATHEMATICS

The grammar used for mathematical discourse is essentially the grammar of the natural language used as substrate, but with several mathematics-specific peculiarities.

Most notably, the mathematical notation used for formulas has its own grammar, not dependent on a specific natural language, but shared internationally by mathematicians regardless of their mother tongues. This includes the conventions that the formulas are written predominantly left to right, also when the writing system of the substrate language is right-to-left, and that the Latin alphabet is commonly used for simple variables and parameters. A formula such as

$\sin x + a \cos 2x \geq 0$ is understood by Chinese and Israeli mathematicians alike.

Such mathematical formulas can be a part of speech in a natural-language phrases, or even assume the role of a full-fledged sentence. For example, the formula above, an equation, can be considered a sentence or sentential phrase in which the greater than or equal to symbol has the role of a verb. In careful speech, this can be made clear by pronouncing "≥" as "is greater than or equal to", but in an informal context mathematicians may shorten this to "greater or equal" and yet handle this grammatically like a verb.

Mathematical formulas can be vocalized (spoken aloud). The vocalization system for formulas has to be learned, and is dependent on the underlying natural language. For example, when using English, the expression "$f(x)$" is conventionally pronounced "eff of eks", where the insertion of the preposition "of" is not suggested by the notation per se. The expression "$\frac{dy}{dx}$" on the other hand, is vocalized like "dee-why-dee-eks", with complete omission of the fraction bar, in other contexts often pronounced "over".

Characteristic for mathematical discourse – both formal and informal – is the use of the inclusive first person plural "we" to mean: "the audience (or reader) together with the speaker (or author)".

THE LANGUAGE COMMUNITY OF MATHEMATICS

Mathematics is used by mathematicians, who form a global community composed of speakers of many languages. It is also used by students of mathematics. As mathematics is a part of primary education in almost all countries almost all educated people have some exposure to pure mathematics. It is interesting to note that there are very few cultural dependencies or barriers in modern mathematics. There are international mathematics competitions, such as the International Mathematical Olympiad, and international co-operation between professional mathematicians in commonplace.

MATHEMATICS IS A LANGUAGE

"My own attitude, which I share with many of my colleagues is simply that mathematics is a language. Like English, Latin or Chinese, these are certain concepts for which mathematics is particularly well suited, it would be as foolish to attempt to write a love poem the fundamental theorem of Algebra using the English language."

—RLE Schwarzenberger (2000)

Mathematics can communicate a range of meanings that is as wide as (althought different from) that of a natural language. Here are there broad categories:

- **Mathematics describes the real world:** Many areas of mathematics originated with attempts to describe and solve real world phenomena from measuring farms (geometry) to falling apples (calculus) to gambling (probability). Mathematics is widely used in modern physics and engineering, and has been hugely successful in helping us to understand more about the universe around us from its largest scales (physical cosmology) to its smallest (quantum mechanics). Indeed, the very success of mathematics in this respect has been a source of puzzlement for some philosophers.
- **Mathematics describes abstract structures:** On the other hand, there are areas of pure mathematics which deal with abstract structures, which have no known physical counterparts at all. However, it is difficult to give any categorical examples here, as even the most abstract structures can be co-opted as models in some branch of physics.
- **Mathematics describes mathematics:** Mathematics can be used reflexively to describe itself—this is an area of mathematics called metamathematics.

As a language mathematics has own symbols, word and rules of sentence. Which is based on a certian consistant set of assumptions and built up from there according to the rules of logic. Such logic is necessary for developing mathematical thought. It's understanding and applications depend upon the level of development of ordinary language. *e.g.,* "Every rectangle is a parallelogram but every parallelogram is not a rectangle. Here, only after developing the use of conjuctions *i.e.* but, hence, so therefore, or and etc. the children become ready for or ordinary language are also used in mathematics. But these words have an exact mathematical meaning. For example — sum, difference, addition, power, multiplication, division, subtraction etc.

Alternative views

Some definitions of language, emphasize the spoken nature of language. Mathematics would not qualify as a language under these definitions, as it is primarily a written form of communication. However, these definitions would also disqualify sign languages, which are now recognized as languages in their own right, independent of spoken language.

Other linguists believe no valid comparison can be made between mathematics and language, because they are simply too different.

EVALUATION

"Evaluation is systematic, continuous process of determining the effectiveness of the learning experiences provided in the class room."

—NCERT

"Evaluation is a continuous process; it forms an integral part of the total system of education and is intimately related to educational objectives. It exercises a good influence on pupils study habits and the teacher's methods of instruction and thus helps not only to measure educational achievement but also to improve it. The techniques of evaluation are means of collecting evidences about the students' development in desirable directions."

—Kothari Commission

"Evaluation is relatively a new technical term, introduced to designate a more comprehensive concept of measurement that is implied in conventional test and examinations."

—The Encyclopaedia of Education Research

"Evaluation may be defined as a systematic process of determining the extent to which educational objectives are achieved by the pupils."

—Dandekar

"Evaluation is an inclusive concept which indicates all kinds of means to ascertain the quality, value and effectiveness of desired outcomes. It is a compound of objective evidence and objective observation. It is total and final estimate. It is a valuable, an indispensable guide to the modification of policies and to further action." —Wesley

Evaluation is consistently identified in the professional literature as both a critical component and a weak link in the delivery of professional development, but it must not be overlooked. Any effective evaluation should concern itself with changes that take place in instructional practices.

Both formal and informal methods of evaluation can be employed in determining the impact of the Workshop/Presentation on instructional behaviour. More formal methods use some type of instrument to assess changes in instructional behaviour, before and after the workshop. Practitioners can complete self-evaluations, or a peer or supervisor can complete an evaluation instrument after classroom observations. Analysis of the completed instruments enables practitioners and supervisors to identify areas of strength and weakness and to work on improving instruction. Other less formal or more qualitative approaches include maintaining records/journals of an instructor's own reflections of what occurs in the classroom, or conducting ethnographic studies that describe what happens in the classroom when new instructional strategies are implemented.

In the Indian education system, the term evaluation is associated with examination, stress and anxiety. All efforts at curriculum definition and renewal come to naught if they cannot engage with the bulwark of the evaluation and examination system embedded in schooling. We are concerned about the ill effects that examinations have on efforts to make learning and teaching meaningful and joyous for children. Currently, the board examinations negatively influence all testing and assessment through out the school years, beginning with pre-school.

At the same time, a good evaluation and examination system can become an integral part of the learning process and benefit both the learners themselves and the educational system by giving credible feedback. This section addresses evaluation and assessment as they are relevant to the normal course of teaching-learning in the school, as a part of the curriculum.

RELATIONSHIP BETWEEN OBJECTIVES, LEARNING EXPERIENCES AND EVALUATION

The objectives, learning experiences and evaluation are all interrelated to each other. Evaluation is based on objectives of teaching and learning experiences and also evaluates the objectives at the same time. Thus, in the classroom teaching the teacher organises suitable teaching- learning activities in order to promote desired expected changes in behaviour. It is much broader term than text or examination. It concerned not only with assessment of the students but also with the whole process of education. After deciding what to teach? (content) and how to teach? (Methods). Why to teach? (object). The question arises what has been achieved? Thus evaluation helps to answer the question what has been achieved by the student? Thus evaluation is the process through which assessment, achievement and effectiveness of educational programme is determined.

Objectives
[Knowledge, Understanding Application, Skills]

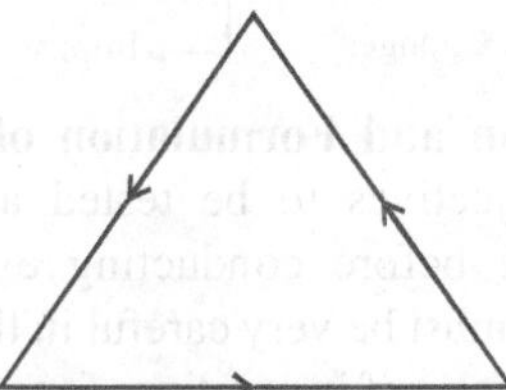

Learning Experiences
[Lecture, Problem Solving Discussion, Text book]

Evaluation
[Essay type, Oral, Written, Rating scale etc.]

Objectives
(Why to teach?)

Content
(What to teach?)

Methods
(How to teach?)

Evaluation
(What has been achieved?)

IMPORTANT FEATURES OF EVALUATION

1. It may be used to improve curriculum, instructions, methods and examination etc.
2. It is diagnostic so that it may provide basis for remedial teaching.
3. It measures the direction and extent behavioural change.
4. Evaluation offers feedback to the entire educational system.
5. It is pupil oriented and activity based programme.
6. It is directly related with the teaching process.
7. It is continuous process.
8. It helps in determining the potentialities and interests of children.
9. It not only measures the educational achievement of the students but also helps in their progress.
10. There is a close relationship between instructional objectives, teaching process and evaluation.
11. It is helpful to a teacher in diagnosing children's difficulties.
12. It makes the reaching-learning process dynamic and innovative.
13. It is a wider concept than testing examination and measurement.
14. It becomes easy to know the present status of the children from their day-to-day record.
15. Evaluation is comprehensive (complete) as it includes everything that can be evaluated.
16. Evaluation is systematic and scientific.
17. Evaluation is both quantitative and qualitative aspects.
18. It is a judgment giving process.
19. Evaluation makes education purpose-centred.
20. Evaluation is concerned with growth and development of the student and not with the status in the group.

PURPOSE & FUNCTION OF EVALUATION

1. **Motivation :** To motivate the children for better learning.
2. **Present Status of the Children :** Evaluation helps in determining the present status of the children in the teaching-learning process.
3. **Guidance and Counselling :** Evaluation provides basis for guidance and counselling to children, by recognising individual differences of children.
4. **To Diagnose the Problems :** Evaluating procedures help the teacher to know the shortcomings of his students, and to diagnose children's weaknesses and strength for further instructions.
5. **Measure Examination System :** Evaluation helps the teacher to measure examination system *i.e.* the topper in the class or failure in the class, etc.
6. **Rate of Progress in Children :** Evaluation helps to determine the rate of progress in children *i.e.* how much marks did Ritu achieved in her 1st term examination and final examinations etc.
7. **Classification of Students :** Evaluation helps in the classification of students into different categories *i.e.* gifted, backward or average students.
8. **Basis for Selection :** With the help of various aptitude and attitude test for selection in various course of study, placement etc. evaluation plays a vital role.

9. **Discover Innovative and Effective Teaching Methods :** Evaluation helps to discover innovative and effective teaching methods by diagnosing children's weakness and strengths.
10. **Improvement in Curriculum :** By evaluation the teacher collect evidences for improvement in curriculum.
11. **Success in Teaching :** Evaluation helps the teacher to assess the success in her teaching.
12. **Improvement in Teaching-learning Process :** Evaluation helps to know the teacher the weaknesses of the student and on those base she brings improvements in teaching-learning process.
13. **Grading the Students :** Evaluation helps in grading the students on the basis of their quarterly, half-yearly and annual examinations and thus knowing the rank of the students of a class.
14. To measure behavioural changes of the children *i.e.* their interest, physical, emotional, moral and social development, etc.
15. **Encourage Teachers for Action Research :** The teacher adopt new strategies for action research on the basis of evaluation.
16. **Feedback to Teacher & Students :** Evaluation helps to give reinforcement and feedback to both the teacher and pupils.
17. **For Remedial Work :** Evaluation helps the students to find out remedies for the problems, so that better results can be achieved.
18. **Clarification of Objectives of Education :** Evaluation is based on objectives. The teacher tries to understand the objectives of each topic in the light of their utility in education.
19. **Basis of Admission :** The students's progress is evaluated by various method *i.e.* tests, annual examination and on its basis the students is given admission in the next class.
20. **In Giving Scholarships :** Evaluation helps in judging the progress of the students and on the basis of this scholarships are provided to students with very high grade.

PROCESS OF EVALUATION

Evaluation process involves the following steps:

1. Selection and formulation of objectives.
2. Defining objectives in terms of behavioural changes.
3. Selection of tools and techniques of evaluation.
4. Interpretation and generalisation of results.
5. Feedback the results for improvement of teaching learning process.

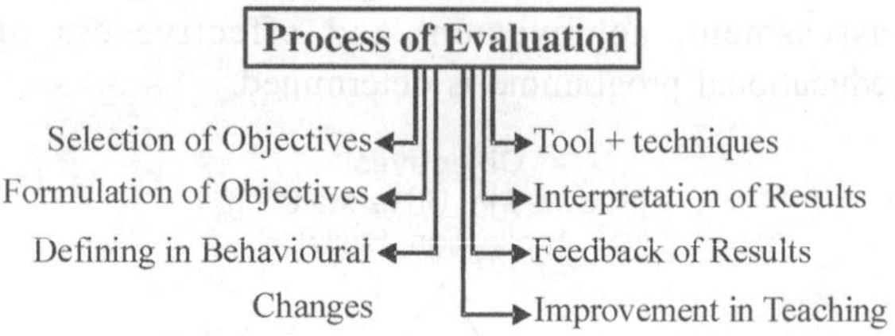

1. **Selection and Formulation of Objectives :** The objectives to be tested are selected in advance before conducting evaluation. The teacher must be very careful in the instructions. On the basis of instructions for objectives given the test items are constructed.
2. **Formulation of Objectives :** A teacher has to be very careful about the instructional objectives of various classes and on that basis of the objective specified various test items are formed for various classes, etc.
3. **Defining Objectives in Behavioural Terms :** After determining and formulation of objectives to be tested teacher should define the objectives clearly in terms of expected changes in pupils' behaviour *i.e.*
   (a) Knowledge
   (b) Understanding
   (c) Application
   (d) Skills
4. **Selection of Tools and Techniques of Evaluation :** Selection of suitable tools and techniques depends upon the types of evidence required. Tools and techniques must provide evidence to the teaching objectives to which they are concerned. They should also satisfy criteria of a good measuring rod or good evaluation.
5. **Use of Tools and Techniques and Making Results :** After selecting and developing the tools, teacher applies them in testing situations, she scores or other evidence regarding the behavioural changes are recorded. On the basis of recorded evidences and information conclusions are drawn.
6. **Interpretation and Generalisation of Results :** The evidence which we get through various tools and technique of evaluation are not meaningful to the learner, the teacher or the parents unless the scores are interpreted properly. Then the results are analysed in terms of objective to rate the progress of an individuals's comparative performance in the class. This collected data helps to generalise the level of achievements required for each class or individual student etc.

7. Feedback of the Results for Improvement of Teaching Learning Process : On the basis of analysis of test results or evidences recorded, pupil's progress is made and shown to the parents. This is necessary for parents to know child's self-evaluation strengths and weakness of their ward for proper diagnosis.

8. Improvements in Teaching-Learning Process: On the basis of the feedback of the results, and after for diagnostic measures, re-teaching and remedial teaching is arranged and the teacher tries to adopt some new strategies in her teaching-learning process for better achievements in student's progress.

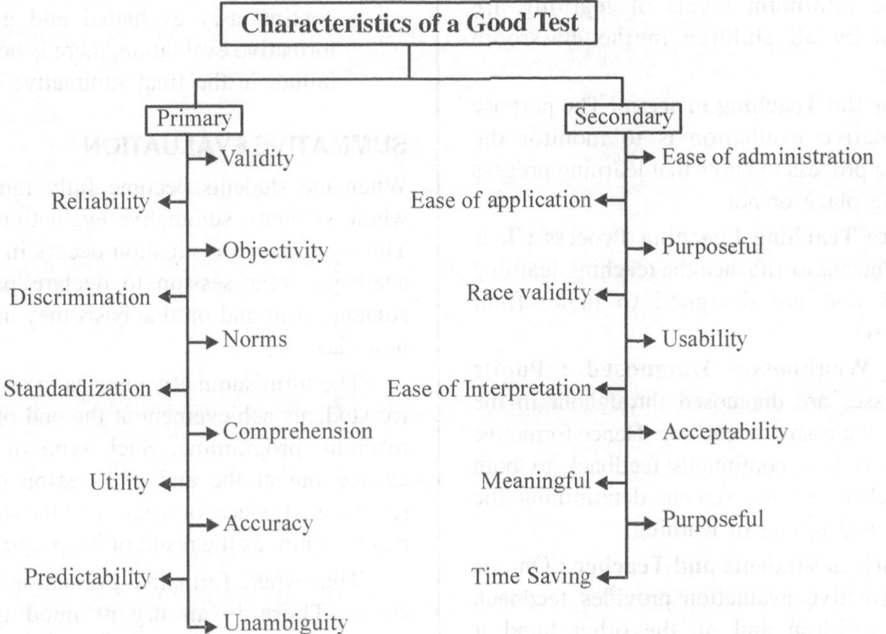

BASIC PRINCIPLES OF EVALUATION

The foundation or base of any building should be very strong, if the building is very beautiful but the foundation or base *i.e.* the pillars on which the building stands are weak, the building will collapse. Similarly, if evaluation is not based on certain basic principles, the evaluation system cannot said to be effective and teaching aims will not be achieved. Some of the basic principles of evaluation are:

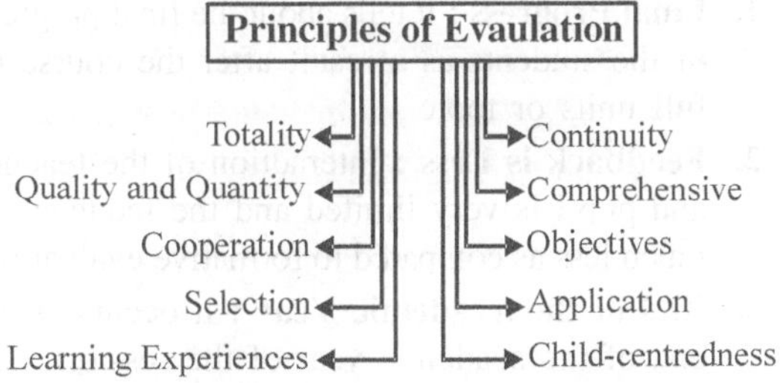

TYPES OF EVALUATION

1. Diagnostic Evaluation
2. Prognosis Evaluation
3. Formative Evaluation
4. Summative Evaluation
5. Comprehensive Evaluation
6. Continuous Evaluation

FORMATIVE EVALUATION

When a teacher has taught a part of unit or some topics or content or any learning concepts he or she wants to judge the outcome of the students. In the same manner the student also need to know their progress in the path of learning. The formative evaluation is a great help to the teacher as well as student as it provides the information to both about the strength and weakness of their teaching and learning.

The term formative means the ongoing or systematic assessment of student's achievement in the course of teaching programme. Formative evaluation occurs between the formative stage that it when the process of teaching and learning is going on and not after it is completed.

According to New Education Policy (1986)—Formative evaluation is an integral part of teaching-learning process. The formative evaluation also is helpful in the process of curriculum construction at the formative stage.

The formative evaluation is carried out both in formal [*i.e.*, question-answer, assignments, tests, quizzes, draft-work, concept maps, peer response, groups porfolio, reviews, conference etc) as well as informal (*e.g.*, listening students comments, conversations, observations etc.)

FEATURES/NEED/IMPORTANCE OF FORMATIVE EVALUATION

1. **Minimum Level of Learning :** The formative evaluation can be used by the teachers to ensure that the minimum levels of learning are attained by all children in the classroom teaching.
2. **Monitor the Teaching Process :** The purpose of formative evaluation is to monitor the teaching process to know that learning process is taking place or not.
3. **Enhance Teaching Learning Process :** It is mainly meant to enhance the teaching-learning process and not designed to make final judgements.
4. **Pupils Weaknesses Diagnosed :** Pupils weaknesses are diagnosed throughout in the process of classroom teaching. Hence formative evaluation is a continuous feedback to both the teacher and the student determining the success and failure of learning.
5. **Feedback to Students and Teacher :** On one side formative evaluation provides feedback to the children and on the other hand it provides feedback to the teacher also and can modify her teaching process accordingly.
6. **Monitoring Pupil's Learning Process :** It is helpful in monitoring pupils learning progress.
7. **Helps to Increase Retention :** It makes easy for the students and helps to increase retention and transfer of learning of the unit or topic being taught.
8. **Self Evaluation :** Formative evaluation can also be used as a self-evaluation. Can also be used as a self-evaluation devices by the children.
9. **Correcting Learning Deficiencies :** It also helps the teacher for correcting her learning deficiencies and weaknesses.
10. **Keep Students Attentive :** Formative test also keep the students attentive.
11. **Immediate Decision Making :** Formative evaluation is most useful for the immediate decision making that students face.
12. **Variety of Techniques Used :** This is a continuous and integral part of teaching where one uses variety of techniques *i.e.* attitude, aptitude, inventories, rating scale, checklists, etc. and alert listeners, and students remain informative for the topic being taught.
13. **Assimilation of Various Concepts :** Formative evaluation determines how well the students are assimilating various concepts, skills and behavioural changes.
14. **Helps to Improve Instructional Behaviour :** Formative evaluation helps to improve the instructional behaviour in the development phase, rather than being in trouble over its failure after the programme is completed.
15. **No Reason for Failure :** When student is continuously evaluated and guided through formative evaluation, there is no reason for the failure in the final summative evaluation.

SUMMATIVE EVALUATION

When the students become fully familiar with the whole syllabus, summative evaluation is conducted. Thus summative evaluation occurs in the end of the academic year session to declare pass/fail of the student result and on that basis they are promoted to new classes.

The turm summative means to assigning a grade for students achievement at the end of a term of the teaching programme. Such type of evaluation is carried out at the end of a lesson or unit, and it represent a find test or measure of the students progress made by him as the result of his progress of teaching.

Thus where formative evaluation reaches its last stage. There is an urgent need of summative evaluation. It occurs at the end of a term or a sesson to measure the success of students and to know what has been achieved by him. For summative evaluation both types of techniques *i.e.*, formal and informal techniques may be used. The formal techniques includes—standardised as well as teacher made test, questionaire, interviews, rating scale, assignments etc. Internal techniques include—observations, discussions, comments and feedback given by the student etc.

FEATURES/NEED/IMPORTANCE OF SUMMATIVE EVALUATION

1. **Final Progress :** It tells about the final progress of the students as a result after the course of full units or topic.
2. **Feedback is Less :** Interaction of the teacher and pupil is very limited and the feedback is much less as compared to formative evaluation.
3. **End of the Academic Year :** It occurs at the end of the academic year of the session.
4. **Declared Pass or Fail :** The students are declared pass or fail on the basis of summative evaluation and on its basis they are promoted to new classes.
5. **Examination Conducted :** It is in the form of annual examination, terminal examination, external examination (board examination *i.e.* CBSE etc.).

6. **Promotion of Students :** Helps in the classification of grades and promotion of students.
7. **End of Course :** It is treated as an end of the course activity.
8. **Results Help to Choose Career :** The result of the students helps them to choose their careers, placements and are predictions for their future success.

On the basis of above description it is clear that formal and informal methods are techniques which are equally used in formative and summative evaluation. But objectives of the techniques are different in both the evaluations.

Why Evaluate?

Effective teachers use a variety of means, some formal and others informal, to determine how much and how well their students are learning. For example, to formally evaluate student learning, most teachers use quizzes, tests, examinations, term papers, lab reports, and homework.These formal evaluation techniques help the instructor to evaluate student achievement and assign grades.

To evaluate classroom learning informally, teachers also use a variety of techniques. For example, teachers pose questions, listen carefully to student questions and comments, and monitor body language and facial expressions. Informal, often implicit evaluations permit the teacher to make adjustments in their teaching: to slow down or review material in response to questions, confusion, and misunderstandings; or to move on when student performance exceeds expectations.

When teaching at a distance, educators must address a different teaching challenge than when teaching in a traditional classroom. For example, instructors no longer have:

- A traditional, familiar classroom.
- A relatively homogeneous group of students.
- Face-to-face feedback during class (*e.g.*, students' questions, comments, body language, and facial expressions).
- Total control over the distance delivery system.
- Covenient opportunities to talk to students individually.

For these reasons, distance educators may find it useful to not only formally evaluate students through testing and homework, but to use a more informal approach in collecting data determine.

PROBLEMS OF TEACHING

Any analysis of mathematics education in our schools will identify a range of issues as problematic. We structure our understanding of these issues around the following four problems which we deem to be the core areas of concern:

1. A sense of fear and failure regarding mathematics among a majority of children,
2. A curriculum that disappoints both a talented minority as well as the non-participating majority at the same time,
3. Crude methods of assessment that encourage perception of mathematics as mechanical computation, and
4. Lack of teacher preparation and support in the teaching of mathematics.

Each of these can and need to be expanded on, since they concern the curricular framework in essential ways.

Fear and Failure

If any subject area of study evokes wide emotional comment, it is mathematics. While no one educated in Tamil would profess (or at the least, not without a sense of shame) ignorance of any Tirukkural, it is quite the social norm for anyone to proudly declare that (s)he never could learn mathematics. While these may be adult attitudes, among children (who are compelled to pass mathematics examinations) there is often fear and anxiety. Mathematics anxiety and 'math phobia' are terms that are used in popular literature.

In the Indian context, there is a special dimension to such anxiety. With the universalisation of elementary education made a national priority, and elementary education a legal right, at this historic juncture, a serious attempt must be made to look into every aspect that alienates children in school and contributes towards their non-participation, eventually leading to their dropping out of the system. If any subject taught in school plays a significant role in alienating children and causing them to stop attending school, perhaps mathematics, which inspires so much dread, must take a big part of the blame.

Such fear is closely linked to a sense of failure. By Class III or IV, many children start seeing themselves as unable to cope with the demands made by mathematics. In high school, among children who fail only in one or two subjects in year-end examinations and hence are detained, the maximum numbers fail in mathematics. This statistic pursues us right through to Class X, which is when the Indian state issues a certificate of education to a student. The largest numbers of Board Exam failures also happen in mathematics.

There are many perceptive studies and analyses on what causes fear of mathematics in schools. Central among them is the cumulative nature of mathematics. If you struggle with decimals, then you will struggle with percentages; if you struggle with percentages, then you will struggle with algebra and other mathematics subjects as well. The other principal reason is said to be the predominance of symbolic language. When symbols are manipulated without understanding, after a point, boredom and bewilderment dominate for many children, and dissociation develops.

Failure in mathematics could be read through social indicators as well. Structural problems in Indian education, reflecting structures of social discrimination, by way of class, caste and gender, contribute further to failure (and perceived failure) in mathematics education as well. Prevalent social attitudes which see girls as incapable of mathematics, or which, for centuries, have associated formal computational abilities with the upper castes, deepen such failure by way of creating self-fulfilling expectations.

A special mention must be made of problems created by the language used in textbooks, especially at the elementary level. For a vast majority of Indian children, the language of mathematics learnt in school is far removed from their everyday speech, and especially forbidding. This becomes a major force of alienation in its own right.

Disappointing Curriculum

Any mathematics curriculum that emphasises procedure and knowledge of formulas over understanding is bound to enhance anxiety. The prevalent practice of school mathematics goes further a silent majority give up early on, remaining content to fail in mathematics, or at best, to see it through, maintaining a minimal level of achievement. For these children, what the curriculum offers is a store of mathematical facts, borrowed temporarily while preparing for tests.

On the other hand, it is widely acknowledged that more than in any other content discipline, mathematics is the subject that also sees great motivation and talent even at an early age in a small number of children. These are children who take to quantisation and algebra easily and carry on with great facility.

What the curriculum offers for such children is also intense disappointment. By not offering conceptual depth, by not challenging them, the curriculum settles for minimal use of their motivation. Learning procedures may be easy for them, but their understanding and capacity for reasoning remain underexercised.

Crude Assessment

We talked of fear and failure. While what happens in class may alienate, it never evokes panic, as does the examination. Most of the problems cited above relate to the tyranny of procedure and memorization of formulas in school mathematics, and the central reason for the ascendancy of procedure is the nature of assessment and evaluation. Tests are designed (only) for assessing a student's knowledge of procedure and memory of formulas and facts, and given the criticality of examination performance in school life, concept learning is replaced by procedural memory. Those children who cannot do such replacement successfully experience panic, and suffer failure.

While mathematics is the major ground for formal problem solving in school, it is also the only arena where children see little room for play in answering questions. Every question in mathematics is seen to have one unique answer, and either you know it or you don't. In Language, Social Studies, or even in Science, you may try and demonstrate partial knowledge, but (as the students see it), there is no scope for doing so in mathematics. Obviously, such a perception is easily coupled to anxiety.

Amazingly, while there has been a great deal of research in mathematics education and some of it has led to changes in pedagogy and curriculum, the area that has seen little change in our schools over a hundred years or more is evaluation procedures in mathematics. It is not accidental that even a quarterly examination in Class VII is not very different in style from a Board examination in Class X, and the same pattern dominates even the end-of chapter exercises given in textbooks. It is always application of some piece of information given in the text to solve a specific problem that tests use of formalism. Such antiquated and crude methods of assessment have to be thoroughly overhauled if any basic change is to be brought about.

Inadequate Teacher Preparation

More so than any other content discipline, mathematics education relies very heavily on the preparation that the teacher has, in her own understanding of mathematics, of the nature of mathematics, and in her bag of pedagogic techniques. Textbook-centred pedagogy dulls the teacher's own mathematics activity.

At two ends of the spectrum, mathematics teaching poses special problems. At the primary level, most teachers assume that they know all the mathematics needed, and in the absence of any specific pedagogic training, simply try and uncritically reproduce the techniques they experienced in their school days. Often this ends up perpetuating problems across time and space.

At the secondary and higher secondary level, some teachers face a different situation. The syllabi have considerably changed since their school days, and in the absence of systematic and continuing education programmes for teachers, their fundamentals in many concept areas are not strong. This encourages reliance on 'notes' available in the market, offering little breadth or depth for the students.

While inadequate teacher preparation and support acts negatively on all of school mathematics, at the primary stage, its main consequence is this: mathematics pedagogy rarely resonates with the findings of children's psychology. At the upper primary stage, when the language of abstractions is formalised in algebra, inadequate teacher preparation reflects as inability to link formal mathematics with experiential learning. Later on, it reflects as incapacity to offer connections within mathematics or across subject areas to applications in the sciences, thus depriving students of important motivation and appreciation.

Other Systematic Problems

We wish to briefly mention a few other systematic sources of problems as well. One major problem is that of compartmentalisation. There is very little systematic communication between primary school and high school teachers of mathematics, and none at all between high school and college teachers of mathematics. Most school teachers have never even seen, let alone interacted with or consulted, research mathematicians. Those involved in teacher education are again typically outside the realm of college or research mathematics.

Another important problem is that of curricular acceleration: a generation ago, calculus was first encountered by a student in college. Another generation earlier, analytical geometry was considered college mathematics. But these are all part of school curriculum now. Such acceleration has naturally meant pruning of some topics: there is far less solid geometry or spherical geometry now. One reason for the narrowing is that calculus and differential equations are critically important in undergraduate sciences, technology and engineering, and hence it is felt that early introduction of these topics helps students proceeding further on these lines. Whatever the logic, the shape of mathematics education has become taller and more spindly, rather than broad and rounded.

While we have mentioned gender as a systematic issue, it is worth understanding the problem in some detail. Mathematics tends to be regarded as a 'masculine domain'. This perception is aided by the complete lack of references in textbooks to women mathematicians, the absence of social concerns in the designing of curricula which would enable children questioning received gender ideologies and the absence of reference to women's lives in problems. A study of mathematics textbooks found that in the problem sums, not a single reference was made to women's clothing, although several problems referred to the buying of cloth, etc.

Classroom research also indicates a fairly systematic devaluation of girls as incapable of 'mastering' mathematics, even when they perform reasonably well at verbal as well as cognitive tasks in mathematics. It has been seen that teachers tend to address boys more than girls, which feeds into the construction of the normative mathematics learner as male. Also, when instructional decisions are in teachers' hands, their gendered constructions colour the mathematical learning strategies of girls and boys, with the latter using more invented strategies for problem-solving, which reflects greater conceptual understanding. Studies have shown that teachers tend to attribute boys' mathematical 'success' more to ability, and girls' success more to effort. Classroom discourses also give some indication of how the 'masculinising' of mathematics occurs, and the profound influence of gender ideologies in patterning notions of academic competence in school. With performance in mathematics signifying school 'success', girls are clearly at the losing end.

RECOMMENDATIONS

While the litany of problems and challenges magnifies the distance we need to travel to arrive at the vision articulated above, it also offers hope by way of pointing us where we need to go and what steps we may/must take.

We summarise what we believe to be the central directions for action towards our stated vision. We group them again into four central themes:

1. Shifting the focus of mathematics education from achieving 'narrow' goals to 'higher' goals,
2. Engaging every student with a sense of success, while at the same time offering conceptual challenges to the emerging mathematician,
3. Changing modes of assessment to examine students' mathematisation abilities rather than procedural knowledge,
4. Enriching teachers with a variety of mathematical resources.

ERROR ANALYSIS

ERRORS BY STUDENTS

Identification of students' specific errors is especially important for students with learning disabilities and low performing students. By pinpointing student errors, the teacher can provide instruction targeted to the student's area of need. In general, students who have difficulty learning math typically lack important conceptual knowledge for several reasons, including an inability to process information at the rate of the instructional pace, a lack of adequate opportunities to respond (*i.e.*, practice), a lack of specific feedback from teachers regarding misunderstanding or non-understanding, anxiety about mathematics, and difficulties in visual and/or auditory processing.

Lack of Knowledge

Students' lack of knowledge could be a major reason why they cannot solve certain problems consistently. As noted above, there are three types of errors: procedural, factual, and conceptual. When a student has not followed the correct steps (or procedures) to solve a problem, this is a procedural error. Factual errors are mistakes that students make when they cannot recall a fact required to solve a problem or if they have not mastered basic facts. Procedural and factual errors (also known as 'slips') are generally not due to inherent misunderstandings; slips may be due to memory deficits, impulsivity, or visual-motor integration problems and are easier to identify than conceptual errors. Conceptual errors (or 'bugs') may look like procedural errors, but they occur because the student does not fully understand a specific math concept, such as place value. As such, bugs are more serious errors. To determine if an error is conceptual, teachers should check by asking the student to represent the problem with concrete objects or show and explain the steps used to solve the problem.

Poor Attention and Carelessness

Other possible causes of student error are poor attention and carelessness. To address this issue, teachers should first consider the alignment between the instruction, student ability, and the task. For example, lack of attention is more likely to occur during a long-division lesson when the students have not learned division or mastered necessary pre-requisite skills (*i.e.*, there is a mismatch between the instruction and student ability). Inattention could occur during parts of lesson where students are required to listen for an extended period of time. In such cases, teachers should consider delivering the materials in a brisk, enthusiastic manner, making sure that students are given ample opportunities to engage and respond to questions. When lack of attention occurs during independent work, teachers should provide clear expectations for completing tasks, monitor student work, and provide corrective feedback.

To Conduct Error Analysis

The following steps describe the error analysis process, applied to mathematics:

1. Collect a sample of student work for each type of problem (*e.g.*, single-digit addition; two-digit multiplication with regrouping), with at least three to five items for each problem type.
2. Have the student verbalize or think aloud as s/he solves the problems without providing any type of cues or prompting.
3. Record all student responses in written and verbal format.
4. Analyse the responses and look for patterns among common problem types.
5. Look for examples of "exceptions" to an apparent pattern (accurate "exceptions" could signal that the student does not fully understand the procedure or concept).
6. Describe the patterns observed in simple language and the possible reasons for the student's problems (*e.g.*, if a student did not regroup double-digit addition problems, it could be a sign that the student does not understand the concept of place value).
7. Interview the student by asking him/her to explain how s/he solved the problem to confirm suspected error patterns.

ERRORS IN EVALUATION

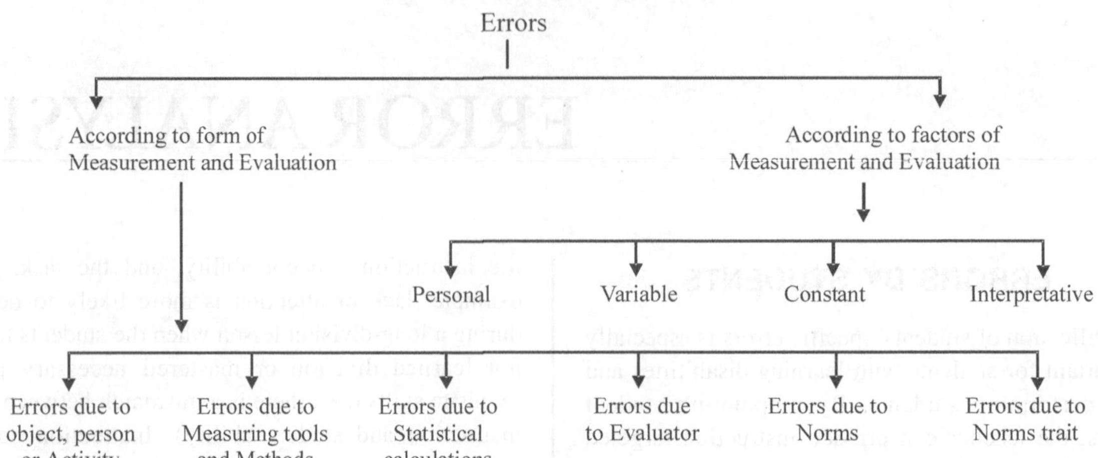

Errors due to Object, Person or Activity

The errors which occur due to object, person or activity of whose quality has to be measured and evaluated. For example, it would be difficult to measures and evaluate the actual ability of a student if he or she is not mentally or physically normal or he or she is tired or frightened or suffering from diseases and not experienced that how the test to be conducted.

Solution: Such type of errors should be reduced by providing the complete information about the test to the student and sympathetically treatment also.

Errors due to Measuring Tools and Methods

Such errors takes place if inadequate tools and methods are used in measuring the qualities of students. For example, if an achievement test is not used to measure the ability, the measurement result will not be correct.

Solution: Such type of errors can be rectified by construction of appropriate tools and methods that should be objective, valid and reliable.

Errors due to Statistical Calculations

If an evaluator commits an error in selecting the appropriate statistical calculation then the evaluation results also get incorrect. Such error is included in this type.

Solution: Such type of errors should be removed by a clear knowledge of statistics and calculations.

Errors due to Evaluator

If the measurer or evaluator is not able to use the tools and methods as well as suitable statistical norm then in this case errors arise. For example, if the evaluator is agitated or prejudiced then he or she can not measure and evaluate correctly.

Solution: Such type of error should be eradicated being objective during measurement and evaluation.

Errors due to Norms

When an evaluator does not have clear knowledge of norms of analysis of the evaluation results then he or she can not analyse the results of measurement correctly.

Solution: Such type of error should be rectified providing the clear knowledge of the norms to the evaluation.

Errors due to Trait

If an evaluator is not aware of measuring trait (quality). He or she is not clear that which kind of ability of the student has to be measured then he or she can not be able to construct an appropriate test. Consequently, he or she can not measure the ability suitably.

Solution: Such type of errors should be eradicated by determining the measuring qualities.

Personal Errors

Evaluator's physical and mental state, his/her personal view point, his/her liking and prejudices effect directly or indirectly the measurement and evaluation process. Such type of errors are generally found in descriptive type answers.

Solution: Such type of errors should be corrected by making the test objective.

Variable Errors

This type of errors occur due to administration of meansuring object, person, activity, quality, tools or methods. Errors are committed due to abnormal physical or mental state of students, unsuitability of tools and methods, enadequate administration and unclarity of measuring variables.

Solution: Such type of errors should be eradicated by dealing with the students sympathetically, select most suitable method, adequate administration and understand clear measuring qualities.

Constant Errors

These type of errors occurs in the form of tools or methods and their use. Marks obtained by all the students are affected by the errors.

Solution: Such type of errors can be eradicated by making the methods more valid.

Interpretative Errors

The errors occuring in analysis of measurement results.

Solution: Such type of errors can be done away with the development of suitable norms and correct statistical calculations.

DIAGNOSTIC TESTING & REMEDIAL TEACHING

Our main role as a teacher is to promote quality learning among the students. This is possible only when we act as a guide and the students actively participate in the process of learning. During the teaching-learning process, we have to locate and identify the areas where the learner commits mistakes. It is the crucial stage of the teaching-learning process where we have to diagnose and prepare instructional material for Remedial Teaching to ensure the desired quality of learning.

At this stage the role of a teacher is just like a doctor's. The doctor takes all the steps necessary to diagnose the disease by performing different tests and then prescribes medicines for the particular disease.

In the case of education the process of diagnostic testing is the step and remedial teaching is the prescription. Hence diagnostic testing and remedial teaching are very essential for ensuring effective learning and in improving the quality of education.

TYPES OF DIAGNOSTIC TESTS

Educational	**Physical/Clinical**
[These tests diagnose disorder of study material according to level of class.]	[These tests diagnose the hearing, vision and other thing that cause hindrance in the course of learning.]

OBJECTIVES OF DIAGNOSTIC TESTING

- To understand the meaning and importance of diagnostic testing;
- To understand the nature and purpose of diagnostic testing;
- To follow the steps and stages of diagnostic testing in the classroom teaching-learning process; and
- To conduct remedial teaching in mathematics in classroom situations

FEATURES OF DIAGNOSTIC TEST

- It is an effective tool for teachers that helps in planning and organising remedial teaching.
- If finds out deficiency and weakness of student in learning of a contents.
- It is a base to form tutorial groups so as helps the poor students to develop their performance removing their differences.
- It is a qualitative test not a quantitative.
- In these tests no scores are made for correct answers only wrong responses are taken into view in the sequence of contents.
- It adopts objective type tests only.
- In needs an expert or specialist to identify the cause for wrong answers.
- It fully emphasises on all learning and teaching points.
- It arranges the items in hearing sequence so as to help transfer of learning position.

FUNCTIONS OF DIAGNOSTIC TEST

Classification	Assessment of Specific Abilities with Regard to	Remediation	Etology
(*i*) Aptitude/Musical level	(*i*) Level of Abnormality	(*i*) Special education for handicapped	(*i*) Study of diagnosis
(*ii*) Vocational level	(*ii*) Level of Adjustment	(*ii*) Counselling for mental Ailment	
(*iii*) Intellectual level	(*iii*) Level of Depression and Anxiety	(*iii*) Remedial teaching for learning weakness	
		(*iv*) Clinical treatment for Physical Ailment	

DIAGNOSTIC TESTING : MEANING AND IMPORTANCE

In general, after completing a particular unit/topic we conduct a test to assess the achievements of learners. After evaluation we draw some conclusions and we find that some of the students have fared very well and a particular group of students have achieved below your expectations. Now we will have to find out the causes for this low achievement or slow learning. There would be certain reasons for this low achievement. Now it is very essential to find out the particular area where the difficulty lies or the particular concept where the learner commits errors. To locate and identify the areas of learning difficulties leads to Diagnostic Testing.

After identifying the areas where the error lies, we have to find out the reasons due to which the particular child/group of students have not responded well. At this stage we have to play the role of a doctor. If a patient visits the doctor's clinic he suggests different tests relevant to the symptoms observed by him. After getting reports he is in a position to identify and diagnose the disease and then prescribe the medicine for it.

Likewise, as a teacher, we have to first identify and locate the area where the error lies. The process adopted for this purpose in educational situations is known as diagnostic testing. We may say that diagnostic testing implies a detailed study of learning difficulties.

In diagnostic testing the following points must be kept in mind:

(*i*) Who are the pupils who need help?

(*ii*) Where are the errors located ?

(*iii*) Why did the error occur ?

Suppose we have taught the simple method of subtraction of two-digit numbers without borrowing and then conducted a test which indicates the solutions as follows :

Student's name—Anshu.

98	77	85	81	97
– 62	– 52	– 35	– 40	– 67
36	25	5(5)	41	3(7)

After conducting test we are in a position to assess the whole group. This assessment is followed by an analysis *i.e.*, we have to find out about each individual the area of difficulty or the concept where the learner commits errors. For example, Student 'Anshu' has solved all the questions of subtraction of two-digit numbers without borrowing correctly except for the subtraction of one digit from another one-digit number. We find that her answers are 5 – 5 = 5, 7 – 7 = 7. We are in a position to diagnose the particular concept which Anshu could not understand. This is known as diagnostic testing.

While performing a diagnostic test you have the specific aim to analyse the exact nature of the progress made by the learner in a particular topic/ unit and to know the particular area of weakness/ error which requires a series of carefully graded tests. The main aim of diagnostic testing is to analyse not to assess. It will be more clear in the following example.

Student's name – Ashish

370	590	860	870
– 210	– 230	– 330	– 353
160	360	530	52(0)

513	654	845
– 206	– 352	– 203
307	(2)02	6(0)2
	Careless slip	

260	280	370
– 109	– 140	– 143
1(0)(0)	240	23(0)

Skill analysis of subtraction performance

We have conducted a test in the classroom to assess subtraction skill. After this assessment we have to find out how many students have not acquired this skill and who they are. For that particular group we will have to prepare a list to find the concept which is not clear to the learner or the particular step where the learner makes mistakes. For instance, in Ashish's case we have found that he makes a mistake when the question involves subtraction of zero from a number or of a number from zero through borrowing from the next digit. Ashish knows how to subtract zero from zero. You can conclude from this analysis that Ashish's makes a mistake only when the concepts of zero and a number come together in subtraction. This is identification of the area of learning difficulties, and the process involved in identifying and testing the problem is called diagnostic testing.

CONSTRUCTION OF DIAGNOSTIC TEST

- Formulate the objectives or outline of contents.
- Analyise the contents into subtopics and its elements.

- Identify the difficulties in the orders of sub-topics.
- Analyse the items and modify them.
- Prepare the final draft of the test.
- Prepare manual of test.
- Remedial devices and measures.

NATURE AND PURPOSE OF DIAGNOSTIC TESTING

If we consider arithmetical attainments from both a qualitative and quantitative standpoints, we can distinguish four main points (*i*) accuracy, (*ii*) speed of writing, (*iii*) methods of work and (*iv*) extent of the arithmetic process mastered.

It is obvious that we will try to find the feedback through the medium of class work or through weekly or monthly tests which indicate pupils' ability in each of the four aforesaid directions. But it is not enough for teaching purposes particularly with those pupils/learners who are slow learners. With this group of learners we are required to have a more analytical estimate of their achievements. Let us take the following example :

After teaching basic operations (addition, subtraction, multiplication and division) to a group of students, we conduct a test of say 10 items and the results are summarized as below :

Items	Errors	Items	Errors
1	2	6	10
2	1	7	8
3	3	8	9
4	2	9	32
5	3	10	32

From the above data it is possible to analyse the test items. It is clear that items 9 and 10 have been missed by most of the students. At this stage we have to re-think to make some modifications in items 9 and 10. This is the stage where we have identified and located the problem and hence diagnosed the area of error committed by the learners. Similarly, for items 6, 7 and 8, we will re-think and evolve instructional material to improve the quality of learning.

The above example suggests that Diagnostic Testing is analytical in nature where the teacher has to look at the performance of pupils in order to examine why they have not learned or mastered the particular concept or competency. For each pupil individually one has to pinpoint the specific kind of mistake he makes. This analysis is based on the date of performance rather than the general opinion of the teacher. It may be interpreted in terms of each students, a group of students, each concept/ competency and for each of the questions.

Why should the teacher undertake this kind of probe into the performance of pupils? The obvious response is that he/she wants to ensure the quality of learning (at the level of mastery) and is curious to know what specific action should be taken to obtain the desired results. Thus the main purpose of diagnostic testing is to spot the learning difficulties of pupils with a view to developing corrective measures, termed as remedial teaching.

STEPS AND STAGES IN DIAGNOSTIC TESTING

The essential steps in educational diagnosis are:

(*i*) Identifying the students who are having trouble or need help.

(*ii*) Locating the errors or learning difficulties.

(*iii*) Discovering the causal factors of slow learning.

(*i*) Identifying the students who are having trouble or need help

First, one must know the learners who require help. For this we can administer a general achievement test based on the topics already taught. After evaluation we will be in a position to make lists of students who are below average, average or above average. Next, one has to locate the area where the error occurs in order to have a deeper insight into the pupils' difficulties.

(*ii*) Locating the errors or learning difficulties

After identifying the students who need help and visualising the necessity of additional instructional material to improve the quality of learning, our main role is to find out the area where the learner commits mistakes or which is the area where learning difficulties lie. For example we examine the pupils' responses as follows:

(*i*) $\frac{3}{4}+\frac{5}{4}=\frac{8}{4}$ (*ii*) $\frac{7}{12}+\frac{4}{12}=\frac{11}{12}$

(*iii*) $1+\frac{3}{4}=\frac{\textcircled{4}}{4}$ (*iv*) $5+\frac{1}{7}=\frac{\textcircled{7}}{7}$

(*v*) $\frac{1}{2}+\frac{1}{3}=\frac{\textcircled{2}}{\textcircled{5}}$ (*vi*) $\frac{3}{7}+\frac{4}{5}=\frac{\textcircled{7}}{\textcircled{12}}$

From the above example we would realise that the learner has the knowledge of adding fractions having the same denominator but the concept of addition of fractions having different denominators is not clear to him even though it was taught in the classroom. Thus we have located the area where the learning difficulty lies.

(*iii*) Discovering the causal factors of slow learning

In some cases of learning difficulties, the causal factors are relatively simple. A student may be inattentive during teaching-learning or may be committing errors due to insufficient practice or irregular attendance.

Sometimes the cause is ill-health or faulty work habits etc. It has also been observed sometimes that the basic cause of low achievement is a feeling of helplessness or the complexity of the subject-matter which perhaps is much above the level of their comprehension.

Sequential presentation in below shows how diagnosis leads to improved quality of learning.

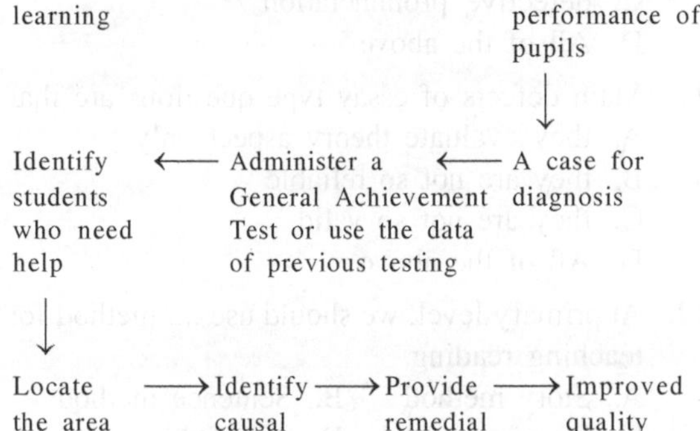

REMEDIAL TEACHING

While diagnosis is the process of investigating the learners' difficulties and the reasons for this, its follow up leads to actions that may help children make up their deficiencies. This step is generally termed Remedial Teaching. So you have to be skilled in preparing or arranging for such materials which may be used to undertake corrective instruction and thus enhancing the quality of learning.

Selection of Materials

The following points should be kept in mind while selecting appropriate instructional material:

(*i*) The corrective material should be designed to correct the students' individual difficulties.

(*ii*) You have to analyse the work of slow learners by means of observation, interview and diagnostic testing. A careful consideration of the three may help decide what kind of corrective material is to be designed and whether material will be adequate to correct the specific difficulties of learners.

(*iii*) The corrective material should be graded, self-directive and should permit students to work independently. Written directions, which accompany the material, should be easily readable and comprehensible by the students.

(*iv*) The corrective material must permit individuals to progress according to their pace.

(*v*) The material should encourage systematic recording of evidence of pupils' progress.

The following examples will illustrate the points discussed above.

For preparing the material for remedial teaching, let us explain the example discussed above. (steps and stages in dignostic testing) In this we had diagnosed that the learners had not understood the concept of adding fractions of the following type:

$$1+\frac{3}{4}, 2+\frac{5}{7}, 3+\frac{6}{7}, \text{etc.}$$

On the other hand, they had attained mastery over adding fractions of the type

$$\frac{1}{2}+\frac{3}{2}; \frac{3}{2}+\frac{5}{2}; \frac{3}{4}+\frac{5}{4}; \frac{4}{5}+\frac{7}{5}; \text{etc.}$$

Accordingly, now, we will have to prepare material where the learner should have plenty of opportunity to exercise on equalization of denominators in the given fractions.

(*i*) $1+\frac{3}{4}=\frac{1}{1}+\frac{3}{4}=\frac{1\times 4}{1\times 4}+\frac{3}{4}=\frac{4}{4}+\frac{3}{4}=\frac{4+3}{4}=\frac{7}{4}$

(*ii*) $2+\frac{5}{7}=\frac{2}{1}+\frac{5}{7}=\frac{2\times 7}{1\times 7}+\frac{5}{7}=\frac{14}{7}+\frac{5}{7}=\frac{14+5}{7}=\frac{19}{7}$

Enough practice should be provided to pupils on similar questions until they attain mastery. While selecting and implementing the instructional material the most important thing is the individual need of the student in a particular area. We have to give differential treatment. Different methodologies have to be adopted for different kinds of students. Other modes of interaction such as learner-learner interaction and learner-material interaction may also be utilized, besides the traditional teacher-learner interaction, using appropriate instructional material.

We have learnt about diagnostic testing which is the most important part of the teaching-learning process. It implies a detailed study of learning difficulties. Its aim is to analyse, not to assess. The nature and purpose of diagnostic testing is to identify the areas of difficulties where the learner commits errors.

After locating the area where the difficulty lies, as a teacher we will devise some strategy to remove problems in learning and the causes due to which the learner has faced the difficulties. The strategy used by us to remove the weakness of the learner is known as remedial teaching. Diagnostic testing leads to remedial teaching in which we have to prepare instructional material for quality learning, adopting different methodologies as per needs of the individual or a particular group.

PRACTICE PAPER

1. Which material can you use for teaching reading at primary stage?
A. Flannel Board B. Lecture by experts
C. Flash cards D. All of these

2. Objective type questions have
A. reliability B. validity
C. coverage D. All of these

3. Which is not related to affective domain?
A. Knowledge B. Characterisation
C. Valueing D. Receiving

4. Which one is the teaching technique?
A. Interview B. Note making
C. Review D. All of the above

5. The devices used to make teaching method more effective are known as
A. principle of teaching
B. techniques of teaching
C. methodology of teaching
D. None of the above

6. We, as mathematics teacher, evaluate pupil performance for
A. upgrading the students
B. motivating the students
C. assessing teacher's performance
D. All of the above

7. The introductory questions should
A. be based on previous knowledge of the students
B. be easy and not difficult
C. have linkage
D. All of the above

8. Internal qualities of a good mathematics book are
A. good printing
B. psychological presentation of the subject-matter
C. suitable font type and size
D. All of the above

9. Which one of the following is not the principle of teaching
A. exposure B. gradation
C. review D. phonology

10. Solving mistakes take place due to
A. poor text books
B. lack of writing exercises
C. defective pronunciation
D. All of the above

11. Main defects of essay type questions are that
A. they evaluate theory aspect only
B. they are not so reliable
C. they are not so valid
D. All of the above

12. At primary level, we should use .... method for teaching reading.
A. Story method B. Sentence method
C. Phonic method D. All of these

13. Which is not a method of teaching mathematics?
A. Grammar B. Translation
C. Direct method D. Enquiry method

14. Giving assignment of the students is a
A. Technique
B. A.V. Aids
C. Principle of teaching
D. Maxim of teaching

15. What are the points of informative and summative assessment?
A. Objectives
B. Tests
C. Level of Generalisation
D. All of the above

16. The teacher should ask the questions
A. Standing amidst the pupils
B. Speaking loudly
C. Following the principle of variety
D. All of the above

17. Which one of the following is not a teaching technique?
A. Seminar B. Symposium
C. Film and Chart D. Interview

18. At Primary stage, which method for teaching of writing is useful?
A. French method
B. Kindergarten method
C. Play way method
D. All of the above

19. Which teaching technique is not suitable for primary stage?

A. Symposium B. Explanation
C. Drill D. Questioning

20. For evaluation, teacher should use
A. essay type questions
B. oral testing
C. objective type questions
D. All of the above

21. The administration of a teaching unit involves
A. introduction B. presentation
C. evaluation D. All of these

22. An ideal lesson plan is
A. Objective based
B. Based on Previous knowledge
C. Based on Teaching levels
D. All of the above

23. The curriculum means
A. Courses of Study
B. Race Course
C. Syllabus
D. Educational Programme

24. Type of curriculum used in our education is
A. Learner-centred
B. Teacher-centred
C. Objective-centred
D. Content-centred

25. The curriculum is developed in view of
A. Educational objectives
B. Child development
C. National development
D. All of the above

26. What is characteristic of essay type examination?
A. Validity
B. Reliability
C. Objectivity
D. Depends on memory

27. Which is the main remedial teaching strategy?
A. Tutorial B. Supervised
C. Both 'A' and 'B' D. None of these

28. The more comprehensive plan is
A. Resource Plan B. Unit Plan
C. Lesson Plan D. All of these

29. A unit Plan should
A. be flexible
B. provide a variety
C. consists of familiar topics
D. All of the above

30. Preparation of daily lesson planning includes
A. determination of objectives
B. selection of content
C. determination of methods
D. All of the above

31. Achievement tests are
A. teacher-made B. standardised
C. Both 'A' and 'B' D. None of these

32. What is the basis of remedial teaching?
A. Diagnosis
B. Weakness of the students
C. Individual difference
D. All of the above

33. The function of measurement is
A. prognosis B. diagnosis
C. research D. All of these

34. In team teaching, the participant teachers decide their
A. objectives B. activities
C. ideas D. All of these

35. Error of evaluation is
A. personal error B. constant error
C. variable error D. All of the above

36. Evaluation is a process of
A. qualitative B. quantitative
C. Both 'A' and 'B' D. None of these

37. Mathematics is the sciences of
A. space B. numbers
C. calculations D. All of these

38. Who said that, 'Mathematics is the science which draws necessary conclusions'?
A. Hogben B. Locke
C. Benjamin Peirce D. None of these

39. The nature of mathematics is
A. ornamental B. logical
C. difficult D. not for common

40. Which work is not related with a teacher?
A. Planning B. Teaching
C. Guidance D. Budgeting

41. What is characteristic of the unit approach of curriculum?
A. Child centred
B. Content centred
C. Objective centred
D. Teacher centred

42. The team teaching is a method of
A. playing game
B. teaching
C. physical exercise
D. None of these

43. Characteristics of good questions are
A. realisation of aims
B. thought provoking
C. brief and direct
D. All of the above

44. What is the basis of teaching method?
A. Objective B. Content
C. Both 'A' and 'B' D. None of these

MATHEMATICS

45. The most effective teaching aid
A. Non-projected B. Direct experience
C. Projected D. None of these

46. The most useful teaching aid in mathematics is
A. visual aid B. audio aid
C. audio visual aid D. None of these

47. The most use of teaching aids are in
A. arithmetic B. algebra
C. science D. trigonometry

48. A good objective should be
A. related to teacher
B. testable
C. small
D. attractive

49. Introductory questions are asked
A. in the beginning of the lesson
B. in midway
C. at the end
D. at every stage

50. Memory questions are used to test
A. previous knowledge of pupils
B. present knowledge of pupils
C. interest of the pupils
D. discipline

51. The aims of questioning are
A. to motivate the pupils
B. to create interest and curiosity
C. to test the previous knowledge
D. All of the above

52. Which is the teacher-centred method?
A. Source method
B. Lecture method
C. Project method
D. Socialised Recitation

53. Micro-teaching helps in
A. controlling indiscipline
B. encouraging indiscipline
C. Both 'A' and 'B'
D. None of the above

54. Achievement test for
A. test of minimum performance
B. test of maximum performance
C. test of natural performance
D. test of performance

55. Which problem in classroom is due to curriculum?
A. Cleanliness B. Indiscipline
C. Teaching D. Discipline

56. In the scope of educational diagnosis use is made of
A. interview B. diagnostic test
C. observation D. All of these

57. The lesson plan helps in
A. applying theoretical knowledge in class
B. giving practical shape to the concept of management of teaching-learning
C. Both 'A' and 'B'
D. None of the above

58. What are the tests of performance?
A. Essay type tests B. Objective tests
C. Test of skills D. None of these

59. Multiple choice tests require thinking the ..... alternative.
A. incorrect
B. correct
C. Both 'A' and 'B'
D. None of the above

ANSWERS

1	2	3	4	5	6	7	8	9	10
C	D	A	D	B	D	D	D	C	D
11	**12**	**13**	**14**	**15**	**16**	**17**	**18**	**19**	**20**
A	B	D	A	D	D	C	D	A	D
21	**22**	**23**	**24**	**25**	**26**	**27**	**28**	**29**	**30**
D	D	B	C	C	D	C	C	D	D
31	**32**	**33**	**34**	**35**	**36**	**37**	**38**	**39**	**40**
C	D	D	B	D	B	D	C	B	D
41	**42**	**43**	**44**	**45**	**46**	**47**	**48**	**49**	**50**
B	D	D	B	A	A	C	B	A	A
51	**52**	**53**	**54**	**55**	**56**	**57**	**58**	**59**	
D	B	A	D	B	D	C	C	B	

Environmental Studies

ENVIRONMENTAL STUDIES

FAMILY AND FRIENDS

The basic unit of the social structure in every society is the family. The easy and classical definitions emphasized that the family was a group based on marriage, common residence, emotional bonds, and stipulation of domestic services. The family has also been defined as a group based on marital relations, right and duties of parenthood, common habitation and reciprocal relations between parents and children. Some sociologists feel that the family is a social group characterised by common residence, economic cooperation and reproduction.

Nowadays the concept of a family is viewed in terms of certain criteria applicable to all societies. For instance, it is felt that the family is a primary kinship unit which carries out aspects of the sexual, reproductive, economic and educational functions. Keeping in mind these definitions, we generally picture a family as a durable association of husband and wife with or without children. The wide variety of family forms, noticed in societies throughout the world in the course of human history is a cultural phenomenon of considerable interest. For example, with regard to residence in some societies, family are 'matrilocal', where a young married couple takes up residence at the home of the bride's parents. While in 'patrilocal' family, the couple takes up residence at the home of bridegroom's parents.

Another distinction is made between the conjugal family which is also called family of procreation, and consanguineous family which is also called family of orientation.

One can also classify families into nuclear, extended and joint types based on the way they are organised.

The nuclear family consists of a married couple and their children. The extended family is commonly defined as the nuclear family plus all kinds belonging to either side, living together. It may be pointed out that a consanguineous family implies ties of blood.

Universal Nature of Family

The family is the most permanent and pervasive of all social institutions. There is no human society without any family system. All societies both large and small, primitive and civilised, ancient and modern have institutionalised the process of procreation of the species and the meaning of the young.

The same type of family is not found everywhere. There are several types of family. In the west nuclear family is found. This comprises the husband and wife together with their children. In Indian villages and in small towns the extended or joint family is found. This has people in it of two to three or more generations under the same roof.

Main Characteristics of Family

1. **Universality:** There is no human society in which some form of the family does not appear. Malinowski writes the typical family a group consisting of mother, father and their progeny is found in all communities, savage, barbarians and civilized. The irresistible sex need, the urge for reproduction and the common economic needs have contributed to this universality.
2. **Emotional basis:** The family is grounded in emotions and sentiments. It is based on our impulses of mating, procreation, maternal devotion fraternal love and parental care. It is built upon sentiments of love, affection, sympathy, cooperation and friendship.
3. **Limited size:** The family is smaller in size. As a primary group its size is necessarily limited. It is a smallest social unit.
4. **Formative influence:** The family welds an en-

vironment which surrounds trains and educates the child. It shapes the personality and moulds the character of its members. It emotionally condition the child.

5. **Nuclear position in the social structure:** The family is the nucleus of all other social organizations. The whole social structure is built of family units.
6. **Responsibility of the members:** The members of the family has certain responsibilities, duties and obligations. MacIver, points out that in times of crisis men may work and fight and die for their country but they toil for their families all their lives.
7. **Social regulation:** The family is guarded both by social taboos and legal regulation. The society takes precaution to safeguard this organisation from any possible breakdown.

Functions of a Family

The function can be discussed as under:

1. According to **Kingsley,** there are four major social functions of family. These are: reproduction, maintenance, placement, and socialization. MacIver divided the functions of the family into two categories—essential and non-essential. Under the essential he includes three functions:

   (a) stable satisfaction of sex need,

   (b) production of rearing of children, and

   (c) provision of a home.

   Under the non-essential functions he mentions religious, educational, economic, health and recreation. These, he says, have now been transferred to specialized agencies in society.

2. **Lundberg** has enumerated four basic functions of family:

   (a) The regulations of sexual behaviour and reproductions,

   (b) Care and training of children,

   (c) Co-operation and division of labour and

   (d) Primary group satisfactions, etc.

3. **Ogburn and Nimkoff** have divided family functions into six categories:

   (a) Affectional,

   (b) Economic,

   (c) Recreational,

   (d) Protective,

   (e) Religious and

   (f) Educational.

WORK AND PLAY

Work and Play is a part of fun and learn system of education during elementary school level. It is still extrinsically motivated. Its aim is to make an overall development of a child. It's emphasis is to grow a child into an independent and responsible citizen. Like play, work is sometimes freely chosen but the option to avoid work rarely available in our society. Here we provide some basic knowledge of games and sports, childs are required to know.

ATHLETICS

There are several events in which the participants have to jump, run or throw. The important events are:

(a) ***High Jump:*** The competitor, after running a small distance, jumps over a horizontal rod without dislodging it. Highest jump wins the gold medal.

(b) ***Long Jump:*** The competitor, after running a small distance, takes off from a designated spot and lands in a sand pit. The distance covered in the jump is measured.

(c) ***Triple Jump:*** There are three steps in this jump. The competitor comes running and first makes a hop so that he lands on the foot with which he took off. In the second step, he takes another step to land on the other foot and finally jumps to land on both feet. The total distance covered in three steps is measured.

(d) ***Races:*** In the ordinary races, all the competitors take off at the same time and whoever finishes first is the winner.

(e) ***Hurdle races:*** All the competitors take off at the same time. During the course of the race, they have to jump over several hurdles, placed at regular distances.

(f) ***Relay races:*** Each team has four players. Each team has a baton, which is carried by the runner during his/her lap. Once the lap is finished, the baton is passed on to the other member of the team who then carries it over the next lap. The team finishing first is declared the winner. The lap for each individual is either 100 m or 400 m.

(g) ***Steeple chase:*** In this race, individuals not only have to cross the hurdles but also the water jumps.

(h) ***Javelin throw:*** A Javelin, long stick with a pointed edge, is thrown from a fixed point. The one, who throws the maximum distance, is the winner.

(i) ***Shot put:*** The competitors throw the shot which is an iron ball.

(j) ***Pole Vault:*** All the competitors use a pole to get support and jump over horizontal bar, suspended with the help of two supports.

BADMINTON

On the either side of the net, players assemble with their rackets, they hit shuttle cock over the net.

Scoring is by single point and only the services score. A point is made if the opponent is not able to return the shuttle or throws it out of court or commits a foul. It can be played either in singles or doubles.

BASEBALL

The game is played on a field containing four bases. The object of each team is to score more runs than the other. A run is scored whenever a player circles all the bases and reaches home without being put out. Ordinarily, a game consists of nine innings but an extra inning is played in case of tie. The players take runs batting from home plate in regular rotation. The opposing pitcher throws the ball and batter tries to hit it as far as possible.

BASKETBALL

Two teams of five players each face each other in the rectangular court. The game consists of two halves of 20 minutes each. Each team tries to put the ball in the opponent's basket which is open at both ends, suspended from a metal ring and is hung on the backboard from the floor. A team scoring the greater number of points in the playing time is declared winner.

BILLIARDS

It is played with just three balls on the table. There are six open-mouthed pouches in the table, called pocket. The players attempt to drive small balls against one another into pockets with a cue. The game at the championship level is usually played in two hour sessions and generally two sessions are held.

BOWLING

In this game, each player's object is to knock down pins with a ball. The winning player or team has the highest score at the end of ten frames, one point is scored for every pin knocked over and one bonus point is given if all pins are bowled down with the first rolled ball.

BOXING

Each boxer scores blows with the knuckle part of the closed glove of either hand on the front or sides of the head or body above the belt of the opponent. The boxer who strikes his opponent the greater number of scoring blows becomes the winner. Sometime the bout is decided on knockout or disqualification basis. The number of rounds can vary, depending on the category and the competition.

CRICKET

There are two teams and each team has eleven players. One team bats while the other team fields and bowls. A bowler throws the ball from one end of the pitch and the batsman, at the other end, tries to hit the ball with the bat. A batsman can be out by being bowled, caught, leg before wicket, hit wicket, stump out or run out. A team scoring more runs wins the match. The match can be of limited overs, one inning or two innings. A match is declared draw if innings of both the sides are not completed within stipulated time period which can be 3 to 5 days.

HOCKEY

It is played by two teams with eleven players on each side. The game is started from the centre line with both sides facing each other. Each side tries to push the ball into the opponents' goal, situated on the either end of the field. The goal is scored from the striking circle which includes the semicircle around the goal post with 16 yards radius. The winning side is the one which scores more goals in the regulated 70 minutes consisting of two halves. Sometimes extra time and penalty shoot outs are used to decide the match.

TABLE TENNIS

It is played on singles or doubles basis, on a table 9' × 5'. A 6" high net is put in between the table. Each player has a racket which is used for hitting the ball in such a manner that it crosses the net and lands on the opponents side of the table. A player scores a point if the opponent fails to hit back properly on the table or commits a foul. Each player gets 5 services after which the opponent is given 5 services. In doubles games, each player of the team alternate in hitting the ball. A game is won by the player or pair first scoring 21 points, unless both have scored 20 points. In that case, winner shall be one who first scores two points more than the opposition. A match can be of best of three or best of five games.

SOCCER

There are two teams with eleven players on each side. In the middle of each end is a goal which stands 8 feet high and 24 feet wide, backed with net. A halfway line, parallel to the goal-line, bisects the field. Soccer is played with an inflated round leather ball, of 27 to 28 inches circumference. The players can use their body parts, except hand, to hit the ball. However, the preferred part is foot. So, the game is also called football. The object of the game is to move the ball down the field and past the defending goalkeeper into the opposing team's goal for a score. The game is played in two halves of 45 minutes, with teams changing sides after the first half.

TENNIS

The game can be played indoors or outdoors, either on grass, clay or cement court. It can be played on singles or doubles basis. The playing court is

78' × 27' for singles and 78' × 36' for doubles. In the middle of the court, a net is put between two posts in such a way that it is 3½' at the corner and 3' at the middle. The game is started by serving the ball over the net from the service side. When a player wins the first stroke in a game, his score is 15. The score becomes 30 with the second winning stroke and 40 with the third winning stroke. The fourth winning stroke can win the match for a player if the opponents score is not 40. If both the players have scores of 40, deuce is applied. A player winning six games first wins the set. The match is decided on the "best of three" or "best of five" sets.

VOLLEYBALL

The 60' × 30' rectangular volleyball court is divided into two equal parts by a centre line. A net 3' high is suspended across the centre line with its upper edge 8' from the floor. A point is scored on the service only. If the opposing team commits an error or foul, the serving team gains receives one point. But if the serving team commits an error or foul it loses the service. After service, the ball every time must be sent back to the other side, with not more than three touches. A game is won when the team leads by two points with a minimum of 15 points. A match is played in "best of three" or "best of five" games.

GOLF

The golf course consists of 18 holes or 9 holes played twice. The hole is 4½ inches in diameter and 4 inches deep. The competitors club a rubber cord ball into an ordered series of holes and one doing in lesser strokes, is the winner.

PLANTS AND ANIMALS

Plants and animals are like our friends and are essential for any ecosystem. They are very useful for human life. They provide us food, milk and other basic things of life. Plants provide us clean air and make the environment cool. Here we study about Plants, animals, ecosystem and biomes.

PARTS OF PLANTS

Roots: Root is an underground cylindrical part of the plant which develops from radicle and grows vertically down into the soil. Root lacks leaves, nodes, internodes and buds. Root is colourless. Root possesses root hairs. The primary functions of the root is to fix the plant firmly with the soil and to absorb water and mineral nutrients. In some plants, roots help in synthesis of food, respiration, storing food, helping the weak stem climb and vegetative reproduction. Nodulated roots of Gram, Groundnut, Beans, etc. have nitrogen fixing bacteria. Some plants have roots above the ground level also.

Stem: Stem is the main axis of plants. It develops from plumule of embryo, grows in the upward direction, towards the sun. Its main function is to conduct water, mineral and food material, to produce and support of leaves and reproductive structure. Some stems remain underground or are weak and need some support to help climbing. Stem bears leaves, flowers, fruits and buds. Based on nature of stem, height of plants and duration of life, plants are categorised as herbs, shrubs or trees. Based on life span of a plant, it can be distinguished as annuals (plants completing life cycles in a single seasons), biennials (plants completing life cycle in two growing seasons) and perennials (plants which grow for many seasons and bear fruits every year).

Leaf: Leaves are the food manufacturing organs of the plant. Each leaf has & stalk and an expanded blade like position called lamina which can be of various shapes. On leaves various veins and veinlets are distributed. Green leaves contain chlorophyll which is responsible for manufacturing food. Loss of water takes place from leaf surface, called transpiration, which creates tension needed for ascent of food, water and nutrients. Through leaves exchange of gases between the environment and the plant takes place. In some plants, leaves store food and water, protect from grazing animals, help in vegetative reproduction, help in climbing the plants with weak stem.

Photosynthesis: It is the only process on Earth by which solar energy is trapped by autotrophic organisms and converted into food. Inorganic compounds carbon dioxide and water form carbohydrates in the presence of chlorophyll and sunlight with liberation of oxygen. The chemical equation is

$$6CO_2 + 6H_2O \xrightarrow[\text{Chlorophyll}]{\text{Sunlight}} C_6H_{12}O_6 + 6O_2$$

Photosynthesis is important for human beings existence as it forms food-stuffs and oxygen. Photosynthesis in plants depends on intensity, quality and duration of light, availability of sufficient carbon dioxide and water, optimum temperature (20°C to 35°C), content of chlorophyll and structure of leaves.

Asexual Reproduction in Plants

Some plants are able to multiply by asexual or vegetative methods, which involve the production of new plants without the act of fertilization. New individuals arise from any vegetative part of the parent and possesses exactly the same characteristics of the parent plant. Some plants like sugarcane, banana, pineapple, etc. grow by this method. Vegetative parts like roots, stems or leaves may be involved in natural propagation. Artificially, it can be done by cutting, layering, grafting or tissue culture.

Sexual Reproduction in Plants

A flower is the branch of stem specially modified for sexual reproduction. The stamens and carpels represent the male and female sex organs respectively. Calyx and corolla are the non-essential parts of flower, as they do not take part in sexual reproduction. Pollengrains are formed in the stamen while eggs are formed in the carpel. When pollens and egg meet, fertilization takes place. The embryo or zygote starts developing. After fertilization, the petals, stamens and style wither away and seeds and fruits formation occurs.

Pollination

The pollengrains, shed from anther, are spread by various agencies. This transfer of pollen from anther to stigma of pistil is called pollination. Pollens may transfer to stigma of the same or the other flower. To other flowers, pollen grains may be migrated with the help of external agencies like wind, water, animals, birds and insects. Depending on the size, shape and other properties of pollen-grains, flowers and plants, anyone of the above mode may be used. Coconut's pollen-grains are spread through water.

Germination

The process by which the dormant embryo works up, grows out of the seed coat and establishes itself as a seedling is called germination. When necessary conditions for germination are supplied, the seed may start to sprout. Sufficient supply of water, nutrients and air must be provided to the seed for germination.

ANIMAL KINGDOM

The animal kingdom is divided into about 24 large groups of phyla. Ten of the more important ones are as follows:

1. **Protozoa:** Microscopic, Unicellular forms of great variety. Some are uninucleated and others have a large number of nuclei. Many can swim by waving hair - like flagella or cilia. They are found in the sea, fresh water and the soil. Some are microscopic and cause diseases in animals and man.
2. **Porifera:** Sponges, very primitive, multi-cellular animals. Largely marine, the body which may become branched and plant-like is supported by a framework of spicules and fibres.
3. **Coelenterates:** Simple animals, largely marine, e.g., Hydra, Jellyfish. Coral reefs are formed from the calcareous skeletons of these animals.
4. **Platyhelminths:** Flat worms which are free living in water and tapeworms which are parasitic. Mesoderm, a third layer, is formed in them.
5. **Nematodes:** Roundworms. The body is smooth and pointed at each end. They are free living in all environments and as parasites.
6. **Annelids:** Segmented worms such as earthworms and leeches. They have a developed body cavity and several systems.
7. **Arthropods:** A very large and diverse group including Crustaceans such as crabs, shrimps; myriapods such as centipedes and millipedes; insects; and arachnids such as spiders and scorpions. They possess a jointed, hard exoskeleton, walking legs and grown muscles within the skeleton.
8. **Molluscs:** Oysters, Octopods and snails etc. They have complex body form. The unsegmented body is protected by shell.
9. **Echinoderms:** Starfish, sea urchins, sea lilies. They are marine, radially symmetrical. Move by hundreds of tube feet projecting from under surface.
10. **Chordates:** They are most advanced. Include Pisces, Amphibians, Reptiles, Birds and Mammals. Those animals with a backbone are called vertebrates and others invertebrates. Fish, Amphibians and Reptiles are cold blooded while Birds and Mammals are warm blooded. Cold-blooded animals have body temperature in equilibrium with the environment. However, warm-blooded animals have a fixed body temperature. Mammals youngsters are suckled by milk producing mammary glands.

Tissue

A group of cells which coordinate to perform a specific function is called tissue. They may be similar in form, structure and origin. Depending on the basis of their function there are four types of animal tissues - epithelial (for protection), muscular (for movement and locomotion), connective (for binding different structures of body) and nervous (for conduction of nerve impulses).

Glands

These structures secrete useful chemical substances. If the secretion is sent to the site of action through ducts, they are called glands e.g. salivary glands, liver, sweet glands. If glands secrete hormone directly into the blood which transports them to their target organs, they are called endocrine glands e.g. thyroid, pituitary, adrenal, parathyroid.

Bones

Bone is the hardest tissue of the body and form the largest section of the body weight. Bones contain organic as well as inorganic matters. With advancing age, the inorganic matter's share increases, causing the bones to become more brittle. Long bones such as humerus and femur are hollow while small bones are solid. Bones are attached to tendons and muscles.

Blood

It is red, opaque, somewhat sticky and viscous fluid in the body of animals. It is slightly alkaline (pH = 7.4), heavier than water (sp gr = 1.05) and five times more viscous than distilled water. Blood forms 6 to 10% of the body weight.

An adult, on average, has about 6.8 litres of blood. Blood contains plasma and blood corpuscles with the former occupying 55-60% of the volume. Plasma is a faint yellow coloured non-living fluid, containing water, inorganic salts, organic compounds and plasma proteins. Plasma transports food components, metabolic wastes and hormones; keeps constant level of pH of blood, maintains body temperature and helps in blood clotting. Erythrocytes or red blood corpuscles (RBCs), leukocytes or white blood corpuscles (WBCs) and blood platelets are other parts of the blood. RBCs are non-nucleated in human beings. There are about 30 trillion RBCs in adult man. Due to the presence of iron containing pigment haemoglobin, RBCs are red in colour. The RBCs are crucial for ex-change of oxygen and carbon dioxide. WBCs are nucleated and non-pigmented cells. They are larger in size than RBCs but far less in number (1 : 600). WBCs play an important role in immune system of the body. Blood platelets cause the coagulation of blood and clot formation to prevent excessive bleeding. Human blood is divided into four main Groups—A, B, AB and O. The plasma of Group A blood contains an anti-B factor and vice-versa, so that people of Groups A and B cannot accept each other's blood. Group AB contains neither anti-A nor antiB factor and people with this group can receive transfusions from both but can give to neither. Group O contains both anti-A and anti-B and can receive blood only from Group O but can donate blood to all Groups. Group O is called universal donor because they can donate to all the Groups. Group AB is called universal acceptor because they can accept blood from all Groups. Group A or B can accept blood from either their Group or Group O. They can donate to their Group or Group AB. Apart from the ABO blood group system, there is another system designated the Rhesus system or Rh-System. Everybody is Rh-positive or Rh-negative depending on the presence of the Rhesus factor. This system of blood factor is inherited separately from the ABO groups.

BIOMES

A biome is a large community unit characterized by the kinds of plants and animals present. This may be contrasted to the ecosystem, which is a natural unit of living and non-living components that interact to form a stable system in which the exchange to materials follows a circular path. Thus, an ecosystem might be a small pond or a large area coextensive with a biome, but it includes the physical environment as well as populations of animals, plants and micro-organisms.

The definition of biome includes not only the actual climax community of a region, but also the several intermediate communities that precede the climax community. Further, there is usually no sharp line of demarcation between adjacent biomes; instead each blends with the next through a fairly broad transition region termed as **ecotone.** There is, for example, an extensive region in Northern Canada where the tundra and coniferous forest blend in the tundra-coniferous ecotone. Some of the biomes recognized by ecologists are **tundra biome, alpine biome, forest biome, grassland biome, desert biome.**

Tundra Biome

Tundra presents the most common example of "fragile ecosystem". Tundra which means "marshy plain" lies largely north of latitude 60°N (*i.e.,* between the Arctic ocean and polar ice-caps and the forests to the south) and is characterizes by the absence of trees, the presence of dwarfed plants, and an upper ground surface that is wet, spongy and uneven, or hummocky, as a result of freezing and thawing of this poorly drained land. Some five million acres of tundra stretch across Northern America, Northern Europe and Siberia. Although there is variation from place to place within the biome, temperature, precipitation, and evaporation are characteristically slow, the warmest months averaging below 10°C and the wettest with about 25 mm of precipitation. Despite the small amount of precipitation, water is usually not a limiting factor because the rate of evaporation is also very low.

The ground usually remains frozen except for the uppermost 10 to 20 cm, which thaw during the brief summer seasons. The permanently frozen deeper soil layer is called **permafrost** . The permafrost line which may exist at a depth of a few centimetres to several metres, is the ultimate limit of plant root growth, but the immediate control is the depth to which soil is thawed in summer. The rather thin carpet of vegetation of tundra biome includes few species : grasses and sedges are characteristic of numerous marshes and poorly drained areas, but large areas consist of ericaceous heat plants (bilberries and dwarf huckleberries), low flowering herbs, and lichens.

Perhaps the most characteristic arcitc tundra plant is the lichen known as "reindeer moss" *(Cladonia).* The animals that have adapted to survive in the tundra are caribou or reindeer, the arctic hare, arctic fox, polar bear, wolves, lemmings, snowyowls ptarmigans and during the summer, swarms of flies, mosquitoes and a host of migratory birds.

Further, certain animals such as caribou and reindeer are highly migratory because there is not enough vegetation produced in any one local area to support them. Though tundras are barren areas yet a surprisingly large number of organisms have become adapted to survive the cold. During the long daylight hours of the brief summer, the rate of primary production is quite high. The production from the vegetation on the land, from the plants in the many shallow ponds that dot the landscape and from the phytoplankton in the adjacent Arctic Ocean provides enough food to support a variety of resident mammals and many kinds of migratory birds and insects. Diversity is very low, and despite the extreme hardiness of the tundra organisms, their growth rate tends to be very low, and the community as a structural unit is exceedingly vulnerable.

Alpine Biome

The region of mountain above the timber line contains a distinct flora and fauna and is referred to as the **alpine zone.** Alpine zone remains conspicuous in those mountains whose peaks reach up to the niveal or snow zone, as in the Himalayas. The alpine zone (zone which lies between timber line and snow zone) includes in the descending order, a **sub-snow zone** immediately below the snow zone a **meadow zone** in the centre and a **shrub zone** which gradually merges into the timber zone. According to **Mani** (1957) snow zone of Himalayas lies over 5100 m above mean sea level and alpine zone exists at a height of 3600 m. From an ecological view point, the zone above the limits of tree growth (timber line) exhibits extreme environmental conditions which greatly influence the biota of this region.

The characteristic features of high altitude environment are following– a low air density, low oxygen and carbon dioxide contents and water vapour, high ozone content, high atmospheric transparency affording greater penetration of light, cold, snow cover, increased rate of desiccation, high, wind velocity, insolation of high intensity during the day and rapid radiation during the night, the high glare from the sky and snow, high intensity of ionizing rediation and the exclusion of trees. Alpine zone of Himalayas is characterized by a sparseness of animal groups, the scarcity being relatively important as far as tropical Indian, South Chinese, Indo-Chinese and Malayan derivatives are concerned. Important constituents of the fauna of this zone are cold-adapted palaearctic forms.

A large number of insects and arachnids remain best adapted to Himalayan alpine zone and at 6900 metres height. The torrential streams which are the products of melting snow contain many mayflies, stoneflies and caddisflies. Some of common insects of this zone are—stonefly *Rhabdiopteryx lunata;* grasshoppers like *Bryo-dema* and *Gomphomastax;* apterous species *Conophyma; Dicranophyma; Sphingonotus;* tettigonid *Hypsinomus fasciata;* earwigs like *Anechura;* bugs like *Dolmacoris, Tibetocoris,* and *Nysius ericae;* aquatic beetle *Amphizoa;* carbides like *Bembidion.*

Forest Biomes

The word **forest** is derived from Latin *'foris'* meaning outside, the reference being to village boundary fence, and must have included all uncultivated and uninhabitated land. Today a forest is any land managed for the diverse purposes of forestry whether covered with trees, shrubs, climbers, etc., or not. The forest biomes include a complex assemblage of different kinds of biotic communities. Optimum conditions of temperature and ground moisture responsible for the growth of trees contribute greatly to the establishment of forest communities. In addition, 50 mm rainfall is a pre-requisite for the growth of trees. The nature of soil, wind and air currents determines the distribution (abundance or sparseness) of forest vegetation. Normally ecologists recognise among forest communities such features as their evergreen nature, whether deciduous or indeciduous, as well as their shape, whether broad-leaved as in temperate forests of more needle-like as in the conifers. On the basis or these features the forest biomes of the world have been classified into following biomes- **coniferous forest, tropical forest,** and **temperate forest.** All these forest **biomes** are generally arranged on a gradient from north to south or from high altitude to lower altitude.

Coniferous Forest: Cold regions with high rainfall and strongly seasonal climates with long winters and fairly short summers are characterized by boreal conifer forest which is transcontinental. For example, adjacent to the tundra region either at latitude or high altitude is the **northern coniferous** or **boreal forest,** which stretches across both North America and Eurasia just south of the tundra *(i.e.,* Canada, Sweden, Finland, Siberia and Mussoorie). The term **taiga** is applied to the northern range of coniferous forests. This is characterized by evergreen plant species. Large size is common, both in the trees, which range up to some 40 m in height, and in vertebrates, which include the giants of several groups of animals, such as moose, caribou, elk, grizzly bear, wolverine beaver, and several large species of birds. Species diversity is low, and pure stands of trees and shrubs are common, as are outbreaks of defoliating insects of several sorts (*e.g.,* bark beetles, saw flies, geometrid moths, etc.). Understory trees are uncommon as a result of the continual low light penetration. Among common understory associates are orchids and ericaceous shrubs like the blue berry.

Boreal forest soils are thin podozols, and are rather poor both because the weathering of rock proceeds slowly in the cold environments, and because the litter derived from conifer needle is broken down very slowly and is not particularly rich in nutrients. These soils are acidic and mineral deficient, the result of the movement of a large amount of water through the soil; in the absence of a significant counter upward movement of evaporation, soluble essential nutrients like calcium, nitrogen, and potassium are leached sometimes beyond the reach of roots thereby leaving no alkaline-oriented cations to encounter the organic acids of the accumulating litter. The productivity and community stability of a boreal coniferous forest are lower than those of any other biome.

Temperate Deciduous Forest: The temperate forest biomes are characterized by a moderate climate and broad-leaved deciduous trees, which shed their leaves in fall, are bare over winter and grow new foliage in the spring. These forests are the characteristics of North America, Europe, Eastern Asia, Chile, part of Australia and Japan, with a cold winter and an annual rainfall of 75–150 cm and a temperature of 10–20°C. In these biomes the precipitation may be fairly uniform throughout the year. In India, at elevations of 9000–12,000 feet in Himalayas occur temperate vegetation including pines, fir, yew and juniper trees with and undergrowth of scrubby rhododendrons.

Soils of temperate forests are podozolic and fairly deep. Trees are quite tall—about 40–50m in height their leaves are thin and broad. the predominant genera of this biome are maple, beech, oak, hickory, basswood, Chestnut, cottonwood, sycamore, elm and willow. There are not many epiphytes or lianas save for some species of mosses, algae and lichens growing on tree trunks, and a few vines, notably *Vitis,* the grape. The understory of shrubs and herbs in the deciduous forest is typically well-developed and richly diversified, with a considerable portion of the photosynthesis and flowering attuned to the short days of the spring season, prior to the leafing out of and consequent shading by the tree canopy. One consists of spring flowers, which bloom before the trees have expanded their leaves and are gone by summer, and the other is adapted to the low light levels of the forest floor and lasts into the fall.

The animals originally present in temperate forests are deer, bears, squirrels, gray foxes, bobcats, wild turkey and wood peckers. Other common animals of this region are invertebrates like earthworms, snails, millipedes, Coleoptera and Orthoptera and vertebrates like amphibians such as newts, salamanders, toads, and cricket frogs; reptiles such as turtles, lizards and snakes; mammals such as racoon opossum, pigs, mountain lion, etc., and birds like horned owl, hawks, etc. All these animals and plants show a profound seasonality; some may even hibernate throughout the winter. The range of animal size and adaptations is wide; the largest animals include such forms as the deer and black bear. The dominant carnivores are large, including the wolf and mountainlion, although smaller carnivores such as fox and skunk are also common. Diversity of fauna is lower than in any of the rain forests and a few species seems clearly to the dominant.

Temperate Evergreen Woodland: Many parts of the world have a Mediterranean-type climate with warm, dry summers and cool, moist winters. These are commonly inhabited by low evergreen trees with small hard needles or slightly broader leaves. The most important area of tropical evergreen woodland in North America is the **'Chaparral'** of the Pacific Coast, the Mediterranean **'maquis',** Spanish **'encinar'** and **'melle scrab'** on Australia's South Coast are the same type of community. In such a woodland, trees are essentially lacking, although shrubs may range upto 3–4 m in height. Species diversity is roughly intermediate between that of a temperate deciduous forest and a drier grassland. Fire is an important factor in this ecosystem, and the adaptations of the plants enable them to regenerate quickly after being turned. The characteristic animals of temperate evergreen woodland or chaparral are mule deer, brush rabbits, wood rats, chipmunks, lizards wem-tits and brown towhees. Small-hooved cursorial ungulates are the dominant herbivores. Saltatorial (jumping) animals and many fast moving ungulates are also common in this fauna.

Temperate Rainforests: The temperate rainforest is a colder ecosystem than any other rainforest. Such a forest has a definite seasonality, with both temperatures and rainfall varying throughout the year. Rainfall is high, but fog may be very heavy and actually more important as a source of water than rainfall. The diversity is much lower, both in plants and animals, in comparison to warmer rainforests, yet it remains still higher than other temperate forest types. The dominant trees (canopies) are coast redwood of the Pacific coast of North America and the alpine ash of Australia and Tasmania, both of which reach more than 100 m in height. Epiphytes and lianas are common but are not abundant like those of other rainforests. The animals of temperate rainforests are similar to those of deciduous forests, but show a somewhat higher-diversity.

Tropical Rainforests: Tropical rainforests occur near Southeast Asia (parts of India and Malaysia), Malaya, Borneo, New Guinea and Northwest Australia. Tropical rainforests are among the most diverse communities on earth. Both temperature and humidity are high and constant. The annual rainfall which exceeds 200 to 225 cm is generally evenly distributed throughout the year.

The flora is highly diversified: a square mile may contain 300 different species of trees, a diversity unparalleled in any other biome. The extremely dense vegetation of the tropical rainforests remains vertically stratified with tall trees often covered with vines, creepers, lianas, epiphytic orchids and bromeliads. Under the tall trees is a continuous evergreen carpet, the canopy layer, some 25 to 35 metres tall. The lowest layer is an understory of trees, shrubs, herbs like ferns and palms, all of which become dense where there is a break in the canopy. Nearly all plants are evergreen, and those that do lose their leaves entirely do so at irregular intervals with no apparent regard to the climatic regime. The leaves of most plants are of moderate size, leathery and dark green in colour.

Soils of tropical rainforests are red latosols, and they may be exceedingly thick. The high rate of leaching makes these soils virtually useless for agriculture purposes, but if they are left undisturbed the extremely rapid cycling of nutrients within the litter layer (due to decomposition) can compensate for the natural poverty of the soil. It is the nature of the soil, both its potential for high leaching as well as its chemical composition that promotes a rock-like quality when exposed to air, that largely has prevented western style agriculture from being applied to the tropical forests.

Invertebrate density and abundance are very high in tropical rainforests, but while vertebrates are diverse, they are not as abundant as in many other communities. The common invertebrates of these forests are worms, snails, millipedes, centipedes, scorpions, isopods, spiders, insects, planarians and leeches. Among insects, heteropterans, orthopterans, blattids, mantids, phasmids, bees, termites and ants are most common. Nocturnal and arboreal habits are most common in many mammals such as insectivores, leopards, jungle cats, ant-eaters, giant flying squirrels, monkeys and sloths. But in New Guinea and Northern Queensland, where monkeys are absent, there are arboreal kangaroos despite the fact that the basic anatomy of the kangaroo is not particularly well-suited to arboreal life. Further, in the foot hills of the forest zone of peninsular India covered with dense tropical vegetation, we have the tiger, the elephant samber deer swamp deer as the major ground dwelling mammals.

Tropical Seasonal Forests: Tropical seasonal forests occur in region whose total annual rainfall is very high, but segregated into pronounced wet and dry periods. Tropical seasonal forests are found in Southeast Asia, Central and South America, Northern Australia, Western Africa and the tropical islands of the pacific as well as India and Southeast Asia. In exceedingly wet tropical seasonal forests, commonly known as **monsoon forests,** the annual precipitation may be several times that of the tropical rainforests. Trees may reach heights over 40 m, but are more commonly 20–30 m high. Stratification is of a relatively simple type with a single understory tree layer, canopy is deciduous and understory is evergreen. Teak is often a major large tree in the best-known tropical seasonal forests, those of India (Central India) and Southeast Asia. Bamboo is also an important climax shrub in these areas although in other areas it is important only in earlier stages of the succession.

Tropical Savanna Biomes

Savannas are tropical **grasslands** with scattered, drought-resistant trees which generally do not exceed above ten metres in height and do not form a canopy. Thus, a savanna is an intermediate between a forest and a grassland. Savannas constitute extensive areas in Eastern Africa, which support the richest diversity of grazing mammals in the world, and also occur in Australia, South America and Asia. The climate is generally characterized by a rainy (May to October) and dry (November to April) season; in the llanos of Venezuela, for example, nearly 90 per cent of the annual rainfall of 130 cm falls during the rainy season. The latosol soil of savannas are nutrient poor owing a heavy leaching. Quite widely distributed in savannas are soils called literite which when dried harden to rock-like consistency thereby precluding their use in western style agriculture. Although climate and soil are significant regulating factors in this biome, the controlling factor appears to be fire, which gives grass and certain species of trees a powerful advantage over other tree species.

The trees of savannas are resistant of desiccation, and may be either deciduous or evergeen. Their leaves are often hard and drought-resistant. Grasses are the most conspicuous plants, and may reach heights of 1.5–2 m. Gigantism of certain animal groups in these tropical savannas is as pronounced as it is in the boreal forest including such giants as many antelope, giraffes, elephants, buffalo and lions. In addition, a rich insectan fauna especially those with strong mandibles capable of mastication are conspicuous in this biome. Grasshoppers and termites are encountered in large numbers.

Grassland Biomes

The grassland biome is found where rainfall is about 25 to 75 cm per year , not enough to support a forest, yet more than of a true desert. The seasonality of grasslands is pronounced, both with respect to rainfall, which is concentrated in the summer and to temperature. The grassland communities are open land communities with limited moisture conditions irregular rainfall, sharp seasonal and diurnal variations and very high radiation. Since tall trees or other thick vegetations are excluded from these communities there is a free movement of air. These winds carry the particles of sand or dust. These open habitats provide natural pasture for grazing animals (herbivore) which are excluded from predation by predators which hide in thick vegetation and prey upon them.

In grasslands, the stratification is reduced essentially to a single story, but within that level, species diversity may be as high as in a deciduous forest-especially for the tall grass prairies. Only along the streams are trees to be found, but the "gallery forests" within a few metres of stream bank are characteristics of grasslands. The grasses comprising of the grasslands can be divided into two basic groups, the tall grasses more than 1 m high, which are found in moist portions of the grassland, and the short grasses less than 1 m high, which are found in the drier regions.

Since the precipitation–evaporation ratio is below 1 in the grassland, leaching is considerably less. The soils of the grasslands are rich, fertile prairie soils (black-earths) and chernozems. Organic matter (humus) accumulates in the upper portion of the soil, rendering it dark; this upper portion remains neutral to slightly alkaline because of the continued replenishment of cations like calcium and potassium through the upward movement associated with evaporation.

Typical animals of grasslands tend to be quite small, with the exception of a few very large cursorial herbivore mammals such as the bison and pronghorn in North America, the wild horse, ass, and saiga antelope of Eurasia and zebra and antelops of Southern Africa. The large herbivores are no where near as diverse as they are in savanna areas. Likewise, carnivores are relatively small such as are coyotes, weasels, badgers, foxes, ferrets, owls and rattle snakes, Rodents such as prairie dogs, rabbits, and ground squirrels are common. Most herbivores characteristically aggregate into herds or colonies; this aggregation provides some protection against predators. The characteristic birds of grasslands are prairie chickens, meadow larks, and rodent hawks. Further, saltatorial motion is widespread, not only in mammals such as rabbits and kangaroo rats, but also in insects, such as grasshoppers and crickets. This probably has to do with increasing rate at which animal can move through or over the tall grassess, as well as making it harder for a predator to catch the animal. Visibility in the grasslands is exceedingly good and the premium placed on efficiency including predators is very high.

The common insects of steppes are termites, locusts, bees, burrowing wasps, mutilid wasps, bumble bees and blister bees. The steppes also harbour an undisturbed reptilian fauna. Lizards and steppes also harbour an undisturbed reptilian fauna. Lizards and snakes are met with in large numbers and possess, remarkable diversity. Most of them are fossorial, insectivorous and carnivorous.

Desert Biomes

Deserts are the biome formed in the driest of environments. Temperature may range from very hot as in **hot deserts** to very cold as in **cold deserts.** Major hot deserts of the world are situated near the tropics of cancer and capricon, with a rainfall of less than 10 mm. The most important hot deserts of world is the Sahara-Arabia-Gobi desert complex extending from Africa to Central Asia and contains highly irregular and very insignificant rainfall, and low humidity due to excessive evaporation. Fairly extensive hot deserts also occur in India (Sind-Rajasthan deserts), South America (Chile), North America and Australia. The cold deserts occur at high elevations where the temperatures are low and rainfall scanty as the air losses all its moisture content as it ascends higher and higher. Cold deserts occur in Ladakh regions of Himalayas, Tibet, and Bolivia Arctic. The hot and cold deserts may also be distinguished by differences in plant population which are mostly succulent type (*e.g.*,cactus, palo verde trees, creosote bush, etc.). Most cold deserts have sage bush.

Low erratic precipitation coupled with soil and air temperatures that are extremely high by day and drop abruptly by night, low humidity, and high insulation are the major desiccating environmental factors to which desert vegetation and animals have adapted. Desert plants which tend to be shrubs are adapted to drought conditions through reduced leaf size and the dropping or leaves in dry conditions, both reducing water loss via evapotranspiration. The roots of most desert plants remain well developed and occur in the top metre of the soil to take maximum possible advantage of any rainfall. Further, the root hairs on many desert plants are ephemeral, drying back under drought conditions and thereby reducing potential water loss by osmosis. Yet other species are short lived annuals that complete their life cycles during the short-moist period. In most hot deserts, there occur plants such as cacti, water-storing succulents such as acacias, euphorbias, cacti, prickly pears, etc., which are adapted by their protoplasmic colloids, which enable the accumulation of substantial water reserves, as well as by a reduced leaf surface, which obviates water loss via evapotranspiration.

The animals present in the desert are reptiles, insects and burrowing rodents. All these animals possess special morphological, physiological and ethological adaptations for deserts. In general, large animals are very uncommon except mule, dear and some species of gazelle and all animals have cursorial, fossorial and or saltatorial adaptations. Some desert animals are nicely adapted for high extremes of temperature. For example, the lethal the temperature for different species of insects found to be following– for the canal spider *Galcodes granti* it is 50°C, for the *Gryllus domesticus* it is 40°C and for the forficulid *Labidura riparia* is is 38°C. Diurnal rhythms are perhaps the best method of avoiding the heat. While some desert plants close their petals at night, manu blossom only at night. Some insects like tenebrionid bettle *Akis spinosa* remain active during the day, and the centipede *Scolopendra clavipes* restricts its activities to night time.

Further, certain reptiles and certain insects are well adapted for survival in deserts because of their thick, impervious integuments and the fact they excrete dry waste matter. A few species of mammals have become secondarily adapted to the desert by excreting very concentrated urine. They avoid the sun by remaining in their burrows during the day. Kangaroo rat and pocket mouse, both are able to live without drinking water by extracting the moisture from the seeds and succulent cactus they eat. The camel and the desert birds (Ostrich, etc.) must have an occasional drink of water but can go for long periods of time using the water stored in the body. Most insects of deserts are herbivores and as a correlation the number of small insectivorous lizards found in the desert is usually high.

THREATS TO BIODIVERSITY

One of the measure threat to Biodiversity is space, food and raw material for expanding human and plant establishment. Wilson 1985 described the losses of biodiversity as ''*Crisis*' and this is more serious for developing countries like India. Since 1600 there have been over 1000 recorded extinctions of plants and animals species. Probably early humans were directly reponsible for extinction of many large and smaller mammals. But the elimination of species is a normal process of the natural world. When species die or extinct, they will replace by others. Due to human population and its impact an ecosystems, thousands of species and sub-species become extinct every year. According to E.O. Wilson, we are losing 10,000 organisms a year i.e. 27 per day. If this will continue, we may destroy millions of plants, animals and microbes in next few decades. It is studied that 99% of all species of fossil that ever existed are now extinct.

Before man's appearance on this planet the rate of extinction was one species per thousand years. However, the pressure of human activity has drastically changed the picture. Between 1650 AD and 1950 AD about 30 species of higher animals were lost. Studies show that about 50,000 invertebrates species are losing every year. Almost one recorded as threatened. Indian wild life act 1972 schedule-I provides a list of about 150 endangered species. Disappearance of Dinosaurs along with about 50% of exististing species at the end of Cretaceous period is the best example of extinction. In India 33% of reptiles and 42 of bird species are endemic. It is said that, the current extinction rates are possibly 4 or 5 times more than the rates in the fossil record.

Habitat Loss

Habitat loss due to human activities and other disturbances are welknown factor. Varying human disturbances are changing ecosystems and are thus threatening the biodiversity. Due to habitat degradation wild population become more volnerable to predators and diseases. This is especially true for wildlife, which suffer due to habitat loss and fragmentation. Habitat loss is in instalments so that the habitat is divided into small and scattered patches i.e. *habitat fragmentation*. The natural forests and grasslands, which were the natural homes of thousands species including wild life species, are going cleared day by day for conversion into agriculture lands, pastures, settlements or for development projects. Thus these species are perished due to loss of their habitat.

Due to pollution and the presence of toxic and hazardous pollutants, our fresh water resources have suffered and many species of aquatic birds, fish and mammals have been threatened. Electric power plants, which causes thermal pollution in biosphere affected all aquatic communities and their natural food chains. Marine biodiversity is also under serious threat due to human intervention. If the present rate of deforestation continue, there will be loss of about 12% birds species and about 15% plant species in South and Central America. Huge amount of habitat are lost each year as the world's forests are cut down. Rain forests, tropical dry forests, wet lands, mangroves and grasslands are threatened habitats and leading to desertification. Problems of acid rains and global climate change are also wellknown for habitat loss.

Poaching of Wildlife

Poaching is another threat to wildlife. As an ancient period, hunters, collectors, and smugglers (traders) are the measure threat to a number of species including endangered species. They collected furs, hides, horns, tusks, and some live specimens, herbal products and smuggled to others for millions of dollars. The alarming point in this case is that for one animal they killed more than one. It is an illegal trade and internationally banned.

The cost of these animal parts are surprising. The cost of Bengal tiger coat is more than one lac dollars. South American ocelot costs more than 50,000 dollars, a single orchid cost more than 5000 dollars, horns of rhinoceros cost their weight in gold. These are some examples by which we can understand the situation of trading wildlife products, which is highly profit making for poachers.

Over collection and over exploitation are the main causes of disappearance of plants of scientific and medicinal value. The reduction of genetic diversity among the cultivated species drastically limit possibilities of creating new cultivar in the future, which could be disastrous for human race. It is advisable that do not purchase the parts and products made from wild animals specially endangered species.

Man-Wildlife Conflicts

Struggle for existence. This is applicable for both, man and wild animal. Due to habit loss animals come out of the forest and destroy the crops later on they become danger to human being. Villagers and affected people kill them. There are so many cases of conflict between man and wild life. In these cases forest department could not pacify, resulted to lack of non co-operation for wild life conservation from affected people.

Animals are prone to infection when they are under stress. Animals held in captivity are also more prone diseases. The elephants and other wild animals suffer pain and turn violent when they come to destroy the electric fancied crop field. It is noted that ill, weak and injured animals have tendency to attack man. Man and wild life conflicts also occur during human encroachment into forest area.

There are number of cases, when man eating tiger was reported several men because they like human flesh rather than animals flesh.

CONSERVATION OF BIODIVERSITY

The geological history of biodiversity is about 3.5 to 4 billion years old. The first appearance of multicellular organism was perhaps a mile stone in the history of biodiversity which did not diversify until about 600 million years ago. It is true that biodiversity is a source, once extinct can not be regenerated again. Due to human activities and over exploitation of ecosystem, the most severe extinction has occured. This is our one of the first and most important requirement *i.e.*, conservation. From biological point of view, its our responsibility to conserve plants, animals (including cultivated plants and domestic animals, and their wild relatives.

In view of the importance of biodiversity (economic, environmental, scientific and medical) the urgent need for conservation of biodiversity was felt in Rio conference. The World Summit on sustainable development held in Johannesburg in August 2002 reiterated that the conservation of biodiversity was necessary for the survival of human race on this earth. In the Convention on Biodiversity (CBD), which has 42 Articles, Articles, 8 and 9 are about in-situ conservation and *ex-situ* conservation respectively. The objectives of CBO clearly stated the conservation of biological diversity, the sustainable use of its components, and the fair and equitable sharing of the benefits arising from the utilization of genetic resources. The conservation has to be *ex-situ* as also in-situ. Both are complimentary to each other.

Conservation of Biodiversity in India

Dr. M.S. Swaminathan (1983) reviewed the scientific aspects of conservation. He suggested that the first step in conservation should be defining the categories of materials (plants/genes) for preservation and the major methods preserving them. He suggested that the following categories should be usually regarded as important.

1. Cultivated varieties in current use.
2. Obsolete cultivars.
3. Primitive cultivars or land races.
4. Wild species and weedy species closely related to cultivated varieties.
5. Wild species of potential value to man.
6. Special genetic stock developed by man.

The principle of any technology designed for germplasm conservation should be to preserve the maximum possible genetic diversity of a particular plant or genetic stock for future use. Diversity in plants is at the level of species, varieties and individuals. Special genetic stocks may include the material (mutant or breed lines with identified gene or gene combination) developed and used in on going breeding programme. It has been estimated that the survival of approximately 9,000 wild species of plants is some way threatened and that the majority of these are from tropical regions. This further highlights the need for a positive approach to conservation of endangered plants. When new cultivars replace the primitive or conventionally used agricultural crops, it becomes especially important that the crop be properly documented and conserved.

According to Swaminathan (1983) conservation methodologies can take the following three forms :

1. Entire biomass
2. *In situ* preservation
3. *Ex situ* preservation

Many ways are being suggested for preserving biodiversity,

1. No undisturbed land use.
2. Catalogues of genetic resources and national biological inventories be prepared.
3. Measures should be taken to reduce emission of green house gases and ozone destroying compounds. Some of them include following:
4. Effective measures for the conservation of biodiversity be developed and strengthened in all countries.

The details of these conservation methods made a separate sub-discipline of biodiversity studies called *conservation biology*. These techniques of conservation of biodiversity include:

1. *In situ* conservation
2. *Ex situ* conservation

Conservation of biodiversity can be achieved in a number of complementary ways. These methods, all of them falling within the broader concepts of gene banks.

Ex-situ Conservation

''*Ex-situ*'' conservation: It means the wild-life conservation in captivity under human care. In this, the endangered plants and animals are collected and bred under controlled conditions in gardens, zoos, sanctuaries etc., wild-life management in captivity have the following advantages:

(*i*) The organisms are assured of food, water, shelter and security and hence can have longer life span and longer span of breeding activity, thereby increasing the possibility of having more number of offsprings.

(*ii*) The chances of survival of endangered species increase because of human care under secure conditions.

(*iii*) This offers the possibility of using genetic techniques to improve the species concerned.

However, there are some disadvantages and limitations of wild-life management is captivity:

(*i*) Since maintenance and breeding of plants and animals under captivity is very expensive, it can be adopted only for a few selected species.

(*ii*) Wild-life captivity only under a set of favourable environmental conditions deprives the organisms the opportunity to adopt to ever-changing natural environment. Therefore, new life forms cannot evolve and thus the gene-pool gets stagnant.

Ex-situ conservation, using sample populations, is done through establishment of gene banks which include genetic resource centres, zoo's, botanical gardens, culture collections etc.

Ex-situ conservation, is the chief mode for preservation of genetic resources, which may include both cultivated and wild material. Generally seeds or in-vitro maintained plant cells, tissue and organs are preserved under appropriate conditions for long term' storage as gene banks. This requires considerable knowledge of the genetic structure of population sampling techniques, methods of regeneration and maintenance of varietal genepools, particularly in cross pollinated plants.

The Methods of *Ex-situ* Conservation

The practice of ex-situ conservation involves technique which are essentially meant to maintain, multiply or help the species to survive under natural conditions. These include—

(*i*) Long term captive breeding

(*ii*) Short term propagation and release

(*iii*) Animal translocations

(*iv*) Animal Reintroduction

Instead of the above methods there are three techniques also used for ex-situ conservation. They are —

(*i*) Seed banks

(*ii*) Gene banks

(*iii*) In-vitro

(*iv*) In-vivo

Certain conservation agencies, botanical gardens and many research institutions are also working in this field. Establishment of ''Central Zoo Authority'' by Govt. of India is another milestone in the way of *Ex-situ* conservation.

In-situ Conservation

In-situ conservation is the conservation of ecosystem where all the flora, fauna and wildlife survive in tandem with nature. Development of gene sanctuaries, biosphere reserves, national parks, protected areas and reserve forests, where wildlife could grow and multiply, constitutes the vital forms of in-situ conservation. Development of biosphere reserves (in-situ conservation) has more than one advantage. It allows natural agencies of creating variation to act unabatedly, thus the range of natural variation continues to reshuffling and replenishing the plantation is never exhausted. The reserves are instrumental in preserving much of wildlife in the vicinity of human establishments.

Approximately 42% of the total geographical area of the country has been earmarked for extensive in-situ conservation of habitats and ecosystem. A protected area network of 99 National Parks and 523 wildlife sanctuaries has been created. The results of this network have been significant in restoring viable population of large mammals such as tiger, lion rhinoceros, crocodiles, elephants etc. Ten biodiversity rich areas of the country have been designated as biosphere reserves.

In-situ means in the natural, original place or position, as in the location of the explant on the mother plant prior to excision. In-situ conservation which include conservation of plant and animals in their native ecosystems or even in man made ecosystem, where they naturally occur. This type of conservation applies only of wild fauna and flora and not to the domesticated animals and plants, because conservation is achieved by protection of populations in nature. This method of conservation mainly aims at preservation of land races with wild relatives in which genetic exists and/or in which the weedy/wild forms present hybrids with related cultivars. These are evolutionary systems that are difficult of plant breeders to stimulate and should not be knowingly destroyed.

The *in-situ* conservation of habitats has received high priority in the world conservation strategy programmes launched since 1980. Institutional, arrangement, especially in countries of the developing world, have been emphasized. This mode of conservation has some limitations however, there is risk of material being lost due to environmental hazards. Further the cost of maintaining a large portion of available genotypes in nurseries or fields may be extremely high.

In-situ conservation includes a system of protected areas of different categories e.g. National parks, Sanctuaries, National Monument, Cultural landscape, Biosphere Reserves etc. One of the best methods to save wildlife species, which is on the road to extinction, is to put it in a special enclosure to reproduce. Sanctuaries and National Parks, whose legal definition varies from country to country, best illustrate this.

National Parks, Wildlife Sanctuaries and Biosphere Reserves

National Parks or a Sanctuary may be defined *as an area, declared by state, for the purpose of protecting, propagating or developing wild life therein, or its natural environment for their scientific educational and recreational value. Human activities like hunting, firewood, collection, timber harvesting etc. are restricted in these areas.*

The creation of National Parks, Wildlife Sanctuaries and Biosphere Reserves in an attempt to manage wildlife by defining protected areas. Wildlife therein is regularly monitored and necessary management strategies for their perpetuation and preservation are formulated and implemented. These protected areas not only benefit wildlife, but indirectly humans too. Their protection means the protection of entire ecosystem, which is necessary to continue to enjoy the benefits that we may now receive from it.

A National Park is an area dedicated to conserve the scenery (or environment) and natural objects and the wildlife therein. In national parks, all private rights are non-existent and all forestry operations and other usages such as grazing of domestic animals are prohibited.

'The national reserve or biosphere reserve are usually large protected areas with boundaries circumscribed by legislation and are usually more than 5000 sq. kms in area. The protected area network in India includes 99 National Parks and 523 Wildlife Sanctuaries, 43 Conservation Reserves and three Community Reserves. Realizing the gigantic task of managing our protected areas The National Wildlife Action Plan (2002-2016) was adopted in 2002, emphasizing the people participation and their support for wildlife conservation.

Important National Parks and Wildlife Sanctuaries in India

States	National Parks and Wildlife Sanctuaries
Andhra Pradesh	Pakhal Wildlife Sanctuary, Pocharam Wildlife Sanctuary, Kawal Wildlife Sanctuary, Kolleru
Arunachal Pradesh	Namdapha Pelicanary Wildlife Sanctuary
Assam (Asom)	Kaziranga National Park Manas Wildlife Sanctuary
Jharkhand	Hazaribagh National Park, Betla National Park
Goa	Mollen Wildlife Sanctuary
Gujarat	Gir National Park, Velavader National Park Wild Ass
Haryana	Sultanpur Lake Bird Sanctuary
J & K	Dechigam Wildlife Sanctuary

Karnataka	Bandipur National Park, Nagarhole National Park, Ranganthitto Bird Sanctuary, Silent Valley National Park
Kerala	Periyar Wildlife Sanctuary Wynad Wildlife Sanctuary
Madhya Pradesh	Kanha National Park, Shivpuri National Park, Bandhavgarh National Park, Panna National Park
Maharashtra	Tadoda National Park, Yawal Wildlife Sanctuary
Manipur	Keibul Lamjao National Park
Meghalaya	Balpakram Sanctuary
Mizoram	Dampa Wildlife Sanctuary
Nagaland	Intangki Wildlife Sanctuary
Orissa	Simlipal National Park, Chilka Lake Bird Sanctuary
Punjab	Abohar Wildlife Sanctuary
Rajasthan	Ranthambore National Park, Sariska Wildlife Sanctuary Ghana Bird Sanctuary
Sikkim	Kanchenjunga National Park
Tamil Nadu	Mudumalai Wildlife Sanctuary, Vedanthangal Water Bird Sanctuary
Uttar Pradesh	Dudhwa National Park
Uttarakhand	Corbett National Park, Rajaji National Park
West Bengal	Jaldapara Wildlife Sanctuary

Biosphere Reserves in India

S. No.	Name	Date of Estbl.	Area (in km²)	Location
1.	Achanakamar-Amarkantak	2005	3835.51	Covers parts of Anupur and Dindori districts of M.P. and parts of Bilaspur districts of Chhattisgarh State
2.	Agasthyamalai	2001	1828	Neyyar, Peppara and Shendurney Wildlife Sanctuaries and their adjoining areas in Kerala
3.	Dehang-Dibang	1998	5111.50	Part of Siang and Dibang Valley in Arunachal Pradesh
4.	Dibru-Saikhowa	1997	765	Part of Dibrugarh and Tinsukia Districts (Asom)
5.	Great Nicobar	1989	885	Southern most islands of Andaman and Nicobar (A&N Islands)
6.	Gulf of Mannar	1989	10,500	Indian part of Gulf of Mannar between India and Sri Lanka (Tamil Nadu)
7.	Kachchh	2008	12,454	Part of Kachchh, Rajkot, Surendra Nagar and Patan Civil Districts of Gujarat State
8.	Khangchendzonga	2000	2619.92	Parts of Khangchendzonga hills and Sikkim.
9.	Manas	1989	2837	Part of Kokrajhar, Bongaigaon, Barpeta, Nalbari, Kamrup and Darang districts (Asom)
10.	Nanda Devi	1988	5860.69	Part of Chamoli, Pithoragarh, and Bageshwar districts (Uttarakhand)
11.	Nilgiri	1986	5520	Part of Wayanad, Nagarhole, Bandipur and Madumalai, Nilambur, Silent Valley and Siruvani hills (Tamil Nadu, Kerala and Karnataka)
12.	Nokrek	1988	820	Part of Garo hills (Meghalaya)
13.	Pachmarhi	1999	4926	Parts of Betul, Hoshangabad and Chindwara districts of Madhya Pradesh
14.	Simlipal	1994	4374	Part of Mayurbhanj district (Orissa)
15.	Sunderbans	1989	9630	Part of delta of Ganges and Brahamaputra river system (West Bengal)
16.	Seshachalam	Sep. 2010	---	Contains eastern ghat in the southern part of Andhra Pradesh.

FOOD

It is a nutritive substance taken by an organism for growth, work, repair and maintaining life processes. It provides energy to do work and maintain body heat, provides materials for the growth of the body, makes necessary materials for reproduction and provides materials for the repair of damaged cells and tissues of our body. Food has many different components and each one is necessary for one or the other function. Major ones are — carbohydrates, fats, proteins, minerals, vitamins, water and roughage.

- **Carbohydrates:** They are made up of three elements - carbon, hydrogen and oxygen, the proportion of hydrogen and oxygen being the same as in water. Glucose $C_6H_{12}O_6$ Sucrose, $C_{12}H_{22}O_{11}$ and Starch $(C_6H_{10}O_5)_n$ are examples of carbohydrates. They are the main source of energy in our body, with 1 gm of carbohydrates producing about 17 kilojoules of energy upon oxidation. For a normal person, 400 to 500 gms of carbohydrates are required daily but for sportspersons, growing children and nursing mothers, it is on higher side. Cellulose, which forms the cell walls of plants is also a carbohydrate but not a food for human because the enzyme capable of digesting cellulose is not produced in human beings. Cellulose, however, helps in maintaining a healthy digestive system. Sugar is a type of carbohydrate which is sweet in taste. Glucose, Fructose and Sucrose are examples of sugar. The carbohydrates in our food is obtained mainly from plant sources like wheat, rice, maize, potatoes, peas, beans and fruits. During respiration, oxidation of carbohydrates takes place. It is represented as

$$C_6H_{12}O_6 + 6O_2 \rightarrow 6CO_2 + 6H_2O + \text{Energy}$$

- **Fats:** They are esters of long chain fatty acids and an alcohol called glycerol. Fats also contain atoms of carbon, hydrogen and oxygen. However, fats contain less proportion of oxygen as compared to carbohydrates. The main function of fats in the body is to provide a steady source of energy and for this purpose, they are deposited within the body. One gm of fat gives 37 kilojoules of energy which is more than double of that given by carbohydrates. Fats, the richest source of energy to our body, can be stored in the body for subsequent use. Fats, soluble in organic solvents and insoluble in water, also supply fat-soluble vitamins to our body. Fats, as such cannot be absorbed by our body due to insolubility in water and needs to be hydrolysed into simpler substances, soluble in water. A normal diet should contain about 75 gms of fat per day. Fats are supplied to our body by butter, ghee, cheese, milk, egg-yolk, meat, nuts, soyabean and cooking oils. Fats containing saturated fatty acids are solid at ordinary room temperature while those containing. unsaturated fatty acids are in the liquid form. Saturated fats are stable and hence get deposited in the body. Our body can convert carbohydrates into some fatty acids but a few others have to be taken with the food as they cannot be synthesised within the body. These fatty acids, which have to be supplied through the food, are called essential fatty acids. These are unsaturated in nature. Therefore, it is better to use unsaturated fats in our diet.
- **Energy Requirements:** The energy requirement of a body varies according to age, sex, lifestyle, occupation, climate and special situations like pregnancy and lactation. Lesser intake of food gives insufficient energy and leads to sick-ness. Excess intake of food also creates problems. Following table gives average daily requirements of energy, with women generally needing less energy than men of the same age group.

Age	*Energy requirements*
5 years	6000 kJ per day
11 years	9000 kJ per day
18 years	11000 kJ per day
Adult (normal work)	9600 kJ per day
Adult (heavy work)	12000 kJ per day
Adult (very heavy work)	16000 kJ per day

- **Proteins:** They are complex organic compounds made up of carbon, hydrogen, oxygen and nitrogen. The building blocks of Protein are Amino acids and there are large number of amino acids. Some proteins also contain sulphur and phosphorus. Proteins are essential for the growth of children and teenagers, and for maintenance and making good the wear and tear of the body tissues in adults. Proteins are made up of nitrogen containing compounds called amino acids. An adult needs about 1 gm of protein per kg of body weight. Proteins can be obtained from the plant as well as animal sources, with groundnuts, beans, whole cereals like wheat and maize and pulses belonging to the former category and fish, eggs, milk, cheese and lean meat belonging to the latter. Milk, meat and eggs contain all the amino acids required by our body.
- **Minerals:** Our body also needs some inorganic substances like metals, non-metals and their salts, though in small amounts. These minerals are needed to build bones, teeth, formation of Red Blood Corpuscles, coagulation of blood, functioning of muscles, nerves and glands, etc. Some of the important minerals needed by our body are — iron, iodine, calcium, phosphorus, sodium, potassium, zinc, copper, magnesium, chloride, fluoride and sulphur. We get most of the minerals in combined form from plant sources. Deficiency of these minerals causes many diseases. The quantity of minerals required vary with about 30 milligram of iron requirement, 1 milligram of iodine requirement and 1 gm of calcium and phosphorus requirement daily for a normal person.
- **Vitamins:** They are complex organic compounds which are necessary for normal growth, good health, good vision, proper digestion and healthy teeth, gums and bones. They act as catalysts in certain chemical reactions of metabolism in our body. They don't provide energy to our body nor form body tissues. Vitamins are needed in small quantities and their deficiency effects eyes, skin, bones, hair and general growth. More than 15 types of vitamins are known and only 2 vitamins — D and K can be formed in our body. Rest are either provided through our diet or taken separately in synthetic form. Vitamin B-complex and C are water soluble vitamins while vitamin A, D, E and K are oil soluble. Vitamin B-Complex is a mixture of 11 vitamins. Following table gives necessity and sources of vitamins.

Vitamin	Necessity	Source
Vitamin A	For maintaining healthy eyesight, normal skin and hair	Cod liver oil, fish, eggs, milk, carrot, leafy vegetables.
Vitamin B_1	For growth, carbohydrate metabolism, functioning of heart, nerves and muscles.	Milk, soya-food, meat, whole cereals, green vegetables.
Vitamin C	For keeping teeth, gums and joints healthy, for increasing resistance of body to infection	Citrus fruits, guava, tomatoes.
Vitamin D	For normal growth of bones and teeth	Milk, eggs, butter, cod liver oil, sun light.
Vitamin E	For normal reproduction, functioning of muscles and protection of liver	Green leafy vegetables, milk, butter, tomato.
Vitamin K	For normal clotting of blood and normal functioning of liver	Green leafy vegetables, soyabean, tomato.

- **Water:** It is essential for our body because it helps in the assimilation of food. About two-thirds of a man's body is the water in his tissues. Water also helps in digestion, transport, excretion and regulating body temperatures. The survival time without water is very short. Amount of water needed depends on one's age, type of work and the climate. Dehydration is caused by excessive loss of water from the body.
- **Roughage:** It is the fibrous material present in plants and their products. It mainly consists of the indigestible plant carbohydrates called cellulose. Though it does not provide any energy to the body, yet keeps the digestive system in order, by helping in retaining water in the body and preserving constitution. The main source of roughage are salads, cabbage, corn cob, porridge, vegetables and fruits with stems.

DISEASES

Communicable Diseases

They are the diseases which can be transmitted from reservoirs of infection or infected person to the healthy but susceptible persons. The disease causing agent or the pathogen can be transmitted directly or indirectly. Direct transmission occurs:

(i) By direct contact with an infected person, e.g., chickenpox, smallpox, measles, leprosy, ringworm, gonorrhea, syphilis etc.,

(ii) Through sneezing, coughing, talking with infected person or spitting, e.g., diphtheria, influenza, common cold, measles, tuberculosis, pneumonia, mumps, whopping cough.

(iii) Through contact of injuries with soil, e.g., tetanus.

(iv) Through animal bites, e.g., rabies.

(v) Through placenta from mother to the foetus, e.g., German measles.

Indirect transmission takes place through some intermediate agents:

(i) Through agency of some vectors, e.g., African sleeping sickness is spread by Tse Tse fly, Kala-azar by sand fly, malaria by female Anopheles, Yellow fever by Aedes mosquito, Filariasis by Culex mosquito, Bubonic plague by Rat flea and Typhoid, cholera, amoebic dysentery by housefly.

(ii) By agencies like blood, water, food, e.g., cholera, dysentery, typhoid, AIDS.

(iii) Through contaminated articles like towels, handkerchief, toys, soap, utensils, surgical instruments.

(iv) By wind currents, aerosol sprays and dust.

(v) Through unclean hands, e.g., Enterobiesis.

Deficiency Diseases

These occur due to deficiency of some nutrients in the diet or some hormone due to hypo activity or damage to endocrine glands.

Diet Deficiency	Disease	Symptoms
Protein	Kwashiorkor	Swelling of abdomen and feet; enlarged liver; skin becomes dark and scaly.
Protein-energy malnutrition	Marasmus	Rapid weight loss; body growth and brain weight lowered.
Vitamin A	Night-blindness,	Inability to see in dim light; defective teeth formation; dry skin;
	Xerophthalmia	retarded growth.
Vitamin B_1	Beri-Beri	Swelling and Pain in legs, loss of appetite; weakness; palpitation; headache.

Diet Deficiency	*Disease*	*Symptoms*
Vitamin B_2	Cheilosis	Cracking of skin; inflammation of mouth and tongue; retarded growth.
Vitamin B_5	Pellagra	Skin eczema; swelling of gums; mental disturbances; disturbance of digestive tract.
Vitamin C	Scurvy	Swelling and bleeding of gums; pain in the muscles and joints; General weakness and fatigue; decreased resistance to cold; long time for wound healing.
Vitamin D	Rickets (in children), (in adult) Osteomalacia	Twisting of bones; bending of bones.
Vitamin K	Hypothrombinemia	Reduced capacity of clotting.
Iron	Anaemia	Loss of appetite; loss of weight; body looks pale; early tiredness.
Iodine	Goitre	Retarded growth; mental disability; enlargement of thyroid gland.
Fluoride	Dental caries	Loosing of teeth; swelling and bleeding of gums.
Calcium and phosphorus	Affects formation of bones and teeth	Weakening of bones; loss of teeth enamel; pain in the bones
Insulin	Diabetes	Sugar level in blood increases; person be-comes more susceptible to infections.
Thyroxine	Cretinism (child), Goitre	Mental retardation; physical growth stunted; small skeleton.
STH	Dwarfism	Diminished growth of the bones; person becomes dwarf, caused by lower activity of pituitary gland.
	Gigantism	Hyperactivity of pituitary gland causes excessive growth of the bones; person becomes abnormally tall.

Allergic Disease

In these diseases, body becomes hypersensitive to some foreign agents, allergens, which cause inflammation when come in contact with the body or enter inside the body. Foreign agents can be dust, pollens, certain-foods, serum, certain drugs or fabrics. The unfavourable response of the body to allergens is called allergic reaction. Asthma and hay fever are allergic diseases.

Degenerative Diseases

These occur due to degenerative changes in some vital organs of the body. Deposition of calcium salts or cholesterol in the walls of the blood vessels, hypertension or high blood pressure, reduced blood supply to heart muscles, clot formation in the coronary artery and back flow of blood from the ventricles to auricles are degenerative diseases of heart and blood vessels of the body. Obstruction of blood circulation to brain and stroke, epilepsy and inflammation of joints (arthritis) also belong to this category of diseases.

Cancer: It is characterised by uncontrolled growth and division of certain body tissues, forming a tumour. The rate of cell division is much higher than that of normal cells. All tumours are not cancerous. These cells have less survival capability than the normal cells and due to less adhesiveness, generally wander through the tissues to cause cancerous growth in different parts of the body. Cancer is neither contagious nor hereditary disease. The agents inducing cancer growth fire called carcinogens. Cancer can be caused by radiations (X-rays, gamma rays and particulate radiations); physical irritants (certain foods causing continued abrasion of the linings of the intestinal tract), chemical agents (caffeine, polycyclic hydrocarbons, heavy metallic ions, hormones), biological agents (viruses). The body organs, affected by cancerous cells are breast, stomach, lung, skin, pancreas, bones, muscles, lymph nodes, urinary bladder, vagina, liver and blood. Blood cancer is called Leukaemia. It is characterised by increased WBC count of the blood. The malignant tumour that grow rapidly and damage the normal cells, needs to be removed immediately otherwise could cause death. Danger signs of cancer are: persisting tumour, any wound not healing, any wound with continuous bleeding, persistent indigestion, rapid change in appearance of warts, persistent changes in bowel movements, persistent hoarseness in voice or coughing or swallowing or unexpected loss of weight.

Congenital Diseases

These are inborn diseases which are present from the birth. These are inheritable and are generally caused by gene or chromosomal mutations. These are Albinism, Sickle cell anaemia, Thalassemia, Hemophilia, Wilson's diseases and Anophthalmia. Some genetic disorders are caused due to changes in chromosomes number in the offsprings e.g. Dow's syndrome (mongolism), Klinefelter's syndrome, Turner's syndrome or super males/females.

Bacterial Diseases

Bacteria are minute organisms which are known to cause a number of diseases:

Disease	*Incubation period*	*Spread through*	*Symptoms*
Tuberculosis	2-10 weeks	Air-borne, droplet infection	Fever, coughing, chest pain and bloody sputum. Any part of body can be effected but lung is most common.
Diptheria	2-6 days	Air-borne droplet infection	Inflammation of mucus membrane of nose, throat and tonsils. In severe cases respiratory tract is blocked. Generally affects children below the age of 5 years.
Cholera	6 hours to 2-3 days	Contaminated food and water. House flies are the vectors	Acute diarrhoea, muscular cramps, sunken eyes, low blood pressure, dehydration, loss of min-erals in urine.
Leprosy	Upto 5 years	Prolonged and intimate contact	Deformity of fingers and toes, formation ulcers, scaly and nodulated skins, infected skin becomes senseless.
Whopping cough	7-14 days	Droplet infection	Mild fever, severe coughing, vomiting, accumulation of muscles in respiratory track, interfering in respiration.
Tetanus	3-21 days	Entry of cysts through any wound made by sharp object, dog bite or fall on the road	Restlessness, pulling pain in the wound, convulsions, stiffness of neck, rigid jaw muscles, contraction of muscles and paralysis.
Typhoid	1-3 weeks	Directed and Contact	Headache, classic typhoid fever, haemorrhage and ulceration of intestines, lashes on chest and upper abdomen.
Plague	2-6 days	Rats and bedbugs transmit the germs	High fever, extreme weakness, enlargement of lymph nodes, haemorrhage of bronchi and lungs.
Pneumonia	1-3 days	Air-borne	Collection of lymph, mucus in the bronchioles and alveoli. Reduced respiratory efficiency.

Gonorrhoea, syphilis, diarrhoeal diseases, food poisoning and meningitis are also caused by bacterias.

Viral Diseases

Disease	*Incubation period*	*Spread through*	*Symptoms*
Chicken-pox	12-20 days	Direct contact with infected persons or infected objects	Fever, headache, loss of appetite followed by dark red coloured rashes on the whole body. After some days rashes dry forming crusts which finally fall and patient recovers. Children below age of 5 years are more likely to catch the virus.
Smallpox	12 days	Droplet infection	Sudden high fever, headache, painful whole body followed by rashes. Rashes change into postulates with fluid. Rashes dry up leaving permanent pockmarks.
Poliomyelitis	7-14 days	Direct and oral	Headache and fever followed by stiffness of neck and convulsions. Finally, legs become paralysed. If respiratory centres are damaged, breathing fails and causes death.
Measles	10 days	Droplet infection	Common cold, headache, fever followed by coughing, sneezing, skin eruptions, conjuctivitis.
Mumps	12-26 days	Droplet infection	Painful enlargement of salivary gland high fever, difficulty in the movement of jaws and opening of mouth.
Rabies	1-3 months	Bite of rabied animal like dogs, monkeys, cates	100% fatal disease, causes severe headache, high fever and painful contraction of muscles ofz throat and chest. Patient fears from water. So, the disease is also called hydrophobia.
Influenza	24-28 hours	Air-borne	Bronchitis, coughing, bronchopneumonia.

AIDS

Acquired Immuno Deficiency Syndrome (AIDS) is caused by a virus which weakens the human body's immunity or self defence mechanism. Since natural immunity of the body gets reduced, AIDS makes body prone to many other infections. The patient suffering from AIDS actually die from other infections or diseases. AIDS disease usually spreads through sexual contact, transfusion of infected blood, use of infected needles for injections or from infected mother to the foetus. No medicine or vaccine has been developed to cure AIDS. Precaution is recommended to avoid AIDS.

Diseases Caused by Protozoa

Amoebiasis (Amoebic dysentery), Malaria, Kala-azar, Trypanosomiasis and Giardiasis are main diseases caused by protozoans. Malaria is a parasitic infection. When mosquito bites man to suck blood, it introduces the saliva containing the malarial parasite into blood stream of the man.

FOOD CHAIN

Flow of energy in an ecosystem is one way process. The sequence of organism through which the energy flows, is known as food chain. Plants are eaten by insects, insects are eaten by frogs, the frogs are eaten by fish and fishes are eaten by humans. The pattern of eating and being eaten forms a linear chain called food chain. Such a food chain can always be traced back to the producers.

The primary producers trap radiant energy of the sun and transfers to chemical or potential energy of organic compounds like proteins, fats and carbohydrates. The formation of ATP during photosynthesis is the first nutritional level. ATP is stored in food matter which is utilized by herbivores, the plant eaters. This process constitutes the second trophic level. When a herbivores animal eats the plant, the organic compounds are oxidised and the energy is liberated. Some of the energy is produced as heat which is not a useful energy. Flow of energy is greatly reduced at each successive level of nutrition because of the energy utilisation by the organisms and heat loses at each step in transformation of energy. This accounts for the decrease in biomass at each successive levels.

A typical food chain of an Indian rivers is as follows :

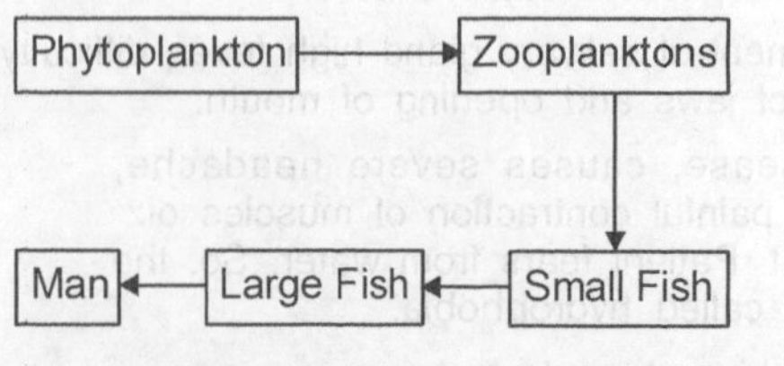

A typical food chain of an Indian river.

It should be noted that the number of steps in a food chain are always restricted to maximum four or five steps. Humans are at the end of a number of food chains.

Types of Food Chain

There are three types of food chain in the nature.

(*i*) Grazing Food Chain

The consumers (which starts the food chain) utilising the plant as their food, constitute grazing food chain. This food chain begins from green plants and the primary consumer is herbivore. Most of the ecosystem in nature follows this type of food chain. From energy view point such chains are very important. For example:

Grass → Grasshopper → Birds → Falcon.

(*ii*) Detritus Food Chain

The organic wastes exudates, and dead matter derived from grazing food chain are termed as detritus. This type of food chain starts from dead organic matter of decaying animals and plant bodies to the micro-organisms and then to detritus feeding organism and to other predators.

The food chain depends mainly on the influx of organic matter produced in another system. It represent an important component in the energy flow of an ecosystem. The organism of the food chain include algae, bacteria, fungi, protozoa, insects, nematodes etc.

In a community of organisms in a shallow sea, about 30% of the total energy flows via detritus food chain. However, in a forest with large biomass of plants and a relatively small biomass of animals even larger portion of energy flow may be obtained via detritus pathways.

Significance of Food Chain

The knowledge of food chain helps in understanding the feeding relationship as well as the interaction between organism and ecosystem. Besides its also help in understanding the mechanism of energy flow and circulation of matter in ecosystem. In addition to these, it also helps to understand the movement of toxic substance and the problem associated with biological magnification in the ecosystem.

Food chains are not always as simple as it looks. Quite often several different species of food organism.

FOOD WEB

A food chain represents only one part of energy flow through an ecosystem, whereas the ecosystem may consist of several interrelated food chains. But for simplicity, in general, a food chain implies a simple isolated relationship which rarely occurs in ecosystems. The same food resource may be a part of more than one chain. This is possible when the resource is at the lower trophic level. Accordingly the inter connected networks of feeding relationships is known as food webs. Most animals in nature utilize more than one species for their food. Therefore, food chains in an ecosystem become interconnected with each other which are summarised in Fig. below.

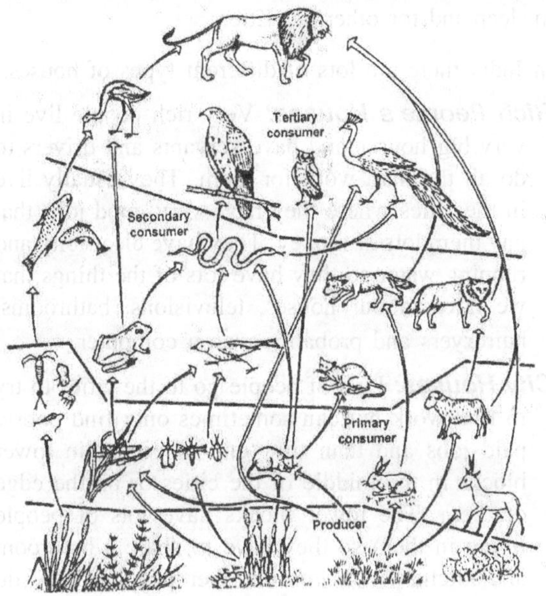

Food web

Several different trophic levels are recognised in any complex food webs. This is mentioned as under:

(*i*) Producer	Green plants	First trophic level
(*ii*) Primary consumers	Herbivores	Second trophic level
(*iii*) Secondary consumers	Carnivores	Third trophic level
(*iv*) Tertiary consumers	Higher carnivores	Fourth trophic level

An example of food web may consist of as many as food chain.

For example:

(*i*) Grass → Grasshopper → Hawk
(*ii*) Grass → Grasshopper → Lizard → Hawk
(*iii*) Grass → Rabbit → Hawk
(*iv*) Grass → Mouse → Hawk
(*v*) Grass → Mouse → Snake → Hawk

SHELTER

A place giving temporary protection from bad weather or danger is called shelter. It is also place providing food and accommodations for the homeless.

COMPONENTS OF SHELTER

The Outside Walls

The siding that gives a home its curb appeal may be vinyl, brick, wood, concrete or many other materials. In conventional construction, you'll find "sheathing," or exterior wall board behind the siding. And behind that is an insulated support system-typically wood framing stuffed with insulation, though alternative systems such as steel framing and prefabricated panels are becoming increasingly popular.

Whatever the outside wall is made of, it should be well sealed and well insulated (more on sealing and insulating later). If you're fortunate enough to tour your home during construction, you may have the chance to inspect the walls yourself. "Studs"-the boards or metal forms that make up the framing system-should be straight, with no significant cracks or twists, and no breaks. The sheathing should fit together tightly. From the outside you shouldn't see spaces where sheathing comes together. From the inside, before the insulation is added, you should not see cracks where sunlight pours in.

Windows, Doors, and Skylights

The good news about windows and skylights: they bring light, warmth and beauty into homes and give a feeling of openness and space to living areas. The bad news: they can also let in the cold in the winter and heat in the summer. Buying the right windows, doors and skylights will probably cost a little more, but don't compromise on these upgrades. They'll keep the temperature in your home more comfortable, prevent drafts and block outdoor noise better. They'll also protect against sun damage to your carpet, wood floors, furniture, fabrics and artwork. And even better: they can substantially reduce monthly heating and cooling bills.

The Foundation

The foundation is usually made of cement blocks or concrete. If you have a basement, the foundation walls double as the outside walls of the basement, and a concrete "slab" is poured to form the basement floor. Sometimes, even if you do not have a basement, a slab is poured and the house is built directly on top of the slab. Either way, the outside of the foundation must be waterproofed (it will look like thick paint has been applied). Otherwise, the concrete, which is porous, will soak up moisture, which may lead to mold and other problems.

The best way to insulate the basement on a new home is by using rigid insulation on the outside. If insulation is applied only on the inside walls, dampness-and mold-will likely build up between the walls and the insulation. Also, many basement walls are damp anyway, or become damp during periods of high rainfall. This dampness will often cause moisture and mold problems if it is isolated behind inside insulation. Insulation on the outside of the basement will add to the comfort of the space in a second way: it may actually reduce the inherent dampness of a basement wall because it provides another layer of sealing, and less condensation will occur on the inside wall.

The same applies to a house that is built on a concrete slab. Surprisingly, just by insulating the outside edge of the slab, you can reduce heating bills by 10 to 20 percent and keep your floor warmer than it would be otherwise.

Walls and Ceilings

Did you know that air leaks in a home can be responsible for as much as 30 percent of heating and cooling costs-and also contribute to moisture, noise, dust and pest problems? Proper air sealing can prevent these problems, but it takes time.

Air leaks usually occur at wall intersections, where the walls meet the ceiling, and around doors, windows and other outside penetrations such as plumbing and electrical. Before interior molding is added, and before the inside walls are finished and painted, look for cracks or openings in these areas. A crack can mean a drafty corner, or a mold problem in the making.

Another benefit of a tight home: builders can install smaller heating, ventilation and air-conditioning (HVAC) systems-up to 40 or 50 percent smaller, in some cases. That means you save both in the lower purchase price of these systems, and in your monthly energy bills.

Insulation

No matter how well sealed the walls are, and no matter how good the heating and cooling system is, expect drafts and uneven temperatures if the insulation is inadequate.

Insulation is rated according to its R-value, with a higher R-value indicating greater thickness and better insulation. Since most heat will escape through the ceiling the ceiling should be the most heavily insulated area: from as low as R-13 in the warmest U.S. climates to as high as R-60 in the coldest areas. Recommended wall insulation varies from R-11 to R-21, and floor insulation from R-11 to R-30.

All varieties of commonly used insulation work well when used properly. Be sure to check for gaps in the insulation. Do not skip over the hard-to-reach places, such as wall corners and around electrical outlets and switches.

HOUSING

A **house** is a building or structure that has the ability to be occupied for dwelling by human beings. The term house includes many kinds of dwellings ranging from rudimentary huts of nomadic tribes to free standing individual structures. In some contexts, "house" may mean the same as dwelling, residence, home, abode, lodging, accommodation, or housing, among other meanings. The social unit that lives in a house is known as a household. Most commonly, a household is a family unit of some kind, though households can be other social groups, such as single persons, or groups of unrelated individuals. Settled agrarian and industrial societies are composed of household units living permanently in housing of various types, according to a variety of forms of land tenure. English-speaking people generally call any building they routinely occupy "home". Many people leave their houses during the day for work and recreation, and return to them to sleep and for other activities.

In India there are lots of different types of houses.

Rich People's Houses: Very rich people live in very big houses and have servants and drivers to do all the hard work for them. They usually live in the cities where they have very good jobs that pay them lots of money. They have electricity and running water so they have lots of the things that we have in our houses, televisions, bathrooms, hairdryers and probably even a computer.

City Houses: Lots of people go to the cities to try to find work but can sometimes only find poorly paid jobs and than they end up living in tower blocks in the middle of the cities or on the edge of them. The tower blocks have lots of people living in them so they have to share a bathroom and kitchen with lots of other people. They do usually have water and electricity but they don't have all the technology that we have. The houses on the edge of the cities tend to be smaller but still cramped together and are no nicer to live in.
Lots of people go to the city to find a job and can't so they end up sleeping on the street instead.

Village Houses: Three-fourth of the population of India live in villages. The houses there are usually made from a mixture of clay, straw and cow dung. This mixture goes really hard when it is dry so it is very useful and also cheaper than bricks or stone. The houses have thick walls and this keeps the houses cool in the summer because the heat can't get through. Even though the families do all they can to keep cool they often sleep outside on the flat roofs where it is breezy and cool at night. Most houses in India have 2 rooms and a courtyard where they keep their animals if they have any. They don't have lots of furniture in village houses just some shelves or storage bins to keep their food in and some mats for the floor where people can sit.
The kitchen is usually in the corner of 1 room and has a stove low down on the floor. They gave very few tools for the kitchen, some pots and pans, utensils and a flat pan for cooking chapattis. The floor is kept very clean because they get food ready while sitting or crouching on the floor. A traditional Indian family eats on the floor in a circle but the men eat first.
These houses do not have running water, indoor toilets, fridges and hairdryers like we do. Most

houses have a radio but if they want to watch the television they have to go to their local community centre with lots of other people. More and more villages are beginning to get their own electricity supply.

Houses Near Water: Houses in India near water are in danger of being flooded when the monsoon rain comes. Some farmers are lucky and can afford to build houses that are higher up on stilts so that when the rain comes it washes underneath and doesn't destroy the houses. These houses are very useful but more expensive than ordinary village houses.

Some people in India are very poor and don't live in a village or in the middle of towns. They build their houses where ever they can and build them out of whatever they can find. They use bits of old wood, fabric, straw, anything at all.

WATER

Water is our most abundant resource, covering about 71% of the earth's surface. This precious film of water—about 97% salt water and the remainder fresh—helps maintain the earth's climate and dilutes environmental pollutants. Essential to all life, water makes up 50% to 97% of the weight of all plants and animals and about 70% of your body. Water is also a vital resource for agriculture, manufacturing, transportation, and countless other human activities.

Because of differences in average annual precipitation, some areas of the world have too little fresh water and others too much. With varying degrees of success, we have attempted to correct some of these imbalances. We have captured fresh water in reservoirs behind dams, transferred fresh water in rivers and streams from one area to another, tapped underground supplies, and attempted to reduce water use, waste, and contamination.

Despite these efforts, water is one of the most poorly managed resources on earth. We waste it and pollute it. We also charge too little for making it available, encouraging even greater waste and pollution of this potentially renewable resource.

Supply and Use of Water Resources

World Supply: The world's fixed supply of water in all forms (vapour, liquid, and solid) is enormous. If we could distribute it equally, every person on earth would have 280 billion liters. However, about 97% of the earth's water is found in the oceans and is too salty for drinking, growing crops, and most industrial uses except cooling.

The remaining 3% is fresh water. However, all but 0.003% of this supply is highly polluted, lies too far under the earth's surface to be extracted at an affordable cost, or is locked up in glaciers, polar ice caps, atmosphere, and soil. To put this in measurements that we can understand, if the world's water supply were only 100 liters, our usable supply of fresh water would be only about 0.003 liter.

That tiny fraction of usable fresh water still amounts to an average of 8.4 million litres for each person on earth. This supply is continually collected, purified and distributed in the natural hydrologic (water) cycle. This natural recycling and purification process works as long as we don't use water faster than it is replenished and as long as we don't overload it with slowly degradable and nondegradable wastes.

Surface-water Runoff: The fresh water we use comes from two sources : groundwater and surface-water runoff. Precipitation that does not infiltrate into the ground or return to the atmosphere by evaporation or transpiration is called **surface water** and becomes **runoff**—fresh water that flows on the earth's surface into streams, rivers, lakes, wetlands, and reservoirs. The land area that delivers runoff, sediment, and water-soluble substances to a major river and its tributaries is called a **watershed**, or **drainage basin**.

Surface water can be withdrawn from streams, rivers, lakes, and reservoirs for human activities, but only part of the total annual runoff is available for use. Some of it flows in rivers to the sea too rapidly to be captured, and some must be left in streams for wildlife and to supply downstream areas. In some years the amount of runoff is reduced by below-average precipitation.

Ground water: Some precipitation seeps into the ground, where it accumulates as **soil water** and partially fills pores between soil particles and rocks in the upper layers of the earth's crust. Most of this water is eventually lost to the atmosphere by evaporation from the upper layers of soil and by transpiration from leaves.

Under the influence of gravity, some infiltrating water slowly percolates through porous materials deeper into the earth. There it fills pores and fractures in spongelike, or permeable, layers of sand, gravel and porous rock such as sandstone. This area, where all available pore spaces are filled by water, is called the zone of saturation. These porous, water-bearing layers of underground rock are called **aquifers** and the water in them is **groundwater**.

Aquifers are recharged or replenished naturally by percepitation, which percolates downward through soil and rock in what is called a **recharge area**. The recharge process is usually quite slow (decades to hundreds of years) compared to the more rapid replenishment of surface water supplies. If the withdrawal rate of an aquifer exceeds its recharge rate, the aquifer is converted from a slowly renewable resource to a nonrenewable resource on a human time scale.

There are two types of aquifers: confined and unconfirned. An **unconfined aquifer**, or **water table** aquifer, forms when groundwater collects above a layer of impermeable rock or compacted clay. The top of the water-saturated portion of an unconfined aquifer is called the **water table**. Groundwater is the part of underground water in the zone of saturation below the water table. Soil water is the part of underground water above the water table, sometimes called the zone of aeration. A shallow unconfined aquifer in recharged by water percolating downward from soils and materials directly above the aquifer.

To get water from an unconfined aquifer, a well is drilled below the water table and into the unconfined aquifer. Then a pump must be used to bring water to the surface. The height of the water table in an area rises during prolonged wet periods and falls during prolonged drought. The water table also falls when water is pumped out by wells faster than the natural rate of recharge. This overdrafting creates a waterless volume known as a cone of depression.

A **confined aquifer** forms when groundwater is sandwiched between two layers of impermeable rock, such as clay or shale. This type of aquifer is saturated with water under a pressure greater than that of the atmosphere. In some cases pressure from the weight of water higher in the aquifer is so great that when a well is drilled into the confined aquifer, water is pushed to the surface without the aid of a pump. Such a well is called a flowing artesian well. With other confined-aquifer wells, called nonflowing artesian wells, pumps must be used because there isn't enough pressure to force the water all the way to the surface.

The recharge areas for confined aquifers can be hundreds of miles away from wells where water is withdrawn. Thus, the rate of natural recharge for such aquifers may not be based on local precipitation at the point of withdrawal as it is for unconfined aquifers.

Water Resource Problems

Too Little Water: A number of experts consider the availability of enough fresh water to meet human needs one of the most serious long-range problems confronting many parts of the world and in India. During the 1970s, major droughts affected an average of 24.4 million people and killed over 23,000 a year—a trend continuing in the 1980s. A **drought** occurs when an area does not get enough water because of lower than normal precipitation, higher than normal temperatures that increase evaporation, or both.

At least 80 arid and semiaird countries, where nearly 40% of the world's people live, have serious periodic droughts. These countries, mostly in Asia and Africa, have great difficulty growing enough food to support their populations. A prolonged drought affected much of Africa between 1982 and 1986. It led to widespread starvation and disease and forced at least 10 million people to abandon their homes in a desperate search for food and water.

Between 1984 and 1988 there were major droughts in parts of China, India, and North America. In the summer of 1988, about 43% of the continental United States experienced severe droughts, comparable to those that created the Dust Bowl in the Midwest in the 1930s. The grain harvest dropped by 31% and crop losses amounted to about $15 billion, one of the costliest natural disasters in U.S. history.

Reduced precipitation, higher than normal temperatures, or both usually trigger a drought. But rapid population growth and poor land use intensify its effects. In many less developed countries large numbers of poor people have no choice but to try to survive on drought-prone land. To get enough food and fuelwood, they strip the land of trees, cultivate poor soils let their livestock overgraze grassland, and grow crops at higher, more erosion-prone elevations. This land degradation increases the severity of long-term drought by reducing the amount of rainfall absorbed and slowly released by vegetation and soils. Each new drought can lead to a downward spiral of further land degradation and desertification, lower food and fuelwood productivity, and more poverty. Water scarcity and clashes over water rights will intensify in many areas if the world's climate warms up as a result of an enhanced greenhouse effect.

In many parts of India, the major water problems are flooding, inability to supply enough water to some large urban areas, and increasing pollution of rivers, lakes, and groundwater. For example, 3 million residents must draw all their water from an underground aquifer. This aquifer is becoming severely contaminated by industrial wastes, leaking septic tanks and landfills, and ocean salt water, which is drawn into the aquifer when fresh water is withdrawn faster than it is naturally recharged.

The major water problem in the arid and semiarid areas of the western half of the country is a shortage of runoff caused by low and variable average annual precipitation, high rates of evaporation, and prolonged periodic drought. As a result, water tables are dropping rapidly as farmers and cities deplete groundwater aquifers faster than they are recharged.

Because most areas in the region have too little precipitation to grow crops without irrigation, 85% of the western water supply is used in agriculture.

Federally subsidized dams, reservoirs, and water transfer projects provide water to farms and cities as such low prices that there is little incentive for conservation. Experts project that present shortages and conflicts will get much worse as more industries and people migrate west and complete with farmers for scarce water.

Water Resource Management

Methods for Managing Water Resources: Although we can't increase the earth's supply of water, we can reduce the impact and spread of water resource problems by managing the supply better. The two major approaches to water resource management are to increase the usable supply and to decrease unnecessary loss and waste. Most water resource experts believe that any effective plan for water management should combine these approaches.

Water problems and available solutions often differ between most developed countries and Less Developed Countries less developed countries may or may not have enough water, but they rarely have the money needed to develop water storage and distribution systems. Their people must settle where the water is.

In most developed countries people tend to live where the climate is favourable and bring in water through expensive water diversion systems. Some settle in a desert and expect water to be brought to them at a low price. Others settle on a floodplain and expect the government to keep flood waters away.

Methods for Managing Water Resources

Increase the Supply	Reduce Unnecessary Loss and Waste
Build dams and reservoirs	Decrease evaporation of irrigation water
Divert water from one region to another Tap more groundwater	Redesign mining and industrial processes to use less water
Convert salt water to fresh water (desalination)	Encourage the public to reduce unnecessary water waste and use
Tow freshwater icebergs from the Antarctic to water-short coastal regions	Increase the price of water to encourage water conservation
Seed clouds to increase precipitation	Purify polluted water for reuse

Constructing Dams and Reservoirs: Rainwater and water from melting snow that would otherwise be lost can be captured and stored in large reservoirs behind dams built across rivers. Damming increases the annual supply by collecting fresh surface water during wet periods and storing it for use during dry periods.

By controlling river flow, dams reduce the danger of flooding in downstream areas and allow people to live on the fertile floodplains of major rivers below the dam. They also provide a controllable supply of water for irrigating arid and semiarid land below the dam. Hydroelectric power plants, which use the energy of water flowing from dam reservoirs, generate more than 20% of the world's electricity. This is a renewable, non-polluting source of electricity. Reservoirs behind large dams can also be used for outdoor recreation such as swimming, boating, and fishing.

But the benefits of dams and reservoirs must be weighed against their costs. Dams are expensive to build and may give developers and residents in a floodplain a false sense of safety from major floods that can overwhelm the ability of a dam to control flood waters. The reservoirs fill up with silt and become useless in 20 to 200 years, depending on local climate and land-use practices. The permanent flooding of land behind dams to form reservoirs displaces people and destroys vast areas of valuable agricultural land, wildlife habitat, white-water rapids, and scenic natural beauty. China's massive Three Gorges Dam project will submerge 10 cities and partially flood another 8. Over 3.3 million people will have to be resettled.

The storage of water behind a dam also raises the water table. The higher water table often waterlogs the soil on nearby land, decreasing its crop or forest productivity. A dam can decrease rather than increase the available supply of fresh water, especially in semiarid areas. This happens because water that would normally flow in an undammed river evaporates from the reservoir's surface or seeps into the ground below the reservoir. Evaporation also increases the salinity of reservoir water by leaving salts behind, decreasing its usefulness for irrigation. The sheer weight of the water impounded in reservoirs increases the likelihood of fault movements, which cause earthquakes.

By interrupting the natural flow of a river, a dam disrupts the migration and spawning of fish. By trapping silt that would normally be carried downstream, dams deprive downstream areas and estuaries of vital nutrients and decrease their productivity. In the opinion of some outdoor-sports enthusiasts, a dam replaces more desirable forms of water recreation (white-water canoeing, kayaking, rafting, stream fishing) with less desirable, more "artificial" forms (motorboating, sailboating, lake fishing).

Water Diversion Project: In most development Countries local government often increase supply of fresh water in water-poor populated areas by transferring water from water-rich areas. One such project in the United States is the California Water Plan-the world`s largest reservoir and distribution system and in India, Bhakhra Dam (Punjab), the highest reservoir. It transports water from water- rich parts of northern California to heavily populated parts of northern California and to mostly arid and semiarid, heavily populated southern California.

Although several large urban areas use lots of water, about 90% of the water withdrawn in U.P. and Bihar is used by agriculture. The basic problem is that two-thirds of all the precipitation in India in the northern mountains, while 70% of the water is used in central and southern parts.

Another example of large-scale water diversion is in Soviet Central Asia, where so much water has been diverted from the Aral Sea for irrigation that the lake bed has dried up. Now massive amounts of salt and sand are blown into the air by winds, disrupting agriculture as far away as India. According to Soviet scientists, this water project may be one of the world's greatest human-caused ecological disasters.

Tapping Groundwater: Another solution to water supply problems is to rely on groundwater. In India about half of the drinking water (96% in rural areas and 20% in urban areas), 40% of the irrigation water, and 23% of all the fresh water used is withdrawn from underground aquifers. In Delhi, Uttar Pradesh, Maharashtra, Gujarat, and other states more than 90% of the population depends on groundwater for drinking water supplies.

Overuse of groundwater can cause or intensify several problems: aquifer depletion, subsidence (sinking of land when groundwater is withdrawn), intrusion of salt water into aquifers, and groundwater contamination. **Aquifer depletion** occurs when groundwater is withdrawn faster than it is recharged by precipitation.

Currently, about one-fourth of the groundwater withdrawn in the United States is not replenished. In the arid and semiarid Texas region up to 77% of the groundwater withdrawn is not replenished. The major groundwater overdraft problem is in parts of the huge Ogallala Aquifer, extending under the farm belt from northern Nebraska to northwestern Texas. Groundwater levels often slowly recover when withdrawals are reduced.

Aquifer depletion is also a serious problem in northern China, Mexico City, and parts of India. The most effective solution is to reduce the amount of groundwater withdrawn by wasting less irrigation water and by not growing crops in dry areas.

When groundwater in an unconfined aquifer is withdrawn faster than it is replenished, the soil of the aquifer becomes compacted and the land overlying the aquifer sinks, or subsides. Widespread subsidence in the San Joaquin Valley of California has damaged houses, factories, pipelines, highways, and railroad beds. Some areas have sunk almost 9 meters (30 feet).

When fresh water is withdrawn from an aquifer near a coast or near an inland deposit of salt water faster than it is recharged, salt water intrudes into the aquifer. Saltwater intrusion threatens to contaminate the drinking water of many towns and cities along the Atlantic and Gulf coasts and in the coastal areas of Israel, Syria, and the Arabian Gulf states.

Unnecessary Water Waste: An *estimated 20% to 40% of the water used in India is unnecssarily wasted.* This explains why many water resource experts consider water conservation the quickest and cheapest way to provide much of the additional water needed in dry areas.

A major cause of water waste in the United States is that elected officials have kept water prices artificially low, hoping to stimulate economic growth and get reelected by keeping consumers happy. Until the late 1980s, government funds were used to build large dams and water transfer projects, especially in the West. These subsidized projects provide low-cost water for farms, industries, and homes. Outdated laws governing access and use of water resources also encourage unnecessary waste.

Water subsidies are paid for by all taxpayers in the form of higher taxes. Because these indirect costs don't show up on monthly water bills, consumers have little incentive to conserve. Raising the price of water to reflect its true cost would provide powerful incentives for water conservation.

Another reason that water waste in the many countries is greater than necessary is that the responsibility for water resource management in a particular water basin is divided among many state and local governments rather than being held by one authority. For example, the Chicago metropolitan area has 349 separate water supply systems, divided among some 2,000 local units of government over a six-county area.

In sharp contrast is the regional approach to water management used in England and Wales. The British Water Act of 1973 replaced more than 1,600 separate agencies with 10 regional water authorities based on natural watershed boundaries. In this integrated approach, each water authority owns, finances, and manages all water supply and waste treatment facilities in its region. The responsibilities of each authority include water pollution control, water-based recreation, land drainage and flood control, and inland navigation, inland fisheries. Each water authority is managed by a group of elected local officials and a smaller number of officials appointed by the national government.

Reducing Irrigation Losses: Since irrigation accounts for the largest fraction (70% worldwide) of water use and waste, more efficient use of even a small amount of irrigation water frees water for other uses. Worldwide, only about 37% of the water used for irrigation contributes to crop growth; the other 63% is wasted. Most irrigation systems distribute water from a groundwork well or a surface canal by gravity flow through unlined field ditches. This method is cheap as long as farmers in water-short areas don't have to pay the real cost of making this water available. But it provides far more water than needed for crop growth, and at least 50% of the water is lost by evaporation and seepage. Such overwatering with inadequate drainage causes land-degrading salinization and waterlogging. Farmers could prevent seepage by placing plastic, concrete, or tile liners in irrigation canals. But as long as government-subsidized water is available to low cost, they have little incentive to conserve it or to switch to crops that need less water.

Many farmers served by the dwindling Ogallala Aquifer have switched from gravity flow canal systems to center-pivot sprinkler systems, which reduce water waste from 50% or more to 30% Some farmers are switching to new, precision application sprinkler systems, which spray water downward, closer to crops, rather than high into the air. These systems cut water waste by 2% to 5% and energy use by 20% to 30%.

Another way to irrigate more efficiently is to bury small plaster-of-Paris (gypsum) blocks in the soil with two wires leading to the surface. As the soil loses or gains water, the electrical resistance between the electrodes changes. A simple clip-on electrical meter can then be used to determine soil moisture. This enables farmers and ranchers to schedule irrigation based on precise measurements of soil mositure rather than on guesses.

In the 1960s highly efficient trickle or drip irrigation systems were developed in arid Israel. A network of perforated piping, installed at or below the ground surface, releases a small volume of water and fertilizer close to the roots of plants, minimizing evaporation and seepage. These systems are expensive to install but are economically feasible for high-profit fruit, vegetable, and orchard crops. But as long as farmers can get water at an abnormally low cost, they don't find it profitable to invest in drip irrigation systems.

Irrigation efficiency can also be improved by computer-controlled systems that set water flow rates, detect leaks, and adjust the amount of water to soil moisture and weather conditions. Farmers can switch to new, hybrid crop varieties that need less water or that tolerate irrigation with saline water. Also, organic gardening techniques produce higher crop yields per acre and require only one quarter of the water and fertilizer used by conventional farming. Since 1950, Israel has used many of these techniques to decrease waste of irrigation water by about 84%, while expanding the country's irrigated land by 44%.

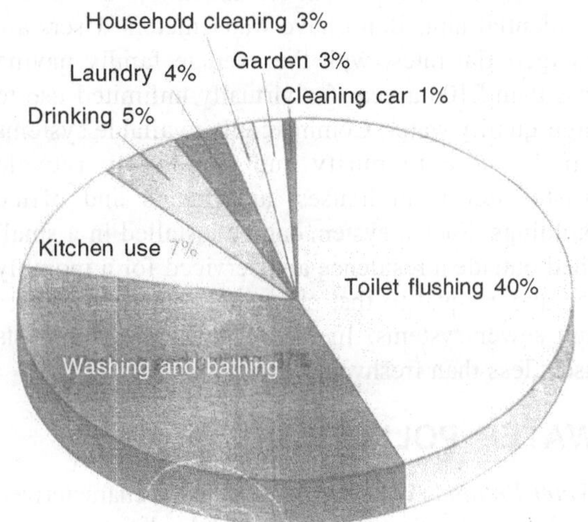

Domestic uses of water.

Wasting Less Water in Industry: Most manufacturing processes can use recycled water or can be redesigned to use and waste less water. For example, depending on the process used, manufacturing 0.9 metric ton (1 ton) of steel can use as much as 199,250 litres (52,800 gallons) or as little as 4,980 liters (1,320 gallons) of water. To produce 0.9 metric ton (1 ton) of paper, a paper mill in Hadera, Israel, uses one-tenth as much water as most paper mills. Manufacturing aluminium from recycled scrap rather than virgin ores can reduce water needs by 97% per cent.

Industry is the largest conserver of water. But the potential for water recycling in many countries manufacturing has hardly been tapped because the cost of water to many industries is subsidized by taxpayers through financed water projects. Thus, industries have little incentive to recycle water, which typically accounts for only about 3% of total manufacturing costs. A higher, more realistic price would greatly stimulate water reuse and conservation in industry.

Less Use of Water in Homes and Offices

Flushing toilets, washing hands, and bathing account for about 78% of the water used in a typical home in India. Much of this water is unnecessarily wasted. Leaks in pipes, water mains, toilets, bathtubs, and faucets waste an estimated 20% to 35% of water withdrawn from public supplies.

Because water cost so little, in most places leaking water faucets are not repaired and large quantities of water are used to clean sidewalks and streets and to irrigate lawns and golf courses. Instead of being a status symbol, a green lawn in an arid or semiarid area should be viewed as a major ecological and economic wrong and replaced with types of natural vegetation adapted to a dry climate.

Many cities offer no incentive to reduce leaks and waste. In New York, for example, 95% of the residential units don't have water meters. Users are charged flat rates, with the average family paying less than $100 a year for virtually unlimited use to high-quality water. Commercially available systems can be used to purify and completely recycle wastewater from houses, apartments and office buildings. Such a system can be installed in a small shed outside a residence and serviced for a monthly fee about equal to that charged by most city water and sewer systems. In Japan recycled water costs users less than freshwater.

WATER POLLUTION

Water Pollution is a phenomenon that is characterized by the deterioration of the quality of land water (rivers, lakes, marshes and ground water) or sea water as a result of various human activities. In the past, if we take a look then as long as the human pollution was small and communication was scattered over large areas of land, the disposal of human waste created no problems. But as communities became more concentrated and villages and towns grew, such a mode of disposal by natural agencies got replace by organized disposal, though again through the agency of natural land and soil columns.

Water pollution is any physical or chemical change in the water that can adversely affect organisms. It is a global problem, affecting both the industrialized and the developing nations. Heat, toxic metals, acids, sediment, animal and human wastes, and synthetic organic compounds foul the waterways of developed nations. Human and animal wastes, sediment and pathogenic organisms head the list in the industrialized nations. In these countries, unsanitary water and malnutrition account for most of the illness and death. Like air pollutants, water pollutants come from mumerous natural and anthropogenic sources, Likewise, water pollutants produced in one nation may take into others, creating complex international control problems that may take decades to solve.

Sources of Water Pollution

Water, the most abundant and wonderful natural resource, is extremely essential for survival of all living organisms. But today clean water has become a precious commodity and its quality is threatened by numerous sources of pollution which are as follows:

1. Sewage and Domestic Wastes

Sewage is commonly a cloudy dilute aqueous solution containing minerals and organic matter. About 75% of water pollution is caused by sewage, domestic wastes and food processing plants. It also includes human excreta, soap, detergents, metals, glass, rubbish, garden waste and sewage sludge. Domestic sewage and other wastes are often untreated or partially treated and dumped into the water bodies such as ponds, lakes, streams and rivers. Since the dumping is uncontrolled especially near big cities, the water bodies are not able to recycle them and lose their self regulating capacity.

If domestic waste of sewage is not properly handled after it is produced or if the sewage received at the end of sewage treatment plants is not of the adequate standards, there are chances of the water being polluted. The indiscriminate method of handling the domestic sewage may also cause pollution of underground sources of water such as wells. If sewage or partially treated sewage is directly discharged into water bodies such as rivers, the water of such gives is polluted or contaminated.

2. Industrial Effluents

Industrial Effluents discharged into water bodies contain toxic chemicals, hazardous compounds, phenols, aldehydes, ketones, amines, cyanides, metallic wastes, plasticizers, toxic acids, corrosive alkalies, oils, greases, dyes, biocides, suspended solids and thermal pollutants from numerous industries. The effluents i.e. discharges from the industries such as that of pharmaceuticals, breweries, tanneries, dyeing, textiles, paper, plastic, chemicals, metallurgical, fertilizers etc. are some of the most important agents of water pollution. These effluents when discharged through the sewage system posion the biological purification mechanism of sewage treatment and pose several pollution problems.

3. Agricultural Discharges

Plant nutrients, pesticides, fertilizers, farm wastes, manure slurry, sediments, drainage from silage, plant and animal debris, soil erosion containing mostly the inorganic materials are reported to cause heavy pollution to water sources. In modern agricultural pesticides NPK fertilizers containing nitrates and phosphates are added to soil. Some of these are washed off through the rainfall irrigation and drainage into water bodies, where they severely disturb the aquatic ecosystem. The excessive use of plant nutrients leads to the disruption of nitrogen and phosphorus balance in water affecting plant growth. Organic wastes increase the BOD of receiving water.

4. Fertilizers

Modern agriculture relies heavily on artificial fertilizers, including several biocides. Although these chemicals enhance vegetation but they disrupt the entire natural aquatic ecosystem. They acutely pollute the water. Indiscriminate and excessive use of fertilizers on land has also created on adverse ecological effect on aquatic ecosystem because some of them are washed off land into rivers and lakes through irrigation, rain, seepage and drainage. One of the ingredients of fertilizers is phosphate salts which cause algal bloom.

5. Detergents

Detergents are of recent origin, used as cleansing agents and derived from surfactants (10-30%), builder (15%) and other ingredients. Household detergents contain several pollutants which severely affect the water bodies. They contain surface active agents and contribute to phosphates of Sodium (Na), sodium silicates, sodium sulphates etc. the most important disadvantage of detergents is the environmental pollution caused by the factory refuse discharged of nearby water sources.

6. Toxic Metals

Amongst the industries with the highest emission of heavy metals are the mining industry, metallurgical industry, leather industry, distilleries, battery industry and thermal power plants. Toxic metals are added in aquatic system from industrial processes and domestic sewage discharge.

Harmful Effects of Water Pollution

1. Harmful Effects of Sewage and Domestic Waste

(*a*) Sewage is an excellent medium for the growth of pathogenic bacteria, viruses and protozoa.

(*b*) Domestic sewage, which is primarily composed of spent water containing wine, soapy water, food material, makes water completely unfit for drinking and domestic use.

(*c*) Several pathogenic microorganism introduced into the water cause deleterious effects and chronic diseases in man and animals.

2. Harmful Effects of Industrial Pollutants

(*a*) It causes deleterious effects on living organisms and may bring about death of sub lethal pathology of kindness, liver, brains, lungs.

(*b*) Disinfectants, which are added in water to control algal growth and bacteria may persist in water bodies and may cause mortality of fish.

(*c*) Effluents containing acids and alkalies make the water corrosive.

3. Effects of Fertilizers

(*a*) **Effects on Humans and Animals—**Excessive application of nitrogen fertilizers to the soil often leads to accumulation of nitrates in the water which when drunk by cattle and man get reduced to toxic nitratres by the intestinal bacteria, Nitrates enter the blood stream and react with hemoglobin which has a stronger affinity for nitrates than for oxygen to form methanoglobin. This causes damage to the respiratory and vascular systems, because of which suffocation and death may occur.

(*b*) **Effects of plants—**Agricultural fertilizers crowd out essential nutrients present in the top soil layers. The microbe enriched humus enhances plant growth. But fertilizer enriched soil cannot support the microbial life for a long time. Fertilizers used to increase in growth of crops also increase the algal growth in surface water into which they are washed.

4. Effects of Thermal Pollutants in Water

The rise in temperature in aquatic system has a profound effect on organisms as well as on water quality. These detrimental effects are as follows:

(*a*) Reduction in dissolved oxygen
(*b*) Increase in BOD
(*c*) Excessive eutrophication
(*d*) Decrease in solubility of gases in water
(*e*) Rapid setting of sediment load in water affecting aquatic food supply

5. Effects of Radioactive Pollutants in Water

(*a*) Polluted water containing radioisotopes produces a set of syndromes characterized by nausea, vomiting, diarrhoea, epilation and general weakness which is known as radiation sickness.

(*b*) It destroys biological immune system *i.e.*, body becomes less resistant towards a variety of diseases.

(*c*) It causes somatic genetic disorders, gene mutations and blood abnormalities in higher animals including man.

(*d*) Radioactive elements present in water accumulate in soil sediments, air and aquatic ecosystems.

Strategies For Water Pollution Control

We are now in a state when water pollution has become a global problem partly because of the pupulation explosion and partly due to the phenomenal advancement in industrialization. Pollution control methods are an investment that ensures long time profits. It is fact that damage caused by pollution is much greater than the investment required to setting up adequate and sustainable pollution control measures. Pollution is an indication of an inefficient process. It represents wastage of world resources, an economic burden on a nation and a financial loss to an enterprise. The pollution can be reduced and minimized by reducing the inefficiencies. The overall efficiency of an energy use in most industrialized or developed countries is 40%. Over 50% of the energy used is wasted and appears in one form or the other as other as waste heat that has an impact on the climate as well as aquatic ecosystems. As a result, industries are facing increasing opposition from the civic society.

A great deal to time and money is wasted in building effluent treatment plants and systems. In many cases, a change of process or raw materials would ensure the problem is removed with minimum costs and without affecting the quality of the product. But the traditional pollution control system does not solve the problem. It may however, complicate it. For example, purification of wastewater creates sludge, but on incineration of chemical wastes creates toxic gases as well as particulate matter. Thus what emerges is an environmental paradox. It takes resources to remove pollution. Pollution removal generates residues. It takes more resources to dispose of this residue and disposal or residue also gives rise to pollution.

So certain strategies are to be adapted to control and prevent water pollution, which are the following:

1. The structural dimensions of non-waste technology requires to be improved and should consist of a linking up of several different industrial, agricultural and urban activities in such a manner that the waste of one industry becomes the raw material to another. Such technology will rely on multiple use of resources and internal transfer if wastes from one section to become the raw materials for another.

   The objectives should be:

   (*a*) Prevention of waste.

   (*b*) Minimizing that wastes which cannot be prevented, and

   (*c*) Rendering harmless the waste ultimately released into the environment.

2. Pollution prevention through cleaner production techniques should be adopted, as they are safer because polluting waste is eliminated at the source.

3. The most reliable way to prevent and control water pollution is undoubtedly to stabilize the aquatic ecosystem by balancing the input and output of energy and nutrients. Practical devices to increase the stability of ecosystem include reduction of waste inputs, controlling hazardous industrial effluents and municipal sewage, harvesting of Biomass, trapping of nutrients, aeration and fish management to protect aquatic flora and fauna.

4. Wastes can be treated by inexpensive as well as efficient methods. For example; where sufficient land is available, by taking the advantage of plentiful sunshine and hot climate that exist in most areas in India, oxidation or stabilization ponds can also be used. In oxidation ponds, domestic or industrial wastes are stored in large, well-detined shallow ponds and kept in it for a few days. Because of the presence of sufficient sunlight and organic nutrients in waste, a healthy bloom of algae flourishes along with colonies of bacteria. In this mutual process, the bacteria speedily digest the organic waste and render it harmless.

5. Treatment of sewage yields irrigation water that contains all the essential nutrients such as nitrogen, phosphorous and potassium to make it a good fertilizer. Now metals like Zn can be extracted from the wastewater of rayon manufacturing industry and lignosulphonate can be recovered from paper and pulp wastewater. The treated sewage can also be used for air-conditioning purpose.

Ground Water Pollution

Over 98% of the fresh water earth lies below the surface. The remaining 2% is what we see in lakes, rivers, streams and reservoirs. Of the fresh water below about 90% satisfies the description of ground water, that is water that occurs in saturated materials below the water table. About 2% water occurs as soil moisture in the unsaturated zone above the water table and is essential for plant growth.

Ground water acts as a reservoir by virture of Large pore space in earth materials, as a conduit which can transport water over long distances and as a mechanical filter that improves water quality by removing suspended solids and bacterial contamination. It is the source of water for wells and springs that is the recommended source of rural domestic use. It is replenished by precipitation through rain, snow, sleet and hail. Today, Human activities are constantly adding industrial, domestic and agricultural waters to ground water reservoirs at an alarming rate. Ground water contamination is generally irreversible *i.e.* once it is contaminated; it is difficult to restore the original water quality of the aquifer. Although the soil mantle through which water passes acts as an adsorbent retaining a large part of colloidal and soluble ions with its cation exchange capacity, but ground water is not completely free from the menace of chronic pollution.

India has a good industrial infrastructure in core industries like metals, chemicals, fertilizers, drugs and petroleum, industries like plastics, pesticides, detergents, fuels, solvents, paints, dyes and food additives, released effluents and emissions, polluting soil water-plant ecosystem. The disposal of solid and liquid wastes containing heavy metals like lead, nickel, chromium, molybdenum and mercury in land or water bodies, leads to heavy metal contamination of the soil-water-plant-animal ecosystems.

Factors Affecting Ground Water Pollution

1. Rainfall Pattern
2. Depth of water table
3. Distance from the source to contamination
4. Soil properties such as Texture, structure and filtration rate

Sources of Contamination In Ground Water

1. Domestic wastes
2. Industrial wastes
3. Agricultural wastes
4. Run off from urban areas

1. Domestic Wastes

Domestic wastes and methods of their disposal are of primary concern in urban areas. Prime factors responsible for deteriorating the water quality include pathogenic organisms, oxygen demand, nutrients and solids from domestic wastes. Solid wastes are the potential source of contamination as they are partly burned and partly incorporated into the soil and pose serious danger to the ground water.

2. Industrial Wastes

Most industries generally produce wastes containing toxic heavy metals along with hazardous organic and inorganic effluents. These chemicals contaminate with the ground water and severely pollute it. Over 500 factories in North Delhi are severely polluting the ground water, which is used for domestic purposes. The steel re-rolling mills and pickling factories are dumping heavy metals and acids into open cesspools or drains, and from here these pollutants permeate into the water table. The worst affected are the people which work in these factories or live around them, most of whom depend on hand pumps for potable water.

3. Agricultural Wastes

Fertilizers, pesticides, insecticides, herbicides, processing wastes and animal wastes etc. are constantly added to the water. Leachates from agricultural land containing nitrates, phosphates and potash, move downward with percolating water and join the aquifers below posing danger to the ground water. Nitrate causes eutrophication of the rivers also although in India phosphate is more blamed for this as phyxiation of water bodies.

Recent researchers showed that all pesticides were found in higher concentrations in ground water compared to surface water. The report explains that the high pesticide residue concentration in ground water might be because ground water flows non-turbulently and experiences limited dilutions as compared to surface water and also due to higher stability of organochlorine pesticides residue concentration in ground water. The soil becomes a reservoir for these pesticides thereby steadily transferring them to ground water. This is a dangerous condition and must be prevented because, people depend on groundwater more than sources particularly rural people because they believe it to be safer than surface water.

4. Urban Areas

1. Effluents from urban areas contain large concentration of oils, greases, nutrients, heavy metals and detergents. The detergents being soluble can pass through the soil and pollute ground water.
2. Raw sewage dumped in shallow soak pits and seepage from polluted lake, pond or stream also pollutes water.
3. Rainfall could pick up substantial contaminants from dust and air and join the aquifer below. The infiltration of liquids containing toxic pollutants may cause pollution in sandy soils and well waters.

5. Soluble Effluents

1. Several soluble effluents pollute the ground water critically. The extent of pollution is more in sandy soils and humid regions having high water table conditions.
2. A direct impact of this has been on the levels of ground water. Increasing use of groundwater has pushed the water table lower.
3. Along the coasts, increasing ground water withdrawals have led to the ingress of saline water into ground water.
4. Pollution is another major factor that is reducing water quality and thereby the availability of clean water.
5. The amounts and types of wastes discharged have outstripped nature's ability to breakdown pollutants into less harmful elements.

Sewage Irrigation

Sewage irrigation is one of the method by which land treats the sewage. The water of the sewage percolates in the ground and the suspended solids remain on the surface of the ground. The organic suspended solids remain at the surface of the ground. The organic suspended solids, are partly acted upon by bacteria, and are partly oxidized by exposure to atmosphere actions of heat, light and air.

Irrigation Water Quality

The quantity of water for irrigation is determined by the effect of its constituents both on the crop and the soil. The deleterious effect on the constituents of the irrigant on plant growth can result from:

(*i*) Direct chemical effects upon the metabolic reactions in the plants.

(*ii*) Direct osmotic effects of salts in preventing water uptake by plants.

(*iii*) Any indirect effect through changes in soil structures, permeability and aeresation.

Sewage Farming

When the sewage is used for growing corps, it is called sewage farming. The roots of the corps consume the fertilizing elements of sewage. The mineral salts of sewage such as nitrates, sulphates and phosphates are the main fertilizing constituents of sewage. By the sewage farming a good income can be done, which is always profitable.

The nutrients of sewage like nitrogen, phosphorus and potassium along with micro-nutrients as well as organic matter present in it could be advantageously employed for sewage farming to add to the fertility of the fields, along with the irrigation potential of water content. Even the application of the treated effluent to land should be carried out with certain precautions, because it is not completely free from this risk. The good sewage farm should run on scientific lines with effluent supervision with the primary objective of disposal of sewage combined with its utilization to the possible extent in a good sanitary manner without polluting the soil, open watercourses or under ground water or contamination of the crops, or impairing the productivity of the farm. The sewage farming should be done such that hygienic safety to the staff is protected against the infection by pathogenic organisms and helminthes. Though the sewage after primary treatment can be applied to the farm, the main reason of providing only primary treatment and eliminating secondary treatment merely depends on cost consideration.

TRAVEL & TOURISM

Tourism is concerned with pleasure, holidays, travel and going or arriving somewhere. These are the motivations that make people leave their 'normal' place of work and residence for short-term temporary visits to 'other' places. According to the WTO, tourism is the movement of people away from their normal place of residence and work for a period of not less than 24 hours and not more than one year. Tourism in fact is a leisure activity because it coexists with its opposite, that is regulated and organised work. This shows us that in modern societies work and leisure are organised as separate and regulated areas of social practice. They are located in specific places and periods of time.

Tourism involves the movement of people to, and their stay at various destinations. This involves a journey and services like transport, accommodation, catering and viewing etc. The journey to and stay at a site is outside the normal place of work and residence for a short period. There is a clear intention when 'going away' to 'return home', we must remember that tourism sites are not connected with paid work and they preferably offer some contrast with sites where a person's work and residence are located.

TYPES OF TOURISM

Alternative Tourism

Alternative tourism can be defined as 'forms of tourism that set out to be consistent with natural, social and community values and which allow both hosts and guests to enjoy positive and worthwhile interaction and shared experience'. **Butler** identified several characteristics of alternative tourism. He observed it to be of small scale and developed and owned by local people. It involves traveling to relatively remote, undisturbed natural areas with the objective of admiring, studying and enjoying the scenery and its wild plants and animals and cultural attributes. It also considers the conservation of the environment and sustenance and well-being of local people. Further, clients are expected to be individuals. Accommodations are locally owned and small scale.

Sustainable Tourism

According to the WTO, "Sustainable tourism development meets the needs of present generation tourists and host regions while protecting and enhancing opportunities for the future." It is expected to lead to management of all resources in such a way that economic, social and aesthetic needs are fulfilled while maintaining cultural integrity, essential ecological processes, biological diversity, and life support systems (WTO, 2002). The WTO paper further explains the need for achieving several objectives for ensuring sustainable tourism.

- The natural, historical, cultural and other resources for tourism are conserved for continuous use in the future, while still bringing benefits to the present society.

- Tourism development is planned and managed so that it does not generate serious environmental or socio-cultural problems in the tourism area.
- The overall environmental quality of tourism areas is maintained and improved where needed.
- A high level of tourist satisfaction is maintained so that tourist destinations retain their marketability and popularity.
- The benefits of tourism are widely spread throughout society.

The guiding principle for sustainable development emphasizes the management of natural and human resources for maximisation of visitor enjoyment and local benefit and at the same time minimising the negative impacts upon the destination site, community and local population.

Community Based Tourism

Community based tourism occurs when decisions about tourism activity and development are driven by the host community. It usually involves some form of cultural exchange where tourists meet with local communities and witness aspects of their lifestyle. Many such remote ethnic communities may be vulnerable to outside influences and decisions about the way tourists are hosted must be owned by the community for successful and sustainable tourism.

Community based tourism can generate a sense of pride in the local population and make funds available for maintaining or upgrading cultural assets e.g. archeological ruins, historic sites, traditional crafts production. The aims of community based tourism largely depend on the issues, problems and needs of the community. In general it serves as a tool for conservation and, at the same time, a tool for improving the quality of life. It also serves as a tool to bring the community together to consult, discuss and work together in solving community problems. Further, such tourism provides opportunity for exchange of knowledge and culture between tourists and the community and helps to provide supplementary income for individual members of the community and for community development.

Responsible Tourism

Responsible tourism refers to the type of tourism where tourism organisations take care of tourist destinations while providing visitor Satisfaction. As a result, the resources and attractions – both natural and cultural – are not spoiled for local people or future visitors. Further, it denotes care for the environment and cultural resources, and opportunity for locals in terms of employment or other kinds of involvement, sufficient information regarding local resources for visitors, and implementation of the policy of Corporate Social Responsibility.

Pro-Poor Tourism

Pro-poor tourism is another form of tourism where the benefits to the poor are greater than the costs that tourism entails to them. Pro-poor tourism strategies emphasize on unlocking opportunities for the poor within tourism, rather than expanding the overall size of the tourism business.

Village Tourism

Village tourism denotes tourists visiting villages and staying in or near the villages. The special feature of this kind of tourism is that the visitors become part of the village for the period of their stay. In other words, they rely on locally available accommodation and food. A house in the village serves as an accommodation for the visitor. Visitors are served local food and cultural programmes are organised for entertainment. Such an opportunity allows visitors to immerse themselves in the local socio-cultural environment. It also allows them an opportunity to get to know local social, cultural and religious practices.

Cultural Tourism

The earliest accounts of cultural tourism can be traced back to ancient history. One such visitor was Huen Tsang from China who visited Nepal and India in the 5th Century AD. One of the important things he did during his visit was to describe the cultural sites of Nepal and India. However, cultural tourism as we know it today was conceptualized by UNESCO during the 1970s. Cultural tourism is regarded as a "Force for cultural preservation". It is also defined as "the absorption by tourists of features resembling the vanishing lifestyles of past societies observed through such phenomena as house styles, crafts, farming equipment, dress, utensils and other instruments and equipment that reflects the lifestyle of any particular community during a particular time."

Although cultural tourism is different from other forms of tourism, it often becomes an integral part of the total visit. For instance, one of the main interests for tourists to Kathmandu is to see the temples and historical monuments in Kathmandu Valley.

SOME OTHER FORMS OF TOURISM

- ***Adventure Tourism:*** tourism involving travel in rugged regions, or adventurous sports such as mountaineering and hiking (tramping).
- ***Agritourism:*** farm based tourism, helping to support the local agricultural economy.
- ***Ancestry Tourism:*** (also known as genealogy tourism) is the travel with the aim of tracing one's ancestry, visiting the birth places of these

ancestors and sometimes getting to know distant family.

- ***Armchair Tourism*** **and** ***Virtual Tourism***: not travelling physically, but exploring the world through internet, books, TV, etc.
- ***Audio Tourism***: includes audio tours and other audio guided forms of tourism including museum audio guides and audio travel books.
- ***Backpacker Tourism***: is a term used to denote a form of low-cost independent international travel, differentiating it from other forms of tourism notably by the following typical attributes: minimal budget use, longer duration traveling, use of public transport and multiple destinations/countries. The origin of the name comes from the backpacks that budget travelers generally carry in the interests of mobility and flexibility.
- ***Creative Tourism***: is a new form of tourism that allows visitors to develop their creative potential, and get closer to local people, through informal participation in hands-on workshops that draw on the culture of their holiday destinations.
- ***Coastal Tourism***: involves tourist products located along Coastal Environments - due to the limited extent of coastal environments they often are amongst the first places to experience tourist congestion for a region.
- ***Dark Tourism***: is the travel to sites associated with death and suffering. The first tourist agency to specialise in this kind of tourism started with trips to Lakehurst, New Jersey, the scene of the *Hindenburg airship disaster.*
- ***Educational Tourism***: may involve travelling to an education institution, a wooded retreat or some other destination in order to take personal-interest classes, such as cooking classes with a famous chef or crafts classes.
- ***Extreme Tourism***: tourism associated with high risk.
- ***Heritage Tourism***: visiting historical (Rome, St. Petersburg, Athens, Cracow) or industrial sites, such as old canals, railways, battlegrounds, etc.
- ***Health Tourism***: usually to escape from cities or relieve stress, perhaps for some 'fun in the sun', etc. Often to Sanatoriums or "health spas".
- ***Pilgrimage Tourism***: pilgrimages to ancient holy places (Rome, and Santiago de Compostela for Catholics, temples and stupas of Nepal for the Hindus and Buddhist, Mount Athos or Painted churches of northern Moldavia for the Orthodox), religious sites such as mosques, shrines, etc.
- ***Sex Tourism:*** travelling solely for the purpose of sexual activity.

CAUSES OF RAPID GROWTH OF TOURISM

The basic causes of this rapid growth are economic, social and technological.

Economic Causes

Rising per capita incomes leading to higher purchasing power and an increase in discretionary incomes have made tourism accessible to a large majority of people. Today in advanced countries, a large majority of people can afford an annual holiday. In fact many can even afford to take 'second holiday' of longer or shorter duration. In the case of more affluent members of the society, establishment of what may be called "recreation homes", e.g., seaside flatlets, country cottages, caravans cruising boats, etc., have become a fashion and a status symbol.

Secondly, more and diverse type of holiday and recreation are becoming popular. For example in addition to comparatively recent developments such as the holiday camps, Caravans and coach tour, there are even newer fashions such as yachting, train riding, safari and archaeological holiday.

Increased mobility as a result of use of motor car for travel is another important economic factor which is responsible for growth in tourism in Europe and North America.

Social Causes

The Social Causes of the rapid growth of tourism are linked with new attitudes towards travel and leisure. The entire concept of pleasure travel has changed quite drastically. Foreign travel in the pre-war days was reserved for the more affluent and leisured who enjoyed travel for its own sake and who were content to enjoy scenery, works of arts and theatres in foreign places. This concept has now changed with change in attitudes towards travel.

The present day tourist has a different kind of background, and his ideas about travel are very different. The present day traveller comes from a wider social background and his tastes and desires are much more varied. His leisure time is much more restricted and, accordingly, he desires to pack into it as much as possible. 'Democratisation' of leisure pursuits is yet another factor responsible for growth in tourist traffic. Winter Sports, for example, were not so very long ago in activity almost exclusively confined to wealthier members of the society. Some of the other exclusive pursuits such as riding, boating, yachting, surf-riding, shooting, etc., is now available to a ordinary man who is interested in these. Large number of people are now going abroad to participate in more exciting and exotic activities like mountaineering, water skiing, trekking, under water swimming and the like.

Technological Causes

The impact of the modern transport technology, specially in aviation field has brought about a completely new meaning to tourism. Travel to even remote destinations has now become a reality. During the last twenty years there has been a remarkable increase in the number of long distance journeys undertaken by tourists.

The technological developments in transport have made it possible for millions of people to travel to far-away places, places which only a few generations ago were regarded as being almost entirely—inaccessible.

Today holiday-makers can be transported a thousand miles or more in a matter of few hours. The gradual evolution of the originally homogeneous air travel market into two separate and distinct segments—charters and schedule air travel has greatly increased the demand. The newer marketing methods like the 'package tour' is a major contributing factor to the growth of tourism. By preparing organised holiday trips complete with all arrangements like transport, accommodation, sight-seeing-tours etc. and selling these on a large scale to the public, the average price per tour has been significantly reduced. This price is much below the price of the trip arranged individually.

Opening up of new travel destinations particularly in developing countries, creation of new facilities to receive larger flow of tourists, and increasing tourism promotion efforts by tourist service enterprises and by official tourist organisations have increased the tourist flows. The participation of a large number of people in tourism activities as we have seen in highly developed industrialised countries as essentially a manifestation of prosperity. As great number of people in these countries enjoy higher living standards they can afford to set aside a proportion of incomes for holidays.

Since the mid-1960s international tourism has become one of the leading items of international trade and exceeds many other commodities including wheat, automobiles and machine tools. The biggest advantage, which tourism has for many countries more especially the developing countries is the lure of foreign exchange. Most developing countries suffer from a more or less acute shortage of foreign currency. As a result they have difficulties in obtaining the goods and services necessary for development. For a significant number of developing countries in many parts of the world, international tourism has thus become major and in many instances the largest source of foreign exchange earnings, with the result these countries are getting more and more interested in the development of tourism.

Presently in the developing world, over one hundred countries are getting increasingly interested in tourism. Some of these countries are calling upon international consulting firms to prepare their tourism development plans, asking the World Bank group to grant loans to finance tourism projects and also putting in requests to United Nations' Development Programme to Finance technical assistance projects for tourism. Almost all developing countries set aside substantial financial allocations every year for the development and promotion of tourism.

ACCOMMODATION

The business of setting up, operating and promoting tourist accommodation facilities is a complex affair. It involves a relationship between "host" cultures and "guest" cultures, ecological and environmental considerations and a fine balance between factors pertaining to leisure and those pertaining to efficiency. These factors are, of course, in addition to the usual commercial aspects of the business.

In a world that is increasingly being reduced to a "global village" the tourist as a consumer is also conscious of the need to be sensitive to the needs and demands of the "host" cultures they are visiting. It should be recognized that in this context there is a healthy tension that can develop between the interests of the host culture, the interests of the tourists and the interests of the commercial organizations such as hoteliers, tour operators and other agencies.

Five Star Deluxe Hotels

These are usually to be found in the metropolitan city areas and have anywhere between 200 to 800 rooms. Some hotels in this category have over a thousand rooms in their inventory. They are categorized by certain international standards which include a given number of restaurants, a particular size of lobby, business centre facilities, a swimming pool etc, including, of course, very strict standards of quality control. These hotels are usually used primarily by the business executive (often 90 per cent of the customers are businessmen and women) and the very upscale tourists.

There are also other star categories like three star, one star etc. However, categorisation into stars is not mandatory in India. Hotels offer themselves for categorisation which is based on certain criteria and inspection by officials.

First Class Hotels

These are a step down from the above category, but contain most of the facilities that are provided in the "Five Star Deluxe" hotels. These are also located usually in the large, metropolitan cities and some mid-sized cities as well. These hotels are also used by a combination of business executives and tourists.

Non-Star Hotels

At every tourist destination you come across many small hotels who don't come under classified categories. Yet many tourists stay there as per their budget adjustments. For example at Kovalam beach there is the ITDC Ashoka group hotel. But many tourists cannot afford it and they stay in small staying places near the beach. Such examples are abundant at every destination be it a hill station or a pilgrimage centre.

Resorts and Lodges

These are meant almost exclusively for the tourists and more often are found in so-called "off the beaten track" destinations. In some countries, where the economic dependence on tourism is very great, such accommodation can also be found in the cities or just outside the cities. Thus, in Kenya for example, one can find very elaborate lodges even in Nairobi, the capital city where most tourists enter the country.

The Resorts and Lodges usually have certain features such as elaborate swimming pools, a balcony or patio overlooking each room and entertainment facilities.

In India we have Beach resorts, Hill resorts and Wild Life resorts. These resort hotels commonly cater to tourists of different tastes and budgets. Whether luxury or low budget resorts they primarily offer a stay in the natural surroundings. These resorts are generally seasonal.

Tented Camps

While most of the types of accommodation discussed so far involve solid structures, a type that is fast gaining popularity around the world is the tented camp variety. These involve relatively low investment. These are ecologically very friendly in that they do not threaten to spoil the landscape too much and can be set up seasonally to reduce expenditure by not having to spend too much on the upkeep of the place when the tourist season is over.

Tented camps are usually set up in very remote places such as near a game park or reserve (some countries allow such camps even within the game reserve) and they have anywhere from 10 to 80 rooms. Their bathrooms are either attached or set up separately, depending on the level of luxury that is intended to be provided. In addition to game parks, which are associated with wildlife viewing and safaris, tour operators have set up tented camps in conjunction with other activities such as fishing tours, white-water rafting tours and canoeing.

Another variation of the tented camp is the mobile tented camps which are used when trekking in various parts of the world.

Heritage Hotels

Tourists visiting a historical city are very fond of historical palaces. Often they dream of staying in the same way and style as that of Rajas. Keeping in view this tourist interest the Government of India's Tourism Department started encouraging Heritage Hotels. By providing financial incentives to the owners of Forts, Palaces and Havelis the Tourism Department encourages the owners to convert their properties into Heritage Hotels. Responding to this scheme Heritage Hotels have come up in many areas.

Guest Houses

The guest house is to be found in cities, towns and even remote destinations. Usually those who use these facilities are individuals who travel on their own, spend relatively longer periods of time in a particular destination, wish to get to know the host culture intimately and want their expenditure to be modest. Therefore, they may have only one or two meals a day and spend the rest of the time outside the guest house. More often than not, the guest house is run by a family and although they may do so in a very efficient manner, the operations are not what might be called "professionally" managed and the tourist is often living, literally, as a "guest" of a family. The House Boat accommodation is a unique example of this category.

Recently in different tourist places the system of paying guest accommodation is gaining much popularity. This has two basic purposes:

Firstly tourists coming from outside India or from various regions of India are generally fond of local etiquette, household, culture and home made food. Compared to staying in hotels which provide typical hotel culture, more or less same everywhere, staying with a local family at tourist places is both economical and informative for knowing the local people and their culture.

Secondly, paying guest accommodation provides the local people with a source of earning without any investment as well as the opportunity to learn different cultures.

Alternative Accommodation

While the above are some of the broad categories into which the types of accommodation are divided, there are a whole range of other types of accommodation such as the small boarding houses which are converted into so-called "guest houses", the YMCA and YWCA facilities, lodges managed by tourism departments and "tourist camps." Some of these could also be termed the unorganized sector of the hospitality industry and should be kept in mind when a professional in the tourism industry is informing his or her potential customer of the options available for accommodation purposes. One can also recommend for short or overnight stay the rest rooms of the railways or dharamshalas.

In concluding this Section it is important to keep in mind that generally speaking the tourist spends approximately 40 per cent of his funds on room and board. Thus it is imperative that any advice, suggestion or recommendation that is given in this regard must be carefully considered and discussed in great detail. The burden of accomplishing this rests with the tourism professional and not necessarily with the customer, who is not always aware of the options available at a given destination.

THINGS WE MAKE AND DO

Avoiding Some Common Traps: Sustaining the earth requires each of us to make a personal commitment to live an environmentally ethical life. We must do this not because it is required by law but because it is right. It is our responsibility to ourselves, our children, our neighbours, and the earth.

Start by being sure that you have not fallen into some common traps or excuses that lead to indifference and inaction:

- *Gloom-and-doom pessimism:* the belief that the world is doomed by nuclear war or environmental catastrophe, so we should enjoy life while we can.
- *Blind technological optimism:* the belief that human ingenuity will always be able to come up with technological advances that will solve our problems. This is the most seductive and dangerous trap. It is something that we would like to believe: Don't worry, be happy, don't change your life-style, there are no limits, and technology will save us.
- *Fatalism:* the belief that whatever will be, and we have no control over our actions and the future.
- *Extrapolation to infinity:* the belief that "If I can't change the entire world quickly, I won't try to change any of it." This rationalization is reinforced by modern society's emphasis on instant gratification and quick results with as little effort as possible.

All of these traps represent various forms of *denial.* To avoid facing up to problems and the need for change, we stick our heads in the sand and engage in activities that divert us from facing up to reality. With our present power to destroy ourselves and most other species, denial is a recipe for disaster.

Becoming Earth Citizens: The good news is that we can sustain the earth and lead more meaningful and joyful lives. To do this begin with yourself.

1. Evaluate the way you think the world works and sensitize yourself to your local environment: Look around, experience what is going on in the environment around you, compare what is with what could and should be. Examine your room, your home, your school, your place of work, your street, and your city, state, country, and world. What things around you improve and what things detract from the quality of your life and that of other people? Where do the water you drink and the air you breathe come from? What kind of soil is around your home? Where does your garbage go? What forms of wild plants and animals live around you? What species have become extinct in your area and what ones are threatened with extinction? What is the past history of land use in your area and what are the projected future uses of this land? What are your environmental bad habits? What is your worldview? Do the assumptions on which it is based represent a valid view of the real world?

2. Become Ecologically Informed: Give up your throwaway thinking and immerse yourself in sustainable-earth thinking. Specialize in one particular area of environmental knowledge and awareness, relate this to sustainable-earth thinking, and share your knowledge and understanding with others (networking). Consider going into an environmental profession or starting or working in an environmentally responsible business. Everyone doesn't need to be an ecologist or a professional environmentalist, but you do need to "ecologize" your lifestyle. Deep in mind Norman Cousins' statement: "The first aim of education should not be to prepare young people for careers but to enable them to develop respect for life."

3. Become emotionally involved in caring for the earth by experiencing nature directly and by trying to find a place that you love and must defend because you are part of it and it is part of you: Intellectual ecological knowledge of how the world works is vitally important. But it will not be enough to bring about a change in the way you live unless it is combined with a sense of place–a feeling of oneness with and thankfulness for some piece of the earth that you truly love and respect. Poet-philosopher Gary Snyder urges us to "find our place on the planet, dig in, and take responsibility from there."

4. Choose a simpler lifestyle by reducing resource consumption and waste and pollution production: Do this by distinguishing between your true needs and your wants and by using trade-offs. For every high energy, high waste, or highly polluting thing you do (buying a car, living or working in an air-conditioned building), give up a number of other things. Such a lifestyle will be less expensive and should bring you joy as you learn how to break through the technological barriers that artificially separate most of us from other people, from other parts of nature, and from our true selves.

5. Become more self-sustaining by trying to unhook yourself from dependence on large, centralized systems for your water, energy, food, and livelihood: You can do this in the country or in the city. Use organic, intensive gardening techniques to grow some of your own food in a small plot, roof garden, or windowbox planter. Get as much of your energy as possible from renewable sources such as the sun, wind, water, or biomass. An organic garden of any size, a solar house, or solar window collectors in an appartment save energy and money on a lifetime cost basis. They also put you in direct contact with nature by bringing the sun, soil, and plants into your life.

6. Remember that environment begins at home: Before you start trying to convert others, begin by changing your own living patterns. If you become an earth citizen, be prepared to have everyone looking for and pointing out your actions force people to look at what they are doing–a threatening process. People are most influenced by what we do, not by what we say.

7. Avoid the four do-nothing traps: gloom-and-doom pessimism, blind technological optimism, fatalism, and extrapolation to infinity: Jump in and become a doer, not a bench sitter or toe dipper.

8. Become politically involved on local and national levels: Start or join a local environmental group, and also join and financially support national and global environmental and conservation organizations whose causes you believe in. Learn how to cooperate with others to amplify or synergize your efforts. Work to elect sustainable-earth leaders and to influence officials once they are elected to public office.

9. Do the little things based on thinking globally and acting locally: Environmental problems are caused by quadrillions of small, unthinking actions by billions of people. They will be cured by quadrillions of small actions in which you and others substitute environmentally beneficial.

PEDAGOGICAL ISSUES

CONCEPT AND SCOPE OF EVS

The word environment is derived from French word *'environ'*, means to encircle or surround. It is a composite word for the surrounding in which organism or group of organisms live. The environ-ment consists of *biotic* and *abiotic* substances, *i.e.*, consists of air, water, food, sunlight, temperature, electricity etc. So, one can define the environment as, *"it is the sum of all social, economical, biological, physical or chemical factors which constitute all surroundings of men or living organism, who is both creater and modular of this environment."*

As other organisms, man is also affected by environmental changes. These changes in environment may harm or benefit the man or other organisms living in it. *Environmental Science is the application of all fields of natural science toward solving environmental problems.* Biology, Geology, Chemistry, Physics, Meteorology and many other disciplines are included in the environmental science. Economics, Sociology, Education and Mass-Communication do help in understanding the socio-economic aspects of environment. Mathematics, Statistics and Computer Science also help in modeling and management of environment.

The *Environmental Science* is, therefore, a multidisciplinary science, which may require attention of experts from different branches of science when decisions regarding environmental matters have to be taken. The craze of progress in agriculture, industry, transportation and technology is taken as the general criterion of development of any nation. Such activities of man has created adverse effects on all living organisms in the biosphere. Today environment has become very unpleasant, contaminated and harmful for living organisms.

Environmental Science courses at both the basic and the advanced level are the most rapidly growing courses at many universities in the India. Individual disciplines are developing Environmental Chemistry, Environmental Biology, Environmental Geology and many similar courses to address society's changing needs. Many colleges now recognise majors in *Environmental Science* and CBSE has also started this course at senior secondary level.

History of Environmental Impact and Movements

Considering the age of the Earth and even the human species, the massive environmental impact of humans is a very recent development. Indeed, our relationship with the environment has evolved as we and our technology have evolved.

Environmental historians often identify five basic stages in this evolution. These stages are largely determined by the economic activity in which humans engage using the technologies available. This activity, in turn, affects how humans impact the environment.

1. Hunting and gathering. Early humans were largely at the mercy of their environment, so they generally viewed it in adversarial terms. Weather, predators, food shortages, and disease were constant threats.

2. Agriculture and conservationism. The shift from hunting and gathering to cultivating food is one of the most profound milestones in human evolution. It allowed a great increase in population size and permitted people to settle down in large towns and cities. But agriculture also had a major impact on the environment. People began to view land as a resource to be exploited wherever needed. As land was cleared and cultivated, however, the wilderness vanished. Toward the end of the agricultural stage, the loss of wilderness became so great that alarmed citizens began conservation movements to set up preserves for the remaining wilderness. Today many developing countries still have agricultural economics, and their vanishing wilderness, especially tropical rainforests, has stimulated the growth of conservationism.

3. Industry and environmentalism. The Industrial Revolution began in England around 1800. As nations industrialize, population grows faster, and the environment is perceived more and more as a place to dispose of the concentrated waste by-products of industry. The result is a rapid increase in air and water pollution, as well as problems with solid and hazardous waste disposal. Toward the end of the stage, pollution becomes so widespread that antipollution social movements emerge. In many countries, these social movements began in the early 1960s and peaked in the 1970s. When people talk about "environmentalism." this antipollution movement is often what they mean. Several early books heralded this new awareness including *Silent Spring* (1962) by Rachel Carson, which warned of pesticide pollution; *The Population Bomb* (1968) by Paul Ehrlich; and *The Limits to Growth* (1972) by Donella H. Meadows and others. These efforts and rising public concern led to the passage of landmark environmental legislation throughout the world.

4. Transition and sustainability. Although some forms of pollution have been reduced, many other environmental problems have increased. In India, for example, species of wildlife are becoming imperiled at increasing rates as habitat is destroyed. Groundwater contamination has worsened, and there are many thousands of hazardous and radioactive waste sites that will likely not be cleaned up for centuries. Despite recycling and precycling efforts, the amount of solid waste produced per person continues to climb. Globally, we see global warming, ozone depletion, and increasing species extinction as the greatest environmental threats to future generations. These problems are caused in large part by rapidly increasing population in developing countries, which also leads to local food shortages and the loss of billions of tons of soil to erosion each year.

We are currently in this fourth stage—the transition. Environmental problems have become so widespread that they demand large-scale solutions that involve many aspects of society. Beginning in the early nineties, a sustainability movement has emerged to try to deal with these problems. Unlike the conservation and antipollution movements of the past, which emphasized specific problems, this movement seeks long-term coexistence with the environment. **Sustainability** means meeting the needs of today without reducing the quality of life for future generations. This includes not reducing the quality of the future environment. Sustainability is achieved through sustainable ("green") technologies that use renewable resources such as solar power and recycle many materials. These technologies allow a **sustainable economy** that produces wealth and provides jobs for many human generations without degrading the environment.

The sustainability movement uses three approaches not attempted by previous environmental movements. First, it focuses explicitly on trying to reduce society's use of all resources. Emphasis is thus on input reduction, as opposed to end-of-pipe solutions *Waste is viewed as a symptom, not a cause, of the environmental crisis.*

Second, the sustainability movement is more holistic. It realizes the necessity of addressing the social, and especially economic, causes environ-mental degradation. This has led to at increasing appreciation of the role of poverty and other economic factors that cause people to deplete resources and pollute. Market-based solutions are becoming more popular, and less emphasis is placed on the legal solutions used in that past. For example, many experts now agree that it is often more effective and cheaper for society to tax coal, gasoline, and other polluting substances than to pass laws specifying how much pollution may be emitted. The higher gasoline prices encourage people to drive less or buy fuel-efficient cars, for instance. Such economic approaches acknowledge that, far from being anti-environmental business can greatly benefit the environment. It is what people produce and sell that can cause environmental problems, not the acts of producing and selling in themselves. Producing and selling furniture made from tropical rainforest timber will harm the environment whereas Brazil nut, rubber, and many other rainforest product may be extracted and sold with little or nil long-term damage.

Components of the Environment

Environment consists of all living and non-living things which surround us. Therefore, the basic components of the environment are:

1. Atmosphere
2. Hydrosphere
3. Lithosphere
4. Biosphere

Atmosphere

Atmosphere consists of a complex mixture of a number of gases, water vapour and a variety of fine particulate matter. The gaseous mantle which surrounds the globe is constituted by about 5.15×10^{15} metric tonnes of gas which exerts a pressure of about 1 kg per sq.cm. on earth's crust. Most of these gases are compressed in the lowermost layer due to the pressure of lower layer above it. Pressure decreases as we move upward.

The composition of earth's atmosphere

Gas	Parts per million	Relative percentage
Nitrogen	780832.00	78.08
Oxygen	209460.00	20.95
Argon	9340.00	00.93
Carbon dioxide	403.00	00.03
Neon	18.00	00.0018
Ozone	0.07	00.000007

Structure of Atmosphere

Based primarily on the temperature pattern, earth's atmosphere can be roughly divided into four major zones:—

1. **The troposphere:** The zone immediately above earth's surface is known as the *troposphere* which extends upto a height of about 20 kms above the equator and about 8 kms over the poles. The temperature in this zone drops with height being as low as – 60°C at its upper extremity.
2. **The stratosphere:** The layer next to troposphere is called the *stratosphere.* It is about 30 kms in thickness and is a very important zone of atmosphere as it contains the vital ozone layer. The temperature in this zone rises from – 60°C to about 0°C in its upper layers. The rise in temperature is due to the formation of ozone under the influence of ultra-violet radiation.
3. **The mesosphere:** It is a zone of about 40 kms in thickness which lies next to the stratosphere. This zone is characterised by gradual decline in temperatures to about – 90°C.
4. **The Thermosphere:** It is the zone next to mesosphere in which temperature increases with height. Most of the constituents of this zone are in ionized state.

Importance of Atmosphere

It is the typical structure and composition of earth's atmosphere which is responsible for creating conditions suitable for the existence of a healthy biosphere on this planet. Atmosphere's role in maintenance of the biosphere in a healthy state can be summed up as follows:

1. Atmosphere regulates the temperature of earth's crust. The presence of gases capable of absorbing long wavelength radiations, is responsible for maintaining the temperatures under which life activities are possible. Moon for example, has no atmosphere. At its equator, surface tempe-ratures rise to 101°C in the day. In nights they drop down to –180°C. No life can survive at these temperatures.
2. The incoming solar radiations are filtered high above earth's surface. Harmful ultra-violet radiations are absorbed in the stratosphere by the vital ozone layer. These rays can severely damage the terrestrial life.
3. Constant mixing of the contents of atmosphere occurs due to air currents and the vertical temperature gradient. This prevents accumulation of harmful gases and vapours at any particular spot. Atmosphere is therefore, a quick and effective media for transfer, transport and dissemination of gaseous wastes.
4. Pollutants in the atmosphere are removed by a much more effective mechanism than that operating on land or in water. As the troposphere derives its heat from earth's surface, warm air being lighter rises and cools down adiabetically. Cooling condenses water vapours. The entire load of pollutants is brought down with snow, dew or rains which cleans the atmosphere.

Hydrosphere

Water is absolutely essential for life on this planet. It is a natural resource of fundamental importance. The atomic structure and unique properties of water seem to be especially designed for the biosphere.

Importance of Water for the Biosphere

Without water life as it exists on our planet is impossible. The importance of water in sustaining a healthy biosphere on our planet can be summed up as follows:

1. Water is the very medium in which all biochemical reactions within a living organism and a large number of chemical reactions involving components of rocks, soil and pollutants of environment occur. It is the availability of water which determines the nature, composition and abundance of terrestrial life. Regions with very low rainfall become deserts. Lush green vegetation develops where water is in abundance.
2. Due to its high specific heat, changes in its temperature need large amounts of heat energy or its withdrawal as compared to other objects. This causes temperature differences between land and sea when heated by solar radiations and an active air circulation is maintained. The air circulation in turn determines precipitation pattern and climatic conditions of locality.
3. A high latent heat of vaporisation causes a large amount of solar energy to be used up in evaporation of water. The solar heat could

have, otherwise, raised global temperatures significantly.

4. The unique property of expansion, when cooled below 4°C causes water to freeze from top downwards as aquatic bodies lose or gain most of their heat energy from the surface in contact with air above. Aquatic life stays safe under the ice-sheet.
5. Water is an efficient means of transfer and transport of the material dissolved or suspended in it. Low lying regions of the world, river basins, land along sea coasts are, therefore, much more productive than upland areas. Water transports dissolved materials, silt, debris, nutrients and pollutants etc. from upland areas to low lying regions. Nearly 90% of world population is, therefore, concentrated in these areas.
6. Water also plays an important role in reducing the atmosphere burden of particulate matters and gaseous pollutants. Water vapours condense around fine particulate matter and gaseous materials dissolve in water and the entire load of waste materials and gases is brought down with rains or snow. This cleans the atmospheric air.

Lithosphere

Earth's crust consists of rocks the loose materials derived from these rocks, most of which is modified into soil. There are about a dozen elements which constitute the bulk of earth's crust-nearly 99% by weight. These elements go into the formation of minerals which in turn form rocks from which all soils are derived.

Elementary composition of earth's crust

Elements	Percentage
1. Oxygen	46.6
2. Silicon	27.7
3. Aluminium	8.1
4. Iron	5.0
5. Calcium	3.6
6. Sodium	2.8
7. Potassium	2.6
8. Magnesium	2.0
9. Hydrogen	0.9
10. Titanium	0.41
11. Chlorine	0.20
12. Carbon	0.19
13. Others	1.00

SIGNIFICANCE OF EVS

The environment studies enlighten us, about the importance of protection and conservation of our indiscriminate release of pollution into the environment.

At present a great number of environment issues, have grown in size and complexity day by day, threatening the survival of mankind on earth. We study about these issues besides and effective suggestions in the Environment Studies. Environment studies have become significant for the following reasons:

1. **Environment Issues Being of International Importance:** It has been well recognised that environment issues like global warming and ozone depletion, acid rain, marine pollution and biodiversity are not merely national issues but are global issues and hence must be tackled with international efforts and cooperation.
2. **Problems Cropped in The Wake of Development:** Development, in its wake gave birth to Urbanization, Industrial Growth, Transportation Systems, Agriculture and Housing etc. However, it has become phased out in the developed world. The North, to cleanse their own environment has, fact fully, managed to move 'dirty' factories of South. When the West developed, it did so perhaps in ignorance of the environmental impact of its activities. Evidently such a path is neither practicable nor desirable, even if developing world follows that.
3. **Explosively Increase in Pollution:** World census reflects that one in every seven persons in this planted lives in India. Evidently with 16 per cent of the world's population and only 2.4 per cent of its land area, there is a heavy pressure on the natural resources including land. Agricultural experts have recognized soils health problems like deficiency of micronutrients and organic matter, soil salinity and damage of soil structure.
4. **Need for An Alternative Solution:** It is essential, specially for developing countries to find alternative paths to an alternative goal. We need a goal as under:

   (1) A goal, which ultimately is the true goal of development an environmentally sound and sustainable development.
   (2) A goal common to all citizens of our earth.
   (3) A goal distant from the developing world in the manner it is from the over-consuming wasteful societies of the "developed" world.
5. **Need To Save Humanity From Extinction:** It is incumbent upon us to save the humanity from exinction. Consequent to our activities constricting the environment and depleting the biosphere, in the name of development.
6. **Need For Wise Planning of Development:** Our survival and sustenance depend. Resources

withdraw, processing and use of the product have all to by synchronised with the ecological cycles in any plan of development our actions should be planned ecologically for the sustenance of the environment and development.

INTEGRATED ENVIRONMENT STUDIES

An ever-increasing world population demanding food, water, energy, health care, and education puts unprecedented pressure on both, the "Earth System" that is its natural environment and resource, and the institutions that design the framework organizing access to and distribution of resources and education. Successful sustainable management of these global challenges, therefore, requires an integrated approach which combines elements from the natural and engineering sciences with those from social, political and economics studies. The Integrated Environmental Studies provides a broad and interdisciplinary education in these diverse fields within the multicultural environment.

ENVIRONMENTAL STUDIES AND ENVIRONMENTAL EDUCATION

Status of Environmental Education in School Education

The education system in India had incorporated certain aspects of environment in school curricula as early as 1930. The Kothari commission (1964-66) also suggested that basic education had to offer EE and relate it to the life needs and aspirations of the people and the nation. At the primary stage, the report recommended that " the aims of teaching science in the primary schools should be to develop proper understanding of the main facts, concepts, principles and processes in physical and biological environment" Environmental education at primary, secondary, higher secondary levels was treated in a different way. Environmental education is an essential part of every pupil's learning. It helps to encourage awareness of the environment, leading to informed concern for active participation in resolving environmental problems. It was introduced without any delay from class –1 as EVS, as a subject so that right from their childhood, the right attitudes towards environment will be nurtured in the young minds.

It is important that we capture this enthusiasm and that no opportunity is lost to develop knowledge, understanding and concern for the environment through school education. The curricular, cross-curricular attempt of environmental education also should be a joy for the learner. In this direction, NCERT has published in collaboration with the Centre for Environmental Education, Ahemadabad a book titled "Joy of learning" with lot of environmental activities, a handbook for teachers. Similarly, several workshops were conducted to orient school teachers and educational functionaries of the state boards on various aspects of environmental education. Strategies for successful implementation of EE in schools were discussed in detail in these interactions.

A curricular framework of environmental education:-

- It envisages the place of EE in the school curriculum.
- Place of EE vis-à-vis other subjects of study.
- Mode and strategy of inclusion of chapters at different levels.
- EE in terms of time and allocation of marks.
- Development of syllabi and instructional material for dissemination at different levels of school education.

In order to supplement the analysis of individual and institutional consultations it was decided to organise two face-to-face National Consultations on Environmental Education in Schools. The First Consultation on the academic aspects of Environmental Education (EE) in schools was organised by NCERT on 13-14 February 2004 in New Delhi . Seventy participants comprising eminent scientists, environmentalists, officials of central and state govt. departments dealing with environment, senior academicians attached to Departments/Centres of environmental studies, environmental science, environmental ecology, botany, regional development, geography, marine biology, etc. of different universities, teacher educators, principals of teacher training colleges, prominent Non-Governmental Organisations (NGOs) and NCERT faculty took part in deliberations. The second consultation on the implementation of EE in schools was held on 13th March 2004 . Seventy-two officials comprising Presidents/Chairpersons of Boards/ Councils of school education, Directors of State Councils of Educational Research and Training (SCERTs), Directors of Education in the states, eminent scientists, environmentalists and NCERT faculty participated. The initial draft prepared by NCERT faculty presented in the First Consultation was revised as per the suggestions received. This revised version was presented in the Second Consultation and suggestions for further improvement were received. Various issues were deliberated in these Consultations through plenary presentation, open house discussion, interaction in groups and consolidation of recommendations.

Aims & Objectives of Environmental Education:

The objectives of environmental education is to increase public awareness about environmental issues, explore possible solutions, and to lay the foundations for a fully informed and active participation of individual in the protection of environment and the prudent and rational use of natural resources. The resolutions provide the following guiding principles for environmental education:

- The environment as a common heritage of mankind.
- The common duty of maintaining, protecting & improving the quality of environment, as a contribution to the protection of human health and safeguarding the ecological balance;
- The need for a prudent and rational utilisation of resources;
- The way in which each individual can, by his own behavior and action, contribute to the protection of environment;
- The long-term aims of environmental education are to improve management of environment and provide satisfactory solutions to environmental issues.
- Provide opportunities to acquire the knowledge, values, attitudes, commitment and skills needed to protect and improve the environment.
- Encourage pupils to examine and interpret the environment from a variety of perspectives-physical, geographical, biological, sociological, economic, political, technological, historical, esthetic and ethical.
- Arouse pupil's awareness and curiosity about the environment and encourage active participation in resolving environmental problems.
- Environmental education is closely linked to the other cross circular themes of other subject areas.

LEARNING PRINCIPLES

The Learning principles of environmental education are:

1. Environmental education should consider the environment in its totality – natural and man-made, ecological, political, economic, technological, social, legislative, cultural and esthetic.
2. Environmental education should be a continuous life-long process, both in-school and out-of-school.
3. Environmental education should be interdisciplinary in its approach.
4. Environmental education should emphasise active participation in preventing and solving environmental problems.
5. Environmental education should examine major environmental issues from a world point of view, while paying due regard to regional differences.
6. Environmental education should focus on current and future environmental situations.
7. Environmental education should examine all development and growth from an environmental perspective.
8. Environmental education should promote the value and necessity of local, national and international cooperation in the solution of environmental problems.

RELATION TO SCIENCE & SOCIAL SCIENCE

Environmental Studies is a student- centred syllabus drawing together the disciplines History, Geography and Civics in a thematic approach to learning. This systematic study of environmental and social issues will enable young people to reflect on the world in which they live and to develop the skills and competencies required for active participation in society.

Environmental studies is the academic field which systematically studies human interaction with the environment. It is a broad interdisciplinary field of study that includes the natural environment, built environment, and the sets of relationships between them. While distinct from ecology and environmental science, the discipline encompasses study in the basic principles of those two fields of learning as well as the associated subjects, such as: policy, politics, law, economics, sociology and other social aspects, planning, pollution control, natural resources, and the interactions of human beings and nature.

A big aspect of environmental studies is the sciences. Students in this discipline may study things like biology, chemistry, geology, and engineering in order to understand more about the natural environment. Some people may also pick a specific field, like forestry or fisheries management, probing more deeply into this facet of interaction between humans and the natural world. Most environmental studies programs have a very demanding science component, to ensure that students have a thorough grounding in the sciences and to show them how to think like scientists.

ESS is a multidisciplinary course with an integrated methodology. Themes are used to provide a context within which the knowledge and understanding of History, Geography and Civic Education can be applied and within which young people are introduced to the work of historians, geographers, archaeologists, cartographers, meteorologists, ecologists and town planners.

ESS is constructed on the rationale that:

- themes of immediate and obvious relevance to students can provide important motivation for further learning;
- the multi-focal perspective provided by the thematic approach allows concepts from the separate disciplines to interact in mutually enriching ways;
- each concept is explored both in space and time by coordinating the geography and history inputs;
- the study of real-world issues requires an integrated approach since many disparate disciplines must be simultaneously brought to bear to understand such issues. Thus an integrated methodology is relevant to the vocational needs and life-experience of students;
- the pedagogical principle of integration, introduced in the Primary school can be continued into second level and used as a springboard for specific disciplines.
- integration of the separate subjects allows the expertise of teachers of the disparate disciplines to interact positively;
- a multidisciplinary approach based on a small number of well-defined subjects can provide the basis for the further development of links with other areas of the curriculum;
- the specific skills of the integrated subjects can be taught in an issues-focused manner, so that their relevance is clear to students.

APPROACHES OF PRESENTING CONCEPTS

What are some strategies to teach environmental topics, particularly controversial ones, without coming up against affective barriers to learning? How can you help students learn the science and the policy without getting weighed down by feeling guilty or defiant?

- **Teach the science first:** Even though most environmental topics are a blend of science, policy, economics and human impacts, it may be helpful to separate these into three distinct sub-topics. First, present the science objectively, using data and relevant examples. Next, discuss the policy and economic issues related to this topic. Once those subjects are covered thoroughly, students will often be interested to learn what their own personal stake may be. By setting the stage deliberately, students are more likely to be receptive to the information and are less likely to get turned off.
- **Teach with data:** Statements like *"species are going extinct at an alarming rate," "wetlands are being turned into strip malls,"* and *"the climate is getting hotter"* are emotional statements (even if true) and will elicit emotional responses in your students. Rather than risk sounding like an alarmist, let the data speak for itself. Have students work through data sets, and they can discover for themselves the rate and extent of environmental change. In some cases, they still may end up being surprised or emotional, but it's because they reached their own conclusion, not because you told them to be alarmed.
- **Use active Learning Techniques:** Students learn better when they can learn it for themselves, and this is especially true for topics that are potential turn-offs for students. Environmental issues lend themselves to teaching techniques like using local examples, gathering data from the field, using role-playing or debates, or participating in environmental projects.
- **Controversy, ambiguity, and topics with incomplete or missing evidence can be used constructively (but need to be introduced judiciously):** Engaging controversial topics, or topics that have no clear-cut answers, can create an environment where students are motivated to learn more out of curiosity or imminent need. Students can be encouraged to review what is known, to identify what additional information is needed to solve the problem, and to continue the search to find and critically examine new information. Learning goals for students can include development of "scientific habits of the mind", to be critical consumers of information, and to be able to create, present and rebut arguments based on evidence. A supportive environment needs to be created to encourage scholarly and open review of the arguments and ideas, and provisions need to be put in place to prevent interpersonal (ad hominem) attacks in reporting results in class activities.
- **It's not all doom and gloom:** Certain environmental topics can be downright depressing. However, there are also many environmental success stories. Strive for a balance in which students do not feel overwhelmed by

a preponderance of "bad news." After all, environmental successes provide relevant examples of how problems can be overcome.

- **Clearly define your role and your teaching approach:** There are many ways to teach environmental issues. Before jumping into your curriculum, consider what your desired outcomes are and what approach you will take. Is your intent to teach just the relevant scientific processes, to promote an awareness of environmental issues, or to lead students toward a shift in their own environmental behavior? In the classroom, do you assume the role of environmental guardian, a free-marketeer, or a devil's advocate? There are advantages to various approaches, but it's important to consciously consider what your goals are and how you can best achieve them.
- **Lead by example, but don't preach:** We all know the stereotype that college professors drive tiny, efficient cars and live an eco-minded lifestyle. Regardless of whether or not this describes you, it's best to avoid talking down to your students for their own personal choices. Preaching to the class about what's "good" and what's "bad" will likely have the opposite effect than you intended; it can be a major turn-off for students. If your goal is to promote environmentally-favorable behavior in your students, consider a hands-on project that will challenge students to consider the environmental impacts of their own actions.

ACTIVITIES

Human activities are deeply related to environment and its degradation. In many ways environment decides human behaviour. To make the child aware of environment many activities should be included—

1. Aforestation and Gardening: The knowledge of flora and fauna, their uses, importance and effects should easily be given to child.
2. Arranging debate and seminars on environmental issues of social importance like Earthquake, Tsunami, Flood, Pollution, Global Warming, Deforestation, Acid Rain and Ozone Depletion.
3. Prepare Chart and Models related to environment related topics.
4. Travelling of environmental sites.

EXPERIMENTATION/PRACTICAL WORK

1. Observe a newly grown potted plant for 20 days. Observe the changes that take place. Record your observations in the table give below:

Number of Days	***Changes in the Plant***		
	Height of the Plant	Number of leaves	Other Changes
1st day			
3rd day			
5th day			
7th day			
10th day			
13th day			
15th day			
17th day			
20th day			

Plant also give rise to new plants. New plants are generally grown from seeds. Find out in what other ways we can grown new plants?

2. Make a list of thirteen natural things which you see in and around your house. Group them into living and non-living things.

	Living things	***Non-living things***
(i)		
(ii)		
(iii)		
(iv)		
(v)		
(vi)		
(vii)		
(viii)		
(ix)		
(x)		
(x)		
(xii)		
(xiii)		

3. Select five plants from your surrounding. Carefully look at each plant. Feel the stem. It is hard or soft. does it stand erect? What is the colour? Observe other parts.

Note down your observations in the table given below.

Local Name of The Plant	Type of stem: hard/soft and erect/ not erect	Flowers: colour and shape	Leaves: colour and shape	Fruits: Present/ Absent	Seeds: Present/ Absent
1					
2					
3					
4					
5					

4. Observe the animals in your surrounding. Which of these animals are four footed? compare these with five common types of birds. In what way are the four footed animals different from the birds? In what way are they similar?

5. Given below are names of some parts of a plant and an animal. Group them into parts of a plant and parts of an animal.

Neck, flower, root head, stem, leg, chest, fruit

Parts of a plant	***Parts of an animal***

6. Draw a picture of any local plant. Write down the names of different parts of the plant.

DISCUSSION

Sustainable Development

Sustainable development is the concept of needs and limitations imposed by technology and society on the environment's ability to meet the present and future need. The term sustainable development was brought into common use by the world commission on environment and development in its reports (WCED). According to WCED sustainable development means a process of change in which the exploitation of resources, the direction of investments, the orientation of technological development and institutional change are all in harmony and enhance both current and future potentiality to meet human needs and aspirations.

Sustainable development is a development that meets needs of the present without compromising the ability of future generations to meet their own needs. For achieving sustainable development what is needed in global movement as well as significantly increased political will and public pressure in order to persuade industry, governments and institutions to take responsibility for their action.

It must be borne in mind that development should not endanger the natural system that support life on earth. With this attitude towards nature technological advances increase our ability to use earth resources and thus increase the damage. However, the realisation is growing fast that we are in a world of limits and ever increasing growth of material consumption can only damage the life giving physical components of the environment.

The concept of sustainable development was highly appreciated at the United Nations Conference on Environment and Development (UNCED) at a Rio de Janero in Brazil, commonly known as Earths Summit.

Sustainable development also needs understanding the basic needs of deprived people of the world. It is necessary to provide opportunities in order to satisfy their aspirations for a better and secured life. Sustainable development can be successfully achieved by (1) conservation or reduction of excessive resource use (II) recycling and reuse of materials and (III) more use of renewable resources like solar energy, rather than non-renewable resources such as oil and coal.

Urban Problems Related to Energy

Urbanisation is a global phenomenon in the developed countries of the world. It is now taking a steady stride in developing countries. The degree of urbanisation has increased tremendously. It means that (A) the proportion has increased (B) the population density of towns has increased and (C) the percentage of growth of population has increased in countries like India.

These three parameters which are related with volume, spatial spread and growth from the three indices of degree of urbanisation is largely due to a steady migration of rural population from rural to urban areas.

The main reason for heavy concentration of urban population in large metropolitan cities is that they are the centres of major industrial and commercial activities. They offer much attraction for migration of people and this accounts for rapid increase in their population.

Factors contributing to urbanisation are (A) Industrialisation (B) Transportation (C) Socio-economic changes all of which have impact on environment and health. The management of urbanisation involves an extremely range of problems and thus effecting all aspects of social life.

The urbanisation and proliferation of urban slums presents a challenge to public health. This situation has become a global concern and future of entire mankind is at stake due to phenomenal rise in population, rapid urbanisation, degradation, of environment, ever increasing pollution and over exploitation of natural and non-renewable resources.

Urbanisation has brought into associated problems related with the energy. Energy is an essential impact for urban development. Energy is produced from commercial sources like cow dung, fuel wood and agricultural wastes. Per capita consumption of commercial energy is sometimes used as an index of the consumption of economic advancement. India's per capita commercial energy, however is very low. It is one eighth of the world average commercial energy accounts for a little over of the total energy used in the country, the rest coming from non-commercial sources.

Global Warming

The accumulation of global warming coincides with a rise in the concentration of green house gases in the atmosphere. More heat and infrared reactions are trapped by the gaseous mantle around the globe which accelerates the pace of global warming.

The globe system and atmosphere is a state of dynamic equilibrium with the rate of absorption of solar radiation and its emission back to space as infrared and heat waves, which balance each other. Such gases and vapours which allow free passage to radiations are of relatively shorter wave length (2900-7000 Å) onwards, play very important role in maintaining surface temperature within a range in which heat can exist. They form a blanket around the globe which checks the passage of infrared and heat wave from earth crust back to space and keep it warm. The word green house is nothing but a glass house which is constructed to grow specific tropical plants in cold areas of tropical climate.

Green House Gases

There are number of gases present in the atmosphere which are capable of absorbing effectively heat waves and infrared rays while being transparent to radiation of lower wave lengths. Trace gases such as water vapour, carbondioxide, methane, chloroflurocarbons, ozone, nitrous oxide are some of the gases which constitutes troposphere. Amongst these five gases having rising concentration's of which has been implicated in causing noticeable rise in the mean global temperature. These gases are carbondioxide, methane, chlorofluorocarbons, nitrous oxide and water vapours, other gases such as sulphur dioxide, ozone are not able to contribute much as they are quickly cleared from atmosphere.

The sources of major green house gases are given below.

The Sources of Major Green House Gases

S. No.	Green House Gases	Sources
1.	Carbon Dioxide	Fossil fuels combustion, deforestation and land use changes.
2.	Methane	Enteric fermentation in cattle and insects. Biomass burning and garbage,land, fuels, coal mines and natural gas leaks, rice, paddies, swamps, bogs.
3.	Chlorofluorocarbons	Aerosol, refrigeration and air conditioning, plastic foams, industrial solvents.
4.	Nitrous oxide	Fertiliser use, fossil fuel combustion, biomass burning.

An additional 1.1 to 2.2 billion tones (1–2 billion metric tonnes) of carbon (4–8 billion tonnes [3.6–7.3 billion metric tonnes] of CO_2) are emitted into the atmosphere each year due to deforestation. Like the fossil fuels, which were once living organisms, the extant forests hold vast stores of carbon. When the trees and other plants die and are either burned or allowed to decay, this carbon is converted into CO_2. Furthermore, trees serve the vital function of removing CO_2 from the atmosphere as they grow, unless deforested areas are quickly replanted, not only is CO_2 emitted directly into the atmosphere, but a vital mechanism for removing excess CO_2 from the atmosphere is also destroyed.

Although not yet considered a serious threat, there is another aspect of excess CO_2 production: the oxygen portion of CO_2 comes from the atmosphere, and we (along with all living aerobic creatures) need this oxygen to breathe. For every tonne of carbon burned, 2.66 tonnes of oxygen are taken from the atmosphere. Since the atmosphere is composed of about 20.9% oxygen, the supply may seem virtually unlimited. Yet measurements indicate that the oxygen content of the atmosphere is currently decreasing at a rate of about 13 ppm annually. Oxygen is being lost from the atmosphere, and as more plants are destroyed, it is not being replaced as fast as it once was. The most serious immediate concern is that falling oxygen levels may adversely affect oxygen concentrations in the oceans and other standing bodies of water. Slight decreases in oxygen concentrations could have severely disruptive effects on many marine organisms. Although carbon dioxide is blamed for 50 to 70% of the current abnormal global warming, (depending on the authority consulted and how "global warming" is calculated), it is not the only major greenhouse gas. The other major culprits are chloroflurocarbon (CFCs), methane (natural gas, CH_4), tropospheric ozone, and nitrogen oxide (NO_x).

The chlorofluorocarbons that promote global warming are the same CFCs that are destroying stratospheric ozone. Indeed, they are up to thousand of times more efficient at absorbing heat and promoting global warming than CO_2. At present, CFCs account for 15 to 25% of the human contribution to global warming. This number would have been even higher if steps had not been taken to reduce the CFCs released into the atmosphere. Thus, there are two good reasons to reduce our reliance on CFCs: to save the ozone layer and to reduce global warming. Methane accounts for an estimated 15 to 20% of current global warming.

It has been estimated that carbon dioxide will account for about half of the temperature increase while methane, nitrous oxide and chloroflurocarbons will be responsible for the rest.

Green house gases are provided both by industrial and biological processes but the industrial emission are fairly well documented but the knowledge of the production rates of green house gases through biological processes and the factors regulating emissions are still in adequate.

Consequence of Global Warming

The earth surface temperature has increased by about 0.5°C but it is suggested that mean global temperature will rise by 2-6°C. During the next century and the concentration of CO_2 will reach 600 ppm.

The rise in global temperature and consequently unfavourable climatic conditions will also affect number of species. The loss of genetic resources may take place on a large scale. The change in wind a precipitation pattern will play an important role in altering the biotic communities. Insects and pests may increase and coupled with higher humidity, pathogenic diseases will multiply. The increase in temperature will also affect agriculture in different parts of the world. In order to cape with alteration in cropping pattern, pest resistance varieties will have to developed. Some of the serious consequences of global warming are:

(i) Increase in surface temperature of earth.
(ii) Sudden changes in rainfall and temperature pattern.
(iii) Rise in sea level causing increased wave attacks and inundation of waste lands.
(iv) Changes in rainfall and temperature patterns.
(v) Increase in frequency of hurricanes, floods and erosion.
(vi) Increase in tropical fever diseases and other health problems.

Green House Effect and Ozone Layer Depletion: The green house gases in the troposphere provides thermal insulation while these gases are considered responsible in causing ozone depletion in the stratosphere. The depletion of ozone layer could neutralise some of the warming effect caused by higher concentration of green house gases.

Global Warming and Human Health: Temperature changes may have an impact on several categories of diseases including cardiovascular, cerebrovascular and respiratory diseases. High temperature overload the thermoregulating system of the body.

Communicable Diseases: The distribution of range of diseases which correlated with temperature could be affected by global climate changes. It occurs likely that communicable diseases problems will be aggravated by climate change.

Immune System: The UV Radiation affects the immune system of the skin and hence these might be an increased number of cases of skin cancer.

Water, Food and Changing Climate: The ability of the earth to produce food depends heavily on elements such as ground water, the genetic diversity of human species and productive soil. Fertilise soil is losing its productivity in many parts of the world because of erosion and salinization. The direct effect of CO_2 on plant growth and use of water complicate efforts how future climate change effect, agriculture, forests and other ecosystems.

Rise in Sea Level: Rising sea level may be one of the most widely felt and easily recognized consequences of warmer global climate. Currently, sea level rising, it is estimated that sea level may rise from about 0.5 to 1.5 metres in response to 3 to 5° C increase in temperature. The issue of global warming is important because an increase in the average temperature of only a few degrees could lead to the melting of glacial ice, a rise in sea level, and flooding of coastal regions.

Acid Rain

Acid rain refers to any precipitation hence a pH value less than that of a normal rain water, when pH value is around 5 or 6. Normal rain water is weakly acidic, because atmospheric carbon dioxide combines with rain water to form weak carbonic acid.

The severe acidic nature of water occurs due to massive pollution caused by industrialisation. Oxides of sulphur, nitrogen and hydrocarbons are the major contributing factors to acid rain.

The gases and aerosols accumulate high up in the atmosphere, water vapours condense on aerosol surface and form a fine film providing suitable level as catalysts for the oxide of sulphur and nitrogen to dissolve in water and react to form corresponding acids which form salts such as nitrates and sulphates when come in contact with basic aerosols. As water vapours continue to condense on these aerosols, large droplets of water are produced which rain down as acid rains.

Sulphuric acid, nitric acid and various sulphates and nitrates are the major chemical constituents of acid rain, small amount of hydrochloric acid and its salt may also be present.

Most areas are susceptible to acid rain. The buffering capacity of water or soil determines its susceptibility. In general, lower the buffering capacity of soil or water are produced which rain down as acid rains.

Effects of Acid Rain

The effects of acid rain depends on the route of deposition (Wet/Dry) as well as on the level of contact with plants, building and water course. Acid rain exerts both direct and indirect influence on organisms and materials. The direct effects are determined by the concentration of pollutants in air and generally they decline with increasing distances from the source of emission. On the other hand the indirect effects include its secondary and tertiary products. They are known to affects and material with more harmful consequences at a distance upto hundreds and some times thousand kilometers.

Dry deposition has direct effects on the environment. It attacks building materials such as sand stone, lime stone, marble, steel while/wet deposition has both direct and indirect effects. It increases the acidity of lakes and rivers, aquatic and terrestrial ecosystem. Acidity kills fish, bacteria and algae.

Acid rain has several effects on fish and fishery resources. Fish kills are a common feature in highly acidified water. A sublethal levels fishes may fail to reproduce. The population may gradually extinct because of negligible recruitment of young fish to replace older ones as they die. They die because of accumulation of heavy metals.

Many direct and indirect effects of acid rain on productivity and survival of wildlife population have been documented. Wildlife is affected indirectly because of loss of alteration of food habit resources. Acid rain can directly affect eggs and tadpoles of frogs and salamanders that breed in small forest ponds. As plants and wildlife are directly related any affect on the former will be disadvantageous to the later.

Ozone Layer Depletion

Ozone is a gas which is composed of three atoms of oxygen. The ozone concentration at earth surface is usually present in the range of 0.02 ppm to 0.04 ppm. Ozone varies globally with concentration of more than 1 ppm and is continuously present on upper atmosphere.

The pressure of ozone in the atmosphere plays as dual role. At ground level ozone enters the body through inhalation and exerts toxic effects directly on the lung. Exposure of ozone has been associated with being cancer, DNA breakage and visual impairment. However, the stratosphere ozone forms a protective shield against harmful UV radiation.

The atmospheric ozone is obtained in its two layers. The bottom layer extends up to 15 km from the earth and is known as troposphere, where as the top layer which extends from 15 to 50 km is known as stratosphere ozone.

Depletion of ozone layer has appeared, first over Antarctica in Northern hemisphere and polar regions. The primary cause for ozone loss is due to chloroflurocarbons (CFC's). During the year 1980 and 1987 it was established that direct involvement of chlorine and some heterogenous chemicals were responsible for depletion of ozone.

It has been established that various kinds of gases which are released in the atmosphere by human activity are main causes for depletion of ozone layer.

Depletion of Ozone Layers Over Poles

The stratosphere ozone is formed mist of equator which is displaced over the polar regions. It is because of this reason that the concentration of ozone is found to be maximum at poles. At these poles and Antarctic and Arctic regions the depletion of ozone has been found to be fastest. This is due to strong westerly winds around the poles moving at a speed of 90 to 100 metre per second.

Depletion of Ozone Layer by Chloroflurocarbons (CFC's)

Out of many reactions sequences which lead to the destruction of ozone, one of the most important reaction is associated with the breakdown of stable organic chlorine compounds of CFC's where air active chlorine atom can catalytically destroy ozone.

Its Impact on Earth

Accelerating ozone layer depletion has serious impact on most of the life forms. For every 10% depletion of the ozone layer, one can expect 20% increase in U.V. radiation arriving on earth. This radiation could change genetic character, after immune systems, damage crops, disrupt marine food web and enhance green house warming by affecting the CO_2 absorption capacity of planktons in the ocean. The incidence of human cancer would increase and the sight of millions could be affected as more intense UV radiation damages eyes and causes cataracts. Immune response may be depressed in people exposed to increased radiation levels, vaccination programmes may become less effective and infectious diseases may become more common and more severe. Plant growth may be inhibited and crop yields may be reduced. Adverse effects on nitrogen fixing bacteria in rice paddies may result in drastic drops in production.

Immune System and Vaccination

UV radiation suppresses allergic reaction of the skin and affects the immune system. As a result skin cancer is developed along with many infectious diseases. These include measles and other viral diseases, herpes, parasite diseases, malaria, tuberculosis leprosy and fungal infection.

Skin Cancer

It has been estimated that five per cent decrease in ozone would mean 14% increase basal cell carcinoma and 25% increase in the carcinoma. It has also been estimated that every one per cent decrease in stratosphere ozone could mean that 2% of world population will develop the type of cancer.

Cataracts and Blindness

Cataracts and blindness are also expected to increase with depletion of ozone layer. Ultra violet radiation damages cornea, lens and to a lesser extent the retina. It has been estimated that one per cent radiation of the ozone layer can cause 150 thousands cataracts. Exposure to sunlight has been established as factor in the development of intraocular in melanoma.

Impacts on Oceans

Depletion of ozone layer disrupts oceans life. The most significant effect of increasing amounts of UV radiation is on plankton and other tiny marine organisms. Planktons produce more than one-half of earth biomass. UV radiation reduces the amount of phytoplankton and zooplankton. In addition it leads to 5% disease in fish yield.

Damage to Materials

Depletion of ozone layer causes many materials to degrade more rapidly. Plastic outdoors will have much shorter life times. Polyacrmyl shedings, window pipes, gullies and trims used in buildings are likely to degrade faster along with cable coverings. Developing countries will suffer the most because plastics are cheap and popular in building materials.

Green House Effect

The haloalkanes not only deplete ozone layer but they are also known as potential green house gases. Phytoplanktons in the oceans normally absorb half of the CO_2 of the atmosphere. Such quality of phytoplankton is considerably decreased when exposed to UV radiation such a process result in the increased level of CO_2 in the atmosphere which in effect will contribute to global warming and hence will have house effect.

CONTINUOUS AND COMPREHENSIVE EVALUATION

Continuous and Comprehensive Evaluation refers to a system of school based assessment that covers all aspects of student's development. It emphasizes two fold objectives.Continuity in evaluation and assessment of broad based learning.

CCE helps in reducing stress of students by :

- Identifying learning progress of students at regular time intervals on small portions of content.

- Employing a variety of remedial measures of teaching based on learning needs and potential of different students.
- Desisting from using negative comments on the learner's performance.
- Encouraging learning through employment of a variety of teaching aids and techniques.
- Involving learners actively in the learning process.
- Recognizing and encouraging specific abilities of students, who do not excel in academics but perform well in other co-curricular areas.

Teachers should Keep in Mind

- Use a variety of tools (oral, projects, presentations).
- Understand different learning styles and abilities.
- Share the assessment criteria with the students.
- Allow peer and self assessment.
- Give an opportunity to the student to improve.

Important Points

- CCE will cover the scholastic and co scholastic areas of school education.
- The two types of assessment referred to in the circular are formative and summative. The periodicity of the two types of assessment are four and twice a year respectively.
- Formative Assessment totals to 40% weightage.
- Summative Assessment totals to 60% weightage.
- There are nine grades in Part A of Scholastic assessment and Part B of the same assessment has five grades.
- Summative assessment covers non academic areas like attitudes and skills and there are three grades.
- If a student secures Grade 6 in the academic areas his/her marks would range from 51% to 60%.
- CCE advocates absolute grading. This means that Grade 9 would imply an A2 grade.
- The academic term will be divided into two terms.

TEACHING MATERIAL/AIDS

Text Book

Text book is the area in which the language material is presented prescribed for teaching and learning English.

Characteristics of Good Text Books

A good text books not only teaches but it also tests. A few essential characteristics of good text books are given below:

1. The size of text book should be handy for the students.
2. The binding should be proper and strong.
3. The subject matter should be printed on good quality paper.
4. Heading and subheading should be printed on title page in bold form.
5. Illustration should be attractive. For every young pupil, the picture should be well drawn and realistically coloured and not in black and white.
6. Clear and unambiguous instruction should be given along side the test and practice and exercise.
7. The introduction at the beginning and conclusion at the end of the chapter should be given in the text book.
8. The words and structure are carefully graded.
9. No difficult words and new words are given in good text book.
10. The words and structure already learnt are repeated in the coming pages so that the students could revise them making them stable in their memory.
11. The subject matter of text book should provide new information so that students could get new knowledge.
12. There should be both practice and text exercise at the end of the chapter.
13. The practice should be low which the majority of students could solve them easily.

Chalkboard

It is the closest friend of a teacher in the class and about 50% teaching task is completed with the help of the blackboard. Advantages of using a chalkboard in the class are as follows :

(*i*) It is a cheap material aid which does not cost much on its maintenance.

(*ii*) When a teacher writes important points of the lesson on the chalkboard along with his oral teaching and lectures, aural and visual both the senses of students work simultaneously. It increases learning many times.

(*iii*) Writing meaning of difficult words, drawing graphs or diagrams, solving the sums of mathematics, preparing the summary of the lesson, all these works can be done on the chalkboard and they help the students understand the facts, events or terminologies.

(*iv*) Blackboard works as a model for students. This can help the students mend their ways if they imitate the model.

Models

Models are the reflection or copy of the real objects. They are used in the class to clarify the concepts when either real objects are not available or it is not possible to bring real objects to the class. They are also the abbreviated version of real objects. Elephants, lions or other animals or birds can not be brought to the class, hence, it is better to use the models of these objects. Globe is the best example of model to be used in the class.

Through models knowledge of all types of historical, geographical and scientific facts and concepts can be given to students. Models are especially useful for teaching visually handicapped children who perceive the objects by touch. Since, clear dimensions of length, breadth and height are given in the model in a proportionate manner, they are more useful for concept formation than pictures.

How to use models :

(*i*) Scale should be used for showing size, shape or structure of the real objects. Apart from this, teacher should also clarify the real shape, size or structure of the real object.

(*ii*) Students should be given opportunity to have a critical view on the model and their views on it.

(*iii*) All students should be given chance to have a close look at the model in the class.

(*iv*) Models should have direct relevance to the lesson and they should develop scientific temperament among learners.

(*v*) Models should be properly explained in the class in order to make the use of models effective.

Pictures

Pictures are used in the class as material aids when neither real objects nor models can be arranged. They are cheap and easily available in the market, therefore, a teacher should not be miserly in using them. Pictures are actually the outlines of the real objects and when they are shown in the class, they give clear concepts about the colour, physique, shape and size of the real objects. Attention of students can easily be drawn to the lesson through them. If pictures related to the lesson are not available in the market, the teacher should sketch them by using pencils and water colours. Pictures are used as material aids for teaching all the school subjects.

Diagrams

They are another option and used when even pictures can not be arranged. They can also clarify the concepts like models or pictures but at a lesser degree. Diagrams are drawn on the chalkboard by using coloured chalks and then students copy it on their notebooks. The biggest advantage of this material aid is that teacher need not spend even a single pie in using this material aid.

They help in clarifying the concepts, laws and principles of science and social sciences. Their role in teaching languages is very limited.

Graphs

Graphs are especially used in history, geography, science and mathematics. They help the teacher and the students to study, analyse and compare the data, facts or events. Whenever action research is made by a teacher in the class, graphs are used to show the data.

Maps

Maps are the flat representation of the surface of the earth on a paper where many informations are presented through lines, symbols dots, points or letters. They have special significance in teaching history and geography. We can also get information about the size and physical features of a country, state or continent through these maps and distance between different parts of the country or the world can also be read from them. Though printed maps of all states or countries are available in the market yet a teacher draws them also on roler boards. This will enable the students to draw such maps themselves.

Slide Projector

Simple 'slide projector' was known as "magic lantern" in the olden days. The principle here is that when we put the transparent slide on the socket and throw light from behind, the light passes through it and projects the image on the screen.

A slide projector typically consists of a quart, three halogen lamps, light to be reflected by the reflector, a heat filter and lastly, condenser lenses. The heat filter is a thermo crystal which absorbs most of the heat produced by three lamps. A cooling system is also needed which consists of a fan for convecting off the heat, filter and other components. The fan is thermostatically controlled. When projector is switched off, the fan is also switched off.

Classroom uses of the Slide Projector : Slides are prepared for selected topics and the informations contained by them may be in the form of written words, pictures, graphs, sketches, etc. The topic selected should be arranged frame by frame. The ideal ratio of length and breadth of slides is 2 : 3. Each frame should have only one concept for the ease of understanding.

The slides and the film strips are arranged in a sequential order. This arrangement is also coordinated with the teaching learning activity of the class. When slides are shown in the class, curtains are drawn on the windows in order to reduce the entry of natural light in the class.

Before showing these slides, teacher elaborates important points. Once the film is over, the teacher gives his own comments and relates the aid with the lesson to be taught.

Film Strips

They are used before a large group of students either for introducing a lesson or for elaborating some minute object not seen in ordinary situations. Film strips are projected on a big screen through a film projector and then the projector is switched on. Here, very minute objects look very big on the screen and we can study their parts. For example, knowledge about bacteria and viruses can be given to students through these film strips. Sometimes, sound recording is also used along with the film to clarify important points.

Advantages of Film Strips :

(*i*) The order or sequence of film strips is fixed and a teacher can prepare the relevant material to supplement the film according to the sequence.

(*ii*) We can have any part of the film on the screen as long as we desire so. As a result, a teacher can discuss a single topic as long as he needs. Thus, complete control over the equipment and the material is possible.

(*iii*) Handling of film projectors is also not complex. There is no problem of storing them because of their small size. Precautions are, however, needed against fungi or physical damage.

(*iv*) They have become very cheap today and any school can afford the cost of these projectors.

(*v*) They do not require complete darkness in the room as we do in using epidiascope or motion film projectors.

Limitations of Film Strips:

(*i*) They can be used only in small sized classes because of limited focal length. Modern projectors are, however, having large focal length.

(*ii*) Slide projection is not as effective as film projection. Inventions of 3D films have reduced the use of slides even further. In spite of this, fixed order of the film strips creates problem in handling individual frames.

(*iii*) Many schools do not have audio-visual workshops and thus, they depend on the cheap and unstandardized materials available in the market.

Film Projector

16 mm films are generally used for the purpose of training or teaching. These films are planned and executed by a pannel of experts who endeavour to prepare films of good quality.

As far as use of film projector for classroom teaching is concerned, it is very easy. Everything is automatic here. If electricity supply is not restricted, the film will not stop in the middle, after it is put on the projector.

Advantages of Motion Pictures :

(*i*) Motion pictures can especially be used for training purposes. Take the example of games and sports. If some actions of a player is wrong leading to defeat in the game, it can be corrected by viewing the films. After the game is over, the film of the game is later analysed to be discussed by the experts to bring in new strategies and tactics to counterplay.

(*ii*) In all training courses, perfection is needed everywhere. If action is recorded on films, we can see our own performance and remove our defects.

(*iii*) In the classroom teaching, motion pictures can highlight those aspects also that would have otherwise been missed. For example, by enlarging, close up and action replay techniques, motion pictures can highlight those movements also which are very minute and can be missed in ordinary situations.

(*iv*) Motion pictures are **multi-sensory technique** of instruction. It is because a combination of light, sound and actions are seen here.

(*v*) Motion pictures can develop imaginative and observational capacities of students simultaneously.

(*vi*) Whatever ideals are shown by the models in motion pictures are imitated by pupils and thus, good ideals and etiquettes can be developed in them.

(*vii*) They are helpful in giving clarity of concepts through concreteness and accuracy.

(*viii*) Facts and events related to industry, politics, history and geography and knowledge about scientific inventions, discoveries, laws and principles can be communicated to pupils very effectively through these motion pictures.

Kinescope

It is a sight and sound recording that can be made in the studio from the television screen for repeated use. What transcription is to radio, the kinescope is to TV. They are used for the following purposes :

(i) For delayed telecast.

(ii) For retelecast of the same programme.

(iii) For repeating the telecast when programme could not be seen due to failure of network.

(iv) For sending programmes abroad.

Only limitation of kinescope is that live element or spontaneity does not exist here.

It can be used in teaching learning process in the same way as television is used.

Epidiascope

Epidiascope is an equipment that can project all types of materials whether transparent or non-transparent (opaque). It has thus a twin facility and separate mechanism for projecting transparent and opaque materials.

In epidiascope, the word epi means 'upon' dia means 'through' and scope means 'projected material to be seen'.

While projecting a slide, beams pass through the slide and projects its image on the screen. In this way, transparent material is projected.

While projecting the opaque material the light bits upon the object which reflects the image on a very sensitive mirror and reflects the image of the opaque objects on the screen.

Despite the multipurpose functioning of this device, it is not very popular in educational institutions because of its poor quality image, total room darkening, very high need of energy, complexity of its use and poor range. It is to be installed in the middle of the class due to its low range, therefore, causing more interference than aiding something to the lesson. Because of its ability to project opaque objects on the screen, it is also known as opaque projector.

Overhead Projector (OHP)

Built on the basic principle of periscope, OHP is an important audio visual equipment. In the classroom it is placed in front of the teacher above his head to reflect an image on the screen (blackboard). This device consists of a strong energy source, (bulbs), fixed reflectors (mirrors), projection lens and a platen. This projector is called over head because the image goes over the head of the teacher and falls on the screen behind him. The teacher puts one slide over the other in order to give a sense of continuity of the subject matter projected on the screen.

Advantages of OHP : Its advantages lie in its special characteristics given below :

(i) No special training is required by the teacher to operate a projector.

(ii) OHPs are not very costly as compared to computers or film projectors.

(iii) It is handy and portable.

(iv) The image formed by the projector is also very bright and every pupil can see it. A 4 × 4 inches slide gives an image of 4 × 4 feet. This enlarged image is very easy to understand.

(v) It can create interests in pupils and hence it is a good motivator.

(vi) It is the best visual aid available to a teacher to supplement his oral teaching. He uses the screen of OHP as a blackboard without looking back. Transparencies, drawing, diagrams, figures and outlines etc. can be shown on the screen.

Television

TV differs from the radio in the sense that it is audio and visual both. We can see the incident occurring round the globe on it immediately after the occurrence of the incident through telecast. Thus, it is bisensory (multisensory) media. We get news, views and recreation through television in the same way as we do through the transistor but in a more compact and concrete way due to the facility of vision here.

As far as application of TV in education is concerned, it is still in the stage of infancy in India. It was only in 1961 that Indian television (Doordarshan) started a special service for schools in collaboration with the directorate of Education. This programme aimed at supplementing the regular classroom teaching in selected subjects. By 1972 only 400 schools of the capital received this telecast and two lakh students benefited from them. These programmes were telecast in the evening and on Sundays but there was no mechanism developed at that time to measure the effectiveness of such transmitting programmes.

After the introduction of distance education system in India, television is now regularly used as an instructional media. The enactment of Prasar Bharti Act is expected to boost the role of TV in the teaching learning process.

Advantages of Television :

(i) It heightens the reality more than the physical presence. For example, if someone is watching a cricket match in a stadium, even then he can not see certain situations despite being present there. On the other hand, if he is viewing a match on a TV, he can see and analyse every situation by close up action replay. Thus, television experience may be more real than the actual one. It can show even those details which we can not see with the help of direct experiences. Thus, television can be used for all training programmes and behaviour of the trainees can be modified in the desired manner.

(*ii*) TV experiences are new and versatile. So, they can bring variety to classroom teaching by breaking monotony and strengthening the learning structures by its multisensory approach.

(*iii*) It widens the horizon of pupils' experiences by giving them upto date knowledge of the real situation and by making them conversant with the opinions of others.

(*iv*) It can motivate the pupils for learning by arousing and retaining their interest in the learning situation.

Limitations of Television:

(*i*) Speed of a television can not be changed as we can do in motion pictures.

(*ii*) A TV programme can not be adjusted to teaching and vice versa will have to be done. A teacher can take the help of video recording in such cases.

Tape Recorder and Audio Cassettes

Cassette type audio taps are available now which can play for 90 minutes on both sides. We can listen to our own recorded voice, recorded speeches of politicians and learned people, recorded poems of great composers, songs, music etc by the tape recorder.

Audio cassette recorder is used for the following purposes :

Such types of recording serve the following purposes:

(*i*) **Analysis of verbal messages :** Accuracy, speed and tone of verbal messages are studied here and if perfection is seen, reinforcement to the presenter is given.

(*ii*) **Drill and practice :** Accurate verbal messages are presented before the trainee for drill and practice.

(*iii*) **Teaching of specific skills :** Impressive oral presentation is actually a skill. This skill is taught to students through audio-recording in the individual and group situations.

(*iv*) **Speech improvement :** Style of speaking and phonetics can also be improved by using this technology.

(*v*) **Improvement in vocabulary :** Recorded verbal messages are full of many new words which pupils can learn by listening to the message.

(*vi*) **Recreation :** Many recorded songs and music entertain the listeners and remove their fatigue.

Radio

It is an important and easily accessable audio aid serving three important general purposes "news, views and recreation". It is the cheapest equipment of all and radio broadcast is now reachable to 100% population of the country. Pupils can get information about the incidents in any part of the globe immediately through radio. This increases their general awareness of the world. Students listen the ideas of learned people, politicians and educationists from across the world on the radio. This extends their own views and way of thinking. Apart from these, there are hundreds of programmes of music, songs and plays broadcast on the radio which entertain them round the clock.

Instructional Value of the Radio :

(*i*) It is a powerful means of developing listening comprehension.

(*ii*) It can also help the pupils to acquire correct pronunciation and phonetics like tape recorders.

(*iii*) Conversational style and language can be learned on the radio.

(*iv*) It improves word power of learners.

(*v*) Mass education goals can be achieved through radio broadcast. It was the realization of the people when radio came into being in 1917.

(*vi*) News listened on the radio can improve our general knowledge.

(*vii*) Radio listening does not require literacy. Even illiterates can take the benefit of it.

Radio Broadcast in India : The first radio station was established in India in July 1927 in Mumbai followed by one more station in Kolkata in the same year. This media is now able to penetrate to the remotest villages of the country and is covering more than 99% of the population.

School broadcasting in India was started in 1937. Radio broadcasting is now very much used for mass education as well as the education of school going children in selected areas. Central Institute for educational technology (CIET) under the supervision and control of NCERT produces quality radio broadcast programmes. Adult education Radio Programmes also started in 1956 to educate the adults in the age group of 15-35 in the vicinity of Pune as a project sponsord by UNESCO. Today, broadcast of adult education programmes are many under different titles. When Consumer Protection Act was passed in 1986, consumer education through radio was also given recognition. Today, it is a regular programme of all the radio stations in India. One more regular radio programme is the radio counseling programme of IGNOU which is broadcast from 4-5 pm on every Sunday.

Apart from these, radio broadcast is also making the people aware about various social and economic problems and people are also educated about how they can solve these problems.

Computer

It is the latest electronic device that is audio and visual both. It accepts data, performs operations on that data in sequence (decided by a programme) and outputs the results.

Computer in education : From input devices to output and its storage, computer has a wide range of applicability in education. In computers inputs are converted into output by a programme. Thus, input (data) plus programme form software or instructional programme. Inputs are converted into output in the CPU of the computer.

Computer always works according to the programme given to it. Whatever instruction or programme the students gives to the computers, it will always act accordingly and output will also come out on the same line. Application of computers in education can be understood by the following lines.

Videodiscs

This system is comprised of videodisc, where the information is stored, a video player and a TV set.

It is helpful in teaching learning process in the following ways :

(*i*) Students can get more informations through effective way of presentation.

(*ii*) By forwarding or reversing the CD player, learners can have access to any informations as many times as possible. This repeated action is necessary in understanding complex materials.

(*iii*) Live coverage given by the CD player can provide higher degree of motivation.

(*iv*) Auto stop system provided in the system can help those learners who study till late hours of night.

(*v*) The materials prepared by the effective teachers can be made available in the market for wide use.

Videotext

This system provides an interactive information retrieval service. It allows the home television to work as a computer terminal, which retrieves the textual material and graphic information from a remote data base.

Advantages of Videotext:

(*i*) It is useful for downloading the required information from a remote data base.

(*ii*) It raises the general awareness of learners.

(*iii*) The principal of a school can have access to any information about his or other schools any time if this system is available in the school.

(*iv*) It is especially useful for distance learning. A learner can connect himself with his study centre or regional office any time.

(*v*) It is free from time schedule. We can have any information any time.

(*vi*) Two way interaction between the teacher and the taught is possible here with the help of alphanumeric keyboard. The learner can address to his tutor by typing questions and sending it to the tutor. Once he receives the answer, he gets immediate feedback.

(*vii*) It is faster than telephone or telegram because user need not wait here in queue.

Teleconferencing

Teleconferencing is a two way broadcast system in which learners can interact with the programme through a local telephone. It is a powerful medium of instruction for distance education. In this system three or four subject experts sit at different places and participate in the discussion on the given subject matter. Here learners do not take part in the teaching-learning process directly. They only hear the programme on their radio set or TV. They can however, interact with the experts through telephone which is connected to the radio or TV station where the discussion is being organised.

Thus, teleconferencing involves the use of many media and allows interactive group communication by means of a two way broadcast. All such conferencing need good quality audio device to facilitate immediate interaction among the participants for exchange of views.

Advantages of Teleconferencing :

(*i*) **Effective for distance learning :** When groups of students are scattered over a large area of the country and it is not possible for them to interact with their teachers personally, then learning through teleconferencing is the best option for them.

(*ii*) **Interaction between the teacher and the taught possible :** As far as interaction between teachers and learners are concerned, this approach does not differ in any way from classroom teaching.

(*iii*) **High quality instruction :** Since, very learned people and experts of the subject take part in these discussions, the quality of the programme is never questionable.

(*iv*) **Immediate feedback :** Learners get answer of their questions immediately from the experts and their problem is solved. In this way, they get immediate feedback.

(*v*) **Flexibility :** Experts do not teach here on a pre-determined track. Their instruction and its way of presentation always changes according to the questions asked by learners. Thus, this approach is very flexible.

Internet

It is the abbreviation of international network. The computers connected to this system are automatically connected to world wide website(www). Due to this we can hear and see any programme available on website any time when we want to do so. If we have missed any television or radio programme, we can not have access to that programme again but if that programme is loaded on the website, we can repeatedly hear and see the programme. We will only have to log on the website of the programme producer and it will be available for us. The major advantage of this system is that it has made 24 hour communication possible especially between those countries which have great differences in their local timings such as India and America have a time difference of 10 ½ hours. When there is day time in India, offices are closed in America.

Applications of internet in education :

(*i*) We can get any information any time at home through internet on one hand and we can store the information by creating our own website on the other. Thus, it is not necessary to have immediate print out of the textual matter.

(*ii*) The two talking persons can see each other in face to face situations also through internet. Thus, a teacher can teach millions of students scattered across the world together.

(*iii*) Many educational institutions have created their educational websites. We can download any information about them any time by logging on these websites.

(*iv*) Internet has also its role to play in classroom teaching. Teacher can show any educational programme through internet any time according to his own convenience and he will not have to adjust his time table according to the programme as he does while using radio or television as aids.

(*v*) Latest teaching strategies and latest researches in different fields can be obtained through internet immediately and we need not have to wait for their publication in magazines and journals.

(*vi*) Books, magazines and newspapers are also published on internet and it has made our access to them easy. Any Indian living in Canada even can read "Amar Ujala" or "Times of India" daily.

(*vii*) Research material and encyclopaedias are also published on internet to facilitate learning process.

PROBLEMS

Teaching of Environmental Studies is a complex human activity. At the one end it is related to fixation of national goal and on the other end it is related to the daily activity of a minor child in the classroom. Environmental study is not only related to a particular subject but a group of subjects. Therefore its content is so wide and varied. The major problems of Environmental studies are—

1. The Syllabus of Environmental Study is not properly arranged.
2. Community Resources are not properly used.
3. Lack of Resources.
4. No scope for Personal experiences in environmental Curriculum.
5. Attitude of Students towards the subject.
6. Lack of well experienced teachers.
7. Methods of teaching is not adaquate.
8. Lack of Practical experiences.

PRACTICE PAPER

1. Environmental Studies are very important for :
   (*a*) getting clean drinking water
   (*b*) hygienic living conditions
   (*c*) clean and fresh air
   (*d*) All of the above
2. Which of the following is telling us what we should and should not do–what is right and wrong, good and bad–within the context of a certain ethical system?
   (*a*) Philosophical ethics
   (*b*) Normative ethics
   (*c*) Descriptive ethics
   (*d*) None of the above
3. The different levels of environmental and conservation awareness are :
   (*a*) Pollution and Environmental degradation
   (*b*) Consumption overpopulation
   (*c*) Sustainable earth
   (*d*) All of the above
4. Which of the following is still a very important source of energy for millions of Indians living in villages?
   (*a*) Oil (*b*) Coal
   (*c*) Fossil fuels (*d*) Fuel wood
5. The characteristic/s of a community is/are :
   (*a*) diversity (*b*) periodicity
   (*c*) dominance (*d*) All of these
6. The criteria for the selection of species under *ex-situ* conservation is/are :
   (*a*) vulnerability of the species of extinction
   (*b*) ecological importance of the species
   (*c*) economic and aesthetic importance of the species
   (*d*) All of the above
7. The establishment of national parks and sanctuaries came under :
   (*a*) *in-situ* conservation of biodiversity
   (*b*) *ex-situ* conservation of biodiversity
   (*c*) Natural development Plan of Biodiversity
   (*d*) All of the above
8. Major pollutants of motor vehicular emission in India are :
   (*a*) Oxides of nitrogen and lead
   (*b*) Diesel particulates and carbon monoxide
   (*c*) Ozone and carbon dioxide, other toxics
   (*d*) All of the above
9. Exposure to UV radiations cause :
   (*a*) damage to eye sight
   (*b*) sun burn
   (*c*) cancer of skin
   (*d*) All of the above
10. Sewage water treatment that involves bacteria is called :
    (*a*) Primary treatment
    (*b*) Activated sludge treatment
    (*c*) Tertiary treatment
    (*d*) Cyclic treatment
11. Sewage water is purified for recycling by the action of :
    (*a*) Light
    (*b*) Micro-organisms
    (*c*) *Eichhornia* aquatic plants
    (*d*) Fishes
12. Most important causative pollutant in soil is :
    (*a*) Plastic (*b*) Glass junk
    (*c*) Iron Junk (*d*) Detergents
13. Green Petrol is :
    (*a*) Leaded petrol
    (*b*) Unleaded petrol
    (*c*) Gasohol
    (*d*) Low sulphur Diesel
14. Photochemical smog related to air pollution is related to :
    (*a*) oxides of sulphur
    (*b*) oxides of nitrogen
    (*c*) oxides of oxygen
    (*d*) oxides of carbon
15. Which is the major source of harmful radiations in the house?
    (*a*) Tubelight (*b*) Colour TV
    (*c*) Oven (*d*) Heater
16. Newsprint making tree of India is :
    (*a*) *Boswellia* (Salai)
    (*b*) *Eucalyptus*
    (*c*) *Diospyros* (Tendu)
    (*d*) *Abies* (Fir)

17. Poor man's Timber is :
(*a*) Pines (*b*) Bamboos
(*c*) Firs (*d*) Junipers

18. Which is the largest bird ever known that is extinct now?
(*a*) Great Indian Bustard
(*b*) California Condor
(*c*) Aephorins
(*d*) Cassowary

19. A pond/lake is :
(*a*) A biome
(*b*) A natural ecosystem
(*c*) An artificial ecosystem
(*d*) A community of plants and animals only

20. Primary consumers in detritus food chain are :
(*a*) Harbivores
(*b*) Bacteria, fungi etc.
(*c*) Insect larvae, nematodes
(*d*) All of the above

21. Detritus food chain in comparison to grazing food chain is :
(*a*) Generally longer
(*b*) Generally equal
(*c*) Generally shorter
(*d*) None of these

22. Putrefying organisms are :
(*a*) Producer organisms
(*b*) Reducer organisms
(*c*) Consumer organisms
(*d*) Parasitic organisms

23. The most important organisms for an ecosystem are :
(*a*) Herbivores (*b*) Carnivores
(*c*) Green plants (*d*) Protozoa

24. A peacock eats snakes which eat frogs. These eat hoppers which in turn thrive on leaves of the plants. The peacock is :
(*a*) Primary consumer
(*b*) Secondary consumer
(*c*) Decomposer
(*d*) Apex of the food pyramid

25. A food chain is :
(*a*) Group of organisms which eat the same type of food
(*b*) Animals eating the plants
(*c*) Series of plants/animals which are interrelated in the form of organism being eaten as food by the other
(*d*) None of these

26. A food chain consists of :
(*a*) Producers (*b*) Consumers
(*c*) Decomposers (*d*) Both (*a*) and (*b*)

27. Trophic levels in a food chain are formed by :
(*a*) Producers (*b*) Consumers
(*c*) Decomposers (*d*) All of these

28. A food chain always starts with :
(*a*) Photosynthesis (*b*) Respiration
(*c*) Nitrogen fixation (*d*) Decay

29. Primary consumers are :
(*a*) Green plants
(*b*) Herbivores
(*c*) Carnivores
(*d*) All of the above

30. Which of the food chain directly depends on solar radiations :
(*a*) Predator
(*b*) Grazing
(*c*) Detritus
(*d*) None of these

31. Producers in any grazing food chain :
(*a*) Feed the herbivores
(*b*) Feed the carnivores
(*c*) Clean the atmosphere
(*d*) Capture solar energy

32. Food web is constituted by :
(*a*) Various interlinked food chains in a community
(*b*) Relationship between animals and plants
(*c*) Relationship between organisms and their environment
(*d*) Relationship between animals, plants and microbes

33. The typical feature of tourism is that
(*a*) the tourist spot is neat, clean and attractive
(*b*) tourists have to pay lots of money to visit various tourist spots
(*c*) the tour operator helps its customers
(*d*) tourists have to be physically transported to tourist spots.

34. Which one of the following is not a part of the infrastructure of tourism?
(*a*) Natural spots
(*b*) Sarais
(*c*) Rope ways
(*d*) Government-owned factories

35. Which one of the following has emerged as a new tourist destination of South Asia during the last decade?
(*a*) Shimla (*b*) Ooty
(*c*) Mauritius (*d*) Barbados

36. In order to earn foreign exchange, a country should concentrate on
(*a*) exports
(*b*) international tourism operations imports
(*c*) imports
(*d*) Both (*a*) and (*b*)

37. Which one of the following is essentially needed by a domestic tourist?
(*a*) Medicines
(*b*) Foreign currency
(*c*) Local currency
(*d*) Passport

38. Educational tourism can be exemplified by the following
(*a*) The tourist starts studying in the Oxford university
(*b*) The tourist learns the art of making and serving tea in Japan
(*c*) The tourist applies for an educational visit at the university of California (Irvine).
(*d*) All of these

39. Which one of the following is a part of adventure tourism?
(*a*) Swimming
(*b*) Bowling
(*c*) Bungee Jumping
(*d*) Chess

40. A person who sits in the transit lounge of an airport and waits for a connecting flight, is a tourist.
(*a*) Yes
(*b*) No
(*c*) May be
(*d*) Cannot comment

41. The fresh water we use comes from—
(*a*) ground water
(*b*) surface water runoff
(*c*) sea water
(*d*) *(a)* and *(b)* only

42. The percentage of fresh water form of water on the earth is—
(*a*) 9% (*b*) 7%
(*c*) 5% (*d*) 3%

43. The precipitation reaching the ground distribute in different ways as—
1. evaporate & reach the atmosphere
2. infiltrate the soil
3. detained in catchment area
4. become a form of run-off

Select the correct answer from the codes —
(*a*) 1, 2 & 3
(*b*) 2, 3 & 4
(*c*) 1, 3 & 4
(*d*) All the four

44. The great ocean currents are set in motion by—
(*a*) rotation of moon
(*b*) rotation of sun
(*c*) dragging of wind over-vast areas of sea surface
(*d*) rise & cooling of air

45. The complexity of any food web depend upon—
(*a*) length of the food chain
(*b*) diversity of organisms in the system
(*c*) alternatives at different tropical levels
(*d*) All of the above

46. Most important work of teacher is
(*a*) to organize teaching work
(*b*) to deliver lecture in class
(*c*) to take care of children
(*d*) to evaluate the students

47. At primary level, it is better to teach in mother language because
(*a*) it develops self-confidence in children
(*b*) it makes learning easy
(*c*) it is helpful in intellectual development
(*d*) it helps children in learning in natural atmosphere

48. A teacher should be
(*a*) honest
(*b*) dilligent
(*c*) dutiful
(*d*) punctual

49. Environmental education should be taught in schools because
(*a*) it will affect environmental pollution
(*b*) it is important part of life
(*c*) it will provide job to teachers
(*d*) we cannot escape from environment

50. What is most important while writing on blackboard?
(*a*) Good writing
(*b*) Clarity in writing
(*c*) Writing in big letters
(*d*) Writing in small letters

51. It is advantage of giving home work that students
(*a*) remain busy at home
(*b*) study at home
(*c*) may be checked for their progress
(*d*) may develop habit of self study

52. Women are better teacher at primary level because
(*a*) they behave more patiently with children
(*b*) they are ready to work with low salary
(*c*) higher qualification is not needed in this profession
(*d*) they have less chances in other profession

53. A student comes late in your class. Then you will
(*a*) inform to parents

(*b*) punish him
(*c*) try to know the reason
(*d*) not pay attention there

54. A teacher has serious defect is he/she
(*a*) is physically handicapped
(*b*) belongs to low socio-economic status
(*c*) has weak personality
(*d*) has immature mental development

55. A Deepawali fair is being organized in your school. What would you like to do?
(*a*) Only to visit the fair
(*b*) To take part in function
(*c*) To take a shop to sell something
(*d*) To distribute free water to visitors

56. The purpose of basic education scheme is
(*a*) universalization of primary education
(*b*) to vocationalise the education
(*c*) to fulfill basic need of persons through education
(*d*) to make education compulsory for all

57. If a student does not pay any respect to you, then you will
(*a*) ignore him
(*b*) award less marks in examination
(*c*) talk to his/her parents
(*d*) rebuke him

58. To maintain interest among students in class, a teacher should
(*a*) use blackboard
(*b*) discuss
(*c*) tell stories
(*d*) ask question

59. To raise the standard of education, it is necessary
(*a*) to evaluate students continuously
(*b*) to give high salary to teachers
(*c*) to revise curriculum
(*d*) to make good school building

60. Why students should play games in school?
(*a*) It makes them physically strong
(*b*) It makes work easier for teachers
(*c*) It helps in passing time
(*d*) It develops co-operation and physical balance

61. What will you do in leisure time in school? You will
(*a*) take rest in teacher's room
(*b*) read magazines in library
(*c*) talk to clerks in office
(*d*) check home work of students

62. How the students should be motivated to get success in life?
(*a*) Selected study
(*b*) Incidental study
(*c*) Intensive study
(*d*) Learning by recitation

63. The experienced teachers do not require the detailed lesson plan of a topic because
(*a*) they can teach in a good manner without its help
(*b*) the number of curious students is very poor in the class
(*c*) when they commit some mistake, they do not face any challenge from their students
(*d*) they can equip themselves with brief outline as they gain specialisation in it through experience

64. The best method of checking student's homework is
(*a*) to assign it to intelligent students of the class
(*b*) to check the answers in the class in group manner
(*c*) to check them with the help of specimen answer
(*d*) to check by the teacher himself in a regular way

65. The priority to girls education should be given because
(*a*) the girls are more intelligent in comparison than the boys
(*b*) the girls are lesser in number than boys
(*c*) the girls were badly discriminated in favour of boys in the past
(*d*) only girls are capable of leading for social change

66. In recent years, there has been an increasing incidence of floods in Northern India because—
(*a*) there has been an increase in annual rainfall
(*b*) the rate of silting of dams has gone up
(*c*) there has been increased deforestation in the catchment areas
(*d*) increased areas of land is being self cultivated

67. Match the following —

Column A	Column B
1. Labour	A. physical & mental talents of people
2. Natural resources	B. plants, animals, water, air nutrients, etc.
3. Intermediate goods	C. tools, machinery, factory, buildings, etc.

Codes :

	1	2	3
(a)	A	B	C
(b)	C	B	A
(c)	B	C	A
(d)	B	A	C

68. The market value in current rupees or dollars of all goods and services, for final use, produced by an economy during a year is—
(a) Economic Growth (EG)
(b) Gross National Product (GNP)
(c) Gross State Economy (GSE)
(d) None of the above

69. The Earth capital is/are—
(a) Air, water & soil
(b) Wildlife, raw materials & minerals
(c) Energy resources & degradation
(d) All of the above

70. Which of the following is still a very important source of energy for millions of Indians living in villages?
(a) Oil (b) Coal
(c) Fossil fuels (d) Fuel wood

71. National Biodiversity Strategy and Action Plan (NBSAP) was established in—
(a) 1986 (b) 1988
(c) 1999 (d) 2004

72. Major health effects due to depletion of ozone layer is/are—
(a) increase in eye cataracts & mutation
(b) increase in skin cancer & melonema
(c) decrease in growth of ocean flora & fauna
(d) All of the above

73. Fluorosis can lead to—
(a) severe skeletal problems
(b) prevent dental caries
(c) stiffness & pain in joints
(d) (a) & (c) only

74. Goitre is an enlargement of—
(a) Pancreas (b) Thyroid gland
(c) Testes (d) Spleen

75. Disposal of flyash is carried out in—
(a) ash ponds (b) air tumbler
(c) thermal plants (d) None of these

76. Biotic community can be grouped into—
(a) producers (b) consumers
(c) decomposers (d) All of these

77. Organisms of an ecosystem are linked together in—
(a) food chains
(b) food webs
(c) biotic communities
(d) All of these

78. Ecology of individual species and its population including the effect of other organisms and environmental conditions on every stage of life cycle, is known as—
(a) Autoecology (b) Genecology
(c) Synecology (d) None of these

79. Which **one** of the following is a direct ecological factor?
(a) Light (b) Temperature
(c) Atmosphere (d) All of these

80. Plants requiring low calcium amount or found in acidic soil is—
(a) Calciphytes (b) Halophytes
(c) Oxylophytes (d) All of these

81. Types of forests found near equator are—
(a) Tropical rain forests
(b) Deciduous forests
(c) Grasslands
(d) Coniferous forests

82. When food is derived by killing the host, this sort of interaction is—
(a) Predation (b) Parasitism
(c) Antibiosis (d) None of these

83. The main source of CO in the atmosphere is—
(a) incomplete burning of automobile petrol
(b) conversion of limestone into cement
(c) decomposition of dead organic matter
(d) respiration & burning of fossil fuels

84. The precipitation reaching the ground distribute in different ways as—
1. evaporate and reach the atmosphere
2. infiltrate the soil
3. detained in catchment area
4. become a form of run-off

Select the correct answer from the codes :
(a) 1, 2 & 3
(b) 2, 3 & 4
(c) 1, 3 & 4
(d) All the four

85. The energy flows in an ecosystem is—
(a) cyclic
(b) unidirectional
(c) multidirectional
(d) square

86. Which of the following is **must** to sustain life on earth?
(a) Energy resources must be preserved
(b) Biodiversity must be reserved
(c) Only essential plant & animal species must be preserved
(d) None of the above

87. Colourless, odourless and non-corrosive air pollutants are—

(*a*) ozones
(*b*) sulphur dioxide
(*c*) carbon dioxide
(*d*) carbon monoxide

88. The concept of environments is based upon—
1. globalisation
2. environmental degradation
3. dimensions of totality of the environment

Of these
(*a*) 1, 2 are correct
(*b*) 1, 2 and 3 are correct
(*c*) only 2 is correct
(*d*) only 1 is correct

89. Which is *NOT* correctly matched?
(*a*) CNG → Compressed Natural Gas
(*b*) GDP → Gross Domestic Product
(*c*) GNP → Gross National Product
(*d*) LPG → Local Petroleum Gas

90. Which of the following cause damage to blood?
(*a*) Iron (*b*) Lead
(*c*) Calcium (*d*) Arsenic

91. Why the ozone is necessary?
(*a*) It acts as a shield that absorbs biologically dangerous UV-radiation
(*b*) It acts as a chemical reactant
(*c*) It is easily combined with CFCs
(*d*) All of the above

92. All the following contribute to pollution *except*
(*a*) Thermal power plant
(*b*) Automobiles
(*c*) Hydroelectric power plant
(*d*) Nuclear power plant

93. In a food chain, herbivores are—
(*a*) primary consumers
(*b*) primary producers
(*c*) secondary consumers
(*d*) decomposers

94. BOD stands for—
(*a*) Biochemical Oxygen Demand
(*b*) Biotic Oxygen Dropping
(*c*) Biochemical Oxygen Dressing
(*d*) None of above

95. Fresh water needed for humans, animals, and plants is only provided by—
(*a*) rain
(*b*) oceans
(*c*) precipitation
(*d*) ground water

96. Water is most common and most important chemical compounds for living organisms as—
1. the life has been originated in the waters of oceans
2. it makes a large proportions of the animal tissues
3. it has valency of + 4 , + 3 etc.
(*a*) Only 1 & 2 are correct
(*b*) Only 2 is correct
(*c*) Only 3 is correct
(*d*) None of these

97. In particular, humans had been injecting enormous quantities of ozone - destroying substances into atmosphere, especially a class of chemical known as—
(*a*) Aerosol spray
(*b*) Chlorofluorocarbons
(*c*) Freons
(*d*) Radionuclides

98. Which statement is *TRUE*?
(*a*) Magneto-hydrodynamic generators convert solar radiation into electricity
(*b*) Coal can be converted to gaseous, liquid or low sulphur, low ash solid fuels
(*c*) Sunlight depend on photosensitive layer
(*d*) None of the above

99. The term 'ecosystem' was coined by—
(*a*) AG Tansley
(*b*) Paul Erlich
(*c*) Rachel Carsen
(*d*) DH Meadows

100. Lead is mainly comes from—
(*a*) Vehicular pollution
(*b*) Water pollution
(*c*) Increasing population
(*d*) All of the above

ANSWERS

1	2	3	4	5	6	7	8	9	10
(*d*)	(*b*)	(*d*)	(*d*)	(*d*)	(*d*)	(*a*)	(*d*)	(*d*)	(*b*)
11	**12**	**13**	**14**	**15**	**16**	**17**	**18**	**19**	**20**
(*b*)	(*d*)	(*b*)	(*b*)	(*a*)	(*a*)	(*b*)	(*c*)	(*b*)	(*b*)
21	**22**	**23**	**24**	**25**	**26**	**27**	**28**	**29**	**30**
(*c*)	(*b*)	(*c*)	(*d*)	(*c*)	(*d*)	(*d*)	(*a*)	(*b*)	(*b*)

31	32	33	34	35	36	37	38	39	40
(d)	*(a)*	*(d)*	*(d)*	*(c)*	*(d)*	*(c)*	*(b)*	*(c)*	*(b)*
41	**42**	**43**	**44**	**45**	**46**	**47**	**48**	**49**	**50**
(d)	*(d)*	*(c)*	*(c)*	*(a)*	*(a)*	*(d)*	*(c)*	*(b)*	*(a)*
51	**52**	**53**	**54**	**55**	**56**	**57**	**58**	**59**	**60**
(d)	*(a)*	*(c)*	*(d)*	*(b)*	*(c)*	*(a)*	*(d)*	*(a)*	*(d)*
61	**62**	**63**	**64**	**65**	**66**	**67**	**68**	**69**	**70**
(d)	*(c)*	*(d)*	*(d)*	*(d)*	*(c)*	*(a)*	*(b)*	*(d)*	*(d)*
71	**72**	**73**	**74**	**75**	**76**	**77**	**78**	**79**	**80**
(d)	*(d)*	*(b)*	*(b)*	*(a)*	*(b)*	*(a)*	*(a)*	*(b)*	*(c)*
81	**82**	**83**	**84**	**85**	**86**	**87**	**88**	**89**	**90**
(a)	*(a)*	*(b)*	*(d)*	*(c)*	*(d)*	*(b)*	*(a)*	*(d)*	*(d)*
91	**92**	**93**	**94**	**95**	**96**	**97**	**98**	**99**	**100**
(a)	*(c)*	*(a)*	*(a)*	*(a)*	*(a)*	*(b)*	*(b)*	*(a)*	*(a)*

English

COMPREHENSION

INTRODUCTION

Reading Comprehension determines the ability of an examinee to grapple with abstract thoughts hidden in the text. It also judges his ability to draw conclusions from the given set of information that is in the form of running text. This test can be solved by reading the given paragraph and answering the questions that are given below it. Answers may be given either by ticking the right choices in the question paper or filling the relevant boxes (showing options) in the answer sheet with pencil. The passage can vary in length; it could be as small as a paragraph of 50 words or, it could be a type of small essay of nearly 500 words, conveniently divided into some paragraphs. Single paragrpahs are also given in many a test. The topic of the paragraph generally deals with abstract subjects whereas figures or tables are generally avoided.

Reading Comprehension is an art. Our readers will do well to answer this test by:

(*a*) developing a broad frame of reference;

(*b*) reading as many passages as is possible and answer questions given below them;

(*c*) developing the reading habit and imbibing the "flow of English language" throughly to understand its style and grammatic intricacies.

While treating the test from an artistic viewpoint, readers will have to develop the sense of making logical conclusions. These conclusions must be based on the text given in the passage; they cannot imagine phenomenon, conclusions or facts. They have to limit their imagination and the power to comprehend the abstract points (the "fine things" stated in the topic) to the passage only.

Reading Comprehension is a science too. In order to solve this test in a scientific manner, readers will have to proceed according to the following steps:

(1) Read the passage at fast pace.

(2) Now, read the passage again at slow pace and also underline important points.

(3) Read those words carefully that are in bold face letters. Try to connect them to the lines in which, they have been carefully embeded.

(4) Now, read the first question given below the passage. If you know the answer fully well, tick the relevant option in the answer sheet.

(5) Now, go to next question and answer it. Proceed in a similar manner and answer all the questions.

(6) If you find a question to be too difficult to answer, skip it and go to the next question. In the end, you can read the passage (only in parts) and answer these question that were left by you.

(7) If the examination has a system of negative marking, do not answer the difficult questions through guess- work or your imagination. It is better not to answer those questions if negative marks are likely to be earned by you by answering them.

(8) Many passages have tests of antonyms and synonyms appended in the end of their questions. Do not imagine the antonym or synonym of the given word or the bold-faced word of the passage. Instead, link that word to the line in which, it is embedded. Try to find out what the author is saying in that line. Now, answer the question (antonym or synonym) keeping in mind the "true spirit" of the word in its sentence.

(9) In many tests, you may be asked to give a suitable title to the passage. Scan through the passage quickly and read the underlined

phrases carefully. Give such a title to the passage as would encompass all the vital points of the passage. Do not go beyond the "real essence" of the given passage. Do not use difficult words in the title decided by you.

As an artist, you have to comprehend the fine aspects of the text that you will read. As a logician, you will be required to deduct and conclude.

Practice will make you perfect.

PASSAGE–1

Indians have a long history of travelling, trading and establishing settlements abroad. Buddhist pilgrims and missionaries penetrated most of Central and East Asia. Several Hindu dynasties ruled parts of Indonesia and South East Asia, and Hindu businessmen established themselves in Afghanistan and parts of Central Asia. Indian contacts with East Africa were among the oldest and the closest. According to one Arab tradition Aristotle advised Alexander the Great to establish a Greek colony on the island of Sokorta off north eastern Africa. The enthusiastic Greeks subdued the Indians who were established there, took possession of Sokorta and removed a colossal idol to which Indians paid homage. As the famous *Periplus of the Erythraean Sea* makes clear, Indian traders continued to visit trading centres along the East African coast well into the first century A.D. Chinese blue-and-white porcelain that found its way to East African during the mediaeval period owed its origin largely to Gujarati ships. Gujarati commercial establishments existed in Africa from the thirteenth century onwards, and Gujarati businessmen, many of them Muslims, acted as bankers. money changers and money-lenders. Their business acumen endeared them to the Arabs who had acquired a hold over the coastal areas of East Africa and who offered them protection and commercial immunity in return for finance and successful economic management. Indian merchants, mainly Muslims, also financed some of the Arab slave traders. By 1860 they are said to have controlled almost the whole of Zanzibari trade. Indian traders married or had liaisons with African women, and their offsprings were to be found not only on the East African coast where they were called 'Chotara', but also in the coastal regions of Gujarat where their racially mixed features earned them the name of 'habsi' or habsi-like' people.

1. Buddhist pilgrims went to different parts of Asia
   A. to remove the Hindu rulers
   B. to establish colonies
   C. to propagate Buddhism
   D. to enhance Indian commercial interests
2. In the long past Indians travelled
   A. for trade and commerce
   B. for labour
   C. for missionary activities
   D. A and C
3. The interest of the Hindus in Indonesia, South East and Central Asia was
   A. religious
   B. commercial
   C. political
   D. both political and commercial
4. Gujarati ships sailed to East Africa as early as
   A. prehistoric period
   B. mediaeval period
   C. modern period
   D. none of these
5. India's relations with East Africa date back to
   A. the Pre-Christian era
   B. the third century A.D.
   C. the thirteenth century A.D.
   D. the eighteenth century A.D.
6. Most of the Gujarati businessmen in Africa in the thirteenth century were
   A. Muslim businessmen
   B. Hindu businessmen
   C. Buddhist missionaries
   D. Hindu and Muslim money-lenders
7. The Indian merchants in Afrcia
   A. discouraged slave trade
   B. encouraged slave trade
   C. financed slave trade
   D. kept themselves away from slave trade
8. 'Chotara' are
   A. offsprings of the immigrants
   B. offsprings of the local people
   C. offsprings of the local people and the Arabs
   D. offsprings of the local people and the immigrants
9. The Indian immigrants were endeared to the Arabs because of their
   A. liberal view of life
   B. strong religious sentiment
   C. wealth
   D. business acumen
10. The Gujarati traders in Africa were offered protection by
    A. the Africans
    B. the local businessmen
    C. the rulers
    D. the Arabs

PASSAGE–2

The happy man is the man who lives objectively, who has free affections and wide interests, who secures his happiness through these interests and affections and through the fact that they, in turn, make him an object of interest and affection to many others. To be the recipient of affection is a potent cause of happiness, but the man who demands affection is not the man upon whom it is bestowed. The man who receives affection is, speaking broadly, the man who gives it. But it is useless to attempt to give it as a calculation, in the way in which one might lend money at interest, for a calculated affection is not genuine and is not felt to be so by the recipient.

What then can a man do who is unhappy because he is encased in self? So long as he continues to think about the causes of his unhappiness, he continues to be self-centred and therefore does not get outside the vicious circle, if he is to get outside it, it must be genuine interests, not by simulated interests adopted merely as a medicine. Although this difficulty is real, there is nevertheless much that he can do if he has rightly diagnosed his trouble. If, for example, his trouble is due to a sense of sin, conscious or unconscious, he can first persuade his conscious mind that he has no reason to feel sinful and then proceed, to plant his rational conviction in his unconscious mind, concerning himself meanwhile with some more or less neutral activity. If he succeeds in dispelling the sense of sin, it is possible that genuine objective interests will arise spontaneously. If his trouble is self pity, he can deal with it in the same manner after first persuading himself that there is nothing extraordinarily unfortunate in his circumstances.

If fear is his trouble, let him practice exercises designed to give courage. Courage has been recognised from time immemorial as an important virtue, and a great part of training of boys and young men has been devoted to producing a type of character capable of fearlessless in battle. But moral courage and intellectual courage have been much less studied, they also, however, have their technique. Admit to yourself everyday atleast one painful truth, you will find this quite useful. Teach yourself to feel that life still be worth living even if you were not, as of course you are, immeasurably superior to all your friends in virtue and in intelligence. Exercises of this sort prolonged through several years will at last enable you to admit facts without flinching and will, in so doing, free you from the empire of fear over a very large field.

1. Who according to the passage is the happy man?
   A. who is encased in self
   B. who has free affection and wide interests
   C. who is free from wordly passions
   D. who has externally centre passions
   E. None of these

2. According to the passage, calculated affection
   A. appears to be false and fabricated
   B. makes other person to love you
   C. turns into permanent affection over a period of time
   D. leads to self-pity
   E. gives a feeling of courage

3. Which of the following virtues, according to the passage, has been recognised for long as an important virtue?
   A. Patriotism B. Sacrifice
   C. Courage D. Self-consciousness
   E. None of these

4. Which of the following, according to the passage, has not been studied much?
   A. Feeling of guilt and self-pity
   B. The state of mind of an unhappy man
   C. How to get absorbed in other interests
   D. Moral and intellectual courage
   E. None of these

5. If a man is suffering from a sense of sin
   A. he should invite opinion of others
   B. he should admit his sin at once
   C. he should consciously realize that he has no reason to feel sinful
   D. he should develop a fearless character
   E. he should develop an internal locus of control

6. What happens to a man who demands affection?
   A. His feelings are reciprocated by others
   B. He tends to take a calculated risk
   C. He becomes a victim of a viscious circle
   D. He takes affection for granted from others
   E. None of these

7. What should a man do who is suffering from the feeling of self-pity?
   A. He should control his passions and emotions
   B. He should persuade himself that everything is alright in his circumstances
   C. He should seek affection from others
   D. He should develop a feeling of fearlessness
   E. He should consult an expert to diagnose his trouble

8. How to get out of the viscious circle mentioned in the passage?
   A. By practicing skills of concentration
   B. By inculcating the habits of self-absorption
   C. Being true to others and one's internal circumstances
   D. Admitting to oneself that others could be right.
   E. None of these

9. Which of the following statements is not true in the context of the passage?
   A. Happy man has wide interests

B. Courage has been recognized as an important virtue
C. Unhappy man is encased in self
D. A man who suffers from the sense of sin must tell himself that he has no reason to be sinful
E. Issue of intellectual courage has been extensively studied

10. Which of the following words is SIMILAR in meaning of the word 'bestowed' as used in the passage?
A. Conferred B. Accommodated
C. Trusted D. Withdrawn
E. Directed

11. Which of the following statements is true in the context of the passage?
A. All passions stem from unhappiness
B. The happy man lives in subjectively
C. Any virtue has a dark side also
D. One feels happy if one receives affection
E. Any affection is always genuine

12. Which of the following words is SIMILAR in meaning to the word 'flinching' as used in the passage?
A. Wincing B. Convincing
C. Explaining D. Providing
E. Debating.

13. What happens when you think about cause of your unhappiness?
A. You try to introspect and look critically at yourself
B. You realize that the life can be lived in different ways
C. You try to practice exercise designed to give courage
D. You remain a self-centred person
E. None of these

14. What according to the passage is the real cause of happiness?
A. Material rewards and incentives received
B. Critical analysis of the happy state of mind
C. Affection received from others
D. Calculated risks taken
E. None of these

15. Which of the following words is OPPOSITE in meaning of the word 'dispelling' as used in the passage?
A. Giving B. Accumulating
C. Projecting D. Scattering
E. Receiving

PASSAGE–3

The Constitution of India ensured woman an equal position with man in regard to her rights and responsibilities; inheritance and other laws were enacted to safeguard her and to give her economic and psychological stability. We see how fragile legislation can be when it is not backed by **sturdy** and passionate human beings who ensure that legislation is translated into action.

In the last few years we find an erosion of woman's position not only in India but all over the world. There is a growing materialism and an increasing fundamentalism which seeks to **entangle** woman through an emphasis on tradition, heritage, custom, the Shastras, religious texts and so push her back centuries, through a man-made social code that limits woman's initiative, creativity and **growth**.

With the explosion in technology, in computer literacy and an increasing search for extending areas of artificial intelligence, new challenges have appeared on the horizon. Labour based on the male physique which dominated employment and defined a woman's role for centuries is being replaced by skill and intelligence-oriented systems for creating wealth. It is possible in the coming decades to erase **discrimination** based on gender; but in India to introduce such systems that render the human beings less and less important in the production processes, when seen against a scenario of exploding populations, of growing unemployment, can only accentuate tension and conflict. As of today no social, economic and psychological solutions to the problem of employment are available. Reservations for women remain valid on paper. The woman remains a victim.

Economic freedom and the independence that arises from it is essential for women. We have to ensure through field studies, through education, through right use of franchise, through an **observing** eye and ear to **unravel** this knot of employement for women. This is only possible with a right use of technology and the examination and strengthening of existing technologies.

A growing fundamentalism is evident in the horrors that have been perpetrated on woman. We are aware how through TV, radio, advertising, magazines, visual and language traps are set up in which woman inevitably falls. This is further accentuated through an educational system, through outdated values and through a close-box culture which binds woman to her man-made role as daughter, wife and mother, so that she exists only in relation to man. In our culture the woman has no independent existence.

Can we create a new agenda for woman based on skill, creativity, knowledge, austerity, compassion and responsibility?

1. Why could legislation not give women their due share?
A. Because legislation has remained merely on paper

B. Men have resisted legislation in a vehement way
C. Women's position has deteriorated all over the world
D. Women have been denied economic opportunities
E. None of these

2. Why does the Constitution give equal position to woman with man?
A. To enable her to carry out her domestic responsibilities in a better way
B. To help her enjoy more rights over ancestral property
C. To make her monetarily independent and psychologically stable
D. To maintain the dominance of males as per the social demand
E. None of these

3. Why has women's status been worsening these days?
A. There is more emphasis on superficial aspects of life
B. The social codes have always remained gender-biased
C. Society expects women not to do what they did centuries ago
D. Women have been unwilling to do anything creative
E. The religious texts recommend that women should remain merely home-makers

4. How does growing unemployment in India come in the way of upliftment of women?
A. There are no solutions to the socio-psychological problems of unemployment
B. There are no special reservations for women
C. It makes the use of modern techniques which are gender-biased
D. Human beings have become less important in the present industrial world
E. None of these

5. What is one of the ways of attaining self-sufficiency for women according to the passage?
A. Gaining respect in the eyes of men
B. Being financially independent
C. Learning new skills
D. Doing some productive work at home
E. Getting higher education

6. Why do women have no independent existence in our country?
A. We have an obsolete educational system
B. The mass media project her in the wrong light
C. Men are bent on exploiting women for their benefit
D. She has to play the roles men assign to her
E. None of these

7. Which of the following is the result of technological explosion?
A. The Act of Indian Constitution to give equal status to women
B. Growing fundamentalism and its undesirable results
C. Physical activities can now be replaced by skill and intelligence-oriented systems
D. Outdated educational system and its implementation
E. None of these

8. What was the basis of differentiation between the male and female roles?
A. Intellectual superiority of males
B. Skills that men possessed and women did not
C. Technological innovations
D. Superior physical attributes of males
E. None fo these

9 . Which of the following statements is **NOT TRUE** with reference to the above passage?
A. Gender inequality should be eliminated
B. Legally men and women have equal rights
C. The present educational system needs to be revamped
D. The importance of physical strength in comparison to intellectual power has decreased
E. Tackling the social, economic and psychological problems of unemployment, is very easy

Directions (Qs. 10 to 12): *Which of the following is most nearly the SAME in meaning as the word given in bold as used in the passage?*

10. **Growth**
A. increase B. development
C. enlargement D. expansion
E. cultivation

11. **Observing**
A. looking B. watching
C. adhering D. examine
E. critical

12. **Sturdy**
A. bold B. vigorous
C. spontaneous D. stout
E. rugged

Directions (Qs. 13 to 15): *Which of the following is the most* ***OPPOSITE*** *in meaning of the word given in* ***bold*** *as used in the passage.*

13. **Discrimination**
A. equality B. incrimination
C. partiality D. justice
E. honour

14. **Entangle**
A. arrest B. wrap

ENGLISH

C. free D. relief
E. escape

15. Unravel

A. real B. fictitious
C. lose D. solve
E. tighten

PASSAGE–4

For years now, George W. Bush has told Americans that he would increase the number of troops in Iraq only if the commanders on the ground asked him to do so. It was not a throwaway line : Bush said it from the very first days of the war, when he and Pentagon boss Donald Rumsfeld were criticized for going to war with too few troops. He said it right up until last summer, stressing at a news conference in Chicago that Iraq commander General George Casey "Will make the decisions as to how many troops we have there." Seasoned military people suspected that the line was a dodge—that the civilians who ran the Pentagon were testing their personal theory that war can be fought on the cheap and the brass simply knew better than to ask for more. In any case, the president repeated the mantra to dismiss any suggestion that the war was going badly. Who, after all, knew better than the generals on the ground?

Now, as the war nears the end of its fourth year and the number of Americans killed has surpassed 3,000, Bush has dropped the generals-know-best line. Sometime next week the President is expected to propose a surge in the number of U.S. forces in Iraq for a period of upto two years. A senior official said reinforcements numbering "About 20,000 troops," and may be more, could be in place within months. The **surge** would be achieved by extending the stay of some forces already in Iraq and accelerating the deployment of others.

The **irony** is that while the generals would have liked more troops in the past, they are **cool** to the idea of sending more now. That's in part because the politicians and commanders have had trouble agreeing on what the goal of a surge would be. But it is also because they are worried that a surge would further erode the readiness of the U.S.'s already stressed ground forces. And even those who back a surge are under no **illusions** about what it would mean to the casualty rate. "If you put more American troops on the front line," said a White House official, "You're going to have more casualties."

Coming from Bush, a man known for bold strokes, the surge is a strange half-measure—too large for the political climate at home, too small to crush the **insurgency** in Iraq and surely three years too late. Bush has waved off a bipartisan rescue mission out of pride, **stubbornness** or ideology, or some combination of the three. Rather than reversing course, as all the wise elders of the Iraq Study Group advised, the Commander in Chief is betting that more troops will lead the way to what one White House official calls "Victory."

1. Bush and Rumsfeld had received brickbats for—

A. waging a war against Iraq
B. testing their personal theories
C. their assertion in the news conference in Chicago
D. turning down the demands of General George Casey
E. None of these

2. George Bush gave an impression to his subjects that his army commanders were given the autonomy to decide—

A. when to start or stop the war in Iraq
B. the reasonable requirement of American troops to fight the war in Iraq
C. how many troops should Iraq use to fight against the Americans
D. the Pentagon policies regarding war in Iraq
E. None of these

3. From the content of the passage, which of the following can be definitely inferred?

1. The U.S. troops in Iraq are happy with their victory
2. The troops already fighting the war in Iraq are sufficient enough to combat the situation effectively.
3. The generals who were earlier not in favour of increasing troops in Iraq are now insisting on surge.

A. (1) and (2) only B. (2) and (3) only
C. (1) and (3) only D. None
E. All the three

4. Which of the following best describes Bush's persistent reaction to the observations that the Iraq war strategy was not effective due to inadequate American forces?

A. Such strategies are better left to Army Commanders to decide on the ground
B. Civilians are the best assessors of such strategies
C. Wars can be fought on the cheap
D. The brass knew better of war but not of politics
E. None of these

5. The author of the passage appears to be

A. in favour of enhancement of American troops in Iraq
B. critical about Bush's strategy of handling situation in Iraq
C. an impartial assessor of the US strategy related to the situation in Iraq

D. an indifferent onlooker of what is happening in Iraq

E. inclined to the idea of withdrawal of American troops to save casualty

6. Which of the following is the assessment of the Commander-in-Chief of U.S. forces in Iraq on the present situation there?

A. America's desired goal will be achieved if more troops are deployed in Iraq

B. Withdrawal of troops from Iraq is essential to raise the morale of the U.S. Army

C. Further strengthening of U.S. army in Iraq will be suicidal as it means more destruction of U.S. forces

D. Pentagon's civilians should not have been allowed to interfere with the army commanders' strategies

E. None of these

7. Which of the following strategies would achieve the desired increase in American forces in Iraq?

1. Continuation of stay of troops for a further period.
2. Expeditious deployment of additional troops
3. Seeking additional input from politicians and commanders of neighbouring friendly countries

A. (1) and (2) only B. (3) only
C. (2) only D. (1) and (2) only
E. None of these

8. Why do the army commanders disfavour enhancement of troops now?

1. More force means more casualties
2. Difference of opinion between politicians and commanders about the aim of the troop enhancement
3. Probable adverse psychological impact on ground forces

A. Only (1) and (2) B. Only (2) and (3)
C. All the three D. Only (1) and (3
E. None of these

9. Which of the following made Bush change his thinking about the requirement of forces in Iraq?

1. The unreasonably long period for which the war continued
2. The large number of American soldiers killed in the war
3. Demand from the Army Commanders

A. Only (1) and (3) B. Only (1) and (2)
C. Only (2) and (3) D. All the three
E. Only (3)

Directions (10 – 12) : Which of the following most OPPOSITE in meaning of the word given in **bold** as used in the passage ?

10. Cool

A. Warm B. Enthusiastic
C. Unwelcome D. Intemperate
E. Indifferent

11. Surge

A. Enhancement B. Trivializing
C. Reduction D. Strengthening
E. Upgradation

12. Stubbornness

A. Uncertainty B. Weakness
C. Acceptability D. Infirmity
E. Flexibility

Directions (13 – 15) : Which of the following is most nearly the **SAME** in meaning as the word given in **bold** as used in the passage ?

13. Illusion

A. Reality B. Reflection
C. Fantastic D. Delusion
E. Deviation

14. Insurgency

A. Rebellion B. Ingredient
C. Combat D. Debacle
E. Violation

15. Irony

A. Levelling B. Precaution
C. Controversy D. Mockery
E. Perception

PASSAGE–5

It all started twenty-five years ago. I was teaching Economics at a university in Bangladesh. The country was in the middle of a famine. I felt terrible. Here I was, teaching the **elegant** theories of Economics in the classroom with all the **enthusiasm** of a brand-new Ph.D. from the United States. But I would walk out of the classroom and see skeletons all around me, people waiting to die.

I felt that whatever I had learned, whatever I was teaching, was all make-believe stories, with no meaning for people's lives. So I started trying to find out how people lived in the village next door to the university campus. I wanted to find out whether there was anything I could do as a human being to delay or stop the death, even for one single person. I **abandoned** the bird's-eye view that lets you see everything from above, from the sky. I assumed a worm's-eye view, trying to find whatever comes right in front of you-smell it, touch it, see if you can do something about it.

One particular incident took me in a new direction. I met a woman who was making bamboo stools. After a long discussion, I found out that she made only two U.S. pennies each day. I couldn't believe anybody could work so hard and make such beautiful bamboo stools yet make such a tiny amount of profit. She explained to me that because she didn't have the money to buy the bamboo to make the stools, she had to borrow from the trader-and the trader imposed the condition that she had to sell the product to him alone, at a price that he decided.

And that explains the two pennies—she was virtually in bonded labour to this person. And how much did the bamboo cost? She said, "Oh, about twenty cents. For a very good one twenty-five cents." I thought, "People suffer for twenty cents and there is nothing anyone can do about it?" I debated whether I should give her twenty cents, but then I came up with another idea—let me make a list of people who needed that kind of money. I took a student of mine and we went around the village for several days and came up with a list of forty-two such people. When I added up the total amount they needed, I got the biggest shock of my life : It added up to twenty-seven dollars! I felt ashamed of myself for being part of a society which could not provide even twenty-seven dollars to forty-two hard-working, skilled human beings.

To escape that shame, I took the money out of my pocket and gave it to my student. I said, "You take this money and give it to those forty-two people that we met and tell them this is a loan, but they can pay me back whenever they are able to. In the meantime, they can get a good price. After receiving the money, they were very excited.

1. Which of the following can be inferred about the author?
A. He studied in Bangladesh
B. He also belonged to a poor family
C. His Ph.D. was on poverty in Bangladesh
D. His Ph.D. was in Economics
E. He started teaching in Bangladesh 25 years after getting his Ph.D. from the United States

2. The author of the passage seems to have–
A. inspired several people through his lecture to make a living
B. transformed himself into an action-oriented person to eradicate poverty
C. continued his teachings excellently and with a lot of enthusiasm
D. helped his students in their endeavour to eradicate poverty
E. contributed money for the needy

3. Which of the following is **most opposite** of the word **"Elegant"** as used in the passage?
A. Irrelevant B. Diluted
C. Crude D. Ill proportioned
E. Ignoble

4. The contents of the passage prove that poverty can be alleviated if ....
1. there is a strong will to do so.
2. some funds and/or other resources are available.
3. there is a vision to identify and remedy the problems
A. Only (1) and (2) B. Only (2) and (3)
C. Only (1) and (3) D. All the three
E. None of these

5. The woman described in the passage could not earn reasonably good money because ....
A. the quality of the goods she made was short of excellence
B. the sale of her products was very scanty
C. the raw material required to make finished products was in short supply
D. there were very few buyers for her goods due to the devastating famine
E. None of these

6. The trader's act to compel the woman to sell the stools only to him can be termed as...........
A. an act of kindness towards the needy woman
B. an ethical business strategy to maximize profit
C. sheer exploitation of the hopeless and needy people
D. contributing some help to the famine-stricken victims
E. None of these

7. What made the author feel ashamed of himself?
A. He lacked in thorough knowledge of Economics and therefore wanted to study more
B. He was ignorant of the fact that even a small help was also going to be significant
C. He was a party to the exploitation of the poor by the trader
D. He was not in a position to take the culprit trader to task
E. He was providing a small amount as a loan and not as donation

8. The survey conducted by the author revealed that............
A. the amount needed to help the village poor to make a living was not very big'
B. it was an unmanageable task for the author to help the needy people of the village
C. there were forty-two traders who were engaged in the act of exploitation of the poor
D. the number of the needy people in the village was very large
E. none of these

Directions (9-10) : *Choose the word/group of words which is most nearly the* ***SAME*** *in meaning as the word given in bold as given in passage.*

9. Abandoned
A. Gave up B. Escaped from

C. Accepted D. Took away
E. Enabled

10. Enthusiasm
A. Excellence B. Happiness
C. Force D. Effervescence
E. Zeal

PASSAGE–6

Comfort is now one of the causes of its own spread. It has now become a physical habit, a fashion, an ideal to be pursued for its own sake. The more comfort is brought into the world, the more it is likely to be valued. To those who have known comfort, discomfort is a real torture. The fashion which now **decrees** the worship of comfort is quite as imperious as any other fashion. Moreover, enormous material interests are bound up with the supply of the means of comfort. The manufacturers of furniture, of heating apparatus, of plumbing fistures cannot afford to let the love of comfort die. In modern advertisements they have found a means for compelling it to live and grow. A man of means today, who builds a house is in general concerned primarily with the comfort of his future residence. He will spend a great deal of money on bathrooms, heating apparatus, padded furnishings, and having spent he will regard his house as perfect. His counterpart in an earlier age would have been primarily concerned with the impressiveness and magnificence of his dwelling—with beauty, in a word, rather than comfort. The money our contemporary would spend on baths and central heatings would have been spent on marble staircases, frescoes, pictures and statues. I am inclined to think that our present passion for comfort is a little exaggerated. Though I personally enjoy comfort, I have lived most happily in houses **devoid of** everything that Anglo-Saxons deem **indispensable**. Orientals and even South Europeans who know not comfort and live very much as our ancestors did centuries ago seem to go on very well without our elaborate apparatus and padded lusuries. However, comfort for me has a justification; it facilitates mental life. Discomfort handicaps thought; it is difficult to use the mind when the body is cold and aching.

1. Choose the word that is **SIMILAR** in meaning of the word **'devoid of'** as used in the passage.
A. available B. lacking
C. empty D. false
E. deficient

2. How people manage to keep the love of comfort alive?
A. By pumping in more comfort goods in the market
B. By sacrificing high profits on comfort goods
C. By targeting youth in the sales campaign
D. By appealing to the emotionality of people
E. None of these

3. What is the author's prediction about comfort?
A. The value of comfort will increase
B. People will value more spirituality thus reducing the value of comfort
C. People will desire simple life style
D. The advertisements will play down the comfort aspect of goods
E. None of these

4. What was the characteristic of affluent man of an **earlier age**?
A. He used to put higher premium on comfort
B. He was relying much on advertisements
C. He believed more in simple and cheaper things
D. He was more qualitative in his emphasis rather than being quantative
E. His emphasis was on beauty

5. What change according to the author has taken place in the attitude to comfort?
A. It is taken for granted in the modern way of living
B. It has become now an ideal to be pursued for its own sake
C. It is now believed that discomfort handicaps thought
D. It is thought that comfort helps body and mind to function effectively
E. None of these

6. Choose the word which is **SIMILAR** in meaning of the word **'decree'** as used in the passage.
A. order B. spread
C. projected D. attract
E. exhibit

7. Why does the author value comfort?
A. It helps to project one's image
B. It helps to project your values
C. It facilitates mental life
D. It encourages a blend of materialistic and spiritual thinking
E. None of these

8. Why would manufacturers of various devices not permit comfort to die?
A. The want to manufacture more and more comfort goods
B. Manufacturers are mainly interested in creating new things
C. Manufacturer's emphasis is on producing beautiful things
D. Their prosperity is closely linked with the people's desire for comfort
E. None of these

9. Choose the word which is **MOST OPPOSITE** in meaning of the word **'Indispensable'** as used in the passage.

A. unattractive B. avoidable
C. favourable D. inelegant
E. comfortable

10. Which of the following statements is **NOT TRUE** in the context of the passage?
A. Discomfort is not liked by those who live in comfort
B. The affluent man of an earlier age was interested more in beauty than in comfort
C. Discomfort handicaps thought
D. Orientals and South Europeans love comfort immensely
E. Author of the passage enjoys comfort

PASSAGE–7

Amnesty International's charge that 'tens of thousands' of political prisoners, including prisoners of conscience, are **languishing** in Indian jails and that prisoners are routinely tortured in this country has to be seen in a much wider contest than the organisation's annual report cares to do. In its overall appraisal of 151 countries, Amnesty has accused 112 of torturing prisoners, 63 of harbouring prisoners of conscience, 61 of resorting to political killings and 53 of detaining people without a trial. Of these apparently **overlapping** categories, India seems to have been excluded from the list of the 61 which undertake political killings. The report has, however, pointed out that **scores** of people in India die for torture in police and military custody and that many also simply disappear. Clearly, only a thin line separates the 61 charged with political murder from the rest. Before coming to such conclusions, however, it may also be necessary to classify the various countries according to their political systems. Torture by the security forces and killings at the behest of the government make no different to the victims whether they are in a democratic country or a totalitarian one. It is also nobody's case that a democratic country is less **culpable** than a dictatorship in the vent of human rights violations. But the point perhaps still needs to be made that torture or 'disappearances' represent a failure of the system in a democracy in contrast to being an integral part of state policy in a country ruled by an autocrat who in answerable to no one.

India may be guilty of keeping 'tens of thousands' behind bars and of the other human rights abuses mentioned by Amnesty, but it still remains a qualitatively different place from a totalitarian country. It is in this respect that Amnesty has been less than fair. It has chosen to ignore the distinctions between the good, the bad and the ugly. The openness of Indian soceity will be evident to anyone who spends half an hour in one of its chaotic market-places or visits the law courts or watches a political rally or reads a newspaper or **strikes up** a conversation with any person on the roads. There is no sense of fear in India, as in a dictatorship. There is also scope for securing relief from the heavy-handed behaviour of the authorities, even if the human rights commission has not yet lived up to expectations. Unless such points are recognised, Amnesty's assessment will seem to be a dry recital of statistics which may **pillory** India simply because of its larger population. Mercifully, Amnesty nowadays at least notes that the terrorists also indulge in human rights violations and that India has to cope with several insurgencies **fomented** by a country where the military does not always seem to be under the control of the elected government. True, there is much that is wrong in India's prison system and with the way the terrorist challenge in sometimes meet, but the stress should be on activating the self-correcting mechanism within a democracy and not merely on painting a grim, even biased, picture.

1. The author suggests classification of various countries on one additional dimension. Which of the following is that dimension?
A. Economic progress
B. Industrial progress
C. Political systems
D. Human rights
E. None of these

2. According to the passage, through which media or forum Amnesty International has hurled the charges?
A. Its International Meet
B. Its Annual Report
C. Seminar on Human Rights
D. Its Regional Meet
E. None of these

3. The author of the passage
A. agrees with the report
B. disagrees with the report
C. disagrees that conditions of prisons in India is bad
D. supports the totalitarian approach
E. disagrees with report on terrorists

4. The Amnesty International report is based on the information of how many countries?
A. 112 B. 63
C. 131 D. 115
E. None of these

5. In the report, India has been excluded from which of the following categories of violating human rights?
A. Political killings
B. Torturing prisoners
C. Detaining without trial
D. Harbouring prisoners of conscience
E. None of these

6. According to the passage, what does political murder in a democratic country signify?
A. Policy of the country
B. Need for autocratic rule
C. Openness of society
D. Failure of system
E. Heavy-handed behaviour of the authorities

7. Which of the following seems to be the main purpose of writing this passage?
A. To highlight the role of Amnesty International
B. To further the cause of human rights
C. To highlight the sufferings of prisoners
D. To condemn political killings
E. None of these

8. Which of the following is *not* true in the context of the passage?
A. There is overlapping of cases in the categories of human rights abuses
B. India was one of the countries appraised by Amnesty International
C. India is guilty of some human rights abuses
D. Amnesty International appraised all the democratic countries
E. The report notes that the terrorists also violate human rights

9. Which of the following is the meaning of the phrase *strike up* as used in the passage?
A. discussion B. hit sharply
C. protest D. initiate
E. undertake

10. According to the author, among the good, the bad and the ugly, what at worst is the situation in India?
A. Good B. Bad
C. Ugly D. Good or Ugly
E. Bad of Ugly

11. Which of the following is *true,* according to the passage?
A. The Human Rights Commission has done commendable service
B. There is a need to check political killings in India
C. There is a need to improve India's prison system
D. India is not at all guilty of human rights violations
E. None of these

12. Which of the following human rights violation is most prevalent among the countries?
A. Torturing prisoners
B. Detaining without trial
C. Killing with political motive
D. Harbouring prisoners of conscience
E. None of these

PASSAGE–8

The most important reason for this state of affairs, perhaps, is that India was the only country in the world to truly recognise the achievements of the Soviet Union—rather than merely focus on the debilitating faults that Communism brought to its people. The people of India realised that the achievement of one hundred per cent literacy in a country much, much larger than its own and with similarly complicated ethnic and religious groupings, the rapid industrialisation of a nation that was a primarily agrarian society when the Bolshevik revolution took place in 1917, the attendant revolutionary steps in science and technology, the accessibility of health care (primeval according to Western standards, perhaps, but not according to Indian ones) to the general population, and despite prohibition of the government of the time the vast outpourings in literature, music, art, etc., are momentous and remarkable feats in any country.

In contrast, all that the West focussed on were the massive human rights violations by the Soviet State on its people, the deliberate uprooting and mass migrations of ethnic peoples from one part of the country to another in the name of industrialisation, the end of religion ..... in short, all the tools of information were employed to condemn the ideology of Communism, so much at variance with capitalist thinking.

The difference with the Indian perception, I think here is, that while the Indians reacted as negatively to what the Soviet governments did to its people in the name of good governance (witness the imprisonment of Boris Pasternak and the formation of an international committee to put pressure for his release with Jawaharlal Nehru at its head), they took the pain not to condemn the people of that broad country in black and white terms; they understood that mingled in the shades of grey were grains of uniqueness. (The Russians have never failed that characteristic in themselves; they have twice experimented with completely different ideologies, Communism and Capitalism both in the space of a century).

1. Which of the following statements according to the passage is correct ?
A. India took heed on the weak faults of Russian policies and system
B. India seriously commended the achievement of Russia, *i.e.,* cent per cent literacy and rapid industrialization
C. The process of industrialization had already started when Russian revolution took place in 1917
D. The literature, art and music received a

setback during the communist regime in Russia

2. The West did not focus on:
   A. rapid growth of nuclear weapons in Russia
   B. Massive human rights violation by the Soviet state on its people
   C. deliberate uprooting and mass migration of ethnic people in the name of industrialization.
   D. Both B and C
3. The India perception of the USSR was always
   A. negative
   B. neutral
   C. counter-reactionary
   D. applauding
4. The passage is
   A. descriptive B. paradoxical
   C. analytical D. thought provoking

PASSAGE–9

India's role on the international stage was moulded by history rather than by the pomp and circumstances of war. As a separate entity of the British empire, India became a founder member of the League of Nations in the same way as Australia and Canada, and thus acquired a somewhat unique international status long before independence. During the days of the League when India's interests were affected, such as in matters of trade or the position of Indians overseas, the Indian delegation did not hesitate to make known its independent position, for what it was worth. Some Indian delegates were in demand for chairing meetings riddled with contention and controversy, because of their reputation for impartiality and talent for mediation.

These were the small beginnings of India's later entry into the United Nations in 1945, again as a founder member before independence. The drafting of Chapter IX and X of the UN Charter, which deal with international social and economic cooperation, was entrusted to a group that was presided over by an Indian. It is important, however, to bear in mind that fact that the Government of independent India had no part in the drafting of the UN Charter, although in accepted the obligations contained therein. The UN was primarily the creation of three powers—The USA, UK and Russia.

The size, population, resources and potential of India lent it the weight of a medium power in the functioning of the United Nations. The fact that India was among the first nations to liberate itself from the imperialist domination through non-violent means endowed it with a moral obligation to work in and outside the UN for the independence of nations still under colonial rule. India has served on the Security Council for 10 years or 5 terms, on the Trusteeship Council for 12 years or 4 terms and on the Economic and Social Council for 21 years or 7 terms.

1. The title below that best expresses the ideas of the passage is:
   A. India's role at the United Nations
   B. India and Her Neighbours
   C. India's International Prestige
   D. British Colonial Expansion
2. Through a part of the British Empire, India enjoyed great prestige at the League in as much as Indian delegates were in demand for chairing meeting to consider controversial issues. It was because:
   (I) Indian delegates were well known for their impartiality.
   (II) Indian delegates had talent for mediation.
   (III) India was considered a power to reckon with.
   A. I and III are correct
   B. I and II are correct
   C. I and III are correct
   D. only I is correct
3. Which articles of the UN Charter deal with International, Social and Economic Co-operation ?
   A. Articles IX and X
   B. Articles XI and XII
   C. Articles VIII and XIII
   D. Articles VI and VII
4. Which of the following countries does not find any coverage in the passage ?
   A. The USA B. Britain
   C. The Russia D. Sri Lanka

PASSAGE–10

Some religious teachers have taught that Man is made up of a body and a soul: but they have been silent about the Intellect. Their followers try to feed the body on earth and to save soul from perdition after death : but they neglected the claims of the mind. Bread for the body and Virtue for the soul: these are regarded as the indispensable requisites of human welfare here and hereafter. Nothing is said about knowledge and education. Thus Jesus Christ spoke much of feeding the hungry, healing the sick, and converting the sinners: but he never taught the duty of teaching the ignorant and increasing scientific knowledge. He himself was not a well educated man, and intellectual pursuits were beyond his horizon. Gautam Buddha also laid stress on morality, meditation and asceticism, but he did not attach great importance to history, science, art or literature. St. Ambrose deprecated scientific studies and wrote, "To discuss the nature and position of the earth does not help us in our hope for life to come". St. Basil said very frankly and foolishly, "It is not a matter of interest for us whether the earth is a sphere or a cylinder or disc." Thomas Carlyle also followed the Christian traditions when he declared that he honoured only two men and no third: the manual labour and the religious teacher. He forgot the scientist, the scholar and the artist. The cynics of Greece despised education at last ?

1. What have the religious teachers taught in the past ?
A. That man is made up of body only
B. That man is made up of soul only
C. That man is made up of bubbles
D. That man is made up of body and soul together

2. What is food for the soul ?
A. Bread B. Virtue
C. Vice D. Education

3. The following philosophers occur in the passage. But they are not in correct order. Correct the order.
(I) Jesus Christ (II) Gautam Buddha
(III) St. Ambrose (IV) Thomas Carlyle
(V) St. Basil
A. I, II, III, IV, V B. I, III, IV, V, II
C. I, II, III, V, IV D. II, I, III, IV, V

4. Intellectual pursuits have been neglected because:
(I) they are unnecessary and superfluous
(II) they make people dwarf
(III) they lead people to hell
A. Only I is correct
B. Only II is correct
C. Only III is correct
D. Only I and II are correct

5. The style of the passage is
A. narrative B. expository
C. critical D. Analytical

PASSAGE–11

The impact of technical advancement in armaments on man, needs to be analyzed with a rational mind, and heart free from prejudices of any kind towards modernisation. The most noticeable impact of this development certainly has been the loss of immunity from violence for successive generations ever since the invention of gunpowder. In modern times, the presence of technically advanced arms, not only at the fronts but also among the civilian population, has vastly undermined the value of human life, and endangered the very entity of those virtues of self restraint and discretion, on which a peaceful and amiable society rests. However, an unbiased view of the present scenario, would refrain one from attributing the rising trends of violence to the availability of technically superior weapons, for one must not overlook the fact that "Necessity is the mother of invention".

Every stage in the development of armaments has been marked by its distinct impact on society. When man fought with stones and his bare hands, the society was not yet compact. The discovery of metal and the use of spears, knives and arrows indicate the stage of the formation of small kingdoms. Fire continued to be an effective weapon of destruction. When man introduced the cavalry into the army and improved the strategies of making war, some small kingdoms gave away to form empires, but with no revolutionary advances in armaments forthcoming, the political structure of society remained more or less stagnant for the many coming centuries.

The next significant development was the use of gunpowder, which could be used to perform acts which were then thought to be impossible. Gunpowder was used to form the ammunition of several guns and canons. This sudden advances in weaponry not only facilitated the control of a large mass of people by relatively few armed men that helping to form strong empires, but the availability of the new technology to a select few nations enabled the formation of colonies in continents which did not have access to the modernized technologies of warfare. Modern technological advances in armaments aided the formation of nation states in Europe. The extensive use of the fire-power lent a lethal edge to the naval power which proved to be the greatest asset to any nation in the 19th century. Small United Nations States of Europe with strong navies, modern arms and disciplined men gained control of lands in foreign continents far greater in areas than the parent countries.

1. Necessity is the mother of invention means
A. where there is mother there is invention
B. when necessity arises invention is done
C. most of the invention are preplanned
D. nothing happens without creating congenial environment

2. The invention of modern weapons have resulted into
A. loss of immunity from war in the society
B. successive wars for the last two centuries
C. arms race among the nations
D. loss of life and property every now and then

3. Small kingdoms turned into big empires, after
A. the invention of cavalry and canons and its introduction into the army
B. the introduction of nuclear arms into the army

C. the end of the use of knives, arrows and swords

D. the end of the 19th century

4. The style of the passage is

A. informative B. analytical

C. retrospective D. provocative

PASSAGE–12

It was during one of the most dreadful smallpox epidemics in England that Edward Jenner, a country doctor, made a discovery which was to alter the course of history. Jenner noticed that the disease seldom struck those who lived in rural areas and worked around cattle. Most farmers and dairy workers had contracted cowpox and had recovered with nothing more serious than a putsule which left a scar. This observation led Dr. Jenner to think: Why not vaccinate people with cowpox to protect them from smallpox ? On May 14, 1876, Dr. Jenner took a healthy boy, James Phillips, to a dairy maid, Sarah Nelmes, who had a cowpox putsule on her hand resulting from an infection from her master's cow. Dr. Jenner made two shallow cuts on James Phillips' arm and inoculated them with matter taken from the cowpox sore. A putsule developed on the boy's arm formed a scab and healed. In July of the same year. Dr. Jenner inoculated James with matter from a smallpox putsule. During the next two weeks, the doctor watched for signs of smallpox. They did not develop. The vaccination was successful. Dr. Jenner wrote a paper explaining his method of vaccination. At first the doctors were hostile and would not listen to a ridiculous procedure. Many towns people organised anti vaccination campaigns. Gradually, however, the doctors and their patients accepted vaccination.

1. The fact that Edward Jenner was a country doctor, was important in the discovery of smallpox vaccine, because

A. he had enough time to pursue his research in the rural areas

B. he noticed that the disease was prevalent where people worked around cattle

C. he noticed that the disease seldom struck people who worked around the cattle

D. he found that he could convince rural people more easily than city people

2. Dr. Jenner was successful as cowpox virus produces

A. severe infection in humans resulting in deaths

B. a mild infection in humans which is not enough to produce active immunity

C. a mild infection in humans which is enough to produce active immunity

D. no infection in humans

3. Dr. Jenner made his experiment on a healthy boy who

A. died after experimentation

B. could not be relieved of his mark of putsule

C. developed the sings of putsule on his body when he was injected the matter of cowpox

D. was paid for it

4. Passage here is having a/an

A. narrative style

B. analytic style

C. provocative style

D. idiomatic style

PASSAGE–13

The Indian culture of our times is in the making. Many of us are striving to produce a blend of all cultures that seem today to be in clash with one another. No culture can live, if it attempts to be exclusive. There is no such things as pure Aryan culture in existence in India today. Whether the Aryans were indigenous to India or were unwelcome intruders, does not interest me much. What does interest me is the fact that may remote ancestors blended with one another with the utmost freedom and we of the present generation are a result of that blend. I do not want my house to be walled in, on all sides and my windows to be stuffed. I want the cultures of all lands to be blown about my house as freely as possible. But I refuse to be blown off my feet by any. I would have any young men and women with literary tastes to learn as much of English and other world-languages as they like, and then expect them to give the benefits of their learning to India and the world alike like a Bose, a Ray or Tagore. But I would not have a single Indian forget, neglect or be ashamed of his mother tongue, or feel that he or she cannot think or express the best thoughts in his or her own vernacular. Mine is not a religion of the prison house.

1. The author views Indian Culture as

A. pure Aryan culture.

B. a clash of cultures.

C. a continual blend of cultures.

D. the culture of remote ancestors.

2. The author thinks that

A. the Aryans were indigenous to India.

B. the Aryans were unwelcome intruders.

C. the question whether the Aryans were indigenous or not is not of interest.

D. the culture that we have inherited is the Aryan culture.

3. The author wants

A. the cultures of others to be kept out.

B. the cultures of others to replace our old culture.

C. the freedom to blend other cultures with our own.
D. the preservation of the culture of our ancestors.

4. The author wants Indians to
A. learn only English, as much as they like.
B. learn English and other world languages.
C. learn only the mother tongue or the vernacular.
D. English and other world languages in addition to the mother tongue.

PASSAGE–14

As civilization proceeds in the direction of technology, it passes the point of supplying all the basic essentials of life, food, shelter, clothes, and warmth. Then we are faced with a choice between using technology to provide and fulfil needs which have hitherto been regarded as unnecessary or, on the other hand, using technology to reduce the number of hours of work which a man must do in order to earn a given standard of living. In other words, we either raise our standard of living above that necessary for comfort and, happiness or we leave it at this level and work shorter hours. I shall take it as axiomatic that mankind has, by that time, chosen the latter alternative. Men will be working shorter and shorter hours in their paid employment.

1. "Then we are faced with a choice..." what does "then'' refer to?
A. When automation takes over many aspects of human life
B. The present state of civilization
C. The past stage of civilization
D. After having provided the basic essentials of life

2. What does the passage suggest about the use of technology?
A. It creates new and essential needs for mankind
B. It is opposed to the basic essentials of life
C. It is complementary to a raised standard of living
D. It is responsible for man's love of comfort and happiness

3. What does increased use of technology imply?
A. An advanced stage in human civilization
B. A backward step in human culture
C. Unnecessary comfort and happiness for mankind
D. Man's zest for more and more work

4. What does the author suggest?
A. Man will gradually rise above his present stage in civilization
B. Man will gradually settle down to the same stage with fewer hours of work
C. Man will gradually raise his standard of living by working longer hours
D. Man will gradually earn a given standard of living with the help of technology

PASSAGE–15

It is said that ideas are explosive and dangerous. To allow them unfettered freedom is, in fact, to invite disorder. But, to this position, there are at least two final answers. It is impossible to draw a line round dangerous ideas, and any attempt at their definition involves monstrous folly. If views, moreover, which imply disorder are able to disturb the foundations of the State, there is something supremely wrong with the governance of the State. For disorder is not a habit of mankind. We cling so eagerly to our accustomed ways that, as even Burke insisted; popular violence is always the outcome of a deep popular sense of wrong.

1. What is the central point that the passage emphasizes?
A. It is unnecessary to define dangerous ideas
B. Dangerous ideas are born out of the enjoyment of freedom
C. A well-governed State is unaffected by dangerous ideas
D. Dangerous ideas originate from man's preoccupation with politics

2. From a close study of the passage, which one of the following statements emerges most clearly?
A. The author is against the exercise of political freedom
B. He is indifferent to dangerous and explosive ideas
C. He welcomes violence as a method to change governments
D. He warns that violence is the outcome of popular dissatisfaction with the government

3. The author says, 'we cling eagerly to our accustomed ways'. Which one of the following statements may be considered as the assumption of the author?
A. We are afraid of social changes
B. Mankind is averse to any disorder
C. We have developed inertia that makes us incapable of social action
D. There is an all-round lack of initiative in the society

4. Which of the following statements may most correctly bring out the significance of the opinion of Burke quoted in the passage?
A. Burke advocated violence against injustice

B. Burke's opinion coincides with the author's opinion on explosive and dangerous ideas
C. Burke hated any popular uprising
D. Burke had no belief in political liberty

PASSAGE–16

The psychological causes of unhappiness, it is clear, are many and various. But all have something in common. The typical unhappy man is one who, having been deprived in youth of some normal satisfaction, has come to value this one kind of satisfaction more than any other, and has therefore given to his life a one-sided direction, together with a quite undue emphasis upon the achievement as opposed to the activities connected with it. There is, however, a further development which is very common in the present day. A man may feel so completely thwarted that he seeks no form of satisfaction, but only distraction and oblivion. He then becomes a devotee of "pleasure". This is to say, he seeks to make life bearable by becoming less alive. Drunkenness, for example, is temporary suicide - the happiness that it brings is merely negative, a momentary cessation of unhappiness.

1. Who is a typical unhappy man?
   A. One who has been deprived of normal satisfaction in youth
   B. One who finds life unbearable and attempts suicide
   C. One who does not mind momentary unhappiness
   D. One who seeks every form of satisfaction
2. "One sided direction" refers to the pursuit of which one of the following?
   A. Drinking and forgetfulness
   B. The satisfaction one had been deprived of
   C. Activities leading to happiness
   D. Every form of psychological satisfaction
3. Which one of the following is the correct statement?
   Drinking helps the unhappy only to
   A. forget their dissatisfaction
   B. get sublime happiness
   C. get the motivational needs fulfilled
   D. concentrate harder
4. What does "becoming less alive" imply?
   A. Neglect of health
   B. Decline in moral values
   C. Living in a make-believe world
   D. Leading a sedentary way of living

PASSAGE–17

What is to be the limit of forgiveness? It would probably have been allowed by many of the ancients that an unforgiving temper was not to be commended. They would have said, we are not to exact a penalty for every nice offence; we are to overlook some things; we are to be blind sometimes. But they would have said at the same time, we must be careful to keep our self-respect, and to be on a level with the world. On the whole, they would have said, it is the part of a man fully to requite to his friends their benefits and to his enemies their injuries.

1. Which one of the following is the correct statement?
   According to the writer we must
   A. ignore an offence if it is nice
   B. forgive people if they bring us nice presents
   C. forgive pretty offenders
   D. not punish each and every offence
2. Which one of the following is the correct statement?
   We must
   A. be blind if we want to forgive others
   B. be blind to the faults of our friends
   C. be indifferent to what others do
   D. overlook certain things
3. Which one of the following is the correct statement?
   In ancient times people were
   A. ordered to lose their tempers
   B. permitted to lose their tempers and not forgive their enemies
   C. told that it was not good to have an unforgiving temper
   D. advised to forgive each and every offence committed by both friends and foes
4. What is the underlying tone of the passage?
   A. We must be forgiving in general
   B. We must forgive our friends
   C. There is no limit whatsoever to our duty to forgive
   D. We must always punish the wrongdoer

PASSAGE–18

We should preserve Nature to preserve life and beauty. A beautiful landscape, full of green vegetation, will not just attract our attention but will fill us with infinite satisfaction. Unfortunately, because of modernization, much of nature is now yielding to towns, roads and industrial areas. In a few places some Natural reserves are now being carved out to avert the danger of destroying Nature completely. Man will perish without Nature, so modern man should continue this struggle to save plants, which give us oxygen, from extinction. Moreover, Nature is essential to man's health.

1. What does "Nature" in the passage mean?
   A. Countryside covered with plants and trees
   B. Physical power that created the world
   C. Inherent things that determine character
   D. Practical study of plants and animals
2. Which one of the following is the correct statement?
   According to the passage
   A. Beauty is only skin-deep
   B. Everything is beautiful in its natural state
   C. There is beauty in Nature
   D. Nature is a moral teacher
3. What does the writer suggest?
   A. We should not modernize, so that Nature can be preserved
   B. While modernizing we should be careful not to destroy Nature completely
   C. All Nature has been destroyed by modern living
   D. Carving out Natural reserves will hamper the growth of industries
4. What does "Struggle" in the passage mean?
   A. Man's Struggle to exist in the world
   B. Man's Struggle to save Nature
   C. Man's Struggle to catch up with modern trends
   D. Man's Struggle to conserve oxygen
5. Why a beautiful landscape will fill us with infinite satisfaction'?
   A. We love beauty
   B. It is full of green vegetation
   C. It will ensure our future existence
   D. It will show our command over Nature

PASSAGE–19

Finally, there arises the question as to our leadership potential. Although the entire younger generation by the very definition is a potential storehouse of leadership, I feel that our universities provide the richest reservoir from which the future leaders of this country will be forthcoming. I have had occasion to travel fairly extensively and to visit a number of university centres in the country. It is deeply encouraging to see that despite the economic and other difficulties which these young men and women have to face they are full of energy and idealism. The real question is whether we have the ability and imagination to tap this reservoir, to fan the sparks of youthful idealism into bright flames that would illumine the future of India — the India of our dreams for the building of which countless generations have struggled and sacrifed; an India socially emancipated, economically prosperous, politically integrated, militarily strong and spiritually dynamic.

1. Which one of the following is correct?
   The writer believes that India is
   A. socially emancipated
   B. economically prosperous
   C. spiritually dynamic
   D. None of the above
2. What is the author's tone in the passage?
   A. Optimistic B. Autocratic
   C. Pessimistic D. Partisan
3. Where will the future leaders of the country mainly come from?
   A. The families of present political leaders
   B. The community of social scientists
   C. The universities
   D. The entire younger generation
4. Which one of the following is correct?
   For realizing the India of our dreams,
   A. we should have the imagination to exploit our budding leadership potential
   B. we should admire the sacrifices made by several generations
   C. we should bring about more technological advancements
   D. we should provide better facilities for sports
5. Which one of the following is correct?
   What is deeply encouraging about educated young men and women of India is that
   A. they come from the richest reservoirs of potential leaders
   B. they are full of energy and idealism because of quality education
   C, they are full of youthful idealism and imagination
   D. they are full of energy and idealism in spite of economic and other difficulties they face as students

PASSAGE–20

My own recollection is that I had not had any high regard for my ability. I used to be astonished whenever I won prizes and scholarships. But, I very assiduously guarded my character. The least little blemish drew tears from my eyes. When I merited, or seemed to the teacher to merit, a rebuke, it was unbearable for me. I remember having once received corporal punishment. I did not so much mind the punishment, as the fact that it was considered my desert. I wept piteously. That was when I was in the first or second standard. There was another such incident during the time when I was in the seventh standard. Dorabji Edulji Gimi was the Headmaster then. He was popular among the boys, though he was a disciplinarian. He was a man of method and a good teacher. He had made gymnastics and cricket compulsory for the boys of the upper standards. I disliked both. I never took part in any exercise, cricket or football, before they were made com-pulsory. My shyness was one of the reasons for this aloofness, which I now see as wrong. I then had the false notion that gymnastics had nothing to do with education. Today I know that physical training should have as much place in the curriculum as mental training.

1. Why did the author say that he did ***not*** have any high regard for his ability?
A. He was a dunce
B. He always used to miss his classes
C. He never did well in studies or sports
D. He was full humility

2. The author's idea that character is a treasure is revealed in which of the statements?
A. "I won prizes and scholarships"
B. "When I merited, or seemed to the teacher to merit, a rebuke, it was unbearable for me"
C. "I very assiduously guarded my character"
D. "I wept piteously"

3. Why did the author weep piteously?
A. He felt insulted
B. Punishment was considered his due
C. He felt the physical pain
D. He took the punishment to heart

4. Why did the author dislike gymnastics and cricket?
A. They cut into his study time
B. He had to spend money in buying bats, etc.
C. He felt that physical education could cause injury
D. He was shy

PASSAGE–21

According to the research findings of a team of American scientists published recently, the sea waves contain as much energy as the world is consuming at present. Scientists have found that through the application of two major devices called land-based systems and offshore devices, this source of energy can provide huge amount of electricity without cooling towers and pollution.

Land-based systems include tapered channels and fixed oscillating water column (OWC) devices whereas offshore devices include floating OWC devices, buoys, etc. Through these devices the mechanical energy of ocean waves is absorbed and converted into electrical energy. The wave power potential depends on numerous factors such as the device's capability to harness long wavelengths, period of waves and depth of water where they arise.

Compared to conventional power stations which require greater space and are difficult to maintain in critical situations, wave power devices are highly modular, cost effective and easier to upgrade. As the recent findings suggest, sea wave energy has much greater potential to be used for electricity generation than the hitherto known sources of renewable energy. Moreover, most of the renewable energy systems require hundreds of square acres of useful land for their installation. But in case of wave energy devices, space crunch' can never be a serious problem.

1. Which one of the following statements is correct?
Harnessing energy from sea waves
A. undermines ecological balance.
B. requires huge capital.
C. requires high technical expertise.
D. results in saving of useful land area.

2. Which one of the following statements is correct?
Wave power devices
A. convert wind energy into mechanical power.
B. convert mechanical energy of ocean waves into electrical energy.
C. require costly transmission mechanism
D. entail risk to human life.

3. Which one of the following statements is correct?
A. Fixed as well as floating oscillating water column devices are required to harness ocean wave energy.
B. Fixed oscillating water column devices are required for off shore based system.
C. Floating oscillating water column devices are required for land-based system.
D. Electricity generated from oceans is independent of the depth of water where waves arise.

4. Which one of the following statements is correct?
The capacity of system to generate electricity from ocean waves
A. can be increased only at exorbitant cost.
B. can be easily upgraded.
C. can be increased but it requires a great space.
D. is only a few megawatts.

5. Which one of the following statements is ***not*** correct?
A. Conventional power stations require cooling towers.
B. Power generation from ocean waves also adds to pollution like conventional power stations.
C. Ocean wave energy can meet all the present energy of the world.
D. Period of waves is one of the relevant factors in power generation from ocean waves.

PASSAGE–22

The most important fact, which a leader who wishes to motivate others should bear in mind, is that an individual has an incessant and gnawing craving for importance. There is no exception to this psychological need. Barring his biological needs, practically all his actions are directed at satisfying his continuing need to feel important. According to William James, the deepest principle in human nature is the craving to be appreciated. The individual who can honestly satisfy this burning hunger for importance on the part of his fellow human beings can literally rule the world. He can motivate and influence any person, big or small, high or low, educated or uneducated, rich or poor, man or woman, provided he is capable of making the other person feel truly important. By discovering the special and particular gifts of an individual, by giving due recognition and sincere appreciation to that singular gift or talent, you can win him or her over to your side easily.

You have to create an eager want on the part of the other individual if you wish to motivate him. In other words, you have to make the horse feel thirsty if your aim is to make it drink. Fortunately for you, there is an inborn, ever-present, gnawing hunger on the part of every human being to gain recognition and appreciation. This want is already there and you don't have to create it. All you have to do is to satisfy this hunger. If you objectively analyse your own motives and needs you will find that this need for recognition is the strong driving factor behind your aspiration to become a leader. It was this urge for importance which made Alexander and Great embark on a world conquest, and made many emperors wage innumerable battles and wars. This urge has driven artists, authors, scientists, inventors and others to attain great heights in their chosen fields and produce the best results.

1. Which one of the following statements is correct?

A. Many scientists and inventors have excelled because of the availability of research facilities.

B. Artists and authors have made contribution to society because of their innate genius.

C. Many athletes have won gold medals in the Olympics because of their coaches.

D. People in different areas have been successful because of the need of recognition.

2. Which one of the following statements is ***not*** correct?

A. Hunger for recognition has to be developed over the years in one's personality.

B. Need to gain recognition is an inborn trait.

C. Many wars have been waged to satisfy the need to get importance.

D. Craving for importance is a natural psychological need of every human being.

3. Which one of the following statements is correct?

A. A successful leader must be able to identify the need of importance of others.

B. Need for recognition is a trait only of high professionals.

C. To motivate a person, an increase of his salary is the best strategy.

D. Monetary success is the driving force for a leader.

PASSAGE–23

Because goldfish can be kept easily in small ponds and aquariums, they make good pets, but like many other pets, they must have proper care and the right kind of place to live.

A two-inch fish requires a minimum of two gallons of water containing sufficient oxygen to support life. Some oxygen will make its way into the water of an aquarium from the air that touches the surface. Plants in an aquarium also help to furnish oxygen. Snails help to keep an aquarium clean. Thus, with plenty of plants and snails the water is an aquarium does not have to be changed frequently. A large lake may prove to be a quite unsuitable abode for goldfish.

It is important that goldfish not be overfed. They can be fed such things as dried insects in addition to commercially-prepared goldfish food, but they should never be fed more than once a day. Even then, they should not be given more food than can be consumed in about five minutes. This ensures prolonged life.

1. Which one of the following statements is correct?

A. Snails eat up the goldfish in an aquarium

B. A large lake may not be a suitable place for goldfish

C. Plants provide food to the snails in an aquarium

D. Goldfish come above the surface of water to get oxygen from air

2. Which one of the following statements is *not* correct?

A. Goldfish can be made goods pets

B. Plants in an aquarium provide oxygen to goldfish

C. Goldfish must never be given too much food

D. Snails make the aquarium clean by eating up goldfish

3. Which of the following helps supply goldfish with oxygen?
   A. Snails
   B. Dried insects
   C. Goldfish food
   D. Plants
4. Which one of the following statement is *not* correct?
   A. Water in an aquarium has to be changed frequently because of plants and snails
   B. Commercially-prepared goldfish is available
   C. The place for the goldfish should be selected with care
   D. Dried insects make good feed for goldfish
5. What is important to remember when feeding goldfish?
   A. Goldfish should be fed more than once a day at regular intervals
   B. Goldfish should be fed with plants and snails
   C. Goldfish should be fed only once a day
   D. Goldfish should be fed only in the evenings

PASSAGE–24

Ah ! whatever could be said was said. All held him guilty. Even his own mother who claimed to understand him the best. All had betrayed him in his hour of need. Yet, there he was, still with a sparkling hope and knew that the truth must prevail. In the cold, dark and damp cell he never for a moment lost faith in God and goodness and was waiting anxiously for an angel to come, plead non guilty for him and free him of his miseries.

1. Three of the following statements indicate that he had a sparkling hope. Which statement does not?
   A. He had never lost faith in God.
   B. He was sure there was goodness.
   C. He could have evidence in his favour.
   D. He knew that the truth must prevail.
2. Whatever others said about him, he
   A. betrayed no one.
   B. thought over the problem.
   C. never lost faith in goodness.
   D. raised his voice against injustice.
3. In the dark dungeon he always waited for
   A. his mother.
   B. the jailer.
   C. the verdict freeing him of his miseries.
   D. the angel to come and plead for him.
4. The truth must prevail means
   A. he was true.
   B. angel will reveal truth.
   C. truth always wins in the end.
   D. we must plead for the truth.

PASSAGE–25

Once while travelling by the local bus, I got a seat beside a very strange man. He seemed interested in every passenger aboard. He would stare at a person, scribble some odd mathematical notations on his long notebook and then move on to the next. Being quite interested in what he was doing I asked him what all those notations meant and then came the startling reply. He saw a man's face not as a single unit but as thousands of squares put together. He was in fact a statistical expert and a budding artist learning the art of graphics.

1. The man was scribbling down
   A. the figures of co-passengers.
   B. the details of thousands of squares put together.
   C. some mathematical formulae and calculations.
   D. some mathematical signs.
2. The man caught author's attention because
   A. he was sitting next to him.
   B. he was staring at every person in the bus.
   C. he would stare at every person and then scribble down some mathematical notation.
   D. he was a budding artist learning the art of graphics.
3. The author found that man's reply quite startling because
   A. a statistical expert cannot be a budding scientist.
   B. a budding artist cannot be a statistical expert.
   C. graphics is still a rare art form and he was learning it while travelling in a bus.
   D. the fact that "a man's face can be analysed as thousands of squares" was a strange concept.
4. From the passage we gather that
   A. the author is very inquisitive.
   B. the author tries to poke his nose in other people's business.
   C. the author is interested in mathematical notations.
   D. the author wants to talk to fellow passengers in the bus.

PASSAGE–26

With the inevitable growth of specialisation I see the universities facing two great dangers. First, it is very easy to get so involved in the technical details of education that the object of education is lost. And secondly, in an effort to condition a university to the needs of its students and to the needs of the state it may lose its power to make or mould those students into responsible men, capable of thinking for themselves and capable of expressing the results of their thoughts to others.

1. The author calls growth of specialisation 'inevitable'. Which one of the following statements is likely to be the most correct reason for this inevitability?
   A. Universities give grants only to do specialised work in different disciplines.
   B. The professors and researchers in universities are competent only for specialised work.
   C. Specialisation helps economic growth of the nation.
   D. In an age of science and technology specialisation becomes necessary.

2. Which one of the following statements most correctly suggests the central theme of the passage?
   A. The aim of education is specialisation.
   B. The aim of education is to mould the youth to work for the state.
   C. The aim of education is to make the youth capable of independent thought and expression.
   D. The aim of education is to enable the youth to earn a comfortable living.

3. Which one of the following statements most correctly suggests the warning implied in the passage?
   A. University education should not be concerned with technical details.
   B. Universities should not subordinate themselves to the interests of tile state.
   C. Universities should be concerned only with the needs of students.
   D. Universities should not go in for any specialisation.

PASSAGE–27

We shall go on to the end; we shall fight in France, we shall fight on the seas and oceans, we shall fight with growing confidence and strength in the air, we shall defend our island whatever the cost may be, we shall fight on the beaches, we shall fight on the landing grounds, we shall fight in the fields and in the streets, we shall fight in the hills. We shall never surrender, and even if this island or a large part of it were subjugated and starving, then our empire beyond the seas would carry on the struggle, untill the New World steps forth to the rescue and the liberation of the Old.

1. On the basis of the passage which of the following statements may be said to be correct?
   A. The speaker is encouraging his men for the conquest of France
   B. The speaker is aggressive and maniacal war-monger
   C. The speaker is not satisfied with the conquest of the island
   D. The speaker is a patriot urging the defence of his motherland

2. The speaker in the passage wants to go on fighting because
   A. he is a raving lunatic
   B. he is in a state of utter despair
   C. he expects help from other quarters
   D. he is the leader of a suicide squad

3. Which of the following pairs of the phrases helps best to bring out the intention of the speaker?
   A. "Go on to the end"; "shall never surrender"
   B. "Growing confidence"; " subjugated and starving"
   C. "Subjugated and starving"; "fight on the landing ground"
   D. "Fight in the streets"; "subjugated and starving"

4. The passage consists of repetitive patterns in syntax and vocabulary. The effect of this style is that it
   A. reveals the speaker's defects in giving a speech
   B. produces the impression of bad poetry
   C. conveys the speaker's helpless situation
   D. reinforces the speaker's basic intention

PASSAGE–28

It is said that once three old men set out on a Journey together. One of them was bald, the second was a philosopher and the third was a barber. At nightfall they decided that each one of them should sit for watch *turn* by turn. The *barber* was to keep watch first of all, the *philosopher* after that and the *bald* man last of all. So, the philosopher and the blad man went to sleep and the barber was on watch. For some time he kept awake but in the end, he felt tired of it and he thought of some *diversion* as otherwise it was difficult for him to *pass* time. Then he took out the razor from his box and shaved the head of the philosopher. At the fixed time he woke up the philosopher and himself went to sleep. when the philosopher got up and felt his head all over, he was startled and said in surprise, "It was my trun but this *wretched* fellow has *awakened* bald man."

1. Why did the philosopher get up?
   A. He realised that his head was being shaved off
   B. It was his turn to keep watch
   C. He was awakened by the barber
   D. he had a bad dream

2. Who went to sleep first?
   A. The philosopher and the barber
   B. The barber and the bald man
   C. The bald man and the philosopher
   D. The barber
3. Why did the barber shave off the head of the philosopher?
   A. The barber was jealous of the philosopher
   B. The barber wanted to indulge in some fun
   C. The barber wanted the philosopher to keep watch
   D. The barber was feeling drowsy
4. Which one of the following is the correct sequence decided upon the three to keep watch turn by turn?
   A. Barber – bald man – philosopher
   B. Bald man – philosopher – barber
   C. Barber – philosopher – bald man
   D. Bald man – barber – philosopher
5. Which one of the following statements is ***not*** correct?
   A. All the three men decided to keep watch one by one
   B. The barber woke up the bald man
   C. The head of the philosopher was shaved off
   D. The philosopher was startled on feeling his head all over

PASSAGE–29

There can be only two explanations why countries like UK, US, Germany and Japan are willing to spend up to 5.5 million to make the Next Generation Linear Collider (NGLC) : Intellectual snobbery or complete indifference to the problems of the real world. To plan a 20-mile-long tunnel merely to go about smashing atoms, so as to recreate the Big Bang, is a frightful waste of public money. The project has no foreseeable practical application. Already, cyber-savvy cosmologists are engaged in simulating the Big Bang, or the beginning of the universe, in the virtual world, through number crunching and reverse engineering. Thye have successfully created a black hole on the desktop. So why go in for prohibitively expensive experimentation, when the virtual world is just a mouse-click away? Scientific ingenuity, remember, is not confined to reallife experiments; many of today's break-throughs have been inspired by research conductd almost entirely in cyberspace. Moreover, virtual research is 'clean'— without such fallouts as lab accidents and chemical leakages—and costs next to nothing.

1. Countries like UK, US, Germany and Japan wish to spend lot of money.
   A. to attend to the problems of humanity.
   B. to control AIDS.
   C. for defence research.
   D. to carry out atomic research.
2. Virtual research is carried out
   A. on computers.
   B. by experimentation in the field.
   C. by spending up billions of dollars.
   D. by experimentation in space.
3. Scientific research is not prohibitively costly when conducted
   A. by simulation in the virtual world.
   B. smashing atoms in a tunnel.
   C. making real-life models.
   D. using satellites.
4. Reverse engineering
   A. is commonly practised in research.
   B. is prohibitively expensive experimentation.
   C. is not used by cosmologists in the virtual world.
   D. is independent of analysis using computers.

PASSAGE–30

Failure and success are the ways of life. Constant efforts despite initial setbacks have brought us from the chrysalis of failures into the bright opportunity of triumphs. The conquest of Everest is a fitting example. Success eluded men for nearly twenty-five years. The leader of an unsuccessful expedition started, "Everest cannot add to its height, but spirit of man heightens even under repulse." Subsequent conquest of Everest has proved the truth of this. Indeed every newborn day is in itself an opportunity teeming with splendid chances for those who are alert, wide awake and aspiring.

1. According to the writer, the conquest of Everest proves that
   A. the spirit of man heightens under demanding circumstances.
   B. man cannot attain the unattainable.
   C. success is always elusive.
   D. the nature is most potent.
2. In this passage, "chrysalis of failure" means that
   A. failure involves a closed situation from which one cannot escape.
   B. failure can be compared to the pupa of the gold-coloured butterflies.
   C. failure is a transitional state.
   D. as an insect emerges in a different shape from chrysalis, so a human being changes after every failure.
3. The very style of the prose suggests that the writer intends the last sentence of the passage to be
   A. poetic

B. inspiring
C. vague
D. contradictory to the first sentence of the passage.

4. The expression "teeming with" in the passage can be replaced by
A. multiplying B. abounding
C. fruitful D. promising

5. Every new day brings fresh challenges for a person
A. who is young
B. whose head is teeming with bright ideas
C. who has come out of the chrysalis of failure
D. who is watchful and daring.

PASSAGE–31

Pisa offers a quiet holiday. Apart from the Leaning Tower Square where the tourists flock, the city is free of the kind of crowds one sees at Florence. An 11-km bus ride brings us to Marina de Pisa, the coastal extension of the city, where the Ligurian Sea and quaint buildings provide a few hours of relaxed walks. However, there is not much of a beach.

Gone is the tension of the previous night, when, flying into Italy in the late hours, my wife and I were a little apprehensive. Compared to Germany where we had spent three weeks, Italy, one thought, was 'unsafe'. The fears were compounded when the night bus from the airport terminated at the railway station, instead of going all the way to our hotel. "Ten Euros,'' said the cab driver at the station when asked how much the ride to the hotel would cost. Quite sure he was overcharging, we got in nevertheless. At 11.30 p.m. we anyway had little choice. The streets were dimly lit and the driver was uncommunicative. Stopping at a desolate building after we had clearly gone out of the city limits, he announced : "Your hotel." I gave him a 10-Euro bill and turned away. But the cabman stopped me. "Your change, sir," he said, pointing to the meter which read 8-20 Euros.

The small change I got back that day was like receiving the certificate of a nation's honesty. Italy, as it turned out, was just fine.

1. The author and his wife were
A. thrilled at the idea of travelling to Italy.
B. concerned about safety.
C. worried because of high cost.
D. worried because of language problem.

2. The author
A. was cheated by the taxi driver.
B. did not like the etiquette of the taxi driver.
C. was pleasantly surprised by the rectitude of the driver.
D. was irked because the driver was very talkative.

3. Pisa
A. has many traffic jams.
B. is full of business houses.
C. is a quiet town.
D. has major pollution problems.

4. Marina de Pisa
A. is known for its beautiful beaches.
B. is full of churches.
C. has many shopping centres.
D. is a coastal city.

PASSAGE–32

Much of our adult state of fear is linked up with the feeling that I, an individual, have to cope single-handed with a hostile world, the details of which have become far too complicated for me to understand. This feeling of isolation is in part a by-product of the way we have been educated and the stress that is pure on passing examinations. The more 'successful' your education, the more likely you are to feel alone, because the process of segregation has been more complete at every stage you proved how much cleverer you are than all those other fellows, until in the end you stand quite alone and afraid. It ought to be possible to manage things in a different way so that we go forward into the future, collaborating as a team instead of looking around for every possible opportunity to knife each other in the back.

1. An adult in the modern world is in a state of fear because
A. he has developed an individuality.
B. he feels lonely in an unfriendly world.
C. his life has become complicated.
D. he cannot understand the challenge.

2. The modern man feels isolated
A. because he has passed through the stress of examinations.
B. because he is the by-product of 'successful' social system.
C. because he fails to receive education.
D. because he nurses his feeling of isolation.

3. The writer thinks that fierce competitiveness in the modern educational system
A. makes them neurotic.
B. makes man clever.
C. does not make man care for his fellows.
D. makes man hostile to his environment.

4. Modern education makes man feel segregated
A. because of its emphasis on materialism.
B. by making him distrustful of others.
C. by making him stand on his own.
D. by inculcating the fear of society in him.

5. It would be a better educational system
A. if it would manage things differently.

B. if it inculcates the spirit of togetherness.
C. if it teaches collaboration with a team.
D. if it does not allows us to knife each other in the back.

PASSAGE–33

Diversity typically provides fresh perspectives on issues, but it makes it more difficult to unify the team and reach agreements. The strongest case for diversity on work teams is when these teams are engaged in problem-solving and decision-making tasks. Heterogeneous teams bring multiple perspective to the discussion, thus increasing the likelihood that the team will identify creative or unique solutions. Additionally, the lack of a common perspective usually means diverse teams spend more time discussing issues, which decrease the chances that a weak alternative will be chosen. However, keep in mind that the positive contribution that diversity makes to decision-making teams undoubtedly declines over time. Diverse groups have more difficulty working together and solving problems, but this dissipates with time expect the value-added component of diverse teams to decrease as members become more familiar with each other and the team becomes more cohesive.

1. Diversity on work team leads to
A. human problems.
B. creative solutions.
C. economy in manufacturing.
D. higher turnover.

2. With diversity in work-force there is
A. difficulty in reaching a solution quickly.
B. difficulty in designing wage formula.
C. difficulty in managing international market.
D. difficulty experienced in shop-floor management.

3. Advantages of diversity
A. are sustained over long periods of time.
B. lead to furhter increase with time.
C. decline as the members come to know each other.
D. decline as the absenteeism increases.

4. Problem-solving tasks can be handled by
A. homogeneous groups.
B. heterogeneous groups.
C. management graduates.
D. consultants.

PASSAGE–34

The world of today has achieved much, but for all its declared love for humanity it has based itself far more on hatred and violence than on the virtues that make man human. War is the negation of truth and humanity. War may be unavoidable sometimes but its progeny are terrible to contemplate. Not more killing, for man must die, but the deliberate and persistent propagation fo hatred and flasehood, which gradually become the normal habits of the peole. It is dangerous and harmful to be guided in our life's course by hatreds and aversions, for they are wasteful of energy and limit and twist the mind, and prevent it from perceiving the truth.

1. According to the author, the achievements of the world are not impressive because
A. there is nothing much to boast of.
B. they are mostly in the field of violence.
C. its love of humanity is a pretence.
D. the world has not made any achievement.

2. War is the negation of truth means
A. wars do not exist.
B. wars are evil.
C. wars spread and advertise falsehood.
D. wars kill human beings.

3. According to the author, the world's declared love of humanity is
A. false.
B. true.
C. non-existent.
D. not to be taken seriously.

4. Man should be guided by
A. scientific discoveries.
B. practical wisdom.
C. generous human feelings.
D. materialism.

5. Hatred and aversions are unwholesome as they are
A. dangerous.
B. harmful.
C. narrow.
D. barries in seeing the truth.

PASSAGE–35

Few people ask from books what books can give us. Most commonly we come to books with blurred and divided minds, asking of fiction that it shall be true, of poetry that it shall be false, of biography that it shall be flattering, of history that it shall enforce our own prejudices. If we could banish all such preconceptions when we read, that would be an admirable beginning.

1. According to this passage, most readers think that poetry is essentially
A. imagination B. unrealistic
C. realistic D. didactic

2. The author's reference to biography being viewed as something 'flattering' suggests that he thinks that it should be

A. offensive B. critical
C. truthful D. subjective

3. According to the passage, most books of history are
A. an objective of the past events
B. the author's views on the past events
C. reproduction of the records available from the past
D. an objective interpretation of the past records

4. According to this passage, most readers
A. expect too much from books
B. ignore the objective of the writer
C. do not know what to expect from a book
D. are positively inclined towards the author

5. The main intention of the author is to
A. point out the faults of the readers
B. define what various kinds of books are
C. suggest the correct approach to books
D. enumerate the readers' preconceptions

PASSAGE–36

I couldn't sleep that night. A vague feeling of impending misfortune affected me. My sister and I were twins, and you know how subtle the linsk are between such people. It was a wild night. Suddenly, there bursts forth the wild scream of a terrified woman. I knew that it was my sister's voice. I rushed into the corridor. By the light of the corridor lamp, I saw my sister at the door of her room, her face pale with terror, and her hands groping for help, and her whole figure swaying unsteadily. I ran to her and threw my arms around her, but her knees gave way and she fell to the ground.

1. The author couldn't sleep because
A. the night was wild
B. she apprehended some trouble
C. she knew that some calamity would befall her
D. she felt uneasy

2. It was well known that
A. she and her sister were twins
B. twins have a special bond between them
C. the relationship between twins is always cordial
D. twins can sense danger more easily than others

3. She rushed into the corridor because
A. she heard a terrifying cry
B. her sister called her to the room
C. she recognised the voic,e of the person who screamed
D. she dreamt that her sister needed her help

4. She realised that her sister
A. was in a state of excitement
B. needed support
C. was too weak to walk
D. was gripped with fear

5. She threw her arms around her sister to
A. express her affection
B. prevent her from running away
C. prevent her from falling down
D. save her from danger

PASSAGE–37

Because millions of years ago, a little tarsier-like creature began to use its hands and became inquisitive, the long trail of evolution towards man began. Those things are among man's characteristic features. Every year he delves deeper and deeper into the secrets of nature and his responsibilities grow more serious. In an age of mass production and machines, collective reason must control mass hysteria and mass instinct. That is the problem. The atomic bomb has only thrown it into higher relief. In the atomic bomb, man has used the fundamental energy process of the universe for destructive purposes, but that is largely an accident of the time and place. All around we have abundant evidence that without this energy, life itself could not exist.

1. The author believes, that man has evolved from a little tarsier-like creature because
A. his face resembles that of a tarsier
B. he uses his hands and walks like a tarsier
C. he is curious and walks like a tarsier
D. he is curious and uses his hands like a tarsier

2. The increasing human knowledge of the secrets of Nature has given rise to a problem which
A. involves a huge expenditure
B. makes man more and more irreligious and irreverential
C. is both a boon and a bane
D. necessitates a rational and humane approach to individual and social life

3. The invention of the atomic bomb has made this problem
A. more obscure
B. more prominent
C. more controversial
D. insignificant

4. Man has used atomic energy for destructive purposes because
A. it has no constructive purposes at all
B. he does not know how to sue it constructively
C. its constructive use is too expensive to be practicable
D. the force of circumstances compelled him to do so

5. The author thinks that the use of atomic energy
   A. will affect the society adversely
   B. is needed for the enrichment of life
   C. will ultimately destroy our civilization
   D. will lead to the end of the universe

PASSAGE–38

The jobs do not get changed around from time to time. I started off on one of the nicer ones. I sat at a conveyor belt slipping a piece of cardboard under each cake as it came down the line. At first it was difficult to keep up. An uneconomic movement, a fumble and four cakes have gone without cards. I got up to chase the four cakes, eight more appeared and for five minutes or so I had to work at twice the speed to work my way back to where I was sitting before. But it takes half a day or so to learn how it's done and soon it becomes quite automatic. The frenzy had quite worn off by the end of the first day and then there was only the monotony and the aching arms. Later I moved to another job on the line, as the girl who usually did it had left. I wasn't surprised. It was the nastiest job in that department. As the cake came out of a machine that had sliced it in three layers, two streams of artificial cream were poured over the layers. I had to stack the layers up again—a messy and very tiring job. The cakes are heavy and the cream is slippery. Anyone who has worked at all in a factory knows how deathly conveyor belt work is. At first it is difficult to keep up, and when you're tired it is quite merciless. After a while, when you have become fairly used to it, the fact that you can't work faster is also infuriating.

1. The writer's purpose in writing this piece is to
   A. make people who don't work in factories realise what it is like to work there
   B. plead to abolish manual labour from factories
   C. plead to get unskilled jobs made easier
   D. explain to young people how to handle a job in an automatized production unit
2. When the writer 'was moved to another job' she wasn't surprised to find that
   A. she had been moved
   B. her new job was very unpleasant
   C. the cream in the cakes was artificial
   D. the girl before her had left
3. The writer found it a messy job to
   A. separate the three layers of the cake
   B. pour artificial cream ove the layers
   C. stack the layers up again
   D. put the cake back on the conveyor belt again
4. The writer calls the conveyor belf 'merciless' because it
   A. could cause an injury if one makes a mistake
   B. is devoid of human feelings
   C. does not slow down even when the worker is tired
   D. is a hard taskmaster
5. After some time the writer got annoyed at the conveyor belt because
   A. she found it dull and monotonous to work with it
   B. she wanted to change her profession
   C. she found it merciless
   D. it always had the same speed

PASSAGE–39

The arrival of the train did not disturb Sir Mohan lal's sang-froid. He continued to sip his Scotch and ordered the bearer to tell him when he had moved the luggage to a first class compartment. Excitement, bustle, and hurry were exhibitiosn of bad breeding, and Sir Mohan was eminently well-bred. he wanted everything 'tickety-boo' and orderly. In his five years abroad, Sir Mohan had acquired the manners and attitudes of the upper classes. He rarely spoke Hindustani. When he did, it was like an Englishman's—only the very necessary words and properly anglicized. But he fancied his English, finished and refined at no less a place than the University of Oxford. He was fond of conversation and like a cultured Englishman he could talk on almost any subject—books, politics, people. How frequently had he heard English people say that he spoke like an Englishman!

1. Sir Mohan Lal is portrayed as
   A. an indophile B. a true Englishman
   C. a Hindu D. an anglophile
2. When Sir Mohan Lal spoke Hindustani it was
   A. Colloquial Hindi B. Literary Hindi
   C. Indian English D. Anglicized Hindi
3. According to Sir Mohan Lal, a well-bred person would
   A. remain aloof from the crowd
   B. like to drink only Scotch in public
   C. always be calm and orderly
   D. speak like an Englishman
4. From his description in this passage, Sir Mohan Lal appears to be
   A. a man of culture B. an aristocrat
   C. a snob D. a scholar
5. According to the passage, a cultured Englishman is able to talk effortlessly on
   A. art and culture
   B. human civilization
   C. modern science
   D. almost any subject

PASSAGE–40

The first and decisive step in the expansion of Europe overseas was the conquest of the Atlantic Ocean. That the nation to achieve this should be Portugal was the logical outcome of her geographical position and her history. Placed on the extreme margin of the old, classical Mediterranean world and facing the untraversed ocean. Portugal could adapt and develop the knowledge and experience of the past to meet the challenge of the unknown. From the seamen of Genoa and Venice, the had learned the organisation and conduct of a mercantile marine and from Jewish astronomers and mapmakers the rudiments of navigation. Largely excluded from the share in Mediterranean commerce, at a time when her population was making heavy demands on her resources. Portugal turned southwards and westwards for opportunities of trade and commerce. But ocean navigation was not the same as navigating the land-locked Mediterranean. The earliest of the band had neither the benefit of sailing directions nor traditional lore. Even the familiar heavenly constellations had been left behind. The challenge was formidable.

1. According to the passage, the most important step in the expansion of European power was
   A. the emergence of Portugal as a power
   B. the growth of Mediterranean commerce
   C. the contact of Europeans with Jewish astronomers
   D. the conquest of the Atlantic Ocean
2. The most important advantage that Portugal had, was its
   A. geographical location
   B. contact with the Arabs
   C. contact with Genoa and Venice
   D. cultural history
3. The Portuguese sailors were ready to explroe the world by sea because they
   A. knew about many countries
   B. had rich patrons to finance them
   C. were prepared for the hazards of sea voyage
   D. were in touch with seamen from Genoa and Venice
4. Portugal was motivated to pioneer ocean navigation because
   A. it was encouraged by other European powers
   B. it faced strong rivals in land-based trade
   C. it collaborated with Venetian merchants
   D. its limited resources could not support its growing population
5. The earliest group of Portuguese navigators going across the Atlantic did not find the venture
   A. different from land-locked navigation
   B. more difficult than coastal navigation
   C. easy and comfortable
   D. challenge and demanding

PASSAGE–41

Literature and history are twin sisters, inseparable. In the days of our own grandfathers and for many generations before them, the basis of education was the Greek and Roman classics for the educated, and the Bible for all. In the classical authors and in the Bbible history and literature were closely intervolved and it is that circumstances which made the old form of education to stimulating to the though and imagination of our ancestors. The read the classical authors and to read the Bible was to read at once the history and the literature of the three greatest races of the ancient world. No doubt the classics and the Bible were read in manner we now consider uncritical but they were read according to the best tenets of the time and formed a great humanistic education. Today the study both of the classics and of the bible has dwindled to small proportions. What has tkane their place? To some extent the vacuum has been filled by a more correct knowledge of history and a wider range of literature. But I fear that the graeter part of it has been filled up with rubbish.

1. Which of the following statements best reflects the underlying tone of the passage?
   A. Literature and history and mutually exclusive
   B. Literature and history and complementary to each other
   C. The study of literature is meaning less without any knowledge of history
   D. Literature and history are inseparably linked together in the classics and the Bible
2. The author of the above passage says that in the past the basis of education for all people, irrepsective of their intellectual calibre, was
   A. Greek and Roman Classics
   B. The Bible
   C. A correct knowledge of history
   D. A wider range of literature
3. The author of the above passage says that the classics and the Bible were read by his ancestors
   A. methodically and with discretion
   B. in a manner that broadened their view of life
   C. with great emphasis on their literacy values
   D. without critical discrimination but in the light of their humanistic culture
4. According to the author of the above passage the old form of education based the study of the classics and of the Bible, has
   A. succeeded in creating interest in history
   B. laid the basis of human civilization

C. had a gradual decline in our time
D. been rejuvenated in the context of modern education

5. The author of the above passage fears that the greater part of the vacuum created by lack of interest in the classic and the Bible has been filled up by
A. a richer sense of history
B. a wider range of literature
C. worthless ideas
D. a new philosophy of life

PASSAGE–42

During the early days as editor of the popular magazine, Saturday Evening Post, George Lorimer did much of the reading of unsolicited stories. This meant endless hours of sitting at the desk, pouring over big stacks of manuscrips, trying to decide which were worthy of publication and which were not. Lorimer became an expert at making these decisions.

One day he received a huffy letter from a wouldbe writer who had a omplaint. "Last week you rejected my story," she wrote. "I am positive you did not read it, because, as a test, I pasted together pages 14, 15 and 16. The manuscript came back with the pages still pasted. These is no question in my mind but that you are a sham and a disgrace to your profession."

Lorimer's reply was succinct: "Madam, at breakfast when I crack open an egg, I don't have to eat the whole egg to know it is bad."

1. Lorimer did much reading of the stories
A. if they were solicited ones
B. when they apeared to be bad
C. when they were from women writers
D. when they came unsolicited

2. Lorimer was a good editor because
A. his reply to the angry writer was polite
B. he apologized for rejecting the story without reading it
C. he could find the worth of a story with a little effort
D. he was promt in writing letters

3. The lady wrote a huffy letter because
A. her story was rejected
B. her story was rejected unread
C. her story was rejected although it was good
D. Lorimer was biased in his decision

4. Lorimer's reply was
A. irrelevant B. rude
C. wity D. funny

5. Lorimer read the stories
A. because he enjoyed reading them
B. in order to publish them
C. only to find fault with them
D. in order to review them

PASSAGE–43

As the tortoise tucks its feet and head inside the shell and will not come out even though you may break the shell into pieces, even so the character of the man who was has control over his motives and organs, is unchangeably established. He controls his own inner forces, and nothing can draw them out against his will. By this continuous reflex of good thoughts and good impressions moving over the surface of the mind, the tendency to do good becomes strong, and in consequence, we are able to control the Indriyas or sense organs.

1. The author uses the phrase 'inner forces' in this passage. Which of the following would be its most correct meaning in the context?
A. Emotional disturbances in man
B. Strength of the internal organs
C. Forces produced by sense organs
D. Reflection of the intellect

2. Which of the following statements would illustrate the metaphor in the passage?
A. Man is slow-moving and slow-witted
B. A man of character refuses to be influenced by outside compulsions against his will
C. Man confines himself to a life of isolation
D. Man cannot have a good character or strong will

3. Which of the following statements may be assumed to reflect the central theme of the passage?
A. Good thoughts lead to the control of the sense organs
B. Control of the sense organs leads to good thoughts
C. Character, though established, may be disturbed by outside forces
D. No man can achieve success in destroying the inner forces

4. Which of the following statements would be most correct in explaining the metaphorical meaning of 'break the shell into pieces'?
A. Destruction of the human body
B. Breaking of the physical environment of man
C. Attempt to destroy man's character
D. Inflicting physical and mental agony on man

5. The passage consists of two long sentences and a short one. The purpose of this style should be to suggest that
A. it is impossible for man to attain perfection of character

B. the attainment of perfect character is the result of a long process of mental discipline
C. the whole life process is clumsy
D. there is a lot of confusion in our understanding of sense organs, character, etc.

PASSAGE–44

One of the most serious problems confronting our country is that of a fast-growing population. In fact, it is at the root of many other problems. At the moment, thanks to planning, we are able to produce food and cloth sufficient for our people and even in some excess. But if the population continues to grow at this rate, it will not be long before the surplus turns into a bare minimum and even a deficit. The position in regard to accomodation is even now far from satisfactory in spite of our efforts.

1. "It is at the root of many other problems" means that
   A. it is found along with many other problems
   B. it is caused by many other problems
   C. it give rise to many other problems
   D. it is buried under many other problems
2. The present satisfactory position in regard to food and cloth is due to
   A. the fact that the population has been controlled
   B. our good luch
   C. good rainfall
   D. our economic planning
3. If the population of India continues to increase at this rate, the situation in regard to food and cloth
   A. is likely to reamain the same
   B. is likely to become less satisfactory
   C. is likely to improve
   D. is likely to vary up and down
4. The situation in respect of accommodation
   A. is less than satisfactory
   B. is quite satisfactory
   C. is improving rapidly
   D. is the result of total neglect
5. At present Indians have
   A. more provision for cloth than accommodation
   B. more provision for accommodation than cloth
   C. abundance of cloth and accommondation
   D. scaracity of cloth and accommondation

PASSAGE–45

Punctually at midday he opened his bag and spread out his professional equipment, which consisted of a dozen cowrie shells, a square piece of cloth with obscure mystic charts on it, a note book, and a bundle of Palmyra writing. His forehead was resplendent with sacred ash and vermilion, and his eyes sparkled with a sharp abnormal gleam which was really an outcome of a continual searching look for customers, but which his simple clients took to be a prophetic light and felt comforted. The power of his eyes was considerably enhanced by their position placed as they were between the painted forehead and the dark whiskers which streamed down his cheeks : even a half-wit's eyes would sparkle in such a setting. To crown the effect he wound a saffron-coloured turban around his head. This colour scheme never failed. People were attracted to him as bees are attracted to cosmos or dahlia stalks.

1. From the description of this passage one can make out the person to be a:
   A. Snake Charmer B. Footpath vendor
   C. Astrologer D. Priest
2. The eyes of the person described sparkled because:
   A. He was sitting under midday sun
   B. He was always looking for possible clients
   C. His forehead was bright with ash and vermilion
   D. He was full of joy
3. The person opened his bag
   A. to search for something he needed
   B. to indicate the start of his work
   C. to keep his professional equipment
   D. to take out things for display
4. The tone of the description is
   A. sad B. neutral
   C. ironic D. sympathetic

PASSAGE–46

Fortunately it is as yet only through fantasy that we can see what the destruction of the scholarly and scientific disciplines would mean to mankind. From history we can learn what their existence has meant. The sheer power of disciplined thought is revealed in practically all the great intellectual and technological advances which the human race has made. The ability of the man of disciplined mind to direct this power effectively upon problems for which he has not specifically trained is proved by examples without number. The real evidence for the value of liberal education lies in history and in the biographies of men who have met the valid criteria of greatness. These support overwhelmingly the claim of liberal education that it can equip a man with fundamental powers of decision and action, applicable not only to boy-girl relationship, to tinkering hobbies, or to choosing the family dentist, but to all the great and varied concerns of human life ...... not least, those that are unforeseen.

1. Liberal education enables a person to
   A. read with more discernment than others
   B. apply general principles to resolve issues
   C. gain prestige
   D. develop a clearer understanding of history than others
2. In this passage, the author stresses the importance of
   A. education for living
   B. technological advances
   C. increased interest in the study of history
   D. satisfying the desire for security
3. In this passage, the expression 'specifically trained' refers to
   A. characteristically trained
   B. particularly trained
   C. peculiarly trained
   D. ostensibly trained
4. According to the author, 'the great and varied concerns of human life' are about
   A. fundamental rights
   B. challenges facing mankind
   C. tinkering hobbies
   D. liberal education

PASSAGE–47

A male jackdaw's courtship behaviour is astonishingly human. All his movements are consciously strained and his proudly reared head and neck are permanently in a state of self-display. He provokes the other jackdaws continually if the female jackdaw is looking on and he purposefully becomes embroiled in conflicts with otherwise deeply respected superiors. Above all, he seeks to impress his loved one with the possession of a potential nesting site, from which he drives all other jackdaws, irrespetive of their rank.

1. A 'courtship behaviour' may best be described as
   A. the behaviour of a jackdaw who shows off his feathers
   B. the behaviour of a male bird to attract a female bird
   C. the behaviour by which a male bird displays its beauty to the female bird
   D. the behaviour of any male to win a female of the same species
2. Which of the phrases best helps to bring out the precise meaning of 'consciously strained'?
   A. Proudly reared and exhibited
   B. Permanently in a state of display
   C. Purposefully put in a state of display
   D. Possession of nesting sight
3. The most important 'trick' of the jackdaw to win his female is:
   A. displaying his head and neck
   B. to be like a human being
   C. to become embroiled with other birds
   D. to possess a place for building a nest
4. The jackdaw fights with other jackdaws because:
   A. he does not respect the senior birds
   B. he wants to fight with his rivals
   C. he does not like to be challenged
   D. he wants to show off
5. Which of the following statements best describes the central theme of the passage?
   A. The courtship behaviour of birds
   B. The similarities between the courtship behaviour of birds and man
   C. The astonishing facts about the jackdaw's love life
   D. The scientific study of the jackdaw's life

PASSAGE–48

Young seekers after peace know that only equal trust shown to all the peoples of the earth and not just to a few of them, can lead to the healing of the wounds that tear them apart and so it is essential never to humiliate the members of a Essential also is boundless concern for so many men and women who today, as exiles or immigrants, live on foreign soil. If every home was open to somebody of foreign origin, the racial problem would be partially solved.

1. For the reconciliation and unity it is essential:
   A. to have no discrimination in the trust shown to the people of the earth
   B. to have young seekers after peace
   C. to have confidence in at least a few of the people
   D. to punish the leaders who committed inhuman sins
2. To make the members of a nation responsible for the inhuman acts of their leaders is:
   A. unimportant
   B. understandable
   C. unjust
   D. undesirable
3. Boundless concern should be shown to:
   A. one's own country men alone
   B. the people belonging to our friendly nations only
   C. the foreigners who just visit our country
   D. all the exiles living away from their native lands

4. The theme of the passage is:
   A. rigid nationalism alone can help peaceful co-existence
   B. trusting all the people of the earth may lead to serious problems
   C. being cautious of others is a must to live in peace
   D. concern for everyone irrespective of the race or country

ANSWERS

PASSAGE–1

1	2	3	4	5
C	D	D	B	A
6	7	8	9	10
D	C	D	D	D

PASSAGE–2

1	2	3	4	5
B	A	C	D	C
6	7	8	9	10
E	B	E	E	A
11	12	13	14	15
D	E	D	C	B

PASSAGE–3

1	2	3	4	5
A	C	B	C	C
6	7	8	9	10
D	C	D	E	B
11	12	13	14	15
B	B	A	C	E

PASSAGE–4

1	2	3	4	5
C	B	D	A	B
6	7	8	9	10
A	D	C	B	B
11	12	13	14	15
C	E	A	A	E

PASSAGE–5

1	2	3	4	5
D	B	E	C	E
6	7	8	9	10
C	B	A	A	E

PASSAGE–6

1	2	3	4	5
B	A	A	E	B
6	7	8	9	10
E	C	D	B	D

PASSAGE–7

1	2	3	4	5	6
D	B	B	E	A	D
7	8	9	10	11	12
C	D	D	D	C	A

PASSAGE–8

1	2	3	4
B	A	D	C

PASSAGE–9

1	2	3	4
A	B	A	D

PASSAGE–10

1	2	3	4
D	B	C	A

PASSAGE–11

1	2	3	4
B	A	A	C

PASSAGE–12

1	2	3	4
C	C	C	A

PASSAGE–13

1	2	3	4
C	C	C	D

PASSAGE–14

1	2	3	4
D	D	A	B

PASSAGE–15

1	2	3	4
B	D	C	B

PASSAGE–16

1	2	3	4
A	B	B	C

PASSAGE–17

1	2	3	4
D	D	C	C

ENGLISH

PASSAGE–18

1	2	3	4	5
A	C	B	D	C

PASSAGE–19

1	2	3	4	5
D	A	C	A	D

PASSAGE–20

1	2	3	4
D	C	A	D

PASSAGE–21

1	2	3	4	5
D	B	A	B	B

PASSAGE–22

1	2	3
D	A	A

PASSAGE–23

1	2	3	4	5
B	D	D	A	C

PASSAGE–24

1	2	3	4
C	C	D	C

PASSAGE–25

1	2	3	4
A	C	D	A

PASSAGE–26

1	2	3
D	C	B

PASSAGE–27

1	2	3	4
D	C	A	D

PASSAGE–28

1	2	3	4	5
C	C	B	C	B

PASSAGE–29

1	2	3	4
D	A	A	A

PASSAGE–30

1	2	3	4	5
A	D	B	B	D

PASSAGE–31

1	2	3	4
B	C	C	D

PASSAGE–32

1	2	3	4	5
B	B	B	B	B

PASSAGE–33

1	2	3	4
B	A	A	B

PASSAGE–34

1	2	3	4	5
C	C	A	C	D

PASSAGE–35

1	2	3	4	5
C	B	D	B	C

PASSAGE–36

1	2	3	4	5
B	B	C	D	C

PASSAGE–37

1	2	3	4	5
D	D	B	D	B

PASSAGE–38

1	2	3	4	5
D	B	C	C	D

PASSAGE–39

1	2	3	4	5
D	D	C	A	D

PASSAGE–40

1	2	3	4	5
D	A	D	D	C

PASSAGE–41

1	2	3	4	5
D	B	D	C	C

PASSAGE–42

1	2	3	4	5
D	C	A	C	D

PASSAGE–43

1	2	3	4	5
D	B	A	C	B

PASSAGE–44

1	2	3	4	5
C	D	B	A	A

PASSAGE–45

1	2	3	4
C	B	D	C

PASSAGE–46

1	2	3	4
B	A	B	B

PASSAGE–47

1	2	3	4	5
D	C	D	D	C

PASSAGE–48

1	2	3	4
A	C	D	D

PEDAGOGY OF LANGUAGE DEVELOPMENT

English is not the most widely spoken language in the world in terms of the number of native speakers. There are many more Chinese speakers than native English speakers but Chinese is spoken little outside of Chinese communities. However English is the most widespread language in the world.

For Governance and Career

In many former British colonies, English is still used in the government and as a medium of communication among people who do not have another language in common. In some cases, it is a neutral language that is used to avoid giving any one indigenous language too much prestige. English is often used in India, because it is neutral. It is the language of the government. People who speak English have a certain status in society. It is used for books, music and dance. In Singapore, English is a second language, but it is necessary for daily life. Many companies there use English. In addition, sixteen countries in Africa have retained English as the language of the government. Now standard English is taught in schools in those countries, because it is necessary for careers.

For News and Information

English is commonly used as a medium for the communication of information and news. Three quarters of all telex messages and telegrams are sent in English. Eighty percent of computer data are processed and stored in English. Much satellite communication is carried in English. Five thousand newspapers, more than half of the newspapers published in the world, are published in English. Even in many countries where English is a minority language, there is at least one newspaper in English. In India alone, there are three thousand magazines published in English. In many countries, television news is broadcast in English. Because of the power of television, demonstrators in every country use signs printed in English for the benefit of the international press.

For Business, Diplomacy, and the Professions

English is a major language of international business, diplomacy, science and the professions. It is the language that an Iranian businessman and a Japanese businessman are likely to use to communicate. Important commodities such as silver, tin, and hard currency are traded in English. English is also an official language of many professional and international organizations including the United Nations.

For Entertainment

Popular culture has also played an important part in spreading English. American and British popular music are heard all over the world. American movies are seen in almost every country. Books in English are available even in countries where very few people actually use English. One reason that students give for learning English is to understand these songs, movies and books.

For Travel

English is also very important for international travel. Much of the information, countries disseminate about themselves outside of their borders, is in English. English is spoken in large hotels and tourist attractions, at airports, and in shops that tourists frequent. There are travel brochures printed in English, and TV news is available in English.

LEARNING

A considerable change in the behaviour of the organism is called learning. When organism comes in contact with his environment certain necessary adjustment in the behaviour is needed. This adjustment in behaviour is the result of acquision of various habits, skills, attitudes and knowledge which is actually learning in simple term.

Thus, learning means change in response or behaviour (modification, elimination or acquisition of responses involving some degree of performance) caused partly or wholly by conscious or unconscious experiences. This learning does not include physiological changes such as fatigue, temporary sensory resistance or non functioning even after continued stimulation.

Definition of Learning

It is very difficult to give a universally acceptable definition of learning because psychologists have defined the concept from different angles on the basis of their experiments. The common feature among these definitions is that learning in psychology has the status of a construct which means an idea or image that can not be directly observed like electrons or genes but they are inferred from the behaviour of the organism.

Melvin H Marx has defined learning in the following words;

"Learning is a relatively enduring change in behaviour which is a function of prior behaviour (usually called practice).

Explanation : According to the definition given above learning has three attributes:

1. Learning is a some what permanent change in behaviour. Changes occurred due to illness, fatigue, maturation or the consumption of intoxicants is not learning.
2. Learning is not directly observable. It is inferred from the behaviour of the organism in the form of construct.
3. Learning is a function of practice and experience. Experiences adds learning and practice gives it an enduring nature.

Some other **definitions** of learning are given below;

"Learning is modification of behaviour through experiences." — **Gates**

"Learning involves the acquisition of habit knowledge and attitudes". —**Crow and Crow**

"Learning is any change in behaviour resulting from behaviour." —**Guilford**

"Learning includes both acquisition and retention." —**Skinner**

Characteristics of Learning

On the basis of the meaning and definitions given above following characteristics of learning can be derived:

1. **Learning is a relatively permanent change in behaviour :** Temporary changes in behaviour brought about due to some accidents or consuming any drugs is not learning at all. Learning is a relatively permanent change in behaviour. It is in this context we can say that reading some selected material to pass an examination is not learning. It is because learnt material is forgotten immediately after the exam.
2. **Learning is a progress or growth of the organism :** Learning is a fundamental need of life. Without it, no progress or growth is possible. This process of growth is unending also. One achievement of the organism motivates him to go for further achievement and thus excellence in many cases is achieved.
3. **Learning is a life long process :** An organism needs learning (behavioural change) at every moment of life to adjust to new situations at every moment. He can not sit idle at any time. Situations all the time force him for the acquisition of new learning.
4. **Learning is not directly observable :** How much learning has taken place in an organism can not be directly observed. It is inferred from his behaviour which is manifested by some activities, mental or physical.
5. **Learning is the result of experiences :** Experiences are gained at every moment of life. Learning is the other name of these experiences.
6. **Learning is a goal directed process :** Learning is a purposeful activity. It is a goal directed process. Learning which is the result of unconscious efforts of the individual is not learning in actual sense.
7. **Learning is retained through practice :** Practice or exercise is a must to retain learning. If practice is not made, learning will be forgotten and the nature of learning will no longer remain permanent. Thus, learning is acquisition and retention both.
8. **Learning is aroused by individual and social needs :** Learning depends upon our social needs, problems, desires, and ideals. There are certain persons who learn very fast whereas others are slow in learning. It should be noticed that social environment affects learning. It is impossible to learn in the absence of environment.
9. **Learning is active and creative :** Learning is active and creative i.e. learning depends upon the active involvement of the learner. It is said that if the learner is not self active, he cannot learn.

   It is, therefore, said that learning is the result of active involvement and experience from the sender and the receiver both.
10. **Learning is universal :** Humans are not the only organism that learn ie, react to the

environment for adjustment. Animals also go through the process of learning though their speed of learning may be slower than humans.

ACQUISITION

Language acquisition is the process by which the language capability develops in a human. It is the process by which a child acquires its mother tongue. It is the most wonderful feat we perform in our whole life and we do it at an age when we can hardly do anything else. It is an active process by which children, taking cues available to them, construct their own utterances and say things they have never heard of. Language learning is a behaviour acquired by making conscious efforts. It involves certain skills – learning to understand when it is spoken, speaking, reading and writing. It is also forming a certain set of habits. It is acquired by imitation and practice. Since language is a learned activity, we have to learn it and teach it properly.

Distinction between Acquisition and Learning

There are many distinctions between the processes of acquisition and learning.

1. Children within 5 years of age learn their mother tongue through acquisition. A second language, is through conscious effort of learning.
2. Acquisition is an unconscious process where no formal classroom instruction is involved. Learning, however is about conscious knowledge and the application of rules and structures.
3. In language acquisition, the focus is on communication or reception of a message. But in language learning the thrust is on syntax and grammar.
4. The context is usually crucial and meaningful in language acquisition but it need not be important to that extent in language learning.
5. Motivation is a matter of urgent necessity for acquisition. It is not so for second learning.
6. Most importantly, the usual outcome of language acquisition is fluency which is by no means guaranteed in language learning.

It is the process by which humans acquire the capacity to perceive, produce and use words to understand and communicate. This capacity involves the picking up of diverse capacities including syntax, phonetics and an extensive vocabulary. This language might be vocal as with speech or manual as in sign. Language acquisition usually refers to first language acquisition, which studies infants' acquisition of their native language, rather than second language acquisition, which deals with acquisition (in both children and adults) of additional languages.

The capacity to acquire and use language is a key aspect that distinguishes humans from other organisms. While many forms of animal communication exist, they have a limited range of nonsyntactically structured vocabulary tokens that lack cross cultural variation between groups.

A major concern in understanding language acquisition is how these capacities are picked up by infants from what appears to be very input. A range of theories of language acquisition has been created in order to explain this apparent problem including innatism in which a child is born prepared in some manner with these capacities, as opposed to the other theories in which language is simply learned.

Social interactionist theory consists of a number of hypotheses on language acquisition. These hypotheses deal with written, spoken, or visual social tools which consist of complex systems of symbols and rules on language acquisition and development. The compromise between ''nature'' and ''nurture'' is the ''interactionist'' approach. In addition, for years, psychologists and researchers have been asking the same question. What are the language behaviours that nature provides innately and what are those behaviours that are realized by environmental exposure, which as nurture.

The relational frame theory (Hayes, Barnes-Holmes, Roche, 2001), provides a wholly selectionist/ learning account of the origin and development of language competence and complexity. Based upon the principles of Skinnerian behaviorism the relational frame theory posits that children acquire language purely through interacting with the environment. The relational frame theorists introduced the concept of functional contextualism in language learning, which emphasizes the importance of predicting and influencing psychological events, such as thoughts, feelings and behaviours, by focusing on manipulable variables in their context. The relational frame theory distinguishes itself from Skinner's work by identifying and defining a particular type of operant conditioning known as derived relational responding, a learning process that to date appears to occur only in humans possessing a capacity for language. Empirical studies supporting the predictions of relational frame theory suggest that children learn language via a system of inherent reinforcements, challenging the view that language acquisition is based upon innate, language-specific cognitive capacities.

Emergentist theories, such as Mac Winney's competition model, posit that language acquisition is a cognitive process that emerges from the interaction of biological pressures and the environment. According to these theories, neither nature nor nurture alone is sufficient to trigger language learning; both of these influences must work together in order to allow children to acquire a language. The proponents of these theories argue that general cognitive processes subserve language acquisition and that the end result of these processes is language-specific phenomena, such as word learning and grammar acquisition. The findings of many empirical studies support the predictions of these theories, suggesting that language acquisition is a more complex process than many believe.

PRINCIPLES OF LANGUAGE TEACHING

1. Consider the whole person : Teacher should take into consideration who the student is. Know different aspects of the individual. (Student's psychology, social background, etc.) Consult with the guiding and class teachers. Don't grade only by looking at his learning English.
2. Language learning is both forming habit and also utilizing the student's innate capacity. Cognitive school of Psychology using the student's innate capacity for the language. The student uses his creative mental power.
3. Keep the students involved. Try to have a student centered class as far as possible. Keep the appropriate ratio of teacher talk and student talk.
4. Language learners learn to do by doing. Items of language should be practised. Practice is extermely important in foreign language learning. Practice, especially drilling, helps with habit formation.
5. Teach all 4 language skills : Listening, Speaking, Reading, Writing. Listening and reading are receptive, speaking and writing are productive skills. All four language skills should go hand-in-hand. They should be integrated. All people understand far more than they can produce. The child has the move following order in acquiring the four skills Listening-Speaking-Reading-Writing.
6. All learning should be functional and have meaning for the students in terms of their needs and life values. Start with their experiences.
7. Go from the known to the unknown. Build on what the students know either in their native language or in English. Compare and Contrast where possible. As a principle, try to have as meaningful language material as possible.
8. Teach only one thing at a time. Don't teach vocabulary and structure at the same time. Teach a new grammatical pattern with the known vocabulary items. While teaching new vocabulary items, use known grammatical patterns in your illustrated sentences.
9. Teach beginning (elementary) students only the forms most frequently used in normal speech. Help them realize that there may be more than one way of expressing the same ideas. But in the beginning, teach them only one form. e.g. the most commonly used request pattern is : Please open the door, Open the door please.
10. Errors will naturally occur in language learning. It is not necessary to correct every error. Be selective in error correction. Be gentle in error correction. Errors are a natural, necessary, and inevitable part of learning. Never interrupt your student while he is talking or reading for a correction. Wait until he finishes his part of talking or reading. Gentle correction should be a principle. Correct only common mistakes.
11. Recognize individual differences. All students learn at different roles. In every class there will naturally be slow, average, and bright students. Give opportunity to all the students to participate in class activities. Do not let the bright students monopolize. You can give bright students difficult tasks to keep their interest alive. To form mixed ability groups we should do anything possible not to foster the feeling of impriority.
12. Keep the pace alive. Provide a variety of activities. Class activities should not go at a monotonous rate. There will be boredom and little or no learning. The activities should go dynamically not monotonously. If the students are not interested with the activity, stop that activity.
13. Teach with examples. Examples speak louder than language explanation. Examples can help the students learn much better than complicated explanations.
14. Relate form to meaning and contextualize. All class activities should be meaningful. Meaning should always be in the foreground. Whatever activity the students are involved in, the students should be able to understand the meaning of what they hear, say, read, or write. Teach new vocabulary items or a grammatical pattern or pronunciation in context. In teaching vocabulary give the meaning and pronunciation. Smallest context is a sentence meaning arises out of the situation. We can use dialogues, anectodes in the spoken form as context.

15. Assign tasks in class. Involve the students as much as possible. A variety of tasks can be assigned in class.
16. Give students a feeling of confidence and success and encourage them. Education should be geared on success. When the grading time comes at the first semester, if there is a student on borderline, pass him.
17. Use Audio-visual aid as much as possible.
18. Teach well before you test. Students often fail because of poor teaching, poor testing, poor evaluation of the exams.

ROLE OF LISTENING

Listening is an active process that has three basic steps.

- **Hearing :** Hearing just means listening enough to catch what the speaker is saying. For example, say you were listening to a report on horses, and the speaker mentioned that no two are alike. If you can repeat the fact, then you have heard what has been said.
- **Understanding :** The next part of listening happens when you take what you have heard and understand it in your own way. Let's go back to that report on horses. When you hear that no two are alike, think about what that might mean. You might think, "Maybe this means that the colour is different for each horse."
- **Judging :** After you are sure you understand what the speaker has said, think about whether it makes sense. Do you believe what you have heard? You might think, "How could the colour to be different for every horse.

How to Become a Good Listener

- Give your full attention on the person who is speaking. Don't look out the window or at what else is going on in the room.
- Make sure your mind is focused, too. It can be easy to let your mind wander if you think you know what the person is going to say next, but you might be wrong! If you feel your mind wandering, change the position of your body and try to concentrate on the speaker's words.
- Let the speaker finish before you begin to talk. Speakers appreciate having the chance to say everything they would like to say without being interrupted. When you interrupt, it looks like you aren't listening, even if you really are.
- Let yourself finish listening before you begin to speak! You can't really listen if you are busy thinking about what you want say next.
- Listen for main ideas. The main ideas are the most important points the speaker wants to get across. They may be mentioned at the start or end of a talk, and repeated a number of times.
- Ask questions. If you are not sure you understand what the speaker has said, just ask. It is a good idea to repeat in your own words what the speaker said so that you can be sure your understanding is correct.
- Give feedback. Sit up straight and look directly at the speaker. Now and then, nod to show that you understand. At appropriate points you may also smile, frown, laugh, or be silent. These are all ways to let the speaker know that you are really listening. Remember, you listen with your face as well as your ears!

ROLE OF SPEAKING

Speaking English is the main goal of many learners. Their personalities play a large role in determining how quickly and how correctly they will accomplish this goal. Those who are risk-takers unafraid of making mistakes will generally be more talkative, but with many errors that could become hard-to-break habits. Conservative, shy students may take a long time to speak confidently, but when they do, their English often contains fewer errors and they will be proud of their English ability. It's a matter of quantity vs. quality, and neither approach is wrong. However, if the aim of speaking is communication and that does not require perfect English, then it makes sense to encourage quantity in your classroom. Break the silence and get students communicating with whatever English they can use, correct or not, and selectively address errors that block communication.

Speaking lessons often tie in pronunciation and grammar which are necessary for effective oral communication. Or a grammar or reading lesson may incorporate a speaking activity. Either way, students will need some preparation before the speaking task. This includes introducing the topic and providing a model of the speech they are to produce. A model may not apply to discussion-type activities, in which case students will need clear and specific instructions about the task to be accomplished. Then the students will practice with the actual speaking activity.

These activities may include imitating (repeating), answering verbal cues, interactive conversation, or an oral presentation. Most speaking activities inherently practice listening skills as well, such as when one student is given a simple drawing and sits behind another student, facing away. The first must give instructions to the second to reproduce the drawing. The second student asks questions to clarify unclear instructions, and neither can look at each other's page during the activity.

Some ideas to keep in mind as you plan your speaking activities.

- **Content :** As much as possible, the content should be practical and usable in real-life situations. Avoid too much new vocabulary or grammar, and focus on speaking with the language the students have.
- **Correcting Error :** You need to provide appropriate feedback and correction, but don't interrupt the flow of communication. Take notes while pairs or groups are talking and address problems to the class after the activity without embarrassing the student who made the error. You can write the error on the board and ask who can correct it.
- **Conversation Strategies :** Encourage strategies like asking for clarification, paraphrasing, gestures, and initiating ('hey,' 'so,' 'by the way').
- **Teacher Intervention :** If a speaking activity loses steam, you may need to jump into a role-play, ask more discussion questions, clarify your instructions, or stop an activity that is too difficult or boring.
- **Quantity vs. Quality :** Address both interactive fluency and accuracy, striving foremost for communication. Get to know each learner's personality and encourage the quieter ones to take more risks.

It is very important that teachers are aware if the aim of a speaking activity is fluency or accuracy, because the role of the teacher is radically different in each activity type.

In accuracy activities, the teacher needs to correct the students if they make mistakes. The whole point of the activity is to form correct sentences, so if a student gets it wrong, it needs to be immediately addressed in the form of correction.

In process oriented fluency activities, however, correcting students can be very counter productive indeed. If we want our students to communicate, we need to give them time and space to do so, in order that they can start to learn to deal with all the demands of oral interaction.

In fluency activities, the teacher becomes more of an organiser, a facilitator, a manager, a guide, a guru. The teacher sets up the activity, explains what needs to be done, organises the necessary groupings, and then lets the learners get on with it.

FUNCTIONS OF LANGUAGE

Six major functions of the English language are:

- A means of conveying information, example, "The Kyneton train is now approaching on platform 4." This example is conveying to those waiting for the Kyneton train that it has now arrived.
- An instrument of action, example, "Don't forget to feed the dog." This example is telling the second person in the conversation to do something.
- To maintain social relationships example, "Good Morning, how are you?" Here we see that this function allows us to make and keep friends. This function is usually more informal than others.
- Acting as a marker of groups example, "He was out for a duck." This example would only be heard by someone talking about the cricket, therefore establishing that the people involved in the conversation are involved with cricket in one way or another, marking them as a group.
- As an instrument of cognitive and conceptual development. This is the power of language to influence thinking. This is why we have many words that mean basically the same thing, because they all have slight differences or are used in different circumstances. For example if you could only say you were happy, but not excited, thrilled, etc, then you would not be able to give as much detail.
- As an art form, language can be purposed towards beauty for beauty's sake.

THE ROLE OF GRAMMAR IN LEARNING A LANGUAGE

One question always arise in my mind is learning grammar necessary for picking up a new language? Some linguists think grammar rules are usually considered core of any language learning class, without which a student would be completely lost. However, a language acquisition theory from Dr. Stephen Krashen, a renowned linguistics professor, suggests picking up a new language doesn't require any conscious knowledge of grammar; instead, the best and most effective methods of acquiring a new language occur through regular and useful conversation.

Dr. Krashen actually separates the way people learn languages into two separate categories: the ''acquired system'' and the ''learned system''. The acquired points to learning a new language in an

ENGLISH

almost subconscious manner, mostly through regular communication and interaction using the target language. The learned system, on the other hand, points to the traditional method of learning that many of us are used to, in which we learn conjugations, grammar rules, tenses, etc. The most important conclusion of Krashen's hypothesis, however, is that the ''acquired system'' is more effective and indeed better the ''learned system'' used by most language schools worlwide.

Language, which includes grammar, would emerge as a result of interaction and communication or that it would emerge as a result of comprehensible input. Krashen holds that given a ''natural order'' in acquistion, grammar teaching is unnecessary.

However, the acquisition of a second language is usually achieved in an acquisition—rich environment. In an acquisition—poor environment like China, there isn't much natural exposure to the target language. We cannot expect the students to achieve grammatical competence solely through interaction and communication.

In communicative language teaching, students could assimilates new structures through active practice and use. However, some also felt that ''more able and/or elder pupils wanted, and could benefit from systematic and explicit oresentation of grammatical rules and explanations, and also that grammatical expositions could assist pupils in shifting from rote learning to a more creative use of the target language''. Wilkins (1976) points out that acquiring the grammatical system of the target language is of central importance, because an inadequate knowledge of grammar would severely constrain linguistic creativity and limit the capacity for communication.

CHALLENGES OF TEACHING LANGUAGE IN A DIVERSE CLASSROOM

Language Difficulty

Students in bilingual and ESL classrooms manipulate more than one language and are influenced by more than one culture. Their experiences with these languages and cultures influence their learning. The more we understand the personal, socio-cultural, and linguistic backgrounds of bilingual students, the better equipped we will be to provide these students with an effective learning environment. This environment should be one that supports learning in a second language and culture, while fostering a positive attitude and respect for the other language and culture.

The responsibility for English language learning, academic progress, and integration of bilingual and ESL learners into the school community should be assumed by *all* personnel at the school, not just by the bilingual and ESL staff. School administrators should make certain that bilingual students have opportunities to integrate both socially and academically with monolingual English speakers. The following practices promote the inclusion of all students in a supportive, educational environment:

1. Create participatory, inquiry-based classrooms
2. Maintain high expectations for all students
3. Teach ESL through content-area instruction
4. Use thematic units
5. Incorporate culturally familiar learning strategies
6. Use a variety of strategies when teaching literacy
7. Provide appropriate and valid assessment
8. Recognize that students use both languages to learn

Errors

English is such a complex language, it is fraught with traps that we all frequently fall into. With this list I hope to clear up at least a few of the confusing words we use every day. This is a list of some of the more common errors people make with English.

Its / It's

As in the case above, the apostrophe denotes an abbreviation: it's = it is. Its means "belongs to it". The confusion arises here because we also use an apostrophe in English to denote possession – *except* in this case; if you want to say "the cat's bag" you say "its bag" not "it's bag". "It's" always means "it is" or "it has". "It's a hot day." "it's been fun seeing you."

Your / You're

Your means "belonging to you". You're means "you are". The simplest way to work out the correct one to use is to read out your sentence.

Practice / Practise

In US English, practice is used as either a verb (doing word), or noun (naming word). Hence, a doctor has a practice, and a person practices the violin. In UK english, practice is a noun, and practise is a verb. A doctor has a practice, but his daughter practises the piano.

Bought / Brought

Bought relates to buying something. Brought relates to bringing something. For example, I bought a bottle of wine which had been brought over from France.

Desert / Dessert

This is a confusing one because in English an 's' on its own is frequently pronounced like a 'z' and two 's's are usually pronounced as a n 's' (for example: prise, prissy). In this case, desert follow the rule – it means a large stretch of sand. However, dessert is pronounced "dez-urt" with the emphasis on the second syllable – ie, something we eat as part of our meal. To make matters worse, when a person leaves the army without permission, it is spelt desert.

Dryer / Drier

If your clothes are wet, put them in a clothes dryer. That will make them drier. A hair dryer also makes hair drier.

Chose / Choose

This is actually quite an easy one to remember – in English we generally pronounce 'oo' as it is written – such as "moo". The same rule applies here: choose is pronounced as it is written (with a 'z' sound for the 's') – and chose is said like "nose". Therefore, if you had to choose to visit Timbuktu, chances are you chose to fly there. Chose is the past tense, choose is the present tense.

Lose / Loose

This one is confusing. In this case, contrary to normal rules of English, the single 's' in loose is pronounced like an 's' – as in wearing trousers that are too loose. Lose on the other hand, relates to loss – for example: "I hope we don't lose this game". A good way to remember this is that in the word "lose" you have lost the second 'o' from loose. If you can't remember a rule that simple, you are a loser!

Literally

This one is not only often used in error, it is incredibly annoying when it is used in the wrong way. Literally means "it really happened" – therefore, unless you live on a parallel universe with different rules of physics, you can not say "he literally flew out the door".

Disorders

Children who have a condition of incomplete or less than normal mental development so that they are unable to adjust to day to day living in a normally efficient, useful, productive and harmonious manner are called mentally retarded. They are, hence, in constant need or care, protection, supervision and help.

Thus, mental retardation is a serious disability. It creates a lot of learning problems before mentally retarded children. These learning problems create obstacle in other areas of life as well. Thus, total life activities are affected by mental retardation.

General Characteristics of Mentally Retarded

On the basis of the definitions given above following common characteristics of mentally retarded children (less than 18 years of age) can be derived:

1. **Limited functioning :** Their level of functioning is very limited. They have difficulty not only in learning but also doing routine life job due to significant loss of conceptual, practical and social intelligence.
2. **Sub average intellectual functioning :** Their intellectual functioning is less than average (below 80 IQ) on an intelligence test. This is the fundamental criterion of diagnosing a mentally retarded child.
3. **Poor performance level :** If someone falls short in his performance of certain tasks from the performance of the majority of children of his own age, he is said to have low mental age or sub-normal intellectual functioning. For example, If eight years old child performs equal to the child of 6 years, his IQ will be (Mental Age/Chronological age × 100) or (6/8) × 100=75
4. **Slow acquisition of skills :** Academic (content related) and non academic (action related) both types of skills are acquired by them at a very slow rate.
5. **Low level of adaptive skills. :** They are not only slow in acquiring skills but they are always poor in adaptive skills also.
6. **Early manifestations :** Mental retardation manifests itself before the age of 18. From this perspective, mental retardation is viewed as a disorder of the life period characterized by the slow rate of development.

Identification (Diagnosis) of Mental Retardation

For early detection of mental retardation of a child, the parents and the teacher refer the cases to child guidance centres so that their mental level may be ascertained and they may be classified for the purpose of placement (education and training).

Following symptoms will help the teacher and the parents to decide whether the child should be sent to child study centres for screening or not. Screening test results must be interpreted and matched in terms of following clinical diagnostic symptoms.

1. **Social adjustment criterion :** If a person is functioning adequately in all socio-economic conditions as compared to his peers or age mates, there is no need of sending the person

to child guidance centres (CGC) for proper screening. Mentally retarded person will surely exhibit adjustment problem in social situations.

2. **Learning ability criterion :** Failure in educational endeavours or low level of general aptitude is another criterion of mental retardation but effects of socio-economic and physical factors should also be taken into account because poor academic achievement is caused due to these factors also.

3. **Development criterion :** The developmental history of the suspected child should also be taken into account, e.g., when the child began to sit, crawl, stand, walk and talk, whether it is normal or not. Delayed development is generally seen in mentally retarded children so, retardation in these areas is certainly helpful in diagnosing the child.

4. **Academic achievement criterion :** These children are generally very slow in academic achievement due to low level of retention power and understanding ability. When they constantly perform poorly in content related skills despite repeated remedial measures adopted by the teachers, they are suspected to be mentally retarded.

5. **Size of the family criterion :** Larger the size of the family, lower will be the IQ scores of the family. Hence, it should also be taken into consideration while taking a decision of M.R.

6. **Medical examination :** It is generally done by experts in the field in CGCs.

   Important physical symptoms of mentally retarded children are given below :

   I. He has lips fairly apart with his tongue visible in between the teeth with saliva.

   II. He has a vacant look and a clumsy gait.

   III. He has flattered skull, stanting eyes and broad nose.

   IV. He has unusually large heads.

7. **Proper screening :** After identifying all the above symptoms, suspected mentally retarded children are properly screened by using different tests.

   The description of some of these tests are given below :

   (a) **Siguin Form Board Test :** This form board test was developed by Seguin a French physician in 1907 to identify and screen mentally retarded children. Here ten boards of different sizes are kept in different shelves of respective sizes in a tray. These boards are taken out of the tray at the time of testing. Then testee is asked to put these boards in the tray again in the same sequence as it was before in as less time as possible. This process is repeated three times and least time taking effort is taken for the purpose of scoring.

   (b) **Developmental Screening Test :** This test is used to measure the mental development of children from the age of 3 months to 15 years.

   Here different types of activities are given to children according to their ages to do. Mental development of the child is calculated on the basis of performance on these activities. Children and their parents and relatives are also interviewed here to gather some more informations about the child.

   (c) **General Mental Ability Test** : This test was developed by RP Srivastava and Kiran Saxena in 1985. Verbal and non-verbal both types of items have been included here. Both these sections have 50 items each. These sections have further been divided into five sub sections namely, analogy, classification, number series, reasoning problems and absurdities. Each item has four multiple choice responses out of which only one option is correct.

   Time allotted for verbal and non-verbal items is 15 minutes and 10 minutes respectively. One mark is given for every correct response and thus a child can score maximum 100 marks. This test can be administered in individual and group situations both.

Purpose of Diagnosing Mental Retardation

Diagnosis of mental retardation serves the following purposes:

1. It provides an estimate of the individual's present level of functioning in terms of the test performance, social adjustment and so on.
2. It provides information regarding the cause of the individual's inadequacies.
3. It helps us to provide them proper care and treatment.
4. It provides some predictions of the probable outcomes in future.
5. It helps us to take decision regarding their

placement in proper special educational programmes.

Mental Retardation and Age

Incidence of mental retardation rises with the increasing age, reaches at its peak at about 14-18 years and then drops off sharply.

Causes of Mental Retardation

Underlying causes of mental retardation can be divided into two categories :

(A) Endogenous causes

(B) Exogenous causes

(A) Endogenous causes

Endogenous literally means originating within the body of the organism, and should refer to those forms of mental retardation that are genetically determined. Heredity is the primary casual factor here. Important genetic factors active to cause mental retardation are given below :

1. **Action of dominant gene** : The transmission of defective dominant gene from one generation to the next is very rare but in some cases some of these conditions may occur in mild form in one generation or in certain members of the family of that generation and in more severe form in another generation or in other members of the same family.
2. **Action of recessive gene** : Such defective children typically come of normal parents. This defect occurs due to child's receiving two similar recessive genes one from each parent.

(B) Exogenous causes

They are also known as secondary, acquired or environmental causes. Some of these causes of mental retardation are given below :

(a) **Prenatal causes :** They work before the birth of the child, and are related to pregnant mothers. Important prenatal causes of mental retardation are as follows:

1. *Physical trauma :* Unsuccessful attempt at trauma and accident to pregnant mother so injure the fetus as to lower the child's mental level.
2. *Nutrition :* Malnutrition during the period of pregnancy may lower mental level of the child.
3. *Infectious diseases :* Infectious diseases of the mother during pregnancy may affect physical and mental development of the fetus and lower mental ability of the child.
4. *Blood incompatibility :* Incompatibility between maternal and fetal blood may cause the child severely jaundiced and mental deficiency is a possible accompaniment.
5. *Radioactivity :* Radiation may affect the germ cells in three ways.
   - They may be killed.
   - Their chromosomes maybe broken up.
   - They may be mutated.

   All these changes may lower mental ability of the child.
6. *Toxic agents :* Toxins such as lead, nicotine, and morphine affect the developing embryo and lower the mental level of off springs.
7. *Consumption of drugs and alcohols :* Consumption of wine, LSD, heroine etc., by the mother during pregnancy is also very fatal for the fetus development and it may cause permanent mental retardation of the child after birth.

(b) **Perinatal (natal) causes :** These causes are associated with the delivery of the child. Important likely causes of mental retardation are as follows:

1. *Pre-mature-birth :* Studies have shown that a large number of people born pre-maturely are mentally retarded. The brain structure of the premature infant is more fragile and thus it can be very easily damaged.
2. *Traumatic Birth injuries :* It is estimated that birth injuries are responsible for 1.5% of the total mental retardation in western countries.
3. *Delivery Complications :* If complications have emerged during the period of delivery, it may cause mental retardation to some extent.

(c) **Post-natal causes :** Important post natal causes of mental retardation are given below :

1. *Brain injury :* Traumatic brain injury from gun shot, wounds or fall is a rare cause of mental retardation.
2. *Infections :* Brain infection causes permanent brain damage or mental retardation. They include encephalitis of various types, meningitis, hydrocephally and the like infections.
3. *Severe malnutrition :* Deficiency in any particular nutrient like vitamins or minerals causes deficiency diseases

which may cause mental retardation in the long run.

4. *General health :* Mental and physical health are most of the time found associated though mental retardation due to poor physical health is not permanent. Heavy mental shock may also cause mental deficiency temporarily. However, good physical health does not necessarily mean good mental health.
5. *Cultural factors :* Low IQ does not always mean low level of intelligence. It is because intellectual level is influenced by the child's cultural background. If an intelligence test includes items representing a particular culture, children alien to that culture are not supposed to perform well on this test of intelligence and hence their IQ level will be low.
6. *Home and family background :* It also affects mental level and intellectual power but so far as mental retardation is concerned, its role is very limited.
7. *Social deprivation :* When a child is deprived of social environment for a very long period of time he is likely to become mentally retarded.

Methods of Identification of Mentally Retarded Children

Different criteria are used to classify mentally retarded into different categories. These criteria are given below:

1. **Normal distribution criterion :** In a normally distributed population, mentally retarded population is found beyond 2SD from the mean, i.e., about 2% of the population is generally found mentally retarded. If this population is tested on intelligence test, their IQ will be less than 90.
2. **IQ criterion :** American Association of Mental Deficiency has classified mentally retarded children on the basis of their IQ scores. Several other educationists have also classified them on this basis. Four broad categories of mentally retarded children are given below:
   - *(a)* Border line cases or dullers : (IQ = 70-90)
   - *(b)* Morons or feeble minded (IQ = 50-70)
   - *(c)* Imbeciles (IQ = 25-50)
   - *(d)* Idiots (IQ less than 25)
3. **Medical criterion :** Medical personnel and physician classify mentally retarded children on the basis of their physical/mental characteristics caused by a damage in the functioning of the brain due to genetic or environmental reasons. Some of these categories are given below:
   - *(a)* Brain damaged child : It is a type of organic malfunctioning in the body which is caused by any serious disease or damage of the brain.
   - *(b)* Mongoloids : These slow learners are very peculiar in the physical characteristics and behaviour such as they are very humble and friendly, they are very poor in taking initiative, they are obstinate in behaviour and they are so simpleton in their behaviour that we call them as cow of the God. Mongols are moderately mentally retarded whose IQ ranges 50-70.
   - *(c)* Cretin child : Mental retardation in these children are caused due to any deformation in thyroid gland. They can be cured by the physician by correcting thyroid gland provided that they are identified in the early stage. They are similar to monogoloids in behaviour and characteristics.
   - *(d)* Phenylketonurin (PKU) : This problem is caused due to metabolic disturbances but its incidence is very rare. When body fails to metabolise phelinylenin protein, a toxic material reaches the brain and enters it through blood circulation and brain cells are damaged resulting in mental retardation.
   - *(e)* Microcephally and hydrocephally : The head becomes short in microcephally and large in hydrocephally, as a result cerebro spinal fluid which is responsible for mental action stops causing mental retardation permanently.
   - *(f)* Cerebral palsy : It is a type of disease which causes uncontrolled action of some muscles and mental retardation is caused due to inadjustability of muscles.
4. **Social deprivation criteria :** Mental retardation is also caused when a person is deprived of social environment and interaction for a long period of time. When these children comes to the environment they fail to adjust there which again increases their mental retardation.

LANGUAGE SKILLS

There are, in general, four language skills, each based upon the modality of emphasis. These are the Listening, Speaking, Reading, and Writing skills.

Listening Skill

Listening in English is attending to and interpreting oral English. Listening is necessary to develop the speaking skill. The student listens to oral speech in English, then separates into segments the stretch of utterances he hears, groups them into words, phrases, and sentences, and, finally, he understands the message these carry. Listening prepares the students to understand the speech of the native speakers of English as they speak naturally in a normal speed and normal manner.

There are three approaches to listening: interactive (listening to a message and doing something as a consequence) and one-way communication or non-interactive (just listening and retaining the message, in activities such as conversations overheard, public address announcements, recorded messages, etc.) and self-talk. Listening to radio and watching TV and films, public performances, lectures, religious services, etc., generally reflect non-interactive listening. Responding to the commands given reflects interactive listening, which, in fact, is equally widespread in communicative situations. Self-talk is also an important process by which internal thinking and reasoning is carried out.

Role of Listening : In the classroom, students listen in order to repeat and to understand. In listening to repeat, students imitate and memorize linguistic items such as words, idioms, and sentence patterns. This is an important beginning task and focus of listening exercises. However, it is listening to understand that is real listening in its own right.

Students listen to understand as part of using English for communication purposes. In listening to understand, students may be involved in the question-oriented response model of learning or in the task-oriented model of learning. In the question-oriented response model, students may be asked to listen to a sentence, a dialogue, a conversation, a passage, or a lecture and asked to answer questions which may be presented in the form of true/false statements, multiple choice questions, fill in the blank, or short answers. In the task-oriented response model, students may be asked to listen to a passage and accomplish the task described in the passage through interaction with others or by themselves.

Listening Comprehension

The listening skill is the most neglected one, both in first and second language teaching. Teachers tend to focus on the rudimentary elements of listening briefly, and pass over to other aspects of language teaching. Discrimination of sounds and intonations often form the major part of listening practice in the classroom. Listening for content is often assumed. In reality, the listening skill is fundamental to the entire process of mastering and using a language, whether first or second or foreign.

In the past, listening was labeled as a passive skill, along with reading. No doubt, it is a receptive skill like reading. Speaking and writing were considered to be productive skills, but also active skills. While this categorization is somewhat justifiable because the focus of listening is on reception of information, listening itself cannot be fully and correctly characterized only as a passive skill.

There is a need for an active involvement of the self for the efficient performance of listening. The listener is often forced into guessing an approximation to what the speaker is communicating. The listener expects and anticipates what may be the form and content of the immediate message being delivered. He actively avoids the redundancies in the process of listening, focuses himself on the relevant, interesting and/or crucial points, and engages himself in some critical analysis of content. Listening becomes the stepping stone for action. In view of all these and other activities that are involved in listening, we should consider listening as an active skill demanding active participation of the listener.

In essence, listening is not mere recognition of linguistic units and their meanings. It comprises an ability to predict information based on linguistic context, and the situation and topic of the message conveyed by the linguistic code, as well as the expectations about the world. Listening helps also to understand and act according to the emotional state of the speaker.

No one should think that listening comprehension exercises are miniature tests. These generally come in the form of questions to be answered, action to be performed, or objects to be identified, etc. Because this format demands response in the form in which tests are generally prepared and presented, we tend to treat the exercise as a test. Consider listening comprehension only as practice and look for progress in student performance.

Brief listening comprehension exercises with content interesting to the student and which focus upon and incorporate his communicative needs will develop his listening comprehension to a satisfactory level. Students need to be attentive to the tone of the conversation, and should ask questions whenever they find it difficult to understand the conversation.

What is the generally followed form of listening comprehension exercises? Students are given a specific task such as answering questions or solving problems. They listen to the teacher or the recorded material and perform the task asked for. Thus the teacher as well as materials on tape/cassette recorders become the major means to train the students in listening comprehension.

Speaking Skill

Imitation and repetition are important elementary steps in developing speaking skill in English. Imitation and repetition are inter-related, and yet they are distinct.

Imitation helps students to pronounce and produce the English utterance they hear from the teacher as closely as possible to the utterance produced by her. Imitation is not restricted to mere production of the sounds, phrases, and sentences. It includes also the capacity to produce the utterances in the contexts in which the original utterances were produced.

Some of the imitation and repetition exercises may be organized in the following manner: Present some simple sentence, phrase, or word and ask students to repeat after you. If you want them to understand and repeat a conversation, say the questions and the answers and have the students repeat the latter, or perhaps both, signaling the meaning in some way. The meaning can be demonstrated with realia (real objects brought into the classroom), pictures, gestures, or translating.

The teacher may use pictures, gestures, pantomime, translation, guessing, and drawing on the board to make the students understand the meaning. It is important that you use only meaningful words, phrases, and sentences for imitation and repetition. The props you use to explain or demonstrate the meaning should enable the student to learn the meaning with ease, along with the pronunciation.

Substitution of a word, phrase, or sentence by another is an elementary method which helps students to produce new utterances and to develop speaking skill.

Expressions of greeting, gratitude, small talk, introductions and making acquaintance, leave-taking, appreciation, expressions of regret and asking to be excused, etc., are very important communicative acts students need to master. For one thing, such expressions may take on different form and import in English than the ones students are accustomed to in their language and culture.

Simple question-answer dialogues around a given context and object/objects is another elementary method to develop speaking skill in students.

How does a teacher teach a dialogue? There are three types of drills one could use in the class: **choral drill** in which the entire class participates in one voice with the teacher modelling the utterance; **chain drill** in which one student asks the question and another answers, and in this way the entire class participates as a chain; and **individual drill** in which individual students are pointed out and asked to produce the utterance modelled by the teacher.

Eliciting is an important process which teachers must employ to get the class involved in what is going on in the class. For speaking practice eliciting is highly essential. It helps students to focus their attention, to think, and to use what they already know. It helps teachers to assess what the class already knew.

Translation is another helpful device to encourage students to speak in English. The students may be given some sentences in their own native language and asked to translate them and use these to answer or ask questions. There are several other ways of using translation as a tool to develop speaking skill.

Reading Skill

Scholors classify reading into three kinds: extensive reading, intensive reading, and oral reading. Extensive reading is used "to refer to the teaching of reading through reading. In this approach, there is no overt focus on teaching reading. Rather, it is assumed that the best way for students to learn to read is by reading a great deal of comprehensible material." Intensive reading is used to refer to the actual teaching skills in an instructional setting. Students are exposed to a variety of materials and asked to perform activities such as answering comprehension questions on the passage read. They may be trained to look for critical information in the passage they read, and make inferences, etc. Intensive reading is instruction-based and forms the core of teaching reading in the classroom. Oral reading does attract much attention from many teachers, but it is "an integral part of reading.

At the beginning level, the focus is on the mechanics of reading. The beginner needs to be taught the relationship and the correspondence between the letters of the alphabet and the spoken language.

In a sense, the letters are all abstract symbols. The letter functions as a tag to the sounds it represents. By seeing (reading) the letter, the beginner identifies the appropriate sound value for that letter in that context.

This is not an easy task even for the adult learner. It is possible that the learner may come from a language in which the Roman alphabet similar to the one used in English is being used. And yet the sound values of letters in his language may vary context to context in his language also, which in their turn may be in conflict with the sound values of the letters as used in English.

Or, the learner may come from a language background in which syllabaries are used. That is, he may be accustomed to reading the syllables which more or less retain the same values wherever they are used. However, he will find that in character and chat, cha needs to be read differently.

Or, he may come from a language background where pictograms are used, as in Chinese in which there is no easy and manifest correspondence between the "letter" and the sound.

Keep the following in mind when you begin teaching reading at the beginner's level.

1. The background of the beginner: a child, an illiterate, a moderately educated person.
2. The Reading task involves decoding the system of abstract symbols to discover its relation to the spoken language system.
3. The time taken to master this relationship varies with age, maturation, previous experience, and other social factors.
4. With primary emphasis on mechanics one may master the mechanics of reading in four months.
5. Some recognition problems in English: capital, small, italics, handwriting, left to right, distinction between letters, mirror image problems.
6. Choose the words which express familiar meanings or meanings which can be recognized and retained in memory.
7. Choose only those words which focus on the item to be learned.
8. Do not choose those words which may have the same spelling in English as well as in the learner's language, but are read (pronounced) differently.
9. Do not ignore the stress.

Writing Skill

Writing is an individual effort. Individuals compose their thoughts often in privacy and then reduce their thoughts to writing, using the strict conventions followed in the language. Writing is an individual effort or work, but it must follow the rules laid down. The development of writing even in native English speaking children is conscious and is thus non-spontaneous.

In writing, the discrete nature of linguistic signs should be appreciated consciously. The learner must recognize the sound structure of each word, dissect it and reproduce it in alphabetical symbols, which he must have studied and memorized before. This same deliberate preparedness is needed to put words in a certain sequence to form a sentence.

"Writing is more an individual effort than speaking, while at the same time more rule-bound and therefore more error-prone. . . The speaker does not have to pronounce each word exactly according to one standard of pronunciation or one model of structure, while the writer is expected to produce according to one model of spelling, and usually a reduced range of structures, with 100 percent accuracy".

The writing classes have the potential to help consolidate and improve the students' speaking and reading skills. However, it is important for us to remember that writing is an important skill which can be taught as an end in itself, although none of the language skills is far removed from the other language skills. Focusing on writing as an independent skill helps us to identify the specific problems faced by the learners, and to identify the specific needs of the learners relating to writing. Mechanics of writing are distinct from the mechanics of other skills such as speaking and reading. While reading involves seeing and pronouncing, writing involves association of sounds with mental composition of thoughts and their orderly presentation, and hand movements.

Raimes classifies approaches to teaching writing into five types: controlled to free, free writing, paragraph pattern, grammar-syntax-organization, communicative, and process approaches. In the controlled to free approach, "students are first given sentence exercises, then paragraphs to copy or manipulate grammatically by, for instance, changing questions to statements, present to past, or plural to singular. They might also change words or clauses or combine sentences" (Raimes 1983).

In the free writing approach, students are asked to "write freely on any topic without worrying about grammar and spelling for five or ten minutes. . . . The teachers do not correct these short pieces of free writing; they simply read them and perhaps comment on the ideas the writer expressed" (Raimes 1983). In the paragraph pattern approach, "students copy paragraphs, analyze the form of model paragraphs, and imitate model passages. They put scrambled sentences into paragraph order, they identify general specific statements, they choose or invent an appropriate topic sentence, they insert or delete sentences" (Raimes 1983). In the communicative approach to writing, students are asked to assume the role of a writer who is writing for an audience to read. Whatever is written by a student is modified in some way by other students for better communicative effect.

In the process approach to writing, students "move away from a concentration on the written product to an emphasis on the process of writing" (Raimes 1983).

Note that a proper blend of these approaches to writing will give us best results. For example, the controlled to free approach to writing helps us to focus on proper mechanics in the beginning level, whereas communicative approach to writing will be very effective once our students have some control over the mechanics and have acquired a good number of words and sentence structures to help them match these with their thoughts. All successful texts and teachers have always tried to take the best and relevant aspects of every method to suit the learner's level and need.

EVALUATING LANGUAGE COMPREHENSION

Meaning of Evaluation

Evaluation is the criteria of success or failure of a task done. If it is done at the end of a task, total efforts, including the investment of time and money may be a failure but if it goes side by side of the task, immediate feedback received might alarm the performer to rectify his mistakes and thus there is 100% chance of success of the programme.

Education is also an investment in the sense that time, energy and money are spent to bring about behavioural change in learners. That is why when a teacher performs his teaching works in his class, he also simultaneously finds out whether the changes in behaviour of learners are in concurrence with the learning objectives or not. If it is not so there, then what types of modifications are needed and at what steps of teaching. He also finds out whether the problem lies in his teaching strategies or techniques or it is there in the students itself. Thus, teaching and evaluation run-hand in hand. Evaluation determines the behaviour of students on one hand and testifies to the teaching of the teacher on the other. This very purposeful behaviour of the teacher is called evaluation in education.

Characteristics of Evaluation

On the basis of the definitions given above, the following characteristics of evaluation can be derived.

1. **A Comprehensive Process :** All the three domains of human behaviour, cognitive, affective and psychomotor, can be accurately measured by evaluation. Apart from student's behaviour, teacher's behaviour (his task of teaching) is also evaluated.
2. **A Systematic Process** : Evaluation is a preplanned and systematic process which goes ahead keeping in view the pre-determined objectives. By this process we find out how much change has occurred in the behaviour of students and teachers and how much change is yet to be brought about by the task ahead.
3. **A Continuous Process** : Evaluation process can not be separated from teaching and both go side by side. By this process whatever changes take place in the behaviour of learners, its proper record is maintained and on this very base students are either ranked in a particular class or decision is taken to promote them to the next higher class.
4. **A Social Process** : Education is a purposeful activity fulfilling the requirements of learners and the society. Evaluation tells us to what extent teaching is fulfilling the requirements of both.
5. **An Information Collection Process** : When students progress step by step in the school system, all the informations regarding their progress are gathered by using a number of tests and by going through various techniques of measurement. After that these informations are interpreted in terms of predetermined objectives.
6. **A Combined Process :** While taking the final decision regarding a student and declaring him fail or pass, the reports of all the concerned teachers of school are taken into account. No such decision is taken by the evaluation report of one or two teachers. Thus, evaluation becomes a comprehensive process.
7. **A Process of Value Judgement** : Scoring 60 or 70 percent in any subject by any of the students in a class does not have any meaning unless the scores of the student is compared either with other students of his own class or it is presented with reference to any outside criterion. When it is done and stated that student has secured first division by scoring 60% or more marks or his rank is third or tenth in his class it becomes evaluation. Thus, evaluation is a value judgement process and tells how far a student is away from his destination.
8. **Evaluation includes Measurement** : Evaluation actually starts from some sorts of measurement then symbols are assigned to students by comparing the performance with cultural or scientific standard. It shows that evaluation reports may vary from culture to culture.

Purpose of Evaluation

Evaluation has following purposes to serve:

1. **Giving Details of Students' Progress** : Evaluation tells where a student is standing on the way to his destination of learning, how much he is ahead or behind his classmates, to what extent the behavioural changes occurred in him are acceptable, how far he can apply his present acquired knowledge to his future life or learning situations, at what point he is facing any difficulty and why and so on. Thus, evaluation here works like the diagnostic function of measurement.
2. **Predicting Future Achievement** : When evaluation covers the aptitude aspect of behaviour, it can predict the future performance of a student or a teacher on the basis of his present performance.
3. **Guidance and Motivation** : When a student comes to know about the actual position of his achievement, he gets motivated to do better. Besides, strengths and weaknesses of students become manifest through evaluation and a teacher can guide them accordingly.
4. **Improvement in the System** : Once proper guidance is given to students by the teacher after evaluation, teaching-learning process gets improved. A teacher can also come to know his own strength and weakness by the process and can change his own behaviour accordingly. Once he gets acquainted with his own shortcomings, he can remove them. Thus, process of evaluation is concerned with inputs and output both.
5. **Discovery of Effective Teaching Strategies** : Evaluation opens the new avenues of action researches in the class. When a teacher does not get the desired result by adopting a particular combination of teaching strategies, he adopts another combination and this process continues until a final effective combination of teaching strategies is discovered.
6. **Classification of Students** : By evaluation process we can classify students into different groups like talented, bright, average, slow learners and poor and adopt different strategies of teaching for different groups. We can also give remedial treatment to weak students in the class only after thorough evaluation of them.
7. **Providing Feedback to Students and Teachers Both** : When a teacher comes to know the results of his efforts he gets feedback. If result is good, he is motivated if result is not satisfactory, feedback pushes him to change his behaviour. Similarly, knowledge of progress and the feedback received thereof motivate the students also.

Steps in Evaluation

An evaluation is comprised of the following steps to be followed in order :

1. **Identification of Objectives** : First of all, a teacher decides which domain of behaviour of a student and upto which level he has to cover by his tests and what advantages he wants to gain by these tests.
2. **Matching the Objectives with the Content:** After identification of objectives a teacher matches the objectives with the subject-matter that he has to teach in the class. He also determines the level of teaching accordingly.
3. **Writing Objectives in Terms of Behavioural Change of Learners** : In the third step objectives are written in such a language which is clear and represent the change of students' behaviour.
4. **Taking the Students to the Environment of Testing** : Teacher takes the students from teaching environment to the testing one very smoothly so that students express their behaviour freely.
5. **Selection of Tools and Techniques** : At this step the teacher decides whether the test will be written, oral or practical and if written test is to be administered, it will be objective or subjective.
6. **Construction of the Test** : Here teacher constructs the test keeping in view the objectives already determined by matching them with the content.
7. **Administration of the Test :** Students are given the test constructed by the teacher and they take the test in stipulated time.
8. **Scoring :** Whatever changes have occurred in the behaviour of students are converted into numerals or grade by scoring.
9. **Interpretation of Result :** At this stage the marks obtained by the students are analysed by the teacher in order to see whether the changes in behaviour are in accordance with the objectives or not.
10. **Value Judgement :** At this step, teacher compares the behaviour of students with any internal norm or outside criteria in order to give it a value judgement, i.e., upto what level the achievement of students is satisfactory, average, excellent or poor.

ENGLISH

11. **Feedback :** After preparing the result, it is sent to students and their guardians in order to give them feedback. Teachers also get feedback by the results and they come to know the strengths and weaknesses of their teaching.

Techniques of Evaluation

Evaluation is broader concept than measurement but no exact evaluation is possible without going through the process of measurement. All the three domains of behaviour are covered by evaluation, e.g.,

1. **Cognitive Domain :** Oral, written, essay type, objective type tests, practical examinations and observation techniques etc. are used for evaluating cognitive domain.
2. **Affective Domain :** This domain is evaluated by interest inventory, attitude scale, check list, rating scales and observation techniques.
3. **Psychomotor Domain :** Performance tests, practical examinations and observation techniques are used to evaluate this domain (See optional paper II for Educational Objectives).

There are basically two techniques of evaluation:

A. Quantitative : These techniques are highly reliable and valid. Important such techniques are as follows:

1. **Oral :** These techniques are basically used at lower grades of teaching. At higher level of education too viva voce is used to test the lower levels of cognitive behaviour. Debates or drama can also be used for this purpose.
2. **Written :** Objective type tests, essay type tests and short answer questions are important written techniques to evaluate cognitive achievement of students. They give more accurate results than oral tests.
3. **Performance Tests** : Here some works are assigned to students to accomplish them. Students practically do these works and then output is evaluated.

B. Qualitative : These techniques evaluate the quality of attributes and hence they are highly subjective. Important such techniques are given below:

1. **Cumulative Records :** Such records are prepared by the school to show all-round development of students individually. They reflect the total personality of the child, i.e., marks obtained by students in sessional tests and examinations, their participation in games, sports cultural programmes and other co-curricular activities, their regularity, punctuality, their etiquette.
2. **Anecdotal Records :** These records maintain the description of significant events or works of students. Here informations regarding the behaviour, attitudes or interests of students are systematically cumulated.
3. **Observation :** This is the most common technique of qualitative assessment of students. It is mostly used at lower grades of education. This is the only technique for the evaluation of classroom interaction.
4. **Check List :** This technique is used for evaluating attitude and affective domain of students. Here questions are given to students and they are asked to answer them in yes or no, e.g.,

   Item : 'Do you like doing mathematical sums-Yes/No.'
5. **Rating Scales :** Here some statements are given to students and agreed, indifferent or disagreed are written before the statements. Then students are asked to tick the option according to their own choice.

Types of Evaluation

1. Formative Evaluation : The purpose of formative evaluation is to monitor instructional process to know whether learning is taking place or not. It is designed to enhance and improve teaching-learning process and thus it becomes a continuous process in the school system.

These tests diagnose the weaknesses of students as well as teachers and thus, both of them can get feedback from these tests. Students and teachers both after identifying their difficulties change their behaviour and remove these difficulties. Thus, function of this evaluation is remedial in nature.

The second function of this evaluation is that if evaluation finds teaching-learning process satisfactory, it motivates the teachers and students to work harder for better results.

Tanner (1972) has defined formative evaluation in the following words :

"Formative evaluation refers to the use of tests and other evaluative procedures while the course and instructional programme is in progress."

Both criterion referenced and norm referenced tests are used to take the students to the mastery of the content. These tests are given in the following stages of learning.

(i) At the end of each unit of the lesson.

(ii) At the end of each whole lesson.

(iii) At the end of each unit of the total course.

Advantages of Formative evaluation :

(i) It provides sufficient information to teachers for modifying teaching.

(ii) It helps in formulating individual and group remedial programmes.

(iii) It provides feedback to students as well as teachers.

(iv) It facilitates retention and transfer of training.

(v) It enables the teacher to readjust his teaching according to the needs of the students.

(vi) Students can also modify their behaviour after getting feedback from this evaluation.

(vii) It gives reinforcement to high achievers.

(viii) It can work as a self-evaluation device for learners.

2. **Summative Evaluation** : This evaluation takes place at the end of the session to measure over all achievement of pupils. Annual, internal or external examinations are the examples of summative evaluation. The purpose of this evaluation is to certify fail or pass of the product. If formative evaluation is related to the process of teaching, it is related to the product of teaching. Here students are evaluated from the whole syllabus. On the basis of this evaluation, a decision is taken whether a student should be promoted to the next class or he should be kept in the same class again.

On the basis of above discussions we can say that summative evaluation works as a complement to formative evaluation and both of them combined together are necessary for all educational system.

TEACHING LEARNING MATERIALS

Text Book

Text book is the area in which the language material is presented prescribed for teaching and learning English.

Characteristics of Good Text Books

A good text books not only teaches but it also tests. A few essential characteristics of good text books are given below:

(i) The size of text book should be handy for the students.

(ii) The binding should be proper and strong.

(iii) The subject matter should be printed on good quality paper.

(iv) Heading and subheading should be printed on title page in bold form.

(v) Illustration should be attractive. For every young pupil, the picture should be well drawn and realistically coloured and not in black and white.

(vi) Clear and unambiguous instruction should be given along side the test and practice and exercise.

(vii) The introduction at the beginning and conclusion at the end of the chapter should be given in the text book.

(viii) The words and structure are carefully graded.

(ix) No difficult words and new words are given in good text book.

(x) The words and structure already learnt are repeated in the coming pages so that the students could revise them making them stable in their memory.

(xi) The subject matter of text book should provide new information so that students could get new knowledge.

(xii) There should be both practice and text exercise at the end of the chapter.

(xiii) The practice should be low which the majority of students could solve them easily.

Chalkboard

It is the closest friend of a teacher in the class and about 50% teaching task is completed with the help of the blackboard. Advantages of using a chalkboard in the class are as follows :

(i) It is a cheap material aid which does not cost much on its maintenance.

(ii) When a teacher writes important points of the lesson on the chalkboard along with his oral teaching and lectures, aural and visual both the senses of students work simultaneously. It increases learning many times.

(iii) Writing meaning of difficult words, drawing graphs or diagrams, solving the sums of mathematics, preparing the summary of the lesson, all these works can be done on the chalkboard and they help the students understand the facts, events or terminologies.

(iv) Blackboard works as a model for students. This can help the students mend their ways if they imitate the model.

Models

Models are the reflection or copy of the real objects. They are used in the class to clarify the concepts when either real objects are not available or it is not possible to bring real objects to the class. They are also the abbreviated version of real objects. Elephants, lions or other animals or birds can not be brought to the class, hence, it is better to use the models of these objects. Globe is the best example of model to be used in the class.

Through models knowledge of all types of historical, geographical and scientific facts and concepts can be given to students. Models are especially useful for teaching visually handicapped children who perceive the objects by touch. Since, clear dimensions of length, breadth and height are given in the model in a proportionate manner, they are more useful for concept formation than pictures.

How to use models

(*i*) Scale should be used for showing size, shape or structure of the real objects. Apart from this, teacher should also clarify the real shape, size or structure of the real object.

(*ii*) Students should be given opportunity to have a critical view on the model and their views on it.

(*iii*) All students should be given chance to have a close look at the model in the class.

(*iv*) Models should have direct relevance to the lesson and they should develop scientific temperament among learners.

(*v*) Models should be properly explained in the class in order to make the use of models effective.

Pictures

Pictures are used in the class as material aids when neither real objects nor models can be arranged. They are cheap and easily available in the market, therefore, a teacher should not be miserly in using them. Pictures are actually the outlines of the real objects and when they are shown in the class, they give clear concepts about the colour, physique, shape and size of the real objects. Attention of students can easily be drawn to the lesson through them. If pictures related to the lesson are not available in the market, the teacher should sketch them by using pencils and water colours. Pictures are used as material aids for teaching all the school subjects.

Diagrams

They are another option and used when even pictures can not be arranged. They can also clarify the concepts like models or pictures but at a lesser degree. Diagrams are drawn on the chalkboard by using coloured chalks and then students copy it on their notebooks. The biggest advantage of this material aid is that teacher need not spend even a single pie in using this material aid.

They help in clarifying the concepts, laws and principles of science and social sciences. Their role in teaching languages is very limited.

Graphs

Graphs are especially used in history, geography, science and mathematics. They help the teacher and the students to study, analyse and compare the data, facts or events. Whenever action research is made by a teacher in the class, graphs are used to show the data.

Maps

Maps are the flat representation of the surface of the earth on a paper where many informations are presented through lines, symbols dots, points or letters. They have special significance in teaching history and geography. We can also get information about the size and physical features of a country, state or continent through these maps and distance between different parts of the country or the world can also be read from them. Though printed maps of all states or countries are available in the market yet a teacher draws them also on roler boards. This will enable the students to draw such maps themselves.

Slide Projector

Simple 'slide projector' was known as "magic lantern" in the olden days. The principle here is that when we put the transparent slide on the socket and throw light from behind, the light passes through it and projects the image on the screen.

A slide projector typically consists of a quart, three halogen lamps, light to be reflected by the reflector, a heat filter and lastly, condenser lenses. The heat filter is a thermo crystal which absorbs most of the heat produced by three lamps. A cooling system is also needed which consists of a fan for convecting off the heat, filter and other components. The fan is thermostatically controlled. When projector is switched off, the fan is also switched off.

Classroom uses of the Slide Projector : Slides are prepared for selected topics and the informations contained by them may be in the form of written words, pictures, graphs, sketches, etc. The topic selected should be arranged frame by frame. The ideal ratio of length and breadth of slides is 2 : 3. Each frame should have only one concept for the ease of understanding.

The slides and the film strips are arranged in a sequential order. This arrangement is also coordinated with the teaching learning activity of the class. When slides are shown in the class, curtains are drawn on the windows in order to reduce the entry of natural light in the class.

Before showing these slides, teacher elaborates important points. Once the film is over, the teacher gives his own comments and relates the aid with the lesson to be taught.

Film Strips

They are used before a large group of students either for introducing a lesson or for elaborating some minute object not seen in ordinary situations. Film strips are projected on a big screen through a film projector and then the projector is switched on. Here, very minute objects look very big on the screen and we can study their parts. For example, knowledge about bacteria and viruses can be given to students through these film strips. Sometimes, sound recording is also used along with the film to clarify important points.

Advantages of Film Strips :

(*i*) The order or sequence of film strips is fixed and a teacher can prepare the relevant material to supplement the film according to the sequence.

(*ii*) We can have any part of the film on the screen as long as we desire so. As a result, a teacher can discuss a single topic as long as he needs. Thus, complete control over the equipment and the material is possible.

(*iii*) Handling of film projectors is also not complex. There is no problem of storing them because of their small size. Precautions are, however, needed against fungi or physical damage.

(*iv*) They have become very cheap today and any school can afford the cost of these projectors.

(*v*) They do not require complete darkness in the room as we do in using epidiascope or motion film projectors.

Limitations of Film Strips:

(*i*) They can be used only in small sized classes because of limited focal length. Modern projectors are, however, having large focal length.

(*ii*) Slide projection is not as effective as film projection. Inventions of 3D films have reduced the use of slides even further. In spite of this, fixed order of the film strips creates problem in handling individual frames.

(*iii*) Many schools do not have audio-visual workshops and thus, they depend on the cheap and unstandardized materials available in the market.

Film Projector

16 mm films are generally used for the purpose of training or teaching. These films are planned and executed by a pannel of experts who endeavour to prepare films of good quality.

As far as use of film projector for classroom teaching is concerned, it is very easy. Everything is automatic here. If electricity supply is not restricted, the film will not stop in the middle, after it is put on the projector.

Advantages of motion pictures :

(*i*) Motion pictures can especially be used for training purposes. Take the example of games and sports. If some actions of a player is wrong leading to defeat in the game, it can be corrected by viewing the films. After the game is over, the film of the game is later analysed to be discussed by the experts to bring in new strategies and tactics to counterplay.

(*ii*) In all training courses, perfection is needed everywhere. If action is recorded on films, we can see our own performance and remove our defects.

(*iii*) In the classroom teaching, motion pictures can highlight those aspects also that would have otherwise been missed. For example, by enlarging, close up and action replay techniques, motion pictures can highlight those movements also which are very minute and can be missed in ordinary situations.

(*iv*) Motion pictures are **multi-sensory technique** of instruction. It is because a combination of light, sound and actions are seen here.

(*v*) Motion pictures can develop imaginative and observational capacities of students simultaneously.

(*vi*) Whatever ideals are shown by the models in motion pictures are imitated by pupils and thus, good ideals and etiquettes can be developed in them.

(*vii*) They are helpful in giving clarity of concepts through concreteness and accuracy.

(*viii*) Facts and events related to industry, politics, history and geography and knowledge about scientific inventions, discoveries, laws and principles can be communicated to pupils very effectively through these motion pictures.

Kinescope

It is a sight and sound recording that can be made in the studio from the television screen for repeated use. What transcription is to radio, the kinescope is to TV. They are used for the following purposes :

(*i*) For delayed telecast.

(*ii*) For retelecast of the same programme.

(*iii*) For repeating the telecast when programme could not be seen due to failure of network.

(*iv*) For sending programmes abroad.

Only limitation of kinescope is that live element or spontaneity does not exist here.

It can be used in teaching learning process in the same way as television is used.

Epidiascope

Epidiascope is an equipment that can project all types of materials whether transparent or non-transparent (opaque). It has thus a twin facility and separate mechanism for projecting transparent and opaque materials.

In epidiascope, the word epi means 'upon' dia means 'through' and scope means 'projected material to be seen'.

While projecting a slide, beams pass through the slide and projects its image on the screen. In this way, transparent material is projected.

While projecting the opaque material the light bits upon the object which reflects the image on a very sensitive mirror and reflects the image of the opaque objects on the screen.

Despite the multipurpose functioning of this device, it is not very popular in educational institutions because of its poor quality image, total room darkening, very high need of energy, complexity of its use and poor range. It is to be installed in the middle of the class due to its low range, therefore, causing more interference than aiding something to the lesson. Because of its ability to project opaque objects on the screen, it is also known as opaque projector.

Overhead Projector (OHP)

Built on the basic principle of periscope, OHP is an important audio visual equipment. In the classroom it is placed in front of the teacher above his head to reflect an image on the screen (blackboard). This device consists of a strong energy source, (bulbs), fixed reflectors (mirrors), projection lens and a platen. This projector is called over head because the image goes over the head of the teacher and falls on the screen behind him. The teacher puts one slide over the other in order to give a sense of continuity of the subject matter projected on the screen.

Advantages of OHP : Its advantages lie in its special characteristics given below :

(*i*) No special training is required by the teacher to operate a projector.

(*ii*) OHPs are not very costly as compared to computers or film projectors.

(*iii*) It is handy and portable.

(*iv*) The image formed by the projector is also very bright and every pupil can see it. A 4 × 4 inches slide gives an image of 4 × 4 feet. This enlarged image is very easy to understand.

(*v*) It can create interests in pupils and hence it is a good motivator.

(*vi*) It is the best visual aid available to a teacher to supplement his oral teaching. He uses the screen of OHP as a blackboard without looking back. Transparencies, drawing, diagrams, figures and outlines etc. can be shown on the screen.

Television

TV differs from the radio in the sense that it is audio and visual both. We can see the incident occurring round the globe on it immediately after the occurrence of the incident through telecast. Thus, it is bisensory (multisensory) media. We get news, views and recreation through television in the same way as we do through the transistor but in a more compact and concrete way due to the facility of vision here.

As far as application of TV in education is concerned, it is still in the stage of infancy in India. It was only in 1961 that Indian television (Doordarshan) started a special service for schools in collaboration with the directorate of Education. This programme aimed at supplementing the regular classroom teaching in selected subjects. By 1972 only 400 schools of the capital received this telecast and two lakh students benefited from them. These programmes were telecast in the evening and on Sundays but there was no mechanism developed at that time to measure the effectiveness of such transmitting programmes.

After the introduction of distance education system in India, television is now regularly used as an instructional media. The enactment of Prasar Bharti Act is expected to boost the role of TV in the teaching learning process.

Advantages of television :

(*i*) It heightens the reality more than the physical presence. For example, if someone is watching a cricket match in a stadium, even then he can not see certain situations despite being present there. On the other hand, if he is viewing a match on a TV, he can see and analyse every situation by close up action replay. Thus, television experience may be more real than the actual one. It can show even those details which we can not see with the help of direct experiences. Thus, television can be used for all training programmes and behaviour of the trainees can be modified in the desired manner.

(*ii*) TV experiences are new and versatile. So, they can bring variety to classroom teaching by breaking monotony and strengthening the learning structures by its multisensory approach.

(*iii*) It widens the horizon of pupils' experiences by giving them upto date knowledge of the real situation and by making them conversant with the opinions of others.

(*iv*) It can motivate the pupils for learning by arousing and retaining their interest in the learning situation.

Limitations of Television:

(*i*) Speed of a television can not be changed as we can do in motion pictures.

(*ii*) A TV programme can not be adjusted to teaching and vice versa will have to be done. A teacher can take the help of video recording in such cases.

Tape Recorder and Audio Cassettes

Cassette type audio taps are available now which can play for 90 minutes on both sides. We can listen to our own recorded voice, recorded speeches of politicians and learned people, recorded poems of great composers, songs, music etc by the tape recorder.

Audio cassette recorder is used for the following purposes :

Such types of recording serve the following purposes:

(*i*) **Analysis of verbal messages :** Accuracy, speed and tone of verbal messages are studied here and if perfection is seen, reinforcement to the presenter is given.

(*ii*) **Drill and practice :** Accurate verbal messages are presented before the trainee for drill and practice.

(*iii*) **Teaching of specific skills :** Impressive oral presentation is actually a skill. This skill is taught to students through audio-recording in the individual and group situations.

(*iv*) **Speech improvement :** Style of speaking and phonetics can also be improved by using this technology.

(*v*) **Improvement in vocabulary :** Recorded verbal messages are full of many new words which pupils can learn by listening to the message.

(*vi*) **Recreation :** Many recorded songs and music entertain the listeners and remove their fatigue.

Radio

It is an important and easily accessable audio aid serving three important general purposes "news, views and recreation". It is the cheapest equipment of all and radio broadcast is now reachable to 100% population of the country. Pupils can get information about the incidents in any part of the globe immediately through radio. This increases their general awareness of the world. Students listen the ideas of learned people, politicians and educationists from across the world on the radio. This extends their own views and way of thinking. Apart from these, there are hundreds of programmes of music, songs and plays broadcast on the radio which entertain them round the clock.

Instructional Value of the Radio :

(*i*) It is a powerful means of developing listening comprehension.

(*ii*) It can also help the pupils to acquire correct pronunciation and phonetics like tape recorders.

(*iii*) Conversational style and language can be learned on the radio.

(*iv*) It improves word power of learners.

(*v*) Mass education goals can be achieved through radio broadcast. It was the realization of the people when radio came into being in 1917.

(*vi*) News listened on the radio can improve our general knowledge.

(*vii*) Radio listening does not require literacy. Even illiterates can take the benefit of it.

Radio Broadcast in India : The first radio station was established in India in July 1927 in Mumbai followed by one more station in Kolkata in the same year. This media is now able to penetrate to the remotest villages of the country and is covering more than 99% of the population.

School broadcasting in India was started in 1937. Radio broadcasting is now very much used for mass education as well as the education of school going children in selected areas. Central Institute for educational technology (CIET) under the supervision and control of NCERT produces quality radio broadcast programmes. Adult education Radio Programmes also started in 1956 to educate the adults in the age group of 15-35 in the vicinity of Pune as a project sponsored by UNESCO. Today, broadcast of adult education programmes are many under different titles. When Consumer Protection Act was passed in

1986, consumer education through radio was also given recognition. Today, it is a regular programme of all the radio stations in India. One more regular radio programme is the radio counseling programme of IGNOU which is broadcast from 4-5 pm on every Sunday.

Apart from these, radio broadcast is also making the people aware about various social and economic problems and people are also educated about how they can solve these problems.

Computer

It is the latest electronic device that is audio and visual both. It accepts data, performs operations on that data in sequence (decided by a programme) and outputs the results.

Computer in education : From input devices to output and its storage, computer has a wide range of applicability in education. In computers inputs are converted into output by a programme. Thus, input (data) plus programme form software or instructional programme. Inputs are converted into output in the CPU of the computer.

Computer always works according to the programme given to it. Whatever instruction or programme the students gives to the computers, it will always act accordingly and output will also come out on the same line. Application of computers in education can be understood by the following lines.

Videodiscs

This system is comprised of videodisc, where the information is stored, a video player and a TV set.

It is helpful in teaching learning process in the following ways :

(*i*) Students can get more informations through effective way of presentation.

(*ii*) By forwarding or reversing the CD player, learners can have access to any informations as many times as possible. This repeated action is necessary in understanding complex materials.

(*iii*) Live coverage given by the CD player can provide higher degree of motivation.

(*iv*) Auto stop system provided in the system can help those learners who study till late hours of night.

(*v*) The materials prepared by the effective teachers can be made available in the market for wide use.

Videotext

This system provides an interactive information retrieval service. It allows the home television to work as a computer terminal, which retrieves the textual material and graphic information from a remote data base.

Advantages of Videotext:

(*i*) It is useful for downloading the required information from a remote data base.

(*ii*) It raises the general awareness of learners.

(*iii*) The principal of a school can have access to any information about his or other schools any time if this system is available in the school.

(*iv*) It is especially useful for distance learning. A learner can connect himself with his study centre or regional office any time.

(*v*) It is free from time schedule. We can have any information any time.

(*vi*) Two way interaction between the teacher and the taught is possible here with the help of alphanumeric keyboard. The learner can address to his tutor by typing questions and sending it to the tutor. Once he receives the answer, he gets immediate feedback.

(*vii*) It is faster than telephone or telegram because user need not wait here in queue.

Teleconferencing

Teleconferencing is a two way broadcast system in which learners can interact with the programme through a local telephone. It is a powerful medium of instruction for distance education. In this system three or four subject experts sit at different places and participate in the discussion on the given subject matter. Here learners do not take part in the teaching-learning process directly. They only hear the programme on their radio set or TV. They can however, interact with the experts through telephone which is connected to the radio or TV station where the discussion is being organised.

Thus, teleconferencing involves the use of many media and allows interactive group communication by means of a two way broadcast. All such conferencing need good quality audio device to facilitate immediate interaction among the participants for exchange of views.

Advantages of Teleconferencing :

(*i*) **Effective for distance learning :** When groups of students are scattered over a large area of the country and it is not possible for them to interact with their teachers personally, then learning through teleconferencing is the best option for them.

(*ii*) **Interaction between the teacher and the taught possible :** As far as interaction between teachers and learners are concerned, this approach does not differ in any way from classroom teaching.

(iii) High quality instruction : Since, very learned people and experts of the subject take part in these discussions, the quality of the programme is never questionable.

(iv) Immediate feedback : Learners get answer of their questions immediately from the experts and their problem is solved. In this way, they get immediate feedback.

(v) Flexibility : Experts do not teach here on a pre-determined track. Their instruction and its way of presentation always changes according to the questions asked by learners. Thus, this approach is very flexible.

Internet

It is the abbreviation of international network. The computers connected to this system are automatically connected to world wide website(www). Due to this we can hear and see any programme available on website any time when we want to do so. If we have missed any television or radio programme, we can not have access to that programme again but if that programme is loaded on the website, we can repeatedly hear and see the programme. We will only have to log on the website of the programme producer and it will be available for us. The major advantage of this system is that it has made 24 hour communication possible especially between those countries which have great differences in their local timings such as India and America have a time difference of 10 ½ hours. When there is day time in India, offices are closed in America.

Applications of internet in education :

(*i*) We can get any information any time at home through internet on one hand and we can store the information by creating our own website on the other. Thus, it is not necessary to have immediate print out of the textual matter.

(*ii*) The two talking persons can see each other in face to face situations also through internet. Thus, a teacher can teach millions of students scattered across the world together.

(*iii*) Many educational institutions have created their educational websites. We can download any information about them any time by logging on these websites.

(*iv*) Internet has also its role to play in classroom teaching. Teacher can show any educational programme through internet any time according to his own convenience and he will not have to adjust his time table according to the programme as he does while using radio or television as aids.

(*v*) Latest teaching strategies and latest researches in different fields can be obtained through internet immediately and we need not have to wait for their publication in magazines and journals.

(*vi*) Books, magazines and newspapers are also published on internet and it has made our access to them easy. Any Indian living in Canada even can read "Amar Ujala" or "Times of India" daily.

(*vii*) Research material and encyclopaedias are also published on internet to facilitate learning process.

REMEDIAL TEACHING

Remedial Teaching (RT) means that help is offered to pupils who need (pedagogical/didactic) assistance. These are often children who function at a lower than average level because of a certain learning- or behavioural problem/disorder, but RT can also be offered to pupils who achieve at a higher than average level, they too can do with the extra attention and care. The best known learning disorder is dyslexia.

The help includes the pupil who is being put forward for RT to the remedial teacher is examined by means of an intake conversation, checks, tests and/or observations. The remedial teacher tries to form a picture of the pupil also by way of talks with the group teacher and the parents in order to discover where the problem lies. When this is clear (diagnosis) a therapy plan is drawn up. In a therapy plan it states amongst others which aims should be achieved. The treatment that ensues is called remedial teaching. It is help that is completely specialized in the problem of the pupil, it is custom-made.

The therapy plan is drawn up for a fixed period of time. Remedial teaching is usually given during 6 weeks to 3 months, once or twice a week at school or in the remedial teacher's own practice. The aim being that the pupil can join his own group again after this period of time (or possibly after a continuation).

Remedial teaching is offered at many schools. However, a school is allowed to establish its own priorities and is not obliged to offer remedial teaching. There has to be a course of care though, the organization of which is determined by the whole team, although the directives and rules are laid down by the Ministery of Education an Science (OC&W).

Quizzing students more often is another commonly used method in a well balanced remedial teaching program. Taking the extra time to check each individual's progress gives the teacher an opportunity to regroup if necessary. It can also take the overall test pressure off students who tend to "freeze" when tested on larger amounts of material. From elementary to college, the best remedial teaching programs will include constant feedback from its students. This kind of communication provides a comfort level between student and teacher which leads to a more proficient, positive and rewarding outcome for both.

Too often, a lack of understanding among parents, school administrators and teaching staff gets in the way. Proper training of teachers and administrators go beyond their degree of specialties. Listening to each other, and to parents and children who live with specific special needs, is a huge first step in creating an exemplary remedial teaching program as opposed to another "one size fits all" classroom. Requesting conferences, discussing individual strengths and weaknesses, and respecting each others expertise and opinions are all important pieces, and are defining points of the best remedial teaching programs.

Remedial Teaching for Slow Learners

Remedial Teaching is identifying slow learners and giving them the necessary guidance to help them overcome their problems, after identifying their areas of difficulty. Contrary to what is said, remedial teaching is done perfunctorily without identifying their areas of difficulty and underlying cause for lagging behind. Some students are unsympathetically branded as 'block heads' without an earnest attempt to know the real cause of their slow learning.

In the present system of education, students are identified as slow learners purely on the basis of their poor performance in the examination, which, in most cases deviates from what is taught. Consequently even talented students are sometimes misconstrued as dullards. So, a slow learner is one whose performance is very dismal in the examination. He is neither mentally retarded nor is on the lower rungs of intelligence scale.

The reasons for some students learning slowly are innumerable. One of the main reasons is the 'no detention system' at the primary and upper primary level. Students are promoted to higher classes on the basis of attendance, even if they score low marks. The heterogeneous composition (mental age & physical age) of over crowded classes in all government run schools and private schools also produces slow learners. So the incapacity of the teacher to pay individual attention to a student over a long period makes a student a slow learner. A slow learner is thus a product of negligence of school at different stages of learning, inspite of his innate capacity to learn.

There are some problems very specific to the individual. Ill health, lack of concentration, less exposure to the subject taught and parental background are some causative factors for slow learning. Talents differ. A childs capacity to learn different subjects varies from student to student. For instance, learning mathematics is a knack. All students do not do well in mathematics just as they do in other subjects. While other subjects can be learnt at any stage, it is very difficult for students to learn mathematics without the basics. Students show interest in the subjects they like and neglect other subjects if not taken care of. An urban child learns languages like English well while a rural child cannot, however well the teacher tries to explain.

Remedial Measures

Learning takes place from simple to complex. If for some reason the student has not learnt the basics, it is futile to teach him the advanced topics. Remedial teaching is not revising the topics taught repeatedly. Careful analysis of the students' performance in the examination and diagnosing the areas of difficulty are key aspects in remedial teaching. Once the difficult areas are identified, the next task is to plan the learning experiences to teach the basics to understand the given topic.

Teachers often feel that what has not been learnt at the primary level, cannot be taught simultaneously with the prescribed topics at the secondary level as they are busy completing the syllabus. Experience shows that once the basics are taught, the learning process is accelerated and the slow learners comprehend and grasp the given topics of the class, since they have already attained the mental age.

In Jawahar Navodaya Vidyalayas nation wide, the students are admitted in class VI based on a selection test consisting of a variety of questions to test intelligence and aptitude of the students.

It has been observed that many students thus selected do not possess the basics which they are supposed to learn at the primary level. But these schools have produced excellent results over the years by introducing bridge courses in their academic planning.

Subjects like physics pose difficulty for students when compared to biology. In biological sciences, students can see and find meaning in what they study. Whereas physics is somewhat intricate and difficult for students without good knowledge of mathematics. Poor performance in physics can be remedied by first teaching the required basic mathematical operations.

Sometimes language becomes a barrier for students to understand the vast areas in subjects like geography. The innumerable new words used to describe various phenomena baffle the students. Students do not find these words in English language textbooks although they learn English language to pursue others subjects in an inter- disciplinary approach. The teacher has to explain all the words and their usage related to his subject before he teaches the concept.

The new words used in questions could confuse students and elicit wrong answers from them. Students should be exposed to a variety of questions with antonyms and synonyms - all the words used to frame a question to test the topic taught. Merely tagging the slow learners with bright students or segregating them into separate sections will not help the slow learners. Slow learners harbour themselves unobtrusively in the group of bright students.

Students learn a lot from the peer group. Unconscious learning does not take place if students are segregated. Keeping the slow learners in the peer group of bright students and paying individual attention to them by the teacher will enable them to overocme their difficulties.

Student is central in the learning process. The learning experiences should be activity-oriented and the teaching should motivate and create interest in the student to learn on his own. When group discussions are held in the classroom, the slow learners are benefited much.

Suitably tailored lesson plan by the teacher and careful monitoring by the school administration will help slow learners have a better grasp of all lessons in schools.

Various Approaches and Tools

Give your older kids a second chance to master grade-level reading.

A comprehensive literacy intervention curriculum for grades 1-12, LANGUAGE ! prepares students to return to conventional curricula by advancing them from current performance levels to grade placement level.

Lindamood-Bell

Lindamood-Bell is an organization dedicated to enhancing human learning. It has developed the sensory-cognitive processes that underlie reading, spelling, language comprehension, math, and visual motor skills. Its Process-Based education programs are for individuals ranging from severely learning disabled to academically gifted–ages 5 years through adult.

Open Court Reading

"Open Court Reading 2002 is a complete elementary basal reading program for Grades K-6. It maintains strong instruction in the areas of decoding (learning how to read), comprehension (understanding what you read), inquiry and investigation (learning how to apply what you have read), and writing (how to communicate with others in print). There are also applications for teaching spelling, vocabulary, grammar, usage, and mechanics, penmanship, and listening, speaking, and viewing."

Orton-Gillingham Approach

"The Orton-Gillingham approach is appropriate for teaching individuals, small groups, and classrooms. It is appropriate for teaching in the primary, elementary, intermediate grades, and at the secondary and college level as well as for adults. The explicit focus of the approach has been and continues to be upon persons with the kinds of language processing problems associated with dyslexia. Early intervention is highly desirable, but it is never too late to begin!"

Phono-Graphix

"The theoretical underpinnings of Phono-Graphix are remarkably straightforward and sensible, no doubt encouraging its rapid spread and popularity among teachers. It is based simply on the nature of the English code, the three skills needed to access that code, and teaching these in keeping with the way children learn.

Project Read

"Project Read/Language Circle is a research based mainstream language arts program for students who need a systematic learning experience with direct teaching of concepts and skills through multisensory techniques."

Reading Mastery Plus

"Reading Mastery Plus gives students the skills and the clear, explicit instruction and guidance they need to master the fundamentals of reading. Oral language, phonemic awareness, and systematic phonics are the starting point.

This program is set up so students are active participants throughout the learning process. Less-structured activities and opportunities for independent work help students develop self-reliance. Ongoing assessment tools are used by the instructor to ensure that no student "falls though the cracks."

Slingerland Institute for Literacy

"The Slingerland Institute for Literacy is a non-profit organization that trains teachers to work with dyslexic students in their classrooms using the Slingerland Multisensory Approach. This methodology is a

ENGLISH

simultaneous, multisensory, structured approach for teaching language arts in the classroom. The Slingerland Multisensory Approach for Teaching Language Arts Training Course is accredited at the Teacher and Instructor of Teaching levels by the International Multisensory Structured Language Educational Council (IMSLEC)."

SFA Components -Reading and Writing Programs

During reading periods, students are regrouped across age lines for 90 minutes so that each reading class contains students reading at one level. This eliminates the need to have reading groups within the class and increases the amount of time for direct instruction. Also, use of tutors as reading teachers during reading time reduces the size of most reading classes. The reading program in grades K-1 emphasizes the development of language skills and launches students into reading using phonetically regular storybooks supported by careful instruction that focuses on phonemic awareness, auditory discrimination, and sound blending as well as meaning, context, and self-monitoring strategies. Students become fluent as they read and reread to one another in pairs.

Reading Wings

A comprehensive, research-based approach to reading and writing for grades two and beyond. Reading Wings consists of four principal elements: listening comprehension, story-related activities, direct instruction in reading comprehension, and integrated writing/language arts. In all of these activities, students work in heterogeneous learning teams. Students are assigned to pairs or triads; then the pairs are assigned to teams. Mainstreamed, academically handicapped, and Title I-identified students are evenly distributed among the teams. All activities follow a regular cycle that involves teacher presentation, team practice, independent practice, peer pre-assessment, additional practice, assessment, and team recognition.

Wilson Language Training

At Wilson Language Training many people, regardless of their age, have not been able to acquire reading and writing skills because their learning needs have never been properly assessed. The majority of these people are subject to a core deficit at the most basic level of language skill: that of phonological coding.

PRACTICE PAPER

ENGLISH

1. Which of the following is not a language skill?
A. Reading
B. Writing
C. Thinking
D. Speaking

2. By which method the students learn to the maximum extent?
A. By seeing
B. By reading
C. By listening
D. By doing themselves

3. Which quality of the teacher is liked the most by the students?
A. Punctuality
B. Impartiality
C. Love for discipline
D. Dominance

4. What should the teacher do to maintain the interest of students in class teaching?
A. Maximum use of blackboard
B. Extensive use of examples from the practical life
C. Extensive use of teaching materials/aids
D. Giving ample opportunity to students for discussion/delibrations

5. Children with disability must get education because—
A. They are vulnerable
B. They have special needs
C. It is a basic constitutional right
D. They are poor

6. Which of the following is a sensory disorder?
A. Hearing Impairment
B. Mental Retardation
C. Cerebral Palsy
D. Neuro Muscular Disorder

7. Learning depends on—
A. Intelligence
B. Parental attitude
C. Peer attitude
D. None of these

8. Which of the following can increase the quality of education?
A. To extend one hour time period
B. Service period teacher training
C. Solution and treatment teaching
D. By help-books

9. Which cannot be the stage of learning?
A. Procedure
B. Difference perception
C. Exercise
D. Imagination

10. Which of the following is decisive for teaching work?
A. To make effective the excellence
B. To educate
C. True management of classes
D. Communication with students

11. What will be the indication when a group of students gets more marks in the question paper made by any teacher?
A. It is a group of high achiever
B. Teacher has tought well
C. Question-paper is good
D. None of these

12. Choose the one which best expresses the meaning of the word 'Condone'.
A. Grieve
B. Endure
C. Forgive
D. Ignore

13. Change the following active voice into passive one :

Does the noise disturb you?

A. You are disturb by the noise.
B. Are you disturbed by the noise?
C. You are disturbing by the noise.
D. Are you disturbing by the noise?

14. A statement that can have a double meaning—
A. Verbose B. Ambivalent
C. Epigraph D. Ambiguous

15. We should always observe from the stand point of others. This is a —
A. Simple sentence
B. Complex sentence
C. Compound sentence
D. Phrase

16. Schools should be concerned with the development of child, which should include—

A. Acquisition of knowledge by the child
B. Acquisition of life skills by the child
C. Acquisition of skills required by the nation
D. Acquisition of skills required by the healthy person

17. A student gives a partially correct respond to your question. Then you will—
A. Seek further information
B. Provide reinforcement
C. Reframe your question
D. Tell the correct information

18. Which of the following is/are productive skill/ skills?
A. Speaking
B. Writing
C. Both A and B
D. None of the above

19. Language acquisition can be automatically attained favoured by—
A. Cognitivists
B. Behaviourists
C. Both of the above
D. None of the above

20. Which of the following grammar teaching method disturbs the teaching of a text book or composition writing at times?
A. Deductive Method
B. Inductive Method
C. Inductive Deductive Method
D. Incidental Method

21. Teaching aids are useful because they—
A. help teacher's work
B. activate all senses
C. help students to be attentive
D. make learning more meaningful

22. Teaching would be more effective if the teacher—
A. Makes his intent purposeful
B. Is master of the subject
C. Uses various instructional aids
D. Declares his objectives in the beginning

23. The word 'Tacit' means—
A. Formal B. Fear
C. Silent D. Celestial

24. One who is well-versed in the science of languages is called a—
A. Philosopher
B. Theologist
C. Philologist
D. Zoologist

25. Choose the correctly spelt word—
A. Coloqial
B. Coloquial
C. Colloqial
D. Colloquial

26. Choose what expresses the meaning of 'Pull the wool over one's eye'—
A. Delay B. Encourage
C. Suppress D. Deceive

27. Student's learning difficulties can be best addressed by—
A. Advising them to work hard
B. Suggesting private tuitions
C. Supervised study in the library
D. Remedial teaching

28. For being successful in life students should be encouraged to—
A. selective study
B. casual study
C. intensive study
D. learning by rote memorisation

29. Students who bring out alternative solutions and cite the books not prescribed by the teacher should be—
A. discouraged
B. encouraged
C. advised to talk to the teacher outside the class
D. advised to follow the class notes to score better in the examinations

30. Problem of school dropouts can be effectively tackled by—
A. reducing curriculum load
B. teachers empathy
C. attractive school environment
D. providing incentives

31. Choose the synonym of voracious—
A. Hungry
B. Wild
C. Quick
D. Angry

32. Choose the misspelt word—
A. Command
B. Appraise
C. Behaviour
D. Mentenance

33. Remedial teachers should observe the following when dealing with the behaviour problems of pupils—
A. should always pay attention to their misbehaviour
B. always observe the performance of pupils in class and their behaviour in groups
C. give positive reinforcement to pupils good behaviour
D. refer the cases to student Guidance Officers/ teachers for follow up action

34. Use stress and rhythmic patterns and intonation patterns of the language and 'use vocabulary appropriately' are the micro-skills involved in which of the following?

A. Speaking
B. Listening
C. Reading
D. Writing

35. Problems in language learning arise due to lack of—

A. methodology of teaching
B. availability of materials
C. teaching of mother tongue
D. teacher's competence

36. Usual teaching-learning processes can be supplemented by the following to improve the quality—

A. Extra coaching
B. Diagnostic and remedial teaching
C. Enrichment programmes
D. Inservice teacher education

37. School based evaluation can solve the problem of—

A. Mass copying
B. Student's indiscipline
C. Unrealistic assessment
D. Teacher's social reputation

38. Choose the correct meaning of the idioms: Hobson's choice—

A. feeling of insecurity
B. accept or leave the offer
C. excellent choice
D. no choice at all

39. Choose the meaning of the **bold** phrase in the sentence—

He has been working **on and off** for several years on this project.

A. at intervals
B. rarely
C. painstakingly
D. continuously

40. Pedagogy is considered to be the—

A. Science of Teaching
B. Art of Learning
C. Science of Communication
D. Art of Assimilation

41. Inductive approach of teaching means—

A. initiating the child to new subject
B. teaching through specific instruction
C. group learning as opposed to individualised learning
D. arriving at generalisations with the help of examples

42. Which of the following is an appropriate order for learning of a language?

A. Listening → Speaking → Writing → Reading
B. Speaking → Listening → Writing → Reading
C. Listening → Speaking → Reading → Writing
D. Listening → Reading → Speaking → Writing

43. The primary functions of language are—

A. Expression of feeling, meaning, communication and thinking
B. To control over other people, as language is a social act
C. Both A and B
D. None of these

44. Which of the following conditions must be satisfied in order to designate a person mentally retarded?

A. Sub-normal intellectual functioning
B. Very poor adaptive ability
C. Dependability on others
D. All of these

45. The best measure of identifying mildly mentally retarded is—

A. Administration of standardized intelligence test
B. Administration of behaviour test
C. Administration of adjustment test
D. A combination of all

46. Physical trauma during pregnancy may cause

A. Mental retardation
B. Blindness
C. Deafness
D. All of these

47. All of the following may cause mental retardation except

A. Blood incompatibility
B. Action of toxic agent
C. Radio-activity
D. None of these

48. Dullers do not differ from normal children in—

A. Physical characteristics
B. Level of social expectancy
C. Both of these
D. None of these

49. Which of the following things is not required for educating mildly mentally retarded children?

A. Regular counselling
B. Remedial teaching
C. Modification in the curriculum
D. Regular evaluation

50. Teaching of which of the following skills is not suitable to borderline cases?

A. Electric fitting
B. Repairing of electric or electronic equipments

C. Oratory skills
D. Activity based skills

51. Morons are slow in—
A. Physical growth
B. Thinking and planning
C. Taking initiative
D. All of these

52. Unsatisfactory relation of a mentally retarded child with the environment is technically called—
A. Autism
B. Maladjustment
C. Pseudo-dullness
D. None of these

53. Learning disabled children are—
A. Deficient in using potentials
B. Low in intelligence
C. Slow in activity
D. None of these

54. Learning disability is related to—
A. low listening and comprehension power
B. poor ability of expression
C. poor ability of mathematical operation
D. All of these

55. Learning disabled children perform very poorly in—
A. Academic areas B. Technical areas
C. Both of these D. None of these

56. Problem of learning disability is more complex than that of other disabilities because—
A. Its causes can not be easily ascertained by applying usual tests
B. It is associated to behaviour problems
C. Both of these
D. None of these

57. Educationally, learning disabled look similar to—
A. Dullers B. Backward children
C. Both of these D. None of these

58. In which of the following physical characteristics learning disabled children differ from the normal ones?
A. They are all the time clumsy and awkward
B. Poor coordination of motor abilities
C. Height, weight and health
D. All of these

59. Which of the following methods is most suitable for learning disabled children?
A. Behaviour guidance method
B. Remedial teaching
C. Brain storming
D. None of these

60. In order to improve work habits of learning disabled what should be done?
A. Unattending behaviour should be penalized
B. Close monitoring of the behaviour is needed
C. Cues and prompt should be given
D. All of these

61. Which of the following situations may lead to educational backwardness?
A. Sensory impairment
B. Motor disability
C. Long diseases and health problems
D. All of these

62. Which of the following is an important cause of educational backwardness at primary level of education in India?
A. Poor school organisation
B. Lack of accountability
C. Attitude of the masses towards education
D. All of these

63. Which of the following measures should be adopted by the teacher to check educational backwardness?
A. Continuous evaluation and regular feedback
B. Remedial teaching
C. Adjustment and behaviour training
D. All of these

64. Teaching by small steps and frequent short assignment techniques are useful for—
A. Slow learners
B. Learning disabled
C. Educationally backward children.
D. Children of all types of disabilities

65. Special schools are required for backward children when—
A. Backwardness is due to any serious physical handicap
B. The size of population of backward children in the society is very large as is the case of Gujarat where the achievement of students in mathematics is always seen very low
C. Both of these
D. None of these

ANSWERS

1	2	3	4	5	6	7	8	9	10
C	D	B	C	C	D	A	B	A	A

11	12	13	14	15	16	17	18	19	20
B	B	B	D	A	B	B	C	A	D
21	**22**	**23**	**24**	**25**	**26**	**27**	**28**	**29**	**30**
D	C	C	C	D	D	D	C	B	D
31	**32**	**33**	**34**	**35**	**36**	**37**	**38**	**39**	**40**
A	D	A	A	D	D	C	D	A	A
41	**42**	**43**	**44**	**45**	**46**	**47**	**48**	**49**	**50**
D	C	C	D	D	D	D	C	C	C
51	**52**	**53**	**54**	**55**	**56**	**57**	**58**	**59**	**60**
D	A	D	D	A	A	B	B	A	D
61	**62**	**63**	**64**	**65**					
D	D	D	D	C					

YOUR SPACE

MANIPUR
General Knowledge

MANIPUR : A PROFILE

The word "Manipur" is being derived from the two Sanskrit Words "Mani" and "Pur", which literally mean 'A Jewelled Land' or 'The Land of Jewels'. Here "Mani" means Jewel and "Pur" means land or place respectively.

Surrounded by blue hills with an oval shaped valley at the centre, rich in art and tradition and surcharged with nature's pristine glory, Manipur lies on a melting pot of culture. It is birth place of Polo. This is the place where Rajashree Bhagyachandra created the famous Ras Lila, the classical dance of Manipur, out of his enchanting dream by the grace of Lord Krishna. His folk dances reveal the mythological concept of creation of Manipur.

Having a varied and proud history from the earliest times, Manipur came under the British Rule as a Princely State after the defeat in the Anglo-Manipuri War of 1891. After independence of India in 1947, the Princely State of Manipur was merged in the Indian Union on October 15,1949 and became a full-fledged State of India on the 21th January, 1972 with a Legislative Assembly of 60 seats of which 19 are reserved for Scheduled Tribe and one reserved for Scheduled Caste. The State is represented in the Lok Sabha by two members and by one member in the Rajya Sabha.

Manipur extends between 23°50' and 25°42' latitudes north and between 92°58' and 94°45' longitudes east. It covers an area of 22,327 square kilometers and is bounded on the north by Nagaland, on the west by Cachar of Assam, on the east by upper Myanmar and on the south by Mizoram and Chin hills of Myanmar.

IMPORTANT FACTS

Capital	:	Imphal
Area	:	22327 sq.km.
Population (2011 Census)	:	28,55,794 (*Males*: 14,38,586; *Females*: 14,17,208)
Decadal Growth Rate	:	24.50%
Density of Population	:	128 (per sq. km.)
Literacy Rate	:	76.94%
Sex Ratio	:	985 (Females per 1000 Males)
Altitude	:	790 mtrs. above MSL (Imphal)
Latitude	:	23°50'N to 25°42'N
Longitude	:	92°58'E to 94°45'E
Rainfall	:	1467.5 mm (Avg.)
Rainy Season	:	May to October
Climate • **Summer** • **Winter**	: :	14°C to 32°C 0°C to 25°C
State Language	:	Manipuri
State Emblem	:	Kangla Sha
State Bird	:	Nongyeen

State Animal	:	Sangai Deer
State Game	:	Sagol Kangjei (Manipuri Polo)
State Flower	:	Siroi Lily
State Tree	:	Uning thou
Assembly Constituencies	:	60
Parliamentary Constituencies	:	2 (One for Inner and One for Outer)
Rajya Sabha Seat	:	1
Districts	:	16—Senapati, Tamenglong, Thoubal, Ukhrul, Bishnupur, Chandel, Churachandpur, Imphal East, Imphal West, Jiribam, Kangpokpi, Kakching, Tengnoupal, Kamjong, Noney, Pherzawl.
Towns	:	51 *(Statutory towns 28, Census towns 23)*
Gram Panchayats	:	165
Highly Populated District (2011)	:	Imphal West
Less Populated District	:	Tamenglong
Most Densely Populated District (2011)	:	Imphal West (998 persons per sq. km.)
Less Densely Populated District (2011)	:	Tamenglong (32 persons per sq. km)
Major Festivals	:	Rath Yatra, Yaoshang (Dol Jatra), Christmas, Diwali, ID, Mahavir Jayanti, Lai Haraoba, Kut, Gan-Ngai, Cheiraoba
Major Cities	:	Imphal, Churachandpur, Kakching, Ukhrul, Andro, Bishnupur, Jiribam, Moirang, Moreh, Ningthoukhong, Thoubal, etc.
Largest City	:	Imphal
Major Tourist Places	:	Shaheed Minar, War Cemetery, Manipur Zoological Garden, Keibul Lamjao National Park, Kaina, Red Hill (Maibam Lok pa Ching), Loukoipat, Shree Shree Govindajee Temple, Phubala, Loktak Lake, Leimaram, Moreh, Tengnoupal, Andro, Khongjom, etc.
Major Crops	:	Wheat, Rice, Pulses, Paddy, Maize, Sugarcane, Potato, Mustard, etc.
Major Fruits	:	Pineapple, Banana, Papaya, Passion Fruit, Orange, Lemon, Mango etc.
Major Vegetables	:	Cabbage, Cauliflower, Peas, French Beans, Tomato, etc.
Major Spices	:	Green Chilli, Ginger, Turmeric, Corriander Seeds, etc.
Major Forest Products	:	Oak, Teak, Pine, Cane, Bamboo, Leihao, Uningthou, etc.
Major Import Products	:	Betel nut, Silk yarn, Pigs, Cotton thread, etc.
Major Export Products	:	Bamboo shoot products (orient food), ginger, pineapple, Maize, Mushrooms, etc.
Chief Rivers	:	Barak, Imphal, Khuga, Maklang, Ithai, Thoubal, Irang, Nambul, Chakpi, Sekmai, etc.
Major Minerals	:	Copper, Nickel, Chromite, Asbestos, Limestone, Lignite, etc.

❑❑❑

ADMINISTRATION

Manipur in its wide territory of 22,327 sq. km. includes 16 districts. The name of districts are Imphal-East, Imphal-West, Senapati, Tamenglong, Thoubal, Ukhrul, Bishnupur, Chandel, Churachandpur, Jiribam, Kangpokpi, Kakching, Tengnoupal, Kamjong, Noney and Pherzawl. Number of Sub-divisions (2019) is 68. For the upliftment and development of the rural areas, the state is sub-divided into community and Tribal Development Blocks and small town committees. The Manipur Legislative Assembly consists of 60 seats out of which, 19 seats are reserved for scheduled Tribes, 1 for Scheduled Caste and 40 for General. Manipur has a two-tier panchayati Raj system. Gram Panchayat at the Village level and the Zila Parishad at the district level. As on 2019 there are 165 Gram Panchayats and 6 Zila Parishads (the Imphal East Zila Parishad, the Imphal West Zila Parishad, the Thoubal Zila Parishad, the Bishnupur Zila Parishad, Jiribam Zila Parishad and Kakching Zila Parishad) in Manipur.

Manipur sends 2 members to Lok-Sabha (Lower House of the Indian Parliament) and 1 member to the Rajya Sabha (Upper House of the Indian Parliament). Manipur was within the jurisdiction of the Imphal Bench of Gauhati High Court till March 25, 2013. Earlier, the Imphal Bench of Gauhati High Court came into existence on 21st January, 1972, the day Manipur attained its statehood. In March 2013, the then Chief Justice of India Altamas Kabir formally inaugurated the Manipur High Court at Imphal and Justice Abhay Manohar Sapre was made the first Chief Justice of the Manipur High Court.

DISTRICTS AND SUB-DIVISIONS OF MANIPUR

Sl. No.	Name of District	Name of Sub-division		
1.	**Senapati**	1. Tadubi 4. Willong 7. Lairouching	2. Paomata 5. Chilivai Phaibung 8. Senapati	3. Purul 6. Song-Song
2.	**Kangpokpi** (Bifurcated from the erstwhile Senapati District)	9. Kangpokpi 12. Kangchup Geljang 15. Lungtin	10. Champhai 13. Tuijang Waichong 16. Island	11. Saitu Gamphazol 14. Saikul 17. Bungte Chiru
3.	**Tamenglong**	18. Tamenglong	19. Tamei	20. Tousem
4.	**Noney District** (Bifurcated from the erstwhile Tamenglong District)	21. Nungba 24. Haochong	22. Khoupum	23. Longmei (Noney)
5.	**Churachandpur**	25. Churachandpur 28. Mualnuam 31. Kangvai 34. Lungthul Suangdoh	26. Sangaikot 29. Singngat 32. Samulamlan	27. Tuibuong 30. Henglep 33. Saikot
6.	**Pherzawl** (Bifurcated from the erstwhile Churachandpur District)	35. Pherzawl 38. Vangai Range	36. Thanlon	37. Parbung-Tipaimukh
7.	**Chandel**	39. Chandel	40. Chakpikarong	41. Khengjoy
8.	**Tengnoupal District** (Bifurcated from the erstwhile Chandel District)	42. Machi	43. Moreh	44. Tengnoupal
9.	**Ukhrul**	45. Ukhrul 48. Jessami	46. Lungchong-Maiphai	47. Chingai

Sl. No.	Name of District	Name of Sub-division		
10.	**Kamjong District** (Bifurcated from the erstwhile Ukhrul District)	49. Kamjong 52. Phungyar	50. Sahamphung	51. Kasom Khullen
11.	**Imphal East**	53. Porompat	54. Keirao Bitra	55. Sawombung
12.	**Jiribam** (Bifurcated from the erstwhile Imphal East District)	56. Jiribam	57. Borobekra	
13.	**Imphal West**	58. Lamshang 61. Wangoi	59. Patsoi	60. Lamphelpat
14.	**Bishnupur**	62. Nambol	63. Bishnupur	64. Moirang
15.	**Thoubal**	65. Thoubal	66. Lilong	
16.	**Kakching** (Bifurcated from the erstwhile Thoubal District)	67. Kakching	68. Waikhong	

MUNICIPALITY

In Manipur there are altogether 9 municipalities which is headed by the Municipality Commission.

Sl. No.	Name of Municipal Council	Total No. of Wards
1.	Imphal Municipal Council	27
2.	Kakching Municipal Council	12
3.	Thoubal Municipal Council	18
4.	Jiribam Municipal Council	10
5.	Moirang Municipal Council	12
6.	Bishnupur Municipal Council	12
7.	Nambol Municipal Council	18
8.	Mayang Imphal Municipal Council	13
9.	Ningthoukhong Municipal Council	

NAGAR PANCHAYATS

There are 18 Nagar Panchayats in the state.

Sl. No.	Name of Nagar Panchayats	Total No. of Wards
1.	Andro	12
2.	Lilong (Thoubal)	9
3.	Lamshang	9
4.	Wangoi	12
5.	Lamlai	9
6.	Sekmai	9
7.	Thongkhong Laxmi Bazar	11
8.	Lilong (Imphal West)	9
9.	Samurou	12
10.	Heirok	12
11.	Wangjing Lamding	9
12.	Shikhong Sekmai	3
13.	Yairipok	9
14.	Sugnu	9
15.	Oinam	9
16.	Kakching Khunou	9
17.	Kumbi	9
18.	Kwakta	9

HISTORY

PERIODS IN THE HISTORY OF MANIPUR

A careful study of a language may reveal a considerable amount of the historical events, the origin, migration, the art and culture of the people. Sir William Jones, a British judge in India in 1786 while studying the Sanskrit literature revealed that it bears a striking resemblance with other two ancient languages — Latin and Greek. The Sanskrit word for father 'Pitar' is astonishingly similar to the Greek and Latin 'Pater'. Similarly, Sanskrit 'Matar' Latin and Greek 'Mater' and English 'Mother' and Hindi 'Mata' share a considerable affinity. Two hundred years of linguistic research had provided evidences that one-third of the human race might have come from this Indo-European "common source", probably between 3500-2500 BC in the central Europe, from where people migrated to the West and East.

In case of the Meitei people, since there were no modern system of recording, where the sense of originality was always contemplated with the modern history, the reconstruction of the ancient manuscripts and languages has yielded a considerable knowledge on the history of ancient Manipur. The following is a brief history or Puwari of some prominent Meitei rulers with a view to bring out an understanding of the various developments in Meitei history, art, culture, tradition, sports, etc. The account is not complete but hope to provide an overall grasp on the history of Manipur.

The history of Manipur may be divided into four main periods: (i) **The Ancient period** (before Christ), (ii) **The early period** (1st-13th AD), (iii) **The Medieval period** (15-18th AD) and (iv) **The Modern period** (19-20th Century AD).

PRESENT MANIPUR

On 21 January 1972, Manipur was granted Statehood after several years of demand by All Manipur Students Union and several political organisations. The ceremony was performed at the Palace Polo ground in Imphal. In 1992, Meitei-lon (Manipuri) was included in the Eighth Schedule as one of the 22 official languages of India. Manipur has yet to see a proper road connection to the rest of India. Air transportations are provided from Kolkata, New Delhi, Guwahati and Silchar but much beyond the reach of commoners.

FAMOUS TITLES OF WELL KNOWN PERSONS

TITLE	NAME
❖ The Lion of Manipur	Bir Tikendrajit
❖ Mahakavi	Hijam Anganghal
❖ Melody King	Nongmaithem Pahari
❖ Melody Queen	Smt. Laishram Mema Devi
❖ Tarzan of Manipur	Irom Leikhendra
❖ Bob	Ralengnao Kathing
❖ Jananeta (leader of the people)	Hijam Irabot
❖ Kaksu	Meidigu Tonkonba
❖ Agayestha of the East	Atombapu Sharma
❖ Thangal General	Kangabam Chitananda Singha
❖ Leipok Keirungba	Leimapokpam Dev Singh

KINGS OF MANIPUR

Name	Period of reign (A.D.)	Number of Years/Months
❖ Nongda Lairen Pakhangba	33-154	121
❖ Khuiyoi Tompok	154-264	110
❖ Taothingmang	264-364	100
❖ Khui Ningonba	364-379	15
❖ Pengsiba	379-394	15
❖ Kaokhangba	394-411	17
❖ Naokhamba	411-428	17
❖ Naophangba	428-518	90
❖ Sameirang	518-568	50
❖ Wura Konthouba	568-658	90
❖ Naothingkhong	663-763	100
❖ Khongtekcha	763-773	10
❖ Keirencha	784-799	15
❖ Yaraba	799-821	22
❖ Ayangba	821-910	89
❖ Ningthoucheng	910-949	39
❖ Chenglie-Ipan-Lanthaba	949-969	20
❖ Keiphaba Yanglon	969-984	15
❖ Irengba	984-1074	90
❖ Loiyumba	1074-1112	48
❖ Loitongba	1122-1150	28

Name	Period of reign (A.D.)	Number of Years/Months
❖ Atom Yoiremba	1150-1163	13
❖ Iyanthaba	1163-1195	32
❖ Thayanthaba	1195-1231	36
❖ Chingthang Lanthaba	1231-1242	11
❖ Thingbai Shelhongba	1242-1247	5
❖ Puranthaba	1247-1263	16
❖ Khumomba	1263-1278	15
❖ Moiramba	1278-1302	24
❖ Thangbi Lanthaba	1302-1324	22
❖ Kongyamba	1324-1335	11
❖ Telheiba	1335-1355	20
❖ Tonaba	1355-1359	4
❖ Tabungba	1339-1394	35
❖ Lairenba	1394-1399	5
❖ Punsiba	1404-1432	28
❖ Ningthoukhomba	1432-1467	35
❖ Kyamba	1467-1508	41
❖ Koiremba	1508-1512	4
❖ Lamkhyamba	1512-1523	11
❖ Nonginphaba	1523-1524	1
❖ Kabomba	1524-1542	18
❖ Tangjamba	1542-1545	3
❖ Chalamba	1545-1562	17
❖ Mugyamba	1562-1597	35
❖ Khagemba	1597-1652	55
❖ Khunjaoba	1652-1666	14
❖ Paikhomba	1666-1697	31
❖ Charairongba	1697-1709	12
❖ Garibniwaj	1709-1748	39
❖ Chitshai	1748-1752	4
❖ Bharatsai	1752-1753	1

Name	Period of reign (A.D.)	Number of Years/Months
❖ Maramba	1753-1759	6
❖ Chingthangkhomba	1759-1762	3
❖ Maramba	1762-1763	1
❖ Chingthangkhomba	1763-1798	35
❖ Labanyachandra	1798-1801	3
❖ Madhuchandra	1801-1803	2
❖ Chourjit	1803-1813	10
❖ Marjit	1813-1819	6
❖ Takuningthou (Herachandra)	1819	1
❖ Yumjaotaba	1820	1
❖ Gambhir Singha	1821	6 months
❖ Jai Singha	1822	1
❖ Jadu Singha (Nongpok Chinslenkhomba)	1823	1
❖ Raghab Singha	1823-1824	1
❖ Nongchup Lamgain-gamba (Bhadrasing)	1824	1
❖ Gambhir Singha (Chinglen Nongdrenkhomba)	1825-1834	9
❖ Chandrakirti (Ningthempishak)	1834-1844	10
❖ Nara Singha	1844-1850	6
❖ Debendra Singha	1850	3 months
❖ Chandrakirti (K.C.S.I.)	1850-1886	36
❖ Surchandra	1886-1890	4
❖ Kulachandra	1890-1891	1
❖ Churachand Singha	1891-1941	50
❖ Bodhachandra Singha	1941-1955	14

IMPORTANT DATES IN MANIPUR HISTORY

33 A.D. – The first king of Manipur was Pakhangba who reigned for 120 years.

154 A.D. – Khuiyoi Tompok ascended the throne and it is belived that during his reign 'Pung' (drum) was first invented.

264 A.D. – Taothing Mang ascended the throne.

568 – Wura Konthouba become a King.

1074 – King Loiyumba came to the throne during his reign many social reform took place.

1247 – Puranthaba became King and in his reign chinese invaded Manipur but was defeated.

1404 – Luwang Punsiba, who introduced the international game of Polo for the first time on the soil of Manipur, ascended the throne.

1467 – Kyamba, who was noted for his military and administration achievement ascended the throne.

1597 – Khangemba become a King and introduced first Manipur coins.

1704 – King Charairongba was initial into Vaishnavism with the result that Vaishnavism become state religion.

1714 – Garibaniwaj ascended the throne.

1736 – Garibaniwaj again with an army crossed Ningthee river and attacked and destroyed the town of Meyedu, on the bank of Yu river.

1762 – The first Alliance become Manipur and East India Company was made.

1765 – The second Burmese invasion took place.

1775 – Occurance of the worst flood known as 'Wang Khem Echao'.

1776 – Set-up the Govindajee Temple at Imphal by king Bheigyachandra.

1819 – 'Seven year Disertation' 1819 to 1825, Magazine wore a deserted look under the tyrancy of invading Burmese.

1826 – Making of the "Treaty of Yandaboo".

1833 – Annexation of Jiribam to Manipur during the reign of Gambir Singh.

1834 – The Kabaw Valley was handed over to Burma.

1885 – First English school was established.

1891 – The Government of India under the British declared war against Manipur; Yuvaraj Tikendrajit and General Thangal were executed by hanging at Pheida Pung (Present B.T. Park).

1904 – First Nupeelal (Women's war against British)

1907 – Manipur State Darbar was established to assist the Maharaja in the administration of Manipur.

1931 – The hanging of Jadonang who was a great Zeliangrong leader.

1939 – Nupeelal, i.e. Second Women's war against the misrule of the British and it continued for about 14 months.

1941 – Maharaj Bodhachandra become the king of Manipur by succeeding to his father Chura Chand.

1944 – The INA Flag Hoisted at Moirang.

1949 – Merger agreement was signed between the government of India and Manipur.

1957 – Manipur become one of the Union Territories under the Union Territories Act, 1956.

1960 – Panchayati Raj System was introduced in Manipur.

1963 – A Legislative assembly of 30 elected and 3 nominated was established under the Govt. of Union Territory Act, 1963; The AIR station of Imphal was inaugurated.

1967 – President's Rule was imposed for the first time in Manipur.

1972 – Manipur became a full fledged state.

1980 – The Manipur university was established.

1987 – TV transmission centre was opened.

1992 – Manipur Language have included in the 8th Schedule of the Constitution of India by the 71st Amendment of Constitution.

1995 – DD-2 metro channel of DDK-Imphal was opened.

1997 – Divided the Imphal East & Imphal West District.

1999 – The 5th National Games were held in Manipur. Manipur overall champion.

2000 – Manipur Cup 2000, 5th International Invitation Polo Tournament at Imphal win Manipur Polo Team.

2002 – The President of India APJ Abdul Kalam, inaugurated the 36 MW Heavey fuel based Power plant at Leimakhong, 20 Km from Imphal.

2004 – Prime Minister Dr. Manmohan Singh handed over the Kangla Fort to the government of India.

2005 – The first Chief Minister of Manipur M.K. Priyobrata passess away at his residence located in Konung Leikei at Palace Compound, Imphal.

2006 – Former Chief Minister of Manipur R.K. Ranabir Singh passes away at his residence at Keishamthong Longiam Leirak, Imphal.

2007 – Manipur gets second position in 33rd National Games held in Guwahati (February 9-18) with 51 gold, 32 silver and 40 bronze medals.

2008 – The Manipur government has decided to construct 25 residential schools in the state with funding from the centre.

2009 – Boxing icon M.C. Mary kom awarded with Rajiv Gandhi Khel Ratna award for 2008-09.

2010 – Manipur won 18th Senior National Women's Football tournament.

2011 – Manipur won Best State Award in 34th National Games-2011.

2012 – Boxing icon M.C. Mary Kom won bronze medal in 2012 London Olympics.

2013 – Chief Justice of India Altamas Kabir inaugurated the Manipur High Court on March 25, 2013.

2014 – Seven Sportspersons from Manipur won medals (3 Gold and 4 Bronze) in Asian Games–2014 held in Incheon, South Korea.

2015 – Binalakshmi Nepram wins L'oreal Paris Femina Women Awards 2015.

2016 – Maurice Yengkhom and Chongtham Kuber Meitei got National Bravery Award; M.C. Mary Kom nominated in Rajya Sabha.

2017 – BJP leader N. Biren Singh became new CM of Manipur.

2018 – The Union Cabinet approved the ordinance of setting India's first National Sports University in Imphal.

2019 – Ms. Bombayla Devi Laishram (Sports—Archery) got Padma Shri Award.

2020 – Government of India approved development of Loktak Inland Waterways improvement project.

2021 – La. Ganesan became new Governor of Manipur.

2022 – N. Biren Singh took oath as the CM of Manipur for a second term.

2023 – Anusuiya Uikey became new Governor of Manipur.

2024 – Machihan Sasa (Art) got Padma Shri Award.

2025 – Ajay Kumar Bhalla became new Governor of Manipur.

2026 – BJP leader Y. Khemchand Singh became new CM of Manipur.

❑❑❑

GEOGRAPHY

Manipur has a total surface area of 22,327 sq. km. forming 0.7% of the total land surface of the Indian Union. It is situated between the parallels 23°50'N -25°42'N and the meridians 92°58'E - 94°45'E. It has a border of 854 km of which 352 km is international border with Myanmar on the east. The remaining 502 km long border separates her from the neighboring states of Nagaland on the north, Assam on the west and Mizoram on the south and the south west. Physiographically the land is divisible into a central valley and the surrounding mountains. The plain or the valley is approximately 2238 sq. km. accounting to 10% of the total state area. Out of this an area of 550 sq. km. is occupied by lakes, wetlands, barren uplands and hillocks. The valley is oval shape with a NNW-SSE orientation and has a gentle slope towards the south measuring 798 m above m.s.l. at the extreme north and 746 m above m.s.l. at the Southern end. The Imphal city stands at an altitude of 790 m above m.s.l.

GEOLOGY

Dayal and Duara (1963) outlined the classification of rocks in Manipur which is more or less in line with that of Oldham (1883) with some modifications after the views of Pascoe (1929) and Evans (1932). The geologic succession according to them is

Age	*Rock Type*
Recent to sub-recent	Alluvium
Oligocene	Barails
Intrusive rocks	Disang Series
Intrusive rocks (Cretaceous to early Eocene)	Surpentinities
Cretaceous	Axials

SEISMOLOGY

The hills of the whole zone of the eastern frontier of India including Manipur were built up during the late Pleistocene period and hence isostatic and seismic balances are yet to be attained. Manipur falls in one of the most seismically active zones of the Trans-Asiatic Earthquake Belt.

CLIMATE

Besides the influence by its locations around the latitudes just north of the Tropic of Cancer, the climate of the state is governed by the relief of land and the rain bearing winds viz. the South-West Monsoon in summer and the North-East Monsoon and the Mediterranean winds in winter. The eastern lowlands along the Indo-Burma border and the Western Assam Manipur border lowlands fall between the altitudes 30-100 metre above m.s.l. and thus reigned by a tropical climate. The Manipur Valley at a height of 780-800 metre above m.s.l. has sub-tropical climate while the higher reaches of the mountains surrounding the valley have a temperate climate.

RIVERS

Rivers along with other natural and man-made sources play an important role in irrigation in the state of Manipur. Irang, Barrak and Turel Achouba are some of the major rivers of the state.

Thoubal River : Thoubal river starts from Huimi hills of Ukhrul and flow westwards upto Yaingangpokpi and turning southwards, joins the Imphal river at Irong Ichin.

Iril River : It rises in the Lamkui and Kadam Hills of the north-eastern Mao. After flowing southwards, it joins the Imphal Rivers at Lilong area.

Barrak River : It is the biggest river of Manipur. Its source is 16 km east of Mao Police Station in Senapati District. Barrak, at its source is known as 'Sanglook'. It leaves Manipur area near Lalpur and flows towards Cachar, Assam. The Makru and the Irang are two main tributaries of this river.

Turel Achouba : Turel Achouba is also known as Imphal or Manipur river. It is the longest river of the state. Its source is Bolen Pat at 197 feet above sea level and 15 km from Kangpokpi area. It also joins the stream of Ningthee or Chindwin river of Burma in its way.

RIVERS IN HILL AREAS

Some of the important rivers of the hill areas of Manipur includes Makru, Barrak, Irang, Leimatak, Tuyungbi, Maklang, Chingai, Chalou, Taret Lok, Lokchao, Chakpi, Khuga and Tuivai river.

MAIN RIVERS : AT A GLANCE

River	Length (km.)	Aspect	Source	Destination
Barrak	84.39	West	Karong-Mao area	Brahmaputra River
Imphal	38	South	Bolen Pat in Kangpokpi area	Chindwin River
Iril	57.27	South	Lakhamai of Pural Block	Imphal River
Irang	28.13	South Western Block	Langka Chongjan area of Kangpokpi	Barrak River
Ithai	24.83	South	Selsi Thoubung area	Iril River

LAKES

The state of Manipur is characterised by numerous lakes. Many of them are also known for its scenic and aesthetic beauty. Loktak lake, the biggest of North East India, is also a part of Manipur. It is also famous for its great beauty.

LAKES IN HILL AREAS

There are two major lakes in hilly areas of Manipur. These are Kachouphung Lake in Ukhrul district and Zailad Lake in Tamenglong district.

MAIN LAKES : AT A GLANCE

- ❖ Loktak Lake
- ❖ Kharung Pat
- ❖ Heingang Pat
- ❖ Kachouphung Lake
- ❖ Waithou Pat
- ❖ Pumlen Pat
- ❖ Utra Pat
- ❖ Zailad Lake
- ❖ Loushi Pat
- ❖ Ikop Pat
- ❖ Ishok Pat
- ❖ Sana Pat
- ❖ Loukoi Pat

WATERFALLS

- ❖ Barrak Waterfalls
- ❖ Sadu Chiru Waterfalls
- ❖ Khayang Waterfalls
- ❖ Leimram Waterfalls
- ❖ Dilily Waterfalls

HILLS

- ❖ Cheirao-Ching
- ❖ Chakka Nungba
- ❖ Somrah
- ❖ Chinganguba
- ❖ Kanpum
- ❖ Kasom
- ❖ Mayangkhang
- ❖ Kopru-Laimatol
- ❖ Nupitel
- ❖ Nunjaibong
- ❖ Khhunho Spurs
- ❖ Hawbi
- ❖ Yomadoung
- ❖ Thumion
- ❖ Koubru Leikha
- ❖ Bharuni
- ❖ Laison
- ❖ Thangjing
- ❖ Kala Naga
- ❖ Sirohi Frar

CAVES

- ❖ Tonglon
- ❖ Sangboo
- ❖ Tharon
- ❖ Khangkhui
- ❖ Hungdung Mangva
- ❖ Khukse

PEAKS

Peaks	*Height (m)*
❖ Leikot	2,832
❖ Tampaba	2,564
❖ Mount Tenipu (Essau)	2,994
❖ Siroi	2,835
❖ Khayangbung	2,833

❑❑❑

ART AND CULTURE

FOLK DANCES

Some Famous folk dances of Manipur are as follows:

Ras Lila : The Ras Lila, the epitome of Manipuri classical dance is inter-woven through the celestial and eternal love of Radha and Krishna as has been described in the Hindu scriptures and reveals the sublime and transcendental love of Krishna and Radha and the Gopies' devotion to the Lord. It is generally performed in an enclosure in front of the temple throughout the night and watched with a deep sense of devotion. Ras performances are seasonal and varied and performed at the temple of Shree Shree Govindajee in Imphal on the nights of Basanta Purnima, Sarada Purnima and Kartik Purnima and at local temples later. Ras performances are mainly of four types—Vasanta Ras, Kunja Ras, Maha Ras and Nata/Nitya Ras. At the temple of Shri Shri Govinda, Vasanta Ras is performed on the full-moon night of Hiyangei (November). After they are performed at the temple of Shri Shri Govinda, they are performed at any time of the year.

Nupa Pala : Nupa Pala which is otherwise known as Kartal Cholom or Cymbal Dance is a characteristic of the Manipuri style of dance and music. The initial movements of this dance are soft and serene, gradually gathering momentum. It is a group performance of male partners, using cymbals and wearing snow white ball-shaped large turbans, who sing and dance to the accompaniment of Mridanga, an ancient classical drum "Pung" as it is called in Manipuri. The Nupa Pala acts as a prologue to the Ras Lila dances, besides an independent performance too, in connection with religious rites.

Pung Cholom : Pung or Manipuri Mridanga is the soul of Manipuri Sankirtana music and Classical Manipuri Dance. Khuyoi Tompok who ruled over Manipur during (154-264 A.D) introduced the pung having only one beating face. Since then, it has developed to the present form of 'Meitei Pung with two beating faces. Today, 'Pung Cholom' which is a traditional dance form of the pung drummers has earned international acclamation for its charming artistic display.

Maibi Dance : During the festival of Lai-Haraoba which is an annual ritual festival of the Meiteis, the inhabitants of the valley of Manipur, the Maibis, the priestesses considered to be spritural mediums, trace through their dances the whole concept of cosmogony of the Meitei people and describe their way of life. Beginning with the process of creation, they show the construction of houses and various occupations of the people to sustain themselves. It is a kind of re-living of the way of life of the past.

Khamba Thoibi Dance : Khamba Thoibi dance is a duet of male and female partners, a dance of dedication to the sylvan deity, Thangjing of Moirang, is the depiction of the dance performed by Khamba and Thoibi, the hero and heroine of the Moirang episode of the hoary past. This, with the "Maibi" dance (Priestess dance), the "Leima Jagoi" etc. form the "Lai Haraoba" dance. The "Lai Haraoba" dance, in many ways, is the fountainhead of the modern Manipuri dance form. This dance is a part and parcel of Moirang Lai-Haraoba. It is believed that the legendary hero - Khamba, and heroin - Thoibi danced together before the Lord Thangjing, a celebrated deity of Moirang, a village in the South-West of Manipur which is known for its rich cultural traditions, for peace and prosperity of the land.

SOME IMPORTANT TRIBAL DANCES OF MANIPUR

1. Kabui Naga Dance
2. Tangkhul Naga Dance – *Tangkhul Hunting Dance, Tangkhul War Dance, Lakhahganui Dance i.e., Virgin Dance etc.*
3. Tarao War Dance etc.
4. Mao Maram Dance
5. Paite Dance – *Dak Lam, Jangta Lam, Phit Lam, Ton Lam and Silam Lam*
6. Thadou Kuki Dance

FOLK SONGS

Some famous folk songs of Manipur are as follows:

Wari Liba : It is an indigenous art form of telling stories prevalent in the State since the 17th century. The Mahabharata and the Ramayana are the themes of such story telling.

Khulang Ishei : Manipuri folk song is known as 'Khulang Ishei'. It is popular for its thematic and romantic contents. The folk songs are commonly sung by the rural folk and hill men at the time of harvesting, collecting firewood, hunting and fishing.

Khongjom Parva : It is a musical narration of the Battle of Khongjom fought between the Manipuris and the British in April 1891. Dhobi Leinou started singing Khongjom Parva by thumping his hands on the knee and some times used an empty tin to thump upon. The Khongjom Parva narrators glorify the Manipuris soldiers who sacrificed their lives for the sake of their motherland. Today the theme of singing Khongjom Parva includes the stories of Khamba and Thoibi, the Ramayana, the Mahabharata and the exploits of the kings of Manipur. The singer uses only a Dholak while singing.

Pena-Ishei : It is an ancient folk song of Manipur which is sung with a musical instrument called "Pena". This song narrates the popular stories of Manipur. Pena is a stringed musical instrument of Manipur. Its origin may be traced back to a hoary past. It is called Bena in parts of Assam. It is made up of two parts viz the penamasa and pena cheijing. Earlier, Pena was usually played by its player to invoke the gods and goddesses. But today, this musical instrument is played in musical concerts and other performances also.

Ougri : This is a very ancient type of song and sung usually in praise of Sun, Moon, Kings etc. It is mostly sung in Lai Haraoba festivals.

Moibung Esei : The conch music of Manipuri is quite distinct and extraordinary. An artist of it can blow two conches simultaneously producing enchanting music.

Nat Esei : It is a peculiar type of song composed and originated by the Manipuris. It is sung in both Manipuri and Bengali languages and the theme is usually of Hindu Gods and Goddesses.

Khubak Esei : This kind of song is performed by two sides of participants standing at opposite sides and facing at each other. The rhythmic clapping of palms is its accompanying music.

Khulang Esei : This kind of song is sung without any musical instrument and the theme of this type of song is related to love & romance. It is known as Heplee in archaic language.

TRADITIONAL MUSICAL INSTRUMENTS

1. Pung (Drum)
2. Kartal (Cymbals)
3. Pena (Sitar)
4. Manjira or Mandilla (Metal jingles)
5. Sipa (Flute)
6. Tingteila (Violin)
7. Mazo (Women's mouth-piece)
8. Khol (Drum), etc.

DANCE & CULTURE TRAINING INSTITUTES

- Government Dance College (Shree Shree Govindajee Natanalya) – Palace Compound, Imphal.
- J.N. Manipur Dance Academy – Near D.M. College Compound, Imphal.

MANIPURI STATE KALA AKADEMI

This Akademi was set up by the Government of Manipur in the year 1971. It is the first of its kind in the eastern region of India. It is an autonomous organization for the promotion and coordinating of cultural activities of the people of Manipur both of the valley and hills.

MUSEUM

MANIPUR STATE MUSEUM

This museum, located near the Imphal Pologround has a fairly good display of the state's heritage and a collection of portraits of Manipur's former rulers. Items of special interests are costumes, arms and weapons, relics and historical documents.

The Manipur State Museum was inaugurated by the late Prime Minister of India, Smt. Indira Gandhi on 23rd September, 1969. During 56 years, this Museum has become a fullfledged multipurpose Museum comprising of various Galleries like—Ethnology, Archeology, Natural History, Painting, Jallan, Children's Gallery and an open air gallery for housing the 78ft long boat called Hiyang Hiren (Royal boat).

Apart from the normal functions of Museum, it took up various activities like Museum awareness programmes, Conservation of Biological specimens, Cultural appreciation course, Science fairs, Thematic exhibition, Mobile exhibition etc.

Manipur State Museum has also taken up numerous sponsor programmes through National and International Museums.

IMPORTANT PLACES OF WORSHIP

All the communities and religions celebrate their respective religious festivals or days with devotion and unflinching commitment. Some of the major worship places are given below:

Kangla Temple	—	4th Assam Rifles Ground
Sanamahee Temple	—	1st Batalion, M.R.
Jain Digamber Temple	—	Paona Road
Govindajee Temple	—	Palace Ground
ISKON Temple	—	Airport Road
Hanuman Thakur Temple	—	Near Palace Ground
Gurdwar Temple	—	Thangal Bazar
Jame Masjid	—	Masjid Road
Hiyangthang Lairembi Temple	—	Hiyangthan
M.B.C. Central Church	—	Deulahland
Moirang Thangjing Temple	—	Moirang

❑❑❑

FESTIVALS

Manipur celebrates a number of peculiar festivals of its own with great pomp and joy. Some of them are:

Lai-Haraoba : Lai Haraoba is one of the most important indigenous ritual festivals celebrated by the Meitei community of Manipur. It is celebrated to propitiate and please the ancestral deities to get their blessings in return. It depicts the act of creating universe and its objects, and unveils the endless journey of universe through its ritualistic performances. It is celebrated in Manipur since time immemorial and is being continued till today.

Yaoshang (Dol Jatra) : Celebrated for five days commencing from the full-moon day of Phalgun (February/March), Yaoshang is the premier festival of Manipur. The Thabal Chongba, a kind of Manipuri folk dance in which boys and girls hold hands and dance away their blues in festive tube-lit ambience is an inseparable part of the festival.

Ratha Jatra : One of the greatest festivals of the Hindus of Manipur, the festival is celebrated for about 10 days in the month of Ingen (June/July). Lord Jagannath leaves his temple in a Rath locally known as Kang pulled by pilgrims who vie with one another for this honour.

Ramjan ID (The premier festival of Manipur Muslims) : Ramjan Id is the most popular festival of the Manipuri Muslims (Meitei Pangal) and is observed in the usual spirits of joy and festivities as in other Muslim world. Ramjan is the ninth month of Hijri year.

Kut (Festival of Kuki-Chin-Mizo) : It is an autumn festival of the different tribes of Kuki-Chin-Mizo groups of Manipur. The festival has been variously described at different places amongst different tribes as Chavang-Kut or Khodou etc. It is a happy occasion for the villagers whose food stock is bountiful after a year of hard labour. The festival is a thanks giving feasts with songs and dances in merriment and joviality for all, in honour of the giver of an abundant harvest, it is observed on the first day of November every year.

Gang-Ngai (Festival of Kabui Nagas) : Celebrated for five days in the month of Wakching (December/January), Gang-Ngai is an important festival of the Kabui Nagas. The festival opens with the omen taking ceremony on the first day and the rest of the days are associated with common feast, dances of old men and women and of boys and girls, presentation of farewell gifts etc. From 1997, it starts from January 21.

Chumpha (Festival of Tangkhul Nagas) : Chumpha, generally the festival of Tangkhul Nagas, is celebrated for seven days in the month of December. It is a great festival of Tangkhul Nagas. The festival is held after harvest. The last three days are devoted to social gatherings and rejoicing. Unlike other festivals women play a special role in the festival. The concluding part of the festival ends with a procession within the village.

Christmas (Festival of Christians) : The Christmas is the greatest festival of all the Christians of Manipur, observed for two days on December 24 and 25. Prayers, reading of Gospels, eating, singing of hymns, lectures on Christ, sports etc., form the major part of the festival. In some villages where the inhabitants are well-off, the celebration continues till January 1 on which the New Years day is also observed.

Cheiraoba (The Manipur NewYear) : During the festival, people clean and decorate their houses and prepare special festive dishes which are first offered to various deities. Celebrated during the month of April, a part of the ritual entails villagers climbing the nearest hill tops in belief that it will enable them to rise to greater heights in their worldly life. The Pangals (Manipuri Muslims) also observe it.

Heikru Hidongba : Celebrated in the month of September, a festival of joy, with little religious significance along a 16 metre wide boat. Long narrow boats are used to accommodate a large number of rowers. Idol of Lord Vishnu is installed before the commencement of the race.

Ningol Chakouba : It is a remarkable social festival of the Meiteis. Married women of the family who were married to distant places come to the parental house along with her children and enjoy sumptuous feast. It is a form of family rejoinder to revive familial affection. The festival is also observed by the Pangals to a certain extent now-a-days. It is observed on the second day of the new moon in the Manipuri month of Hiyangei (November).

Lui-Ngai-Ni : It is a collective festival of the Nagas observed on the 15th day of February every year. This is a seed-sowing festival after which tribes belonging to the Naga group begin their cultivation. Social gathering, songs, dances and rejoicing highlight the festivity. The annual festival also plays a great role in boosting the morale and strengthening the bond of Naga solidarity.

Kwak Jatra : Goddess Durga is propitiated with pomp and ceremony in this festival. It is celebrated in the month of October and represents the victory of righteousness over evil.

FESTIVALS OF MANIPUR : AT A GLANCE

Festivals	Celebrated by	Time of Celebration
❍ Lai Haraoba	Meiteis	May
❍ Rath Yatra	Hindus	July
❍ Yaoshang (Dol Jatra)	Hindus	February/March
❍ Christmas	Christians	25th December
❍ Mahavir Jayanti	Jains	April
❍ Depawali	Hindus	October / November
❍ Cheiraoba	Meiteis	April
❍ Chumpha	Tangkhul Nagas	December
❍ Gan Ngai	Kabui Nagas	16th January
❍ Heikru Hitongba	Meiteis	September
❍ Kwak Yatra (Durga Puja)	Hindus	September / October
❍ Kut	Kuki Chin Mizos	November
❍ Lui-Ngai-Ni	Nagas	15th February
❍ Mera Nongma Panba	Meiteis	September
❍ Ningol Chakkouba	Meiteis	November

SOME TRIBAL FESTIVALS OF MANIPUR

Tribes	*Festivals*
Anal	Sungkhomlkham, Mikhemphan, lkam, Philthabla, Inhla, etc.
Aimol	Reeyan
Chothe	Inampeilin
Hmar	Butu Chonglawa
Kabui	Gan-Ngai
Kharam	Lamtoul Kalouh
Kuki	Chapchar Kut, Mimkut, Chavang Kut
Mao	Chithuni
Naga	Lui-Ngai-Ni
Tangkhul	Shimsak Kasa, Chumpha, Thisham, Yarra, Mangkhap, Luira, Darreo etc.
Thadou	Chon
Zeliangrong	Gudui Ngai, Rih Ngai

❑❑❑

Census 2011

The Census of India 2011, is historic and epoch making being the second census of the twenty-first century. It reveals benchmark data on the state of abundant human resources available in the country, their demography, culture and economic structure at a juncture, which marks a centennial and millenial transition.

Census of India comprises of Population, Population-Density, Sex Ratio and Literacy. One of the important indices of population concentration in census is the density of population which is the number of persons per square kilometre. Sex ratio is the number of females per thousand males while a person aged seven, and above, who can both read and write with understanding in any language, is treated as literate.

The districts of the states play an important role in census. As an administrative unit, district assumes a lot of significance in the context of decentralized planning and implementation of various plans and programmes. Therefore, deciding on an appropriate size of a district in terms of population and geographical area is a vital and essential element in creating an effective administrative set up.

Census 2011 reveals that Tamenglong is the least populous district of Manipur while the Imphal West is the most literate district. Imphal West tops in the category of sex ratio, whereas child population (0-6) years is higher in Thoubal than any other district. Given below are the tables showing population, density, literacy rate etc. district wise for the entire state of Manipur.

Population

Manipur : 2,855,794 (***Males:*** 1,438,586 ***Females:*** 1,417,208)

Sl.No.	*District*	*Population*	*Male*	*Female*
1	Senapati	479,148	247,323	231,825
2	Tamenglong	1,40,651	72,371	68,280
3	Churachandpur	2,74,143	1,38,820	1,35,323
4	Bishnupur	2,37,399	1,18,782	1,18,617
5	Thoubal	4,22,168	2,10,845	2,11,323
6	Imphal West	5,17,992	2,55,054	2,62,938
7	Imphal East	4,56,113	2,26,094	2,30,019
8	Ukhrul	1,83,998	94,718	89,280
9	Chandel	1,44,182	74,579	69,603

Decadal Growth Rate

Manipur (1991-2001) : 24.86%, (2001-2011) : 24.50%

Sl.No.	*District*	*1991-2001*	*2001-2011*
1	Senapati	36.09	68.9
2	Tamenglong	29.23	26.1
3	Churachandpur	29.36	20.3
4	Bishnupur	15.27	13.9
5	Thoubal	23.87	15.9
6	Imphal West	16.70	16.6
7	Imphal East	19.49	15.5
8	Ukhrul	28.83	30.7
9	Chandel	66.62	21.9

SEX RATIO

District Wise Sex Ratio in Manipur (1971-2011)

Sl.No.	District	1971	1981	1991	2001	2011
1	Senapati	950	929	942	928	937
2	Tamenglong	1016	975	935	922	943
3	Churachandpur	976	929	931	993	975
4	Bishnupur	–	–	984	1004	999
5	Thoubal	–	–	980	998	1002
6	Imphal West	–	–	979	1007	1031
7	Imphal East	–	–	966	992	1017
8	Ukhrul	969	917	884	920	943
9	Chandel	975	935	913	986	933
	State	980	971	958	978	985

DENSITY

Manipur (2001) : 97; (2011) : 128

Sl.No.	District	2001	2011
1	Senapati	48	146
2	Tamenglong	25	32
3	Churachandpur	50	60
4	Bishnupur	420	479
5	Thoubal	708	821
6	Imphal West	856	998
7	Imphal East	557	643
8	Ukhrul	31	40
9	Chandel	36	44

LITERACY RATE

Manipur (2001)	: 70.50	Manipur (2011)	: 76.94
Males	: 80.30	Males	: 83.58
Females	: 60.50	Females	: 70.26

Sl.No.	District	2001			2011		
		Total	Male	Female	Total	Male	Female
1	Senapati	59.8	67.9	51.2	63.60	69.21	57.67
2	Tamenglong	59.2	68.7	49.0	70.05	76.09	63.69
3	Churachandpur	70.6	77.7	63.1	82.78	86.97	78.50
4	Bishnupur	67.6	79.6	55.7	75.85	85.11	66.68
5	Thoubal	66.4	80.4	52.5	74.47	85.00	64.09
6	Imphal West	80.2	89.2	71.3	86.08	92.24	80.17
7	Imphal East	75.4	85.5	65.3	81.95	88.77	75.32
8	Ukhrul	73.1	80.1	65.4	81.35	85.52	76.95
9	Chandel	56.2	64.3	48.0	71.11	77.78	63.96

❑❑❑

MULTIPLE CHOICE QUESTIONS

1. What is the total area of Manipur?
   A. 22327 sq. km. B. 22223 sq. km.
   C. 22732 sq. km. D. 22237 sq. km.
2. In which year Manipur became the twentieth state of the Indian Union?
   A. 1970 B. 1971
   C. 1972 D. 1973
3. In Manipur Jadonang was hanged in August, 1931. Who was Jadonang?
   A. A great Naga leader
   B. A great Zome leader
   C. A great Zeliangrong leader
   D. A great Meitei leader
4. In which year revered king Pakhangba ascended the throne?
   A. 30 A.D. B. 31 A.D.
   C. 32 A.D. D. 33 A.D.
5. When was the Manipur Constitution Act passed?
   A. 1947 B. 1948
   C. 1949 D. 1950
6. In which year Nara Singha became the King of Manipur?
   A. 1832 B. 1840
   C. 1844 D. 1848
7. How many states touch the boundary of Manipur?
   A. 3 B. 4
   C. 5 D. 6
8. In which year was the Battle of Khongjom fought?
   A. 1885 B. 1887
   C. 1890 D. 1891
9. In which year did Manipur become a Union Territory?
   A. 1950 B. 1955
   C. 1956 D. 1960
10. When was Shillong Accord signed?
    A. 15 Oct., 1949 B. 20 Sep., 1950
    C. 25 Nov., 1952 D. 15 Aug., 1957
11. Who was the last King of Manipur?
    A. Maharaja Gambhir Singh
    B. Maharaja Tikendrajit Singh
    C. Maharaja Ranjit Singh
    D. Maharaja Purandar Singh
12. During the first world war, which King ruled over in Manipur?
    A. Maharaja Nara Singha
    B. Maharaja Garibniwaz
    C. Maharaja Chandrakirti Singh
    D. Maharaja Koineng Singh
13. During the reign of which King of Kangleipak was the title ''Manipur'' named after it?
    A. Maharaja Churachand Singh
    B. Maharaja Garibniwaz
    C. Maharaja Bhagyachandra
    D. Maharaja Chandrakirti Singh
14. What is the Capital of Manipur?
    A. Imphal B. Bishnupur
    C. Churachandpur D. Thoubal
15. What is the total number of districts in Manipur?
    A. Eight B. Sixteen
    C. Ten D. Twelve
16. What is the total population of Manipur as per the 2011 census?
    A. 30,48,756 B. 28,55,794
    C. 32,27,309 D. 22,18,960
17. When was the census started in Manipur?
    A. 1750 B. 1752
    C. 1757 D. 1760
18. When did Manipur come under the British rule?
    A. 12 April, 1891 B. 12 March, 1890
    C. 10 May, 1885 D. 5 June, 1860
19. Who among the following have got Padma Bhushan Award?
    A. M.C. Mary Kom B. Heisnam Kanhailala
    C. Both 'A' and 'B' D. None of these
20. How many Legislative Assembly Constituencies are there in Manipur?
    A. 50 B. 60
    C. 70 D. 75
21. Which is the biggest river in Manipur?
    A. Iril B. Sekmai
    C. Barrak D. Nambul
22. Which one of the following is not a physical division of Manipur?
    A. Churachandpur B. Manipur Hills
    C. Manipur Valley D. Jiribam Plains

23. How many MLAs are elected from the Hill Districts to the Manipur Legislative Assembly?
A. 20 B. 25
C. 30 D. 35

24. In Manipur Assembly how many seats are reserved for Scheduled Tribes?
A. 15 B. 19
C. 25 D. 30

25. On what date Martyr's Day is observed in Manipur?
A. 10th August B. 13th August
C. 15th August D. 18th August

26. Machi sub-division is located in which district?
A. Chandel B. Tengnoupal
C. Senapati D. Tamenglong

27. Which is the first Manipuri colour feature film?
A. Imagee Ningthem B. Brojendrogi Luhongba
C. Langlen Thadai D. Matamgi Manipur

28. Which is the first Manipuri feature film?
A. Ishanou B. Khonjel
C. Saphabee D. Matamgi Manipur

29. Who is the first Manipuri to win the Arjuna Award?
A. Dingko Singh B. N. Kunjarani Devi
C. M.C. Mary Kom D. Suraj Lata Devi

30. Who is the first Manipuri to win the Sahitya Academy Award?
A. Pacha Meeitei
B. N. Kunjamohan Singh
C. L. Samarendra Singh
D. A. Minaketan Singh

31. Who was the first woman MLA (Member of Legislative Assembly)?
A. Kim Gangte B. W. Leima Devi
C. Hangmila Shaija D. None of these

32. Who was the first Chief Minister of Manipur State?
A. M. Kaireng Singh B. L. Thambou Singh
C. M.K. Priyobrata Singh D. R.K. Dorendra Singh

33. Who was the first Lok Sabha member from the Inner Parliamentary Constituency of Manipur?
A. L. Jugeswar Singh B. L. Achaw Singh
C. S. Tombi Singh D. M. Meghachandra

34. Who was the first Lok Sabha member from the outer Parliamentary Constituency of Manipur?
A. Rungsung Suisa B. Rishang Keishing
C. Paokai Haokip D. Yangmaso Shaiza

35. Heikru Hitongba festival was introduced in Manipur in :
A. 1778 B. 1775
C. 1779 D. 1772

36. Who was the first Governor of Manipur?
A. L.P. Singh B. S.M.H. Burney
C. K.V. Krishna Rao D. B.K. Nehru

37. Who was the first Rajya Sabha M.P. from Manipur?
A. Ng. Tompok Singh
B. L. Lalit Madhob Sharma
C. S. Krishnamohan Singh
D. Salam Tombi Singh

38. How many members represent Manipur in the Rajya Sabha?
A. 1 B. 2
C. 3 D. 4

39. How many members represent Manipur in the Lok Sabha?
A. 2 B. 4
C. 5 D. 7

40. In which year Manipur became a full fledged state?
A. 1970 B. 1972
C. 1973 D. 1974

41. When did the Gauhati High Court come into existence in Manipur?
A. 21-1-1972 B. 21-4-1970
C. 21-4-1971 D. 21-4-1973

42. In which of the following rivers does the Imphal river fall?
A. The Iril river B. The Loktak lake
C. The Brahmaputra D. The Chindwin river

43. In which year Imphal District was divided?
A. 1995 B. 1996
C. 1997 D. 1998

44. When was the ''Khongjom War'' fought in Manipur?
A. 23-7-1891 B. 23-6-1891
C. 23-4-1891 D. 16-9-1890

45. Who is the first olympian from Manipur?
A. P. Nilkamal Singh B. N. Kunjarani Devi
C. H.L. Tangkhul D. Thoiba Singh

46. 'Nongyeen' was declared as the State Bird of Manipur in the year :
A. 1986 B. 1987
C. 1988 D. 1989

47. The first Legislative Assembly was inaugurated in Manipur in :
A. 1961 B. 1962
C. 1963 D. 1964

48. In which lake the Sendra island is situated?
A. Loukai lake B. Waithou lake
C. Ikop lake D. Loktak lake

49. Which is the 'State Bird' of Manipur?
A. Tragopan B. Ashangba
C. Nongyeen D. Langmeidon

50. Who is the first sports person from Manipur to win a gold medal in the Asian Games?
A. N. Kunjarani Devi B. Suraj Lata Devi
C. M.C. Mary Kom D. Dingko Singh

51. In which year Manipuri language was included in the 8th schedule of the Indian Constitution?
A. 1990 B. 1991
C. 1992 D. 1993

52. Pamheiba was the most powerful kings of Manipur in whose reign the state reached the pinnacle as a powerful state. His original name was—
A. Madhuchandra B. Churachand Singh
C. Chandrakirti D. Garibniwaz

53. When did Doordarshan start in Manipur?
A. 30 April, 1990 B. 30 April, 1991
C. 30 April, 1992 D. 30 April, 1993

54. Who is the writer of novel 'Leikangla'?
A. M. Borkamya B. K. Bira
C. S. Biren D. N. Ibabi

55. Who is the poet of ''Dustbin Amagi Warri''?
A. R. Constantine B. T.C. Hudson
C. T. Ibopishak Singh D. Vedaja Sanjenbam

56. Ruins of Citadel was built in the year:
A. 1500 A.D. B. 1611 A.D.
C. 1600 A.D. D. 1550 A.D.

57. How many years Manipur remained as a part state and Union Territory?
A. Twenty B. Twenty one
C. Twenty two D. Twenty four

58. During the reign of which King in Manipur the first Telegraph line and Telegraph office were established?
A. Maharaja Chandrakirti in 1886
B. Maharaja Madhuchandra in 1801
C. Maharaja Yumjaotaba in 1820
D. Maharaja Churachand Singh in 1891

59. Which period was known as the ''Dark Period'' in Manipur?
A. 1730 A.D. to 1750 A.D.
B. 1755 A.D. to 1826 A.D.
C. 1650 A.D. to 1726 A.D.
D. 1820 A.D. to 1850 A.D.

60. ''Manipur is the Jewel of India and Switzerland of the East''. Who said this quotation?
A. Jawaharlal Nehru B. Mahatma Gandhi
C. Subhash Chandra Bose D. M. Kaireng Singh

61. Who introduced Polo in Manipur?
A. Thayanthaba B. Ebudhou Marjing
C. Garibniwaj D. Koiremba

62. Who introduced ''Boat Race'' in Manipur?
A. Thangbi Lanthabu B. Keiphaba Yanglon
C. Ninthou Punshiba D. Gambhir Singha

63. When did Hindu Priest Santidash Goshai come to Manipur?
A. 1550 A.D. B. 1600 A.D.
C. 1760 A.D. D. 1716 A.D.

64. When was Manipur State Film Festival started?
A. 1982 B. 1983
C. 1984 D. 1985

65. What is the state language of Manipur?
A. Manipuri B. English
C. Hindi D. None of these

66. In Manipuri week days 'Nongmaijing' is known as :
A. Monday B. Sunday
C. Tuesday D. Wednesday

67. In which year was 'Meitei Chanu' the first journal of Manipur published?
A. 1920 B. 1922
C. 1924 D. 1926

68. The number of Jila Parishads in Manipur is :
A. 3 B. 6
C. 5 D. 4

69. 'Lhawa Chun Festival' is celebrated by which tribe of Manipur?
A. Aimol B. Kabui Naga
C. Maring D. Kuki

70. How many alphabets were there in the original Meitei language?
A. 20 B. 22
C. 25 D. 27

71. When did Doordarshan's Metro Channel (DD2) start in Manipur?
A. December 23, 1995 B. December 23, 1990
C. December 23, 1991 D. December 23, 1992

72. The historic Kangla Fort Complex was formally handed back to the people of Manipur in the presence of the former Prime Minister Manmohan Singh on :
A. 20th November, 2004 B. 20th November, 2005
C. 20th November, 2006 D. 22nd November, 2006

73. When was the first ''Nupi Lal'' happened in Manipur?
A. 1904 A.D. B. 1905 A.D.
C. 1906 A.D. D. 1907 A.D.

74. In which district of Manipur can we find ''DZUKU LILY''?
A. Imphal East B. Chandel
C. Senapati D. Thoubal

75. Which Manipuri scholar was called the ''Agyestha of the East' by Smiti Kumar Chatterjee?
A. Shyam Sharma B. E. Nilakanta Singh
C. C. Joshua Thomas D. Atombapu Sharma

76. The founder of the Praja Sameleni was :
A. Hijam Irabat Singh B. Lalita Madhop
C. Elangbam Tompok D. Aaiga Bankabihari

77. Who is the author of the book 'Labangalata'?
A. Lucy Zehol B. Khwairakpam Chaoba
C. M.K. Singh D. E.W. Dun

78. The Sangai Deer is found at which National Park/ wild life sanctuary in Manipur?
A. Sirohi
B. Keilam
C. Keibul Lamjao
D. Yaingangpokpi Lakchao

79. Tharon caves are located in which district of Manipur?
A. Chandel B. Thoubal
C. Tamenglong D. Senapati

80. What is the state tree of Manipur?
A. Teak B. Pine
C. Parkia Javanica D. Uningthou

81. Who become the first woman minister in Manipur?
A. R. Apabi Devi B. Kh. Thoibi Devi
C. Kim Gangte D. Khaidem Sakhi Devi

82. The state of Manipur lies between .... and .... east Longitude.
A. 80.20° and 84.35° B. 92.58° and 94.45°
C. 75.10° and 60.20° D. 96.20° and 99.13°

83. In which year Manipur Olympic Association was formed?
A. 1947 B. 1948
C. 1949 D. 1950

84. Who was the founder President of the Manipur Olympic Association?
A. Churachand Singh
B. R.K. Madhuryajit Singh
C. Kalachandra
D. Debendra Singh

85. Who was the founder of the ''Ningthouja Dynasty'' in Manipur?
A. Nongdalairen Pakhangba
B. Atom Yairemba
C. Keiphaba Yanglon
D. Nongchup Lamgaingamba

86. Who was the King of Manipur when the Burmese invaded in the year of 1819?
A. King Loyumba B. King Marjit Singh
C. King Gambhir Singh D. King Kiyamba Singh

87. Who was the first British Political Agent of Manipur?
A. George Gordon B. Grimwood
C. Captain William D. James Hednic

88. Who introduced ''Bell metal currency'' in Manipur?
A. Kyamba Maharaj
B. Maramba Maharaj
C. Khagemba Maharaj
D. Labanyachandra Maharaj

89. Porompat, Keirao Bitra and Sawombung are the sub-divisions of which district?
A. Churachandpur B. Chandel
C. Imphal West D. Imphal East

90. Who among the following was not the Chief Minister of Manipur?
A. Md. Alimuddin B. P. Brojen Singh
C. M.K. Priyobratta D. Rishang Keishing

91. Who introduced 'Vaishnavism' as a state Religion?
A. King Chingthangkhomba
B. King Koiremba
C. King Bhagyachandra
D. King Bharatsai

92. Who may be given the title of the ''First Modern Political Leader of Manipur?
A. Hijam Irabat Singh B. L. Jugeswar Singh
C. Paokai Haokip D. Ng. Tompok Singh

93. The first English Journal of Manipur 'Meitei Leirang' was published in :
A. 1965 B. 1969
C. 1972 D. 1975

94. Which is the first Health Journal of Manipur?
A. Chingtam B. Sanaleibak
C. Meeyam D. Meitei Maiba

95. Who was the first speaker of Manipur Legislative Assembly?
A. T.C. Tiankham B. Sibo Larho
C. M. Koireng Singh D. Tombi Singh

96. What is the literacy rate of Manipur as per the 2011 census?
A. 65.36 per cent B. 72.16 per cent
C. 76.94 per cent D. 75.24 per cent

97. What is the density of population in Manipur as per the 2011 census?
A. 128 B. 110
C. 132 D. 120

98. Who is the first Manipuri girl to become Miss East India?
A. Aparna Jhaveri B. Bonnie Gurumayum
C. Gayatri Heisnam D. Priyanka Kokila

99. The number of Universities in Manipur is :
A. 2 B. 3
C. 4 D 5

100. Manipur University was established in :
A. 1977 B. 1978
C. 1979 D. 1980

101. Board of Secondary Education, Manipur was established in :
A. 1972-73 B. 1974-75
C. 1976-77 D. 1978-79

102. Script of the Grand Prix award winning film 'Imagee Ningthem' is written by :
A. N. Kunjamohan B. M.K. Binodini
C. A.K. Paul D. L.R. Singh

103. 'Seven Years Devastation' (Chahi Taret Khuntakpa) covers the period from :
A. 1810 to 1816 B. 1819 to 1825
C. 1829 to 1835 D. 1827 to 1833

104. When did the Manipur State Archieves set up?
A. 1980 B. 1982
C. 1985 D. 1988

105. Who described Manipur as ''An oasis of comparative civilization amidst the Barbarians?''
A. James Hotten B. William Ban
C. Alfred Lyll D. George Linde

106. Who is known as Queen of Boxing in Manipur?
A. M.C. Meri Kom B. N. Kunjarani Devi
C. Suraj Lata Devi D. Brojeswari Devi

107. During the reign of which King of Manipur the ''Scout Movement'' was started in the state?
A. Maharaja Chalamba Singh
B. Maharaja Chura Chand Singh
C. Maharaja Bharatsai Singh
D. Maharaja Ching Thang Khomba Singh

108. What is the area of Kangla, the ancient palace of Manipur?
A. 240.56 acres B. 350.16 acres
C. 237.62 acres D. 290.48 acres

109. Who is the first chairman of Hill Area Committee?
A. P.K. Mohan B. P.C. Mathew
C. E.P. Moon Jan D. S.P. Henry

110. When was the first Community Development Block established in Manipur?
A. 1952 B. 1953
C. 1954 D. 1955

111. Keilam Wildlife Sanctuary is located in which district?
A. Churachandpur B. Senapati
C. Thoubal D. Ukhrul

112. How many airports are there in Manipur?
A. 1 B. 2
C. 3 D. 4

113. Which is the first railway station of Manipur?
A. Dimapur Railway Station
B. Jiribam Railway Station
C. Toubal Railway Station
D. Karong Railway Station

114. Where is airport of Manipur located?
A. Churachandpur B. Tamenglong
C. Imphal D. Chandel

115. What is the 'State Game' of Manipur?
A. Thang Yannaba B. Mangjong
C. Lamjel D. Sagol Kangjei

116. In which year 'Manipur Hockey Association' was formed?
A. 1976 B. 1977
C. 1978 D. 1979

117. The author of the book 'Bir Tikendrajit Road' is :
A. T.C. Hudson B. Hijam Guno
C. Nilima Roy D. Lal Dena

118. Who is the first Manipuri to appear on postage stamp?
A. Laishram Memma B. Jugeswori Devi
C. Rani Gaidenlilu D. Rashi Devi

119. Who is the first person from Manipur to receive the 'Padmashree'?
A. N. Kunjarani Devi B. Irom Leikhendra
C. P. Neelkamal D. Atombapu Sharma

120. The number of Industrial Training Institutes in Manipur is :
A. Four B. Five
C. Six D. Eleven

121. Manipur Handloom and Handicrafts Development Corporation was set-up in :
A. 1972 B. 1976
C. 1980 D. 1982

122. In which year was the Manipur State Museum established?
A. 1965 B. 1969
C. 1975 D. 1979

123. What is Manipuri Polo called :
A. Yubi Lakpi B. Khong Kangjei
C. Mukna Kangjei D. Sagol Kangjei

124. Who was the first Deputy Chief Minister of Manipur?
A. L. Jugeshwar Singh
B. M. Koireng Singh
C. Irengbam Tompok Singh
D. Yangmasho Shaiza

125. When was the 'Patriot Day'' observed at the first time in Manipur?
A. 1965 B. 1966
C. 1968 D. 1969

126. Which King introduced the system of 'Division of Labour'' in Manipur?
A. King Loyumba
B. King Marjit Singh
C. King Gambhir Singh
D. King Khagemba Singh

127. Who is the writer of the book ''Elisa Amagi Mahao''?
A. E. Nilakanta Singh
B. N. Kunja Mohan Singh
C. G.C. Tongbra
D. A. Minaketan Singh

128. When was the first "District Library established in Manipur?
A. 1950 B. 1952
C. 1955 D. 1958

129. R.K. Chandrajit Singh is related to :
A. painting B. writing
C. music D. sport

130. In which district of Manipur the highest hill mount Tenipu is situated?
A. Senapati B. Imphal East
C. Thoubal D. Bishnupur

131. The largest pineapple producer district of Manipur is:
A. Bishnupur B. Thoubal
C. Tamenglong D. Ukhrul

132. 'Manipur Film Society' was established in :
A. 1955 B. 1960
C. 1962 D. 1966

133. Which is the first Manipuri documentary film?
A. Maipak – the Son of Manipur
B. Meitei Pung
C. Chatldo Eidi
D. Yellhou Jagai

134. Who is the director of first Manipuri documentary film?
A. M.A. Singh B. Aribam Shyam Sharma
C. Devkumar Bose D. Oken Amakcham

135. Nambol sub-division is located in which district?
A. Bishnupur B. Jiribam
C. Ukhrul D. Thoubal

136. When was the Jiribam Railway Station inaugurated?
A. 1990 B. 1982
C. 1987 D. 1992

137. The number of Post Offices (2011) in Manipur is :
A. 1200 B. 1394
C. 1060 D. 970

138. Which is the largest export-oriented agricultural product of Manipur?
A. Maize B. Rice
C. Cotton D. Wheat

139. Manipur State Kala Academy was established in :
A. 1965 B. 1970
C. 1972 D. 1975

140. What is the average height of Imphal valley above MSL (mean sea level)?
A. 790 metres B. 850 metres
C. 990 metres D. 1050 metres

141. Who started the festival of Kang-Chingba (Ratha Yatra) in Manipur?
A. Maharaja Jai Singh
B. Maharaja Madhuchandra
C. Maharaja Churachand Singh
D. Maharaja Gambhir Singh

142. Who among the following is not recipient of Padma Shri Awards from Manipur?
A. Th. Subedar Singh B. Ratan Thiyam
C. Th. Haridas D. M. Kirti Singh

143. When was the last independent war of Manipur fought against British?
A. 20th March 1875 to 25th June 1875
B. 24th March 1891 to 27th April 1891
C. 15th January 1890 to 25th February 1890
D. 10th May 1879 to 27 July 1879

144. What is the serial number of Manipuri as it is listed in the Eight schedule to the constitution of India?
A. 9th B. 10th
C. 11th D. 12th

145. The judges of Manipur High Court are appointed by :
A. The Chief Justice of India
B. The President of India
C. The Chief Minister of Manipur
D. The Governor of Manipur

146. The language spoken by the largest number of people in the Manipur is :
A. English B. Bengali
C. Hindi D. Manipuri

147. What was the old name of Senapati district?
A. Manipur East B. Manipur West
C. Manipur North D. Manipur South

148. What was the old name of Chandel district?
A. Central District B. Manipur West
C. Manipur East D. Tengnoupal

149. The ornament, which is worn around the neck by the Manipuri women, is called :
A. Khonanakpi B. Khuji
C. Khorau D. Kanberi

150. In which year Manipur was included on the Indian Railway Map?
A. 1989 B. 1990
C. 1991 D. 1992

151. As per the 2011 census what is the sex ratio in Manipur?
A. 985 B. 980
C. 975 D. 995

152. Loktak Project was commissioned in :
A. 1983 B. 1984
C. 1985 D. 1986

153. In which district of Manipur Zoological Garden is located?
A. Tamenglong B. Imphal West
C. Churachandpur D. Bishnupur

154. Manipur Agro-Industries Corporation was set-up in :
A. 1989 B. 1990
C. 1991 D. 1992

155. The last Lieutenant Governor of Manipur was :
A. J.M. Raina B. P.C. Mathew
C. D.R. Kohli D. Baleshwar Prasad

156. Which King introduced Kwak Tomba religious ceremony in Manipur?
A. Khuiyoi Tompok B. Keiphaba Yanglon
C. Khui Ningngomba D. Chingthang Lanthaba

157. During the reign of which King in Manipur the game Yubi Lakpi first played?
A. King Thawanthaba
B. King Chingthangkhomba
C. King Lanthaba
D. King Ayangba

158. Mualnuam sub-division is located in which district?
A. Bishnupur B. Churachandpur
C. Chandel D. Ukhrul

159. Jhaveri sisters are famous for :
A. Odissi Dance B. Kathak
C. Manipuri Dance D. Bharat Natyam

160. Manipur Theological college is located at :
A. Thoubal B. Ukhrul
C. Kangpokpi D. Chandel

161. In Manipur INA Museum is located at :
A. Moirang B. Nambal
C. Kakching D. Lilong

162. Where is the state Museum of Manipur situated?
A. Chandel B. Senapati
C. Imphal West D. Tamenglong

163. Who was Manipur's first MBBS Doctor?
A. Dr. Nanda Babu Roy B. Dr. P.K. Rana
C. Dr. J.C. Arya D. Dr. C.L. Mohan

164. Who was Manipur's first lady medical Doctor?
A. Manorama Devi
B. Thangjam Ongbi Bedamani Devi
C. N. Chidambara
D. Payal Ghosh

165. When was the first Operation Theatre opened in Manipur?
A. 1920 B. 1926
C. 1930 D. 1935

166. When was the first Hospital ward opened in Manipur?
A. 1925 B. 1928
C. 1930 D. 1931

167. Who was first Mr. Manipur?
A. P. Jugol B. Irom Leikhendra
C. R. Shyam D. Ranabir Meitei

168. Who is the Manipur's first Mr. India?
A. M. Gopal Sharma
B. K. Dilip Singh
C. Nongthongbam Maipak
D. M. Phanjoubam

169. Who is the author of the book "Manipur: The Jewel of India"?
A. E. Ishwarjit Singh B. S.C. Joshi
C. L.R. Singh D. H. Guno Singh

170. Who is the author of the book "Madhabi"?
A. Kh. Chaoba B. R.K. Shitaljit
C. Dr. Komal Singh D. Lal Dena

171. Who is the author of the book 'Mao : The Naga Tribe of Manipur?
A. Lorho Mary Maheo B. Naorem Sanajaoba
C. R. Constantine D. H. Bhuban Singh

172. Where is Nupi Lal Memorial Complex located in Manipur?
A. Imphal West B. Moirang
C. Churachandpur D. Moreh

173. Ruins of Citadel was built during the reign of :
A. King Jai Singh B. King Khagemba
C. King Marjit D. King Chourjit

174. Ruins of Citadel was built in the year :
A. 1500 A.D. B. 1550 A.D.
C. 1600 A.D. D. 1611 A.D.

175. Where is Shree Shree Govindajee Temple located?
A. Bishnupur B. Imphal East
C. Thoubal D. Ukhrul

176. Who is the first Manipuri Child to get the Best Child Actor Award?
A. Leikhendra Singh B. Ranbir Goswami
C. Shyam Singha D. K. Narsingha

177. A veteran freedom fighter and a great socio-religious leader, Rani Gaidenliu was a living goddess for the manipuri people. Name the great Prime Minister of India who described her as "the daughter of the hills and gave the title "Rani of her people".
A. Lal Bahadur Shastri
B. Pandit Jawaharlal Nehru
C. Smt. Indira Gandhi
D. Morarji Desai

178. Which is the first Manipuri magazine started in 1917-18?
A. Longtai B. Wakhal
C. Meitei Leima D. Athouba

179. Which was the first Manipuri book to be awarded with the Telem Ningol Atoibema Award in children's literature?
A. Sana Kakchao B. Ithak Ipom
C. Jahira D. Ima

180. Who got Padma Shri Award in 2024?
A. M. Borkanya B. T. Amudon Sharma
C. Bipin Singh D. Machihan Sasa

181. Who is the first Manipuri to win a Gold Medal in Asian Games?
A. Ng. Dingko Singh B. Sanamacha Chanu
C. N. Kunjarani Devi D. M.C. Mary Kom

182. Who is the first Manipuri to become a Union Minister?
A. Ng. Tompok Singh B. R.K. Jaichandra
C. R.K. Dorendra Singh D. N. Gouzagin

183. Who is the first Manipuri Film Actor?
A. Leikhendra Singh
B. Robindro Sharma
C. Aribam Shyam Sharma
D. M.A. Singh

184. Who is the first Manipuri Film Actress?
A. Gita Devi B. Manorama Devi
C. Rashi Devi D. Rashmi Devi

185. Who is the first Manipuri to win Rajiv Gandhi Khel Ratna Award (Now Major Dhyan Chand Khel Ratna Award)?
A. Ng. Dingko Singh B. Thaiba Singh
C. M.C. MaryKom D. N. Kunjarani Devi

186. Who is the first Muslim Chief Minister of Manipur?
A. Md. Alimuddin Lilong Turel Ahanbi
B. Md. Abdul Qayum
C. Md. Ali Akbar
D. Javed Ahmed

187. Who is the first Manipuri Muslim Woman Advocate?
A. Noor Bano B. Benazir Majumdar
C. Fatima Shaikh D. Sabnam Noorani

188. What is the percentage of Muslim population as per 2011 census?
A. 22.40 B. 25.50
C. 8.40 D. 15.60

189. What is the area covered by the Manipuri Hockey field?
A. 200 × 20 Yards B. 200 × 40 Yards
C. 200 × 60 Yards D. 200 × 80 Yards

190. The historic 'International Polo Tournament' was held in Manipur in the year :
A. 1985 B. 1987
C. 1989 D. 1990

191. In which year Oak Tassar was introduced in Manipur?
A. 1973-74 B. 1975-86
C. 1977-78 D. 1980-81

192. Who built the famous Vishnu temple situated at Bishenpur?
A. King Kyamba B. King Telheiba
C. King Tonaba D. King Punsiba

193. Sirohi National Park of Manipur got its recognition by the government in the year :
A. 1990 B. 1998
C. 1999 D. 2000

194. In which year was Yaingangpokpi Lakchao Wildlife Sanctuary opened :
A. 1989 B. 1991
C. 1995 D. 1998

195. The Manipur State Museum was inaugurated by which Prime Minister of India?
A. J.L. Nehru B. Indira Gandhi
C. Rajiv Gandhi D. A.B. Vajpayee

196. In which year Manipur University was upgraded as a Central University?
A. 1990 B. 1992
C. 1994 D. 1998

197. Which is the largest and most important mineral resource of Manipur?
A. Chromite B. Coal
C. Lignite D. Limestone

198. Mukna is a:
A. Game B. Fair
C. Festival D. None of these

199. In which year the first Manipur Panchayati Raj Bill was passed?
A. 1972 B. 1975
C. 1978 D. 1980

200. In which year Manipur got its own High Court?
A. 2010 B. 2011
C. 2013 D. 2012

201. In which year the Indian Penal Code was first enacted in Manipur?
A. 1901 B. 1902
C. 1903 D. 1904

202. Who among the following has not worked as the Governor of Manipur?
A. S.K. Sinha B. V.K. Duggal
C. S.S. Siddhu D. V.P. Marwah

203. The area covered by the Jiribam Rubber Farm is :
A. 800 hectares B. 889 hectares
C. 900 hectares D. 1050 hectares

204. Who was the Manipuri Muslim, popularly known as Japan Pitru?
A. Ali Akbar
B. Alauddin Khan
C. Naqi Ahmed Choudhary
D. Mehtab Ali

205. Which river flows from Manipur to Assam?
A. Barrak B. Thoubal
C. Iril D. Makru

206. Which is the largest grown agricultural product of Manipur?
A. Wheat B. Maize
C. Rice D. Orange

207. When was the old Cachar road constructed in Manipur?
A. 1530 B. 1532
C. 1534 D. 1536

208. Who constructed the old Cachar road?
A. Meidingu-Kabomba
B. James Johnstone
C. Yengkham Deksan Singh
D. J. K. Rajan

209. Sandhya Rani is related with which sports?
A. Judo B. Wushu
C. Boxing D. Hockey

210. Who was the first chief commissioner of Manipur?
A. Major General Rawal Amar Singh
B. Himat Singh
C. E. P. Moon Jan.
D. P. C. Mathew

211. Who was the first Lieutenant Governor of Manipur?
A. D. R. Kohli B. Baleswar Prasad
C. J. M. Raina D. E. P. Moom

212. Loktak Lake is located in which district?
A. Bishnupur B. Thoubal
C. Ukhrul D. Tamenglong

213. Kachouphung Lake is located in which district?
A. Ukhrul B. Bishnupur
C. Thoubal D. Tamenglong

214. Barak waterfalls are located in which district?
A. Tamenglong B. Bishnupur
C. Ukhrul D. Senapati

215. Sangboo cave is located in:
A. Chandel B. Ukhrul
C. Churachandpur D. Imphal East

216. Height of Leikat Peak is :
A. 2,832 m. B. 2,760 m.
C. 2,560 m. D. 2,960m.

217. As per the 2011 census, the urban population of Manipur is :
A. 8, 34, 154 B. 9, 50, 325
C. 7, 90, 660 D. 10, 10, 548

218. As per the 2011 census, the rural population of Manipur is :
A. 20, 18, 224 B. 16, 20, 360
C. 20, 21, 640 D. 17, 10, 660

219. The State Emblem of Manipur is:
A. Singda Dam
B. Kangla Shaa
C. Shree Govindajee Temple
D. Khang Khui Cave

220. Kamjong district came into existance in :
A. 2016 B. 2015
C. 2014 D. 2013

221. Which is the new district in Manipur?
A. Mao B. Jiribam
C. Tamei D. Moreh

222. As per the 2011 census which is the highly populated district in Manipur?
A. Thoubal B. Bishnupur
C. Imphal West D. Senapati

223. As per the 2011 census which is the less populated district in Manipur?
A. Ukhrul B. Churachandpur
C. Chandel D. Tamenglong

224. As per the 2011 census which is the most densely populated district in Manipur?
A. Imphal West B. Thoubal
C. Bishnupur D. Imphal East

225. As per the 2011 census which is the less densely populated district in Manipur?
A. Ukhrul B. Tamenglong
C. Chandel D. Churachandpur

226. What is the decadal growth rate (2001-11) of Manipur as per the 2011 census?
A. 20.01% B. 25.02%
C. 24.50% D. 32.03%

227. Which is the largest city in Manipur?
A. Kakching B. Thoubal
C. Lilong D. Imphal

228. Who is known as the "Lion of Manipur"?
A. Bir Tikendrajit B. Hijam Irabat
C. Paona Brajabashi D. Zilla Singh

229. Who is known as 'Mahakavi' in Manipur?
A. H. Guno Singh B. Hijam Anganghal
C. Kh. Chaoba D. Dr. Komal Singh

230. Famous book 'Khudol' is written by :
A. Kh. Chaoba B. Dr. Komol
C. H. Guno Singh D. O. Bhogeshor

231. Where is the headquarters of Imphal East district?
A. Porompat B. Kirao Bitra
C. Sawombung D. Jiribam

232. Where is the headquarters of Imphal west district?
A. Lamsang B. Lamphelpat
C. Patsai D. Wangai

233. Rani Gaidinliu Tribal freedom fighters museum is being set up in which district?
A. Chandel B. Senapati
C. Tamenglong D. Bishnupur

234. Manipur 'Statehood Day' is celebrated on :
A. 25th February B. 13th August
C. 28th September D. 21st January

235. 'Manipuri Language Day' is celebrated on :
A. 20th August B. 28th September
C. 30th September D. 12th September

236. 'Manipur Integrity Day' is celebrated on :
A. 25th September B. 28th September
C. 23rd April D. 25th February

237. When was the State Institute of Journalism established?
A. 15th May 1990 B. 16th June 1994
C. 19th October 1992 D. 20th July 1995

238. When was the Council of Higher Secondary Education, Manipur established?
A. 1990 B. 1991
C. 1992 D. 1993

239. Manipur Human Rights Commission, Lamphelpat was established on :
A. 20th June 1995 B. 27th June 1998
C. 11th May 1990 D. 15th June 1992

240. Bunning wildlife sanctuary is situated in which district?
A. Imphal East B. Tamenglong
C. Chandel D. Churachandpur

241. Which wildlife sanctuary has the largest area in Manipur?
A. Yaingoupokpi Lokchao
B. Keilam
C. Zeliad
D. Jiri Makru

242. Zeliad wildlife sanctuary is located in which district?
A. Chandel B. Tamenglong
C. Bishnupur D. Churachandpur

243. Which was the first English Journal of Manipur?
A. Meitei Chanu B. Manipur Mail
C. Sangai Express D. Manipur News

244. Who is the first Manipuri Film Producer?
A. Debkumar Bose
B. Karam Manmohan Singh
C. Kh. Pramodini
D. Aribam Shyam Sharma

245. Which was the first Manipuri Film to receive the President's Medal in the 20th National Film Festival?
A. Matamgi Manipur B. Langlen Thadoi
C. Imagee Ningthem D. None of these

246. Who is the first Manipuri to win a silver medal in Olympics?
A. N. Dingko Singh B. M.C. Mary Kom
C. Mirabai Chanu D. N. Kunjarani Devi

247. Suraj Lata Devi is related with which sport?
A. Hockey B. Weightlifting
C. Boxing D. Cricket

248. N. Dingko Singh was related with which sport?
A. Cricket B. Football
C. Hockey D. Boxing

249. Anita Chanu has fame in which sport?
A. Mountaineering B. Football
C. Tennis D. Cricket

250. The first National Games were held in Manipur in :
A. 1995 B. 1996
C. 1997 D. 1999

251. Who was the editor of the "Manipur Paojel" in 1939?
A. Keisham Kunjabihari Singh
B. George Gordon
C. Dr. Brown
D. Hijam Irabat

252. Who among the following has got Major Dhyan Chand Khel Ratna Award?
A. N. Kunjarani Devi
B. M.C. Mary Kom
C. Saikhom Mirabai Chanu
D. All of these

253. When was the "Clapped song" sung first time in Manipur?
A. 1830 B. 1847
C. 1857 D. 1870

254. Arjuna Award winner Tombi Devi is related with which sports?
A. Judo B. Boxing
C. Wushu D. Archery

255. When was the Manipur State Transport established?
A. 10th July, 1948 B. 15th August, 1949
C. 13th May, 1950 D. 20th April, 1952

256. When was the Manipur State Transport become a Corporation?
A. 20th July, 1972 B. 14th December, 1978
C. 27th March, 1976 D. 16th November, 1976

257. When does Manipur observe "Save Boundary Day"?
A. August 4, 1987 B. May 6, 1987
C. July 4, 1987 D. October 10, 1987

258. When did the King Gambhir Singh die?
A. 1831 B. 1832
C. 1833 D. 1834

259. When was the second "Nupi-Lal" (Women war against British) took place in Manipur?
A. 1939 B. 1940
C. 1941 D. 1942

260. Where is the Pony Breeding Project established in Manipur?
A. Tamenglong District B. Senapati District
C. Bishnupur District D. Chandel District

261. When was the first Bank opened in Manipur State?
A. 1942 B. 1944
C. 1946 D. 1948

262. Manipur State Bank was opened in :
A. 1942 B. 1944
C. 1945 D. 1947

263. Who was the editor of the weekly jounral "Anouba Yug" in 1947?
A. Hijam Irabat Singh B. George Gordon
C. R.K. Bhubonsana D. Dr. Brown

264. During the reign of which king of Manipur the festival "Ningal Chackouba" was introduced?
A. Maharaja Tangjama
B. Maharaja Chandra-Kirti
C. Maharaja Garibnivaj
D. Maharaja Maramba

265. Who built the famous Lord Krishna temple situated in Imphal?
A. Nara Singha B. King Surchandra
C. King Charairongba D. King Kulachandra

266. When was the famous Lord Sanamahi temple built?
A. 1880 A.D. B. 1885 A.D.
C. 1890 A.D. D. 1891 A.D.

267. Who among the following is the winner of Sahitya Akademi Award from Manipur?
A. Rajkumar Bhubonsana
B. Rajen Toijamba
C. L. Biramangol Singh
D. All of these

268. Which song of Manipur is sung by only women?
A. Nat Ishei B. Nupi Pala
C. Ougri D. Pena Ishei

269. The creator of the Manipuri classical dance 'Ras Leela' was :
A. King Bhagyachandra Singh
B. King Chingthang Khomba
C. King Ningthou Khomba
D. King Madhuchandra

270. Nongthombam Maipak got the 'Mr. India' title in the year :
A. 1967 B. 1968
C. 1969 D. 1970

271. In which year Sougaijam Somorendra Singh became the first graduate from Manipur?
A. 1920 B. 1925
C. 1932 D. 1935

272. M. Bimoljit Singh is related with which sport?
A. Wushu B. Boxing
C. Hockey D. Judo

273. Manipur Agro-Industries Coporation was set-up in :
A. 1992 B. 1993
C. 1994 D. 1995

274. L. Devendro Singh is associated with which sports?
A. Hockey B. Football
C. Boxing D. Wushu

275. Which district is the largest producer of Sugarcane in Manipur?
A. Chandel B. Imphal west
C. Bishnupur D. Thoubal

276. Yangmaso Shaiza was the first tribal :
A. Chief Minister of Manipur
B. Chief Commissioner of Manipur
C. M.P. from Manipur
D. Governor of Manipur

277. How many assembly seats are reserved for scheduled castes in Manipur?
A. 1 B. 2
C. 3 D. 4

278. "Manipur Municipality Act" was introduced in the urban areas of the state in the year :
A. 1971 B. 1973
C. 1976 D. 1978

279. The total area covered by the Manipur Valley is :
A. 1800 sq. kms. B. 1843 sq. kms.
C. 1860 sq. kms. D. 1875 sq. kms.

280. What is the height of Mount Tenipu?
A. 2910 metres B. 2950 metres
C. 2970 metres D. 2994 metres

281. With which country Manipur shares an international border?
A. Myanmar B. China
C. Bangladesh D. None of these

282. Mount Tenipu is located in which district of Manipur?
A. Tamenglong B. Senapati
C. Thoubal D. Bishnupur

283. Jananeta Irabat's birthday is celebrated on :
A. 20th October B. 30th November
C. 30th September D. 18th September

284. The biggest source of the state income of Manipur is:
A. Industry B. Forest Resource
C. Agriculture D. None of these

285. The State Anthem of Manipur was composed by :
A. B. Jayanta Kumar B. K. Kunjabihari
C. A. Thambou Singh D. Sagolsem Indramani

286. L.M.S. Law college stands for :
A. Lairenmayum Seibyasachi Law College
B. Lairenmayum Sobita Law College
C. Longjam Mani Singh Law College
D. Liberal Manipur Society Law College

287. Manipur's first eastern dam Khoupum Dam is situated on which river?
A. Imphal river B. Manchandui river
C. Iril river D. Nambul river

288. In which district Khoupum Dam is located?
A. Bishnupur B. Thoubal
C. Ukhrul D. Tamenglong

289. In which year was the Loktak Hydel Project commissioned?
A. 1980 B. 1981
C. 1982 D. 1983

290. Manipur's premier college Dhana Manjuri College (D.M. College) was established in the year :
A. 1946 B. 1947
C. 1948 D. 1949

291. In which part of Manipur bamboo forests are abundantly grown?
A. Eastern Part B. South western Part
C. South Northern Part D. Northern Part

292. Who is the author of the Jamini Gold Medal award winner novel "Khudol"?
A. Pacha Meitei
B. E. Nilakanta Singh
C. Hijam Guno Singh
D. A. Chitreshwar Sharma

293. Who was the author of the 18th century book called "Sana Manik"?
A. E. Sonamani Singh
B. R.K. Madhubir
C. Wahengbam Madharam
D. Sudhir Naoraibam

294. Who wrote "Elisa Amagi Mahao"?
A. Nilabir Sharma Shastri
B. Arambam Biren Singh
C. G.C. Tongbra
D. N. Kunjamohan

295. Padmashree Award winner author who translated 'Mahabharata' book in Manipuri is :
A. Ch. Kalachand Shastri
B. Birendrajit Naorem
C. Ningombam Sunita
D. N. Ibobi Singh

296. Luira is a festival of which tribe?
A. Thadou B. Tangkhul
C. Kabui D. Kuki

297. Which popular form of festival is observed by Kuki tribes?
A. Chumpha B. Chavang Kut
C. Gan Ngai D. None of these

298. Padma Shri Award winner T. Chaoba Singh is related with which field?
A. Sports B. Arts
C. Public Affairs D. Literature

299. In the reign of which king 'Heigru Hitongba' was started in Manipur?
A. King Irengba
B. King Chandra Kirti
C. King Surchand Singh
D. King Meidingu Loitongba

300. The game of 'Kong' flourished during the reign of :
A. King Ningthou Kongba B. King Laitongba
C. King Keiphaba D. King Khomba

301. How many gold Medals were won by Manipur in the 38th National Games 2025?
A. 20 B. 25
C. 14 D. 30

302. R. K. Singhajit got Padmashree for his work in :
A. Dance B. Literature
C. Drama D. Education

303. As per the 2011 census which district have the highest literacy rate?
A. Imphal East B. Imphal west
C. Bishnupur D. Churachandpur

304. When was Manipur Human Rights Commission established?
A. 25th May 1995 B. 27th June 1999
C. 27th June 1998 D. 28th April 1996

305. As per the 2011 census what is the Males population of Manipur?
A. 1,438,586 B. 1,105,680
C. 1,516,123 D. 1,315,219

306. As per the 2011 census what is the Females population of Manipur?
A. 1,170,338 B. 1,417,208
C. 1,330,216 D. 1,175,670

307. The Kabaw Valley was handed over to Myanmar (Burma) in the year :
A. 1830 B. 1834
C. 1838 D. 1840

308. When was the first English school established in Manipur?
A. 1880 B. 1885
C. 1890 D. 1892

309. Why was Manipur Durbar established in 1907?
A. To assist the British in the administration of Manipur
B. To assist the Government of India in the administration of Manipur
C. To assist the Maharaja in the administration of Manipur
D. None of these

310. The Manipuri Kings who got title of KCSI (Knight Commander Service of India) are :
A. Chandrakriti and Churachand Maharaja
B. Surchandra and Churachand Maharaja
C. Budhachandra and Surchandra Maharaja
D. Chandrakriti and Budhachandra Maharaja

311. What is the full form of MOA?
A. Manipur Olympic Association
B. Manipur Oil Association
C. Manipur Organisation of Adults
D. None of these

312. In which year was 'Manipur women's Football Association' formed?
A. 1972 B. 1976
C. 1980 D. 1982

313. Who was the 'founder patron' of modern sports movement in Manipur?
A. Charairongba B. Keiphaba Yanglon
C. Sir Churachand Singh D. Bhadra Singh

314. Who is the author of the book 'My Experience in Manipur'?
A. Sir James Johnstone B. Lucy Zehol
C. A.K. Paul D. E.W. Dun

315. In Manipur 'Durga Puja' is locally known as:
A. Heikru Hitongba B. Kwak Yatra
C. Yaoshang D. None of the above

316. What is the height of Saheed Minar?
A. 45 feet B. 50 feet
C. 55 feet D. 60 feet

317. L. Nabakishore Singh got Padamshree for his work in:
A. Theatre B. Literature
C. Dance D. Herbal Medicine

318. Ksh. Thouranisabi Devi got Padamshree for her work in :
A. Nat Songkritan B. Mountaineering
C. Cinema D. Boxing

319. Where is Sainik School situated in Manipur?
A. Imphal B. Bishnupur
C. Senapati D. Ukhrul

320. Who is known as the 'Melody King' in Manipur?
A. R.K. Bhogen B. Nongmaithem Pahari
C. S. Devabrata Singh D. L. Lakpati Singh

321. Who is known as the 'Melody Queen' in Manipur?
A. Sabitri Heisnam B. Y. Gambhini Devi
C. Laishram Mema Devi D. Y. Ranjana Devi

322. Who is popularly known as the 'Jananeta' (leader of the people) in Manipur?
A. L. Jugeswar Singh B. N. Tombi Singh
C. Paokai Hao Kip D. Hijam Irabat

323. Which is the biggest Temple in Manipur?
A. Shree Shree Govindajee Temple
B. Vishnu Temple
C. Hanuman Thakur Temple
D. Radha Raman Temple

324. Which is the biggest cave in Manipur?
A. Khu Kse B. Khang Khui Cave
C. Sangboo D. Tonglon

325. Laishram Birendra Kumar got Padma Shri for his work in:
A. Medicine B. Sports
C. Trade & Industry D. Art-Music

326. Which is the highest rainfall area in Manipur?
A. Thoubal B. Ukhrul
C. Tamenglong D. Chandel

327. Which is the lowest rainfall area in Manipur?
A. Senapati B. Imphal
C. Ukhrul D. Churachandpur

328. Where is Orange Festival celebrated in Manipur?
A. Tamenglong B. Ukhrul
C. Senapati D. Bishnupur

329. The present 10+2+3 system of education was started in Manipur from the academic session of :
A. 1985-86 B. 1986-87
C. 1988-89 D. 1990-91

330. What is Jhum cultivation locally called in Manipur?
A. Mono B. Kamlou
C. Pamlou D. Tuwalu

331. Manipur Spinning Mills Corporation, Loitam Khunou, Imphal was established in:
A. 1992 B. 1988
C. 1973 D. 1995

332. In which year Oak Tassar Project was introduced in Manipur?
A. 1973-74 B. 1971-72
C. 1975-76 D. 1978-79

333. "INAMPEILIN' is the annual festival of which tribe of Manipur?
A. Maring B. Tongkhul
C. Chothe D. Tarao

334. What does 'MASLSA' stand for?
A. Manipur State Legal Services Authority
B. Manipur State Legal Society Authority
C. Manipur Strong Legal Society Association
D. None of these

335. When was the status of chief commissioner upgraded to Lieutenant Governor in Manipur?
A. 1968 B. 1969
C. 1970 D. 1971

336. Who is the first Manipuri Women Film Producer?
A. Sabitri Heisnam
B. Y. Ranajana Devi
C. Khaidem Sakhi Devi
D. K. O. Thouranisabi Devi

337. Manipur State Gazette was first launched in the year :
A. 1929 B. 1930
C. 1931 D. 1932

338. Who was the first Teacher (Manipuri) to have taught in School?
A. Mayanglambam Purna Singh (1893)
B. Ch. Kalachand Shastri (1860)
C. R.K. Jhalajit Singh (1870)
D. G. Surchand Sharma (1880)

339. Who was the first Director of Education in Manipur?
A. M.S. Sharma (1960-61)
B. S.D. Bahuguna (1958-59)
C. C. Kirti Singh (1972-73)
D. K.C. Tongbra (1975-76)

340. Which lake is known as the "Kohinoor of Manipur"?
A. Zailad Lake B. Kachouphung Lake
C. Loktak Lake D. Kharung Lake

341. What is the oldest salt mine (brine) in Manipur?
A. Ningel salt mine
B. Sikhong salt mine
C. Chandrakhong salt mine
D. Waikhong salt mine

342. Where is rubber grown in Manipur?
A. Kakching B. Jiribam
C. Nambal D. Machi

343. When does the "Manipur Plantation Crops" establish?
A. 1985-86 B. 1990-91
C. 1979-80 D. 1981-82

344. Who is the author of the Novel 'Imasi Nurabee'?
A. Sudhir Naoroibam B. R.K. Mani
C. B.N. Maisanamba D. Y. Ibomcha

345. Who was the first person to set up NCC in Manipur?
A. L.H. Harnet B. H. Tombi Singh
C. P.K. Suisy D. P. K. Behring

346. Who is the first Manipuri Chief Justice ?
A. P. Jugal
B. R. K. Manisama Singh
C. Ranbir Meitei
D. K. Sanatomba

347. The district of Manipur which is known as the birth place of Christianity in the state is :
A. Thoubal B. Senapati
C. Ukhrul D. Chandel

348. Who among the following has not worked as the chief Minister of Manipur?
A. Rishang Keishing B. Y. Yaima Singh
C. R.K. Ranbir Singh D. R.K. Dorendra Singh

349. In which year Oak Tassar Project was introduced in Manipur?
A. 1971-72 B. 1975-76
C. 1973-74 D. 1978-79

350. Bir Tikendrajit Singh's crusade was against the :
A. Chinese B. Japanese
C. Burmese D. Britishers

351. Takhel Khong (Tripura Canal) was Constructed by :
A. Khabomba B. Punsiba
C. Telheiba D. Bharatsai

352. Manipur state Durbar was established in :
A. 1905 B. 1906
C. 1907 D. 1908

353. In which district Nungba Sub-division is located?
A. Thoubal B. Jiribam
C. Noney D. Ukhrul

354. How many Nagar Panchayats are in Manipur?
A. 15 B. 16
C. 17 D. 18

355. When was the war of Independecne or the Anglo-Manipur war held?
A. 1890 B. 1891
C. 1895 D. 1897

356. When did the Chandel district come into existence?
A. May 13, 1974 B. July 6, 1977
C. June 10, 1978 D. Septerber 5, 1980

357. When was the 'Fast Tract Court' established in Manipur?
A. October 5, 2001 B. November 6, 2002
C. January 7, 2003 D. July 5, 2001

358. When did Manipur Sales Tax Act & Rules come into force?
A. December 10, 1990 B. June 5, 1980
C. May 20, 1985 D. August 6, 1995

359. Manipur Public Service Commission was formed in :
A. 1972 B. 1973
C. 1974 D. 1975

360. Who was the first chairman of the Manipur Public Service Commission?
A. S. K. Behring
B. G. B. K. Hooja
C. K. L. Sharma
D. P. Krishnamohan Singh

361. Who was the first secretary of the Manipur Public Service Commission?
A. Ch. Abhijit Singh
B. Ph. Shyamananda Sharma
C. Karam Goura Kishore Singh
D. Ch. Dhanbir Meitei

362. When was the Manipur Science & Technology Council established?
A. 1980 B. 1985
C. 1988 D. 1990

363. What is the total area of Manipur under forest cover?
A. 20,660.80 sq km. B. 18,560.40 sq km.
C. 16,585 sq km. D. 17,980.50 sq km.

364. The book 'Matamgi Manglan' was written by:
A. L. Premchand B. Lucy Zehal
C. Hijam Angahal D. Lenin Khumancha

365. Thanlon is located in which district?
A. Pherzawl B. Imphal West
C. Senapati D. Tamenglong

366. Phungyar is located in which district?
A. Bishnupur B. Thoubal
C. Kamjong D. Chandel

367. The book 'Fragments of Manipuri Culture' was written by :
A. E. Nilakanta Singh B. G. K. Ghosh
C. R. K. Shitaljit D. M. K. Binodini

368. The book 'Ima' was written by :
A. L. Premchand B. Hijam Angahal
C. Lucy Zehal D. E. W. Dun

369. The book 'Sur Vigyan' recognised by the state government as a text book for music in Manipur is written by :
A. H. Guno Singh B. E. Nilakanta Singh
C. Laishram Memma D. R. K. Madhubir

370. In Manipur who was popularly known as Bob?
A. Birendrajit Naorem
B. Aribam Shyam Sharma
C. M. A. Singh
D. Ralengnao Khaling

371. Who is known as the 'Father of Manipuri Dance and Style'?
A. Guru Amubi Singh
B. Guru T. Amudon Sharma
C. Guru Bipin Singha
D. Guru L. Kaireng Singh

372. Who is honoured with the title 'Nritya Rani'?
A. L. Ibemhal Devi B. Elam Indira Devi
C. H. Ngangbi Devi D. Darshana Jhaveri

373. Who is the first recipient of the Manipuri children's literature award named 'Telam Ningal Atoibema Award'?
A. R. K. Bhubonsana B. S. Surchand Sharma
C. M. Kirti Singh D. M. K. Binodini Devi

374. Which place is called the 'Rice Basket of Manipur'?
A. Kumbi B. Kwakta
C. Kakching D. Samurou

375. The Meitei language has its own script. The name of script is :
A. Meitei Mayek B. Devnagari
C. Sabrai D. None of these

376. Sanjta Chanu have fame in:
A. Tennis B. Football
C. Hockey D. Weightlifting

377. The total length of National Highways in Manipur is:
A. 850 kms. B. 900 kms.
C. 1746 kms. D. 1000 kms.

378. Who was the first General Secretary of the Manipuri Sahitya Parishad established in 1935?
A. Hijam Irabot B. Gokulchandra Singh
C. Laitman Yaima D. A. Thambou Singh

379. Sirohi National Park is located in which district of Manipur?
A. Imphal East B. Chandel
C. Tamenglong D. Bishnupur

380. Where is 'Khansari Sugar Factory' located in Manipur?
A. Khangabok B. Iraishemba
C. Kabowakching D. Kadamtala

381. Where is 'Mechanised Dye House' located in Manipur?
A. Iroishemba B. Takyel
C. Loitang Khunou D. Kabowakching

382. Around which plant all Manipuri marriage ceremonies are conducted?
A. Sirai Lily B. Pineapple
C. Tulsi D. Orange

383. The Gostha Lila dance of Manipur is also known as :
A. Panshenba B. Manshenba
C. Sanshenba D. None of these

384. Which is the biggest festival celebrated by the Kabui Naga tribe of Manipur?
A. Gan Ngai B. Kut
C. Cheiraoba D. Chumpha

385. Manipuri folk dance 'Thabal Chongba' is associated with which festival?
A. Lai Haraoba B. Yaoshang
C. Rath Yatra D. Heikru

386. How many types of Kauna are available in Manipur?
A. Two B. Three
C. Four D. Five

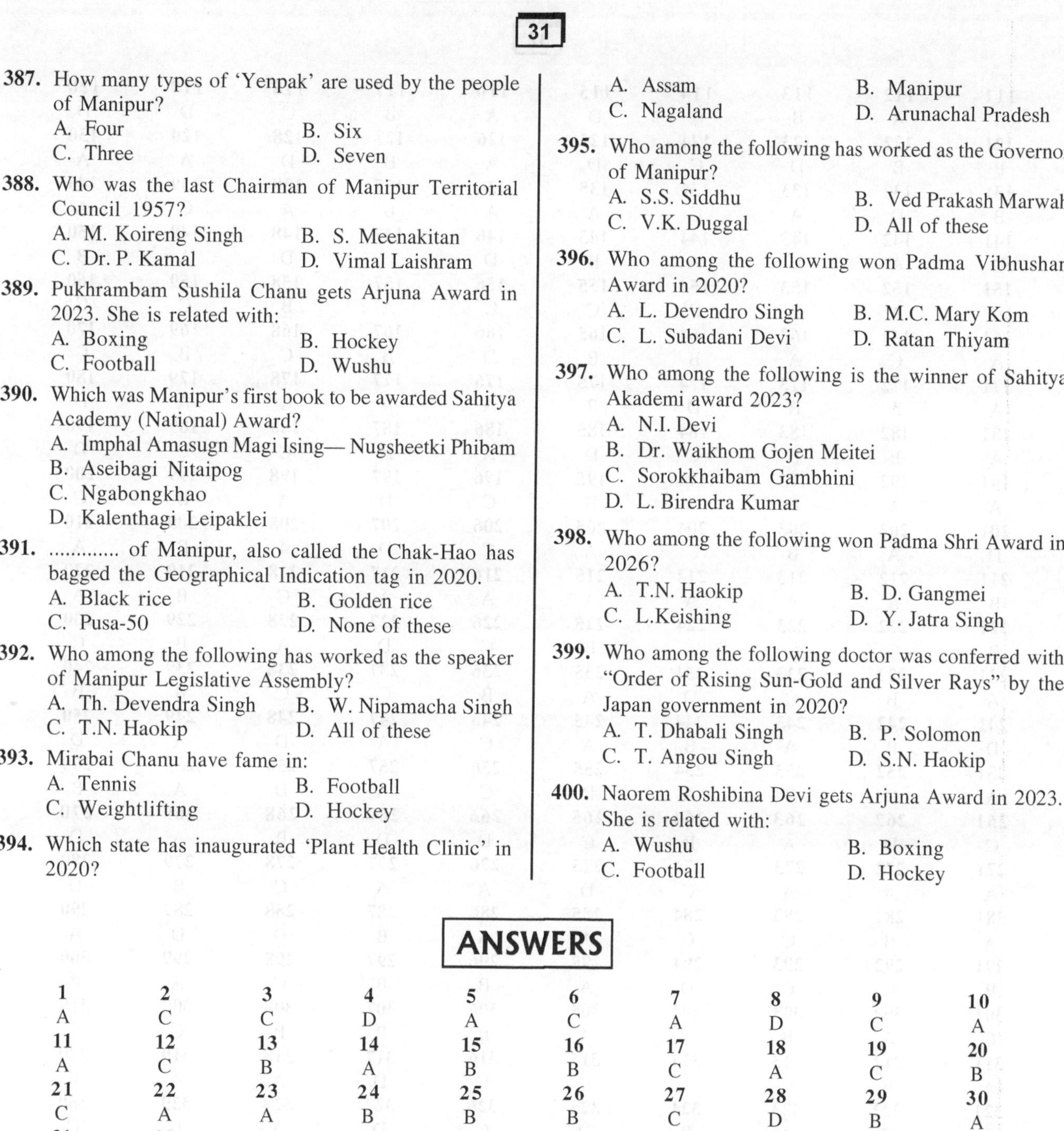

387. How many types of 'Yenpak' are used by the people of Manipur?
A. Four B. Six
C. Three D. Seven

388. Who was the last Chairman of Manipur Territorial Council 1957?
A. M. Koireng Singh B. S. Meenakitan
C. Dr. P. Kamal D. Vimal Laishram

389. Pukhrambam Sushila Chanu gets Arjuna Award in 2023. She is related with:
A. Boxing B. Hockey
C. Football D. Wushu

390. Which was Manipur's first book to be awarded Sahitya Academy (National) Award?
A. Imphal Amasugn Magi Ising— Nugsheetki Phibam
B. Aseibagi Nitaipog
C. Ngabongkhao
D. Kalenthagi Leipaklei

391. .... of Manipur, also called the Chak-Hao has bagged the Geographical Indication tag in 2020.
A. Black rice B. Golden rice
C. Pusa-50 D. None of these

392. Who among the following has worked as the speaker of Manipur Legislative Assembly?
A. Th. Devendra Singh B. W. Nipamacha Singh
C. T.N. Haokip D. All of these

393. Mirabai Chanu have fame in:
A. Tennis B. Football
C. Weightlifting D. Hockey

394. Which state has inaugurated 'Plant Health Clinic' in 2020?
A. Assam B. Manipur
C. Nagaland D. Arunachal Pradesh

395. Who among the following has worked as the Governor of Manipur?
A. S.S. Siddhu B. Ved Prakash Marwah
C. V.K. Duggal D. All of these

396. Who among the following won Padma Vibhushan Award in 2020?
A. L. Devendro Singh B. M.C. Mary Kom
C. L. Subadani Devi D. Ratan Thiyam

397. Who among the following is the winner of Sahitya Akademi award 2023?
A. N.I. Devi
B. Dr. Waikhom Gojen Meitei
C. Sorokkhaibam Gambhini
D. L. Birendra Kumar

398. Who among the following won Padma Shri Award in 2026?
A. T.N. Haokip B. D. Gangmei
C. L.Keishing D. Y. Jatra Singh

399. Who among the following doctor was conferred with "Order of Rising Sun-Gold and Silver Rays" by the Japan government in 2020?
A. T. Dhabali Singh B. P. Solomon
C. T. Angou Singh D. S.N. Haokip

400. Naorem Roshibina Devi gets Arjuna Award in 2023. She is related with:
A. Wushu B. Boxing
C. Football D. Hockey

ANSWERS

1	2	3	4	5	6	7	8	9	10
A	C	C	D	A	C	A	D	C	A
11	12	13	14	15	16	17	18	19	20
A	C	B	A	B	B	C	A	C	B
21	22	23	24	25	26	27	28	29	30
C	A	A	B	B	B	C	D	B	A
31	32	33	34	35	36	37	38	39	40
C	C	A	B	C	D	A	A	A	B
41	42	43	44	45	46	47	48	49	50
A	D	C	C	A	D	C	D	C	D
51	52	53	54	55	56	57	58	59	60
C	D	C	A	C	B	C	A	B	A
61	62	63	64	65	66	67	68	69	70
B	C	D	C	A	B	B	B	C	D
71	72	73	74	75	76	77	78	79	80
A	A	A	C	D	A	B	C	C	D
81	82	83	84	85	86	87	88	89	90
A	B	A	B	A	B	A	C	D	B
91	92	93	94	95	96	97	98	99	100
C	A	B	D	A	C	A	B	A	D
101	102	103	104	105	106	107	108	109	110
A	B	B	B	C	A	B	C	D	A

111	112	113	114	115	116	117	118	119	120
A	A	B	C	D	A	B	C	D	D
121	122	123	124	125	126	127	128	129	130
B	B	D	C	D	A	B	D	A	A
131	132	133	134	135	136	137	138	139	140
B	D	A	C	A	A	B	A	C	A
141	142	143	144	145	146	147	148	149	150
D	A	B	A	B	D	C	D	A	B
151	152	153	154	155	156	157	158	159	160
A	A	B	D	C	C	A	B	C	C
161	162	163	164	165	166	167	168	169	170
A	C	A	B	B	D	B	C	B	C
171	172	173	174	175	176	177	178	179	180
A	A	B	D	D	A	B	C	A	D
181	182	183	184	185	186	187	188	189	190
A	B	B	D	D	A	B	C	D	D
191	192	193	194	195	196	197	198	199	200
A	A	B	C	B	C	D	A	B	C
201	202	203	204	205	206	207	208	209	210
D	A	B	C	A	C	D	A	B	A
211	212	213	214	215	216	217	218	219	220
B	A	A	C	A	A	A	C	B	A
221	222	223	224	225	226	227	228	229	230
B	C	D	A	B	C	D	A	B	C
231	232	233	234	235	236	237	238	239	240
A	B	C	D	A	B	C	C	B	B
241	242	243	244	245	246	247	248	249	250
D	B	A	B	B	C	A	D	A	D
251	252	253	254	255	256	257	258	259	260
A	D	B	A	B	C	A	D	A	B
261	262	263	264	265	266	267	268	269	270
C	D	A	B	C	D	D	B	A	D
271	272	273	274	275	276	277	278	279	280
A	A	A	C	D	A	A	C	B	D
281	282	283	284	285	286	287	288	289	290
A	B	C	C	A	A	B	D	D	A
291	292	293	294	295	296	297	298	299	300
B	C	C	D	A	B	B	C	A	B
301	302	303	304	305	306	307	308	309	310
C	A	B	C	A	B	B	B	C	A
311	312	313	314	315	316	317	318	319	320
A	B	C	A	B	C	D	A	A	B
321	322	323	324	325	326	327	328	329	330
C	D	A	B	D	C	D	A	B	C
331	332	333	334	335	336	337	338	339	340
C	A	C	A	B	C	D	A	B	C
341	342	343	344	345	346	347	348	349	350
A	B	D	C	A	B	C	B	C	D
351	352	353	354	355	356	357	358	359	360
A	C	C	D	B	A	A	A	A	B
361	362	363	364	365	366	367	368	369	370
C	B	C	D	A	C	A	D	C	D
371	372	373	374	375	376	377	378	379	380
C	B	A	C	A	D	C	A	A	A
381	382	383	384	385	386	387	388	389	390
A	C	C	A	B	A	C	A	B	A
391	392	393	394	395	396	397	398	399	400
A	B	C	B	D	B	C	D	A	A

❑❑❑